York City
A Complete Record

1922
1990

S M GAWTHORNE
A D G K N S Y

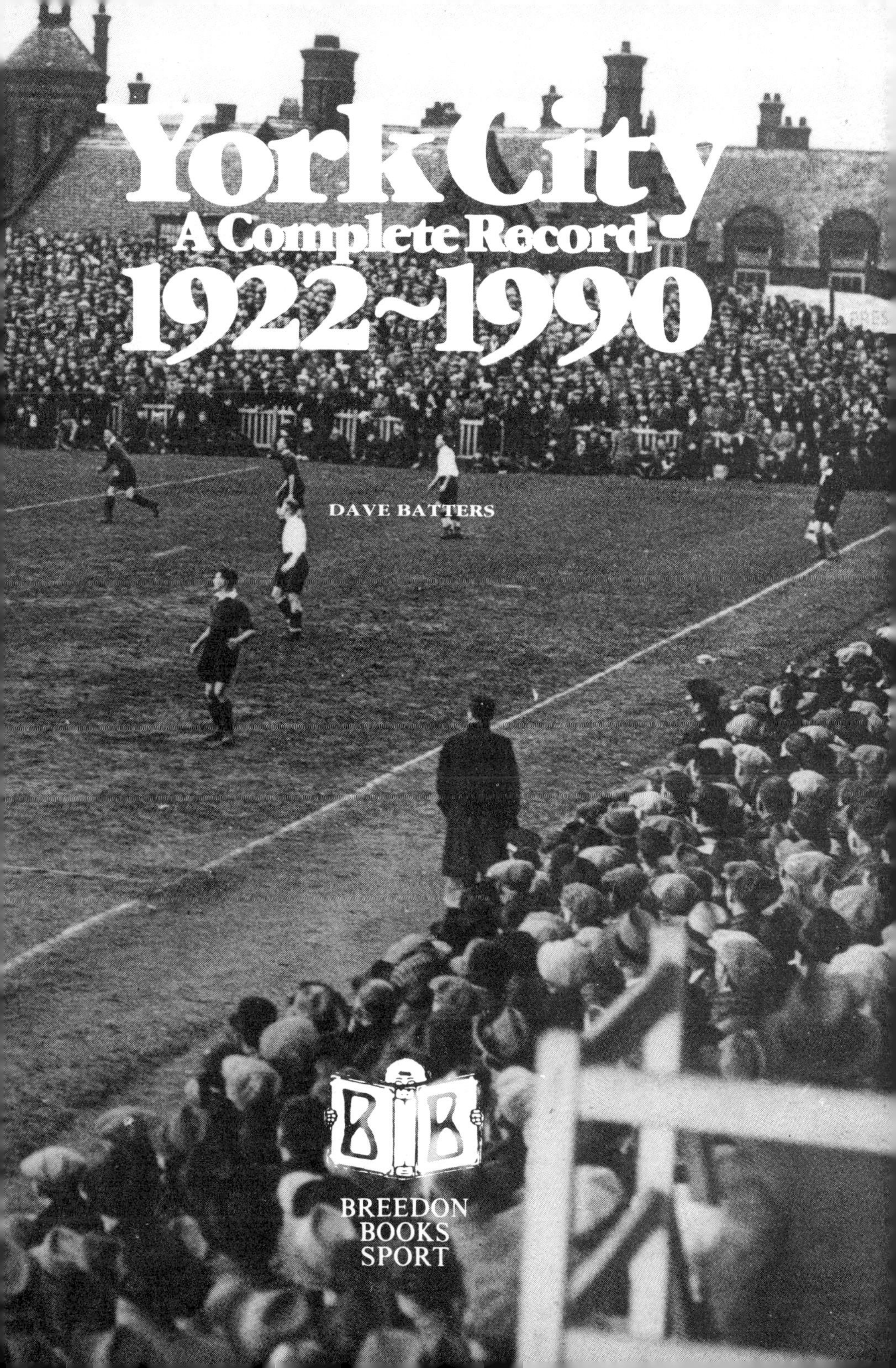

York City
A Complete Record 1922~1990

DAVE BATTERS

BREEDON BOOKS SPORT

First published in Great Britain by
The Breedon Books Publishing Company Limited
44 Friar Gate, Derby DE1 1DA
1990

ISBN 0 907969 69 0

Printed by Butler and Tanner Limited, Frome
Jacket designed by Graham Hales and printed by Arkle Print, Northampton.

Contents

Foreword

AS York City Football Club approaches its 70th birthday, it could be said that the first comprehensive book recording all the historical statistics of the club is long overdue.

It gives me great pleasure, therefore, to congratulate David Batters on his publication, which I am sure will be enjoyed by all those interested in football, young and old.

Certainly it will bring back memories to York City supporters, as former glories and personalities are recalled.

Michael Sinclair
Chairman, York City Football Club

Foreword

ANYONE who has had the good fortune to write about football — amongst other sports — for a living, will know only too well that a great deal can depend on the information at one's fingertips.

It is all very well being able to report, for example, that Bill Smith scored a hat-trick, all of them with headers from centres by Alan Jones. The knack is knowing whether the feat has been achieved before and, if so, when.

It has been my pleasure — some cynics would regard it as otherwise — to write about York City affairs for the *Yorkshire Evening Press* for the past 22 years. It has been a memorable journey, with thousands of miles travelled and millions of words written along the way.

There have been some marvellous moments and some sad ones and the midnight oil has been burned as another chapter was written into York City's history.

Extensive records were kept by my predecessor, Wilf Meek, from the time City were formed in 1922 and I have attempted to follow his example since I took over.

But, despite all the information at arm's length in the office, there have been a great number of occasions when I have been deeply grateful for the knowledge and help of David Batters, who has the most obscure facts and figures at his command.

David and I have shared a great love of the glory game and particularly our local club, which has experienced more ups and downs than most in the Football League.

And every club depends a lot on — and is lucky to have — a man like David, who charts City's history with such meticulous care.

So, with that in mind, you can imagine how nice it was to be asked to write a few words as a foreword to this fine book, which I am sure will be a treasured addition to our soccer bookshelves.

The book is unique as it is the first official history of the club put together in one volume. That history will be added to as time goes on.

I hope that others will get as much pleasure out of it as I am sure David had in writing it.

I commend it to everyone who loves our national game and York City in particular.

Malcolm Huntington
Chief Sportswriter
Yorkshire Evening Press
June 1990

Introduction

IT was in October 1948 that as a nine-year-old I was taken for the first time to Bootham Crescent by my Uncle Les, and for the record, City beat Mansfield Town 2-1. So started for me, on that autumn afternoon over 40 years ago, a fascination and interest in my local club which had never waned.

During this time there have been the highs and lows, the joy and the gloom, the Cup triumphs and promotion successes, the dismal seasons of relegation and the applications for re-election — and the many years of what is termed 'bread and butter' fare.

Arguably, the 1954-5 team was the finest in the club's history. My happiest memories are of that time when my Dad and I travelled far and near, cheering on the 'Happy Wanderers' as Ernie Phillips and his side were known. They were, indeed, unforgettable days.

Other great milestones in the club's history include the outstanding promotion season of the mid-1960s, the glorious drive to Division Two in the 1970s and the magnificent Fourth Division championship triumph of the 1980s. Older followers will also recall with pride the marvellous FA Cup exploits of the 1930s and the wartime successes. Whatever the memories, I hope that this book will revive warm memories of York City Football Club.

David Batters
Haxby
York
August 1990

Acknowledgements

The author wishes to thank the following: The chairman, directors and staff of York City FC for their help and encouragement; Malcolm Huntington, chief sports writer of the *Yorkshire Evening Press*, for writing a Foreword and allowing access to files, especially to Wilf Meek's record of the club's early days; Martin Jarred and the library staff of the *Evening Press*; staff of the York Reference and Information Library; Dave Windross for his invaluable help with statistics; Frank Cawood for sight of his magnificent scrapbooks of the 1930s; Bill Bevan, Chris Forth and Phil Vardy for their help in writing out results charts etc. Thanks also to my family for their encouragement, especially to my wife, Kath, for her great patience and understanding and her tremendous help in typing out much of the material. Many thanks are also due to the publishers for their kind and much appreciated support of the Shipton Street Roof Appeal Fund.

Photographic credits

Grateful thanks to the *Yorkshire Evening Press* for allowing extensive use of photographs from their library. Many thanks also to Mrs Judith Brisby, daughter of Mr Tom Lockie, and Mrs Terry Fowler, daughter of Mr G.W.Sherrington, for allowing photographs from their private collections to be used. Other photographs were supplied by Colorsport of London.

Dedication

To my wife, Kath, and my Dad. Also to the memory of my late uncle, Mr Les Crossley, and the late Mr Cliff Fowler, who was a close friend and colleague of mine on York Hospital Radio.

The York City Story

ASSOCIATION football was played by several clubs in the York area in the latter part of the last century, but with Rugby Union holding sway, the handling code claimed the only representative city side.

In the 1890s, local soccer was not run on an organized basis and as teams were not affiliated to any association or competition, only friendly games were played. Some of the early clubs in the area were York Wednesday, who claimed to be the oldest club in the city, St Clements, Heworth, Ebor Wanderers and school teams Bootham, St John's College and Elmfield College. This latter school produced a great soccer enthusiast, Mr S.R.Slack, who was its headmaster for many years. A fine player in his younger days, he was later president of the York Football Association for more than 30 years, until his death in 1946.

In the 1890s, with leagues developing throughout the country, moves were made to organize such a competition in York and in 1897, the York & District League was established. Ten clubs were divided into two divisions and these pioneers were St Clements, Rowntrees, Acomb, Sycamore, Heworth, Groves Wesley, Selby, Easingwold, Ulleskelf and Ebor Wanderers. Two men who were largely involved in setting up the organization were C.M.Rawes and A.Lumley.

In 1900 the York City & District Football Association was formed and local cup competitions launched — the Riley Smith Cup, which was to become the Junior Cup, and the Faber Cup which became the Senior Cup. A prominent figure in local football at this time was Mr J.A.MacGregor. Under the umbrella of the local FA, the York League was supplemented by the Half-Holiday League which catered for games played on Wednesdays.

The Minor and Junior Leagues were formed and the Schools League and the York FA ran four cup competitions together with two charity cup tournaments. Military clubs entered the competitions — Northumberland Fusiliers, York & Lancaster Regiment, 18th Hussars, 5th Royal Irish Lancers and the Border Regiment.

In those early days the Rowntree club were the most successful and their chief rivals were St Clements, Heworth, St Pauls, Sycamore and Hungate Mission. The league continued to expand and Knaresborough and Malton United joined the fold. By the tenth year of its existence, in 1907, the league operated with three divisions and over two dozen clubs. Amateur soccer was thus prospering in the city.

At this time the York FA council members were Messrs J.Ernest Trees (honorary secretary), J.W.Biscomb (president), C.M.Rawes (vice-president), T.K.Wilson (vice-president), J.Bond, J.W.Cundall, A.Bell, F.Butler, C.H.Page, G.Dinsdale, W.W.Milburn, A.R.Crowe, F.Taylor, G.F.Andrew (honorary treasurer) and J.G.Bruce (assistant honorary secretary).

The demand grew for a club representative of the city and in 1908 the first York City Football Club was formed as an amateur concern. The honorary secretary was Mr Trees and the club entered the Northern League.

The newly-formed club obtained a ground in Holgate Road at the end of Lindley Street and Murray Street. The only stand accommodation was a couple of open stands from York Racecourse. One was canvas-covered and 300 people could be accommodated. The first captain was Tom Hillary, who was born in Guisborough, Cleveland, in 1883 and arrived in York in November 1899, when he joined the St Paul's club. Hillary later appeared for St Clements and NER United, as well as playing for York in inter-city games against Sheffield and Middlesbrough.

City's first game, at home to South Bank, was won 2-1 and opponents that season included West Hartlepool, Saltburn, Bishop Auckland, West Auckland and Leadgate. The club entered the FA Amateur Cup and, after knocking out Withernsea and St Paul's, lost to Scarborough in a replay.

For two seasons they met with average success and in 1910-11, in order to reduce travelling, they competed in the Yorkshire Combination where they were in opposition to West Riding clubs. In 1911, Mr J.E.Wright took over as secretary from Mr Trees. He quickly came to the conclusion that amateur football would not thrive in a Rugby stronghold and he paved the way by signing a professional by the name of Corrighan (amateur clubs in the Yorkshire Combination were at the time allowed to field one paid player). Corrighan therefore became the first professional to play soccer for a club in the city of York, but Wright had bigger ideas and advocated the formation of a limited liability company to run a professional club.

Several well-known citizens expressed interest, including the Lord Mayor, Alderman Norman Green, who became chairman of the board. Frank Marks, who kept The Greyhound Hotel, Bert Rutter, who ran the old Victoria Hall Cinema in Goodramgate, Mr J.T.Clarke, Mr S.R.Slack and Fred Airey were the other directors.

The new professional club was formed in 1912 and 592 five-shilling shares were issued. A plot of rough land in Burton Stone Lane, known as Field View and not far from the present club's headquarters at Bootham Crescent, was obtained. One of the early directors was Alderman Sir William Forster Todd, who later moved over to Clarence Street where he was a very influential figure at York RLFC between the wars.

In May 1912, a deputation went to the Midland League's annual meeting in Nottingham and the club was admitted to that competition. The directors appointed Peter Boyle, a former Sheffield United, Sunderland and Irish international full-back, as player-manager. Another personality to join the club was Roddie Walker, a full-back from Hearts who had represented the Scottish League against the Football League in 1910-11.

The opening of the ground at Field View, with a game against Midland League champions Rotherham Town, was an auspicious occasion. One of York's two Members of Parliament, Sir John Butcher, was in attendance together with the Lord Mayor, General Plumer and General Reade. The ceremony was filmed and the picture shown at the Empire and the Victoria Hall in Goodramgate. For the match there were 5,000 paying spectators —sixpence for men, threepence for boys, ladies admitted free. Season tickets were 7s 6d (37½p).

Players who appeared for the club in those early professional days included goalkeeper Jimmy Atherton and David Melville, a right-back from Bradford City. His left-back partner was Dick Waterworth of Rowntrees. The half-back line was A.Lawson of the Scots Greys, Bob Black, a Scottish Junior international, and George Sykes, who attracted the attention of Herbert Chapman — then manager of Leeds City. In attack was David Galbraith of Raith Rovers, J.McMahon, Scotsman W.Lomas from Bury, who was valued at £500 — a big sum in those days — T.Shanks, an Irish international inside-left, and W.Robertson, a former Portsmouth winger.

Added to these experienced players were a number of notable local lads. Dick Tindall from Rowntrees, Tommy Holmes, who had a long association with Acomb, and Teddy Ledgard a talented inside-forward from Lowther United, a top York amateur side at the time. As part of Ledgard's transfer deal, City sent their professional team to play United at Mille Crux Rowntrees — and lost 4-0.

After the enthusiasm of the introduction of professional football, the club struggled to establish itself and fixture clashing with York RLFC frequently occured. The Rugby hold was formidable. The Football Association granted York a representative North v South fixture, but the receipts totalled only £36. Sir Frederick Wall, the FA secretary, when told of the 'gate', remarked to the City secretary: "Never again sir!"

Tommy Collier succeeded Peter Boyle as manager and after him came Archie Taylor, who had captained Barnsley when they won the FA Cup in 1912. Features in those far-off days were a visit from Newcastle United, for a friendly game, and hard-fought FA Cup tussles against Goole Town. In August 1914, City were invited to a meeting by the Nelson club to discuss the formation of a Third Division of the Football League, but war was declared and this never took place. Otherwise York City might have been original members of the Third Division.

The club completed its third season in the Midland League in 1914-15, but then the competition was suspended because of hostilities. In 1915-16, a few friendly games were played and then in 1917, the club folded. Pressed by a creditor, York City went into liquidation through the bankruptcy court almost overnight. The stand and equipment were disposed of and Field View was turned into allotments and then a building estate. The current overdraft at the bank had only been £518, but with the stand unpaid for and one creditor pressing for payment, the end came after only five years' brief history. It was to be another five years before the new and present York City FC emerged.

Local football continued to prosper and expand after World War One but now, with no professional club in the city, York's Rugby League side had the stage to themselves. Junior soccer was proving popular, however, and so many clubs were springing up that the York League was constantly having to be revised. Local cup competitions, promoted by the York FA, attracted good crowds and receipts exceeding £100 were taken at a Senior Cup Final with an admission fee of 6d (2½p).

Shortly after the war, the Yorkshire League was formed. This catered for clubs with part-time professionals and three York clubs entered the new competition — Acomb WMC, Rowntrees and York YMCA. This brought reserve teams of a number of senior professional clubs, and a good standard of football, to the York area. Acomb, particularly, had a fair degree of success and amongst their players of note were Tom Maskill, later to play for York City, Jack Robson, who was a fine centre-half, Tommy Holmes, 'Sandy' Acklam, the Halder brothers and 'Mike' Dennis. YMCA recruited an Aberdeen full-back, McRobbie, as trainer and it was with this club that Joe Hulme, who went on to have an illustrious professional career with Arsenal and England, played his early football. Without doubt these Yorkshire League games helped to create a demand for another senior team in the city of York. With growing public opinion, a number of private meetings and discussions took place and then on 31 March 1922, Harry Hayhurst called together enthusiasts for a public meeting at the Guildhall.

Great interest was aroused and 400 people attended. Amidst a good deal of enthusiasm the following resolution, proposed by Councillor W.H.Shaw and seconded by J.Hutchinson, was passed:

'That, in the opinion of this meeting, the present is an opportune time for the formation of a York City Association Football Club'.

The chairman of the meeting was C.Horner and amongst those present were Hammond Richmond, who contributed articles in the *Football Press* under the pseudonym of 'Nomad', Arthur Brown, Councillor W.H.Shaw, H.Hayhurst,

H.Rusholme, J.Hutchinson and J.Scott. A committee of 20 was formed with Richmond as secretary. At a further meeting on 4 April 1922, C.Horner was elected chairman and George Robinson of the Blue Bell, Fossgate, became honorary treasurer. A number of early meetings regarding the formation of the club had been held in this public house, which is still a very popular hostelry today. Five trustees were elected, amongst them John Fisher, who was to prove a good benefactor.

On 6 May 1922, the decision was made at a meeting in the Co-operative Hall to form the York City Football and Athletic Club Limited. The meeting fixed the sum of £5 as a minimum share investment for a director's financial responsibility. The first five directors elected were Messrs J.Fisher, G.W.Sherrington, G.E.Robinson, A.Brown and H.Watson. Later additions resulted in W.H.Shaw being elected chairman and secretary Harry Rusholme was put on the board. One of the first things on the directors' agenda was to make what could only amount to a cheeky application to join the Football League.

The following letter was circulated to Football League clubs in support of the application.

YORK CITY ASSOCIATION FOOTBALL & ATHLETIC CLUB.

Headquarters,
Y.M.C.A.
Clifford Street.
York.
24 May, 1922

Sir,

Following a series of public meetings held in the City of York, a Limited Company is being formed for the purpose of raising an Association Football Club.

As you are aware, application has been made for inclusion in the Third Division of the Northern Section.

In seeking your support in furtherance of our election, we beg to place before you the following facts:—

(a) The population of the City of York is approximately 85,000; there is a growing demand for a better class of football & there are at present, some 70 clubs playing the Association Code in the City and neighbourhood of York.

(b) The purchase of a ground covering seven acres, is on the point of completion, and it is intended to equip this in the most up to date style. The ground is conveniently situated on a main tram route.

As the geographical position of York is second to none, and its railway facilities of the best, the travelling expenses of visitors will be reduced to a minimum.

(c) It is the intentions of the club to get together a strong workmanlike team by the commencement of next season, and in this connection it may be stated that applications have already been received from several prominent players.

(d) Financially, the capital of £5,000 is practically assured; already there are upwards of 1,000 shareholders of £1 0s 0d in addition to those of larger amounts.

(e) A strong Supporters' Club has already been formed and is working hard for success in all directions.

We are making application in confidence that we should be able to carry out all that is required of us.

Thanking you in anticipation of your kind support.
Yours faithfully,

(signed) ARTHUR BROWN, Chairman.
(signed) HAMMOND N.RICHMOND, Hon. Secretary.

They had neither ground nor players — yet Fisher and Rusholme were sent to the Football League's annual meeting in London to apply for membership to the Third Division North. Halifax Town and Rochdale were both re-elected and although the infant York City received one vote, the president of the Football League, John McKenna, and committeeman Charles Sutcliffe, told the York delegation — go back home, establish the club, work a bit and then come back another day.

Shortly afterwards directors attended the Midland League annual meeting in Sheffield and on 10 June 1922, York City were elected to that competition. It was a close call, however, as seven clubs competed for six vacancies. City finished sixth, only three votes ahead of Sutton. With the problem of playing in which league now solved, the task of recruiting players was embarked upon. Hughie 'Spud' Murphy, after long service in the Army, became trainer and one of the first players to be signed was Nicol Hendry, who for many years was Hull City's goalkeeper. Other former Hull players acquired were centre-half Billy Smith, who was appointed the club's first captain, and outside-left Joe Harron. There were links with the old Field View club with the signing of 'Ginger' Lynch and Tommy Holmes. From the Acomb club came Tom Maskill, who had been a schoolboy international and 'Sandy' Acklam. There was also a strong contingent of Sheffield players — Ted Thorpe, Charlie Elliott and Charlie Lemmons.

In the summer of 1922 there were financial problems. The formation of a limited liability company had been decided with an authorized share capital of £4,000 in £1 shares. Before the directors could go to allotment it was necessary to raise £1,250 and this capital was very slow in coming. One of the schemes introduced was one whereby shares could be purchased in weekly instalments and, as a result, many supporters became shareholders. The establishment of York City FC arose from a desire to provide sport for the working men of the city and subsequently it was largely the working men who brought it into being. A ground at Heslington Lane, Fulfordgate, was obtained and the necessary minimum capital was raised. The prospectus was published as follows:

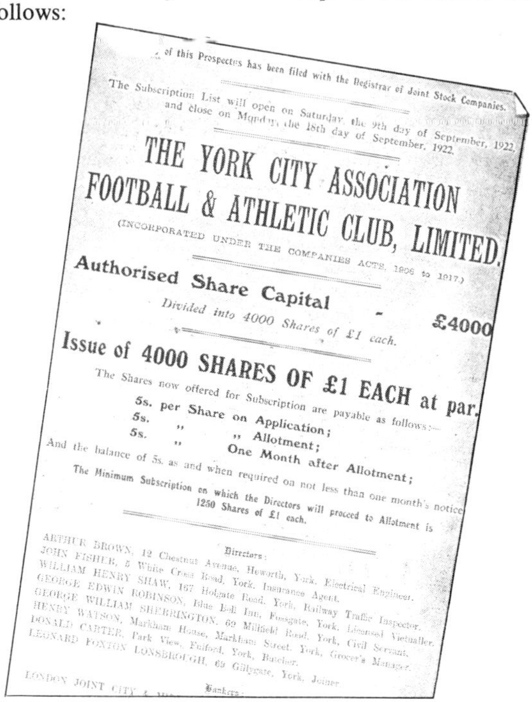
... of this Prospectus has been filed with the Registrar of Joint Stock Companies.

The Subscription List will open on Saturday, the 9th day of September, 1922, and close on Monday, the 18th day of September, 1922.

THE YORK CITY ASSOCIATION FOOTBALL & ATHLETIC CLUB, LIMITED.

(INCORPORATED UNDER THE COMPANIES ACTS, 1908 to 1917.)

Authorised Share Capital - £4000

Divided into 4000 Shares of £1 each.

Issue of 4000 SHARES OF £1 EACH at par.

The Shares now offered for Subscription are payable as follows:—

5s. per Share on Application;
5s. " " Allotment;
5s. " One Month after Allotment;

And the balance of 5s. as and when required on not less than one month's notice

The Minimum Subscription on which the Directors will proceed to Allotment is 1250 Shares of £1 each.

Directors:

ARTHUR BROWN, 12 Chestnut Avenue, Heworth, York, Electrical Engineer.
JOHN FISHER, 5 White Cross Road, York, Insurance Agent.
WILLIAM HENRY SHAW, 167 Holgate Road, York, Railway Traffic Inspector.
GEORGE EDWIN ROBINSON, Blue Bell Inn, Fossgate, York, Licensed Victualler.
GEORGE WILLIAM SHERRINGTON, 69 Millfield Road, York, Civil Servant.
HENRY WATSON, Markham House, Markham Street, York, Grocer's Manager.
DONALD CARTER, Park View, Fulford, York, Butcher.
LEONARD FOXTON LONSBROUGH, 69 Gillygate, York, Joiner

Bankers:

LONDON JOINT CITY & ...

Nicol Hendry was appointed as player-coach at a salary of £4 per week and his duties as spelled out in the club's Minute Book were as follows:

1. To have supervision of all players and trainer.
2. To coach the players in football playing.
3. To attend the directors weekly meeting, and give report of players attending practice.
4. To receive report from trainer as to the fitness or otherwise of players, and report to the directors at their weekly meeting.
5. To act as medium between players and directors.
6. To sign on amateur players on the instruction of the secretary.
7. To induce local lads to sign on for the reserve team, with the object of their becoming fit for the first eleven.
8. To obtain the authority of the secretary for the expending of any money, and obtain his counter signature before issuing orders for work or materials required.
9. To report to directors as to suitability or otherwise of new players.
10. To perform any special duty that may be requested by the directors at any time in the interests of the club.
11. That he be invested with power to settle disputes but in case of any disputes which he settles, the same to be immediately reported to the secretary, so that the same may be put before the directors at their next meeting.

The duties of Hughie Murphy — trainer and groundsman — were as follows:

1. To see that all players are properly prepared before turning out in a match and that they are all supplied with equipment.
2. To see that all players equipment is kept in good condition and ready for use by the players.

York City line up prior to their first home game v Lincoln City Reserves on 9 Sep 1922 at Mille Crux, Rowntrees. Back row (left to right): H.Rusholme (honorary secretary), Tommy Holmes, Nick Hendry, Ted Thorpe, Hughie Murphy (trainer). Middle row: 'Ginger' Lynch, Charlie Elliott, Billy Smith (captain) Charlie Lemmons, Joe Harron. Front row: 'Sandy' Acklam, Jack Woods, Tom Maskill.

3. To give attention to minor injuries.
4. To keep in good condition the rooms and equipment and have the ground marked out for matches, and to do any other work on the ground in the interest of the club, either with or without assistance when authorised or requested to do so by the directors.
5. To report to the player-coach any serious injury.
6. To make requisition to the player-coach for any materials required.
7. To obtain authority from the player-coach before expending any money.

The first match for the club was away to Notts County Reserves on Wednesday, 6 September 1922. Against strong opposition, City put up a good display before losing 4-2. The first City goal was scored by skipper Billy Smith, direct from a free-kick, and Jack Woods, who had previously been with Halifax Town, was the other marksman. That first City team lined up as follows: Hendry, Holmes, Thorpe, Lynch, Smith, Acklam, Elliott, Moult, Woods, Lemmons and J.Harron. The club colours were maroon and white striped shirts, white shorts or knickers as then described.

With Fulfordgate not yet ready, City had to play their first home match three days later at Mille Crux, Haxby Road, the ground of Messrs Rowntree & Company Limited. Lincoln City Reserves were the visitors and York won 3-2 with goals from Acklam, Elliott and Woods. The gate receipts at a 9d fee (just under 4p), were £122 and this figure remained a record for a long time. Rowntrees again kindly loaned their ground a week later, when City lost to Boston Town 2-4, and then on Wednesday, 20 September 1922 the first game was played at Fulfordgate. City celebrated with a 4-1 victory over Mansfield Town and generally that season performed creditably, but after occupying a mid-table position in early March, the side failed to win any of its last 14 fixtures and finished in 19th position.

The team did very well, however, in the North Riding Senior Cup and they reached the Final. A 7-1 victory at Scarborough in a qualifying round match was followed by home wins over Stockton Catholics and Darlington RA. The Final against Middlesbrough Reserves was played at Ayresome Park on 10 March 1923. City took the lead through Jack Woods but eventually lost 4-2 to the experienced and powerful 'Boro side. Joe Harron was the other scorer that day and that was to be his last game for the club.

On 12 March, Harron became the first City player to figure in a transfer when he went to Sheffield Wednesday for £200. At the end of the season local lad, Tom Maskill, moved to Coventry City. Tom was one of two talented local brothers, both of whom gained schoolboy international honours. Younger lad, George, made his senior City debut in January 1924 and moved to Scarborough in 1927. Both players returned to York City in 1932-3 and played in the Third Division North side. Meanwhile the board of directors had been increased to 12 and Leslie Brown had succeeded Rusholme as secretary in December 1922.

Financially, the first season proved disappointing and a little worrying. A loss of £718 was reported and only £1,260 of the share capital had been subscribed. Councillor Shaw relinquished the chairmanship to Arthur Brown and the small band of enthusiasts renewed their efforts to build a successful and soundly based club. On 20 April 1922 the Supporters' Club had been formed and in the summer of 1923, under their sponsorship, many improvements were made to the ground.

In 1923-4 the club entered a reserve team in the Yorkshire League and competed in the FA Cup. The previous season the club had not been formed in time to enter the competition. In the extra preliminary round, Castleford and Allerton United were beaten 2-1 at Fulfordgate. The honour of scoring the first FA Cup goal for York City went to Tommy Rippon.

In the next round City won at Cudworth, but in the first qualifying round they lost to Mexborough in a second replay. Humble beginnings, therefore, in the competition which was to provide so many thrills and excitement for York City in the years to come. Further transfers took place with the departure of goalkeeper Len Boot to Huddersfield for £300 in October 1923 and then in February the following year, teenager Joe Hulme moved to Blackburn Rovers for £250. City received a further £50 after the right winger played in six first-team games and Rovers played a friendly match at Fulfordgate as part of the deal. The 19-year-old Hulme had made a total of only 28 Midland League appearances and scored three penalties, but he had immense natural football ability and quite a few clubs, including Hull City and Barnsley, were very keen on his signature. The Ewood Park club won the race for his services and within 18 months he had been transferred to Arsenal, then managed by Herbert Chapman, for almost £3,000. Hulme went on to be one of the best outside-rights of his generation, winning League and FA Cup honours with Arsenal as well as being capped for England nine times. One player who established himself in the team that season was 'Micky' Albrecht. He had joined the club from Inniskilling Dragoons and was described as being as 'hard as nails' and was quite a character.

Travelling to games in those far off days could be quite difficult as the following experience proved. In December 1923 City were away to Grimsby Town Reserves and they made the journey to Hull to cross the Humber by ferry to New Holland. The boat got off-course and hit a sandbank and the City party were stuck in mid-river for a long time. A belated arrival at Hew Holland caused the rest of the trip to be made by dock tram car and taxi and the match began nearly an hour late. To complete City's woe, Town won 9-0 and the game finished in almost total darkness. City ended 1923-4 again in 19th position with an almost identical record to the previous year. The best performance of the season was a 5-0 win at Rotherham County Reserves with Tommy Rippon netting a hat-trick. Joe Hulme, in what was his last game for the club, scored from the penalty-spot and the other marksman was Arthur Charlesworth.

At the annual meeting in September 1924, shareholders were told of an 'encouraging outlook' by the directors. Wages, salaries and bonuses paid to players in that second season had amounted to £1,494. Travelling expenses and refreshments cost £497 6s 9½d. Items on the revenue side included gate receipts of £2,119 19s 4d and sale of programmes £62. Overall, the loss on the season's working was £350, a big improvement on the first year's figures and the directors felt that they were on the right path. To be able to reduce the loss by nearly £400 in what had only been a moderate playing season was no mean achievement and the directors report concluded: 'The presence of so many York born players with the club should appeal to sportsmen in the city and the directors are looking forward to a very successful season and hope that the public will give them every support in their endeavour to establish and popularise the Association game in the city. There is still one goal ahead namely the Third Division and we appeal to all to give us the necessary financial support to achieve this object at the earliest possible moment'.

During the summer of 1924 the old established Midland League was faced with a crisis. Eight reserve teams of Football League clubs withdrew from the competition to help form the Midland Combination. The split came at such short notice, that to ensure a full complement of fixtures, the Midland League formed a Principal Competition to end in February and then followed this with two subsidiary north and south sections. 1924-5 proved a successful campaign for the club. They finished sixth in the Principal Competition and runners-up to Denaby United in the North Subsidiary Competition. Players who made their mark this season were Jimmy Miller, a clever Scottish inside-forward who finished top scorer with 17 goals; Joe Laws a tubby little outside-left and Fred Walker a local centre-half from Heslington, who made such fine progress that in the summer of 1925 he was transferred to Tottenham. In those days, as City did not pay summer wages to retain players, Spurs got Walker without a fee (as did Coventry with Tommy Maskill in 1923). The London club did, however, agree to make a donation if the young centre-half made the grade in the First Division. This he did do and in November 1925 it was announced that Tottenham had made a generous donation which had been gratefully received by the City directors. A local full-back, Lester Marshall, hit the headlines when he was tried at centre-forward. He hit five goals in the FA Cup tie against Horsforth, five goals in a League match against Castleford and in a North Riding Senior Cup tie he netted six in an 11-1 win over Grangetown St Mary's. In January 1925 he moved to Lincoln for £100. Brothers Joe and Reg Baines also made appearances in the first team. Reg was to play a big part in the club's history in the years ahead. The Reserves side also did well that season, winning the York Senior Cup and York Charity Cup. It was in 1924 that George William Sherrington, one of the directors, took over the task of honorary secretary. He was to serve the club as secretary for 37 years. 'Billy' Sherrington was indeed 'Mr York City'. One of the founder members of the club in 1922, he was born on Tyneside and worked as a civil servant. Upon taking over the secretaryship he inherited a legacy of administrative problems, but he applied all his enthusiasm to the job. When the club did gain election to the Football League in 1929 the secretarial work became much more intensive, as did the financial administration. On 1 February 1930 he was appointed full-time secretary and consequently relinquished his position as a director. He was to give the club outstanding and loyal service and in 1951 he received the Football League long service medal. After his retirement in 1961 he became the club's president and he died in 1977.

The mid-1920s were difficult days economically, especially for football clubs like York City still striving to establish themselves. In the dark days of 1925 the club was only kept going by the enthusiasm of the directors. One of them, John Fisher, who was now chairman, loaned them several sums and it was indeed to men such as this that Sherrington had to turn for the cash to pay wages. York City had to fight to keep their head above water and it was the then directors — the gallant pioneers — in the early days which kept the club in existence.

The Midland League was restored in size in readiness for 1925-6 and new clubs elected included Alfreton, Loughborough, Long Eaton, Sutton, Shirebrook and Ilkeston. With only one point from the first six games, City made a bad start from which they never really recovered and they finished a disappointing 16th. Captain was a strong centre-half by the name of Jimmy Loughran and under his leadership the side did, however, have their best run in the FA Cup to date reaching the third qualifying round before losing to Wath. In the preliminary round at Maltby Main they were winning 7-0 when a violent rainstorm caused the match to be abandoned after 71 minutes. The game was replayed at Fulfordgate and City had to battle hard to win 5-3. With the arrival of the new clubs in the League, City had a number of long trips to make. Invariably for these matches to Nottinghamshire and Derbyshire a small party assembled in York, as few of the players then lived in the city and the team used to be collected *en route*. On a trip to Alfreton on 21 November, City were one man short and Sherrington recruited a man from a local pub who was reported to be useful. Less than an hour before the game he was drinking pints — in the game he scored City's only goal in a 5-1 defeat. During this time there was a prolonged strike in the coal-mines and there was considerable depression. Visiting one mining town, City officials called on a local hostelry which was full of out of work miners before the game. It was customary for the City players to be paid their wages on the day of the match and, to the consternation of the landlord, the director in charge of the party took out his wallet and started to check the wages cash. He was the object of much attention in the crowded pub and after a hint from the landlord the group of City officials grabbed their hats and coats and bid a hasty retreat.

The 1926-7 season was the most successful York City experienced as a non-League club. They finished sixth in the table scoring 96 goals in their 38 League matches and they reached the second-round proper of the FA Cup.

City strengthened their side with more experienced players and this reaped dividends. Goalkeeper George Thompson proved an outstanding discovery. In July 1927 he was transferred to Southampton and in the 1950s his son was to play for City. Former Exeter player, Andy Flynn, proved an excellent right-back. Jimmy Loughran was again an inspiration at centre-half and the ever-reliable Jack Middlemiss was at left-half. At centre-forward was Charlie Flood who had previously been with Plymouth, Hull, Bolton and Nottingham Forest. He rattled in 17 goals in 15 League appearances and was transferred to Swindon in February 1927. Dicky Merritt, ex-Lincoln, was at outside-left and was a match-winner on his day. Skilful inside-forward Sam Ranby was in his second season with the club and Tom Fenoughty, destined to have a long career with City, made his debut. Levi Redfern, a talented half-back recruited from Denaby, was transferred to Huddersfield late in the campaign.

There were some high-scoring performances in the League. Alfreton Town were beaten 7-0 at Fulfordgate, with Len Duckham netting five goals. Flood hit four goals in a six-goal win over Ilkeston and he also grabbed a hat-trick in a 7-1 thrashing of Wath Athletic. The same player also netted three in a 4-4 draw at home to Heanor Town. Another hat-trick scorer was Clayton against Wombwell (7-1). The team suffered only one League defeat at Fulfordgate and that was to runaway champions Scunthorpe United. A young local outside-left, Ron Clancey, made his debut on New Year's Day in 1927 in a home game against Sutton Town. He scored the only goal of the match, but then broke his ankle and, sadly, never played again.

It was, however, the FA Cup run of 1926-7 which put the club on a sound basis. For the first time City were switched geographically from South to North Yorkshire in the qualifying stages. In the early rounds Guisborough Belmont, South Bank and Whitby United were disposed of and then in the fourth qualifying round City entered a bigger geographical area and were drawn away to Ilkeston. They swept to a 5-1 victory, and in the competition proper for the first time in their history, they were drawn at home to Worksop. A 4-1 success in front of 3,500 at Fulfordgate sent City into the second round and a trip to Second Division Grimsby Town. After a tremendous tussle, City lost narrowly, 2-1 in front of 11,000 fans, paying receipts of £750. The demand grew for Third Division football and in 1927 the club made its first serious attempt for election to the Football League. They received much encouragement from outside sources.

Wilf Meek, who was a sports journalist on the staff of the *Yorkshire Evening Press*, reported on City's activities from the club's inauguration in 1922 until his retirement in 1968. For many years he used the pseudonym 'Citizen'. In later years he became a club director. York City received much publicity and support through the columns of the *Yorkshire Evening Press*. In turn Meek received many letters of encouragement from notable football personalities including Ivan Sharpe the editor of the *Athletic News* and from Charles Buchan, the famous Arsenal and England inside-forward.

The application was not successful, however, and both retiring clubs, Barrow and Accrington Stanley, were re-elected. City received only six votes, but at the club's AGM in July the club were able to give an optimistic report. For the first time the balance sheet showed a surplus of income (£850) over expenditure. Gate

City circulated League clubs in May 1927 with the following letter asking for support:

York City Association Football & Athletic Club, Ltd.

(Members of the Midland Counties Football League and Yorkshire League)

Telephone:
Ground: FULFORD, 43.
(During Match).

Secretary:
G. W. SHERRINGTON.

Ground: FULFORDGATE.

Registered Office:
37, MARKET STREET,
YORK.

13th May, 1927.

Dear Sir,

Our application for admission to the Third Division of The Football League – Northern Section has been forwarded to Mr. Charnley, and we give below a few particulars to enable you to judge our merit.

This City itself has a population of 85,000 exclusive of the military, and the area served by the 2d. tram route covers more than 100,000 population. There are not six towns larger that are represented in the Northern Section.

There is no Football League Club nearer than Leeds 26 miles, Darlington 45 miles, Sheffield 50 miles, Hull 45 miles, so that there is no counter attraction to our matches if we are elected. There are a number of smaller towns and villages near at hand from whom we can expect a measure of support if we can provide League Football.

The excellent railway facilities, are a feature in our favour. There is no other place in the section so well situated. There are a number of first class hotels in the City.

Our ground is the property of the Club, splendidly drained, well equipped, spacious and capable of being extended to hold any number up to 40,000 spectators. It is our intention to carry out necessary improvements during the Summer.

The Club is controlled by a popularly elected Board of Directors comprising business men of experience.

For five seasons we have been members of the Midland League and have earned a name for always playing attractive football.

This season we have had an excellent team, having lost only nine League matches, whilst in the second round of the F. A. Cup we played at Grimsby Town to lose 2. – 1.

We honestly believe our Club would be a credit to the League.

We hope you will give us your support, and if we are elected you will have nothing to regret.

Charles Buchan wrote as follows:

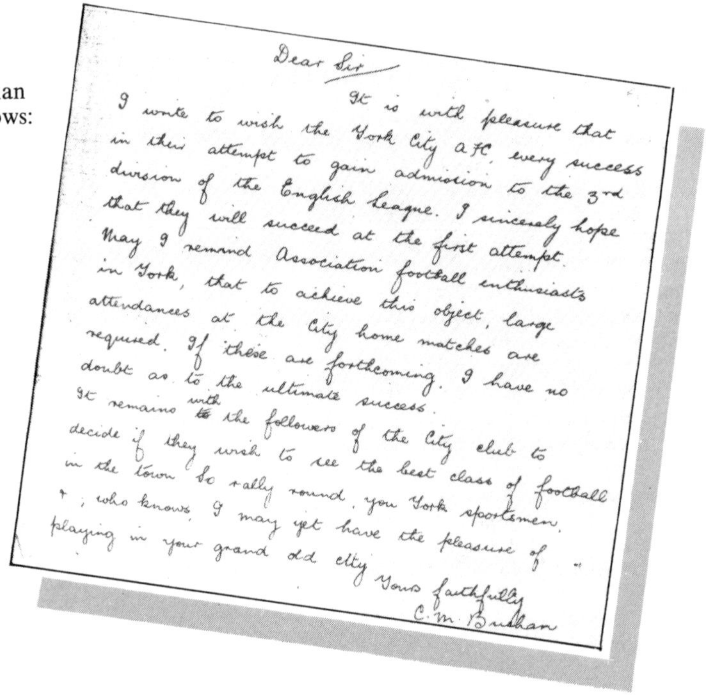

Dear Sir

It is with pleasure that I write to wish the York City A.F.C. every success in their attempt to gain admission to the 3rd division of the English League. I sincerely hope that they will succeed at the first attempt.

May I remind Association football enthusiasts in York, that to achieve this object, large attendances at the City home matches are required. If these are forthcoming. I have no doubt as to the ultimate success.

It remains with the followers of the City club to decide if they wish to see the best class of football in the town. So rally round, you York sportsmen, & who knows, I may yet have the pleasure of playing in your grand old city.

Yours faithfully
C. M. Buchan

receipts for 1926-7 were £2,783 compared with £1,776 for the previous year. One interesting item of expenditure was police charges £3 12s! Considerable improvements, with the co-operation of the Supporters' Club were in hand at the Fulfordgate ground. Summing up, the directors expressed great optimism regarding the club's future and quoting from the report — 'The club has weathered stormy seas and pulled through to calmer waters. Well established York City need not fear the coming years'.

After the excitement and progress made in 1926-7 the following season was a little disappointing, although the side finished a very creditable seventh in the League. The outstanding performance in the League was a remarkable 7-1 win away to Nottingham Forest Reserves in March. City also beat Heanor 7-1 at home, with Hammerton scoring four. There was a controversial game away to Mansfield in January 1928 when City played with only nine men for 75 minutes. Goalkeeper George Crowther was carried off injured and then Tom Fenoughty was sent off. Mansfield won 5-1 and later in the season Town completed the double with a 5-2 win at York. In the FA Cup they were knocked out in the fourth qualifying round replay at home to Shildon. In an earlier round they had been drawn against

Scarborough, who were in their first season of Midland League football. The tie at Fulfordgate attracted tremendous interest and a record crowd of 6,422 (with receipts of £311) saw a 1-1 draw on 15 October 1927. In the replay at Scarborough, watched by 4,073, City won surprisingly easily by 4-0. City relied chiefly on the players who appeared the previous year, but two promising youngsters who sprang to the fore were George Crowther (goalkeeper) and Dunnington-born Jack Everest. In May 1928 these two players were snapped up by Stockport County. That summer City made another bid for League status. With only seven votes they again failed, but Carlisle United were successful at the expense of Durham City.

Arthur Brown again became chairman and he was to hold this position until 1939. Brown had a lifelong interest in soccer and had taken up refereeing in 1894 in the Middlesbrough area. He was appointed secretary of the Middlesbrough League and then, when he moved to Otley at the beginning of the century, he refereed in the Leeds and Bradford area. He came to York in 1905 and continued his 'whistling' taking charge of local cup finals over the years. He went on to complete over 30 seasons as a referee. In 1908 he assisted in the formation of the original York City amateur club and was the first chairman of that organization for a short period. He helped form the present City club and served as a director for 20 years, most of these as chairman. He was also involved for many years on the executive of the York and District Referees Association. In June 1928 the York City Supporters' Club were able to announce at their annual meeting that they had a record membership of 632, with receipts of £837. During the 1927-8 season they had been able to donate £325 to the City club and, in the six years of its existence the Supporters' Club had handed over £1,250 to the parent body. At the time the officials of the Supporters' Club were Arthur Russell (chairman), H. Ward (secretary) and the committee members were Messrs Taylor, Barnes, Dunn, Dungate, Deighton, Houghton, Hardcastle, Innes, Morton, Marshall, Pinder, Pearson, Shepherd, Shaw, Thompson, Topping, Temple, McAdams, Pratt, Ledward, Trebich and Waite.

Although disappointed at their failure to get into the Football League, City planned ahead and in the summer of 1928 appointed John 'Jock' Collier, the former Hull City and Queen's Park Rangers half-back, as player-manager. Scotsman Collier recruited no fewer than seven players from over the border, most notably centre-forward Jimmy Cowie from Raith Rovers. His scoring feats in the last season of Midland League football were legendary. In 49 League games he totalled 49 goals and was top marksman in the Midland League. The cry of 'Give it to Cowie' became a slogan at Fulfordgate. Twice he scored six goals, once five and twice four. In one sequence of seven games in January-February 1929 he scored in every match, netting a total of 17 goals. At the end of the season he was selected for the Rest of the Midland League against the champions, Mansfield Town, as was outside-left Dicky Merritt. Also outstanding that season was Sam Charnley, a centre-half signed from Wolves. A skilful left-half was Johnny Duthie, who had been with Collier at QPR. The club finished ninth in that last season with a total of 50 League games in the newly extended Midland League. No shortage of goals, thanks chiefly to Cowie. The biggest score was 8-2 against bottom-of-the-table Worksop Town. What was to prove the last non-League game for the club was against Gainsborough Trinity, at Fulfordgate on 1 May 1929. Duthie scored the only goal but, to the disappointment of all concerned, Jimmy Cowie failed to get his 50th goal of the season, although according to all reports it certainly was not for the want of trying.

It was the FA Cup which again provided the real excitement. City won their way to the fourth qualifying round and at this stage they had three tremendous tilts with Jarrow. The tie went to a third meeting which was staged at St James' Park, Newcastle, and a crowd of 6,843 saw City win through 3-2. In the first round the club were drawn at home to Third Division Barrow — the first time they had entertained a League club in a competitive match. The attendance of 6,957 (receipts £352) set new club records and the visitors rather luckily scraped home 1-0. The end of the season saw the departure of Jack Middlemiss, who for six seasons had been first choice at right-half. He had given splendid service, travelling from Durham for every game, and he became the first City player to be rewarded with a benefit. Middlesbrough sent a team for the occasion and Jack received a cheque for £111.

City's bid for Third Division football grew stronger and on 24 April 1929 they derived great encouragement when Northern Section clubs, meeting in Manchester, voted that City be elected and Hartlepool re-elected. Although this only recommended the change to First and Second Division clubs, City's hopes were considerably boosted.

In making what was their fourth bid for League status, York City stressed the following points. They owned their own ground which could accommodate 17,000 spectators. Revenue for 1928-9 was almost £5,000 and York was one of the largest places not represented in the Football League. On 3 June 1929 the York City delegation of Messrs D.A.Pratt, H.Rusholme, J.Fisher, G.H.Douglas and G.W.Sherrington made the journey to London for the League meeting in optimistic mood.

The voting for the Northern Section resulted as follows:

Hartlepools United	33 votes
York City	24 votes
Mansfield Town	16 votes
Ashington	14 votes
Manchester Central	2 votes
Prescot Cables	1 vote

Chester, Rhyl and Workington received no support.

So City took the place of Ashington in the Third Division North and, seven years after being told by John McKenna to go back and work, had achieved their great ambition.

The news was received with great enthusiasm. The Lord Mayor of York (Councillor Rymer) telegraphed his congratulations to the York directors at the Hotel Imperial, London, and York MP, F.Burgess, sent his tribute. After the declaration of the result, the York deputation received further congratulation messages especially from representatives of Yorkshire clubs.

The seventh annual meeting of the club was held on 17 July 1929. Seconding the adoption of the report director D.A.Pratt said that the optimism which had been expressed at the last annual meeting had been well justified. York City had been regarded as the most attractive team in the Midland League. By admission to the Football League they were creating history in the ancient City of York. He thought there was a good deal more optimism ahead and every incentive to them to work hard.

The list of directors and officials at York City at the time of their joining the Football League was as follows:

President	Capt H.Whitworth, MFH
Chairman	A.Brown
Directors	Messrs G.H.Douglas, J.Fisher, H.Hayhurst, W.Mason, D.A.Pratt, N.Pratt, G.E.Robinson, J.W.Rosindale, H.Rusholme, G.W.Sherrington, Councillor J.Wilkinson
Hon Secretary	G.W.Sherrington
Manager	J.Collier

The summer of 1929 was a very busy time for the club as they prepared for League soccer. Manager Collier recruited virtually a new team as the Midland League stalwarts departed. Of the side that opened a new era for City as they kicked off their Football League career on 31 August 1929, only Jimmy Cowie had played for City the previous season.

The team that lined up at Wigan Borough that memorable day was as follows:

Jack Farmery (goalkeeper): Signed from Doncaster Rovers having previously been with Hull City and Bradford City.

David Archibald (right-back): Joined the club from Morton.

Sam Johnson (left-back): Previously with Stoke City and Swindon Town.

Harry Beck (right-half): An England junior international player who had been with Walsall and Barrow.

Charlie Davis (centre-half): Signed from Torquay United having started his career with Bath City.

Oliver Thompson (left-half): Captain of the side and formerly with Chesterfield and QPR.

Sam Evans (outside-right): A Scot who had played most of his football in his native land before joining Reading from whom he was signed by City.

Wally Gardner (inside-right): Very experienced forward who had gained England Amateur honours before going on to play for Derby County, Spennymoor United, QPR, Darlington and Torquay United.

Jimmy Cowie (centre-forward): The scoring hero of 1928-9. Signed from Raith Rovers in the summer of 1928.

Tom Smiles (inside-left): Joined the club during the summer of 1929 from local junior soccer.

Reg Stockill (outside-left): Local youngster who was drafted into the side at the last minute owing to an injury to Willie Millar.

In front of a crowd of 8,880 at Springfield Park, City gained a famous 2-0 victory. Scorer of their first-ever Football League goal was Stockill. Born in York on 23 November 1913, he was only 15 years and 281 days old and remains the youngest player to appear for the club in a senior competitive match. He had attended Poppleton Road School and was an England Schoolboy international. He was destined to play only one other League game for the club and that by coincidence was on the opening day of the following season. In 1931 he moved to Scarborough and later was transferred by the Seasiders to Arsenal for a fee of £850, plus £300 if he played in the first team at Highbury. He did just that playing alongside Alex James, Eddie Hapgood and the other local lad made good, Joe Hulme. In 1934 he was signed by Derby County, who then boasted such stars as Sammy Crooks and Hughie Gallacher in their team. He joined Luton Town three years later and his professional career ended just after the war owing to injury. He later played in local football for Ainsty Builders and worked for British Rail. City's other goal at Wigan was appropriately netted by the scoring machine, Jimmy Cowie. The little Scot, however, was unable to reproduce his scoring feats in the months ahead.

The Athletic News summed up City's performance as follows:

'York City justified their election to the Northern Section not only by a win at Wigan, but by their play.

'On their display against Wigan Boro' York City should do well in the Northern Section. Well endowed with physique, they can play the robust kind of game which counts for much in this competition, and they have skill, too.

'In Farmery they have a goalkeeper of more than average ability, and in Archibald and Johnson a fine pair of full-backs, who can tackle and kick with equal facility. Altogether it is a defence which will be a match for the best of attacks.

'The half-back line is more a spoiling force than constructive. Davies, the ex-Torquay man — 6ft 1in and 13st 7lb — is a player who, though not polished, is very effective.

'The attack is speedy and thrustful and always alive to a chance. Evans and Gardner are a dangerous right-wing pair, and Stockill, the outside-left, is always ready to cut in and have a shot'.

The Sunday Despatch reported:

'York City, the newly-elected Third Division Northern Section side, made a great start when they beat Wigan Borough at Wigan by two clear goals. York gave a capital display, showing dash and fearlessness in attack, and a sturdy defence. York well deserved their first points'.

City's first home match was on 4 September against Wrexham and a crowd of 8,726, paying receipts of £433, saw a goalless draw. The club had a very satisfactory debut season in the League and finished in sixth position (it was to remain their highest League placing until the early 1950s). They drew as many as 16 League games and undoubtedly their chief strength was a very strong defence. The half-back line of Harry Beck, Charlie Davies and Oliver Thomson was outstanding and they only missed four games between them.

Other players who figured prominently in that historic first League campaign were:

Billy Bottrill (inside-right): Formerly with Middlesbrough, Nelson and Rotherham United, he topped the scoring charts that season. In a 4-0 win over Wigan Borough at Fulfordgate on 28 December 1929 he recorded the first League hat-trick for the club. At the end of the season he was transferred to Wolverhampton Wanderers where he had a good deal of success.

Willie Millar (outside-left): A much travelled Glaswegian who had seen service with Hearts, Ayr United, Rhyl and Middlesbrough, before signing for City. A very fast and direct winger.

Jack Brooks (right-back): Experienced defender who had previously been with Fulham, Darlington and Nelson.

Tom Fenoughty, who had made his City debut in 1926-7, also played his part that season and made 30 League appearances, scoring 15 goals.

The reserve side, still operating in the Yorkshire League, fielded a number of promising local youngsters, one of them being a right-back by the name of Jack Pinder, who was to have a long and distinguished career with the club.

The biggest win of the season was a six-goal success over Rochdale, whilst the biggest Fulfordgate crowd was 10,120 on Easter Monday, 2 April 1930, to see the Third Division North champions elect, Port Vale, win 2-0. The match between the sides at Burslem on Good Friday had drawn an attendance of 15,346.

Not for the first time, and certainly not the last, the highlight of the season was provided by the FA Cup. City had to compete in the fourth qualifying round of the competition and were drawn to visit Scarborough. An attendance of 8,089 (receipts £446) saw City record a 3-1 victory. In 'Boro's team were the York brothers George and Tom Maskill. In the first round Tom Fenoughty was the hero against Tranmere Rovers. He netted both goals in a 2-2 home draw and then scored the winner at Prenton Park. At the next stage City had to travel to pastures new when they were drawn to visit Southern Section club Southend United. Again Fenoughty produced the goods when he bagged a brace in a remarkable 4-1 success. City were rewarded in round three with a trip to First Division giants Newcastle United.

Saturday, 11 January 1930 goes down as one of the first red letter days in York City's history. What was described as 'the great exodus to Tyneside of 5,000 exuberant and boisterous Yorkshire spirits' witnessed a remarkable City display. The match, watched by 38,674, produced gate receipts of £2,440 and was played in dreadful conditions. A severe snowstorm almost obliterated the line markings and the surface was treacherous. The ball was very heavy, but the game was played at a fast and thrilling pace. City, playing a direct open game, had the edge in the first half and were unlucky not to take the lead in the 20th minute when Gardner hit the post with a fine shot. Farmery made fine saves to thwart Hughie Gallacher and Andy Cunningham and then Gardner was foiled by United's 'keeper, McInroy. Newcastle opened the scoring just before the interval when Gallacher headed home a Sam Weaver cross. City defended stoutly early in the second half and then in the 61st minute drew level with a magnificent goal scored by Wally Gardner. He collected a pass from Sam Johnson and burst through United's defence, finishing with a fine right-foot shot from 12 yards. In the closing stages the First Division side threw everything into attack but City's defence, with Farmery and Davis outstanding, held firm and at the final whistle the team received a great ovation. Crowds clamoured round the entrance to the dressing-rooms. Supporters pursued them to the Station Hotel and then saw them depart back to York on the seven o'clock train. As described at the time 'these happy undaunted enthusiasts then went back into the Tyneside City and revelled in the gayest spirits'. When the team arrived back in York there were a thousand people there to greet them amidst scenes of great enthusiasm at the railway station. The Football League babes had held a team of seven internationals and shown outstanding team spirit and determination.

The replay at Fulfordgate on 15 January attracted tremendous interest. Less than eight years since the club's formation they were entertaining First Division opposition and all the stand seats had been sold within 30 minutes of them going on sale. The gates were closed an hour before the start with many locked out, including over 700 Newcastle supporters who had arrived too late. The playing conditions were vastly different to those at St James' Park and the pitch, although a little on the soft side, had made a good recovery from heavy rain. City started the match at a tremendous pace and threatened to overrun their famous opponents. After Tom Fenoughty missed an easy chance from ten yards City, to the great delight of the home supporters, took the lead in the 23rd minute. Good work by Thompson and Millar set up the chance for Sam Evans who shot the ball into the net. Newcastle struggled to get into the game but in the 36th minute equalized when Gallacher, with one of his famous and remarkable leaps, headed a Hutchinson free-kick past Farmery. In the second half City ran out of steam and the 'Magpies' began to dominate the game. In the 66th minute Davis fouled Gallacher and a penalty was awarded. The Scottish international took the spot-kick but his shot was parried by Farmery and Gallacher hit the rebound wide. Within two minutes, however, Newcastle scored the decisive goal when Hutchinson netted from close range. City fought gallantly and with great credit, but the visitors went on to win and so qualified to meet Clapton Orient at home in the next round.

The attendance of 12,583 (receipts £900) set new club records. The City side was the same for both games and the teams lined up for the replay as follows:

York City: Farmery; Brooks, Johnson, Beck, Davis, Thompson, Evans, Bottrill, Gardner, Fenoughty, Millar.
Newcastle United: McInroy; Fairhurst, Thomson, McKenzie, Hill, Weaver, Hutchinson, Cunningham, Gallacher, Chalmers, Scott.

In the first game Tommy McDonald had played at inside-right for United. This clever Scottish player was later to move to City (August 1931). This cup run yielded a net profit to the club of £1,300 and for the first time all existing liabilities were wiped out. The detailed figures were:

		Attendances	Receipts
Scarborough	(a)	8,089	£446
Tranmere Rovers	(h)	5,550	£308
Tranmere Rovers	(a)	4,882	£281
Southend United	(a)	11,000	£654
Newcastle United	(a)	38,674	£2,440
Newcastle United	(h)	12,583	£900
		80,778	£5,029

A very successful season, therefore, and in the last programme of the campaign it was summed up as follows:

'We in York have reason to remember 1929-30 for in this season City attained Football League status and we realise how well the club has justified the promotion. The memorable cup-ties will never be forgotten nor will the way the team rose to the occasion in the League matches.

Meanwhile the club would like to express its thanks to all who have helped to make this season such a wonderful one. To J.Collier, for his advice and team building; to Oliver Thompson, for the way he has captained the team and earned the distinction of appearing in all games; to the players themselves for the clean, whole-hearted manner in which they have helped to lay such solid foundations in making York a League centre; and lastly, but by no means least, to Trainers Murphy and Duncombe, for the efficient and untiring way in which they have looked after the players in their charge.

To the football public we express our thanks for the wonderfully consistent support, and to all who have in any way helped towards a successful working, not forgetting the backbone of the club — the members of the Supporters' Club. We have all had a great time, a feast of good football, and, what is more important, can await the future with every confidence. Meanwhile, officials, players and supporters can take a little relaxation that has been so fully deserved'.

Total revenue for the season was £10,574, of which £7,531 was taken at Fulfordgate. One important event during that season was the appointment on 1 February 1930 of G.W.Sherrington as full-time secretary. As previously mentioned, Billy Sherrington had been one of the founder members of the club and had acted as honorary secretary since 1924. Election to the Football League had caused extra work and City had been the only club in the competition without a full-time secretary. The appointment was unanimous and was recognition of his excellent and meticulous work. Sherrington relinquished his work as a civil servant and his position as a club director. The following month Jock Collier announced that at the end of the season he was to resign as manager and take over the duties of mine host at The Punchbowl Inn, York. For the next three years Billy Sherrington combined his duties of secretary with those of manager.

City relied chiefly on the same squad of players for 1930-31. They had to be content with a mid-table position, however, averaging a point per game, but again they did well in the FA Cup. City dismissed non-League Gresley Rovers and fellow Northern Section Nelson to reach the third round where they were drawn to visit First Division Sheffield United. At the time the 'Blades' had such stars as veteran Irish international Billy Gillespie, Fred Tunstall and Jimmy Dunne. City gave a fine display at Bramall Lane and in front of 31,821 (receipts £1,932) were a shade unlucky not to win. In the first half especially, they were well in command and United's goalkeeper, Kendall, was kept busy. As one commentator said at the time, if points had been awarded as a boxing match York City would have had a big lead. United resumed in a more positive manner and in the 52nd minute opened the scoring when a centre-cum-shot from Gibson eluded Farmery and went into the net via a post. The home side were handicapped when full-back Hooper went off injured and City staged a strong finish. They deservedly drew level in the 80th minute when, following a corner, Frank Laycock drove the ball past Kendall. Both sides went near to snatching the winner in the last few minutes. City's regular half-back trio of Beck, Davis and Thompson all had outstanding games whilst Laycock and Evans were the pick of the attack.

The replay at Fulfordgate set new attendance and receipt records (12,721 and £1,059). Although City put up a plucky display, the First Division side ran out deserved winners by 2-0 with goals from Gibson and Dunne. The teams lined up for the replay as follows, with City being unchanged from the first match:

York City: Farmery; Brooks, Johnson, Beck, Davis, Thompson, Evans, Laycock, Gardner, Fenoughty, Millar.

Sheffield United: Kendall; Thorpe, Green, Sampy, Carrigan, Gooney, Gibson, Oxley, Dunne, Radford, Tunstall.

Gross revenue for this season was £8,483, with a deficit of £533. At the shareholders meeting in the summer of 1931 J.M.Knowles was elected a director in place of N.Pratt. At the meeting chairman Arthur Brown stated that the club had reached a point when they might consider themselves well established as a company and in the Football League. During that close season a number of changes were made to the playing staff and among the new arrivals was Reg Baines, who returned to the club after a spell with Scarborough. Other new signings included Peter Spooner from Bradford, Tommy McDonald and Joe Harris from Newcastle United and Tom Mitchell, ex-Newcastle and Leeds United.

This season also saw the senior debuts of Stan Fox and Ted Wass, who were to serve the club so well. Another important move was the switch of the reserve side from the Yorkshire League to the Midland League.

The new players settled in quickly and the side played consistently well. They entered the Christmas programme second in the table behind Gateshead with the following record: P 19 W 11 D 4 L 4 Pts 26.

Support proved disappointing, however, with average crowds of only around 5,000. In December the directors issued an official statement making a strong appeal for bigger attendances. It was pointed out by club officials that 'no other football centre has made the progress which has characterized the growth of York City since the club was founded in 1922. The directors feel that with slightly better support and co-operation on the part of the public York City might reach Second Division status after only three years as members of the Football League'. In return for an increase of supporters of at least 1,000 per match the directors would do everything possible to strengthen the side further and try to achieve promotion. There was to be a crowd of over 8,000 for the Boxing Day fixture at home to Doncaster, but three successive defeats over Christmas and New Year dented the promotion challenge and in the end City had again to settle for a mid-table position. Reg Baines was the hero of the season and his 29 League goals set a scoring record which was to remain until 1951-2. He netted three hat-tricks. City were involved in some high-scoring games. They beat Halifax Town 7-2 in what was to be the last League match staged at Fulfordgate but lost heavily to Crewe 8-1, Hartlepool 7-2 and Gateshead 6-0. In October 1931 Wigan Borough dropped out of the League and Rochdale finished at the foot of the table with only 11 points. Over Easter City completed a 5-2 and 5-3 double over the luckless Spotland club and Baines' personal tally from those two matches was five goals.

The League match against Carlisle United on 13 February 1932 was attended by His Grace the Archbishop of York (Dr W.Temple). The event was described as unique in the history of football, as no evidence had been found that any other

Archbishop of York or Canterbury had been to a Football League match before. There was no divine intervention, however, as City lost 4-2!

In the FA Cup, City suffered a disappointing first-round defeat away to lowly New Brighton. Lack of Cup revenue resulted in a deficit of £1,539 over the season, whilst average home crowds of only 4,000 were also a blow. This continued lack of support was one of the chief factors in the move to Bootham Crescent. (See *Homes of York City*.)

The end of the season saw the departure of stalwarts Oliver Thompson, Harry Beck and Jack Brooks, who had served the club so well in those early years of League Football.

During the season W.E.Leckenby was co-opted on to the board and at the AGM in the summer of 1932 two former directors, L.F.Lonsborough and A.H.Shaw, were re-elected. Councillor James Wilkinson, after nine years service on the board, retired owing to ill health. At the meeting the directors were commended by shareholders for the bold policy they had pursued in moving to the new ground in such a short time. With a new permanent home with modern conveniences, and capable of development, a new era had dawned for York City. The club also sported new colours — chocolate and cream striped shirts and white shorts (an association no doubt with the confectionery industry in York).

The 1932-3 campaign started with a defeat at Crewe and then, in the official opening match at Bootham Crescent, Stockport County were the visitors. Over 8,000 saw this historic game and for the record the City team was: Duckworth; Archibald, Johnson, G.Maskill, Harris, Bolton, Williams, Fenoughty, Baines, McDonald, Mitchell.

The match ended in a 2-2 draw and the scorer of City's first-ever goal at the new ground was Tom Mitchell, who was later to manage the club. Reg Baines netted the other goal from the penalty-spot. City lost the next home game to Rochdale 6-2 and went on to experience their worst season to date in the Football League. They struggled near the foot of the table for much of the campaign and only escaped having to apply for re-election on the last day of the season. A 6-1 home victory over bottom club Darlington enabled them to leapfrog on goal-average over New Brighton, who lost at home to Wrexham 2-0 that day. So the team finished with a flourish, but it had been a bitterly disappointing season.

In the FA Cup they again fell at the first hurdle when they lost at Bootham Crescent 3-1 to local rivals Scarborough. To rub salt into the wounds one of 'Boro's scorers was former City player Matt Jenkinson, who was to return to York later in the season, and the other was netted by York-born outside-left Dave Halford. The attendance was 8,958. Reg Baines had another fine season and he again scored 29 League goals. On 4 May 1933, only two days prior to the vital last game of the season, he was transferred to First Division Sheffield United for £500 and a few days later outside-left Peter Spooner followed him to Bramall Lane for a similar fee. Both of these players were eventually to return to Bootham Crescent and figure prominently in a glorious chapter that lay ahead. One of the successes of the season had been the form shown by new goalkeeper Des Fawcett, who had previously been with Darlington, Nelson and Preston North End. Joe Harris also did well in the centre of defence, whilst Jack Pinder established himself at right-back in the second half of the season. The Maskill brothers had returned to the club, but George's appearances were limited to only three matches. Many of the players were released at the end of the term, including full-backs Sam Johnson and David Archibald, who had served the club so well since 1929. Johnson later returned as second team trainer.

The death was announced in April 1933 of the club's president, Sir John Hunt. The club expressed their sense of deep loss to a generous man who had taken an active interest in the club. Subsequent presidents in the pre-war period were Lord Milton MFH and Viscount Halifax. Financially 1932-3 had been a bad one. The deficit on the season was £624 and, with the cost of the removal to the new ground, the total adverse balance carried forward was £3,388. In May 1933 it was decided to reappoint Jock Collier as team manager and he was given the task of rebuilding the side and reviving the club's fortunes. During the close season a number of new signings were made, including Maurice Dando, a centre-forward from Bristol Rovers and half-backs Ted Hathway from Bolton and Stan Wilcockson from Dartford. A fee was paid to Coventry City for inside-forward Walter Lax and another forward, George Ivory, was acquired from Millwall. Last but not least City signed a tall, well-built centre-half from Barnsley by the name of Tom Lockie. He was to have a big influence in the years ahead at York.

Results improved in 1933-4 and the club finished in 12th position, but overall the season was a little disappointing. New men Dando and Hathway scored 39 League goals between them. Three times City netted six goals, twice against Rochdale who again found themselves at the foot of the League. The season's biggest blow was in the FA Cup when Hartlepools United won 3-2 at Bootham Crescent in the first round. It was the third successive season that City had fallen at the first stage. Once again, of course, this was another severe blow to the club's finances and the deficit amounted on the season's workings to £2,051, with a total indebtedness of £5,446. There were a number of changes to the personnel at the end of this rather moderate campaign and one of the players with whom the club reluctantly parted with was Tom Fenoughty. He had spent eight seasons with City, serving the club well in the Midland and Football League and at Fulfordgate and Bootham Crescent. In total he made 252 League and cup appearances and notched 104 goals.

York City Reserves pictured prior to a North Riding Senior Cup tie against Scarborough at Bootham Crescent on 19 December 1936. Back row (left to right): S. Fox, S. Fearnley, T. Lockie, G. Denholme, S. Milton, H. Young, J. Whitelaw. Front: J. Nicol, G. Lee, A. Gray, S. Gledhill, Mascot 'Jimmy'.

As an economy measure it was decided to switch the reserve side back to the Yorkshire League for the forthcoming 1934-5 season. This saved considerably on travelling costs. At the AGM in the summer of 1934 a good deal of anxiety was expressed regarding the finances. Some shareholders expressed the view that the club was now carrying a lot of extra overhead charges at the new ground which they could not afford. The directors stated, however, that the club had had two extraordinary years of expense following the move and also much-needed FA Cup revenue had been minimal. They were confident that the move to Bootham Crescent would prove of great benefit to the club in the years ahead. The chairman said that the widening of the road as an approach to the ground would greatly facilitate the arrival and departure of spectators. The improvement was being done at no cost to the club. Brown also expressed the directors appreciation of the work of the Supporters' Club who were now well on the way to paying for the Popular Stand. The stand had cost £1,500 and the supporters had now raised over £950. Retiring directors Messrs G.W.Halliday, W.E.Leckenby and H.Rusholme were all re-elected but J.M.Knowles did not seek re-election. At the annual meeting of the Supporters' Club the Hon Secretary, H.Ward, announced that membership had dropped from a record 1,100 the previous season to 638. One suggestion to increase membership was to reduce the annual subscription from 1s 3d (6½p) to 1s (5p).

Jock Collier's new recruits for 1934-5 included a new captain in Jack Eyres, an experienced inside-forward from Bristol Rovers, and goalkeeper Joe Cunningham from QPR. Bill Routledge, a powerfully-built centre-half, was also signed from Bristol Rovers and Fred Speed, equally at home at half-back or up front, had previously been on the books of Hull City. The side had a mixed season in the League and finally had to be content with 15th position. Maurice Dando again showed good scoring form and twice hit hat-tricks — in a 5-0 victory over Rotherham United and a 7-0 thrashing of Carlisle United. This latter win was to remain City's record League victory until February 1957. Another high-scoring game was a 7-3 success over Crewe Alexandra.

After three barren years the club again experienced some thrills and excitement in the FA Cup. In the first round they were drawn away to non-League club Burton Town. The game was an exciting, and at times explosive, affair. The small ground was packed to capacity and Burton started at a tremendous pace which put City under great pressure. In the 23rd minute the non-League side took the lead, but within four minutes City equalized through a Ted Hathway penalty after Dando had been fouled. Play was tense and the tackling very hard and as the players left the field at half-time there was a scuffle which included some spectators. Two quick goals midway through the second half kept the game at boiling point. Town took the lead again, but City equalized within a minute when Evan Jenkins headed a George Bowater cross into the net. City were generally on top in the closing stages but Routledge had to make one goal-line clearance. There were further crowd scenes and a policeman was placed behind the York goal to provide Cunningham with protection. With two minutes remaining, City snatched a dramatic winner through Bowater after a Dando shot had rebounded to him. The goal was disputed for offside and at the end of the game hundreds of spectators swarmed on to the pitch and the referee was attacked. The Burton secretary was injured as he tried to protect the official, G.Dutton from Warwick. At least two arrests were made and as described in Press reports 'it was a disgusting final scene as players and officials tried with the utmost difficulty to reach the dressing rooms'. The Burton ground was later closed for a period by the Football Association.

In the second round, New Brighton were beaten at Bootham Crecent thanks to a fine goal by Fred Speed and the reward was a home draw against Derby County. First Division County had three international stars in their attack — wingers Sammy

Crooks and Dally Duncan and Hughie Gallacher at centre-forward who once again crossed swords with City. Former City youngster Reg Stockill, now at the Baseball Ground, missed the match through injury. It was the first big game to be staged at Bootham Crescent and a record crowd of 13,612 (receipts £1,040) were present. City put up a fine effort and defended stoutly with Routledge and Stan Fox outstanding. Cunningham also had a fine game in goal. The attack did not get many chances, although Dando always posed a threat. Derby's pressure told, however, and in the 87th minute their outstanding player, Crooks, shot the winner from six yards. The teams lined up that day:

York City: Cunningham; Pinder, Wass, Fox, Routledge, Speed, Jenkins, Eyres, Dando, Hathway, Bullock.

Derby County: Kirby; Udall, Collin, Nicholas, Barker, Hann, Crooks, Groves, Gallacher, Ramage, Duncan.

City's left winger that day, Arthur Bullock, was an amateur player from Hull who made a handful of appearances for the club. He was an amateur international.

At the end of the season Maurice Dando was transferred to Chesterfield and he helped the 'Spires' to promotion to the Second Division in 1935-6. A number of other players received free transfers. The balance sheet showed a deficit of £229 which was an improvement on the previous years figure. Expenditure had been reduced by £1,400 with savings being achieved in wages, travelling expenses etc. An analysis was given on how the gate receipts of £1,040 for the Derby County cup tie were allocated.

Entertainment Tax £173, printing, posting and advertising £6. Referee and linesmen £8, police £5, visitors' fares £12, sundry expenses £4. This left £415 for both City and Derby. W.H.Sessions, who had recently been co-opted on to the board, suggested that the 'football habit' had still to be cultivated in the city. Discussions also took place regarding the establishment of a trust fund with the idea of purchasing the Bootham Crescent ground before the lease ran out in 1953.

D.A.Pratt, who had been associated with the club since its inception, relinquished his seat on the board owing to business reasons.

The 1935-6 season was a very poor one. Not only did York struggle in the lower reaches of the Northern section throughout the campaign, finally finishing in 19th position, but they were also swept out of the FA Cup by Burton Town. The Derbyshire non-Leaguers gained a sensational 5-1 victory at Bootham Crescent in the first round and thus gained more than full revenge for their home defeat 12 months earlier. It was a black day for City — 30 November 1935 — and as described in reports 'a crowd of 6,182 watched almost mesmerized as Burton banged in the goals'. There were a few more black days that season as City suffered some heavy defeats in the League. Chester (a) 12-0 their record loss, Walsall (a) 6-0, Accrington (a) 7-2, Rotherham (a) and Mansfield (a) both 5-0 and Oldham (a) 6-2. The 95 goals conceded that season has only been exceeded once in their history (106 — 1965-6).

Peter Spooner had returned from Sheffield United in the summer of 1935 and he was an ever present on the left wing that season along with right winger Harry Green, who had been signed from Bristol City. Another personality at the time was Duncan Lindsay, an experienced Scottish campaigner who joined City from Northampton and added some punch to the attack. An interesting character, he was said to know 'every trick in the book'. The loss on the season's workings was £1,352 and the total debt now stood at £7,048. The annual report stated that 'the revenue from League games was insufficient to pay the wages of the playing staff. Increased support from the public must be forthcoming if the club is to retain its Football League status. It was impossible to cut expenses any further if a reasonable state of efficiency was to be maintained'. Individual directors continued to dip into their pockets to help things along. In June 1936, the club launched a 'Shilling Fund' appeal which was inaugurated by the Lord Mayor, W.H.Shaw. Weekly publicity of subscription lists appeared in the *Evening Press* and tremendous work was done by the Supporters' Club in organizing collections and over a period of months a useful sum of money was raised.

No fewer than ten players were given free transfers in May 1936 and come the start of 1936-7 there were several new faces. Goalkeeper Norman Wharton was signed from Doncaster Rovers, half-back Dick Duckworth from Rotherham United and ex-Crystal Palace inside-forward Malcolm Comrie — three players who were to play a big part in the glory days that lay not too far ahead. Promising local youngster George Lee was snapped up on his 17th birthday and a right winger, Alf Agar, came from Oldham.

In the summer of 1936 the club announced the appointment of Tom Lockie as trainer and coach to the reserve team — so started 31 years of outstanding service that he was to give to York City as trainer, coach and manager. Upon leaving City as a player in 1934 he had short spells with Accrington Stanley and Mansfield Town before returning to live and make his home in New Earswick near York. For the third time in their history the club colours were changed and they now sported red jerseys with white collars, white shorts and red stockings.

The season got off to a bright start and they were unbeaten in the first six League games. The visit of Chester on 19 September 1936 drew a crowd of 10,629, paying receipts of £480, which set a new League record for the club. The overall form was a little inconsistent, however, and the final position of 12th fell a little below expectations.

In October 1936 a well-built and powerful centre-forward moved to City from Bradford. Welshman Albert Thompson, who had been a regular soldier, created an immediate impact and went on to score 28 goals in 29 League and cup games. City hit the FA Cup trail this season — a prelude of things to come — and for

City players taking a training stroll in 1936. The dog handlers are Ted Hathway and Eddie Legge.

the first time they reached the fourth round of the competition. They started at the first hurdle with a convincing 5-2 victory over Hull City, with Agar hitting a hat-trick.

In the second round they were once again drawn to visit Southend United — almost seven years to the day since their previous visit to Roots Hall. Manager of Southend at the time was David Jack, a former Arsenal player and scorer of the first FA Cup final goal at Wembley for Bolton back in 1923. A thrilling and exciting game ended 3-3 with Southend equalizing in the 85th minute. For the replay at Bootham Crescent, United fielded at left-back Jack Everest. Born in Dunnington, he had played for City in the Midland League days in 1927-8. He arrived at Southend via Stockport, Blackpool, Rochdale and Cardiff. The replay was a hard-fought affair won by City with a Peter Spooner goal in extra-time.

City were involved in another Yorkshire derby at the next stage — away to Second Division Bradford City. This was the first time that they had met a club from that division. Personality of the Paraders side was centre-half Sam Cowan, who had captained Manchester City in the 1933 and 1934 FA Cup finals. A big following of nearly 3,000 fans made the journey to Valley Parade and they saw City stage a tremendous fight-back to draw 2-2 after being two goals behind after half an hour. Just before the interval, Comrie shot a fine 20-yard goal to reduce the arrears. On the resumption City put the home side under tremendous pressure and fully deserved their 70th-minute equalizer when Spooner headed a Pinder free-kick into the net. City came near to winning the tie near the end and fully deserved their draw.

A Bradford newspaper report read 'York City deserved all the credit that can be given them upon a grand and clean fight together with the skill of their play which accompanied it. The great battle that York fought in the second half was something that will live in the memory. There is no doubt at all that for the greater part of this period they were the better more spirited and more assertive side. From every point of view York thoroughly earned their replay chance and Bradford City obviously have a tremendous task to proceed further in the tournament'.

Albert Thompson, who had missed the game because of 'flu, returned for the replay but early in the game he received an injury which reduced his effectiveness. Undeterred City went on to record a famous victory with an 87th-minute goal scored by Jim Nicol. The club had reached the fourth round of the FA Cup and for the first time had beaten opposition from a higher division. City's reward was a long trip to Swansea Town, also of the Second Division. The game at the Vetch Field was played under terrible conditions. Heavy rain fell throughout the 90 minutes, turning the snow covered pitch into a muddy morass. The markings were washed out and pools of water were everywhere. The referee inspected the pitch at the interval and decided to continue, although conditions were near farcical. In the first half Swansea put tremendous pressure on the City defence but, with Wharton and Wass outstanding, the visitors held on. After the interval the game was more even.

In the closing stages conditions could hardly have been worse and the players could hardly kick the ball more than three or four yards. Amazingly the game was completed and City had gained a memorable draw. Players from both sides were exhausted at the end and Stan Fox collapsed in the dressing-rooms. In view of the ordeal, the City party cancelled the all-night journey home and stayed at a Swansea hotel. This draw at Swansea maintained City's remarkable away record in the FA Cup. Since 1929 they had only lost once in 11 ties — that was at New Brighton in 1931-2.

Albert Thompson, who had missed the match at Swansea, was fit for the replay and again the teams were faced with a heavy, gruelling pitch. The visitors took an early lead, but City fought back to equalize after 35 minutes with a Ted Hathway header. After the interval City got on top and Town's goalkeeper, Moore, made a number of outstanding saves. Ten minutes from the end, however, Swansea scored against the run of play and then notched a third goal on the final whistle. Sunderland beat Swansea in the fifth round and the Rokermen went on to win the FA Cup that season. The Cup run had grossed receipts of £4,666 and at the end of the day a profit of £1,088 helped reduce the overall debt.

Two players who appeared in the first team in the closing weeks of the season were right winger Fred Scott from Bradford and teenager George Lee. During this period two directors died — S.M.Gawthorne, who sadly did not live to see the establishment of the Social Club at the ground which was his brainchild, and G.W.Halliday who was so instrumental in the move to Bootham Crescent. In March 1937 Collier announced that he had decided to leave football to go into a business partnership with a younger brother in his native Scotland. Tom Mitchell, the former Newcastle, Leeds and City outside-left was appointed manager and the club prepared for the new season ahead.

As replacement for Thompson, who had moved to Swansea, City brought back Reg Baines to Bootham Crescent for what was his third spell with the club. After a couple of seasons at Bramall Lane he had helped Doncaster Rovers gain promotion to the Second Division. Claude Barrett, a full-back from Port Vale and Sam Earl, a winger from Bury, were newcomers but basically the team was the same as had done well the previous season.

The memorable events of 1937-8 firmly put the name of York City on the football map. The famous FA Cup run to the quarter-finals is dealt with in another chapter. It was a record-breaking year with attendance records and receipts broken at every stage, culminating in the 28,123 that saw the sixth-round tie against Huddersfield — a Bootham Crescent record that will remain for all time. In the League they started quite well, but four successive defeats in October were a set-back. Then followed a run of 17 League games, nine of which were won and six drawn. When

The winning goal against Middlesbrough in the fifth round of the FA Cup in 1938 scored by Peter Spooner (out in picture).

they were finally knocked out of the FA Cup at the beginning of March, City were on the fringe of the promotion race with games in hand on all their rivals. In the closing weeks the side faltered however, and finishing with five successive defeats the final position was 11th. Reg Baines had lost none of his scoring skill and he topped the charts with 23 League goals. Undoubtedly the strength of the side was in defence, particularly at half-back where Dick Duckworth, Ted Wass and Ted Hathway were a tower of strength. Profit from the FA Cup run amounted to £3,518 and the overall deficit was reduced to £3,674. There was also success for the reserve team that season when they won the Yorkshire League Championship. During the year J.A.Wright was co-opted on to the board. He was to be chiefly responsible for the club carrying on in the early war years, but sadly died in 1943 at the age of 40. At the end of the season Stan Fox, who had served the club so well as a utility player for seven years, retired and he was rewarded with a benefit game.

City retained nearly all their Cup heroes for the 1938-9 campaign. Only Reg Baines, who could not agree terms and went to Halifax Town, and Malcolm Comrie departed from the Bootham Crescent scene. As replacement for Baines a former Blackburn Rovers centre-forward, Bob Mortimer, was signed and he was to prove quite a prolific scorer with 22 League goals. Early in the season he scored in five successive games as City made a reasonable start. A disastrous sequence, however, of seven successive defeats in October and November resulted in a long struggle to avoid having to seek re-election. A win in their penultimate game at Darlington saved that indignity but it had been a very disappointing season and some very heavy defeats were suffered. Crewe Alexandra (a) 8-2, Bradford City (a) 6-0, Oldham (a) 6-0 while Rochdale won 7-0 at Bootham Crescent to inflict on City their biggest ever home defeat.

The reliable Ted Hathway was an ever present whilst wing-men Fred Scott and the ever-improving George Lee did well. A promising young player by the name of Bert Brenen won his place in the first team in the closing weeks of the season. He was to be an influential figure in the early post-war period with the club. As reward for their FA Cup feats of the previous season they were exempt until the

City players and officials outside the Hotel Rotterdam on their visit to Holland in October 1938.

third round of the competition. No glory this campaign, however, as Second Division Millwall swept City out by five goals at Bootham Crescent. The Lions centre-forward, McLeod, scored four of his side's goals.

Another reward for their Cup performances of 1937-8 was an invitation by the Dutch Football Association to visit Holland and play a Dutch National XI at Rotterdam. The City party of players and officials sailed from Harwich on 11 October 1938 and, although they were to lose the game 8-2, they had a very enjoyable trip. In defence of City it had to be stated that this Dutch side had beaten Arsenal and no English team had won at Rotterdam against Holland for five years. The Dutch officials extended every hospitality to their visitors and gifts were exchanged. City came back with good impressions from their continental trip and could report that Holland had little to learn from English clubs, both in regard to ground facilities and playing ability. The City party left Rotterdam on the Berlin boat express back to the Hook and experienced a 'black out' for an air raid test. All stations were blacked out and the train coaches heavily screened — a sign that war clouds were gathering over Europe.

A loss of £1,471 on the season increased the total debt to £5,467 and there was a big clearout of players at the end of the season. Many of the Cup team were to depart, namely Wharton, Barrett, Duckworth, Earl, Hughes, Spooner and Wass.

Although war was uppermost in people's minds in the summer of 1939, preparations went on for the forthcoming season. A number of new signings were made, notably goalkeeper Bob Ferguson from Middlesbrough, Bill Allen, a forward from Chesterfield, and Fred Tilson, an ex-England and Manchester City star. Tilson had won League and cup honours with the Maine Road club and scored both City's goals in their 2-1 FA Cup Final win in 1934 over Portsmouth.

City opened the season with a home draw against Chester 2-2 and then lost at Rotherham 2-1 and Rochdale 1-0. The team that represented the club in these three games was:

Ferguson; Kelly, Boyle, Hathway, Hawkins, Gledhill, Scott, Allen, Thompson, Tilson, Lee.

The City party travelled back home from Spotland that Saturday, 2 September, and the following day war was declared. All the professional players were called together at Bootham Crescent on the Monday morning. Secretary G.W.Sherrington explained that owing to the war all football had been stopped and the club had no prospect of any revenue. In consultation with the newly-appointed chairman, W.H.Sessions, it was decided to give the players their insurance cards after which they were free to return to their homes. They were thanked for their services by the secretary and wished the best of luck in whatever sphere they found themselves.

It was to be seven long years before football was resumed on a normal peacetime basis again.

Upon the declaration of war, football, together with all other sport, was closed down. Within a few weeks the stringent conditions were gradually eased. It was the start of the period known as the 'phoney war' and the Government gave permission to the Football Association for the game to proceed on a wartime footing. The Football League in October 1939 organized regional competitions. One important ruling was that clubs could use the services of 'guest players' ie players who lived or were stationed nearby. Being a military centre, City were to benefit greatly from this. Players were to be paid 30 shillings (£1.50) per match. This was increased to £2 in 1943. As previously stated the City club had effectively closed down on 4 September when all the players were given their cards. The board after long discussions decided unanimously, however, to carry on and so began an interesting, and at times glorious, chapter in the club's history.

The first wartime season was very experimental. City were placed in the North

East League where their opponents included Newcastle United, Middlesbrough and Leeds United.

After a friendly home match against Sheffield United on 14 October, City started their League programme the following week when they lost 3-1 to Middlesbrough at Bootham Crescent. Quite a few of City's regular players were available in this first season, namely Ferguson, Gledhill, Brenen, Allen, Lee, Pinder and Porritt. 'Guest Players' included Jack Everest and Reg Stockill, back in their home City. To add to problems, the winter of 1940 was one of the most severe in modern times. Snow and ice caused a virtual shut down and City did not play a competitive game from Christmas Day until 16 March. The season was subsequently extended until the beginning of June. City finished eighth in their League of 11 clubs, with eight wins and a draw.

A number of friendly games supplemented the programme and in the closing weeks of the season the Football League War Cup was instituted. In the preliminary round City beat Bradford City 6-4 at Bootham Crescent, but then lost 1-2 on aggregate to Hull City in the first round. A deficit of £435 was announced at the end of City's first season of wartime football and the year was described as a difficult one. The club was still active, however, and the directors stated that they intended to carry on and looked ahead with confidence. York City Supporters' Club continued to carry on their activities and the chairman, J.W.Edwards, pledged their full support.

For 1940-41 City grouped in the North Regional League which comprised 36 clubs. As each team did not play each other the League placings were decided on percentages. These percentages were decided not on wins or losses but on goals scored for and against. City finished fifth from the bottom of the League with the following record: P 25 W 7 D 4 L 14 F 49 A 71. Average 0.690. Although results had been disappointing there was some entertaining football played with obviously the emphasis on goals. George Lee continued to make outstanding progress and for the second season he topped the scoring charts.

Bert Brenen, Sam Gledhill and Jack Pinder continued to provide stalwart service. Among the guests that season was a Scottish player by the name of Matt Patrick from Cowdenbeath. In the years to come he was to prove a fine servant. A young local player, Alf Patrick, also made an appearance. Other guests included George Eastham (England and Blackpool), Tommy Dawson (Charlton Athletic), Sam Hodgson (Grimsby Town), Tom Holley (Leeds United) and a centre-half from Wolves, E.Robinson. He was later killed on active service. Another local lad who came into the team was a very talented left-back from Dringhouses, Gordon Jones, and he quickly made a big impression.

The League War Cup was again played on a home and away basis. In the preliminary round, City beat Sheffield Wednesday at home 7-0 with Bert Brenen scoring four goals. They lost the second leg, which was staged at Scunthorpe, 2-1 and were then paired against Bradford. They beat Bradford 3-2 at York and won the second leg 4-3 with guest goalkeeper Arthur Jepson of Port Vale saving two penalties for City. Owing to an unfit pitch at Bradford this match was also played at Scunthorpe. In the second round City were matched with Newcastle United. The teams drew 1-1 at Bootham Crescent but the Magpies won 4-1 at St James' Park. The City team that day was Jepson (Port Vale); Pinder, Jones, Livesley (Crystal Palace), Robinson (Wolves), Gledhill, Brenen, Dawson (Charlton), Hydes (Newport), Eastham (Blackpool), Lee.

In December 1940 the death was announced of City's first manager, Jock Collier.

The second season of war football produced a profit of £27 and the club soldiered on. The format for 1941-2 was as follows. The first half of the season was devoted to the League programme comprising 18 games. The previous years experiment of percentages was scrapped and the points system again operated.

City finished 32nd out of 38 in the Northern League with the following record:
P 18 W 4 D 4 L 10 F 41 A 55 Points 12.

Two famous players each made an appearance in City colours — Raich Carter of Sunderland and England fame and the legendary Dixie Dean played in the home game against Gateshead on 22 November 1941.

Fittingly, Dean scored with a header, although City lost 4-3. The League Cup was run in the second half of the campaign and the qualifying stages were on a league basis. Fifty-four clubs competed and the first 32 qualified. City finished 33rd and so just missed out on competing in the knock-out stages. As a result, in the closing weeks of the season City competed for the Combined Counties Cup along with Chesterfield, Halifax, Bradford City, Middlesbrough and Huddersfield Town and went on to win the trophy. In the final, over two legs, they beat Halifax 5-2. The team that played in these two matches was:
Ferguson; Gledhill, Jones, Hodgson (Grimsby), Wilson (Reading), Atkinson (Bolton), Porritt, Brenen, O'Donnell (Aston Villa), Brown (Charlton), Lee.

At centre-forward was Scotland international star Frank O'Donnell who was stationed in the RAF near York and he made a number of guest appearances. At inside-left was another RAF man, Bert Brown of Charlton and England, and he became a most popular personality in the war years at Bootham Crescent. Nicknamed 'Sailor' because of his rolling gait, he was a very clever inside-forward and helped form a brilliant left-wing partnership with George Lee. He went on to play for Charlton in the 1945-6 FA Cup Final and later played for Nottingham Forest and Villa. Jimmy Rudd (Manchester City) and Len Butt (Blackburn), both to play for the club after the war, made appearances. Early in 1942 Arthur Brown, the former chairman, resigned his place on the board after almost 20 years service. He retired to live in the South of England and Ernest Harwood was co-opted in his place.

A profit of £1,041 was made in 1941-2 during which the level of support, between 4,000 and 5,000, was encouraging. At the club's 20th annual meeting tribute was paid to Arthur Wright for his tireless work as acting team manager and to Tom Lockie the chief trainer. Praise was also given to Wilf Meek (Citizen) for his balanced reporting and judgement in the *Yorkshire Evening Press*. "No one has seen more City matches in the 20 years of existence of the club during which he had missed no fewer than a dozen games" said Sherrington. Being one of the best supported clubs in Yorkshire, the Football League staged a representative match at Bootham Crescent on 17 October 1942 between the League and the Northern Command. At left-back for the League was City's highly-rated Gordon Jones. A great future was predicted for this local lad. Sadly in 1943 he was struck down by a serious illness from which he was never able to recover. This illness lasted several years and in January 1947 he died at a tragically early age.

City's best wartime season was 1942-3 and it was an outstanding campaign. At the club's disposal now was Charlton Athletic's famous goalkeeping personality, Sam Bartram, and he teamed up with his old colleague 'Sailor' Brown. Also continuing to guest were Sam Hodgson, Frank O'Donnell and Reading centre-half Joe Wilson. Pre-war City right winger Fred Scott returned to the fold and at inside-right was a young Bolton player, John Knight. The Arsenal centre-half and Middlesex cricketer, Leslie Compton, also played three games for the club. An appearance was also made by local lad Neville Tutill. Many years later his son, Stephen, was to play for City.

The same fixture format applied as the previous season. In the League North, City finished 17th out of 47. P 18 W 9 D 3 L 6 F 47 A 36 Pts 21.

Two individual scoring feats, both for and against, are worth recalling that season in the League. In the home win over Newcastle on 10 October all four of City's

Cecil McCormack (second left), a guest player from Gateshead, battles it out in the air with Sheffield Wednesday's Walter Millership during the second leg of the Football League War Cup semi-final in 1942-3. Interest was so high in the game that spectators clambered on to the popular stand in City's highest wartime attendance of 16,350.

goals were netted by O'Donnell. On 5 December, Bradford won 6-3 at York and Len Shackleton scored five times.

After the disappointment of the previous season, in which the team narrowly failed to qualify in the League Cup, City made no mistake this time. They sailed through the qualifying games, winning six and drawing one of their nine matches. The knock-out stages were again on a home and away basis and City were paired with Newcastle in the first round. In front of just under 20,000 spectators at St James' Park they lost 3-2, but triumphed 2-0 at home thanks to goals from Wilson and Brenen to go through on aggregate.

In the second round City entertained Bradford in the first leg and won 2-1. Bradford had a strong side with future internationals in their line-up in Billy Elliott and Len Shackleton. In the second leg City swept to a fine three-goal victory and now in the quarter-finals met Chesterfield, who were a Second Division side and a team with a very good wartime record. City established a two goal home first-leg lead in front of a new wartime record crowd of 14,007. They repeated the scoreline at Saltergate and for the first time in their history had reached a semi-final of a major cup competition.

Enthusiasm in the City was on a par with the great days of 1937-8 and Sheffield Wednesday provided the last hurdle before the final. The first leg was at Hillsborough but unfortunately 'Sailor' Brown was unavailable. Charlton Athletic were competing in the League Cup South semi-finals and they required his services. A crowd of 35,253 saw the game and one of the stands was not in use because of a bomb

George Lee nets from the penalty-spot against Wednesday to record his 100th goal for the club.

blast. Wednesday won 3-0 that day but outstanding in goal for them was John Smith, a Sheffield United player! Brown returned for the second leg and also in the City team for the match was Leeds United star Aubrey Powell. The record wartime Bootham Crescent crowd of 16,350 (receipts £1,399) saw the task too hard for City. They drew 1-1 and went out of the competition 4-1 on aggregate. City's goal was scored from the penalty-spot by George Lee. It was his 100th goal for the club and for the fourth successive season he was leading scorer and his tally this year was 25. In the other League Cup North semi-final, Blackpool beat Aston Villa and the Seasiders won the Football League North Cup by beating Wednesday 4-3 on aggregate. The team line-ups for this famous wartime cup run were as follows:

First Round
Newcastle United (a)
Bartram (Charlton); Pinder, Gledhill, Hodgson (Grimsby), Wilson (Reading), Gledhill (Luton), Scott, Dawson (Charlton), Brenen, Brown (Charlton), Lee.
Newcastle United (h)
Ferguson; Pinder, Jones, Hodgson (Grimsby), Wilson (Reading), Campbell (Luton), Scott, Black (Hearts), Brenen, Brown (Charlton), Lee.
Second Round
Bradford (h)
Bartram (Charlton); Pinder, Jones, Hodgson (Grimsby), Wilson (Reading), Gledhill, Scott, Dawson (Charlton), Brenen, Brown (Charlton), Lee.
Bradford (a)
Bartram (Charlton); Pinder, Jones, Hodgson (Grimsby), Wilson (Reading), Gledhill, Scott, Dawson (Charlton), McCormack (Gateshead), Brown (Charlton), Lee.
Third Round
Chesterfield (h) & (a)
Bartram (Charlton); Pinder, Jones, Hodgson (Grimsby), Wilson (Reading), Gledhill, Scott, Dawson (Charlton), McCormack (Gateshead), Brown (Charlton), Lee.

Semi-final
Sheffield Wednesday (a)
Bartram (Charlton); Pinder, Jones, Hodgson (Grimsby), Wilson (Reading), Gledhill, Scott, Dawson (Charlton), McCormack (Gateshead), Brenen, Lee.
Sheffield Wednesday (h)
Bartram (Charlton); Pinder, Jones, Hodgson (Grimsby), Wilson (Reading), Gledhill, Scott, Powell (Leeds United), McCormack (Gateshead), Brown (Charlton), Lee.

Gross receipts from the eight games realized £9,156 and a profit on the years workings amounted to £2,188.

City's Cup run had not only attracted the attention of people at home but many messages of congratulations were received from York servicemen abroad, especially from the victorious Eighth Army in North Africa.

The sad news was announced in June 1943 of the death of Arthur Wright, who had shown so much enthusiasm in his six years as a director. He had been one of York's leading chemists and was proprietor of the Mansion House Pharmacy (Mark F.Burgin). It was Wright who had been instrumental in bringing so many notable guest players to York. On a brighter note benefits were given to Sam Gledhill and Ted Hathway.

The summer of 1943 marked the coming of age of York City. At a special meeting to mark the 21st anniversary a tribute was made to Billy Sherrington. Chairman W.H.Sessions summed it up 'Billy Sherrington is York City and what more can I say than that'. Sherrington's life work had seen the club grow from an idea into a soccer stronghold. At the outbreak of war he had resumed civil service duties but he continued to work tirelessly for the club during this difficult period.

1943-4 again provided some excellent entertainment at Bootham Crescent, watched by sizeable crowds. Benny Fenton of West Ham, Millwall and Charlton fame made a number of appearances. A run of five successive defeats in the pre-Christmas League programme was a set-back, however, and they finished in the lower half of the table. P 18 W 7 D 2 L 9 F 35 A 40 Pts 16.

In the League Cup qualifying group, City went into their last game needing to beat Leeds United by a big score in order to reach the knock-out stages. They did just that by beating United 8-1! In the first round, Barnsley were defeated 5-4 on aggregate with over 14,000 watching the second leg at Oakwell. City fell at the next stage, however, when they lost to a strong Bradford side. Bradford won 5-1 at York and 7-2 on aggregate and Len Shackleton scored four goals in the two matches.

Once again the season produced a profit (£1,230). At the AGM criticism was voiced regarding the high level of entertainment tax clubs had to pay. In 1943-4 City paid a total of £2,354 tax on gross receipts of £8,842. This tax payment was considerably more than the wages and travelling bill. It was pointed out that if clubs like York City were to survive after the war when the wage bill could be trebled, some tax consession would have to be made. Tribute was paid to two players who had lost their lives on active service — Len 'Taffy' Milner and G.Reynolds, a Charlton Athletic centre-half who had guested that season. George Lee joined the Army in March 1944 and his future appearances for City were now to be limited. In April that year a promising young local goalkeeper, Peter Pickering, was signed. One change in the boardroom was made when former director D.A.Pratt was elected to fill the vacancy caused by R.E.Warners resignation.

The sixth season of wartime football caused great selection problems. Many players had left for the war fronts and, with constant troop movements, there were considerable alterations to team personnel. No fewer than 57 players appeared for City during 1944-5. Remarkably there was one ever-present — Joe Wilson, who gave the club fine service during this period. Although 'Sailor' Brown had left, Sam Bartram made over 20 appearances and towards the end of the season he took over the role of penalty taker. There was certainly no shortage of goals this season and on 28 October Gateshead were beaten 10-2, with Harry Hawkins scoring four times. The Southport and ex-Middlesbrough forward had an excellent season and netted over 20 goals.

With only three wins in their ten cup qualifying matches, City did not reach the competition proper. To supplement their programme they competed in the Tyne, Wear and Tees Cup along with Darlington, Middlesbrough, Sunderland and Newcastle. It was in this competition, in a match against Darlington, that Sam Bartram scored twice from the penalty-spot to earn a 2-0 victory.

In March 1945 Harry Hayhurst, who had been involved with the City club since its formation, resigned from the board owing to ill health and Hugh Kitchin was co-opted to succeed him. At the AGM in 1945 Messrs E.J.Pulleyn and W.Newton stood down as directors and their places were taken by Messrs B.Littlefair and D.Blundy.

Although hostilities had finished by the start of the 1945-6 campaign, there was not sufficient time to restore soccer to its pre-war pattern. Changes were made, however, to the format in preparation for the resumption of normal peacetime soccer. For the first half of the season City competed in the Third Division East which comprised ten clubs.

In October 1945 one of City's former players, local lad Albert Bonass, who had played for the club in 1933-4, was killed in a RAF flying accident near York. He guested for the club during the war and in fact, at the time that his death was announced, had been selected to play for City in a game at Halifax a few days later. His other clubs during his career were Hartlepools, Chesterfield and QPR.

The Reserves resumed their programme in the Yorkshire League. City finished mid-table in their Third Division group with a very well balanced record! P 18 W 6 D 6 L 6 F 34 A 34 Pts 18.

In the New Year the same ten clubs played in one group of a qualifying tournament for the Third Division North Cup. The top eight of the group, plus the top eight of the West Division, took part in the knock-out stages of the competition. City qualified on goal-average but, after defeating Accrington Stanley in the first round, they were beaten by Chester.

The highlight of the season was provided in the FA Cup competition, which was restored for the first time since 1938-9. For the first and only time ties were to be settled on a two-legged home and away basis.

City knocked out Halifax Town and Bishop Auckland in the opening two rounds and then were drawn against the powerful Second Division side, Chesterfield, who at the time were current leaders of the League North. Signed just in time to play in the third-round matches was inside-forward Harry Thompson from Sunderland in what, at the time, was the biggest transfer deal in City's history. Thompson, who had guested for the club the previous season, had been signed by Sunderland from Wolverhampton Wanderers for the then very sizeable fee of £7,000.

City put up a tremendous battle in the first leg at Saltergate and fully deserved their 1-1 draw. The return game played at Bootham Crescent on a Wednesday afternoon attracted a crowd of over 14,000. The match was a thrilling and tense affair. After 60 minutes City led 2-0 thanks to an own goal and an Ian Winter header. The League leaders stormed back and with five minutes remaining had levelled the scores. In semi-darkness, 20 minutes of extra-time was played. Amidst great excitement, City regained the lead, when after a fine dribble by Thompson, the ball was volleyed into the net by Winters for the local centre-forward's second goal. In a terrific finish City withstood tremendous pressure and just managed to hold on for a dramatic and famous win — one to rank with their other famous Cup exploits. City had reached the fourth round for the third time in their history. They were swept out of the tournament at this stage, however, by Sheffield Wednesday 11-2 on aggregate. City had written though another exciting chapter in their FA Cup history.

Details of their FA Cup games that season are as follows:

Round 1 (1st leg)
17 November 1945 v Halifax Town (a) 0-1
Ferguson; Pinder, Poole, Gledhill, Bentall, Rodgers, Scott, Robbins, Winters, Green, Routledge.
Attendance: 5,849

Round 1 (2nd leg)
24 November 1945 v Halifax Town (h) 4-2 (agg 4-3)
Lee, Gledhill (pen), Scott 2.
Ferguson; Pinder, Poole, Gledhill, Bentall, Rodgers, Reagan, Scott, Winters, Robbins, Lee.
Attendance: 7,573

Round 2 (1st leg)
8 December 1945 v Bishop Auckland (a) 2-1
Maddison, Winters
Ferguson; Pinder, Poole, Gledhill, Young, Rodgers, Reagan, Scott, Winters, Robbins, Maddison.
Attendance: 5,674

Round 2 (2nd leg)
15 December 1945 v Bishop Auckland (h) 3-0, Aggregate 5-1
Winters, Brenen, Robbins
Ferguson; Pinder, Poole, Gledhill, Young, Rodgers, Scott, Brenen, Winters, Robbins, Routledge.
Attendance: 8,651

Round 3 (1st leg)
5 January 1946 v Chesterfield (a) 1-1
Mahon
Ferguson; Pinder, Rodgers, Brenen, Young, Gledhill, Scott, Robbins, Winters, Thompson, Mahon.
Attendance: 15,025

Round 2 (2nd leg)
9 January 1946 v Chesterfield (h) 3-2 (agg 4-3)
Winters 2, own-goal
Ferguson; Pinder, Rodgers, Brenen, Young, Gledhill, Scott, Robbins, Winters, Thompson, Mahon.
Attendance: 14,207

Round 4 (1st leg)
26 January 1946 v Sheffield Wednesday (a) 1-5
Scott (pen)
Ferguson; Pinder, Rodgers, Brenen, Young, Gledhill, Scott, Robbins, Winters, Thompson, Mahon.
Attendance: 33,363

Round 4 (2nd leg)
30 January 1946 v Sheffield Wednesday (h) 1-6 (agg 2-11)
Allen
Ferguson; Pinder, Rodgers, Brenen, Brentall, Gledhill, Scott, Robbins, Allen, Thompson, Porritt.
Attendance: 10,447

Former chairman and director, Arthur Brown, collapsed and died after attending the 1945-6 FA Cup Final.

The 1945-6 campaign resulted in a loss of £187, but five of the seven wartime seasons had produced a profit. The York public had been well entertained and the decision to carry on back in 1939 had been fully vindicated.

City were indebted to many guest players during those seven seasons, but tribute had to be paid to five of their own players who gave such outstanding service: Sammy Gledhill, who made over 220 wartime appearances for the club; Jack Pinder over 175; Bert Brenen over 125, in the process of which he played in every position, including goal; Bob Ferguson over 100 games and, before his military call up, George Lee, who totalled 140 plus matches and proved a prolific scorer. A big future lay ahead for him. A benefit match on behalf of Pinder was staged on 1 May 1946 when Huddersfield Town provided the opposition. An attendance of almost 6,000 was just reward for the stalwart full-back, who by now had completed 17 years with the club.

Praise was also due to the directors and Sherrington for their yeoman work behind the scenes during the difficult war years and last but not least there was Tom Lockie.

The following letter sent by Sherrington on behalf of the directors in July 1945 paid an apt tribute to the work done by the loyal and dedicated club man.

York City Association Football & Athletic Club, Ltd.

Members of the Football League (Div. III, Northern Section) and Yorkshire League.

Telephones:
Ground: York 4447.
Secretary's House: York 77145.

Secretary:
G. W. SHERRINGTON

Ground and Registered Office:
BOOTHAM CRESCENT,
YORK.

3rd July 1945.

Mr T. Lockie,
19 Almond Grove,
New Earswick,
York.

Dear Tommy,

At a meeting of the Directors held on 26th June 1945, I was requested to convey to you the sincere thanks and appreciation of the Board for the excellent services you have rendered to the club during the war years.

It has been a most difficult time to all concerned with the game and in the case of our club all the work has been carried on during the last six years by Officials during their spare time.

In the limited time at your disposal during this period you have not spared yourself in doing everything possible to assist in keeping the flag flying. Often it has been a nightmare to get a team together, and you have rendered invaluable assistance in obtaining players and encouraging them to do their very best, when at times circumstances appeared to be all against us.

The Directors are well aware of the part you have taken in maintaining a team spirit amongst so many Guest Players as well as our own players, and they appreciate all you have done in the interests of the club.

A big job has to be done to get the club on to normal working conditions and they know that they can rely upon your wholehearted co-operation and support to bring this about.

My I express to you my personal thanks for the ready assistance you have given me at all times since you became associated with the club and to say that I hope we may be able to work together for many years to come.

The soccer flag had been kept flying by York City and the club looked ahead with confidence and eagerness to the resumption of peacetime football in August 1946.

The 1946-7 season was one of reconstruction not only at Bootham Crescent but also throughout the Football League. The seven-year gap had seen a lot of the older players retire from the game. The fixture list remained the same as that for the ill-fated campaign of 1939-40 and City entertained Chester on 31 August 1946. In 1939 the teams had drawn 2-2 and on this occasion it finished 4-4. Bill Allen, who had netted twice in his first game in City colours seven years earlier, scored once on his official debut in 1946 and the other men on the mark were Frank Carr and Ernie Nettleton. Of the side who had played at Rochdale in the last game before the outbreak of war there were four survivors — Bob Ferguson, Sammy Gledhill, Fred Scott and Allen. Also in the team were pre-war players Jack Pinder, Bert Brenen (captain) and Austin Collier, whilst Walter Porritt was still on the books. Tom Mitchell had resumed his duties as team manager following his demobilization from the RAF so, unlike a lot of clubs, there was a good deal of continuity at Bootham Crescent.

Within a week of the start of the season outside-right Fred Scott was transferred to Nottingham Forest for a then record fee received of £3,000. In November, Harry Thompson was transferred to Northampton Town where he took over as club coach. He had joined City in December 1945, but was taken seriously ill whilst on a coaching engagement in Norway in the summer of 1946. On returning to this country he moved to the Midlands to recuperate and City finally released him from his contract.

No fewer than 34 players appeared for City in this first post-war season — a club record. Debuts were made by the two Patricks — Matt and Alf — no relation — who served the club so well in the late 1940s and early 1950s. Local centre-forward Alf quickly made his mark and finished top scorer with 17 goals. Late in the season two of the most skilful ball players to appear for the club joined City. Jimmy Rudd, an Irish will-o'-the-wisp on the left wing from Manchester City, and little Sid Storey who cost the princely sum of £100 when signed from Wombwell. Two Polish Army players made appearances — goalkeeper Eddie Wojtczak and outside-left Eryk Kubicki.

The winter of 1947 was one of the worst of the century and in February and March the country was in the grip of ice and snow — then followed by floods. City did not play between 1 February and 22 March and the season was extended until 7 June. These were the days long before floodlights and there also was a Government ban on midweek football. This was to prevent men from being distracted from working during the early post-war economic crisis.

The season was a mixed one for City, who finished 15th in the Northern Section. They were badly let down by poor home form — only six wins and four draws at Bootham Crescent — and they also lost at home in the first round of the FA Cup to Scunthorpe United, then in the Midland League. The death was announced in January 1947 of former player Gordon Jones. The Supporters' Club held their annual dinner that month and handed over a cheque for 200 guineas to the parent club. Tribute was paid to the secretary, H.Ward, who had held that post for 20 years.

Average attendances for the season were 6,900 and at the club's Silver Jubilee AGM in the summer of 1947 a profit of £3,651 was revealed on gross revenue of £13,425. F.H.Magson was elected to the board in place of J.W.Rosindale, who had resigned. Three former directors, Messrs J.Fisher, H.Hayhurst and G.Simpson, died during the year. For the new season the reserve team transferred back to the Midland League.

Prior to the start of the 1947-8 campaign, George Lee was transferred to Nottingham Forest for a new record fee received of £7,500. At Forest he teamed up with former colleague Fred Scott and his wartime mentor 'Sailor' Brown. Because of his military service, Lee made only one post-war League appearance for City. The season started

Above: *City players engaged in an unusual bowls competition following pre-season training in August 1947. Left to right: Jackson, Rudd, Bradley, M.Patrick, Allen, Butt, Browne, Lee.*
Below: *Alex Jackson (second right) heads over the crossbar when City entertained lowly Tranmere Rovers in January 1948. City lost 2-1.*

York City pictured in 1947-8. Back row (left to right): Pinder, Brenen, Gale, Jackson, Pickering, Browne, McDermott, Lockie. Front row: M.Patrick, Butt, A.Patrick, Storey, Rudd.

well and after six games York were unbeaten and top of the table. A crowd of 13,604 saw an early season midweek win over Rotherham. The side fell away, however, and finally had to settle for 13th position. Again they fell at the first hurdle in the FA Cup when Rochdale won at Bootham Crescent.

Newcomers this season included Tommy Gale, centre-half and captain, and John Simpson who became the first £1,000 signing made by City when he was recruited from Huddersfield Town in March 1948. Two other players who made their debuts this season were Percy Andrews and Ron Spence. Outstanding during the campaign had been goalkeeper Peter Pickering and the local lad had made tremendous progress since making his debut in May 1947. On 11 May 1948 he was transferred to Chelsea for a fee of £6,750. Average crowds rose to 9,006 and takings that season of £16,213 were a record at Bootham Crescent. A net profit was announced of £4,914 and the club were able to carry forward a creditable balance of £1,483.

In September 1948 the club announced the purchase of the Bootham Crescent ground. (See *Homes of York City*.) N.J.Hopwood was elected to the board and the directors were pleased to make the following donations: £75 to former centre-forward Maurice Dando, who was suffering from paralysis, in Bristol and £100 to the York & District League for the advancement of junior football. Former groundsman T.Ledgard, who was suffering from blindness, was granted a benefit match and a year's pay.

The 1948-9 season was the peak of the post-war soccer boom with record attendances throughout the country. City's average League crowd of 10,412 that term remains a club record. On 23 April 1949 the record League crowd of 21,010 saw the visit of champions-elect Hull City, whilst on 20 November 1948 over 19,000 saw the memorable 6-1 victory over Rotherham United when Alf Patrick scored five goals.

City showed outstanding home form in the first half of the season and in one sequence won eight successive League games at Bootham Crescent, scoring 31 goals in the process. With the exception of a 3-2 win at Hull in early April, City fell away badly in the closing weeks and a final position of 14th was disappointing. Early in the New Year the mercurial Jimmy Rudd was transferred to Leeds United and at the end of the campaign Sammy Gledhill hung up his boots. He had served the club spendidly for 13 years. The previous season the other stalwart, Jack Pinder, ended his playing career. In the years to come these two ex-players were to help the club in coaching and scouting roles.

In the FA Cup York lost at home to Southport in a second-round replay. Takings at Bootham Crescent rose to £19,035 and a net profit on the season amounted to £4,987 and a credit balance of £6,470 had accumulated. The death occurred of H.Rusholme, vice-chairman and longest-serving director. Back in 1922 he had been the club's first honorary secretary. J.W.Rosindale resumed his place on the board.

The team made a bad start to the 1949-50 campaign with only one win in their opening 10 matches. They never recovered from this and finished bottom of the Northern Section with only nine wins and 31 points to their credit. They thus had to apply for re-election for the first time in their history. That year the League was increased to 92 clubs. Subsequently City, with the other three retiring clubs — Halifax, Newport and Millwall — were re-elected without having to enter a ballot. Twenty non-League clubs competed for the four available places and Scunthorpe, Shrewsbury, Colchester and Gillingham were the successful ones. Attendances at Bootham Crescent dropped to an average of 8,016. For the fourth successive season Alf Patrick topped the scoring charts and one notable newcomer to the ranks was centre-half Alan Stewart from Huddersfield Town. In February 1950 Tom Mitchell announced his resignation as manager, a post he had held since 1937. Dick Duckworth, who had captained the side during the memorable FA Cup run of 1937-8, was appointed as his successor. In March the death was announced of City's first trainer, Hughie 'Spud' Murphy at the age of 64.

Three members of the backroom staff pictured in 1950. Left to right: Tom Lockie, Jack Pinder and Sam Johnson.

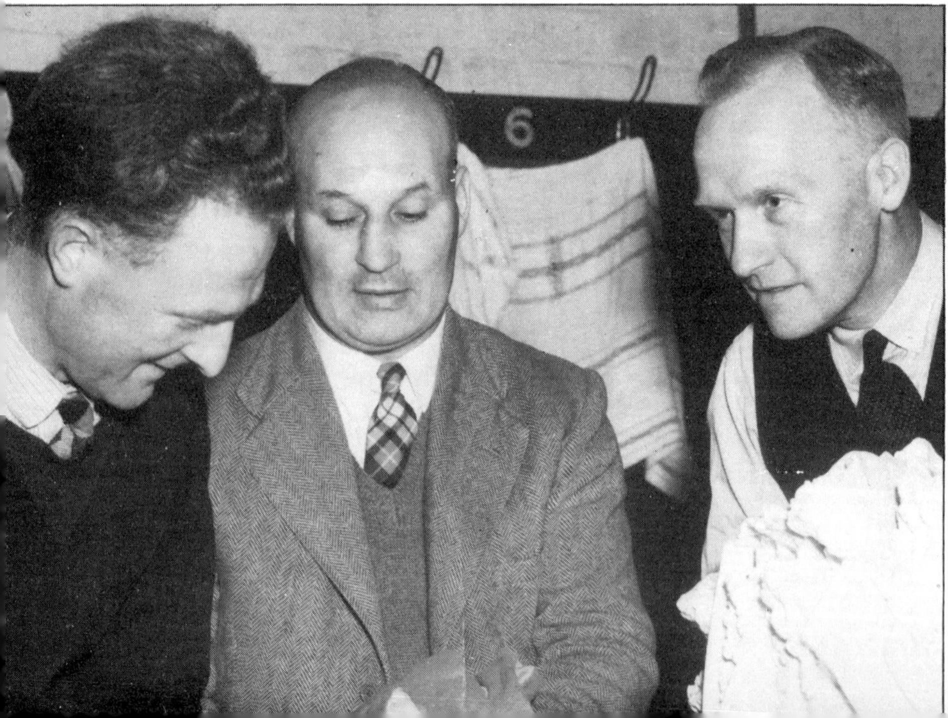

It was not all doom and gloom in 1949-50. The reserve side had a very successful season, finishing in the top six of the Midland League and scoring over 100 goals. They also won the North Riding Senior Cup for the first time in the club's history. On 7 April 1950 they beat Middlesbrough Reserves 3-0 in the final at Ayresome Park. The successful line up was: Frost; Brown, Duthoit, Spence, Burgin, Jackson (captain), Ivey, Coop, Walker, Collins, Birch.

At the AGM in September 1950 a net deficit of £1,556 was reported on the year's workings. At the meeting the new manager outlined his policy. It was a three-year plan at the end of which the aim was to be knocking at the door for promotion. For the first time the club entered a third team in the Yorkshire League. A new scouting system was inaugurated and a number of amateurs received trials. Duckworth emphasized that in the Third Division you had to have a team with determination. He wanted fast, aggressive players who would play open football based on teamwork.

Season 1950-51 got off to a disastrous start with a 7-2 defeat at Tranmere. Making his one and only appearance in goal for City that day was Jimmy Pegg, who had previously been with Manchester United and Torquay. It was to prove a better campaign, however, and the final position was 17th. Notable newcomers were John Linaker a skilful right winger and Gordon Brown, inside-forward, both from Nottingham Forest. Linaker finished joint top scorer with Matt Patrick. In the second half of the season a promising and talented young goalkeeper, Des Thompson, made his debut. Average League attendances at Bootham Crescent were 7,478.

For the first time since 1945-6 the club reached the third round of the FA Cup. Bishop Auckland and Tranmere Rovers were knocked out in the first two rounds and then City were drawn away to Bolton Wanderers. It was their first tilt against First Division opposition since the sixth-round match against Huddersfield 13 years earlier. The game at Burnden Park was played on 6 January 1951 and took place in shocking conditions. Heavy rain reduced the crowd to 26,652. City put up a stubborn and resolute defensive display, but the turning point of the game came when Alan Stewart was injured in a collision with Bolton's international centre-forward Nat Lofthouse. The centre-half and captain was off the field for 15 minutes whilst a deep facial cut was stitched. During this period, when they were short-handed, they conceded the vital first goal in the 65th minute. Stewart returned to play on the right wing and the gallant City team did not concede a second goal until the last minute. The teams lined up that day:

Bolton Wanderers: Hanson; Ball, Kennedy, Howe, Barrass, Edwards, Hughes, Moir, Lofthouse, Webster, Langton.
Scorers: Langton, Lofthouse.
York City: Ashley; Andrews, Simpson, Brenen, Stewart, Spence, Linaker, Brown, A.Patrick, M.Patrick, Ivey.

In April 1951 a benefit match on behalf of Bert Brenen was played between a City XI and Leeds United. He thus became the eighth recipient of a benefit game. The previous ones had been: J.Middlemiss (1929), T.Fenoughty (1934), S.Fox (1938), J.Pinder (1938 and 1946), E.Wass (1939), S.Gledhill (1943 and 1949) and T.Ledgard (1948).

Brenen received a record benefit, a just reward for 13 years outstanding service as a utility player. Failure to agree terms, however, in August 1951 caused him to be placed on the transfer list and he subsequently moved to Scarborough. Thus ended the last pre-war link on the playing side of the club. At the 29th AGM a loss of £3,769 was revealed and the credit balance stood at £1,002. Average League attendances were 7,512.

As part of the Festival of Britain celebrations a series of special matches were played in May 1951. For their part City entertained League of Ireland clubs Sligo

Above: *City meet Bradford for the third time in the FA Cup first round, this time at neutral at Elland Road in December 1951. City players Fred Slater (7) and Alf Patrick look on as the Bradford left-back clears his lines.*
Below: *City play Bradford again, this time in a Third Division North game on Christmas Day 1951. Matt Patrick (centre) challenges the visitors' goalkeeper in York's 1-0 win.*

Rovers and Transport, winning 4-0 and 5-0 respectively. It was in these games that a young outside-right by the name of Billy Hughes made his debut.

In readiness for 1951-2 several new signings were made, notably Billy Fenton an outside-left from Blackburn Rovers and Steve Griffiths an experienced inside-forward who had been on the books of Halifax, Chesterfield, Portsmouth and Barnsley. It was to be City's best post-war season to date as they rose to tenth position and the 49 points they gained set a new club record. Under the skilful leadership of the veteran Griffiths they played some entertaining football and at home proved well nigh invincible with 16 wins and four draws. Some big victories were recorded — Accrington 6-1, Halifax 6-2, Oldham 5-0 and Workington 5-1. During the season Alf Patrick reached the tally of 100 League goals for the club — the first player to achieve this feat.

The scoring hero this term, however, was newcomer Fenton who smashed Reg Baines' 20-year-old club scoring record by notching 31 League goals. Earlier in the campaign John Linaker move to Hull City and Billy Hughes established himself at outside-right. In the last game of the season teenage centre-forward David Dunmore made his debut and scored in a 3-0 home victory over Crewe Alexandra. Average

No play today - Tom Lockie, Des Thompson, John Simpson and a member of the groundstaff survey the watery scene in February 1952.

The York City team which played a Football League XI for Tom Lockie's benefit match in April 1952. Back row (left to right): Andrews, Brown, Thompson, Stewart, Spence, Simpson. Front row: Hughes, A.Patrick, Griffiths, McGoldrick (Rotherham United), Fenton.

home League attendances were 7,968. In the FA Cup they lost to Bradford in a first-round second replay played at Elland Road. In March 1952 T.W.(Wilf) Meek, who had reported City's affairs in the *Yorkshire Evening Press* since the club's formation, was appointed to the board. At the end of the season a benefit match was played for Tom Lockie when City met a Football League XI. Included in the representative side were Sam Bartram, Len Shackleton and a young Sheffield United forward by the name of Arthur Bottom. He was to have a big impact in the years ahead.

For the 1952-3 season City relied on virtually the same playing staff and at the half-way stage were well placed in the promotion race in third position. P 24 W 13 D 6 L 5 F 33 A 20 Pts 32.

In the midst of this impressive run there were two crucial departures from Bootham Crescent. In October 1952 manager Dick Duckworth was reluctantly released from his contract to enable him to take a similar appointment with Stockport County. The following month the former Newcastle United and England centre-half, Charles Spencer, took over the managerial reins. He had been in charge at Grimsby Town for a number of years. The other person to leave was goalkeeper Des Thompson who, rather controversially, was transferred to Burnley for a fee of £7,350 on the eve of a first-round FA Cup-tie against Barrow. Local lad Mick Granger, who at the time was doing his National Service, was pressed into action for the Cup match. He made a very good debut, but Barrow gained a shock victory thanks to a last minute goal.

The turning point of the season was on 3 January 1953 when League leaders Oldham Athletic won 2-1 at Bootham Crescent after a tremendous battle in front of 15,222 spectators. Including this game, City won only one of 11 matches and did not record a victory at home from Boxing Day until 28 March. The promotion dream thus faded, but the final position of fourth with 53 points were new club records. The chief strength of the side was in defence and outstanding were Percy Andrews and Ron Spence, who were both ever-present, and Joe Spence, who missed only one game. Billy Fenton netted 25 goals and the popular left winger had scored 56 times in two seasons. Sadly Charles Spencer's tenure as manager was to be very short as in February 1953 he died. In May that year Jimmy McCormick was appointed as his successor. He was a former Spurs and Fulham player and coach at Sheffield United.

The balance sheet issued in the summer of 1953 showed a net profit of £1,851. It was pointed out to shareholders, however, that without the transfer fee received for Des Thompson there would have been a big deficit. This for a club that had finished as high as fourth was a rather disappointing state of affairs and average League crowds of 8,654 still fell below the requirements to enable the club to pay its way. 'However the item of entertainment tax of £3,433 on the balance sheet should be noted' said the director's report. 'It is a striking plea for a reduction in taxation when a Third Division club enjoying the best League season in its history can only make ends meet by the transfer of one of its best players'.

Three seasons of steady progress had seen the club climb from the foot of the Northern Section to fourth place and hopes were high at the start of 1953-4. Injuries to key players at the beginning of the campaign did not help but the season was to be bitterly disappointing. At the half-way stage they were bottom of the table and only victory in the last game at Halifax avoided the indignity of having to apply for re-election. In the FA Cup they were swept out in the first round at Barnsley 5-2.

The one bright spot had been the progress made by David Dunmore. The powerful young centre-forward had 20 goals to his credit when in February 1954 he was transferred to Tottenham Hotspur for a new record fee received of £10,500. Average League crowds had dropped to 5,636 — the lowest since the war — and as reported 'while the transfer is regretted it is the inevitable outcome of a mounting deficit due to poor gates'. Once again Percy Andrews was an ever-present and a tower of strength in the defence and Alan Stewart returned to the side after a long absence through injury. The end of the season saw the departure of stalwarts John Simpson and Alf Patrick.

In November 1953 W.H.Sessions stood down as chairman after over 14 years in that position. He remained a director, however, and became club president. The new chairman was H.F.W. (Hugh) Kitchin and vice-chairman D.Blundy. Arthur Brown was appointed a director.

With the monies available from the Dunmore transfer, plus financial help from the Supporters' Club, and Auxiliary Supporters' Club a big recruiting drive for new players was embarked upon in the summer of 1954. All the profits were ploughed back and new signings included Tommy Forgan, Ernie Phillips, George Howe, Arthur Bottom, Norman Wilkinson, Les Slatter and Sam McNab.

The new-look team, under the captaincy of Phillips, started in sensational style with a 6-2 victory at Wrexham. A home win over Hartlepools was then followed by a defeat at the hands of Scunthorpe United at Bootham Crescent. After this match a dispute over team selection arose between McCormick and the directors. This was not resolved and a few days later the manager's resignation was accepted.

Above: *Steve Griffiths (left) greets Mick Granger (right) prior to his debut in goal against Barrow in the FA Cup first round in November 1952. Manager Charles Spencer looks on.*
Below: *City team that opened the 1952-3 season during which they finished fourth in Division Three North. The following players accumulated 415 League appearances between in this term. Back row (left to right): Andrews, Brown, R.Spence, Thompson, J.Spence, Simpson. Front row: Fenton, Hughes, Griffiths, A.Patrick, Storey.*

Arthur Bottom (centre) scoring at the Shay in a 3-3 draw against Halifax Town in February 1955.

Team affairs were subsequently handled by Tom Lockie and Billy Sherrington — it was to be 18 months before a new manager was appointed. A run of eight games without a win (two draws, six defeats) saw the club slump to near the bottom of the League and attendances during this time plummeted from 12,000 to under 6,000. With the return to the fold of Billy Hughes, and with Sid Storey restored to the attack, the team started to blend at the beginning of October. The obvious potential in the side began to be realized. York City were on the threshold of great and historic deeds. With the emphasis on the close passing game and attacking football the crowds started to flock back to Bootham Crescent. A run of ten games without defeat put the side in good heart for the start of the FA Cup. Their exploits in the competition that season are legendary as they became the first Third Division club in history to reach a semi-final replay. (See *Cup Glory Days.*)

In the League from mid-September until late April they boasted the following magnificent record: P 33 W 21 D 9 L 3. The only three defeats they suffered in this period were at home to Bradford, Barnsley (eventual champions) and away to Darlington. On Good Friday 1955, just under 20,000 fans saw the promotion clash at Bootham Crescent against Accrington Stanley and the gates had to be closed. The following day there was an attendance of 12,436 for the home game against Grimsby Town. A total of almost 33,000 spectators at Bootham Crescent in the space of 24 hours!

City were just unable, however, to make up for that poor start and a crop of injuries in the closing weeks, plus a crowded fixture list, cost them the chance of promotion. In the end they had to be content with fourth position and 58 points. The Oakwell side completed the double over City and in the final analysis how crucial that was to be.

It had, however, been a memorable campaign — arguably the best in their history. Certainly the standard of football they produced that season was of a quality way

Above: *'The Happy Wanderers'. City pictured in 1954-5, when they won 11 away matches and finished fourth in Division Three North for the second time in succession. Back row (left to right): Wilkinson, Brown, Forgan, Stewart, Spence, Howe, Lockie (trainer). Front row (left to right): Hughes, Bottom, Phillips (captain), Storey, Fenton.*

Below: *Billy Fenton (second left) forces Newcastle's Simpson to make a save in the FA Cup semi-final replay at Roker Park. The other City player is Arthur Bottom.*

above the Third Division. Of the many tributes paid to the club that season was one by the noted sports journalist Henry Rose of the *Daily Express*. Reporting on a City win at Stockport, only two days after the triumph over Spurs, he proclaimed — 'York City are First Division class. On snow covered turf they played top notch football. They found their men, used the open spaces and switched defence to attack with precision passes. There were no weak spots in this First Division team masquerading in Third Division shirts'. This rearranged midweek match drew a number of big club managers — 'the best Third Division side I have ever seen' stated one manager, who was a former famous England captain, and his view was echoed by many.

Average League attendances rose to 9,630 and gross receipts were £38,227 compared to the previous season's £17,960. The revenue account showed a profit for the year of £2,448 and the balance sheet had an accumulated credit balance of £8,907. Benefit cheques of £500 each were given to Alan Stewart, Sid Storey, Ron Spence and Matt Patrick, four players who had given valued and loyal service to the club. At the end of the season City were invited by the East Riding County FA to play Hull City at Boothferry Park for the East Riding Invitation Cup. A crowd of 8,598 saw a goalless draw and both clubs held the trophy for six months.

As a reward for their fine season, the City players embarked on a week's tour of Ireland in May 1955. It was the club's first overseas trip since the visit to Holland back in 1938. City played two matches. At Dalymount Park, Dublin, they shared six goals with Bohemians. The Irish side included a number of guest players from England, including Harry Johnston and Roy Gratrix of Blackpool and Johnny Haynes and Charlie Mitten from Fulham. Fenton, Wilkinson and Spence scored for City. In the other match they beat Linfield 3-1 at Windsor Park, Belfast, with new signing from Leeds United, Clive Colbridge, scoring twice. Reserve player Bob Bainbridge notched the other goal. The City party received characteristic warm Irish hospitality throughout their stay and attended a number of civic receptions.

Needless to say, optimism was sky-high at the outset of the 1955-6 season. Although losing their opening game at home to Wrexham they made a good start and after ten games led the table with 14 points. During this period a young local lad had a meteoric rise. This season City restored their third team in the Yorkshire League (the previous venture had only lasted for one season, 1950-51). Centre-forward Peter Tait (19-years-old) made his debut for the 'A' team and scored twice. He then made two Midland League appearances for the Reserves and netted three goals. He was then called up to make his Football League debut against Hartlepools United and scored in City's 3-0 victory. This sequence of events took place in only three weeks.

A bad run of seven games without a win (two draws and five defeats) halted their progress and they never really got back into the promotion race. The final position was 11th but the support was very good and the average League crowds at Bootham Crescent of 10,291 were the second highest in their history. For the second season in succession Arthur Bottom netted 31 League goals, whilst during the campaign Billy Fenton completed 100 goals for the club.

Although lacking a little consistency the City team again played some fine football and provided tremendous entertainment. It was the FA Cup that again provided the major highlights. In the first two rounds they dismissed Rochdale and Mansfield Town. In the third round they had to visit Swansea — memories of the epic game in 1937! At the time the Welsh club were challenging strongly for promotion near the top of the Second Division. On 7 January 1956 City gained one of their finest-ever Cup victories when they beat the 'Swans', who had eight Welsh internationals in their side, by 2-1. The scoring was opened by Clive Colbridge, deputizing for the injured Billy Fenton, in the 25th minute. Town equalized before half time but City, playing their by now traditional close passing game, took command and won the game with an 80th minute Arthur Bottom goal. As the *Sports Press* headlined the victory — 'City are at it again — Look you!'

City's reward in the fourth round was a home draw against First Division Sunderland, then billed as the 'Bank of England' side. The previous season City and Sunderland had been the beaten semi-finalists. An all-ticket crowd of 22,000 witnessed an epic battle. City had much the better of the goalless draw and Sunderland were lucky to live to fight again. Their 'keeper, Willie Fraser, made a number of fine saves, whilst Wilkinson and Fenton both came within inches of scoring. The replay was staged on an icy pitch at Roker Park in front of 43,928 spectators. Honours were even in the first half with both defences on top, but just before the interval Sunderland took the lead with a fortunate goal when a 35-yard lobbed shot by Stan Anderson was mispunched into his own net by Tommy Forgan. City fought back and in the 54th minute equalized through a Billy Fenton header. Only a brilliant Fraser save prevented a Bottom goal as the game switched from end to end. With extra-time looming the home side snatched an 88th-minute winner when Charlie Fleming beat Forgan with a low shot. For the second successive season City had gone out of the FA Cup at Roker Park, but even in defeat they had added to their prestige. The City team that played in both these games was their usual formation: Forgan; Phillips, Howe, Brown, Stewart, Spence, Hughes, Bottom, Wilkinson, Storey, Fenton.

The Sunderland side for the replay was: Fraser; Hedley, McDonald, Anderson, Daniel, Aitken, Bingham, Fleming, Holden, Elliot, Shackleton.

During the season serious consideration was given to filling the vacant managerial position. In December 1955 Don Roper, who was the current Arsenal captain and inside-forward, was offered the post of player-manager. York were prepared to pay the London club a big fee for his services. Roper was offered a long-term contract and housing accommodation. After prolonged negotiations the Arsenal player turned down the deal, chiefly because of business interests he had in London. Early in 1956 they turned their attention to Charlie Wayman, the Middlesbrough centre-forward, but the transfer fee proved too big. Finally, on 9 March 1956, the club announced the appointment of Sam Bartram as their new manager. The evergreen Charlton Athletic goalkeeper was a popular choice. He had been a great favourite with the Bootham Crescent fans during the war years when he guested for the club. On the short-list was George Hardwick, the former Middlesbrough and England captain.

At the end of the season Gordon Brown received a £500 benefit cheque and long-serving Sid Storey was surprisingly given a free transfer. He duly signed for Second Division Barnsley. City again competed with Hull City for the East Riding Invitation Cup and this time won the competition outright with a 7-4 aggregate win. The second leg at Bootham Crescent, which attracted a crowd of 8,881, was won 5-0 by City.

That season no fewer than ten home League matches drew five-figure attendances with the biggest crowd being that of 14,976 to see the visit of Derby County.

The reserve side finished in the top six of the very competitive Midland League whilst the third team, at the first attempt, won promotion to the First Division of the Yorkshire League. A promising young local inside-forward by the name of Colin Addison made his debut in the third team that season.

At the AGM in September 1956 record gross receipts of £40,582 were reported and a profit of £8,453 was declared. The accumulated credit balance now stood at an impressive £22,121. On the balance sheet the Bootham Crescent ground and equipment was valued at £19,832.

In the summer of 1956 the club spent a good deal of money on new players, Alan Monkhouse, a centre-forward from Newcastle United, Jim Cairney, a centre-half from Portsmouth and Peter Wragg, an ex-Sheffield United inside-forward. A total of £12,000 — big by 1956 standards — was invested in these players. Everything appeared geared to the big promotion drive and a crowd of 7,099 saw the public practice match between the Reds (first team) against the Blues (second team). It was in this game that a youthful Barry Jackson made his first appearance. In December that year he signed professional terms for the club and so began an illustrious career at Bootham Crescent. Enthusiasm was at a new high and 15,318 saw the opening home game against Workington. The team never quite made the impact hoped for, however, and they had to be content with seventh place.

A good run of results early in the New Year — six wins and a draw in eight games — rekindled hopes but the momentum could not be sustained. During this successful period the club's record win — 9-1 against Southport — was achieved. In the FA Cup they fell at the second hurdle to Hull City at Boothferry Park. Arthur Bottom again topped the scorer's list and the average League attendances were 9,414 (six five-figure crowds). At the end of the season a benefit match was staged for Percy Andrews who had given the club ten years excellent service. The reserve team again did well, finishing in the top five of the Midland League, but the third team suffered immediate relegation from the Yorkshire League First Division. Another profit on the season was made, albeit a small one, and the accumulated credit balance was £22,687. A financial position which many clubs in the country would be proud to possess, stated the annual report. Matt Patrick and Alan Stewart both retired after fine careers.

1957-8 was a crucial campaign for Third Division clubs — the last season of regional football. At the end of the term the top 12 clubs in the North and South Leagues would form the Third Division and likewise the bottom dozen clubs in each section would become founders of the Fourth Division.

After three very good seasons, City's form deserted them and at just the wrong time. City went into their Easter programme in an apparently hopeless position. They were 22nd in the table with only 29 points from 36 games. They then staged a tremendous last-ditch effort in a bid to retain their Third Division status. In their last ten games they won seven and drew three and in the end only an inferior goal-average prevented them from attaining the top 12 position — so near yet so far!

In the final analysis three heavy defeats cost them dear. Chester (a) 9-2 their heaviest post-war defeat, Tranmere (a) 6-0 and Carlisle (h) 5-0 the biggest post-war reverse at Bootham Crescent. Amidst all their traumas in the League, however, there emerged more FA Cup excitement and triumph. City reached the third round by defeating Chesterfield and South Shields. They then entertained First Division Birmingham City who, only 18 months earlier, had lost in the Final to Manchester City. The match on the Saturday was postponed owing to an unfit pitch but on the following Wednesday afternoon City rose to the occasion and gained a magnificent 3-0 victory. Goals in the first half hour from Arthur Bottom, Peter Wragg and Norman Wilkinson sank the Blues. Eight of the City team that had reached the semi-final three years earlier were in the team that day and it was a triumph for Ron Spence, who had been sidelined through injury for 18 months. Goalkeeper Mick Granger, playing in his first major cup-tie, had an outstanding game.

The teams lined up:

York City: Granger; Phillips, Howe, Brown, Johnson, Spence, Hughes, Bottom, Wilkinson, Wragg, Fenton.

Birmingham City: Merrick; Hall, Farmer, Watts, Smith, Neal, Hooper, Kinsey, Brown, Murphy, Astall.

In the next round City were drawn at home to Bolton Wanderers, then a powerful First Division outfit. The biggest post-war Bootham Crescent crowd — an all-ticket

23,600 — saw a grim, hard-fought tussle end in a goalless draw. City played with great spirit but constructive football was almost impossible on the treacherous surface which had the players slipping and sliding about. City bowed out in the replay 0-3 in front of 34,062 and Bolton went on to win the Cup, beating Manchester United in the post-Munich final. Shortly after the Cup defeat, Arthur Bottom was transferred to Newcastle United and at the end of the season three more of the famous semi-final side left the club — captain Ernie Phillips, Gordon Brown and Billy Fenton. Jim Cairney emigrated to Canada whilst Tommy Forgan missed most of the season through injury. Seventeen-year-old inside-forward Colin Addison made his senior debut during the season. Average League attendances dropped to 7,270. The Reserves were again well placed in the Midland League.

So ended an era — City now faced the future as a Fourth Division club. The Reserves were also to operate in a new League — North Regional — and so finished the club's long connection with the Midland League.

York City's first-ever game in the Fourth Division was at Boundary Park, Oldham, on 23 August 1958. A Ron Greensmith goal earned the points and the match marked the debut of 20-year-old Barry Jackson at centre-half. Under the captaincy of Peter Wragg they gained promotion (see *Promotion Years*) and so quickly restored their Third Division status.

In the summer of 1959 floodlights were installed at Bootham Crescent. Back in the Third Division, but a very different League to that of the old Northern Section. For the first time in their history they crossed swords with the likes of Norwich City, Southampton, Bournemouth, Reading and Queen's Park Rangers. Apart from John Edgar, a forward from Gillingham, and John Battye an experienced half-back from Huddersfield Town, they relied chiefly on the players who had helped gain promotion. Although finding goals hard to come by, City held their own in the early weeks of the campaign and support was at a good level. The floodlights were first really used for an evening game against QPR in early September when 10,593 saw an exciting 2-1 City win. Nearly 12,000 were in attendance when Grimsby Town were the visitors and a thrilling game ended 3-3. Following a goalless draw at home to Barnsley at the end of February, City were in mid-table with a record of: P 33 W 11 D 11 L 11 F 43 A 48 Pts 33.

A disastrous finale to the season, with only two wins and a draw in their last 12 fixtures, saw the side slump into the bottom four and sadly drop back to the Fourth Division. In the FA Cup they were knocked out in the third round at Bournemouth. Average attendances fell to 7,507 and at the end of the season a number of players were released, including long-serving Ron Spence. Others to depart included Terry Farmer, Ron Greensmith, Billy Hill and Johnny Powell.

The 38th annual report of the club whilst expressing 'keen disappointment' over the playing record of 1959-60, was able to confirm a satisfactory position as to the financial stability of the Company.

The summer of 1960 was one of many changes. Sam Bartram was released from his contract as manager and he took up a similar position at Luton. After careful thought, and without advertising the post, the directors unanimously decided to appoint Tom Lockie as manager. Since 1936 he had been a loyal and enthusiastic clubman, most of the time as chief trainer. Appointed as the new trainer at the same time was former player Sid Storey and the new player-coach of the third team was to be Ernie Phillips. Several new signings were made, including Jimmy Weir ex-Fulham, Alan Woods from Swansea and Walter Bingley and Jack Fountain from Swindon Town. Under the new managerial team, the side playing attractive football, got away to a good start. By November they were well-placed in the top four, but then followed a bad December with five successive defeats. A good run in the New Year revived hopes but, with only one win in the last seven fixtures,

Sam Bartram recuperating from appendicitis in August 1959, attended to by his daughter.

they finished fifth — nine points behind fourth-placed Bradford. During the season Norman Wilkinson reached 100 League and cup goals in his City career. Top marksman was Peter Wragg with 22 League goals. Unfortunately, owing to injury, he missed the crucial last weeks of the campaign.

The biggest crowd of the season was 11,768 in April to see the League's newest club, Peterborough United, who finished as champions. Average League attendances were 6,900. York again reached the third round of the FA Cup knocking out Bradford and Tranmere Rovers after replays in the two early stages. Then followed two keenly-fought games against Second Division Norwich City. At Bootham Crescent the sides drew 1-1, with the visitors snatching a late equalizer. In the replay at Carrow Road, in front of over 27,000, City were beaten rather unluckily by an 84th minute penalty. This match was the last in City colours for Colin Addison. A few days later he signed for Nottingham Forest for a club record fee received of £12,000. The Football League Cup was instituted this season and Addison had scored City's first-ever goal in the competition in a 3-1 first-round defeat at the hands of Blackburn Rovers at Bootham Crescent. This history-making match was played on 10 October 1960 and the attendance was 10,933. The teams lined up:

York City: Forgan; Bingley, Howe, Woods, Boyes, Fountain, Hughes, Scott, Wragg, Wilkinson, Addison.

Scorer: Addison.

Blackburn Rovers: Jones; Bray, Pickering, Clayton, Woods, Newton, Isherwood, Dobing, Dougan, Crowe, Douglas.

Scorers: Crowe, Dougan (2).

The death occurred in December 1960 of Hartas Foxton, who had served as a director for 19 years. In his will he left £1,000 to the club. K Lancaster was co-opted on to the board.

At the end of the 1960-61 season Sherrington retired from his post as secretary. He had filled that position with distinction for 31 years and was one of the best-known and respected officials in the Football League. Previous to 1930 he had been honorary secretary and a director and had helped to establish the club in 1922. Many tributes were paid on his retirement and from the club he received a television set and from the directors a set of cut glass. He was made the first vice-president of York City. His successor was George Teasdale who had served in the RAF for a number of years and had later been manager of Selby Town and then Goole Town. Before taking up his appointment at Bootham Crescent he had been employed in the administration section at RAF Church Fenton. W.H.Sessions and J.W.Rosindale both retired as directors after long and valued service and Tom Mitchell, a former player and manager, joined the board. A profit on the year's workings amounted to £11,923.

New signings for the 1961-2 campaign included Tommy Heron from Manchester United and John Stainsby (ex-Barnsley), whilst Billy Rudd joined the club from Birmingham City for a sizeable fee in November. They were on the fringe of the top four throughout the season but poor away form let them down. Watched by an average home crowd of 6,890 they recorded several big victories at Bootham Crescent, notably 5-0 against Colchester United and Barrow. In a nailbiting finish City went into their last game at home to Aldershot needing a win to ensure promotion. Sadly they failed to rise to the occasion and, in a bitterly frustrating finale, lost by the only goal of the game. Jimmy Weir had a fine season and was top scorer with 29 League and Cup goals.

Cup success this season came in the Football League Cup, as in the first round of the FA Cup, City fell at Bradford City. *En route* to the quarter-finals of the League Cup they dismissed Third Division clubs Bristol City and Watford after two replays and Bournemouth. The outstanding performance came in the second

round when First Division Leicester City were beaten 2-1 at Bootham Crescent in front of 13,273. Match details are as follows:
York City: Forgan; Bingley, Heron, Woods, Jackson, Fountain, Weir, Wragg, Stainsby, Wilkinson, Gould.
Scorers: Wragg (24 min), Stainsby (83 min).
Leicester City: Banks; Chalmers, Norman, McLintock, King, Appleton, Riley, Walsh, Keyworth, Wills, Mitten.
Scorer: Mitten (63 min).

It was a fine display by City and they even allowed themselves the luxury of a missed penalty. Scenes at the end of the match were reminiscent of the FA Cup games of the mid 1950s. Having done so well in the tournament it was a big disappointment when they lost to fellow Fourth Division side Rochdale at Spotland in the last eight.

At the end of the campaign two more of the famous cup giantkilling team departed — Billy Hughes and George Howe. Reliable understudy goalkeeper, Mick Granger, also left club.

The Accrington Stanley club collapsed in March 1962 and one of their players, Alex Hamilton, assisted City in the closing weeks.

A loss of £2,126 on the revenue account for the year was declared. In the 40th annual report, tribute was again paid to the work done by honorary medical adviser Dr J.B.McKenna.

During the 1961-2 season C.Hull joined the board. At the start of the following campaign the City Supporters' Club staged a big membership drive. The annual fee was 2s (10p) and officials and committees for the new season were: chairman J.W.Edwards, vice-chairman A.Butler, honorary secretary and treasurer F.Cawood, committee: Messrs R.Bayes, G.Bodley, J.Constable, J.Duffy, R.Frost, A.Kerr, J.Mortimer, R.Nelson, F.Linwood, R.L.Pearce, W.A.Pearson, R.Robinson, A.Ruddock, D.Scott, W.Scott, F.Taylor, P.Wilmott, J.Wright, A.Newton.

Women's section: chairman Miss M.Theasby, vice-chairman Mrs J.W.Edwards, honorary secretary and treasurer Mrs C.Brown, committee: Mrs E.Coupe, Miss F.Holt, Miss Dunn, Miss Gillis, Mrs Duffy, Mrs Flintoft, Mrs Richards, Mrs Ferriss, Mrs N.Bayes.

After narrowly missing promotion in each of the two previous seasons City started with little change of personnel, but in September Jimmy Weir was transferred to Mansfield Town. The club experienced a disastrous first half to the campaign and defeat at Doncaster on 22 December left them in 23rd position with the following record: P 24 W 5 D 6 L 13 F 28 A 33 Pts 16.

This was the winter of the 'big freeze' and, following this game at Belle Vue, City did not play a League match until 8 March when they entertained Newport County. The rest obviously did City good, for in the second half of the season they showed promotion form: P 22 W 11 D 5 L 6 F 39 A 29 Pts 27.

This enabled them to pull well clear of the re-election zone and they finished in a respectable 14th position. None the less it had been a disappointing term overall and the average League attendance dropped to a new post-war low of 4,515.

In the FA Cup, City reached the third round of the competition, but crashed to a 5-0 defeat at Southampton at this stage. Because of the arctic weather this match was rearranged no less than nine times. Top scorer for the season was the ever-faithful Norman Wilkinson. Departures at the end of the campaign, which was extended until 20 May, included Walter Bingley, John Stainsby and Peter Wragg. The last named had given seven years outstanding service. The annual report stated that the financial position of stability was largely due to the very welcome assistance from the Auxiliary Club, Supporters' and Social Clubs.

The Auxiliary Supporters' club had been formed in 1954 as a special fund-raising branch of the Supporters' Club. The committee included Frank Cawood, Arthur Butler, Jack Burke, Jim Edwards, Eric Thompson, Norman Clay, Tommy Roebuck and Billy Hill. At one time the money-raising scheme boasted 16,000 members and, in a period of over ten years, thousands of pounds were raised.

As an economy measure, however, the third team was withdrawn from the Yorkshire League and disbanded.

Several newcomers joined the club in the summer of 1963. Noel Peyton an ex-Leeds United and Republic of Ireland international, Gerry Baker from Nottingham Forest and Jimmy Goldie from Luton Town. Ron Spence took over as physiotherapist and trainer from Sid Storey. A dreadful start was made and the first four home games were lost. They never recovered from these disasters and struggled throughout the season. They finished in 22nd position and had to apply for re-election for the second time in their history. Average League crowds dropped to 3,937 and the match against Oxford United on 21 December drew only 1,653 spectators — a new record low crowd at Bootham Crescent.

Norman Wilkinson was again leading scorer whilst during the campaign popular wingman Wally Gould, who had been at York for nearly three years, was transferred to Brighton. No joy either in the cup competitions. In the FA Cup they lost 5-2 at home to Carlisle in the first round whilst in the Football League Cup they fell at the second stage in a replay at Lincoln.

Overshadowing everything, however, that season was the football bribery scandal exposed by the *Sunday People* in April 1964. Jack Fountain, City's half-back and former captain, was one of the players named by the newspaper — accused of fixing the results of matches.

The 'Big Freeze' of 1963 and City players slide across an arctic Bootham Crescent. Left to right: Gould, Forgan, Ambler, Woods, Wragg and Jackson.

Reporting the matter in the *Sports Press* Wilf Meek summed up the situation by saying 'without doubt this has been the most unfortunate and sickening week in the 42 years history of York City Football Club'.

The City matches that were allegedly fixed were a home game against Tranmere Rovers on 21 October 1961, which was lost 2-1, and a game at Oldham on 1 December 1962. This latter match ended in a 3-2 win for the home side after City had led 2-0 at the interval. At the time Athletic were Fourth Division League leaders whilst City were next-to-bottom of the table.

Fountain's contract with the club was terminated. He was subsequently found guilty, banned from football for life and served a prison sentence. Amongst other players involved and found guilty were England internationals Tony Kay and Peter Swan.

City polled 48 votes at the Football League's AGM and were re-elected. The annual report refered to the difficult season experienced which had resulted in a loss of £3,181. The year had seen the foundation of the Development Association and donations from the organization concerned with the club totalled £12,865. Praise was given to Bryan Foster, the groundsman, for his fine work. The condition of the ground was now the envy of many visiting clubs.

After the trials and tribulations of 1963-4 the next season saw City rise from the ashes. In the summer of 1964 new recruits included Paul Aimson from Manchester City, Andy Provan (ex-Barnsley), Derek Weddle from Darlington and Dennis Walker who was previously with Manchester United. The side, under the inspired leadership of Billy Rudd, found the right blend and, producing the best football seen at Bootham Crescent since the glory years of the mid-1950s, won promotion (see *Promotion years*). Average League crowds of 7,185 were almost double the previous season. At home 20 League wins were recorded — a club record — and after the darkest hour in the club's history the sun once more shone on York City.

In March 1965 the club's longest-serving director, William Mason, died. He had joined the board in 1927 and had given a lifetimes' devotion to the interests of the club. In tributes paid to him it was said that: 'York City was more than just a pastime occupation to him. He helped to found the club and he worked exceptionally hard to secure admission for City to the Football League.' The City board placed on record his great service to the club. His death took away one of the old personalities in the game and one who was well known far afield among football administrators.

In preparation for their first season back in the Third Division since 1960, York signed a talented young Irish midfield player, Eamonn Dunphy, from Manchester United. Another recurit from Old Trafford was John Pearson and from Manchester City came other young promising forwards, Ken Morton and Bobby Cunliffe. Making a welcome return to the club was David Dunmore who, since leaving Bootham Crescent 11 years earlier, had seen service with Spurs, West Ham United and Leyton Orient. Goalkeeper Harry Fallon was signed from St Johnstone early in September following a serious injury to Tommy Forgan. Hopes were high and early results were encouraging. Victories at Brentford, Southend and a spectacular success at Hull gave grounds for optimism and attendances at Bootham Crescent were the highest for several seasons.

Sadly their home form deserted them and they were to record only five wins at Bootham Crescent all season — in direct contrast to 1964-5. By Christmas the side had dropped into the bottom four of the table and in March they sunk to the foot of the League, where they stayed. Meanwhile Eamonn Dunphy, anxious to better himself, was transferred to Millwall in January 1966 and leading scorer Paul Aimson moved to Bury in March. A season which had started with so much expectation and promise crashed about York's ears as the side suffered a series of heavy defeats. Twice they conceded seven goals and once six and the total number

Tom Lockie (extreme right) conducts a pre-season training session in August 1965. Back row (left to right): Baker, Aimson, Wealthall, Jackson, Dunmore, Cunliffe, Lowe, Pearson, Morton. Front row: Rudd, Heron, Woods, Provan.

of goals let in that season amounted to 106 — a club record. Average League attendances were 5,921. The biggest crowd was that of 19,420 in March to see Hull City gain revenge with a 2-1 victory.

In the Football League Cup they fell to Millwall in the second round, whilst they suffered a humiliating first-round FA Cup defeat away to non-League South Shields. It was their first defeat at the hands of non-League opposition since 1946-7 when Scunthorpe won at York. The end of the season saw the departure of the last two members of the great 1954-5 side — Tommy Forgan and Norman Wilkinson. Between them these two outstanding stalwarts made 830 League and cup appearances and Wilkinson's grand total of 143 goals remains a club record. Other players to leave Bootham Crescent in May 1966 included Billy Rudd, who was transferred to Grimsby Town, Alan Woods, Tommy Heron and Ken Boyes. The latter had served the club loyally for several years, chiefly as understudy to Barry Jackson. In recognition of their fine service Forgan, Wilkinson and Boyes were presented with inscribed gold watches by the chairman.

Recorded in the Minute Book:

'Kitchin said it gave him the greatest pleasure to do this which was the first occasion in the club's history that it had been done. It was a tribute to the loyalty these players had shown at all times and a mark of respect felt for these players by the Directorate and Staff of the club and the supporters. During their time with us these players had shown true sportsmanship and the chairman hoped they would have happy memories of their service with York City'.

After their briefest possible stay in the Third Division, fresh team building was done in the summer of 1966 and several new players joined the club. Goalkeeper Mike Walker was signed from Shrewsbury, as was the new captain and full-back

Ken Turner. New forwards were Roland Horrey from Blackburn, John Goodchild (ex-Sunderland and Brighton) and Tommy Spencer from Southampton, who was to finish top scorer with 23 League and cup goals. York-born John Hawksby, formerly with Leeds United and Lincoln, had been signed towards the end of the previous campaign.

The reserve team switched from the North Region League and joined the Second Division of the Yorkshire League. They won promotion at the end of the season.

In November 1966 the death occurred of W.H.Sessions. For over 30 years he had been associated with York City as a director, chairman and in the latter period as club president. An offical club statement paying tribute said of him: 'A man of great charm, he lent dignity and prestige to the game and the club. We will remember him with affection and esteem.' Upon the death of Sessions the club presidency passed to Billy Sherrington.

The years 1966 to 1969 could be regarded as the 'dark ages' for York City. During this time they had to make three successive applications for re-election under, incidentally, three different managers.

A reasonable start was made to the Fourth Division programme in 1966-7 and they were mid-table in November, but then came a terrible slump with only one victory in 18 games and they dropped to the bottom of the League. During this spell they suffered a sequence of eight successive League defeats — the club's worst-ever run. A brief rally at the end of the season could not prevent them finishing in the bottom four. The away record was dismal, with only one win and six draws, whilst average home crowds of 3,776 were the lowest since the war. A total of ten cup ties were played, including five against Middlesbrough, and these provided the highlights of the season. In the FA Cup three exciting games were played against 'Boro, watched by an aggregate of over 55,000 fans and City were knocked out in the second replay at St James' Park, Newcastle.

At the Football League AGM City received 45 votes and were duly re-elected.

In June 1967 Hugh Kitchin resigned from the board. He had been a director since 1945 and for over 13 years had been chairman. It was with great reluctance that he made this decision, which was due to business commitments. The club's long-serving Honorary Medical Officer, Dr J.B.McKenna, joined the board.

The new chairman was Derek Blundy and vice-chairman F.H.(Eric) Magson. Sixteen months later Magson took over the chairmanship and Wilf Meek became his deputy.

For the first time in 31 years there was a change of club colours. For the 1967-8 campaign they would sport an all-white kit.

Two new additions were made to the attack during the close season. Tommy Ross was signed from Peterborough United and centre-forward Ted MacDougall was a £5,000 capture from Liverpool. City made a disastrous start — their worst ever — when they failed to win any of their first 13 League games (five draws, eight defeats). It was 23 October, when Swansea were beaten at Bootham Crescent, when they finally broke their duck. By then manager Tom Lockie had been dismissed — the first City boss to suffer this fate. He had spent 31 years with the club and Bootham Crescent would never quite be the same without the tall, likeable and much-respected Scot. Joe Shaw, the long-serving Sheffield United centre-half, was appointed as his successor in November. He recruited a Bramall Lane colleague, Billy Hodgson, as player-coach. Results improved and by the beginning of April they had risen from the bottom of the League to 14th position. A bad finish, with two draws and six defeats in the last eight games, saw them drop back into the bottom four. For the first time in their history they were knocked out in the first round of both cup competitions, but average League attendances at Bootham Crescent showed an improvement on the previous season and were 4,578. Departures at the

Joe Shaw (seated) meets City players on his appointment as manager in November 1967. Left to right: Provan, Jackson, Spencer, Baker (partly hidden), Burrows, Hawksby, Joy, MacDougall, Collinson, Fallon, M.Walker, Ross.

end of another disappointing campaign included Dennis Walker, Harry Fallon and John Hawksby. With 46 votes City were re-elected back to the Fourth Division. May 1968 marked the end of an era with the retirement of *Yorkshire Evening Press* journalist Wilf Meek. He had reported on City's fortunes for 46 years since their formation in 1922. Since 1968 Malcolm Huntington has chronicled the club's affairs.

The second team had a bad season, finishing in the bottom six of the First Division of the Yorkshire League. In the summer of 1968 it was decided to scrap the reserve side. There was to be a first-team pool of about 16 professionals and an intermediate side, for players up to the age of 19, would compete in the Northern Intermediate League.

The most notable close-season capture that year was Phil Boyer, a highly-rated young forward from Derby County. He thus teamed up with Ted MacDougall and so started a highly-successful partnership which was in time to take them to Bournemouth and then Norwich City. The 1968-9 campaign was less than a week old when Joe Shaw announced his shock resignation as manager for personal reasons. At the end of October Tom Johnston, former boss of Rotherham, Grimsby and Huddersfield, was appointed manager. He became the ninth person to officially hold this position and in the fullness of time, arguably, he was to be the most successful.

At the time of his arrival, City were struggling in the lower reaches of the League and, chiefly because of continued poor away form, they were unable to escape the re-election zone.

They managed only two wins and three draws on their travels and lost their last 11 away League games on the trot. In the three seasons back in the Fourth Division they had won only five of their 69 away games! In the FA Cup they reached the third round of the competition for the first time since 1962-3. In the

York City pictured in 1968-9. Back row (left to right): Kelly, Baker, Carr, Widdowson, Walker, MacDougall, Jackson, Topping. Front row: Joe Shaw (manager), Spratt, Ross, Provan, Burrows, Hodgson, R.Spence (trainer).

first round they recorded their biggest ever away win (6-0 at South Shields) with Tommy Ross hitting a hat-trick. First Division Stoke City, with a 2-0 win at Bootham Crescent, ended their hopes of a cup run in front of 11,129 fans — the first five-figure crowd for nearly three years.

New signings during the campaign included Archie Taylor from Bradford City, Dick Hewitt from Barnsley and ex-Leeds United defender Bobby Sibbald. In December 1968 17-year-old Chris Topping, the clubs first-ever apprentice, made his senior debut.

Players to leave during the season were goalkeeper Mike Walker to Watford and Andy Provan, who moved to Chester. Full-back Gerry Baker had to retire from the game owing to injury and the following season he was granted a testimonial match in which the current City side played the 1954-5 team. In the last few matches of 1968-9 local amateur 'keeper John Andrews deputized for the injured Bob Widdowson.

There was a very sombre note to the last home game of the campaign against Halifax Town. Early in the match referee Roy Harper of Sheffield collapsed and died after a heart attack. Average League attendances dropped to 3,883.

At the end of the season Ted MacDougall, who for the second time finished leading scorer, was transferred to Bournemouth. So came to an end the fourth consecutive season of disappointment and failure — relegation followed by three cap-in-hand applications for re-election back to the League.

In June 1969 they received 45 votes at the League AGM and again were readmitted to the Fourth Division without any undue anxiety.

Changes in the boardroom saw Chris Hull and Tom Mitchell step down and Dr Angus McLeod and Bernard Kilner take their places. Club colours were changed to maroon shirts and white shorts and the reserve team was restored. They were to operate in the North Midlands League, whilst the intermediate side was maintained.

Paul Aimson (left) on his return to Bootham Cresent in August 1969 with manager Tom Johnston.

After four years in the doldrums 1969-70 was a much better season and the side finished in a comfortable mid-table position. In the early weeks of the campaign a promotion challenge looked likely and, with eight wins in the opening 12 games, they occupied a position in the top four — a welcome change of fortunes. A mid-season slump, however, saw the promotion hopes fade and again it was poor away form which was the bugbear. Just two victories on their travels, which meant only seven away wins in four seasons! Newcomers this term included Ian Davidson (ex-Hull City), John Mackin from Lincoln and Kevin McMahon from Newcastle United. Notable signings were Paul Aimson, who returned to Bootham Crescent after an absence of over three years during which time he had been with Bury, Bradford

City and Huddersfield, and Barry Swallow. The centre-half was signed from Bradford City in October and he was to prove one of the club's finest captures.

After a number of lean seasons in the FA Cup, City gave their supporters some 'Cup cheer' by reaching the fourth round of the competition for the first time since 1957-8. Non-League Whitby Town and Bangor City were defeated in the first two rounds and they were drawn at home to, at the time, high-flying Second Division side Cardiff City. The Welsh team were managed by Jimmy Scoular, an old Cup adversary of York having captained Newcastle United in the semi-final battles of 15 years earlier. In an exciting match the teams drew 1-1. Phil Boyer gave City a second-minute lead with a diving header and in the early stages the visitors were in danger of being swamped. In the 15th minute, however, Barry Swallow had the misfortune to head an own goal and although that was the end of the scoring, thrills abounded in a very lively cup tie. In the last quarter City took command but the Cardiff defence held on and the Welshmen gained a rather fortunate replay.

At Ninian Park the teams were involved in another thriller and City put on a tremendous display by holding the Second Division leaders to a 1-1 draw after extra-time. Cardiff took the lead with a controversial goal in the 33rd minute when John Toshack appeared to handle the ball before shooting past Gordon Morritt. After the interval City stormed into attack and went close on several occasions. Ian Davidson hit the post and then in the 88th minute they got a richly-deserved equalizer when Archie Taylor's lobbed shot found the net. Extra-time failed to produce a result and a few days later the show moved on to St Andrew's, home of Birmingham City, on 15 January 1970. It was quite rightly described as 'York City's Night to Remember' as, after another titanic battle which went into extra-time, they finally knocked-out their Welsh foes 3-1. Peter King put Cardiff ahead in the 40th minute. City, playing some fine football, went near several times before again grabbing a late equalizer. In the 82nd minute following a free-kick, Barry Swallow crashed a tremendous 15-yard shot into the net. It was Swallow's first goal for City and early in extra-time he headed his side into the lead from close range. Paul Aimson clinched a famous Cup victory with a third goal and after 330 minutes City finally reached the fourth round. It had been a magnificent team effort but special praise was due to Barry Jackson, who for the third time, snuffed out Cardiff's rising young star, John Toshack. So much so that the Welsh international was finally substituted.

A crowd of 38,283 at Ayresome Park saw City's run ended by Middlesbrough 4-1 — a scoreline which did not do justice to a gallant York effort. Early in the second half Phil Boyer made the score 2-1 and for a while it was touch and go. It was only in the closing minutes, with two late goals, that 'Boro took complete command. Consolation for City was that their FA Cup run (watched by over 92,000 spectators) had produced a £6,000 profit.

During the season, teenager Chris Topping continued to make good progress, whilst 17-year-old 'keeper Ron Hillyard made his debut. Billy Hodgson was released at the end of the campaign, as was Barry Jackson. He had been a virtual ever-present at the centre of City's defence for 12 seasons and his total of 539 senior appearances is easily a club record. Unfortunately his last season was clouded with controversy. Sent off in a game at Scunthorpe in January, he received a suspension of eight weeks. He had had a magnificent career, however, and his enthusiasm and commitment has rarely been equalled. An outstanding figure and one who ranks high in the club's Roll of Honour.

Average League crowds rose slightly to 3,951.

The 1960s had largely been a disappointing decade for York City. The one bright spot had been the 1964-5 promotion campaign. The 1970s were to provide a highpoint in their Football League career.

The death occurred in August 1970 of Wilf Meek, the vice-chairman of the club

The York City and Workington teams stand in silence in tribute to City vice-chairman Wilf Meek whose death was announced in August 1970.

and a director for over 18 years. He will be best remembered for his reports and articles on York City in the *Yorkshire Evening Press* where he was sports editor. The number of mourners at his funeral was testimony to the high regard in which he was held and the affection so many people had for him. The club's official obituary said this of him:

'Those of us who have followed the fortunes of York City since 1922 will remember 'Citizen' for his faithful reports and it was with eager anticipation that we thoroughly digested his opinion of the match appreciating his views both praiseworthy and critical (if needs be) of the team to which he was so keenly devoted.

'No one did more to try and maintain the interest and impetus of York City supporters, for he realized that the obtaining of Football League status for the City of York was an achievement to be cherished and maintained and his confidence in the Club even in difficult periods, never faltered. His reminiscing of many sporting occasions gave him much enjoyment and his listeners great pleasure but in retrospect one feels that his finest hour was during the wonderful FA Cup of 1954-5, when with great relish he produced his 'Happy Wanderer' brochure and was immensely proud that his team had produced football of quality and power to emulate all other Third Division sides by reaching the semi-final and forcing a replay against the mighty Newcastle United.'

Wilf Meek's philosophy was very aptly contained in a quote, in 1927, from his own suggestions to all Supporters' Clubs.

To see BOTH sides.

To discourage foul play and barracking.

To protect the reputation of the game on the terraces.

To encourage all referees.

To 'stand by' the club in 'bad weather'.

For over 40 years, he helped to compile the City programme. He was also very keenly involved in all aspects of local junior football. His son, David Meek, has reported on the fortunes of Manchester United for several years in the *Manchester Evening News* and has also written a number of books on the Old Trafford club.

In the wake of Wilf Meek's passing, Ken Lancaster was to become vice-chairman and newcomers to the board were Gordon Winters, R.Myles-Gibson and Bob Strachan in place of Mr A.Brown and Dr J.B.McKenna.

The death also occurred of 'Jack' Wright, one of the stalwarts of the Supporters' Club. Going back to the Fulfordgate days he had helped with a wide variety of jobs, including assisting the groundsman. For many years he worked as a match-day steward and he had also helped the Auxiliary Branch as an agent.

For 1970-71 City relied chiefly on the same squad of players as the previous season, but two newcomers were Albert Johanneson from Leeds United and Tommy Henderson from Bradford, who had lost their League place to Cambridge United.

Mid-table early in the New Year, York swept to promotion following a magnificent sequence of results in March and April.

For the second successive season they reached the fourth round of the FA Cup. Non-Leaguers Tamworth and Boston United were knocked out in the first two rounds and then Second Division Bolton Wanderers were beaten 2-0 at Bootham Crescent. Ian Davidson was the hero in this victory with two first half goals. In the fourth round, City were drawn at home to First Division Southampton and the game at Bootham Crescent on 23 January 1971 was a classic — arguably the most exciting Cup tie staged at the ground. At half-time the score was 0-0, but City had outclassed the Saints for long periods and had played some brilliant football. Yet there were blows for City in the second half when, against the run of play, Southampton went 2-0 ahead through Jimmy Gabriel and Mike Channon. In the 80th minute, Kevin McMahon pulled one back with a header but Ron Davies restored the visitors' two-goal lead with only six minutes remaining. City appeared down and out, but in the 87th minute Dick Hewitt cracked in a close-range shot to make the score 2-3. With the crowd roaring them on, York surged forward and in an incredible finish equalized in the last minute when Paul Aimson rose high above the Southampton defence to head home a cross from John Mackin.

A truly magnificent match and a credit to both teams, who received a standing ovation at the end. The line-ups were:
York City: Hillyard; Mackin, Burrows, Davidson, Swallow, Topping, Taylor(Henderson), McMahon, Aimson, Hewitt, Johanneson.
Southampton: Martin; Kirkup, Hollywood, Fisher, McGrath, Gabriel, Paine, Channon, Davies, O'Neill, Walker.

The replay at The Dell was another thrilling affair and City put up another tremendous display before losing 2-3.

Paul Aimson's dramatic last minute equalizer against Southampton in the fourth-round FA Cup tie in January 1971.

Barry Swallow (extreme right) heads in goal number three against Grimsby Town in the first-round FA Cup tie in November 1971.

Back in the Third Division after a five-season absence, City recruited John Woodward, a utility player from Arsenal, midfielders Pat Lally from Millwall and Laurie Calloway from Southport and forward Eddie Rowles, who was involved in an exchange transfer which took Ian Davidson to Bournemouth.

City started the campaign quite well with notable victories at Brighton and Bolton, but an 11-match run without a win (three draws, eight defeats) saw them drop into the bottom four and in the second half of the season they had to wage a long battle against relegation. In a nail-biting finish, only goal-average saved City from the drop. They thus avoided the fate which had befallen them in 1960 and 1966, when they suffered immediate relegation back to Division Four. They were indebted to the back four — John Mackin, Phil Burrows, Barry Swallow and Chris Topping — all of whom were ever-presents. During the season, goalkeeper Graeme Crawford was signed from Sheffield United and winger Dennis Wann came from Blackpool. A local youngster, 17-year-old winger Brian Pollard, made his debut in the closing weeks. City's average home League attendance of 5,597 was the highest for six years.

The Football League Cup provided the highlight of this season and the third round was reached for the first time since 1966-7. In the second round, York had two tremendous tilts with Second Division Middlesbrough. At Bootham Crescent, City let slip a two-goal lead, but in the replay at Ayresome Park they gained a famous victory with goals from Laurie Calloway and Tommy Henderson. In the third round they were drawn away to Sheffield United, who at the time were First Division leaders. A crowd of almost 30,000 at Bramall Lane saw City give the Blades a tremendous fright. Barry Swallow opened the scoring but Tony Currie

Above: *Tommy Henderson (out of picture) cracks in a fine goal against Shrewsbury Town in October 1971.*

Below: *Villa's Willie Anderson scores the only goal of the game from the penalty-spot at Villa Park in February 1972. A paper streamer hangs in the net behind City 'keeper Graeme Crawford.*

City's goals against Sheffield United at Bramall Lane in October 1972. Above: *Barry Swallow (5) celebrates his goal which put City in front.* Below: *Chris Topping fires in the second-half equalizer.*

and an Alan Woodward penalty gave the home team an interval lead. In a thrilling second half, Chris Topping scored a 65th-minute equalizer and with only four minutes remaining, substitute Eddie Rowles missed a glorious chance for City when he miskicked in front of goal. United celebrated their escape by scoring a magnificent winner when Woodward beat Ron Hillyard with a tremendous 25-yard shot in the 88th minute. City had given a wonderful display, however, and had written yet another glorious chapter in their Cup history. The sides lined up at Bramall Lane as follows.

Sheffield United: Hope; Badger, Barlow, Flynn, Colquhoun, Hockey, Woodward, Salmons, Dearden, Currie, Scullion.

York City: Hillyard; Mackin, Burrows, Lally, Swallow, Topping, Henderson, McMahon(Rowles) Aimson, Calloway, Hewitt.

To celebrate the 50th anniversary of the club in 1972, the City Supporters' Club produced a souvenir handbook which provided a condensed history of York City. Committee members Jeff Mortimer and Norman Clay provided the editorial. For several years the latter wrote the Supporters' Club notes in the match-day programme. At the time Arthur Butler was chairman of the Supporters' Club and Frank Cawood the honorary secretary. He had taken over that position in 1959 from Harry Ward, who held that post for 33 years. A lifelong supporter and fund raiser for York City, Frank has worked in the match-day office for many years and is one of the best known and well liked characters behind the scenes at Bootham Crescent.

In preparation for 1972-3, a new centre-forward, Jimmy Seal, was signed from Barnsley and defender John Stone came from Middlesbrough. A nightmare start was made to the campaign and York failed to win any of their opening 11 matches (five draws six defeats). Only three goals were scored in this period and City failed to score in seven consecutive games.

Results improved in mid-season and, by the beginning of March, City were in the top half of the table. But with only two wins in their last 13 matches, City once again walked the tightrope. A dramatic win in the last match at Rotherham saved them from relegation and for the second successive season they avoided the drop on goal-average. Goals were a scarce commodity and City failed to score in half their League games. They were involved in nine goalless draws as their average League attendances dropped to 3,792.

Dennis Wann had the misfortune to break a leg in a Boxing Day fixture at Oldham and Paul Aimson was transferred to Bournemouth late in the season.

Former Middlesbrough and Darlington player, Billy Horner, was appointed trainer-coach at the beginning of the campaign, but in January 1973 he announced his shock resignation. When he left, the players handed a long list of grievances to the directors which amounted to a vote of no confidence in manager Tom Johnston. After a clear-the-air meeting between players, management and directors, the club issued a brief official statement which said: 'The directors have considered the points

Barry Swallow (on ground) scores the first goal in the 2-0 win over Tranmere Rovers at Bootham Crescent in October 1973.

Above: *John Woodward scoring from the penalty-spot against Tranmere Rovers in a 4-1 home win in February 1973.*
Below: *The City team salute the crowd prior to the Oldham Athletic game in April 1974 which clinched promotion to Division Two.*

The last minute winning goal against Orient in the FA Cup third round replay in November 1973. Scorer Ian Butler is out of the picture.

raised by the players and these matters are being dealt with.' It had been a traumatic few days at Bootham Crescent but, thankfully, differences were resolved and the team responded with their best sequence of results that season. They won five of the next six games, including a fine 3-2 victory away to leaders Bournemouth.

A founder member of the Supporters' Club and chairman for many years, Jim Edwards, died during the season, whilst the sudden death of Billy Fenton, one of the heroes of the 1954-5 Cup team, occurred in April 1973. He was the second member of that famous team to pass away within 18 months. George Howe had died suddenly at his home in Wakefield in November 1971.

During the summer of 1973 a number of important signings were made. Ian Butler from Hull City, Chris Jones from Walsall and Ian Holmes from Sheffield United. Early in the season came Barry Lyons from Nottingham Forest. Colin Meldrum was appointed the new trainer-coach. After narrowly avoiding relegation in each of the two previous campaigns, City astounded the football world by winning promotion. After 38 seasons in the Football League, York City had reached the Second Division.

Left-back Phil Burrows, who had played such an important part in the promotion success and had not missed a game in four seasons, was transferred to Plymouth Argyle in the summer of 1974. He was City's first ever 'Clubman of the Year'.

The 1973-4 season was also notable for a good run in the Football League Cup. For only the second time, City got past the third round of the competition. In the second round at Bootham Crescent they gained an excellent 1-0 victory over Second Division Aston Villa, thanks to a goal scored by reserve player John Peachey. At the next stage they defeated another Second Division team, Orient, after a dramatic replay win at York. There was no score after 90 minutes and the visitors took the lead in extra-time, but in a thrilling fight-back City snatched victory with goals from Ian Holmes and Ian Butler, the winner being scored with only seconds remaining. In the fourth round, City were drawn at home to First Division Manchester City. The match — played on a Wednesday afternoon owing to a floodlight ban during the power crisis — attracted Bootham Crescent's biggest crowd for seven years — 15,360. A hard-fought tussle ended goalless and the teams lined up:

York City: Crawford; Stone, Burrows, Lyons, Swallow, Topping, Pollard, Woodward, Seal(Holmes), Jones, Peachey.

Above: *The York City squad in November 1973 prior to their League Cup tie against Manchester City. Back row (left to right): Pollard, Woodward, Seal, Holmes. Middle row: Meldram (coach), Stone, Peachey, Crawford, Topping, Swallow, Spence (physiotherapist). Front row: Wann, Burrows, Calvert, Tom Johnston (manager), Jones, Butler.*

Below: *Action from the Manchester City Cup tie as Barry Lyons (far left) and Jimmy Seal put pressure on the visitors' defence.*

Manchester City: McCrae; Pardoe, Donachie, Doyle, Booth, Towers, Barrett, Bell, Summerbee, Lee, Marsh.

In the replay at Maine Road, York City went down 4-1. Rodney Marsh scored a hat-trick for the home side and Francis Lee netted from the penalty-spot. Brian Pollard got the consolation goal for the visitors.

In January 1974, Bob Strachan took over as chairman from Eric Magson, who remained on the board. As the club celebrated promotion to the Second Division the board of directors were: Messrs R.B.Strachan (chairman), F.H.Magson, K.N.Lancaster, A.G.D.Blundy, B.M.Kilner, G.S.Winters, R.Myles-Gibson and Dr A.I.MacLeod.

New signings for the first season of Second Division soccer included midfielder Micky Cave from Bournemouth, for a then record club fee of £18,000, and Jim Hinch, a centre-forward from Hereford.

In the summer of 1974 the appointment of Keith Hunt as the club's first ever commercial manager was made. He had held a similar position with Bristol Rovers and was to spend a rather stormy five months at Bootham Crescent. In October he resigned, stating that he was 'bitterly disappointed in the obvious lack of faith the board of directors has in my ideas and judgements'. During his short stay he had clashed a number of times with the directors and also with the Supporters' Club. In a statement chairman Bob Strachan said that 'he regretted Mr Hunt's resignation and whilst paying tribute to his drive and energy this was not, however, always to the best advantage'.

One of Hunt's first deeds at Bootham Crescent was, with the help of former City reserve player Peter Turpin, to design a new strip of maroon shirts with a huge white 'Y' on the front. Two seasons later these colours were reversed. He also designed a new match-day magazine-style programme.

One of the club's best known supporters died in September 1974. Raymond 'Nobby' Clarke, who on the big occasion would dress as a 'pearly king' and parade round the pitch.

The Auxiliary Branch of the Supporters' Club was wound up after over 21 years of fund raising. During its existence it had raised approximately £120,000 for York City.

Barry Swallow leads City on to the field for the club's opening Second Division game against Aston Villa on 17 August 1974.

Above: *Jimmy Seal (9) nets the only goal of the game against Norwich City in a Second Division fixture at Bootham Crescent in November 1974.*

Below: *York City's squad in 1975-6. Back row (left to right): Cave, Lyons, Woodward, Hosker, Seal, Wann, Oliver, Butler. Third row: Wilf McGuinness (manager), Jones, Topping, Robb, Neenan, Walker, Hinch, Stone, Baker (coach), Spence (physiotherapist). Seated: McMordie, Holmes, Calvert, Swallow, Pollard, Hunter, Downing. Front row: O'Sullivan, Taylor, Pickard.*

In April 1975, one of the Supporters' Club stalwarts, Albert Ruddock, died. He had been associated with that organization for 40 years and was responsible for the formation and running of the club programme shop.

The two seasons of Second Division football marked an historic and memorable period in the life of York City and the club also had memorable clashes against First Division giants Arsenal and Liverpool during this time.

Exempt until the third round of the FA Cup for only the second time in their history (1938-39 was the other occasion), City were drawn away to Arsenal in January 1975. On their first visit to Highbury Stadium, City gave a splendid performance and fully deserved their draw. Early in the second half, Jimmy Seal shot a magnificent

City in action at Highbury in the third-round FA Cup tie in January 1975. Jimmy Seal challenges Arsenal's 'keeper Jimmy Rimmer. Seal scored in the 1-1 draw which brought the Gunners back to Bootham Crescent for the replay.

25-yard goal, only for Eddie Kelly to equalize shortly afterwards. As the game switched from end to end, Seal, with a brilliant diving header, was only inches wide.

In the replay at Bootham Crescent, after a magnificent match, the Gunners won 3-1 after extra-time. After early Arsenal pressure, which resulted in a sixth-minute Brian Kidd goal, City dominated the game for long periods.

A Barry Swallow header hit the crossbar and Jimmy Rimmer, in the Arsenal goal, was kept busy. In the 69th minute they got a well-deserved equalizer when, after good work by Swallow and Seal, following a Butler free-kick Barry Lyons' low cross-shot beat Rimmer. The game went into extra-time and City conceded two bad goals. A 40-yard pass back by Cliff Calvert to Craeme Crawford saw the goalkeeper lose out in a challenge with Kidd and the ball rebounded off the international forward for a lucky goal. Kidd went on to get his hat-trick when a powerful shot was fumbled by Crawford and trickled into the net. So City rather unluckily were dismissed and had been far from disgraced. The teams for the replay were as follows.

York City: Crawford; Calvert, Ogden, Holmes, Swallow, Topping, Lyons, Woodward(Oliver), Seal, Jones, Butler.

Arsenal: Rimmer; Rice, McNab, Kelly, Simpson, Mancini, Armstrong, Ball, Radford, Kelly, Cropley. Sub: Powling.

Shortly afterwards Tom Johnston's six-year reign as manager ended. He was reluctantly released from his contract, which still had over three years to run, to enable him to take over at Huddersfield Town. Clive Baker, the trainer-coach, took over as caretaker manager. Baker had joined the club earlier in the season, taking over from Colin Meldrum, who left to become manager of Workington. He had coaching experience at Halifax, Rotherham and Hartlepool and he duly applied for the vacant post.

A few weeks later, Wilf McGuinness was appointed the new manager. Strong candidates for the job, apart from Baker, were Stan Anderson, the former boss of Middlesbrough, and Maurice Setters, a former Manchester United and England Under-23 player, who had been in charge at Doncaster.

In 1970, McGuinness had taken over from Sir Matt Busby as manager at Old Trafford. Working in the shadow of the great man did not work out and after leaving Manchester United he had spent two years as a coach and manager in Greece.

For the start of York City's second season in Division Two, the new manager signed Northern Ireland international, Eric McMordie, from Middlesbrough. During the season Steve James, a centre-half from Manchester United, and Peter Scott, a full-back from Everton, joined the club.

City were honoured when chairman Bob Strachan was elected to the Football League Management Committee (1975-6). A Scot, who hailed from Port Glasgow, he later held official positions with the Football Association. He served on the FA disciplinary, executive and financial and international committees. In 1978 he relinquished his position as chairman of York City, but remained on the board until retiring in 1989, after 19 years as a director. In the late 1980s he was a member of the European Football Union committee.

In September, trainer and physiotherapist Ron Spence left the club and retired from the game. As a player and then backroom boy, he had served York City from 1948 to 1975, apart from a short period in the early 1960s.

A new commercial executive, Brian Bateson, was appointed but his tenure of office was to be of relatively short duration. Mrs Maureen Leslie joined the commercial staff and the fund-raising schemes — bingo and lottery competitions — were expanded.

On 10 September 1975 there was another big Cup-tie occasion for York City when they crossed swords with Liverpool for the first time. It was in the second round of the Football League Cup and a dramatic game at Bootham Crescent was

Liverpool's Emlyn Hughes (foreground) congratulates Alec Lindsay after the defender had scored from a controversial, 87th-minute penalty, in the second round of the League Cup in September 1975.

decided by a controversial 87th-minute penalty goal. Chris Topping was adjudged to have fouled Kevin Keegan in the area and from the spot, Alec Lindsay scored the goal which knocked City out. It was an exciting game which was evenly balanced throughout. The best save of the night was made by Ray Clemence to thwart Jimmy Seal, whilst Keegan had a shot pushed on to a post by Graeme Crawford. Other chances fell to both teams and City could consider themselves a little unlucky in not getting the replay their overall play deserved. The teams were:

York City: Crawford; Calvert, Downing, Woodward, Swallow, Topping, Lyons, Cave, Seal, Jones, McMordie.

Liverpool: Clemence; Neal, Lindsay, Thompson, Cormack, Hughes, Keegan, McDermott, Heighway, Kennedy, Callaghan.

Shortly after this game, defender Chris Calvert was transferred to Sheffield United for a club record fee received of £30,000.

Frank Cawood resigned as secretary of the Supporters' Club in October 1975, following a serious illness. He had given over 25 years' valuable and hard working service. The new secretary was Jeff Mortimer, who had been connected with the club for many years.

A disappointing season ended in relegation back to Division Three and a number of players left the club at the end of the campaign, including Barry Swallow, Barry Lyons, John Stone and Dennis Wann. Early in 1976-7, the scoring heroes of the

Above: *Ian Holmes nets a penalty in a Boxing Day 1975 Second Division match against Blackburn. In goal for Rovers was Roger Jones, later to play for City.*

Below: *Mick Channon (right) scores Southampton's goal at Bootham Crescent in February 1976 when City won 2-1. City players (left to right) are Steve James, Brian Pollard and Graeme Crawford.*

promotion season and Second Division days, Chris Jones and Jimmy Seal, were transferred to Huddersfield Town and Darlington respectively.

Long-serving director and former chairman, Derrick Blundy, retired after 31 years on the board in October 1976.

A bad start was made to the season and York were bottom of the table for most of the first half of the campaign. One of the worst defeats was in September when, in front of BBC TV's *Match of the Day* cameras, City crashed 7-2 at Brighton. In the New Year, results improved and by early March, York had moved up to 17th place. However, with only one victory in their last 15 games, City dropped back to the bottom and so suffered a second successive relegation. Average League attendances fell to 2,986 — the first time in the club's history that they dropped below 3,000.

Brian Pollard was top goalscorer and was elected 'Clubman of the Year'. Chris Topping was an ever-present for the sixth successive season and during the campaign made his 300th consecutive League appearance. To mark that occasion he was presented with a silver tray and seven crystal goblets by the club. Gordon Staniforth joined the club from Hull City in mid-term and quickly made his mark.

Talented left-sided midfield player Chris Galvin also came from Boothferry Park on an extended loan. York City's shareholders' annual meeting in December 1976 was a stormy and rather controversial affair. There was strong criticism from the floor led by shareholder, and former Football League referee, Peter Rhodes who almost ten years earlier had, along with a number of York businessmen, made an aborted take-over bid for the club. He wanted to know why, after the club had suffered relegation from the Second Division, the manager had been given a new contract. He also criticized the chairman for stating that the future of York City

Micky Cave (second left) scoring against Bury in the 2-2 draw in August 1976.

was one of survival — that it would continue to exist at its 'proper level' and that the move was towards part-time football at presumably that level, together with regionalization. Rhodes said that Strachan's term of office coincided with a disastrous time for the club.

The chairman replied that since he became chairman the club had had two years in the Second Division — the most successful period in their League history. In his report Strachan said that attendances had been disappointing, especially in the Second Division days, and that was why the money received for the Calvert transfer had been used to help run the club and not been made available for new players. At the meeting Strachan made a strong attack on the *Yorkshire Evening Press* over coverage of the City club. He and the board felt that City were not getting adequate publicity through the Press columns. Replying through Malcolm Huntington, the paper defended itself and suggested that 'Mr Strachan put his own house in order before attacking the newspaper. City's regular fortnightly board meetings rarely produced information for the Press. Can the club complain about lack of coverage if City do not release news?' For the first time since York City's election to the Football League in 1929, the Press did not receive a copy of the balance sheet. The public of York are entitled to know what is going on, said Rhodes. The shareholders voted to send the figures to the newspaper as had been the previous practice.

Myles Gibson did not seek re-election as a director.

In April 1977, Michael Sinclair joined the board. In a new and welcome move he was made director in charge of public relations.

Two great City stalwarts passed away in the summer of 1977 — club president Billy Sherrington and former City player, trainer and manager Tom Lockie.

The club dispensed with the services of coach Clive Baker and appointed as trainer and physiotherapist, former player John Simpson. Another of the heroes of the Second Division days, Graeme Crawford, moved to Scunthorpe.

Two promising 16-year-old youngsters joined the club that summer — Gary Ford and John Byrne — and what an important part they were to play in the 1980s.

Back in Division Four for the first time since 1971, York experienced a traumatic season and completed an unenviable hat-trick. Relegated in 1976 and 1977, City had to apply for re-election in 1978. It was the sixth time in their history that City had to seek readmittance to the League. The season started badly and it was no surprise when Wilf McGuinness was dismissed in October 1977. New signings Kevin Randall and Ian McDonald joined the club from Mansfield and in a flurry of autumn activity, Ian Holmes was transferred to Huddersfield and Brian Pollard moved to Watford for a new club record fee received of £33,000.

In November new boss Charlie Wright was appointed. A Glaswegian, Wright had a long League career as a goalkeeper and was coach at Bolton prior to his move to York. On the short-list had been former City captain, Barry Swallow. The dismal campaign completed its unhappy course and City finished in 22nd position. For only the second time in their history City were knocked out in the first round of both Cup competitions in the same season. In the FA Cup City lost away to then non-League Wigan Athletic. Gordon Staniforth was leading marksman and was 'Clubman of the Year'. At the end of the campaign John Woodward departed after seven years' service and in May 1978, the last link with the Second Division days was broken when Chris Topping was transferred to Huddersfield for £20,000. Since making his debut as a 17-year-old in 1968, he had been a model of consistency in the centre of the defence. He had been an ever-present in his last seven seasons at Bootham Crescent — a magnificent sequence of 355 successive League appearances — and he played in 463 League and Cup games, a total only bettered by that other local central defender and stalwart, Barry Jackson.

Meanwhile, the average League attendance for 1977-8 fell to a new record low of 2,139.

With serious financial problems mounting, there was the biggest boardroom shake up in the club's history in April 1978. Local businessman 36-year-old Michael Sinclair, who had only been on the board for a year, took over as chairman and three directors retired — Ken Lancaster, Dr Angus MacLeod and Gordon Winters. A few weeks earlier, Bernard Kilner had stepped down and as a result only three directors remained — Sinclair, Strachan, who had been chairman since 1974, and Magson, who had been on the board since September 1947 and who was also a former chairman.

Sinclair promised new ideas and a fresh approach. He and his fellow directors were given a boost when York City were given a massive vote of confidence at the League's annual meeting, City receiving the maximum number of 49 votes.

There was a lot of activity at Bootham Crescent in the summer of 1978 and no less than seven new signings were made. Three new defenders were Roy Kay, formerly with Hearts and Celtic, Steve Faulkner, from Sheffield Wednesday, and Jimmy Walsh, previously with Watford. Midfielder Peter Stronach was signed from Sunderland and new forwards were Neil Warnock from Barnsley, Barry Wellings from Everton and the costliest capture was David Loggie, a £20,000 buy from Burnley.

The club's present logo was introduced and, for the seventh time since their formation, the colours were changed. The new strip was red shirts, navy-blue shorts and red stockings. The following year the stockings were changed to white and since then the colours have remained the same. The 'Y' on the front of the shirts, which had been featured in recent years, disappeared. A new weekly lottery under the guidance of Maureen Leslie was launched. A travel club for away matches was instituted. The grandstand was repainted and the car-park was resurfaced.

As the new-look image began to blossom it was announced that City would become the only club in the League to provide spectators with a free match-day programme from the start of the season.

Douglas Craig JP joined the board in September that year and former director Dr Angus MacLeod continued as the club's medical officer. On the field, 1978-9 proved a much better year after three seasons in the doldrums. York finished in the top half of the Fourth Division and reached the fourth round of the FA Cup. Non-League opposition was defeated in the first two rounds and then Second Division Luton Town were beaten 2-0 at Bootham Crescent. At the next stage, City were drawn away to League Champions, Nottingham Forest. On a treacherous and snow-covered surface, York put up a gallant fight at the City Ground but were well beaten by a Forest side, who went on to win the European Cup that season. Outstanding for City was goalkeeper Graham Brown.

The teams lined up that day:

Nottingham Forest: Shilton; Anderson, Bowyer, McGovern, Lloyd, Burns, O'Neill, Gemmill, Birtles, Woodcock, Robertson.

York City: Brown; Kay, Walsh, Pugh, Faulkner, Clements, Ford, Randall, Loggie(Wellings), McDonald, Staniforth.

Average crowds rose to 2,935 and for the second successive season, Gordon Staniforth was top scorer and 'Clubman of the Year'. Seventeen-year-old Gary Ford made his senior debut in October 1978. Peter Scott, who had become City's most capped player with seven appearances for Northern Ireland, was transferred to Aldershot.

In September 1978, George Teasdale resigned because of health reasons. He had been secretary since 1961. Shane Winship, who had worked in the club offices since leaving school, took over as acting secretary and then in August 1979 was officially

City 'keeper Graham Brown makes a brave save at the feet of Garry Birtles (left) and Tony Woodcock in the fourth-round FA Cup tie against Nottingham Forest at the City Ground in January 1979. City's Rob Kay and Forest's John Robertson look on anxiously.

appointed secretary. At the age of 21, he became the youngest secretary in the Football League.

During the season, City were awarded a grant of £18,339 by the Sports Council to enable them to embark on a youth development scheme. A statement from the club said: 'The scheme, which includes the appointment of a full-time youth coach and the provision of a new floodlit training area, will be the club's commitment to a new youth policy'.

In recent years, City had the use of two part-time coaches, John Calpin and Colin Sanderson, with Geoff Taylor acting as a liaison officer between parents and club. They had done a good job but a full-time person would obviously be better equipped to help with the development of local talent. From almost 100 applications for the post of youth coach, Gareth Powell was appointed. A physical education teacher from near Wrexham, he was recommended to City by Welsh team manager Mike Smith. Unfortunately, Powell was unable to settle in the York area and resigned after less than a month. In June 1979, former player Barry Lyons was appointed to that post. He was to be in charge of the youth team and apprentice professionals and the club's ambassador to schools and youth clubs in the Sports Council backed scheme.

Two newcomers to the office administration staff were Bob Godfrey and Sheila Smith.

Just how serious City's financial problems had become was disclosed in the balance sheet that was presented to shareholders at the annual meeting held in January 1979. But for a £54,000 loan from directors, the club would have ended the financial year with a £100,000 overdraft. City had lost £28,589 on the year ending June 1978 (compared to a £14,673 loss the previous year).

It was announced at the meeting that the share capital was to be increased to £100,000. At the time there were only 4,000, £1 shares. The majority of the 96,000

John Byrne (half hidden, extreme right) scoring against Rochdale in the 3-2 win at Bootham Crescent in October 1979.

new shares would be bought by existing shareholders but 20,000 were to be offered to the general public. The directors agreed that the massive loan of £54,000, which ensured the survival of the club, should be converted into shares. "This cleared the club of its obligation to repay the money," said Sinclair.

Before the end of the season, Brian Houghton and Colin Webb joined the board, which now had a complement of six.

The year 1979 marked the 50th anniversary of City's election to the Football League and the *Yorkshire Evening Press* issued a souvenir edition to mark the event.

After the improved performances of the previous campaign, 1979-80 proved disappointing and City had to wage a long battle against having to make another re-election application.

The most notable newcomer was Peter Lorimer, the former Leeds United and Scotland star, and he quickly became a firm favourite with the City fans. He joined the club in September, after playing in Canada, and returned to North America in March 1980. In October 1979, Gordon Staniforth was transferred to Third Division Carlisle United for a new club record fee received of £120,000. Meanwhile, 18-year-old John Byrne made his first-team debut early in the season, whilst new signings during the campaign included Derek Hood, from Hull City, and Terry Eccles, a centre-forward whose previous clubs had included Blackburn Rovers and Huddersfield Town. Midway through the season, Graeme Crawford returned to York City in an exchange deal which took Joe Neenan to Scunthorpe.

The club's annual meeting was held in November and the accounts reflected the general improvements made on the administration side. The loss on the year ending June 1979 was £6,607 — less than a quarter of the previous year's deficit. In the accounts, the sale of two club houses had made a profit of £21,964.

Languishing near the foot of the Fourth Division, City dismissed manager Charlie Wright on 18 March 1980. An official statement issued by the board of directors read: 'Following a board meeting it has been decided to terminate the existing contract of the York City manager Charlie Wright. The responsibilities for team affairs for the rest of the season will be undertaken by Barry Lyons.

Above: *Gordon Staniforth pictured after his hat-trick feat at Wigan in September 1979. A few days later he was transferred to Carlisle for a club record fee received of £120,000.*

Below: *York City's squad pictured in 1979-80. Back row (left to right): Wellings, Harrison, Leaf, Brown, Kamara, Pugh, Stronach, Ford. Middle row: Charlie Wright (manager), Barry Lyons (coach), Loggie, Clements, Foulkner, James, Randall, Byrne, J.Simpson (physiotherapist). Front row: Ferebee, Staniforth, Kay, McDonald, Walsh.*

The decision has been arrived at with much regret and the board of directors extend to Wright their very best wishes.'

City pulled clear of the re-election zone, finishing 17th, and in May, Barry Lyons was appointed as team manager. At the same time Kevin Randall became youth coach. Average attendances were 2,703 and 'Clubman of the Year' was captain and ever-present, Ian McDonald. At the end of the season, Steve James and David Loggie were released.

The death was announced of former chairman and long-serving director Derrick Blundy, at the age of 66. The club's longest serving director, Eric Magson, retired in the summer. He had been on the board since 1947.

At a special dinner held on his behalf he was presented with a silver salver by the chairman. And in recognition of his hard work during his 33 years service he was made club president.

A new decade had dawned and the 1980s were to provide York City with their first major honour.

Before then, however, City were to experience perhaps their worst-ever season when, in 1980-81, they finished at the foot of Division Four. Peter Lorimer's contract had not been renewed at the start of the campaign but newcomers were goalkeeper Eddie Blackburn, from Hull City, and defender Derek Craig, formerly of Newcastle United and Darlington. Graeme Crawford moved to Rochdale in September.

At the annual meeting in 1980, a profit of £31,355 was announced but this was solely due to the transfer of Gordon Staniforth and the operating loss on the football side was £75,330. The board's statement said 'that one of their main responsibilities was to continue to endeavour to contain expenses while improving income from off-the-field activities and so help to ensure the financial stability of the company.'

They started the 1980-81 season brightly (unbeaten in the first seven League and Cup games) in more ways than one with the floodlights having been improved. Early in the New Year, City occupied a mid-table position. Their record for the final 18 matches, however, read: P18, W3, D1, L14, Pts7 and thus York City dropped to the foot and so had to make their seventh application for re-election.

During the campaign, 16-year-old goalkeeper Mike Astbury and 17-year-old Steve Senior made their League debuts. Eddie Blackburn was 'Clubman of the Year' and attendances dropped to 2,245. The crowd of 1,167 for the last game of the season against Northampton was the lowest in City's history. With 46 votes City were once more re-elected to the League.

In August 1981, Barry Swallow was appointed a director of the club. He thus became only the second City player to become a member of the board. The other was Tom Mitchell. Each of the directors had areas of control and responsibility: Bob Strachan, very much involved in FA matters and just appointed chairman of the disciplinary committee, was looking after youth-team affairs: Douglas Craig dealt with the lottery and other financial matters: Brian Houghton looked after the ground and Colin Webb the social club. Swallow now provided the football experience.

City's disastrous 1980-81 campaign was reflected in the balance sheet, which showed a loss of £33,437. During the year the social club premises had been redeveloped and a gymnasium built and these had been principally financed by loans and grants. Shane Winship retired as club secretary to take over the social club and also act as sales executive. The new secretary was 46-year-old Tom Hughes. He had been involved for many years in football administration in the Selby and West Yorkshire Leagues and had been employed by Cochrane's Shipbuilders Ltd, Selby, for the past 30 years in an administrative capacity. Ian Fowler, who was appointed company secretary in 1979, continued his duties.

The 1981-2 season (now three points for a win) proved to be another poor campaign for City. They utilized a total of 27 players and once again walked the re-election tightrope and they lost in the FA Cup to non-League Altrincham. Their problems were chiefly due to a nightmare sequence at Bootham Crescent where City went 12 League games without a win — their worst-ever home run. They did, however, end their home programme with a number of convincing victories, including a 6-0 win over Crewe Alexandra, which was their biggest win since 1964-5. This enabled them to finish in 17th position. New signing, Keith Walwyn, became the first player to top 20 League goals since Paul Aimson in 1970-71 and he was voted 'Clubman of the Year'. Brian Pollard returned to the club after a four-year absence and Malcolm Crosby arrived from Aldershot in an exchange deal which took Ian McDonald to the Recreation Ground. Local lad Richard Dawson established himself in the defence.

On the managerial front this season was one of great upheaval. On 8 December 1981, Barry Lyons was sacked after 18 months in the post. The club's official statement read: 'The directors announce that Barry Lyons has been relieved of his duties of team manager. Kevin Randall has agreed to take over these responsibilities for the immediate future. The directors would like Barry to continue to be associated with the club and recognize his talents, particularly in working with young players. Accordingly he has been offered (*and subsequently accepted*) the post of youth team manager, a position in which he was previously very successful.'

A further run of bad results dropped City into the bottom four and on 3 March 1982, Randall was relieved of his acting managerial duties. Director Barry Swallow took on the role of caretaker manager and was assisted by Gerry Sweeney, a new signing from Bristol City, and former City coach Colin Meldrum. One of their first acts was to get Stoke City centre-half Denis Smith on loan — a move which was to have long-term beneficial effects for the Bootham Crescent club.

The average attendance rose to 2,360. At the end of the season, Ray Kay departed and Sweeney and Peter Aitken, another former Bristol City player, decided not to stay at York. Both these defenders had done a good job for City during the vital closing weeks.

City's caretaker management team in March 1982. From left, Gerry Sweeney, Barry Swallow and Colin Meldrum.

Former City 'keeper Graeme Crawford about to save Derek Hood's penalty kick at Spotland as City go down to Rochdale 2-0 in April 1982.

Careful housekeeping had enabled City, in what had been a disappointing playing season, to show only a net loss of £19,505. Income from the Development Association and other commercial activities raised nearly £100,000.

On 12 May 1982, Denis Smith was appointed player-manager and player-coach was to be Viv Busby. Not since the late 1920s had City had the services of a player-manager (Jock Collier).

City's chief problems in 1981-2 had been in defence. The 91 goals conceded was the worst in the Football League. Smith's chief priority, therefore, was plain to see and during the summer of 1982 he recruited a new defence. In goal Roger

Jones, a 'keeper with vast experience, full-backs Chris Evans, from Stoke, and Alan Hay, from Bristol City, and Ricky Sbragia, a former Birmingham and Walsall player, who would line up alongside Smith in the centre of defence. Later in the campaign John MacPhail was signed from Sheffield United.

The year 1982 marked the Diamond Jubilee of the club and the 50th anniversary of the move to Bootham Crescent and it certainly marked an upturn in City's fortunes. They experienced by far the best season since their return to Division Four in 1977. They were to finish seventh and only just missed a promotion place by four points, chiefly due to indifferent away form, especially in the first half of the season. At home, City were well nigh invincible and had one sequence of 13 successive League and Cup victories at Bootham Crescent, scoring 47 goals in the process. City netted 100 goals during the season — 88 League and 12 Cup. Keith Walwyn again topped the 20-goals mark and 'Clubman of the Year' was the ever-present and versatile Derek Hood.

Average League crowds rose to 3,243, the highest since the Second Division days. During the season, Eddie Blackburn moved to Hartlepool and at the end of the campaign, physiotherapist John Simpson retired and was rewarded with a testimonial match against Leeds United. Long-serving chairman of the Supporters' Club, Arthur Butler, died in July 1983 and Cliff Beckwith became acting chairman. In June 1984, Jeff Mortimer was elected chairman and Ray Wynn became secretary. These two stalwarts of the Supporters' Club still hold those positions.

Early in 1983, Jack Miller was appointed sales consultant. A retired Rowntree Mackintosh executive, his brief was to raise money through programme and ground advertising. At the annual meeting in November 1983, a small profit of £6,052 was disclosed and once again tribute was paid to the commercial and lottery departments for their off-the-field activities.

Hopes were high as City went into the 1983-4 season and these were fully realized.

Keith Walwyn (left) squeezes the ball into the Swindon net in the 2-0 win in March 1984. This game was played on a Saturday morning to aviod a clash with York Rugby League Club's semi-final game against Wigan in the Challenge Cup.

'Clubman of the Year' John MacPhail leaves the field after the final home game against Bury in the Fourth Division championship-winning season of 1983-4.

In a magnificent record-breaking campaign, York finished runaway Fourth Division champions and so won their first major honour. Two newcomers to Bootham Crescent were midfielder Sean Haslegrave, from Crewe Alexandra, and new physiotherapist Gerry Delahunt. Owing to a number of teams switching over to the Central League, the North Midlands League folded and subsequently City did not operate a reserve team this season. Reserve friendly games were arranged as and when necessary.

One sad note, in what was a very good year for the club, was the death in March 1984 of president Eric Magson. He had served York City for a total of 37 years.

City's good season was reflected in the balance sheet and a profit of almost £15,000 was achieved. At the annual meeting in October 1984, optimism was expressed for the future and the club clearly set its sights on further promotion and progress.

The reserve side was resurrected and was elected to the Second Division of the Central League. In readiness for their first season back in the Third Division since 1977, new players Gary Nicholson, from Mansfield, and Hugh Atkinson, formerly of Wolves, were signed to strengthen the squad.

A marvellous start was made to 1984-5 and after eight League games (six wins,

Keith Walwyn (left, on ground) heads City's opening goal in their 2-0 win against Blue Star FC in the first round of the FA Cup in November 1984.

two draws) the club sat proudly at the top of Division Three for the first time. The match that made them leaders was a 1-0 home victory over Bristol Rovers and marked the 100th League game of the Smith-Busby era. They could proudly boast the following record: P100, W59, D23, L18, F200, A104, Pts200. This marked the pinnacle of City's League season. They lost the next game, at home to Bristol City, and in a mini slump with only two wins out of 11, City lost touch with the leaders. One of those victories, however, was a magnificent 7-1 win over Gillingham their biggest score for 20 years. A final position of eighth was generally regarded as very satisfactory.

Average League attendances rose to 5,550 and were the highest since 1974-5. City's Cup exploits were the highlights of the season. They played no less than 14 Cup ties during the campaign and the total of 60 matches played was a club record. In the Milk Cup, City dismissed Doncaster Rovers 8-2 on aggregate. First Division Queen's Park Rangers provided the opposition in the second round. In the first leg at Bootham Crescent, in front of over 10,000, a thrilling match ended in a 4-2 win for the visitors. City twice fought back to equalize but the London club had just a little too much class. In the return game on the Loftus Road plastic pitch, Rangers won 4-1 for an aggregate 8-3 success. A few days later, City's highly-rated striker, John Byrne, was signed by Queen's Park Rangers for a fee of £100,000. In November, Dale Banton was signed as his replacement, from Aldershot for a club record fee paid of £50,000.

By now, the FA Cup was underway and City progressed to the fifth round for only the third time in their history (1937-8 and 1954-5 the previous times). In the opening three rounds Blue Star, Hartlepool and Walsall were beaten without a goal being conceded. Fourth-round opponents were the mighty Arsenal, who travelled to York on a cold and frosty day on 26 January 1985. With a dramatic late penalty netted by Keith Houchen, York City gained one of their most famous FA Cup

Above, left: *Keith Houchen (right) slots home the dramatic late penalty winner against Arsenal.* Above, right: *Keith Walwyn (second right) gets in his shot despite the attentions of David O'Leary.* Below: *City players celebrate the victory over Arsenal.*

victories. It was a well-deserved success for City, who on the day were the better side against their famous opponents, who fielded an all-international line-up. The teams were:

York City: Astbury; Senior, Hay, Sbragia, MacPhail, Haslegrave, Ford, Butler, Walwyn, Houchen, Pearce. Sub: Chippendale.

Arsenal: Lukic; Anderson, Sansom, Talbot, O'Leary, Caton, Robson, Williams, Mariner, Woodcock, Nicholas(Allinson).

A great City team effort but praise was due to two youngsters, Alan Pearce, a former apprentice in his first season as a professional, and 18-year-old Martin Butler, who had joined the club as a YTS lad. Son of former City player Ian Butler,

Above, left: *John MacPhail congratulates Ricky Sbragia after his equalizer against Liverpool, five minutes from time.* Above, right: *Liverpool's Ronnie Whelan (second left) nets Liverpool's third goal in the replay at Anfield.*

he scored against Walsall in the third round, in what was his full senior debut. He was in the side owing to the fact that Dale Banton was Cup-tied.

In the next round they received a plum draw — at home to Liverpool. An all-ticket crowd of 13,485 was fixed and Cup fever struck the city of York. It was the mid-1950s all over again. The office staff of Tom Hughes, Sheila Smith and newcomer Patricia Westland were inundated with requests for tickets. As City launched a voucher scheme, a crowd of 10,940 saw a League game against Wigan, which produced receipts of £22,140. Penalty hero Keith Houchen was injured in this game and subsequently missed the Liverpool tie at Bootham Crescent. In the days before the game, the pitch was protected against frost by straw and polythene. The groundstaff, led by Bryan Foster, did yeoman work to ensure that the game went ahead.

The atmosphere was electric as the game kicked-off and in the seventh minute, Martin Butler shot the ball into the Liverpool net, only to be ruled offside. Honours were even in the first half but the deadlock was broken in the 52nd minute when, following a free-kick, Ian Rush latched on to a Kenny Dalglish header and cracked a first-time shot past Mike Astbury. It was the first goal City had conceded in nine games and the first they had let in during the FA Cup that season. The European Champions began to dictate the game and only a goal-line clearance by John MacPhail prevented them from going further ahead.

City stuck to their task, however, and in the 85th minute scored a dramatic equalizer which sent their supporters wild with delight. Alan Pearce's free-kick on the left was knocked back into the middle by Gary Ford and then in quick succession Ricky Sbragia hit the post, Keith Walwyn's header struck the bar, John MacPhail's shot rebounded off Grobbelaar's legs and, finally, Sbragia hammered the ball into the net.

In a pulsating finale, Liverpool had a Ronnie Whelan goal disallowed. In the end City deserved the draw and a trip to Anfield as reward. Alas, there was some crowd trouble at the final whistle but it did not spoil another great day in City's history. The crowd of 13,485 paid new club receipts of £29,138.

The teams lined up:

York City: Astbury; Senior, Hay, Sbragia, MacPhail, Haslegrave, Ford, Butler, Walwyn, Hood, Pearce.

Liverpool: Grobbelaar; Neal, Kennedy, Gillespie, Nicol, Hansen, Dalglish, Whelan, Rush, MacDonald, Wark.

Nearly 10,000 City fans went to Merseyside for the replay — the biggest exodus for 30 years as FA Cup fever swept York. Keith Houchen returned to the side and Derek Hood was substitute, whilst Liverpool were unchanged.

City's Cup dreams were swept aside, however, as Liverpool hit top gear in front of 43,010, which was Anfield's biggest crowd for two seasons. With John Wark leading the way with a hat-trick, the First Division side won 7-0. It had been a memorable night, none the less, as City strode the famous Anfield pitch for the first time. Manager Denis Smith summed up: "We can't compete at world level. We have a good Third Division side, possibly capable of doing well in the Second, but when you play against the best team in Europe and probably one of the best three or four club sides in the world, you realize what a gap there is."

City were still on the Wembley trail, however, in the Freight/Rover Trophy, but went down in disappointing fashion when they lost at home to Lincoln City in the Northern quarter-finals.

Tony Canham made his debut as an amateur in the closing weeks of the season and scored in his opening game. Promising striker, 17-year-old Marco Gabbiadini made his League debut when he came on as a substitute in a game against Bolton in March. At the end of the campaign, Roger Jones was released after three oustanding seasons with the club. John MacPhail was voted 'Clubman of the Year' for the second successive season.

Bob Baldwin was appointed the new commercial manager, assisted by the continued part-time help of Jack Miller. A former Leeds United advertising and promotions manager, Baldwin had been a freelance journalist before becoming assistant press officer of the Football League in 1968 and was editor of the *League Review*, a popular magazine which was included in club programmes in the late 60s early 70s.

A number of ground improvements were made in the close season and accounts for the year ended 30 June 1985 showed a profit of £6,552. City were saved from a huge deficit by their success in the FA Cup and Milk Cup. They had spent £197,000 on essential safety and improvement work on the ground in recent months and, but for their Cup success, would have had to borrow this money from the bank at a high interest rate. Gate receipts rose to £336,000, an increase of £124,000 on the previous year, and City's share of away receipts rose from £4,000 to £55,000. The balance sheet also showed that the club employed 41 people during the year, with one of them receiving between £30,000 to £35,000.

Ricky Sbragia was made club captain and midfield player Simon Mills was signed from Sheffield Wednesday for a fee of £21,000. Other newcomers were central defender David McAughtrie, from Carlisle, and local goalkeeper Andy Leaning as City embarked on their 50th season in the Football League.

The 1985-6 season followed a remarkably similar pattern to the previous campaign. City completed their fifth successive climb up the League since they finished bottom of Division Four in 1981. The final position of seventh was a little disappointing, however, as promotion hopes were high at the beginning of the season. A good start was made and by the end of November, City were second in the table behind runaway leaders Reading, with 36 points from 20 games. In October, they thrashed

Tony Canham and Keith Walwyn watch as a shot goes over the Bristol City crossbar in the 1-1 draw at Bootham Crescent in September 1985.

Darlington 7-0 to record their equal second biggest win in their League career. A bad mid-term spell, with only ten points out of a possible 39, dented their promotion hopes and only a good finish — unbeaten in the last nine games — enabled City to finish as high as they did. Without doubt, poor away performances cost them dear, for whilst their form at Bootham Crescent was excellent, with 16 wins and 49 goals, City recorded only four victories on their travels. Average League attendances dropped to 4,111.

For the second successive season, York City hit the FA Cup trail and again reached the fifth round. By a remarkable coincidence, they were again pitched against Liverpool and the First Division giants again needed a replay at Anfield to despatch their Third Division opponents. To reach the fifth round, York had the unique experience of being drawn at home to non-League opposition in four successive rounds.

Morecambe, after a replay, Whitby Town, Wycombe Wanderers and Altrincham were all sent packing before the might of Liverpool was again faced at Bootham Crescent. Cup fever again gripped the City and with the weather once again in an icy grip, it was almost an action replay of the events of 12 months earlier. The pitch was declared fit and another epic game was staged. Dale Banton missed a glorious chance in the opening minutes and for much of the first half, the visitors were forced back on defence. Bruce Grobbelaar made a magnificent save to thwart John MacPhail and Liverpool were fortunate to be on level terms at half-time.

The First Division side resumed in more purposeful manner, but then in the 61st minute, the ground erupted when City took the lead. Tony Canham crossed the ball from the left, Dale Banton and Keith Walwyn helped it on and Gary Ford drove it past Grobbelaar. City held their lead for only four minutes. A Kenny Dalglish free-kick was floated into a crowded penalty area and Steve Senior was adjudged to have handled the ball. Jan Molby netted from the resultant penalty and Liverpool could breathe again. Ian Rush almost won the game in the closing stages but City, again, well deserved their draw and another trip to Anfield.

The line ups were:

Above, left: *Whitby's goalkeeper, David Harvey, watches a header from Alan Pearce (out of picture) go into the net in the FA Cup first round in November 1985.* Above, right: *Dale Banton (8) opens the scoring against Altrincham in the fourth round FA Cup tie in January 1986.*
Below: *City players show their reaction to the news that they have drawn Liverpool again in the FA Cup.*

York City: Leaning; Senior, Hood, McAughtrie, MacPhail, Mills, Ford, Banton, Walwyn, Haslegrave, Canham.
Liverpool: Grobbelaar; Lee, Beglin, Lawrenson, Wark, Hansen, Dalglish, Johnston, Rush, Molby, Seagraves.

Liverpool had returned a number of unsold tickets so the attendance was recorded at 12,752 with new record receipts of £38,054.

Once again a big army of travelling fans made their way over the Pennines for the replay. City were unchanged but the Merseysiders brought in Ronnie Whelan and Gary Gillespie for Mark Seagraves and Craig Johnston.

Nearly 5,000 City fans in a crowd of 29,362 saw a famous performance and only a controversial second-half decision robbed them perhaps of their greatest-ever FA

Action from the FA Cup fifth round tie in 1986. Top: *Magic moment – Gary Ford (second right) drives past Grobbelaar to give City the lead at Bootham Crescent.* Middle: *Andy Leaning makes a brave save as Ian Rush (left) waits to pounce.* Bottom: *Keith Walwyn (right) watches as a shot from Tony Canham (out of picture) beats Bruce Grobbelaar for City's equalizer and extra-time at Anfield.*

Cup win. John Wark opened the scoring in the 19th minute but there was to be no repeat of the seven-goal drubbing of a year earlier. After 44 minutes, a superb 40-yard pass from Simon Mills found Tony Canham on the left. He cut in, beat a defender, and his low shot eluded Grobbelaar to put City level. With 25 minutes to go, Walwyn collided with Grobbelaar, Hansen and Gillespie and managed to poke the ball into the net. Referee Howard Taylor disallowed the goal, to Liverpool's great relief.

Johnston came on for Wark as the home team pushed forward. The game went into extra-time and Keith Houchen came on for Sean Haslegrave. In the 94th minute, Molby scored a spectacular goal to beat Andy Leaning, who had an outstanding game. Three minutes later, City's gallant effort was over when Dalglish netted Liverpool's third. It had been another wonderful night and the magnificent York City team received a standing ovation at the end. In the four games against Liverpool, City had held them to a draw three times over 90 minutes.

The Reds got to Wembley and Craig Johnston was quoted in the FA Cup Final programme as follows: 'York earned top marks for taking the game into extra-time. There had been several heart-stopping moments, not least of which was when York appeared to have scored a second goal. Fortunately for us it was not allowed, but I must admit that at the time I could not see a lot wrong with it. In the game at York, we were very glad to earn a replay'.

Shortly afterwards Keith Houchen was transferred to Scunthorpe and other departures that season saw Chris Evans and Mike Astbury go to Darlington.

During the season, 'veteran' Gary Ford became only the tenth player to complete 300 League games for the club and Keith Walwyn reached his century of goals. Simon Mills was elected 'Clubman of the Year' and Marco Gabbiadini continued to show much promise.

In July 1986, the *Sports Press* was printed for the last time. It had first been published in 1905. York City match reports and news had featured prominently in the newspaper over the years. In March 1955, when City played in the semi-final of the FA Cup, 25,000 copies were sold. The match reports of 'Citizen' (Wilf Meek) and Malcolm Huntington were always eagerly awaited and it was a sad day when the decision to terminate publication for economic reasons was announced.

York City made a net profit of £39,064 on the year ended 30 June 1986. They were indebted to income from off-the-field activities. Some £53,000 was received from the promotions and development association and nearly £30,000 from sponsorship and hire of hospitality boxes. Season tickets had shown a big increase from £19,190 to £35,022.

City employed 45 people in the year and the balance sheet showed that Denis Smith's salary was now in the £40,000 to £45,000 range.

Tribute was paid in the annual report to Bob Godfrey, who for the past eight and a half years had very ably dealt with the day-to-day accounting. He would continue to do this, although new director John Quickfall would be responsible for financial affairs at board level.

After the successes and triumphs in League and Cup over the past four seasons, 1986-7 was a very disappointing campaign and City narrowly avoided the relegation play-offs as well as suffering defeat at the hands of non-League opposition in the FA Cup. Malcolm Crosby, who had taken over as reserve-team coach, left in August 1986 to take up a coaching appointment in Kuwait.

By the start of the season, John MacPhail and Alan Hay had departed to Bristol City and Tranmere Rovers respectively. They were never effectively replaced and as a result defensive problems, plus a number of injuries, contributed to the decline.

The campaign opened with a fair degree of hope and optimism and victory over champions-elect Bournemouth on 30 September lifted City into second place with

Gary Ford (second right) scores City's final goal in their 3-1 win against Darlington at Bootham Crescent on the opening day of the 1986-7 season. The Quakers' goalkeeper is former City custodian Mike Astbury.

16 points from the opening eight matches. Defeat followed, however, in the next game against Mansfield Town and from then on it was downhill all the way with only seven victories in the last 38 games. Indeed, City went into their final match still requiring one point to guarantee Third Division status. Their away form was quite appalling with only one victory and 17 defeats on their travels. Only once before in their League history (1966-7) had City completed a season with only one away win and only once before had they lost more away matches (1968-9 — 18 defeats). The best League performance was a 3-1 victory over Middlesbrough on New Year's Day, which was watched by the season's biggest crowd at Bootham Crescent — 8,611. The average League attendance fell to 3,432.

In the previous two seasons, City had experienced FA Cup glory but this time it was the other side of the coin with Multipart League side, Caernarfon Town, winning a second-round replay at Bootham Crescent. It was the first time in the club's history that City had lost at home in a replay to non-League opposition. There was a little more to cheer in the Littlewoods Cup with an exciting success over Sunderland and a first-leg home victory against Chelsea before York bowed out at Stamford Bridge. In the Freight/Rover Trophy, City lost at home to the eventual winners, Mansfield Town, in the first round.

At the end of what was a rather traumatic year there was what proved to be a mass exodus from Bootham Crescent in the summer of 1987.

Players to leave at the end of the term included Sean Haslegrave, who had given four years' excellent service, latterly as captain, and Andy Leaning, who was surprisingly given a free transfer and moved to Sheffield United. Full-back Steve Senior joined Northampton Town and Gary Ford was signed by Leicester City for a fee of £25,000. A local lad, Ford had been at Bootham Crescent for ten years and was a virtual ever-present in the first team in his last seven seasons. Only three players — Barry Jackson, Chris Topping and Tommy Forgan — have made more than his 366 League appearances for the club.

The end of the season also saw the departure to Sunderland of the managerial team of Denis Smith and Viv Busby. They had been in charge for five years and had guided York from the lower reaches of the Fourth Division to the championship

Above: *Keith Walwyn (on ground) scores the dramatic last-minute goal that tied the scores against Sunderland in the Littlewoods Cup in September 1986 at York. City won on the away-goals rule after extra-time.*
Below: *Kerry Dixon (centre) scores Chelsea's second goal in the second leg of the Littlewoods Cup second round match at Stamford Bridge in October 1986.*

in 1983-4, a place in the top eight in Division Three in successive seasons and consecutive appearances in the fifth round of the FA Cup.

The City club were somewhat annoyed about the manner of approach made by Sunderland to Smith. The board held an emergency meeting and the compensation factor for Smith's contract was the major sticking point. After talks between Sinclair and Sunderland chairman Bob Murray, agreement was finally reached. The Roker Park club would pay £20,000 compensation immediately and a further £20,000 if they won promotion to Division Two within the next two seasons. If Sunderland failed to get promotion, Denis Smith promised to pay City £10,000 out of his own pocket. (Sunderland finished Third Division champions in 1987-8).

When the side was going through its bad spell, supporters queried whether any manager in Division Three was worth such a high salary. When Smith went to Roker Park it was revealed that he had volunteered to take a £10,000 cut in wages so that York could afford to take on a full-time youth coach.

The man appointed to the hot seat in June 1987 was Bobby Saxton, former boss of Exeter City, Plymouth Argyle and Blackburn Rovers. Saxton was faced with a massive team building effort as Keith Walwyn joined the list of departures when he signed for Blackpool for a tribunal-fixed fee of £35,000. Walwyn, voted 'Clubman of the Year' for 1986-7, boasted the magnificent scoring record of 140 League and Cup goals in six seasons. This made him the second-highest scorer in the club's history behind Norman Wilkinson. Ricky Sbragia hung up his boots to take over as youth team manager. Ian Hope, as youth development officer, and Jim Lamb, the youth-team coach, continued their excellent part-time duties with the youngsters.

Only one player — Derek Hood — was now left of the championship-winning side of only three years earlier.

There were also changes on the administrative and commercial side. Tom Hughes, who had been secretary for six years, took up a similar appointment with Middlesbrough, and commercial manager Bob Baldwin returned to Leeds United.

The new secretary, only the fifth in City's League history, was Keith Usher. A former policeman, he was secretary of both the York FA and York and District League and a member of the North Riding County FA. He relinquished all these positions upon his appointment with City. For many years he had also been a well-known local referee.

Nick King, who had worked in Sheffield United's commercial department, was appointed the new commercial manager. Just six weeks later, however, he left the club saying that 'he did not feel up to the job'.

Gerry Delahunt, physiotherapist for the past four years, left in the autumn of 1987 to start a private practice in Doncaster. His successor was Jeff Miller, who had previous experience as a physiotherapist in the Northern League with Gainsborough Town, Stockton and South Bank.

At the 65th annual meeting of shareholders in December 1987, it was disclosed that the club had lost £65,578 on the day-to-day football running costs on the year ending June 30 1987. An overall profit of £105,456 was made, however, due to the sale of players, plus compensation received from Sunderland for Denis Smith. At a lively meeting, Sinclair revealed that the club's slide had started in April 1986 when Smith turned down a substantial sum of money to strengthen the side. "The club was ready and needed to go up and we put a lot of money in our terms at his disposal for the purpose of improving the team" said the chairman. "The manager declined the offer, feeling that he had a strong enough squad. During that close season he was unable to agree terms with John MacPhail and his replacement, Mike Pickering, was not good enough." Sinclair added, however, that Denis Smith had put the club back on the map again and had given York City four good years.

The 1987-8 season was always going to be a difficult campaign and, sadly, worst fears were realized with relegation back to Division Four. Statistically it was City's worst season since joining the Football League. Fewest wins — eight; most defeats — 29; and least points — 33 (25 under the old system). Two record sequences were also established during the season — 17 League games without a win and an away record without a League victory was extended to an incredible 38 matches. Indeed, City went 18 months without an away win (from September 1986 to March 1988, drawing six and losing 32).

When Bobby Saxton was appointed, only two players had signed contracts. Thrown in at the deep end, he was faced with the almost impossible task of building a

Tony Clegg (second right) scores against Brentford in the 1-1 draw at Bootham Crescent in December 1987.

strong enough squad in a matter of a few weeks. In the event, City made a nightmare start from which they never recovered, losing their opening five games and not winning their first League match until 31 October, at the 16th attempt.

Marco Gabbiadini, an £80,000 transfer to Sunderland in September, and Simon Mills, £35,000 to Port Vale in December, left the club and with several injuries adding to the problems, City utilized no less than 31 players as they tried in vain to stem the tide. Youngsters Steve Tutill and Gary Himsworth made their League debuts, whilst newcomers during the season included Gary Howlett from Bournemouth, and centre-forward Ian Helliwell from Matlock Town. Gordon Staniforth made a welcome return on a non-contract basis. John Newman, the former Exeter, Grimsby, Derby and Hereford manager, joined the club in mid-season to assist Saxton. He left a few months later.

utility player player Derek Hood. He was rewarded with a testimonial match in November 1988 when many of the 1983-4 championship side appeared.

Mrs Sheila Smith was appointed commercial manager in May 1988. She had joined the club in 1978 as assistant to the secretary and later became the manageress of the club shop. Since Nick King left in September the previous year, she had been acting commercial manager. One of her first accomplishments was to devise a new-style programme. The club received a boost when their sponsorship deal with J.W.Cameron & Company Limited was extended for a further two years from August 1988. The exact cash amount was not disclosed. Camerons, the Hartlepool brewery, first sponsored York City in 1983-4.

The new deal included the continued use of the word HANSA (a lager) on the team shirts, plus use of one of the hospitality boxes. Camerons had a long link with the York area and John J.Hunts, York-based brewers, had become part of their company 30 years earlier. When City moved to Bootham Crescent in 1932 Sir John Hunt was club president.

In the summer of 1988, City announced a £100,000 share issue and Sinclair's family company, Mulberry Hall, agreed to underwrite virtually the whole sum. That took the chairman and his company's stake in the club from 53 per cent to 75 per cent. The City board also stated that they were prepared to go into the red by earmarking £100,000 for the manager to spend on new players in a determined bid to make a speedy return to Division Three. Close-season signings were Chris

Above: *Gordon Staniforth, back in City colours, heads for goal in the 2-0 win over Chester on New Year's Day 1988.*
Below: *Play is halted in the City v Sunderland match in March 1988, owing to crowd disturbance.*

Marples, a £28,000 goalkeeper from Chesterfield, Steve Spooner, a midfielder and new club captain from Hereford for £29,000, and central defender Kevan Smith, who cost £35,000 from Coventry City. Derek Fazackerley, a long-serving player with Blackburn Rovers, became player-coach. The York City Youth Federation was formed. They increased their scouting system, especially in the Manchester area, and signed a number of associate schoolboys. They fully utilized the Youth Training Scheme and ran a centre of excellence and held regular training sessions for young players. Terry Garvey took over as youth development officer.

Back in Division Four for the first time since 1984, York City had to be content with a mid-table position. Considering a nightmare start to the campaign however,

By the end of February, with only two wins in 32 outings, relegation was inevitable and City were 14 points adrift of second-from-bottom Doncaster Rovers. The season ended on a brighter note, however, with six victories and a draw in the last 14 matches.

A win at Brentford in the final game lifted City off the bottom of the League — a position they had occupied since the end of August. The most pleasing and dramatic victory was in March, against Sunderland in front of the season's biggest crowd at Bootham Crescent. In the Littlewoods Cup, after a praiseworthy draw at Elland Road, City crashed at home to Leeds United, whilst Fourth Division clubs Hartlepool and Darlington dispatched York out of the FA Cup and Freight/Rover Trophy respectively. Dale Banton was top scorer and 'Clubman of the Year'. The average attendance dropped to 2,754.

At the end of the season, several players were released, including long-serving with only one point from the opening five games and a place in the bottom four at Christmas, a final position of 11th was generally regarded as reasonably satisfactory.

Following a home defeat at the hands of Scunthorpe on 17 September, and with the club at the bottom of the table, Bobby Saxton announced his shock resignation. He said that he 'had to take this decision for the sake of York City'. He thought he had put the players under too much pressure and felt that a new face in charge was necessary. Club director Barry Swallow took over as caretaker manager, as he had done back in 1982, and vital points were collected.

On 10 October 1988, John Bird became York City's 15th manager. Previously in charge at Hartlepool United, he had done a good job at the Victoria Ground. He brought with him Alan Little as assistant manager and coach.

The club gradually made progress up the table and in the second half of the season showed especially good form on their travels, with five wins and three draws in their last ten away matches. Such a good recovery was made that City went into the last week of the season still with a chance of making the promotion play-offs. A feature of the campaign was that City won away at Crewe, Tranmere and Rotherham — the three teams that won automatic promotion. The disappointment of the season was dismissal in the first round of both the FA Cup and Littlewoods Cup — only the third time that this had happened in their history.

Gary Howlett (extreme right) scoring City's fifth goal against Halifax Town in October 1988.

Dale Banton, still the club's record signing at £50,000, was transferred to Walsall in October 1988 for £80,000. Shaun Reid, brother of England's Peter Reid, was signed from Rochdale in December, for a fee of £32,500. Ian Helliwell was top scorer and voted 'Clubman of the Year', whilst average attendances were 2,613.

At the annual meeting in December 1988, the club announced a £15,000 loss but with a severe warning of worse to come with £135,000 having been spent on new players during the summer. The 'horrendous' implications of the Government's proposed identity-card scheme also cast a dark cloud over Bootham Crescent. York City were facing their toughest time for years but the directors were confident that the club would survive.

John Greenway, MP for Ryedale, who had become club president in the autumn of 1988, together with York's MP, Conal Gregory, had spoken out strongly against the ID card plan. In the light of the Taylor report on the Hillsborough tragedy, the identity card scheme was shelved but in common with other League clubs, York City are likely to have to make Bootham Crescent an all-seater stadium in the 1990s.

In March 1989, a sportsmans' dinner in aid of the Shipton Street Roof Appeal was held at the Viking Hotel. In attendance were 24 former City players (going

Ian Helliwell, 'Clubman of the Year' 1988-9, holds his trophy aloft.

back to the 1940s and 1950s) including Norman Wilkinson, Alan Stewart and Billy Hughes of the semi-final side. During an evening of glorious nostalgia film was shown of the 1954-5 Cup run.

Newcomers in the summer of 1989 included Bob Colville, a striker from Stockport County, Tom Kelly, a full-back from Torquay United, and Ray Warburton, a central defender from Rotherham.

At the shareholders meeting in December, tribute was paid to Bob Strachan, who, after 19 years' service on the board of directors, had retired in July. In the financial year ending 30 June, City lost £190,692, the highest amount in their history. They were not carrying an overdraft, however, thanks to interest-free loans from directors plus the £100,00 share issue made in July 1988. The balance sheet reflected more than two years of bad playing results, but the chairman was not too discouraged or pessimistic as he presented the following report:

'The accounts may, at first sight, cause concern because of the large loss. On closer inspection it will be seen that a large part of this loss arises from exceptional items, principally the cost of bringing new players into the club (which I warned about in my report of last year), the compensation paid for the manager and ground safety work. The reality of the cash position is that the company has traded throughout the year without having to go into overdraft and the board intends to continue endeavouring to manage the company's affairs to preserve that situation if at all possible.

'The financial success of the company usually reflects the success of the playing staff and we are particularly pleased to see the better results which are being achieved by John Bird, Alan Little and the whole of the playing staff. If the team gets the support its efforts deserve, then the club gate receipts, which are the bedrock of its income, will, we hope, have an impact on the overall financial position.

'As a board we will continue in our efforts to meet all the responsibilities during the forthcoming year, as well as supporting to the best of our ability the manager and coach in their quest for success on the field.'

In the summer of 1989, Michael Sinclair was elected unopposed as the Third and Fourth Division representative on the Football League Management Committee. For some time he had been chairman of the Associate members (Third and Fourth Division clubs).

In the first half of 1989-90 results were encouraging and City went into their Christmas programme in fourth place and well poised to make a promotion bid. Successive home defeats over the holiday heralded a disappointing decline, however, and they again had to settle for a mid-table position with the same number of points — 64 — as the previous campaign. Bad luck with injuries did not help, especially when £30,000 capture David Longhurst from Peterborough United in January was sidelined after only four games.

Undoubtedly poor home form in the second half of the season let them down and no less than eight games were lost at Bootham Crescent. For only the second time in their history (previous occasion 1946-7) they did in fact lose more home games than away.

Clubman of the Year was goalkeeper Chris Marples whilst Ian Helliwell was top marksman for the second successive year. Average League attendances were almost identical to 1988-9 at 2,615. Marples and Tony Barratt were ever-presents and in April Tom Kelly returned to Devon where he teamed up with Fourth Division champions elect Exeter City. No joy in the cup competitions although City put up a creditable display against Southampton in the Littlewoods Cup.

An attractive clock in club colours was erected on the top of the popular stand in April 1990. It was presented to the club by the family of Phil Dearlove, a very keen young City fan, who had died a year earlier.

Kevin Dixon (on ground) scores with a diving header in the 4-2 victory over Cambridge in October 1989.

In the Fourth Division Programme of the Year awards the City publication was voted joint second best for 1989-90.

After nearly 25 years, honorary medical officer Dr Angus MacLeod retired from the post and was succeeded by Robert Porter.

New club sponsors were announced in May 1990. Flamingo Land Funpark and Zoo at Kirby Misperton near Malton took over from Camerons who, however, continued their association with City by maintaining their private box at the ground.

For the first time in the club's history an under-16 team was to be fielded in 1990-91. The side, managed by former City player Barrie Tait, was to play in the Yorkshire Conference League. This extended the club's successful youth policy and as Michael Sinclair said: "There is absolutely no question about it — the future of our football club depends to a huge extent on finding young players and bringing them through to the senior ranks."

With a number of good youngsters making progress the chairman believed that the club was set for a healthy future and York City looked ahead with confidence to the 1990s and on into the next century.

Homes of York City

WHEN York City Football Club was formed in 1922, eight acres of land were purchased for £2,000 in Heslington Lane, Fulfordgate. This was in the south-east of the city, away from the centre and not far from where the University is now situated.

It was very much a rural setting and the land was known as Gate Fulford. Hawthorn hedges formed its boundaries and it was very well drained. The name was reversed to be called Fulfordgate. Initially there were no covered stands and the dressing-rooms consisted of an old army hut. Open stands were bought from York Race Committee.

The first match to be played at the ground was on Wednesday, 20 September 1922, against Mansfield Town. The game went ahead only after the necessary requisite deposit, which amounted to £180, was paid. This cash, courtesy of one of the directors, Mr John Fisher, was produced literally at the last minute.

Gradually the ground was built up and improved and, within a couple of years, covered accommodation was available. In the letter of application for admission to the Football League in 1927, York City were able to say that the ground was 'splendidly drained, well-equipped, spacious and capable of being extended to hold up to 40,000 spectators'.

Considerable improvements were made that year. New turnstiles were fitted and stronger fencing was built around the pitch. It was reported that when that fencing was completed, it would be much more difficult for a spectator to surmount it and go on the pitch — an important feature from the referee's view. Behind one of the goals, nine-tier terracing replaced the old banking. The covered 'popular' stand was extended and could now house 1,000. There was also by now a small seated stand.

Before City were elected to the Football League, the biggest crowd housed at the ground was 8,318 (receipts £366) to see the English Schools' Trophy semi-final between York Boys and Brighton Boys on 12 May 1928. In the York team were Reg Stockill and Dave Halford, both of whom went on to have distinguished football careers. By the time of the election to the League the following year, it was estimated that Fulfordgate could accommodate 17,000.

The ground was to stage two big FA Cup third-round replay matches. In January 1930, for the visit of Newcastle United, 12,583 congregated, paying receipts of £900 5s 3d. The following year, Fulfordgate records were set when 12,721, paying £1,058 16s, saw Sheffield United provide the opposition. In November 1931 an Amateur international between England and Ireland was played at the ground.

Towards the end of the third season in the Football League, concern was expressed at York City's poor support. One of the directors, Mr G.W.Halliday, was convinced that the only solution was a change of ground. A major problem about Fulfordgate was the relative inaccessibility of the place. It was a good distance from the railway station and the tram service to Fulford had only a single track. The loop system for tramcars passing one another also restricted the service. The bus routes had not been fully developed and, with general car ownership still a long way in the future, Fulfordgate, without doubt, was not an easy ground for the majority of supporters to reach.

Early in 1932, a ground which was geographically ideally situated near the centre of the city became vacant. For a number of years York Cricket Club had played at Bootham Crescent, but they had decided to move to new headquarters at Wigginton

Aerial view of Bootham Crescent, taken from 1,000 feet in 1983 when York City were playing Colchester United. The ground's main entrance can be seen upper left.

Action from a York City Reserves game at Bootham Crescent in August 1932, just prior to the official opening of the ground. The Members' Stand shown in the above picture was described as 'one of the most modern in the country, it has all the latest apparatus and facilities for players'. Below: View of the Popular Stand 'which holds 6,000 spectators . . .with a tunnel at the rear for speedy exit'.

Road, which is now the site of York & District Hospital. Yorkshire Gentlemen's Cricket Club had previously played at Wigginton Road, but they in turn had transferred to Escrick Park. Cricket had been played at Bootham Crescent for many years. In June 1890, Yorkshire beat Kent by eight wickets on this ground in what remains the only County Championship match played in York.

After preliminary discussions and visits to the Bootham ground, the directors were unanimous of the opinion that a change should be made and a special meeting

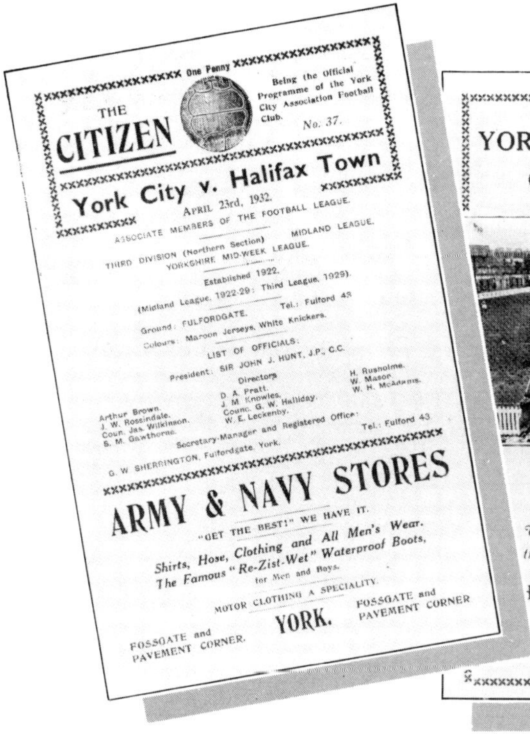

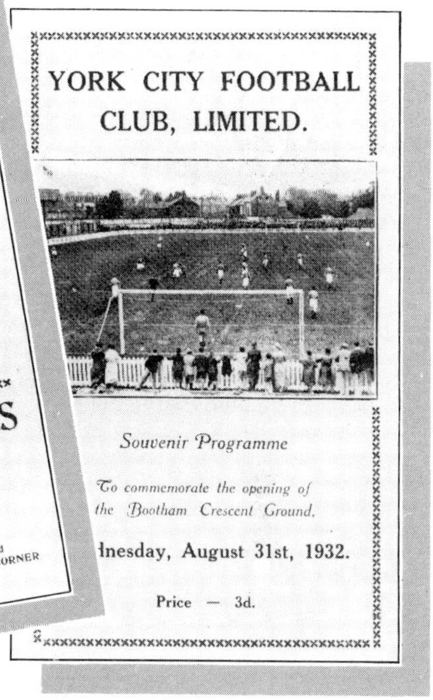

Historic programmes: The last match at Fulfordgate and the first at Bootham Crescent

of the shareholders was held at St George's Hall, Castlegate, on 26 April 1932 to consider and approve the intended move.

At the meeting the chairman, Mr Arthur Brown, drew attention to the 'gate' receipts figures in the three seasons of League football at Fulfordgate, (1929 30 £261; 1930-31 £183; and in 1931-2, when the club were near the top of the table for the first half of the campaign, £198).

This represented average League crowds of approximately 4,000 and at the end of the day a deficit on the balance sheet. The board felt that the class of football had been good enough but the distance to Fulfordgate from the main parts of the city, coupled with the inadequate transport services, had a serious effect on attendances especially in bad weather and when an early kick-off operated.

Mr Halliday pointed out that in a one-mile radius of Bootham Crescent the population was 30,000, whereas for a similar radius at Fulfordgate it was only 3,000. On the question of ownership against tenancy, Mr Brown stated that Fulfordgate was mortgaged as far as possible and the present mortgage, bank interest and overdraft would exceed the rent and rates at Bootham Crescent by £40 per annum.

The directors were satisfied that the new ground would fulfil all requirements. There were no restrictions as to banking, terracing and the erection of stands and the property of the shareholders would be fully protected if the lease, which was for 21 years, expired.

The oldest stand at Fulfordgate needed replacing and it was pointed out that the club could put up a structure three times the size on the new ground. New dressing-rooms were also required at Fulfordgate.

There was some opposition to the move. A former director, Mr J.Fisher, who had proved a benefactor back in 1922, said that during the club's ten years existence it had built a playing history and a ground second to none in such a short time. He pointed out that it had been a bad time for football clubs generally with regard to crowds and that good times would come again to Fulfordgate. He condemned the proposal as a bad policy when it involved renting a ground instead of owning it. The Fulfordgate pitch had an excellent playing surface, whilst the new ground was on land subject to severe flooding. There was also a danger of Bootham Crescent being more heavily-rated once it got valuable equipment on it. Another former director, Councillor W.H.Shaw, also opposed the scheme and expressed doubts regarding the approaches and, looking ahead to the future, car parking limitations at the new ground.

After much discussion, the matter was put to the vote and by a majority of over three to one (115 for, 37 against) the shareholders approved the move to take on lease the Bootham Crescent ground. The Fulfordgate site was subsequently sold and developed as a building estate. There is nothing now to indicate it as the site of the birth of modern football in York in 1922.

The summer of 1932 saw a period of feverish activity as the new ground was equipped. The area was first drained and then built to the design of Messers Ward & Leckenby, architects of York. Two stands were erected — the Main (members') stand and the Popular Stand. The supporters club undertook the responsibility for defraying the cost of the latter stand and there were many willing hands as the club, within four months, set up the new ground in readiness for the 1932-3 season.

The official opening of the ground was on 31 August 1932, for a Third Division

York City (dark shirts) meet Middlesbrough in the FA Cup fifth-round tie at Bootham Crescent in February 1938.

North game against Stockport County. The club president, Sir John Hunt, formally opened the ground by cutting a chocolate and cream coloured ribbon — the colours of the club. Also in attendance were the Sheriff of York (Mr Arnold Rowntree), Mr Roger Lumley MP, Mr Arnold Kingscott, treasurer of the Football Association, and other personalities in the football world. The attendance was 8,106 with receipts of nearly £400 and the result was a 2-2 draw.

The first big match staged at the ground was on 12 January 1935, when Derby County were the visitors in a third-round FA Cup tie. The attendance of 13,612 set a new club record. Three seasons later, when York City reached the quarter-finals of the FA Cup, attendance records were established at four successive stages, culminating in the 28,123 who attended the sixth-round match against Huddersfield Town on 5 March 1938.

During the war the tunnel at the back of the Popular Stand was used as an air-raid shelter for pupils and staff of the nearby Shipton Street School. The ground suffered slight damage after the air-raid on York in April 1942. Houses at the Shipton Street end were bombed. A representative match was staged at the ground on 17 October 1942 when a Football League XI defeated the Northern Command 9-2, watched by 5,500. After the match Mr Fred Howarth, the secretary of the Football League, wrote the following letter to the club:

"May I take this opportunity, on behalf of the League, of congratulating your club, directors and officials alike, for the excellence of the arrangements. You will appreciate that always in representative matches our chief concern is the smoothness of the arrangements. You did your part splendidly.

"The League thanks you for staging the match, which was a complete success, both from the entertainment side and from the financial side. They are grateful for the kindly attention of your directors and will remember with pleasure their first official visit to your lovely city."

In the early post-war period, considerable improvement was made to the ground. Deeper drainage was completed and also the concreting of the banking at the Bootham Crescent end of the ground, together with the installation of loudspeaking equipment.

At the shareholders' annual meeting in September 1948, it was announced that the club had purchased the Bootham Crescent ground which had been on lease since 1932. The chairman, Mr W.H.Sessions, stated that an agreement had been signed and felt that the club now owned one of the best grounds in the Third Division. At the time the club's finances were on a very sound basis.

The company had £6,000 invested in Government stock. There was a balance on transfer deals of £5,570 with donations chiefly from the City Social Club of £2,105. The balance sheet revealed that the ground was bought for £4,075 and the buildings, which cost £7,444, had been depreciated so that the whole ground and equipment was listed at £7,204 at current value in 1949.

To celebrate the purchase of the ground, a dinner was held at the Royal Station Hotel at which the deeds were handed to the chairman. Among those present were past and present directors and many enthusiasts who had worked over the years for the club. Also in attendance was the club's first captain back in 1922, Billy Smith.

In May 1952, England met Ireland in the first Schoolboy international to be played at Bootham Crescent. The attendance was 16,000 and England, who won 5-0, were captained by Wilf McGuinness, who was to become manager of York City some 23 years later.

In the late 1940s and early 1950s, concreting was completed to the terracing in the Popular Stand — thanks to the efforts of the Supporters' Club — and the Shipton Street end. The next major work was carried out in the summer of 1955 when the Main Stand was extended towards Shipton Street. Profits from the FA Cup run, together with a Stand Extension Fund, helped in this project.

The following year a concrete wall was built at the St Olave's Road (Bootham Crescent) end. The project which cost more than £3,000 had a two-fold purpose — a safety precaution and a support for additional banking and terracing. The FA Cup tie in 1955 against Tottenham Hotspur had been restricted to a 21,000 capacity by the police, but with the improvements made the limit had risen to 23,600 when Bolton Wanderers provided the opposition in January 1958.

In the summer of 1959 floodlights were installed at the ground, at the cost of £14,500, a substantial sum of which was raised by the Auxiliary Club. The installation was based on a system of lighting developed by the General Electric Company Ltd, who designed and supervised the project. Messers Shepherds of York were responsible for the concrete bases and erection of the four 100ft towers.

The electrical sub-contractors were Messrs F.H.Wheeler of Scunthorpe. The lights were officially switched on in a match against Newcastle United on 28 October 1959. In an entertaining exhibition game, United won 8-2 in front of a 9,414 crowd.

The year before, in August 1958, a young man by the name of Bryan Foster joined the groundstaff. He duly became head groundsman and, apart from a period 1971 to 1975 when he held similar appointments at Bury and then Preston, he has served the club ever since. For many years the Bootham Crescent pitch has had an excellent playing surface and in recognition of his long and outstanding service, Bryan was presented with a gold watch from the directors in March 1988.

The 1960s were a relatively quiet period in the history of the ground. In 1965 the half-time score-board at the Shipton Street End ceased to be used for that purpose but remained as an advertising hoarding. In March 1966 an attendance of 19,420 saw the Third Division fixture against Hull City and in February 1968, Bootham Crescent staged its first major neutral match when the Tigers played Middlesbrough in a third-round FA Cup second replay. 'Boro won 1-0 in front of 16,524.

The next major alteration to the ground was in the summer of 1974 when seats were installed in the Popular Stand prior to the start of Second Division football. This increased the seating capacity to 2,762.

In 1980, the floodlights were updated and improved at a cost of £20,000. They were officially switched on by former Wolves player and Northern Ireland international, Derek Dougan, prior to a friendly game against Grimsby Town on 1 August. The referee for this game was Keith Usher, who was later to become club secretary.

Early in 1981 a gymnasium was built at the Bootham Crescent end for £50,000. To help towards this City received £15,000 from the Sports Council and £20,000 from the Football League Improvement Trust. In the summer of 1983 improvements were made to the administration facilities. New offices for the manager, secretary, match-day and lottery manager were built together with a vice presidents' lounge. Jack Dunnett, chairman of the Football League, offically opened the lounge prior to a game against Wrexham in November 1983.

In the early 1980s cracks appeared in the concrete wall which had been built in 1956 at the back of the Bootham Crescent end. The rear of the terracing was cordoned off and the capacity of the ground had now been reduced to under 13,500, less than half the attendance record set in 1938. For segregation purposes the Bootham Crescent end was allocated to visiting supporters and before the FA Cup tie against Liverpool in February 1985 fencing was erected for the first time at the ground.

During the successful seasons of 1983-4 and 1984-5 many problems had arisen in handling big crowds. This was due to the old problem of the ground having only two of its four sides available for entry and exit plus the home supporters funnelling through the car-park to the Shipton Street end. In the summer of 1985, therefore, extensive improvements at a cost of approximately £100,000 were made and eight new turnstiles were installed at that end. At the same time the dressing-

Extensive improvements were carried out in June 1985 when turnstiles at the Shipton Street End and groundsman's equipment building were knocked down to make way for new baths and showers, referee's room, physiotherapist's room and toilets.

rooms were refurbished incorporating new baths and showers, plus a new referee's changing room and physiotherapist's treatment room. New toilets were also built at the Shipton Street end.

In 1986-7, hospitality boxes were built into the Main Stand. Video equipment was installed inside the ground and crash-barriers strengthened. Ground safety requirements were met and in September 1989 it was announced that the ground capacity had been increased to 14,628.

Main Stand (seats)	1,102
Popular Stand (seats)	1,957
Shipton Street End	5,105
Shipton Street Enclosure	867
Bootham Crescent End	4,747
Bootham Crescent Enclosure	850

In recent years the following non-football events have been staged at the ground. A pop concert was held in September 1979 and a firework display to celebrate the centenary of the *Yorkshire Evening Press* in October 1982. An American Football match took place in the summer of 1988 and in January 1989, Rugby League football was staged for the first time at Bootham Crescent. York RLFC entertained Leeds and the attendance was 11,347. For the record Leeds won 28-9.

Bryan Foster, York City's groundsman, with the gold watch presented to him in recognition of his 25 years' service to the club.

With the improvements and alterations in recent years the ground is now well-appointed and equipped. A fully stocked and modern club shop, built in 1985, is situated just inside the car-park and this also houses the commercial manager's office. Adjoining this is the social club and players' bar.

Biggest Attendances at Bootham Crescent

28,123	FA Cup 6th round	Huddersfield Town, 5 March 1938
23,860	FA Cup 5th round	Middlesbrough, 12 February 1938
23,600	FA Cup 4th round	Bolton Wanderers, 25 January 1958
22,000	FA Cup 4th round	Sunderland, 28 January 1956
21,010	Third Division North	Hull City, 23 April 1949
21,000	FA Cup 5th round	Tottenham Hotspur, 19 February 1955

Footnote
THE lack of covered standing accommodation is the ground's one major drawback. For many years a stand at the Shipton Street end has been talked about but the prohibitive cost has been the problem. In the spring of 1988, two supporters, Chris Forth and Frank Ormston, launched 'The Shipton Street Roof Appeal Fund' in an endeavour to raise money for the building of a stand. With the blessing of the directors, a committee was formed and various fund raising schemes were put into operation. In August 1989, Middlesbrough played City at York in a special match with all the proceeds going to the fund. A percentage of the sales of this book is also being allocated to the fund. It is to be hoped that in the early 1990s, the stand will have come to fruition 60 years after supporters had raised monies to build the Popular Stand.

YORK CITY Managers

John Collier
July 1928 to May 1930 and May 1933 to March 1937

JOHN 'Jock' Collier was appointed the first official manager of York City in July 1928, prior to the start of what was to be the club's last season in the Midland League.

Born in Scotland in 1899, Collier played for Inverkeithing Juniors and had trials for the Scottish Junior international team. He signed for Raith Rovers and then, in 1920-21, was transferred to Hull City. A right-half, he captained the Tigers for a couple of seasons before moving to Queen's Park Rangers in 1926.

Collier joined York City as player-manager, but a broken ankle ended his playing days after he had made only two senior appearances. He was at the helm as City successfully bridged the gap between non-League and Third Division football, but at the end of that first season of League soccer he left York to become a publican. Collier retained an interest in City's affairs during the time that managerial duties were carried out by the club secretary, Mr G.W.Sherrington.

In May 1933 he was reappointed manager. City's fortunes were at a low ebb, but under Collier's leadership, steady progress was made as York continued to establish themselves at League level. In 1936-7 they progressed to the fourth round of the FA Cup. That season, Collier was very much involved in the coaching side of the game but in March 1937 he announced his retirement from football and went into a business partnership with one of his brothers in Scotland. Sadly, he was troubled by ill health and was only 41 when he died in Hull in December 1940.

Tom Mitchell
March 1937 to February 1950

TOM Mitchell hailed from the North-East and began his playing days as a junior with Tudhoe United and then Spennymoor. An outside-left, he was signed by Newcastle United and competed for the number-11 position with Stan Seymour, who for many years was associated with the Magpies, first as a player and then as a director and chairman.

Mitchell moved to Leeds United and joined York City in 1931-2. In August 1932 he scored the club's first-ever goal at Bootham Crescent, in a 2-2 draw against Stockport County when the ground was officially opened. He retired temporarily from the game at the end of the 1932-3 campaign and was appointed City's manager following the departure of Jock Collier.

Apart from wartime service in the RAF, Mitchell held the job until early 1950. In his first full season (1937-8) he guided the club to the quarter-finals of the FA Cup. He liked to concentrate on coaching and for many years was a Football Association coach, making frequent summer visits to Scandinavia.

Mitchell resigned from the City job in February 1950 and set up a family sports outfitter's shop in York. He later became a director of City before ill health caused him to leave the board. He died in November 1984, aged 85.

Dick Duckworth
March 1950 to October 1952

DICK Duckworth was no stranger to Bootham Crescent when he was appointed manager in March 1950. Twelve years earlier he had captained the City side that reached the sixth round of the FA Cup.

The son of a former England and Manchester United star, he played at right-half, the same position as his father. Duckworth began his career with Second Division Oldham Athletic before moving to Chesterfield. In three seasons at Saltergate he was an ever-present and helped the Derbyshire club to promotion to the Second Division in 1930-31. He subsequently played for Southport, Chester and Rotherham United before joining City in 1936. Duckworth spent three seasons at Bootham Crescent, where his strong and forceful wing-half play had a big influence on City's success during that period.

He was player-manager at Newark at the outbreak of war and, after hostilities ended, became coach at Chesterfield. At the time of his City appointment, Duckworth was the chief northern scout of Birmingham City.

In just over two full seasons at Bootham Crescent he lifted the club from the foot of the Northern Section to a position in the top four by the time he left to take over at Stockport County in October 1952. He remained in charge at Edgeley Park until 1956 and later managed Darlington and Scunthorpe United.

Charles Spencer
November 1952 to February 1953

CHARLES Spencer had an illustrious playing career as a centre-half for Manchester United and Newcastle United. With Newcastle he won an FA Cup winners' medal in 1924 and a First Division Championship medal in 1927 and was twice capped by England.

Spencer, who was born in Washington, on Tyneside, in 1899, was player-manager of Tunbridge Wells after leaving Manchester United. He held a similar job at Wigan Athletic before being appointed manager of Grimsby Town in March 1937. He remained at Grimsby for 14 years and for most of this period the Mariners were a First Division side as well as reaching the FA Cup semi-final on one occasion under his charge. Ill health forced him to retire in May 1951 and the man who took over from him at Blundell Park was Bill Shankly. Recovered from illness, Spencer was appointed York City manager in November 1952 but, sadly, he had a relapse and died in February the following year, after less than three months in office.

Jimmy McCormick
June 1953 to September 1954

BORN in Rotherham in 1912, Jimmy McCormick was a right winger in his playing days and spent 12 seasons with Tottenham Hotspur prior to the outbreak of World War Two. He also played for Rotherham, Chesterfield, Fulham, Lincoln City and Crystal Palace.

McCormick had extensive coaching experience in Norway, Malta and Turkey and, at the time of his appointment as manager of York City, he was coach and assistant trainer at Sheffield United. During what was to be McCormick's only season at Bootham Crescent, local centre-forward Dave Dunmore was transferred to Spurs for a then club record incoming fee of £10,750.

It was with this money that McCormick recruited new players during the summer of 1954. Arthur Bottom, Ernie Phillips, Tommy Forgan, Norman Wilkinson and George Howe were amongst his signings and City were away to a 'flyer' on the opening day of the 1954-5 campaign with a magnificent 6-2 victory at Wrexham. A 1-0 win over Hartlepools United followed, but then came a 3-2 home defeat at the hands of Scunthorpe United.

A dispute then arose between the manager and the board of directors regarding team selection. This was not resolved and early in September, McCormick's resignation was accepted and his contract ended by mutual consent. What followed is history. The team which he had largely built went on to reach the FA Cup semi-final.

In January 1968, Jimmy McCormick was killed in a road accident whilst on holiday in Spain with his wife. At the time of his death he was the licensee of a public house in Hertfordshire.

Sam Bartram
March 1956 to July 1960

FOLLOWING the dramatic resignation of Jimmy McCormick, York City went 18 months without a manager. During this period — the most successful from a playing point of view in their history — managerial affairs were looked after by trainer Tom Lockie and secretary Bill Sherrington. In March 1956, however, the board announced the appointment of Sam Bartram, the former Charlton Athletic goalkeeper who had spent 22 years at The Valley.

Born in the North-East in January 1914, Bartram was generally regarded as the best uncapped goalkeeper in England. He helped Charlton gain promotion from the Third Division South to the First Division in successive seasons in the mid 1930s. During the war, Bartram guested for York for a number of years and proved a most popular player with the fans. When peacetime football returned, he won an FA Cup winners' medal with Charlton in 1946-7 and altogether made 582 League appearances for the club.

During his reign at Bootham Crescent, Bartram experienced mixed fortunes. In 1958, City failed on goal-average to become founder members of the new national Third Division. The following season they gained promotion for the first time in their history, only to suffer immediate relegation in 1959-60. In July 1960, City released Bartram and he took over as manager of Luton Town. He spent two years in charge at Kenilworth Road and then was involved in sports journalism. He died suddenly in London in July 1981, aged 67.

Tom Lockie
July 1960 to October 1967

UPON the departure of Sam Bartram, City turned to their loyal servant, Tom Lockie, to fill the manager's job at Bootham Crescent. Born in Duns, Scotland, in 1906, Lockie started his career with his home-town club before joining Glasgow Rangers, where he spent four years, mostly playing for the Reserves.

A tall, commanding centre-half, he went on to play for Leith Athletic and Barnsley before joining York City in 1933. He spent one season with the club and then played for Accrington Stanley and Mansfield Town before returning to Bootham Crescent as reserve-team trainer in 1936.

Lockie was soon promoted to first-team trainer and obtained qualifications for the treatment of players. He was very much involved with the team that reached the quarter-finals of the FA Cup in 1937-8 and during the war years he did a tremendous amount of work which helped the club during those difficult days. A qualified FA coach, he was granted a testimonial match in 1951-2, in which City played a Football League XI.

Following Jimmy McCormick's departure in September 1954, Lockie shared the managerial duties with Bill Sherrington and played a considerable part in team affairs as City embarked on one of the most glorious chapters in their history.

In his first two seasons as manager, York narrowly missed promotion to the Third Division but then followed a couple of disappointing campaigns with an application for re-election to Division Four in 1963-4. The following season was an outstanding one, however, with some of the best football seen at York since the FA Cup glory days of ten years earlier.

The side gained promotion to the Third Division, finishing only one point behind champions Brighton. Alas, the club was immediately relegated and then had to apply for re-election in successive seasons. The start of the 1967-8 campaign was disastrous and after 12 games, York were bottom of the Fourth Division without a win. Almost inevitably, Tom Lockie was dismissed in October, the first City manager to suffer this fate.

Upon leaving the club he spent a number of years working in the wages office at Rowntree Mackintosh. He lived in the village of New Earswick, near York, for over 40 years and died in July 1977.

Joe Shaw
November 1967 to August 1968

THE choice of Joe Shaw as the next City manager was a popular one. Shaw had enjoyed an outstanding 21-year career with Sheffield United as a fine, ball-playing centre-half. He captained the Blades for a number of seasons and toured Australia with the FA team in 1952 as well as representing the Football League on a number of occasions.

Born in Marton, South Yorkshire, in June 1928, he made well over 600 League appearances for United. In his last two seasons at Bramall Lane he assisted manager John Harris by looking after the Intermediate and Central League sides.

One of Shaw's first tasks after moving to York was to appoint as coach a former Sheffield United colleague, Billy Hodgson. After the nightmare start to 1967-8, results improved and by early April, City had climbed to 14th position. A bad slump in the closing weeks followed, however, and to everyone's bitter disappointment another re-election bid had to be made.

During the summer, a number of new signings were made, notably Phil Boyer from Derby County, and hopes were high for the new season. However, on 16 August 1968, Joe Shaw made the shock announcement of his resignation for personal reasons. His wife had a woollen and baby-clothes shop in Sheffield and they were having difficulties in selling this and purchasing a new house in the York area. This had been causing him considerable worry and he had found the constant travelling a problem. He later returned to football and managed Chesterfield from 1973 to 1976.

Tom Johnston
October 1968 to January 1975

SCOTSMAN Tom Johnston was arguably the most successful manager in York City's history. He took over with the club in the lower reaches of the Fourth Division and, although he could not avoid them having to make another re-election application in May 1969, he was to pilot City to the Second Division for the first, and so far only time, in their history.

Born near Coldstream in December 1918, his English playing career was spent with Nottingham Forest and Notts County, making a total of 332 League appearances and scoring 112 goals. He was in the Notts County side that lost to City in the quarter-finals of the FA Cup in 1955. Four times he was reserve for Scotland before he hung up his boots in 1957.

A fully qualified FA coach, Johnston spent four years in Finland with the Valdokoski Harka club, who won the Finnish Cup during his regime. Upon returning to England, he was appointed manager of Rotherham United. He later became manager at Grimsby Town and Huddersfield Town and took over as York City's chief on 31 October, 1968.

A strong disciplinarian, Johnston gradually improved the squad and after finishing in mid-table in 1969-70, City gained promotion the following year. The next two seasons saw York avoid relegation only on goal-average, but in 1973-4 they astounded the football world by finishing third and winning promotion to the Second Division.

The manager had built an almost impregnable defence led by Barry Swallow. New signings Barry Lyons, from Forest, and Ian Holmes, from Sheffield United, brought skill and inventiveness to the midfield in which former Hull City player Ian Butler also starred. Up front, Jimmy Seal and Chris Jones provided the scoring power. It was a glorious season and a marvellous achievement by the team under Johnston's leadership.

York were holding their own in the higher grade and held Arsenal to a draw in the FA Cup at Highbury when it was announced early in January 1975 that the manager had asked to be released from his new four-year contract, which still had three years and two months to run.

Huddersfield Town, struggling near the foot of the Third Division, wanted his services and after some controversy over his contract, he was allowed to go to Leeds Road as general manager. An official statement made by City read as follows: 'York City FC has accepted, with reluctance, the resignation of Mr T.D.Johnston from his position as manager of the club with effect from January 11, 1975. The directors would like to place on record their appreciation of the services rendered to the club by Mr Johnston during his period as manager and wish him success in his new appointment.' He was to spend two seasons in his second spell at Huddersfield.

Tom Johnston brought considerable success to Bootham Crescent during his six years stay and did very well in transfer deals, achieving just the right blend. Often described as a 'dour and canny Scot', his period as manager was not without controversy. During the 1972-3 season a major row developed between the players and Johnston which amounted to a vote of no confidence in their manager. The matter was eventually resolved by the directors and Tom Johnston went on to create history for York City.

Wilf McGuinness
February 1975 to October 1977

ONE of the most illustrious names to manage York City was Wilf McGuinness, but unfortunately he presided over a bad period in which the club slumped from the Second to Fourth Division. At the time of his departure they were in the bottom four of the League.

Born in Manchester in October 1937, McGuinness was an outstanding wing-half and one of Manchester United's 'Busby Babes'. Owing to injury, he missed the ill-fated trip to Munich in February 1958 but had his career cut short by a broken leg in the early 1960s, soon after being capped twice by England. He went on to coach the England Youth team and helped Sir Alf Ramsey with his preparations for the 1966 World Cup-winning squad.

Reserve-team trainer with Manchester United, he became chief coach at Old Trafford and was appointed to succeed Sir Matt Busby as manager. After only a short spell in charge, however, (and with the shadow of Busby never far away) he was relieved of the post and spent three years in Greece, managing Aris Salonika.

He was appointed manager of York City on 15 February 1975 and helped City stay in the Second Division. From then on, however, it was all downhill as the club finished 21st in the table in 1975-6 and bottom of the Third Division in 1976-7. He was unable to check the slide and when he was dismissed on 20 October 1977, City were 22nd in the Fourth Division. During his period with the club, only 27 League matches were won out of 113, whilst York suffered 60 defeats in that time.

A most likeable and friendly man, it was very sad that Wilf McGuinness did not have success at York. He later became chief coach and physiotherapist at Bury.

Charlie Wright
November 1977 to March 1980

CHARLIE Wright became the fourth Scotsman and second former Charlton Athletic goalkeeper to manage York City when he was appointed on 22 November, 1977. A Glaswegian, he was born in December 1938 and started his playing days with Morton and then had a spell with Glasgow Rangers. Whilst doing his National Service in Hong Kong, Wright represented that country in an international match against Peru. His English clubs were Workington, Grimsby Town, Charlton and Bolton Wanderers and he made a total of 535 League appearances in his career. He became youth coach and looked after the reserve team at Bolton before his move to York.

Wright could not prevent City having to seek re-election in May 1978, but in his first full season there was a considerable improvement as the club finished tenth. In 1979-80 fortunes dipped again and the side was struggling in the lower reaches of the Fourth Division when he was sacked on 18 March 1980.

A hard-working manager, he was never able to quite rebuild the side that had dropped from the Second to the Fourth Division in the mid 1970s. A very loyal man, Wright was at times outspoken and his colourful language was not to everyone's liking. A lively character indeed, he saw his side win 35 of the 111 League games in which he was in charge. After coaching on the continent he managed Bolton Wanderers from January to December 1985.

Barry Lyons
March 1980 to December 1981

UPON the departure of Charlie Wright, youth coach and former City player Barry Lyons was appointed caretaker manager. The re-election threat was beaten off, the side finished 17th and on 4 May 1980, Lyons was officially appointed manager.

Born in Shirebrook in 1945, he began his career with Rotherham and then moved to Nottingham Forest, for whom he made over 200 League appearances. He was transferred to York City in September 1973 and played a big part in the side's promotion drive for the Second Division. Lyons left Bootham Crescent at the end of 1975-6 and joined Darlington before retiring as a player in 1979. He became City's youth coach in June that year.

The team made a good start to his first full season as manager and were unbeaten in their first seven League and Cup games. Alas, a bad slump followed and York finished bottom of the Football League in 92nd position.

During the summer of 1981, a player who was to have a big influence in the years ahead was signed — Keith Walwyn from Chesterfield — but City continued to struggle in the lower half of the table and on 8 December 1981, Barry Lyons was relieved of his duties. He resumed as youth-team coach, but finally left the club in July 1982 and took up employment outside football.

Denis Smith
May 1982 to May 1987

FOR the second half of 1981-2, York City utilized the services of two caretaker managers. Former player and youth coach Kevin Randall was in charge until early March 1982 and then club director Barry Swallow was put in control of team matters until the end of the season which saw City finish 17th. One of Mr Swallow's first acts was to obtain, on a month's loan, the Stoke City centre-half Denis Smith, who was approaching the end of his playing career.

Born in Stoke in November 1947, he made over 400 League appearances for the Potters and won a League Cup-winners' medal in 1971-2. On 12 May 1982, it was announced that the experienced defender was to become York City's first player-manager since Jock Collier in the 1920's.

Smith chose as player-coach and his right-hand man the former Fulham and Norwich City striker, Viv Busby, and a new era was ushered in at Bootham Crescent. A new defence was recruited and City rose to seventh place in 1982-3. The manager hung up his boots at the start of the following season which was to be an historic one for York City as they won their first major title — the Fourth Division championship.

It was a record-breaking campaign as City became the first club in League history to reach 100 points, now that three points were awarded for a win. The next two seasons were also successful as the side finished eighth and seventh in the Third Division and on each occasion reached the fifth round of the FA Cup, losing to Liverpool in replays at Anfield.

After four good campaigns, the 1986-7 season was very disappointing and relegation was only just avoided. At a salary reported to be £45,000 per annum, Smith was believed to be the highest paid Third Division manager at the time, but at the end of May 1987 he accepted the vacant manager's job at Sunderland.

After compensation of £20,000 was agreed between the clubs he moved to Roker Park, along with Viv Busby. In their first season in charge, Sunderland won the Third Division championship and, as a result, City received a further £20,000 compensation. Although the last months of the Smith-Busby regime at Bootham Crescent turned a little sour, overall the pair did an excellent job and put the club back on the footballing map. City won 105 and drew 54 of the 230 League games under their control.

Bobby Saxton
June 1987 to September 1988

WHEN Bobby Saxton became the next York City manager, on 9 June 1987, he was faced with the monumental task of virtually rebuilding the side in a matter of a few weeks. Experienced players Keith Walwyn, Gary Ford and Steve Senior had left Bootham

Crescent and when training for the new season resumed in mid-July, only three players had signed contracts.

Eventually, a squad was acquired but almost inevitably the team struggled and relegation was on the cards from the opening day. New signings were made during the summer of 1988 and when City started their first season back in the Fourth Division since 1984, hopes were reasonably high. A disastrous start was made, however, and with only one point from the opening four games and the side bottom of the League, Saxton resigned on 17 September. He blamed himself for putting the players under too much pressure and openly admitted that he did not know what to do next.

Born in Doncaster in September 1943, Saxton's playing career was spent with Derby County, Plymouth and Exeter. He managed Exeter, Plymouth and Blackburn and had a good deal of success at Ewood Park, narrowly failing to obtain promotion to the First Division. Nevertheless, he was sacked in December 1986 and had a short spell as assistant manager at Preston before joining City. Shortly after leaving Bootham Crescent, Saxton became assistant to newly-appointed manager Jim Smith at Newcastle United.

John Bird
October 1988 to date

BARRY Swallow was again summoned as caretaker boss after Bobby Saxton's dramatic departure. Vital points were gained which lifted City off the foot of the table and on 10 October 1988, John Bird became the 15th person to hold the official post of manager of York City. Like Saxton he was Doncaster-born, in June 1948, and started his playing days with his home-town club. A centre-half, Bird went on to play for Preston, Newcastle and Hartlepool and managed 'Pool before his City appointment. Assisted by coach Alan Little, he set about the recovery and rescue job and at the end of his first season he had lifted York City to 11th position.

For the first half of 1989-90 the team were well placed in the promotion race and hopes were high. A bad run in the New Year both with results and injuries saw them falter and although results improved in the closing weeks the final position of 13th was undoubtedly very disappointing to the manager.

With a settled squad at his disposal and with a number of good youngsters on the fringe of the first team John Bird approached his third year in charge with a measure of some confidence.

York City Stars A-Z

Born in Taunton in 1940, Colin Addison moved with his family to York at the age of 11. He played for York City as a junior in 1956 before becoming a full-time professional at the start of the 1957-8 season and making his League debut in September 1957. He soon made his mark as an attacking inside-forward and played his part in the promotion season of 1958-9. Addison developed into a regular scorer with some of his goals being quite spectacular efforts, especially one against Blackburn Rovers in a Football League Cup tie at Bootham Crescent in October 1960, which was City's first-ever game in that competition. He attracted the attention of a number of First Division clubs and, in January 1961, was transferred to Nottingham Forest for a then record club fee received of £12,000. He went on to play for Arsenal, Sheffield United and was player-manager of Hereford United when they joined the Football League in 1972. After his playing days finished, Addison had an extensive managerial career with Derby County, West Bromwich Albion and Newport County and had a successful spell with Spanish club Celta Vigo before having a short period in charge of Atletico Madrid. In July 1990 he returned to Hereford as manager.

League debut for City v Bury (h) 14 September 1957, Third Division North.

	LEAGUE		*FA CUP*		*FL CUP*		*TOTAL*	
	App	*Gls*	*App*	*Gls*	*App*	*Gls*	*App*	*Gls*
1957-58	8	0	0	0	0	0	8	0
1958-59	25	10	1	0	0	0	26	10
1959-60	31	4	2	1	0	0	33	5
1960-61	23	14	6	1	1	1	30	16
	87	28	9	2	1	1	97	31

COLIN ADDISON

Born in Macclesfield in 1943, Paul Aimson had two very successful spells with York City and figured prominently in the promotion campaigns of 1964-5 and 1970-71. He joined Manchester City as a junior in 1960 and whilst at Maine Road made a total of 16 League appearances, scoring four goals. In July 1964 he was signed by York for £1,000 and scored on his debut on the opening day of the 1964-5 season, against Rochdale. Aimson went on to score 30 League and Cup goals that term as City swept to promotion. The following season he was one of the few successes as the club struggled at the foot of the Third Division and in March 1966 he was transferred to Second Division Bury for £10,000. Aimson went on to have spells with Bradford City and Huddersfield Town before returning to Bootham Crescent in August 1969 for £8,000. His first game back in City colours on 25 August 1969, against Exeter, was watched by 6,200, double the previous home crowd. In 1970-71 he hit 31 League and Cup goals as City again won promotion, finally leaving the club in March 1973 to join Bournemouth for £12,000. He completed his playing career with Colchester United when a serious injury caused his retirement in 1973-4. Aimson scored three League hat-tricks for City, the most memorable being at Hull in September 1965 in a famous 4-1 victory. The others were against Brentford in March 1970 and Chesterfield in April 1972. He also netted two FA Cup hat-tricks against Bangor in November 1964 and Tamworth in November 1970, but his most memorable Cup goal was his dramatic last-minute headed equalizer in the epic 3-3 draw against Southampton in the fourth round at Bootham Crescent in January 1971. Paul Aimson was the complete centre-forward. He could shoot with either foot, was excellent in the air and was a talented, skilful and intelligent leader of the attack. In four of his six seasons he finished top scorer and is the fifth-highest marksman in the club's history.
League debut for City v Rochdale (h) 22 August 1964, Fourth Division.

PAUL AIMSON

	LEAGUE		*FA CUP*		*FL CUP*		*TOTAL*	
	App	*Gls*	*App*	*Gls*	*App*	*Gls*	*App*	*Gls*
1964-65	45	26	2	4	1	0	48	30
1965-66	32	17	1	1	3	3	36	21
1969-70	29/4	8	5	2	0	0	34/4	10
1970-71	42/1	26	6	5	1	0	49/1	31
1971-72	42/1	16	3	0	4	0	49/1	16
1972-73	20/3	5	0/2	0	0	0	20/5	5
	210/9	98	17/2	12	9	3	236/11	113

Born in Newcastle in 1917, Billy Allen was signed from Chesterfield in August 1939 after spending two seasons with the Derbyshire club. He scored both goals on his debut, in a 2-2 home draw against Chester on 26 August, but a week later the League was suspended because of the outbreak of war. It was to be another seven years before Allen made his official debut. He again celebrated by scoring against the same opposition, this time in a 4-4 draw. From 1946 to 1950 he was a regular and consistent performer in the first-team, playing at either half-back or inside-forward. In the summer of 1950 he was transferred to League newcomers Scunthorpe United.
League debut for City v Chester (h) 31 August 1946, Third Division North.

	LEAGUE		*FA CUP*		*TOTAL*	
	App	*Gls*	*App*	*Gls*	*App*	*Gls*
1945-46	0	0	1	1	1	1
1946-47	33	13	1	0	34	13
1947-48	29	4	1	0	30	4
1948-49	33	3	3	0	36	3
1949-50	34	3	0	0	34	3
	129	23	6	1	135	24

BILLY ALLEN

Percy Andrews, who was born in Alton, Hampshire, in 1922, served York City well for 11 years from 1947 to 1958. His football skills were spotted as a schoolboy in Hampshire and he signed as an amateur with Portsmouth, making a number of appearances in the London Senior Football League. Andrews joined the Royal Signals at the age of 16 and had a distinguished Army career. He played regularly in service football competitions and he went on to captain the British Army team, being awarded more than 20 medals as skipper. He joined City shortly after the war and for a number of seasons he was a key member of the defence, filling the right-back or centre-half position. He was an ever-present in 1952-3 and 1953-4 but, following an injury in October 1954, he did not appear again in the first team. He did continue to serve the club loyally and well in the reserve and third teams, helping the younger players until his retirement in 1958. In May 1957 he was rewarded with a testimonial match when a City team played an All Stars XI. Percy Andrews continued to live locally until his death at Pocklington in February 1985, at the age of 62.

League debut for City v Carlisle United (a) 4 September 1947, Third Division North.

	LEAGUE		*FA CUP*		*TOTAL*	
	App	*Gls*	*App*	*Gls*	*App*	*Gls*
1947-48	1	0	0	0	1	0
1948-49	5	0	0	0	5	0
1949-50	27	0	0	0	27	0
1950-51	21	0	3	0	24	0
1951-52	26	0	0	0	26	0
1952-53	46	0	1	0	47	0
1953-54	46	0	1	0	47	0
1954-55	4	0	0	0	4	0
	176	0	5	0	181	0

PERCY ANDREWS

When goalkeeper Mick Astbury made his Football League debut in a Fourth Division game at Bournemouth on 15 November 1980, he became, at the age of 16 years and 298 days, the second-youngest player to appear for York City. Born in Kippax in January 1964, Astbury played for Castleford and Yorkshire Boys and represented the Yorkshire Under-19 team when only 15. He also played for Farsley Celtic in the Yorkshire League and turned down an opportunity of signing for Leeds United by joining City in March 1980, when former goalkeeper Charlie Wright was manager. He became an apprentice professional in June that year and signed full terms in January 1982. His first-team opportunities were limited, however, as he understudied Eddie Blackburn and then Roger Jones. He made only a handful of appearances in the Fourth Division championship-winning season of 1983-4, but the following campaign played in the Cup ties against Arsenal and Liverpool. He had the misfortune to concede seven goals and collect an injury at Anfield, but prior to this he kept a clean sheet for seven successive matches. Following the departure of Jones, Astbury started the 1985-6 campaign as first-choice 'keeper but had the great misfortune to suffer a serious facial injury and depressed fracture of the cheekbone in a match at Bristol Rovers on 2 November 1985 and did not play for the first team again. He left Bootham Crescent at the end of that season, and after a period on loan with Peterborough United, went on to play for Darlington, Chester and Chesterfield before taking up a coaching position in the United States.

League debut for City v Bournemouth (a) 15 November 1980, Fourth Division.

MICK ASTBURY

	LEAGUE		*FA CUP*		*FL CUP*		*OTHERS*		*TOTAL*	
	App	*Gls*	*App*	*Gls*	*App*	*Gls*	*App*	*Gls*	*App*	*Gls*
1980-81	1	0	0	0	0	0	0	0	1	0
1981-82	15	0	0	0	0	0	0	0	15	0
1982-83	4	0	1	0	0	0	0	0	5	0
1983-84	5	0	0	0	1	0	0	0	6	0
1984-85	7	0	4	0	0	0	1	0	12	0
1985-86	16	0	0	0	4	0	0	0	20	0
	48	0	5	0	5	0	1	0	59	0

Locally-born Reg Baines was York City's pre-war scoring hero. He spent a short period with the club in the mid-1920s, making a total of 19 Midland League appearances and scoring seven goals. After spells with Selby Town and Scarborough, Baines returned to York in 1931. He scored on his League debut at Carlisle in October that year and in his first season set a new club scoring record of 29 League goals, a feat he emulated the following campaign. This record stood until 1951-2, when Billy Fenton netted 31 times. In May 1933, Baines was transferred to Sheffield United for £500 and then moved to Doncaster Rovers, helping the Belle Vue club to promotion to the Second Division in 1935. He returned for his third spell with City at the start of 1937-8. This was to be a memorable season with the club reaching the quarter finals of the FA Cup. Baines scored five goals in that memorable Cup run and his finest hour was when he hit a hat-trick in the fourth-round 3-2 win over First Division West Brom. He scored a total of six League hat-tricks for City, a record which was later equalled by Alf Patrick, and finished his playing days with Halifax Town in 1938-9. A typical 'old school' bustling centre-forward, he is number-seven in the club's all-time scoring list. A most popular and friendly character, Reg Baines was also a very good local cricketer and played many seasons for Rowntrees, the company for whom he worked for over 50 years. Reg died suddenly whilst on holiday abroad in 1974, aged 67.

League debut for City v Carlisle United (h) 3 October 1931, Third Division.

	LEAGUE		FA CUP		TOTAL	
	App	Gls	App	Gls	App	Gls
1924-25*	9	1	0	0	9	1
1925-26*	10	6	0	0	10	6
1931-32	32	29	1	0	33	29
1932-33	39	29	1	0	40	29
1937-38	39	23	9	5	48	28
	129	88	11	5	140	93

* Midland League.

REG BAINES

Born in Wigan in 1938, Gerry Baker was on the books of Bolton Wanderers and Nottingham Forest, but did not make his League debut until joining York City. He was signed in July 1963 and for five seasons he was a virtual ever-present, helping the club to promotion in 1964-5. Most of his appearances were at right-back, but he did play a few games at centre-forward with some success. A serious knee injury midway through the 1968-9 season cut short Gerry Baker's career and in October 1969, a testimonial match was staged on his behalf when City's 1969-70 side met the club's 1954-5 FA Cup semi-final team.

League debut for City v Tranmere (a) 26 August 1963, Fourth Division.

	LEAGUE		FA CUP		FL CUP		TOTAL	
	App	Gls	App	Gls	App	Gls	App	Gls
1963-64	33	5	1	0	4	1	38	6
1964-65	41	1	2	0	0	0	43	1
1965-66	43	0	1	0	3	0	47	0
1966-67	40	0	4	0	2	0	46	0
1967-68	41	1	1	0	0	0	42	1
1968-69	16	0	2	1	0	0	18	1
	214	7	11	1	9	1	234	9

GERRY BAKER

When Dale Banton was signed from Aldershot in November 1984, for a fee of £50,000, he became York City's most expensive player. Born in Kensington in 1961, Banton joined West Ham United as an apprentice and made six senior appearances for the Hammers before moving to Aldershot in the summer of 1982. In two and a half seasons with the Hampshire club, he scored 59 goals in 126 League and Cup games. In 1982-3, he was the leading Fourth Division scorer with 28 goals and in May 1983 netted five times in a 6-1 win over Halifax. Banton scored on his debut for City, at Lincoln on 24 November 1984, but it took him a little time to settle down at Bootham Crescent. This was chiefly due to the fact that when he arrived, City had embarked on an FA Cup run that was to take them through to the fifth round. Because he was Cup-tied he spent the first three months in and out of the side. Comparison with former favourite John Byrne, whom he had replaced, together with the big transfer fee, weighed heavily and it was a while before the fans began to appreciate his skill on the ball and his sharp finishing. In his first full season (1985-6) he played a full part as the club once again reached the fifth round of the FA Cup and he struck up a partnership with Keith Walwyn. Injuries caused Banton problems the next season, but in 1987-8 he had his best campaign with the club. Although the side struggled at the foot of the Third Division, he finished top scorer with 18 League and Cup goals and was voted 'Clubman of the Year' by supporters. On 25 October 1988, shortly after the arrival of John Bird as the new City manager, Banton was transferred to Second Division Walsall for a fee of £80,000. He was to experience an unhappy few months at Fellows Park before he returned to his former club, Aldershot, at the start of the 1989-90 season.
League debut for City v Lincoln (a) 24 November 1984, Third Division.

DALE BANTON

	LEAGUE		*FA CUP*		*FL CUP*		*OTHERS*		*TOTAL*	
	App	*Gls*	*App*	*Gls*	*App*	*Gls*	*App*	*Gls*	*App*	*Gls*
1984-85	29/1	12	0	0	0	0	4	1	33/1	13
1985-86	33/2	11	7	1	3	1	2	0	45/2	13
1986-87	24/5	6	3	1	4	0	0	0	31/5	7
1987-88	32/1	16	4	1	4	0	2	1	42/1	18
1988-89	11	4	0	0	2	0	0	0	13	4
	129/9	49	14	3	13	1	8	2	164/9	55

Claude Barrett, a determined, hard-tackling left-back, was born at Rawdon on 5 December 1903 and started his professional soccer career with Bradford, for whom he first signed in February 1932. Barrett made 47 appearances for the Park Avenue club before being transferred to Port Vale in 1936. York City signed him in August 1937 and he made his first-team debut in November that year. Barrett went on to figure in City's run to the quarter-finals of the FA Cup, playing a vital role in defence. He died in August 1976.
League debut for City v Crewe Alexandra (h) 6 November 1937, Third Division.

	LEAGUE		*FA CUP*		*TOTAL*	
	App	*Gls*	*App*	*Gls*	*App*	*Gls*
1937-38	29	0	9	0	38	0
1938-39	12	0	0	0	12	0
	41	0	9	0	50	0

CLAUDE BARRETT

Harold Beck gained a Junior international cap for England against Scotland in 1925, when he played in the Birmingham League. After assisting his home-town club, Walsall, he moved to Barrow, where he was captain. Beck joined York City at the start of their first season in the Football League, making his debut in the opening game at Wigan Borough. A stalwart half-back, he was a virtual ever-present in his three seasons with City, making a big contribution as they established themselves in the Football League. He also figured in the FA Cup ties against Newcastle United and Sheffield United in the early 1930s. There is one amusing story about Harry. He was a rather argumentative player, persistently baiting the referee, but he was once very effectively quietened. In a game at New Brighton, he chuntered to the official over every decision until, finally, the referee called him over, told the surprised Beck to open his mouth and popped in a stick of chewing gum. The implication was obvious and Harry kept quiet for the rest of the game.
League debut for City v Wigan Borough (a) 31 August 1929, Third Division North.

	LEAGUE		*FA CUP*		*TOTAL*	
	App	*Gls*	*App*	*Gls*	*App*	*Gls*
1929-30	41	3	6	0	47	3
1930-31	41	9	5	0	46	9
1931-32	37	0	1	0	38	0
	119	12	12	0	131	12

HAROLD BECK

Born in Sheffield in 1930, Walter Bingley joined York from Swindon Town in the summer of 1960 and proved to be a reliable and steady right-back in his three seasons at Bootham Crescent. He started his League career with Bolton Wanderers in the late 1940s and moved to Sheffield Wednesday in 1955. Bingley made a number of First and Second Division appearances for the Owls before joining Swindon Town in January 1958, for whom he played in over 100 League games. He missed only six games in his period at York and in 1962-3 he was their penalty-kick expert. The previous season he helped his club reach the quarter-finals of the Football League Cup. He concluded his League career with Halifax Town, spending two seasons at The Shay (1963-5).
League debut for City v Millwall (h) 20 August 1960, Fourth Division.

	LEAGUE		*FA CUP*		*FL CUP*		*TOTAL*	
	App	*Gls*	*App*	*Gls*	*App*	*Gls*	*App*	*Gls*
1960-61	44	0	6	0	1	0	51	0
1961-62	44	0	1	0	7	0	52	0
1962-63	42	5	4	0	2	0	48	5
	130	5	11	0	10	0	151	5

WALTER BINGLEY

Born in Houghton-le-Spring in 1957, goalkeeper Eddie Blackburn was manager Barry Lyons' first signing for York City when he was bought from Hull City in May 1980, for a fee of £6,000. He made a total of 68 League appearances for the Tigers. Although City finished bottom of the Fourth Division in 1980-81, Blackburn had an outstanding first season and was elected 'Clubman of the Year'. Upon the signing of Roger Jones at the start of the 1982-3 campaign, he lost his place and in January 1983 moved to Hartlepool, for whom he made over 150 League appearances.
League debut for City v Bournemouth (h) 16 August 1980, Fourth Division.

EDDIE BLACKBURN

	LEAGUE		*FA CUP*		*FL CUP*		*TOTAL*	
	App	*Gls*	*App*	*Gls*	*App*	*Gls*	*App*	*Gls*
1980-81	45	0	2	0	4	0	51	0
1981-82	31	0	3	0	2	0	36	0
	76	0	5	0	6	0	87	0

Arthur Bottom was one of City's all-time scoring heroes and was arguably the best marksman in the club's history, with over 100 League and Cup goals in less than four seasons at Bootham Crescent in the mid-1950s. Born in Sheffield in 1930, Bottom joined Sheffield United as a junior and signed professional terms for the Blades in April 1947. In six seasons at Bramall Lane he made 24 League appearances and scored seven goals. He joined City in the summer of 1954 and made a sensational debut, scoring a hat-trick in a 6-2 win at Wrexham. He scored a total of 39 goals in his first season, equalling Billy Fenton's club record total of 31 League goals, a feat he emulated the following campaign. He was a key figure in the FA Cup semi-final run, scoring a hat-trick at Dorchester, two goals at Bishop Auckland, the winning goal at Notts County and the equalizer against Newcastle United in the semi-final at Hillsborough. His biggest scoring feat was the four goals he netted in the 9-1 victory over Southport in February 1957 and he finished top scorer in each of his three full seasons with the club. In February 1958, he was transferred to Newcastle United and, with ten goals in 11 matches, saved the Magpies from relegation to the Second Division. He moved to Chesterfield in November 1958 and in 18 months at Saltergate scored six goals in 34 League games. He finished his playing days with Midland League club Alfreton Town in the early 1960s. Sixth in York's all-time scoring list, Bottom thrilled the crowds in the 1950s, during City's golden period, with his explosive shooting and aggressive style. A sometimes controversial figure on the field, he was quiet and retiring off it.
League debut for City v Wrexham (a) 21 August 1954, Third Division North.

ARTHUR BOTTOM

	LEAGUE		*FA CUP*		*TOTAL*	
	App	*Gls*	*App*	*Gls*	*App*	*Gls*
1954-55	38	31	8	8	46	39
1955-56	43	31	5	2	48	33
1956-57	37	21	3	1	40	22
1957-58	19	9	5	2	24	11
	137	92	21	13	158	105

Phil Boyer was one of the most talented and skilful players to appear for York City. Born in Nottingham in 1949, he served his apprenticeship with Derby County but did not make a first-team appearance for the Rams before joining City for £3,000 in July 1968. A most exciting and lively player with good ball skills, he quickly proved popular with the fans. In his first season he struck up an effective partnership with Ted MacDougall, which they were to continue in the 1970s at Bournemouth and then Norwich City. In December 1970 Boyer was transferred, for a then club record fee received of £20,000, to Bournemouth. After 140 League games for the Cherries, he moved to Southampton (138 League games 49 goals) and ended his career at Manchester City, where his playing days in the League were curtailed by injury after a further 17 games. Boyer, who won a full England cap whilst at Norwich and also made a number of Under-23 appearances, later played in Hong Kong and was player-manager of Grantham Town.
League debut for City v Chester (a) 10 August 1968, Fourth Division.

	LEAGUE		*FA CUP*		*FL CUP*		*TOTAL*	
	App	*Gls*	*App*	*Gls*	*App*	*Gls*	*App*	*Gls*
1968-69	46	9	3	0	1	0	50	9
1969-70	40/1	9	6	3	0	0	46/1	12
1970-71	22	9	3	1	4	3	29	13
	108/1	27	12	4	5	3	125/1	34

PHIL BOYER

Scarborough lad Ken Boyes was signed from his local club in October 1955 and gave York City 11 seasons of loyal service, despite managing just over 50 Football League appearances in that time. A talented centre-half, he was in the shadow of Barry Jackson for much of his time at Bootham Crescent, but proved a most capable understudy and played in a number of games in the promotion season of 1958-9. He also appeared in the first Football League Cup tie played by York City, in October 1960 against Blackburn Rovers. He returned to Midland League Scarborough in 1966.
League debut for City v Gateshead (h) 26 October 1957, Third Division North.

	LEAGUE		*FA CUP*		*FL CUP*		*TOTAL*	
	App	*Gls*	*App*	*Gls*	*App*	*Gls*	*App*	*Gls*
1957-58	5	0	0	0	0	0	5	0
1958-59	14	1	0	0	0	0	14	1
1959-60	17	1	2	0	0	0	19	1
1960-61	3	0	1	0	1	0	5	0
1961-62	2	0	0	0	0	0	2	0
1962-63	2	0	0	0	2	0	4	0
1963-64	9	0	0	0	0	0	9	0
1964-65	0	0	0	0	0	0	0	0
1965-66	1	0	0	0	0	0	1	0
	53	2	3	0	3	0	59	2

KEN BOYES

A schoolmaster, Bert Brenen was a part-time professional for all his long and distinguished playing career. Born in South Shields in 1915, he played junior football in the North-East before going to St Johns' College, York, as a student at the age of 20. Previously, he had played for South Shields in the Northern League. During his time at St Johns', Brenen was invited by City manager, Tom Mitchell, to have a trial at Bootham Crescent. He duly signed as a part-timer with the club and scored on his Football League debut, on 4 March 1939. He played for City during most of the war and was a virtual ever-present from 1946 to 1951, captaining the side on a number of occasions. Although his best place was at right-half, he had the distinction of appearing in every position for the club and even kept goal in a wartime game. In 1951 he was rewarded with a testimonial match against Leeds United and received a then record benefit of £750. Unfortunately, a dispute over terms at the beginning of the following season caused him to leave and he joined Scarborough. He spent four years with the Seasiders and played against City in the first round of the FA Cup in 1954-5, a game which proved to be City's hardest match in the run to the semi-final. He went on to manage Goole Town and later had a spell coaching City's intermediate and junior teams. For a number of years he was one of the commentators on the York Hospital Broadcasting Service, covering City's home games. An all-round sportsman, he was a boxer in his younger days and played in local cricket for many seasons. In later life he was a keen snooker and bowls player.
League debut for City v Chester (h) 4 March 1939, Third Division North.

	LEAGUE		*FA CUP*		*TOTAL*	
	App	*Gls*	*App*	*Gls*	*App*	*Gls*
1938-39	12	5	0	0	12	5
1945-46	0	0	5	1	5	1
1946-47	36	1	1	0	37	1
1947-48	41	2	1	0	42	2
1948-49	38	1	3	0	41	1
1949-50	41	1	1	0	42	1
1950-51	38	3	3	1	41	4
	206	13	14	2	220	15

BERT BRENEN

HARRY BRIGHAM

Harry Brigham was a very experienced player when he joined York City in the summer of 1948, from Nottingham Forest. Born at Selby in 1914, he first played for Frickley Colliery in the Midland League before joining Stoke City in May 1936. The Potters had first tried to sign him 12 months earlier, but Brigham chose to stay with his local club. He eventually came to the attentions of several clubs and even when he was on the platform of his local railway station, awaiting a train to Stoke, scouts from two League clubs tried to persuade him otherwise. Brigham was transferred to Nottingham Forest in November 1946, for £4,000, and made 35 League appearances whilst at the City Ground. A very dependable, no-nonsense right-back, he was a penalty-kick expert. He left Bootham Crescent in 1950.
League debut for City v Crewe Alexandra (h) 21 August 1948, Third Division North.

	LEAGUE		*FA CUP*		*TOTAL*	
	App	*Gls*	*App*	*Gls*	*App*	*Gls*
1948-49	30	5	3	1	33	6
1949-50	26	0	1	0	27	0
	56	5	4	1	60	6

A talented right-back, Jack Brooks served York City well in their early days in the Football League. Born in Stockton-on-Tees in March 1904, Brooks started his professional career with Fulham, whom he joined from Stillington St John's in the close season of 1924. After making nine Football League appearances for the Cottagers, he was transferred to Darlington in the summer of 1926 and joined Nelson in March 1928. He moved to York in August 1929 and, after making his debut for the club at the end of October, was a regular in the defence for a couple of seasons. A very strong, stocky and speedy player, he had some outstanding games for the club, especially in the FA Cup ties against Newcastle United and Sheffield United. He finished his playing days with Bacup Borough. During his time at Fulham he was awarded a gold medal when he gave blood to help save the life of the Cottagers' trainer, Elijah Morse, who had been badly injured in a car crash on the way to a reserve game. Jack Brooks died at Stockton in March 1973.

League debut for City v Tranmere (a) 26 October 1929, Third Division North.

	LEAGUE		*FA CUP*		*TOTAL*	
	App	*Gls*	*App*	*Gls*	*App*	*Gls*
1929-30	30	0	6	0	36	0
1930-31	42	0	5	0	47	0
1931-32	10	0	0	0	10	0
	82	0	11	0	93	0

JACK BROOKS

Born in Worksop in March 1929, Gordon Brown joined Nottingham Forest as a junior in 1946, but he did not make his League debut until after his move to Bootham Crescent in the summer of 1950. During his early days with the club, Brown played at inside-forward, but switched to half-back with considerable success and was a vital cog in the 1954-5 side which reached the FA Cup semi-final. He gave eight seasons splendid service and figured in all City's FA Cup triumphs in the 1950s. After leaving the club in 1958, he went on to play for non-League sides Sutton United and Shirebrook Miners' Welfare. A fine attacking wing-half, Gordon Brown was one of the four part-timers in the famous City Cup side of 1955 when he worked as a storeman near his Mansfield home.

League debut for City v Tranmere Rovers (a) 19 August 1950, Third Division North.

	LEAGUE		*FA CUP*		*TOTAL*	
	App	*Gls*	*App*	*Gls*	*App*	*Gls*
1950-51	31	8	3	0	34	8
1951-52	42	4	3	0	45	4
1952-53	45	1	1	0	46	1
1953-54	43	1	1	0	44	1
1954-55	44	5	8	0	52	5
1955-56	42	2	5	0	47	2
1956-57	43	3	3	0	46	3
1957-58	32	1	5	0	37	1
	322	25	29	0	351	25

GORDON BROWN

Born in Stockport in April 1946, Phil Burrows was an outstanding left-back and a virtual ever-present in his eight seasons at Bootham Cresent. He played for Stockport Boys and, after leaving school, had a short spell with Bury before joining Manchester City as an amateur at 16. He graduated from the youth team to the Reserves at Maine Road and signed professional terms in 1962, but was unable to break into the first team and joined York in the summer of 1966. Fast and very strong in the tackle, he immediately established himself in the senior side and initially played at left-half. He played a big part in the promotion seasons of 1970-71 and 1973-4, which saw York rise from the Fourth to the Second Division, and did not miss a game in his last four seasons at Bootham Crescent. He became City's first ever 'Clubman of the Year' and received the newly-instituted trophy on the day that promotion to the Second Division was clinched in April 1974. Alas, Burrows was never to play at this level for City. In July 1974 he was transferred to Plymouth Argyle for a fee of £20,000. Two years later he moved on to Hereford United with whom he finished his League career in 1979-80.
League debut for City v Chesterfield (h) 20 August 1966, Fourth Division.

	LEAGUE		*FA CUP*		*FL CUP*		*TOTAL*	
	App	*Gls*	*App*	*Gls*	*App*	*Gls*	*App*	*Gls*
1966-67	32/1	2	6	0	4	0	42/1	2
1967-68	32/2	2	1	0	1	0	34/2	2
1968-69	40	1	3	0	1	0	44	1
1969-70	45/1	1	7	0	1	0	53/1	1
1970-71	46	1	6	0	4	0	56	1
1971-72	46	3	3	0	4	0	53	3
1972-73	46	1	3	1	1	0	50	2
1973-74	46	3	2	0	6	0	54	3
	333/4	14	31	1	22	0	386/4	15

PHIL BURROWS

Although making only a handful of appearances for City, Viv Busby was an influential figure at Bootham Crescent in the 1980s, as Denis Smith's right-hand man. Appointed player-coach in May 1982, he formed with Smith the most successful managerial partnership in the club's history. As a player, Busby started his career with Luton Town and went on to Fulham, with whom he won an FA Cup runners-up medal in 1975. He then played for Norwich City and Stoke City before spending a year with Tulsa Roughnecks in the North American Soccer League. He returned to England to play for Blackburn Rovers before his move to York. In May 1987, he left with Denis Smith for Sunderland.
League debut for City v Torquay (h) 28 August 1982, Fourth Division.

	LEAGUE		*FA CUP*		*TOTAL*	
	App	*Gls*	*App*	*Gls*	*App*	*Gls*
1982-83	9/7	4	0	0	9/7	4
1983-84	0/3	0	2	0	2/3	0
	9/10	4	2	0	11/10	4

VIV BUSBY

Ian Butler was one of a number of important captures City made in 1973 — a prelude to their elevation to the Second Division. A natural and outstanding outside-left, Butler was born in Barnsley in 1944 and played for Yorkshire Boys. He joined Second Division Rotherham United, then managed by Tom Johnston, straight from school and was transferred to Hull City for £40,000 in January 1965. He played a big part in the successful Tigers team in the mid to late-1960s and went on to play in well over 300 Second Division games for Hull. In July 1973 he moved to Bootham Crescent, when he was signed for the second time by Tom Johnston. The fee was, at the time, a club record of nearly £10,000. Although he was to play in less than 50 League games for City, he gave a number of important displays and his experience was invaluable, both in the promotion campaign of 1973-4 and in the first season of Second Division football. He played five games on loan to Barnsley (one goal) in 1975. His son, Martin, was later to play for City 1983-9.
League debut for City v Charlton Athletic (a) 25 August 1973, Third Division.

IAN BUTLER

	LEAGUE		*FA CUP*		*FL CUP*		*TOTAL*	
	App	*Gls*	*App*	*Gls*	*App*	*Gls*	*App*	*Gls*
1973-74	19/3	1	0	0	4	1	23/3	2
1974-75	24	1	2	0	1	0	27	1
	43/3	2	2	0	5	1	50/3	3

Without doubt one of the most talented and skilful players to appear for the club, John Byrne was born in Manchester in 1961 and joined City as an apprentice in July 1977. He had been recommended to the then City boss, Wilf McGuinness, by a taxi driver, who had spotted John playing in a Manchester park. He signed professional terms in February 1979 and made his senior debut later that year. A naturally gifted ball-player, his shooting improved under the guidance of coach Viv Busby and he had an outstanding season in 1983-4, when City won the Fourth Division Championship. He finished top scorer with 27 League goals and was voted 'Top Fourth Division Player of the Season' in the *Sunday People/Bukta Merit Awards.* In October 1984, he was transferred to QPR for £100,000 and went on to be capped for the Republic of Ireland, the country of his father's birth. He later played for French club Le Havre.
League debut for City (sub) v Lincoln (h) 25 August 1979, Fourth Division.

JOHN BYRNE

	LEAGUE		*FACUP*		*FLCUP*		*OTHERS*		*TOTAL*	
	App	*Gls*	*App*	*Gls*	*App*	*Gls*	*App*	*Gls*	*App*	*Gls*
1979-80	5/4	2	1/1	1	0	0	0	0	6/5	3
1980-81	36/2	6	2	1	0/2	0	0	0	38/4	7
1981-82	28/1	6	0	0	2	1	0	0	30/1	7
1982-83	42/1	12	4	1	2	1	0	0	48/1	14
1983-84	46	27	3	1	2	0	1	0	52	28
1984-85	10	2	0	0	4	3	0	0	14	5
	167/8	55	10/1	4	10/2	5	1	0	188/11	64

A Glaswegian, Jim Cairney was born in 1931 and, after playing in Scottish junior football, joined Portsmouth — then First Division champions — in 1949. He spent seven years at Fratton Park, mostly as understudy to England international Jack Froggart. Cairney was one of a number of signings made by new manager Sam Bartram in the summer of 1956 and he quickly impressed with his fine ball-playing ability and his cool, constructive play at either wing-half or centre-half. It was a big disappointment when he decided to emigrate to Canada in the spring of 1958.
League debut for City v Carlisle (h) 3 September 1956, Third Division North.

JIM CAIRNEY

	LEAGUE		FA CUP		TOTAL	
	App	Gls	App	Gls	App	Gls
1956-57	32	0	3	0	35	0
1957-58	21	0	0	0	21	0
	53	0	3	0	56	0

Birmingham-born in 1945, Laurie Calloway served his apprenticeship with Wolves. He did not make his League debut until moving to Rochdale and this was, incidentally, at York on the opening day of the 1964-5 season. He later played for Blackburn Rovers and Southport before moving to Bootham Crescent in May 1971, for a fee of £6,000. A hard-working midfield player, Calloway played an important part in York City's first season back in the Third Division in 1971-2. Midway through the following campaign he was transferred to Shrewsbury Town, for whom he went on to make 82 Football League appearances and score three goals.
League debut for City v Bristol Rovers (h) 14 August 1971, Third Division.

LAURIE CALLOWAY

	LEAGUE		FA CUP		FL CUP		TOTAL	
	App	Gls	App	Gls	App	Gls	App	Gls
1971-72	42	3	1	0	4	1	47	4
1972-73	12/1	0	0	0	1	1	13/1	1
	54/1	3	1	0	5	2	60/1	5

Born in Dunnington, York, in 1954, Cliff Calvert joined City as an amateur in the early 1970s and was capped for England at Youth international level. After a spell as an apprentice, he signed full-time professional terms in July 1972 and made his senior debut towards the end of the 1972-3 season. A very strong and capable player, who could fit in at either full-back or midfield, he figured prominently in the promotion season of 1973-4. He was transferred for a then record club fee received of £30,000 in September 1975 to Sheffield United. He later went to play in the North American Soccer League for Toronto Blizzards and Dallas Tornado.
League debut for City v Plymouth Argyle (h) 26 March 1973, Third Division.

	LEAGUE		*FA CUP*		*FL CUP*		*TOTAL*	
	App	*Gls*	*App*	*Gls*	*App*	*Gls*	*App*	*Gls*
1972-73	6/1	0	0	0	0	0	6/1	0
1973-74	32/2	0	1	0	1/1	0	34/3	0
1974-75	21/3	0	2	0	0	0	23/3	0
1975-76	3	0	0	0	2	0	5	0
	62/6	0	3	0	3/1	0	68/7	0

CLIFF CALVERT

Tony Canham was discovered playing for Harrogate Railway Athletic in the Northern Counties (East) League and appeared in a number of games for City Reserves as an amateur in 1984-5. Earlier in his career he had trials with his home-town club, Leeds United, where he was born in June 1960. He scored on his League debut in March 1985 and that summer turned professional at the ripe old age of 25. He quickly proved a favourite with the fans, with his exciting dribbling and explosive finishing, and in his first full season he was second leading scorer with 14 goals. After a troublesome time with injuries, which caused him to miss much of the 1987-8 campaign, he bounced back and was again second leading marksman in the following season. By the end of the 1989-90 season he had played in over 200 senior games for the club.
League debut for City v Brentford (h) 2 March 1985, Third Division.

	LEAGUE		*FA CUP*		*FL CUP*		*OTHERS*		*TOTAL*	
	App	*Gls*	*App*	*Gls*	*App*	*Gls*	*App*	*Gls*	*App*	*Gls*
1984-85	3	1	0	0	0	0	1/1	0	4/1	1
1985-86	40/1	13	5	1	4	0	2	0	51/1	14
1986-87	36/2	9	3	1	4	1	2/1	1	45/3	12
1987-88	13/5	2	0	0	2	0	0	0	15/5	2
1988-89	40/1	9	1	0	0	0	3	1	44/1	10
1989-90	28/6	3	1	0	0	0	3	2	32/6	5
	160/15	37	10	2	10	1	11/2	4	191/17	44

TONY CANHAM

Micky Cave became City's most expensive signing when he moved to Bootham Crescent in August 1974 from Bournemouth for a fee of £18,000. Born in Weymouth in 1949, Cave started his League career with Torquay United in 1968 and was then transferred to the Cherries three years later. A talented midfield player, he joined York City just prior to the start of the club's first season in the Second Division, making his debut in the opening game against Aston Villa. He was a virtual ever-present in his two and a half years at York and in 1975-6 was 'Clubman of the Year'. In February 1977 he returned to Bournemouth for £10,000. In the late 1970s he went to America and played for teams in Seattle and Los Angeles before taking a coaching appointment in Pittsburgh. He died in tragic circumstances in November 1984, at Aleppo, near Pittsburgh, of accidental carbon monoxide poisoning.
League debut for City v Aston Villa (h) 17 August 1974, Second Division.

MICKY CAVE

	LEAGUE		*FA CUP*		*FL CUP*		*TOTAL*	
	App	*Gls*	*App*	*Gls*	*App*	*Gls*	*App*	*Gls*
1974-75	39	1	0	0	1	0	40	1
1975-76	32/2	8	1	0	3	0	36/2	8
1976-77	23	4	5	2	3	0	31	6
	94/2	13	6	2	7	0	107/2	15

A skilful and talented central defender, Andy Clements served the club well in his four seasons at Bootham Crescent between 1977 and 1981. Born at Swinton, near Manchester, in 1955, he served his apprenticeship with Bolton Wanderers and signed for City in November 1977. During his time at York, he was a regular and consistent performer in City's defence. At the end of the 1980-81 season, he left the club and moved into non-League football.
League debut for City v Southport (h) 12 November 1977, Fourth Division.

ANDY CLEMENTS

	LEAGUE		*FA CUP*		*FL CUP*		*TOTAL*	
	App	*Gls*	*App*	*Gls*	*App*	*Gls*	*App*	*Gls*
1977-78	29	0	1	0	0	0	30	0
1978-79	46	2	5	1	2	0	53	3
1979-80	41/1	3	3	0	2	1	46/1	4
1980-81	30/1	1	2	0	0	0	32/1	1
	146/2	6	11	1	4	1	161/2	8

Winger Clive Colbridge, who could operate on either flank, was signed from Leeds United in May 1955. Born in Hull in 1934, he joined Leeds as an 18-year-old and played in their Intermediate and Central League sides. He made his debut for York City during the trip to Ireland in the spring of 1955 and immediately created a big impression when he scored twice against Linfield at Windsor Park, Belfast, in a 3-1 victory. He gave another good display in the next game, against Bohemians at Dalymount Park, Dublin. He also scored on his League debut, against Hartlepools in September 1955. His fast and skilful play down the wings (chiefly the left) proved popular with the fans, but he was never able to properly establish himself in the first team, owing to the consistent form of Billy Hughes and Billy Fenton. One of his best games was at Swansea in the third round of the FA Cup in 1955-6, when he scored in the 2-1 victory. He was transferred to Workington in September 1957 and after a further move to Crewe Alexandra, his career blossomed with a move to First Division Manchester City in May 1959. He made 62 League appearances for the Maine Road club and finished his playing days with Wrexham in the mid 1960s.

League debut for City v Hartlepools (h) 12 September 1955, Third Division North.

	LEAGUE		*FA CUP*		*TOTAL*	
	App	*Gls*	*App*	*Gls*	*App*	*Gls*
1955-56	22	11	1	1	23	12
1956-57	11	2	2	0	13	2
1957-58	4	1	0	0	4	1
	37	14	3	1	40	15

CLIVE COLBRIDGE

Malcolm Comrie was a typically Scottish scheming inside forward, whose skilful play exercised such a big influence on York City's FA Cup exploits of 1937-8. Born in Denny, he played in Scottish junior football before moving south of the border and with Brentford, Manchester City, Burnley and Crystal Palace he played in all divisions of the Football League. Comrie moved to Bootham Crescent from Palace in June 1936 and in his two seasons at York, he was a key man in the side as the club experienced the best period in its history to date. In these two years, Comrie played in no fewer than 16 FA Cup ties.

League debut for City v Halifax (a) 29 August 1936, Third Division North.

	LEAGUE		*FA CUP*		*TOTAL*	
	App	*Gls*	*App*	*Gls*	*App*	*Gls*
1936-37	42	8	7	2	49	10
1937-38	37	12	9	1	46	13
	79	20	16	3	95	23

MALCOLM COMRIE

When Jock Collier was appointed City manager in 1928, he recruited several new players and established a strong Scottish contingent at Fulfordgate. One of these signings was a 5ft 6ins tall, stocky centre-forward from Raith Rovers by the name of Jimmy Cowie. He proved to be a prolific scorer and averaged a goal per game — 56 League and Cup appearances, 56 goals — in that last season of Midland League football. His scoring feats were remarkable. Twice he netted six goals in a match (against Worksop in the League and in the FA Cup against Stockton). He scored five against Hull City Reserves and twice netted four. At the end of the 1928-9 season he was selected for the Rest of the Midland League XI against the champions, Mansfield Town. Cowie was one of only three players who bridged the gap between the Midland League and Football League. The others were Tom Fenoughty and George Sharpe. In the opening Third Division North game, he scored the second goal in the 2-0 win at Wigan Borough. He was unable to repeat the sensations of the previous campaign, however, and in two seasons played in only 18 League games. In total he scored 66 goals in 77 appearances and his club record of 1928-9 is likely to remain for all time. He died in April 1966.

League debut for City v Wigan Borough (a) 31 August 1929, Third Division North.

	LEAGUE		*FA CUP*		*TOTAL*	
	App	*Gls*	*App*	*Gls*	*App*	*Gls*
1928-29*	49	49	7	7	56	56
1929-30	14	4	3	1	17	5
1930-31	4	5	0	0	4	5
	67	58	10	8	77	66

* Midland League

JIMMY COWIE

One of the outstanding goalkeepers in the club's history, Graeme Crawford was born in Falkirk in 1947 and started his career in his native Scotland with East Stirling. He moved to Sheffield United in 1968 but, in three years at Bramall Lane, his League appearances were limited to two games and in November 1971 he joined City on loan. The following month Crawford signed for the club and for the next five and a half seasons he was a virtual ever-present. During the promotion season of 1973-4 he kept a clean sheet in 11 consecutive League matches, helping to equal a Football League record set up by Millwall in 1926. He played in every game in City's two seasons of Second Division football — Chris Topping was the only other to do this. In July 1977 he was transferred to Scunthorpe United, but in January 1980 he returned to Bootham Crescent in an exchange deal with Joe Neenan. His second spell was only of a short duration and in September 1980 he moved to Rochdale with whom he spent three seasons. His playing days finished with Scarborough in the Gola League, but he did come out of retirement to make an FA Cup appearance for Goole Town at the age of 42.

League debut for City v Tranmere Rovers (a) 5 November 1971, Third Division.

	LEAGUE		*FA CUP*		*FL CUP*		*TOTAL*	
	App	*Gls*	*App*	*Gls*	*App*	*Gls*	*App*	*Gls*
1971-72	28	0	0	0	0	0	28	0
1972-73	42	0	3	0	1	0	46	0
1973-74	43	0	2	0	6	0	51	0
1974-75	42	0	2	0	1	0	45	0
1975-76	42	0	2	0	3	0	47	0
1976-77	38	0	5	0	3	0	46	0
1979-80	17	0	0	0	0	0	17	0
	252	0	14	0	14	0	280	0

GRAEME CRAWFORD

Malcolm Crosby joined York City in an exchange deal with Aldershot which took Ian McDonald to the Recreation Ground in November 1981. A very industrious midfield player, Crosby quickly settled in and played his part in the championship-winning side of 1983-4. Born in South Shields in 1954, he spent over ten years with Aldershot, joining them as an apprentice and making almost 300 senior appearances for the Hampshire club. In his later days at Bootham Crescent he was involved in the coaching of the juniors and in August 1986 he left to take up a coaching appointment in Kuwait. He returned to England two years later and joined the backroom staff at Sunderland where he teamed up again with Denis Smith and Viv Busby. A very likeable personality, he was a big influence on the club during his stay with City.
League debut for City v Scunthorpe (a) 5 November 1981, Fourth Division.

	LEAGUE		*FA CUP*		*FL CUP*		*OTHERS*		*TOTAL*	
	App	*Gls*	*App*	*Gls*	*App*	*Gls*	*App*	*Gls*	*App*	*Gls*
1981-82	19/4	2	3	0	0	0	0	0	22/4	2
1982-83	38	2	4	0	0	0	0	0	42	2
1983-84	31	0	3	0	2	0	1	0	37	0
1984-85	11	0	1	0	0	0	0	0	12	0
	99/4	4	11	0	2	0	1	0	113/4	4

MALCOLM CROSBY

Born in the West Country, Maurice Dando had two successful seasons with York City in the mid-1930s. A lively and energetic centre forward, he was signed from Bristol Rovers. He scored twice on his debut, in a match at Crewe in August 1933, and proved a consistent and reliable marksman during his period at Bootham Crescent. He netted three hat-tricks and at the time only Reg Baines had bettered this for the club. In 1934-5 he was in the team that only narrowly lost to Derby County in the third round of the FA Cup. In June 1935, Dando was transferred to Chesterfield. Later, he was to suffer badly from ill health and died in 1949.
League debut for City v Crewe Alexandra (a) 30 August 1933, Third Division North.

	LEAGUE		*FA CUP*		*TOTAL*	
	App	*Gls*	*App*	*Gls*	*App*	*Gls*
1933-34	41	25	1	0	42	25
1934-35	41	21	3	0	44	21
	82	46	4	0	86	46

MAURICE DANDO

A talented and stylish wing-half, Ian Davidson joined York from Hull City in June 1969. Born in Goole in 1947, he joined the Tigers from school and made a handful of Second Division appearances for the club. Whilst at Hull, he had an extended period on loan with Scunthorpe United. His attacking midfield play was a key factor in City's promotion to the Third Division in 1970-71 and he missed only two games that term. He also played an important part in the FA Cup run that season, scoring the equalizer in the second round at Boston and at the next stage when his two goals knocked out Second Division Bolton Wanderers at Bootham Crescent. In July 1971 he was involved in a player-exchange deal which took him to newly-promoted Bournemouth and brought striker Eddie Rowles to York. After one season down on the south coast, Davidson finished his League playing days with Stockport County.

League debut for City v Newport County (a) 9 August 1969, Fourth Division.

	LEAGUE		*FA CUP*		*FL CUP*		*TOTAL*	
	App	*Gls*	*App*	*Gls*	*App*	*Gls*	*App*	*Gls*
1969-70	39/3	0	5	0	1	0	45/3	0
1970-71	43/1	4	6	3	4	1	53/1	8
	82/4	4	11	3	5	1	98/4	8

IAN DAVIDSON

Born at Bristol in 1905, Charlie Davis was City's regular centre-half in their first couple of seasons in the Football League. He started his playing career with Bath City and then joined Torquay United in 1927, when they were elected to the Football League Third Division South. Two years later he moved to York, just prior to City's baptism in the League. A big, burly man, Davis stood over 6ft 1in tall and weighed nearly 14st. He formed a very effective half-back line, playing alongside Harold Beck and Oliver Thompson. He played in all 11 FA Cup ties in his two-year period at Fulfordgate, giving two outstanding performances against Newcastle United in the third round in January 1930, when in both matches he effectively marked the legendary Hughie Gallacher out of the game. The following season he again played his part in the FA Cup run and rose to the occasion in two matches against First Division Sheffield United. In the summer of 1931, he was transferred to newly-elected Mansfield Town in the Third Division South and finished his playing days in the League in 1934.

League debut for City v Wigan Borough (a) 31 August 1929, Third Division North.

	LEAGUE		*FA CUP*		*TOTAL*	
	App	*Gls*	*App*	*Gls*	*App*	*Gls*
1929-30	41	1	6	1	47	2
1930-31	20	0	5	0	25	0
	61	1	11	1	72	2

CHARLIE DAVIS

Dick Duckworth joined York in July 1936, from Rotherham, and his strong and resolute play was an important factor in City's success in the late 1930s. A very experienced player, his other clubs were Oldham, Southport, Chesterfield and Chester before his move to Bootham Crescent. During the 1937-8 campaign he took over the captaincy and his strong leadership played a big part in City's FA Cup triumphs that year. He left the club in 1939, but was to return as manager 11 years later when, in a two and a half year period, he had considerable success (see *York City Managers).*
League debut for City v Halifax Town (a) 29 August 1936, Third Division North.

	LEAGUE		*FA CUP*		*TOTAL*	
	App	*Gls*	*App*	*Gls*	*App*	*Gls*
1936-37	40	0	7	0	47	0
1937-38	37	0	9	0	46	0
1938-39	11	0	1	0	12	0
	88	0	17	0	105	0

DICK DUCKWORTH

Although born in Whitehaven in 1934, Dave Dunmore was a product of local York football. He attended Canon Lee School, played for York Boys, had a trial with Yorkshire boys, played for North Riding Boys and then went on to play for Cliftonville Minors, who proved such a good breeding team for City in the late 1940s and early 1950s. He arrived at Bootham Crescent in his teens and established himself in the Midland League side in 1951-2. Dunmore made his League debut at the age of 18, in the last game of that season and scored, in a 3-0 victory over Crewe Alexandra. The following season the powerful young centre-forward made steady progress and in 1953-4 he attracted the attention of senior clubs with his strong and, at times, explosive finishing. On 11 February 1954, Dunmore was signed by Tottenham Hotspur for a then record club fee received of £10,500. It was chiefly with this money that, in the summer of 1954, City recruited several players who helped form the team that reached the FA Cup semi-final — knocking out Spurs on the way. Dunmore was to spend six years at White Hart Lane (75 League appearances; 23 goals). He had one season at West Ham (36 games; 16 goals) and then moved to Leyton Orient in 1961. He spent four successful years at Brisbane Road, helping that club to promotion to the First Division in 1962 for the first time in their history. Whilst with the Os, he scored 55 goals in 147 League games. After over 11 years in London, he returned to York in the summer of 1965 for a fee of £5,000. He ended his League days two years later and his career record reads: 396 League appearances and 132 goals. Dunmore later played for Bridlington Trinity.
League debut for City v Crewe Alexandra (h) 3 May 1952, Third Division North.

DAVE DUNMORE

	LEAGUE		*FA CUP*		*FL CUP*		*TOTAL*	
	App	*Gls*	*App*	*Gls*	*App*	*Gls*	*App*	*Gls*
1951-52	1	1	0	0	0	0	1	1
1952-53	16	4	1	0	0	0	17	4
1953-54	31	20	1	1	0	0	32	21
1965-66	38/1	8	0	0	2	2	40/1	10
1966-67	23/1	5	6	0	2	0	31/1	5
	109/2	38	8	1	4	2	121/2	41

Although Eamonn Dunphy was with the club for only five months and made only 26 appearances, his talent and skills left a big impression at Bootham Crescent. Born in Dublin in 1945, Dunphy signed for Manchester United on his 17th birthday. He played regularly in the Central League side, but was unable to win a first-team place at Old Trafford. He joined York in August 1965, just prior to the start of the new season and City's return to the Third Division. Dunphy immediately took the eye with his fine ball skills and his outstanding midfield play and in November 1965 he was capped for the Republic of Ireland against Spain in a World Cup qualifying game. He thus became the first player to gain international honours whilst with York City. Unfortunately, as City continued to struggle near the foot of the Third Division, he became unsettled and in January 1966 was transferred to Millwall for £8,000. He helped the Lions gain promotion to the Second Division and spent eight years at The Den. He then went to Charlton and Reading and was capped for the Republic of Ireland 23 times. He became a literary personality in the game, writing a number of articles and a book on his experiences at Millwall and a book on the pop group 'U2'.
League debut for City v Grimsby Town (h) 27 August 1965, Third Division.

	LEAGUE		*FA CUP*		*FL CUP*		*TOTAL*	
	App	*Gls*	*App*	*Gls*	*App*	*Gls*	*App*	*Gls*
1965-6	22	3	1	0	3	1	26	4
	22	3	1	0	3	1	26	4

EAMONN DUNPHY

Born in Gateshead in 1915, Albert 'Sam' Earl played for Rhyl and Bury before moving to Bootham Crescent in the summer of 1937. An inside-forward, he suffered a loss of form and did not play in the first two rounds of the FA Cup in 1937-8, against Halifax and Clapton. He was recalled to the side at outside-right in time for the third-round game against Coventry and scored in the 3-2 victory. He retained his place in the team and figured in the remainder of the Cup run. He left the club at the outbreak of war and when peace returned, went on to play for Stockport County, Rochdale and New Brighton.
League debut for City v Rochdale (a) 28 August 1937, Third Division North.

	LEAGUE		*FA CUP*		*TOTAL*	
	App	*Gls*	*App*	*Gls*	*App*	*Gls*
1937-38	38	4	5	1	43	5
1938-39	20	5	1	0	21	5
	58	9	6	1	64	10

ALBERT 'SAM' EARL

Born in Barnsley in 1936, John Edgar joined his home-town club as a junior and made his League debut in 1955-6. He was transferred to Gillingham in the summer of 1958 and scored 23 goals in his one season at Priestfield Stadium. He was regarded as an important capture in the 1959 close season, as City faced up to their first season in the Third Division after winning promotion. It was to be a disappointing campaign for the club, culminating in immediate relegation and, although Edgar finished leading scorer, he never quite fulfilled his promise. His best performance came on 3 October 1959, when he netted the quickest hat-trick in the club's history, scoring three times in six minutes in a 3-0 victory over Accrington Stanley at Bootham Crescent. A serious injury curtailed his appearances the following season and in June 1961 he moved to Hartlepool. He finished his League days at Exeter and later played for Scarborough in the Midland League.

League debut for City v Bradford City (a) 22 August 1959, Third Division.

	LEAGUE		FA CUP		TOTAL	
	App	Gls	App	Gls	App	Gls
1959-60	42	15	3	2	45	17
1960-61	5	1	0	0	5	1
	47	16	3	2	50	18

JOHN EDGAR

Born in the Rhondda in 1962, Chris Evans was Denis Smith's first signing for City in the summer of 1982. He was a Welsh Schoolboy and Youth international and was on the books of Arsenal and Stoke City but did not make his League debut until his move to York. He was an ever-present in his first season at Bootham Crescent and impressed with his cool and steady play at right-back. He lost his place to Steve Senior at the start of the 1983-4 campaign, having been injured in a pre-season match and never quite fully established himself in the first team again. In September 1985 he was transferred to Darlington for £13,000. In his second season with the Quakers, a serious leg injury cut short his career. He attempted a comeback and played a few games for City Reserves before retiring. He returned to Wales and took up an administrative job in football.

League debut for City v Torquay United (h) 28 August 1982, Fourth Division.

	LEAGUE		FA CUP		FL CUP		OTHERS		TOTAL	
	App	Gls	App	Gls	App	Gls	App	Gls	App	Gls
1982-83	46	0	4	0	2	0	0	0	52	0
1983-84	16/3	0	0/1	0	0/1	0	1	0	17/5	0
1984-85	24	0	1	0	4	0	1/1	0	30/1	0
1985-86	7	1	0	0	2	0	0	0	9	1
	93/3	1	5/1	0	8/1	0	2/1	0	108/6	1

CHRIS EVANS

Early in the 1965-6 campaign, City were faced with a goalkeeping crisis. Tommy Forgan had broken his hand in a match against Bristol Rovers and Tony Moor had been transferred to Darlington during the close season. The club made a quick dash over the border and signed St Johnstone 'keeper Harry Fallon. He made a magnificent debut in a 3-2 win at Southend and a few days later kept a good goal as City gained a sensational 4-1 victory at Hull. Born in Paisley in 1942, Fallon gained Scottish Junior international honours. In his day he was a very good goalkeeper but he was prone to errors. He remained first-choice 'keeper in 1965-6, but in his second season he had to contest the berth with newcomer Mike Walker. He played his last League game, by coincidence against Southend, in September 1967 and left the club in May the following year.
League debut for City v Southend United (a) 13 September 1965, Third Division.

HARRY FALLON

	LEAGUE		*FA CUP*		*FL CUP*		*TOTAL*	
	App	*Gls*	*App*	*Gls*	*App*	*Gls*	*App*	*Gls*
1965-66	32	0	1	0	0	0	33	0
1966-67	26	0	0	0	4	0	30	0
1967-68	9	0	0	0	1	0	10	0
	67	0	1	0	5	0	73	0

Rotherham-born in 1931, Terry Farmer spent two and a half years at York in the late 1950s and proved a useful goalscorer. He started his League career with his home-town club and scored 25 goals in 61 appearances. Farmer moved to Bootham Crescent and scored on his League debut for the club in a match at Bury. He effectively took over from Arthur Bottom who, a few weeks later, was transferred to Newcastle United. Farmer figured prominently in the promotion season of 1958-9 and it was his goal in a win at Aldershot in April 1959 that clinched the prize. He lost his place to John Edgar at the start of the following season and made only 12 appearances that term. In July 1960 he was transferred to Scarborough.
League debut for City v Bury (a) 18 January 1958, Third Division North.

TERRY FARMER

	LEAGUE		*FA CUP*		*TOTAL*	
	App	*Gls*	*App*	*Gls*	*App*	*Gls*
1957-58	18	12	0	0	18	12
1958-59	36	12	1	0	37	12
1959-60	12	4	0	0	12	4
	66	28	1	0	67	28

John Farmery joined the club in the summer of 1929 and was first-choice goalkeeper in City's first two seasons in the Football League. He had previously played for Hull City, Bradford City and Doncaster Rovers and first came into prominence when serving in the Army and playing for the Military Police team. A big man at 6ft and over 13st, he was extremely nimble for his size. He had some outstanding games for York City, especially the FA Cup matches against Newcastle United in January 1930.
League debut for City v Wigan Borough (a) 31 August 1929, Third Division North.

JOHN FARMERY

	LEAGUE		FA CUP		TOTAL	
	App	Gls	App	Gls	App	Gls
1929-30	38	0	6	0	44	0
1930-31	29	0	5	0	34	0
	67	0	11	0	78	0

A very tall centre-half, Steve Faulkner was born in Sheffield in 1954. He joined Sheffield United as an apprentice, making his Football League debut in the First Division in 1972-3 against Manchester United at Old Trafford. He spent six years at Bramall Lane and was signed by Charlie Wright in the summer of 1978. Faulkner was a commanding figure in the heart of the City defence and was very strong in the air, using his 6ft 3ins to good effect. For two seasons he held a regular first-team place. Sent off in a game at Tranmere in September 1980, he lost his position and never really re-established himself in the senior side. He left the club at the end of his third year at Bootham Crescent and went on to play for Rowntree Mackintosh in the North-Eastern Counties League for a number of seasons.
League debut for City v Rochdale (a) 19 August 1978, Fourth Division.

STEVE FAULKNER

	LEAGUE		FA CUP		FL CUP		TOTAL	
	App	Gls	App	Gls	App	Gls	App	Gls
1978-79	44	1	5	1	2	0	51	2
1979-80	31	5	1/1	0	2	0	34/1	5
1980-81	15	1	0	0	4	0	19	1
	90	7	6/1	1	8	0	104/1	8

Born in Rotherham in 1908, Tom Fenoughty gave the club eight years of excellent service as an inside-forward. He was spotted playing in Sunday School football in Rotherham and joined City during the 1926-7 season, making his Midland League debut at Fulfordgate in March 1927 against Lincoln City Reserves. For the next six seasons he was a regular first-teamer, bridging the gap between the Midland League and Football League and Fulfordgate and Bootham Crescent. A regular scorer, he netted over 100 goals for the club in all competitions. He figured prominently in the 1929-30 FA Cup run. In the first-round tie against Tranmere Rovers he scored three goals in the two matches and netted twice in the second-round 4-1 victory at Southend. He played in the Cup ties against Newcastle United and Sheffield United in the early 1930s. With York experiencing accute financial problems, they reluctantly parted with the player early in 1934. He was given a benefit match against Leeds United and made a very sporting offer as he left the club. Knowing the financial problems, he offered to loan his benefit cheque to help City to tide over a lean time. A fine club stalwart, indeed.

League debut for City v Wrexham (a) 11 September 1929, Third Division North.

	LEAGUE		*FA CUP*		*TOTAL*	
	App	*Gls*	*App*	*Gls*	*App*	*Gls*
1926-27*	12	8	0	0	12	8
1927-28*	35	18	5	1	40	19
1928-29*	35	15	6	1	41	16
1929-30	29	15	6	5	35	20
1930-31	38	17	3	0	41	17
1931-32	30	13	1	0	31	13
1932-33	30	9	1	0	31	9
1933-34	20	2	1	0	21	2
	229	97	23	7	252	104

* Midland League.

TOM FENOUGHTY

Outside-left Billy Fenton was one of the outstanding personalities in the 1950s and is the third-highest scorer in the club's history. Born at Hartlepool in 1926, he played for Horden Colliery Welfare before Blackburn Rovers signed him in December 1948. In two and a half years at Ewood Park, Fenton made 33 Second Division appearances and scored seven goals. In May 1951 he joined York for a small fee and, in his first season, he broke the club's 20-year-old scoring record by netting 31 goals. Fenton was a key member of the 1954-5 FA Cup team and scored vital goals in the victories over Blackpool and Tottenham Hotspur. His best scoring feat was when he netted four goals in a 5-4 victory at Carlisle in November 1954. He played for Scarborough after being released by City at the end of the 1957-8 season. A most popular player, he will be remembered for his tremendous pace down the wing, together with his sharpness in front of the goal. A part-time player during his career, he was a draughtsman by trade. It was a tremendous shock when he died suddenly at his home in York in April 1973 at the tragically early age of 46. His name lives on at the club, however, and 'The Billy Fenton Memorial Trophy' is presented annually to the 'Clubman of the Year'.

League debut for City v Lincoln (a) 18 August 1951, Third Division North.

	LEAGUE		*FA CUP*		*TOTAL*	
	App	*Gls*	*App*	*Gls*	*App*	*Gls*
1951-52	45	31	3	0	48	31
1952-53	44	25	1	0	45	25
1953-54	37	8	1	1	38	9
1954-55	45	22	8	3	53	25
1955-56	29	12	4	1	33	13
1956-57	37	15	1	0	38	15
1957-58	21	5	3	1	24	6
	258	118	21	6	279	124

BILLY FENTON

Darlington-born in 1917, goalkeeper Bob Ferguson played for Middlesbrough in the First Division, making his League debut as a teenager in 1936. He moved to York in the summer of 1939 and played in the three games of the ill-fated 1939-40 season. He appeared for the club many times during the war, although for some time he was understudy to guest player Sam Bartram. He made 26 League appearances in the first post-war season and then, in 1947, joined Midland League club Peterborough United. Ferguson finished his playing days with Goole Town. A very good cricketer, he was a wicketkeeper-batsman and was a prolific run scorer in the Bradford League, where he played as a professional for Bankfoot. He played cricket until his late 40s and in retirement took up bowls with considerable success.

League debut for City v Chester (h) 31 August 1946, Third Division North.

	LEAGUE		*FA CUP*		*TOTAL*	
	App	*Gls*	*App*	*Gls*	*App*	*Gls*
1945-46	0	0	8	0	8	0
1946-47	26	0	1	0	27	0
	26	0	9	0	35	0

BOB FERGUSON

Local lad Gary Ford was born in 1961 and played for York City Boys under-15 team before signing schoolboy forms with Hull City. Upon leaving school, however, it was with York that he became an apprentice professional in the summer of 1977, at the same time that John Byrne joined the club. He made his League debut as a 17-year-old in October 1978 and, apart from season 1979-80, was a virtual ever-present in the first team until 1987. In January 1986 he made his 300th full League appearance so becoming the tenth player to achieve this milestone for the club. He was the second youngest to do this. Chris Topping was a couple of months younger when he reached that target in December 1975. Operating chiefly on the right side of midfield, he was City's Mr Consistency for most of the 1980s and he did not miss playing in a single home game from September 1981 until April 1986. In June 1987 he was transferred to Second Division Leicester City for a reported fee of £25,000. He later moved on to Port Vale, helping this club to promotion to the Second Division in 1988-9. In the club's history only Barry Jackson and Chris Topping have exceeded Gary's total of 435 senior appearances.

League debut for City v Reading (a) 21 October 1978, Division Four.

	LEAGUE		*FACUP*		*FLCUP*		*OTHERS*		*TOTAL*	
	App	*Gls*	*App*	*Gls*	*App*	*Gls*	*App*	*Gls*	*App*	*Gls*
1978-79	32/1	4	5	1	0	0	0	0	37/1	5
1979-80	26/3	2	3	0	2	0	0	0	31/3	2
1980-81	41/2	4	2	0	4	1	0	0	47/2	5
1981-82	40/1	8	3	1	2	0	0	0	45/1	9
1982-83	45	11	4	2	2	0	0	0	51	13
1983-84	46	11	3	0	2	1	1	0	52	12
1984-85	44	5	6	0	4	2	3	0	57	7
1985-86	40	4	7	3	4	0	2	0	53	7
1986-87	45	4	3	0	4	0	3	0	55	4
	359/7	53	36	7	24	4	9	0	428/7	64

GARY FORD

One of the best and certainly one of the most popular goalkeepers to play for York was Tommy Forgan, who was at Bootham Crescent from 1954 to 1966. Born in Middlesbrough in 1929, he joined Hull City from Teesside junior soccer in May 1949. In five years at Boothferry Park he was chiefly understudy to the mercurial Billy Bly and he made only 11 Second Division appearances for the Tigers. He moved to York in June 1954 and quickly became a firm favourite with the fans. He missed the first two rounds of the run to the semi-final, owing to injury, but marked his return to the side at Blackpool in the third round by saving a penalty. As well as the Cup successes, Forgan twice helped York to gain promotion (1958-9 and 1964-5). Apart from 1957-8, when he missed most of the campaign through injury, he was a virtual ever-present for eight seasons and his total of 388 League appearances is a club record for the position of goalkeeper. He played for Gainsborough after leaving City and in 1974 emigrated to Australia.
League debut for City v Wrexham (a) 21 August 1954 Third Division North.

	LEAGUE		*FA CUP*		*FL CUP*		*TOTAL*	
	App	*Gls*	*App*	*Gls*	*App*	*Gls*	*App*	*Gls*
1954-55	39	0	6	0	0	0	45	0
1955-56	41	0	5	0	0	0	46	0
1956-57	46	0	3	0	0	0	49	0
1957-58	12	0	0	0	0	0	12	0
1958-59	46	0	1	0	0	0	47	0
1959-60	32	0	3	0	0	0	35	0
1960-61	41	0	6	0	1	0	48	0
1961-62	38	0	1	0	5	0	44	0
1962-63	30	0	4	0	0	0	34	0
1963-64	20	0	1	0	2	0	23	0
1964-65	29	0	0	0	0	0	29	0
1965-66	14	0	0	0	2	0	16	0
	388	0	30	0	10	0	428	0

TOMMY FORGAN

John 'Jack' Fountain was born in Leeds in 1932 and signed professional terms with Sheffield United in November 1949. He spent seven years at Bramall Lane, during which time he made 31 League appearances. In January 1957 he moved to Swindon Town and after 81 League games for the Wiltshire club, joined City in the summer of 1960. A strong-tackling and hard-working half-back, he was a regular in the first team for three seasons and captained the side on a number of occasions. Injuries restricted his appearances in 1963-4 and then his career ended on a sad and sour note in April 1964 when he was one of the players involved in a bribery scandal which had been exposed by the *Sunday People*. Found guilty, he was imprisoned for 15 months.
League debut for City v Gillingham (a) 21 September 1960, Fourth Division.

	LEAGUE		*FA CUP*		*FL CUP*		*TOTAL*	
	App	*Gls*	*App*	*Gls*	*App*	*Gls*	*App*	*Gls*
1960-61	38	1	6	0	1	0	45	1
1961-62	33	1	1	0	7	0	41	1
1962-63	46	1	4	0	2	1	52	2
1963-64	13	0	0	0	1	0	14	0
	130	3	11	0	11	1	152	4

JOHN FOUNTAIN

Born in Sheffield in 1906, Stan Fox played for Sheffield United and Bury before joining York in 1931. A most versatile player he gave the club several years excellent service. Although chiefly an inside-forward, he was called upon to play in most positions and he proved an invaluable utility player. Upon leaving the club, Fox received a well-earned benefit in a match against Southport in May 1938. He worked for Cooke, Troughton & Sims and then for British Rail until his retirement in 1971. Stan Fox died, aged 73, in York in August 1979.
League debut for City v New Brighton (h) 27 February 1932, Third Division North.

	LEAGUE		*FA CUP*		*TOTAL*	
	App	*Gls*	*App*	*Gls*	*App*	*Gls*
1931-32	5	0	0	0	5	0
1932-33	12	2	0	0	12	2
1933-34	19	1	0	0	19	1
1934-35	35	1	2	0	37	1
1935-36	36	0	0	0	36	0
1936-37	24	0	3	0	27	3
1937-38	5	0	0	0	5	0
	136	4	5	0	141	7

STAN FOX

Born in Nottingham in 1968, of an Italian father and English mother, Marco Gabbiadini spent his childhood in York and attended Nunthorpe Grammar School. He became an apprentice professional with City in November 1984 and soon proved a prolific scorer with the Intermediate and Reserve sides. He made a substitute appearance later that season and made his full League debut on the opening day of the 1985-6 campaign, when he scored in a win against Plymouth. He was blooded gently and the talented player made steady progress. With his pace, strength and powerful shooting, he greatly impressed manager Denis Smith who, before the end of that season, believed he could have a future international player on the books and urged England boss Bobby Robson to call him up in the Under-18 squad before Italy made a claim for him. It was hardly surprising, therefore, that shortly after Smith went to Sunderland, one of his first signings was Marco for £80,000 in September 1987. He was an instant success at Roker Park finishing top scorer as Sunderland won the Third Division championship. In the summer of 1988 he went on a tour of Brazil with an England Under-20 squad and was rated in the £1 million class.
League debut for City (sub) v Bolton Wanderers (h) 28 March 1985, Third Division.

	LEAGUE		*FA CUP*		*FL CUP*		*OTHERS*		*TOTAL*	
	App	*Gls*	*App*	*Gls*	*App*	*Gls*	*App*	*Gls*	*App*	*Gls*
1984-85	0/1	0	0	0	0	0	0	0	0/1	0
1985-86	10/12	4	0	0	0/1	0	2	0	12/13	4
1986-87	24/5	9	0	0	2/2	0	2	3	28/7	12
1987-88	8	1	0	0	2	1	0	0	10	2
	42/18	14	0	0	4/3	1	4	3	50/21	18

MARCO GABBIADINI

Born in Durham in 1920 Tommy Gale played as an amateur for Gateshead before joining Sheffield Wednesday in 1944. He made a number of Second Division appearances for the Owls before joining York City in August 1947 and made his debut in a 6-0 home victory against Halifax Town that month. A strong, powerfully-built centre-half, he spent two successful seasons at Bootham Crescent and captained the club on a number of occasions.
League debut for City v Halifax Town (h) 30 August 1947, Third Division North.

TOMMY GALE

	LEAGUE		*FA CUP*		*TOTAL*	
	App	*Gls*	*App*	*Gls*	*App*	*Gls*
1947-48	40	0	1	0	41	0
1948-49	36	0	3	0	39	0
	76	0	4	0	80	0

A very experienced inside-forward who gave the club invaluable service in its first two seasons of League football, Wally Gardner was born in County Durham in June 1893 and played as an amateur for Bishop Auckland. He appeared in the 1915 FA Amateur Cup Final and won two England Amateur caps in 1920. Gardner turned professional and went on to play for Derby County, Spennymoor United, QPR and Darlington before moving to York from Torquay in July 1929. He figured prominently in the 1929-30 FA Cup run and had an outstanding game in the third round at Newcastle, when he scored City's equalizing goal. Upon leaving York, he played for Crewe Alexandra and Rochdale and then retired from the game to help run a family business in Durham.
League debut for City v Wigan Borough (a) 31 August 1929, Third Division North.

WILLIAM 'WALLY' GARDNER

	LEAGUE		*FA CUP*		*TOTAL*	
	App	*Gls*	*App*	*Gls*	*App*	*Gls*
1929-30	31	16	3	2	34	18
1930-31	20	10	3	0	23	10
	51	26	6	2	57	28

Born at Castleford in 1913, Sammy Gledhill was a miner and joined City as an amateur from Altofts in the summer of 1936. He went on to give the club many years excellent service, playing mostly at half-back. In 1937-8 he played for a Yorkshire League XI in a match against the Corinthians. Gledhill was a regular for City throughout the war years and in 1943 was awarded a benefit by the club. On retiring from the playing side of the game in 1949, he coached City's Yorkshire League side and was a scout for the club for a number of years. He was a very good baseball player and once played for a Rest of England side in a representative match. There is one amusing story about Sammy: City were involved in a gruelling fourth-round FA Cup tie at Swansea in January 1937 and, owing to the condition of some of the players, it was decided to stay overnight. When the team did leave on the Sunday, Sammy slept blissfully in bed until long after the rest had departed and he arrived home alone, hours later.
League debut for City v Port Vale (a) 10 October 1936, Third Division North.

	LEAGUE		*FA CUP*		*TOTAL*	
	App	*Gls*	*App*	*Gls*	*App*	*Gls*
1936-37	9	5	0	0	9	5
1937-38	16	0	0	0	16	0
1938-39	34	0	1	0	35	0
1945-46	0	0	8	1	8	1
1946-47	28	1	1	0	29	1
1947-48	32	0	1	0	33	0
1948-49	4	0	0	0	4	0
	123	6	11	1	134	7

SAMMY GLEDHILL

Fast and direct winger Wally Gould was a popular character at Bootham Crescent in the early 1960s. Born at Rotherham in 1938, he played for Rawmarsh Welfare before turning professional with Sheffield United in March 1958. His first-team appearances with the Blades were limited and he arrived at York in February 1961. Equally at home on either flank, he was a regular first-teamer in his three years with the club. In January 1964, Gould was transferred to Brighton and helped the Seagulls win the Fourth Division championship in 1964-5, pipping York City by just one point. He went on to make 168 League appearances for Brighton and later spent a number of years playing and coaching in South Africa.
League debut for City v Oldham Athletic (h) 18 February 1961, Fourth Division.

	LEAGUE		*FA CUP*		*FL CUP*		*TOTAL*	
	App	*Gls*	*App*	*Gls*	*App*	*Gls*	*App*	*Gls*
1960-61	13	3	0	0	0	0	13	3
1961-62	40	5	1	0	7	1	48	6
1962-63	42	11	3	0	2	1	47	12
1963-64	25	6	1	0	4	0	30	6
	120	25	5	0	13	2	138	27

WALLY GOULD

Goalkeeper Mick Granger was another of the players who joined the club from local junior side, Cliftonville. Born in York in 1931, he signed for City in December 1951 and made his senior debut in an FA Cup tie against Barrow in November 1952. Because of National Service, he did not make his League debut for another two years, in what was a remarkable game at Carlisle which City won 5-4. Whilst in the Forces he was elected 'Footballer of the Year' in Hong Kong. An excellent 'keeper, Granger had the misfortune to be in the shadow of Tommy Forgan, but he proved a capable understudy. Only in 1957-8, however, did he have an extended run in the first team. He left the club in the summer of 1962 and went on to play for Hull City and Halifax Town.
League debut for City v Carlisle United (a) 6 November 1954, Third Division North.

MICK GRANGER

	LEAGUE		*FA CUP*		*FL CUP*		*TOTAL*	
	App	*Gls*	*App*	*Gls*	*App*	*Gls*	*App*	*Gls*
1952-53	0	0	1	0	0	0	1	0
1953-54	0	0	0	0	0	0	0	0
1954-55	7	0	2	0	0	0	9	0
1955-56	5	0	0	0	0	0	5	0
1956-57	0	0	0	0	0	0	0	0
1957-58	34	0	5	0	0	0	39	0
1958-59	0	0	0	0	0	0	0	0
1959-60	14	0	0	0	0	0	14	0
1960-61	5	0	0	0	0	0	5	0
1961-62	6	0	0	0	2	0	8	0
	71	0	8	0	2	0	81	0

Although in the twilight of his career when he joined City in 1951 at the age of 37, Steve Griffiths was an influential figure in his two seasons at Bootham Crescent. A clever, scheming, ball-playing inside-forward, he led the club to their then highest placing in the League when they finished fourth in the Third Division North in 1952-3. Born in Barnsley in 1914, he played for Halifax Town, Chesterfield and Portsmouth before the war and was also with Aldershot and Barnsley before coming to York. Whilst at The Shay, he was in the Halifax side that lost to City in the first round of the FA Cup at the start of the memorable run of 1937-8.
League debut for City v Lincoln City (a) 18 August 1951, Third Division North.

STEVE GRIFFITHS

	LEAGUE		*FA CUP*		*TOTAL*	
	App	*Gls*	*App*	*Gls*	*App*	*Gls*
1951-52	40	6	3	0	43	6
1952-53	34	6	1	0	35	6
	74	12	4	0	78	12

Hard-tackling midfielder Sean Haslegrave was a key man in City's Fourth Division championship-winning side of 1983-4. He moved to Bootham Crescent prior to the start of that record-breaking campaign and gave four years' excellent service to the club. Born in Stoke in 1951, he joined his home-town club as a junior and signed professional terms in November 1968. He spent eight seasons at the Victoria Ground and made over 100 League appearances. After a short spell under Brian Clough at Nottingham Forest, Haslegrave went on to have four years at Preston North End. He joined York from Crewe Alexandra and immediately impressed with his drive and total commitment. He qualified as a full FA coach in the summer of 1985 and took over the captaincy of the club when Roger Jones departed. He left for Torquay in the summer of 1987, as player-coach, and later became the assistant manager at Plainmoor.

League debut for City v Rochdale (h) 3 September 1983, Fourth Division.

	LEAGUE		*FA CUP*		*FL CUP*		*OTHERS*		*TOTAL*	
	App	*Gls*	*App*	*Gls*	*App*	*Gls*	*App*	*Gls*	*App*	*Gls*
1983-84	24/2	0	0	0	1/1	0	0/1	0	25/4	0
1984-85	42	0	6	0	4	0	2	0	54	0
1985-86	37/2	0	4	0	4	0	0/1	0	45/3	0
1986-87	34/1	0	1	0	2	0	3	0	40/1	0
	137/5	0	11	0	11/1	0	5/2	0	164/8	0

SEAN HASLEGRAVE

A native of Bristol, Ted Hathway gave York City six years excellent service in the 1930s. He was with Bristol Rovers and Bolton Wanderers before moving to York in June 1933. A strong and reliable left-half, he was a free-kick expert and had a terrific shot from a dead ball, scoring a number of goals that way. He figured in all the FA Cup triumphs of 1936-7 and 1937-8. Hathway returned to Bristol at the outbreak of war, but received a benefit from the club in recognition of his services in 1943.

League debut for City v Halifax Town (h) 14 October 1933, Third Division North.

	LEAGUE		*FA CUP*		*TOTAL*	
	App	*Gls*	*App*	*Gls*	*App*	*Gls*
1933-34	31	14	1	0	32	14
1934-35	41	6	2	1	43	7
1935-36	39	6	1	0	40	6
1936-37	40	7	7	1	47	8
1937-38	25	1	9	0	34	1
1938-39	42	4	1	0	43	4
	218	38	21	2	239	40

TED HATHWAY

Born in York in 1942, John Hawksby played for York Boys and was an England Youth international. A very talented inside-forward, he joined Leeds United as a junior and signed professional terms in June 1959. He made a total of 36 League appearances for United in the Second Division and was then transferred to Lincoln City in August 1964. In just under two seasons at Sincil Bank, Hawksby played in 64 League games for the Imps and was signed by City in March 1966. In two years in his native city, he never quite fulfilled his obvious potential and in the summer of 1968 moved to non-League King's Lynn.
League debut for City v Hull City (h) 12 March 1966, Third Division.

	LEAGUE		FA CUP		FL CUP		TOTAL	
	App	*Gls*	*App*	*Gls*	*App*	*Gls*	*App*	*Gls*
1965-66	16	2	0	0	0	0	16	2
1966-67	39	4	1	0	4	0	44	4
1967-68	17/2	1	1	0	0	0	18/2	1
	72/2	7	2	0	4	0	78/2	7

JOHN HAWKSBY

Alan Hay was one of manager Denis Smith's early signings and was City's regular left-back in the League and Cup successes in the mid-1980s. Born in Dunfermline in 1958, he won a Scottish Under-16 Cup winners' medal with the Riverside Boys Club. After a short spell with Dundee, he moved south of the border to Bolton Wanderers. It was with Bristol City that he made his Football League debut in 1979-80 and he arrived at Bootham Crescent in August 1982. A natural left-sided player, he was very strong in the tackle and a consistent performer. He moved to Tranmere Rovers in the summer of 1986 and then returned to Scotland where he played in amateur football. Hay moved to the club midway through the 1988-9 season, for a short trial period. After similar trials with Sunderland, he joined Torquay United at the start of the 1989-90 campaign.
League debut for City v Torquay United (h) 28 August 1982, Fourth Division.

	LEAGUE		FA CUP		FL CUP		OTHERS		TOTAL	
	App	*Gls*	*App*	*Gls*	*App*	*Gls*	*App*	*Gls*	*App*	*Gls*
1982-83	42	1	4	0	2	0	0	0	48	1
1983-84	42	0	3	0	2	0	0	0	47	0
1984-85	42/3	0	6	1	4	0	3	0	55/3	1
1985-86	21	1	3	0	2	0	1/1	0	27/1	1
1988-89	1	0	0	0	0	0	0	0	1	0
	148/3	2	16	1	10	0	4/1	0	178/4	3

ALAN HAY

Born in Rotherham in 1962, Ian Helliwell played for Sheffield Wednesday's juniors on leaving school and also had trials with Stoke City. He took up employment with British Steel and played in local football in South Yorkshire before attracting the attention of Chesterfield and in 1982-3 made a number of appearances in their reserve side. In the summer of 1983, Helliwell joined Northern Premier League side, Matlock Town, and in four and a half years at Causeway Lane made 183 appearances and scored 68 goals. In October 1987, he was signed by York City for a fee of £10,000 and made a very promising debut at Sunderland. The tall centre-forward had been a virtual ever-present in his time at York and in 1988-9 was leading scorer and was voted 'Clubman of the Year'. In November 1989 he netted his first hat-trick for the club, in a 7-1 victory over Hartlepool United in the Leyland Daf Cup. With 19 League and Cup goals he was again top scorer in 1989-90.

League debut for City v Sunderland (a) 24 October 1987, Third Division.

	LEAGUE		*FA CUP*		*FL CUP*		*OTHERS*		*TOTAL*	
	App	*Gls*	*App*	*Gls*	*App*	*Gls*	*App*	*Gls*	*App*	*Gls*
1987-88	32	8	0	0	0	0	1	0	33	8
1988-89	41	11	1	0	2	0	3	0	47	11
1989-90	44/2	14	1	0	4	1	2/1	4	51/3	19
	117/2	33	2	0	6	1	6/1	4	131/3	38

IAN HELLIWELL

Before joining City in May 1961, Tommy Heron played football in his native Scotland, in Ireland and spent three years with Manchester United. Born in Irvine in 1936, he began his career as a left winger. Heron played for the Royal Academy School and Ayrshire Boys and after Army service spent two seasons with the famous amateur club, Queens Park, and also played a few games with Kilmarnock. He signed for Irish club Portadown and after only a few matches was recommended by a Manchester United Irish scout to Matt Busby. He duly transferred to Old Trafford in March 1958, but during his time at Manchester made only three League appearances for the Reds. Whilst with United, he was converted to left-back and filled that position when he came to York. He was an instant success at Bootham Crescent and his enthusiastic style of play made him a firm favourite with the fans. As a legacy of his outside-left days, he was very much an attacking full-back. He did in fact play a number of games on the left wing for the club. He was a virtual ever-present in his first four seasons and played a big part in the promotion season of 1964-5. In June 1966 he was transferred to non-League Altrincham.

League debut for City v Bradford City (a) 19 August 1961, Fourth Division.

	LEAGUE		*FA CUP*		*FL CUP*		*TOTAL*	
	App	*Gls*	*App*	*Gls*	*App*	*Gls*	*App*	*Gls*
1961-62	44	0	1	0	7	0	52	0
1962-63	39	3	4	0	2	0	45	3
1963-64	46	3	1	0	4	0	51	3
1964-65	46	0	2	0	1	0	49	0
1965-66	17	0	0	0	2	0	19	0
	192	6	8	0	16	0	216	6

TOMMY HERON

Born in South Elmsall in 1943, Dick Hewitt was signed on amateur forms by Huddersfield Town whilst playing for Moorthorpe St Josephs OB. He represented the England Boys' Clubs XI in matches against Wales, Ireland and Scotland. Hewitt turned professional with Town in May 1961, but did not make his League debut until joining Bradford City at the start of the 1964-5 season. After a period with Barnsley he moved to York in March 1969. A clever inside-forward, he took a while to settle down at Bootham Crescent. His best season was 1970-71 when he played a very important part in the promotion success. At the end of the 1971-2 campaign he went to Scarborough.
League debut for City v Swansea Town (a) 18 March 1969, Fourth Division.

DICK HEWITT

	LEAGUE		*FA CUP*		*FL CUP*		*TOTAL*	
	App	*Gls*	*App*	*Gls*	*App*	*Gls*	*App*	*Gls*
1968-69	14	2	0	0	0	0	14	2
1969-70	17/4	3	3/1	0	1	0	21/5	3
1970-71	37	2	6	2	0	0	43	4
1971-72	19	0	0	0	4	0	23	0
	87/4	7	9/1	2	5	0	101/5	9

Rotherham-born in 1952, Ron Hillyard joined City as a junior and was thrust into the first team in October 1969, when the club were faced with a goalkeeping injury crisis. The youngster did well and signed professional terms in December that year. He established himself in the first team in 1970-71 and made 34 appearances in goal in the promotion season. Hillyard was to suffer a loss of confidence the following year and upon the arrival of new 'keeper Graeme Crawford, his first-team appearances were limited. In May 1974, he went on a free transfer to Gillingham and gave the Kent club splendid service, breaking their appearance record of 571 League games set up by another goalkeeper, John Simpson.
League debut for City v Peterborough United (a) 25 October 1969, Fourth Division.

RON HILLYARD

	LEAGUE		*FA CUP*		*FL CUP*		*TOTAL*	
	App	*Gls*	*App*	*Gls*	*App*	*Gls*	*App*	*Gls*
1969-70	3	0	0	0	0	0	3	0
1970-71	34	0	6	0	0	0	40	0
1971-72	17	0	3	0	4	0	24	0
1972-73	4	0	0	0	0	0	4	0
1973-74	3	0	0	0	0	0	3	0
	61	0	9	0	4	0	74	0

A Glaswegian born in 1935, Billy Hodgson began with St Johnstone before moving to Sheffield United in May 1957. A small, tricky inside-forward, he spent six seasons with the Blades, making 152 League appearances. After two-year spells with Leicester City and Derby County, he had a short period with Rotherham United. One of the first tasks when new boss Joe Shaw took over was to appoint a player-coach and in December 1967, he chose Billy Hodgson, a former colleague of his at Bramall Lane. Hodgson received a full FA coaching badge and when Shaw resigned in August 1968, he took control over team matters until the appointment of Tom Johnston. He was to spend two and a half years with York and his coaching skills and experience helped in the development of the younger players. In July 1970, he returned to Sheffield United to coach.
League debut for City v Workington (a) 16 December 1967, Fourth Division.

	LEAGUE		*FA CUP*		*FL CUP*		*TOTAL*	
	App	*Gls*	*App*	*Gls*	*App*	*Gls*	*App*	*Gls*
1967-68	25	0	0	0	0	0	25	0
1968-69	44	2	3	0	1	0	48	2
1969-70	29	1	5/2	0	1	0	35/2	1
	98	3	8/2	0	1	0	108/2	3

BILLY HODGSON

Born in Wombwell in December 1950, Ian Holmes joined Sheffield United as a junior and signed professional forms for the Blades in January 1968. His League appearances for United were limited to six games before he moved to Bootham Crescent in the summer of 1973. The clever, skilful midfield player took a little time to establish himself, but he became a firm favourite with the fans and his partnership with Barry Lyons was a key factor in City's promotion to the Second Division in 1973-4. He was a penalty-kick expert, showing great coolness with his spot-kicks, none more so than when he netted an injury-time winner in a vital promotion clash against Bristol Rovers in March 1974. In October 1977, he teamed up again with Tom Johnston, when the former City boss signed him for £10,000 for Huddersfield Town. Holmes finished his playing days at Leeds Road.
League debut for City v Charlton Athletic (a) 25 August 1973, Third Division.

	LEAGUE		*FA CUP*		*FL CUP*		*TOTAL*	
	App	*Gls*	*App*	*Gls*	*App*	*Gls*	*App*	*Gls*
1973-74	27/4	5	0/1	0	1/2	1	28/7	6
1974-75	42	9	2	0	1	0	45	9
1975-76	30/1	6	1	0	2	0	33/1	6
1976-77	39/2	7	5	3	3	1	47/2	11
1977-78	14	3	0	0	3	0	17	3
	152/7	30	8/1	3	10/2	2	170/10	35

IAN HOLMES

One of the most popular and versatile players to wear City's colours, Derek Hood was the club's 'Mr Utility' man in the 1980s. Born in Washington, County Durham, in December 1958, he had a period as an apprentice with West Bromwich Albion before joining Hull City, for whom he made his League debut in 1977-8. He moved to Bootham Crescent in February 1980, for what was certainly to prove a bargain buy of £2,000. He was to play in over 350 games for York, mostly at either full-back or in midfield. Twice he was an ever-present (1981-2 and 1982-3) and in the latter season was voted 'Clubman of the Year'. A serious injury caused him to miss the early part of the 1983-4 campaign, but he returned to play his usual energetic and vital role as the Fourth Division championship was won. In May 1987 he was given a free transfer, but re-signed a couple of months later. A troublesome knee injury caused his retirement from full-time football in 1988. A testimonial match was played for his benefit in November 1988, a just reward for the eight years' outstanding service he had given the club.

	LEAGUE		*FACUP*		*FLCUP*		*OTHERS*		*TOTAL*	
	App	*Gls*	*App*	*Gls*	*App*	*Gls*	*App*	*Gls*	*App*	*Gls*
1979-80	16	1	0	0	0	0	0	0	16	1
1980-81	42	0	2	0	1	0	0	0	45	0
1981-82	46	8	3	0	2	0	0	0	51	8
1982-83	46	7	4	2	2	0	0	0	52	9
1983-84	33/1	4	3	0	1	0	1	0	38/1	4
1984-85	27/3	4	2/1	0	0/2	0	3	0	32/6	4
1985-86	29/2	1	5	0	2/1	0	1	0	37/3	1
1986-87	24/3	3	3	0	4	0	1/2	0	32/5	3
1987-88	24/4	4	2/1	1	4	1	1	0	31/5	6
	287/13	32	24/2	3	16/3	1	7/2	0	334/20	36

Hood later played on a part-time basis for Goole Town and Harrogate Town.

League debut for City v Halifax Town (h) 12 February 1980, Fourth Division.

DEREK HOOD

One of the heroes of the 1954-5 FA Cup semi-final side, George Howe gave splendid service at left-back and in seven seasons (1954-61) missed only 15 League games out of a possible 322. He was a most reliable and consistent defender and was a fine positional player. A highlight of his career was when he played the legendary Stanley Matthews out of the game in York's famous FA Cup win over Blackpool in January 1955. In 1961-2, he played for the Reserves, helping the younger players, and at the end of that season retired from the game. Born in Wakefield in January 1924, Howe had joined Huddersfield Town during the war. He made a total of 40 League appearances at Leeds Road before moving to York in June 1954. On leaving the game, he worked in the maintenance section at Pinderfields Hospital, Wakefield. He died suddenly in November 1971, at the age of 47.

League debut for City v Wrexham (a) 21 August 1954, Third Division.

	LEAGUE		*FA CUP*		*FL CUP*		*TOTAL*	
	App	*Gls*	*App*	*Gls*	*App*	*Gls*	*App*	*Gls*
1954-55	46	0	8	0	0	0	54	0
1955-56	44	0	5	0	0	0	49	0
1956-57	45	0	2	0	0	0	47	0
1957-58	44	0	5	0	0	0	49	0
1958-59	36	0	1	0	0	0	37	0
1959-60	46	0	3	0	0	0	49	0
1960-61	46	0	6	0	1	0	53	0
	307	0	30	0	1	0	338	0

GEORGE HOWE

Keith Houchen will always have pride of place in York City's history as the man who scored the dramatic late penalty winner against Arsenal in the fourth round FA Cup tie in 1984-5. He was signed from Orient in March 1984 for £15,000 and made a handful of appearances towards the end of the championship-winning season. He made a dramatic debut when he came on as substitute in a game at Aldershot on 14 April 1984. He scored, missed a penalty and was cautioned. Playing in either midfield or up front, Houchen was leading scorer in 1984-5 with 18 League and Cup goals. He became unsettled the following season, however, and in March 1986 was transferred to Scunthorpe United for a fee of £20,000. He soon moved on to Coventry and scored the Sky Blues' FA Cup-winning goal in 1987 with a spectacular diving header. In 1989 he was transferred to Hibernian, for whom he played in the UEFA Cup.
League debut for City (sub) v Aldershot (a) 14 April 1984, Fourth Division.

	LEAGUE		*FA CUP*		*FL CUP*		*OTHERS*		*TOTAL*	
	App	*Gls*	*App*	*Gls*	*App*	*Gls*	*App*	*Gls*	*App*	*Gls*
1983-84	1/6	1	0	0	0	0	0	0	1/6	1
1984-85	35	12	5	3	3	2	2	1	45	18
1985-86	20/5	6	4/2	0	3	1	2	1	29/7	8
	56/11	19	9/2	3	6	3	4	2	75/13	27

KEITH HOUCHEN

Born in Dublin in 1963, Gary Howlett started his footballing days with League of Ireland club, Home Park before coming to England to serve his apprenticeship with Coventry City. In 1982 he was transferred to Brighton, then in the First Division, and scored on his Football League debut in March 1983, against Liverpool. A few weeks later he played in the FA Cup Final against Manchester United, which went to a replay. He moved to Bournemouth in December 1984 and spent three years at Dean Court, during which time the Cherries won promotion to the Second Division. He joined City in January 1988 and the clever and skilful midfield player soon established himself in the first team. Howlett represented the Republic of Ireland at Under-15, Youth and Under-21 level and received a full cap against Japan in 1983. After a troublesome time with injuries in 1988-9 he was a virtual ever-present the following campaign.
League debut for City v Walsall (a) 30 January 1988, Third Division.

	LEAGUE		*FA CUP*		*FL CUP*		*OTHERS*		*TOTAL*	
	App	*Gls*	*App*	*Gls*	*App*	*Gls*	*App*	*Gls*	*App*	*Gls*
1987-88	18	2	0	0	0	0	0	0	18	2
1988-89	20/3	4	0/1	0	2	0	0	0	22/4	4
1989-90	41/2	4	1	0	4	0	3	0	49/2	4
	79/5	10	1/1	0	6	0	3	0	89/6	10

GARY HOWLETT

Born in Coxhoe, Jimmy Hughes was a regular soldier in the Army and served in the Second Battalion Northumberland Fusiliers. When stationed at Catterick, he played a few games for City Reserves as an amateur in 1933-4. Upon leaving the forces he signed professional for the club in August 1934. He had a short spell with Hartlepool at the start of 1935-6, but soon returned to Bootham Crescent and established himself in the side at inside-right. A versatile and hard-working player, he figured in all the FA Cup ties of 1936-7 and 1937-8. During World War Two, he was a prisoner of war in Germany. He died in January 1966.
League debut for City v Lincoln City (h) 1 September 1934, Third Division North.

JIMMY HUGHES

	LEAGUE		FA CUP		TOTAL	
	App	Gls	App	Gls	App	Gls
1934-35	15	5	2	0	17	5
1935-36	14	7	1	0	15	7
1936-37	28	6	7	0	35	6
1937-38	25	8	9	3	34	11
1938-39	24	4	1	0	25	4
	106	30	20	3	126	33

From 1951 to 1961, Billy Hughes was the regular wearer of the number-seven shirt for City and made a total of 380 League and Cup appearances for the club. Born in Glasgow in March 1929, he was an amateur on the books of Newcastle United. He was spotted by City whilst doing his National Service in the RAF at nearby Rufforth and signed professional terms in May 1951. He made his League debut in October 1951, when John Linaker moved to Hull, and immediately established himself in the side. A very skilful ball player, he was of the old-school dribbling type of winger. He played in all the major FA Cup ties of the mid-1950s and in the promotion season of 1958-9. Upon leaving City in 1962, he played in local football and, like so many other ex-York players, continued to live in the area. By coincidence his last game for the club was at Spotland, almost exactly ten years later — 30 September 1961.
League debut for City v Rochdale (a) 20 October 1951, Division Three North.

BILLY HUGHES

	LEAGUE		FA CUP		FL CUP		TOTAL	
	App	Gls	App	Gls	App	Gls	App	Gls
1951-52	33	4	0	0	0	0	33	4
1952-53	32	6	0	0	0	0	32	6
1953-54	25	2	1	0	0	0	26	2
1954-55	33	5	8	0	0	0	41	5
1955-56	39	7	5	1	0	0	44	8
1956-57	24	4	2	0	0	0	26	4
1957-58	32	7	5	0	0	0	37	7
1958-59	42	7	1	0	0	0	43	7
1959-60	46	7	3	1	0	0	49	8
1960-61	41	5	5	1	1	0	47	6
1961-62	2	1	0	0	0	0	2	1
	349	55	30	3	1	0	380	58

A diminutive winger who could operate on either flank, George Ivey excited the early post-war crowds with his enterprising play. Born in West Stanley in October 1923, he was signed from West Stanley United in June 1948. He made a dramatic debut when he scored twice in a six-goal victory over Carlisle United. An extremely tricky little player — he stood only 5ft 5ins — he was very popular. He was transferred to South Shields in June 1951 and six years later played for Shields against City in the second round of the FA Cup. He died in November 1979.

League debut for City v Carlisle United (h) 11 September 1948, Third Division North.

	LEAGUE		FA CUP		TOTAL	
	App	Gls	App	Gls	App	Gls
1948-49	35	7	3	1	38	8
1949-50	25	2	1	0	26	2
1950-51	19	4	1	0	20	4
	79	13	5	1	84	14

GEORGE IVEY

Holder of the club's appearance record, Barry Jackson played in a total of 539 League and Cup games and gave over 14 years of outstanding service to York City. A local lad, born in February 1938, he was another product of the Cliftonville minor league club. He played a number of games at centre-forward in those days. Converted to centre-half, he signed professional terms on 17 December 1956. He had been on the club's books as an amateur since the start of that season and first made an appearance in a public practice match in August 1956. With enthusiasm still high after the previous years' Cup feats, there was an attendance of 7,000 that day. His first two seasons were spent in the Reserves but at the start of the 1958-9 campaign, regular first-choice pivot, Howard Johnson, was injured and Jackson stepped into the breach. Thus started a remarkable 12 seasons in which he was a virtual ever-present at the heart of the City defence. At 6ft 4ins he was a commanding figure and played with tremendous whole-heartedness and spirit. He captained the side on a number of occasions and twice helped the club gain promotion (1958-9 & 1964-5). Jackson played hard and determinedly and now and again fell foul of the referee. He was sent off in a game at Scunthorpe in January 1970 and received a ban of eight weeks. After his suspension he was unable to regain his first-team place and left the club at the end of that season. He had a short spell with Scarborough before retiring from the game. A testimonial match was played on his behalf when Hull City provided the opposition in February 1970. During his playing days, he had a sweet shop near the City ground and later worked for the Electricity Board. A fine club stalwart, he will never be forgotten by all those who saw him play.

League debut for City v Oldham Athletic (a) 23 August 1958, Fourth Division.

	LEAGUE		FA CUP		FL CUP		TOTAL	
	App	Gls	App	Gls	App	Gls	App	Gls
1958-59	34	0	1	0	0	0	35	0
1959-60	37	0	3	0	0	0	40	0
1960-61	43	2	5	0	0	0	48	2
1961-62	42	1	1	0	7	1	50	2
1962-63	45	2	4	0	1	0	50	2
1963-64	38	0	1	0	4	0	43	0
1964-65	44	0	2	0	1	0	47	0
1965-66	45	0	1	0	3	0	49	0
1966-67	46	1	6	0	4	0	56	1
1967-68	42	1	1	0	1	0	44	1
1968-69	40/1	1	2	0	1	0	43/1	1
1969-70	25	1	7	0	1	0	33	1
	481/1	9	34	0	23	1	538/1	10

BARRY JACKSON

Born in Coseley in 1948, Steve James joined Manchester United from school and signed professional terms for the Reds in December 1966. An England Youth international, he spent nine years at Old Trafford, making 129 League appearances. In 1974-5 he won a Second Division championship medal. He moved to Bootham Crescent in January 1976 but, although his cool and skilful play at centre-half strengthened City's defence, he was unable to prevent the drop from the Second Division. Troubled by injuries, he missed the whole of the 1978-9 season. In May 1980, James moved to Kidderminster Harriers.
League debut for City v West Bromwich Albion (h) 17 January 1976, Second Division.

	LEAGUE		*FA CUP*		*FL CUP*		*TOTAL*	
	App	*Gls*	*App*	*Gls*	*App*	*Gls*	*App*	*Gls*
1975-76	14	0	0	0	0	0	14	0
1976-77	37	1	5	0	3	0	45	1
1977-78	36	0	1	0	3	1	40	1
1978-79	0	0	0	0	0	0	0	0
1979-80	18	0	2	0	0	0	20	0
	105	1	8	0	6	1	119	2

STEVE JAMES

Regular left-back and skipper Paul Johnson did a reliable and steady job for City during two difficult years for the club between 1987 and 1989. Born in Stoke in 1959, he started his career as an apprentice with his home-town club and signed professional forms in 1977. Johnson was given his League debut in 1978-9 and, after making 34 League appearances for the Potters, he moved to Shrewsbury. He spent several years at Gay Meadow, playing in 181 League games before he was signed for York by Bobby Saxton in the summer of 1987. Not retained at the end of the 1988-9 campaign, he was transferred to Macclesfield Town.
League debut for City v Brighton & Hove Albion (a) 15 August 1987, Third Division.

	LEAGUE		*FA CUP*		*FL CUP*		*OTHERS*		*TOTAL*	
	App	*Gls*	*App*	*Gls*	*App*	*Gls*	*App*	*Gls*	*App*	*Gls*
1987-88	39	0	3	0	4	0	1	0	47	0
1988-89	44	1	1	0	1	0	3	0	49	1
	83	1	4	0	5	0	4	0	96	1

PAUL JOHNSON

Born at Kidsgrove in Staffordshire, Sam Johnson joined York City from Swindon Town in the summer of 1929, prior to the start of their initial season in the Football League. He had started his career with Stoke City and, originally a half-back, was converted to left-back. Johnson was a regular in City's defence in their first three seasons in the League and was a very cool and reliable player. On leaving the club in 1933, he had short spells with Crystal Palace and Southport. He retired from the game and took over a pub in York. In 1937, Johnson became City's reserve-team trainer, a position he was to hold until the 1960s.
League debut for City v Wigan Borough (a) 31 August 1929, Third Division North.

	LEAGUE		*FA CUP*		*TOTAL*	
	App	*Gls*	*App*	*Gls*	*App*	*Gls*
1929-30	37	0	6	0	43	0
1930-31	36	0	5	0	41	0
1931-32	38	0	1	0	39	0
1932-33	13	0	1	0	14	0
	124	0	13	0	137	0

SAM JOHNSON

Born in Altrincham in 1945, Chris Jones joined Manchester City as a junior and signed professional terms in May 1964. He made a number of senior appearances whilst at Maine Road and then moved on to Swindon Town. Jones spent four seasons with the Wiltshire club and had an 18-month spell with Walsall before joining York in June 1973. His first season at Bootham Crescent was an outstanding one and he finished top scorer. His striking partnership with Jimmy Seal was very effective as City won promotion to the Second Division. In his second season he was second-leading scorer and his experience stood the club in good stead as they operated at the higher level. He was transferred to Huddersfield Town in August 1976 and then, after spells with Doncaster, Darlington and Rochdale, he ended his League career in 1980. He later played for Rowntree Mackintosh in the North-Eastern Counties League and was chairman of the York Football Coaches' Association.
League debut for City v Charlton Athletic (a) 25 August 1973, Third Division.

	LEAGUE		*FA CUP*		*FL CUP*		*TOTAL*	
	App	*Gls*	*App*	*Gls*	*App*	*Gls*	*App*	*Gls*
1973-74	41	18	2	2	5	0	48	20
1974-75	36/1	12	2	0	0	0	38/1	12
1975-76	17	4	0	0	3	1	20	5
	94/1	34	4	2	8	1	106/1	37

CHRIS JONES

Arguably the best all-round goalkeeper to play for York City, Roger Jones captained the club to their first major honour when they won the Fourth Division championship in 1984-5. Jones was born at Upton-upon-Severn in 1946 and served his apprenticeship with Portsmouth. He made his Football League debut after moving to Bournemouth in 1965 and made 160 League appearances for the Cherries before joining Blackburn Rovers in January 1970. Whilst with Bournemouth, he was capped for England Under-23 against Hungary in 1968. He made 242 League appearances for Blackburn and then, after a short spell at Newcastle, moved to Stoke City in 1977, where he teamed up with Denis Smith. A further 101 League games and then on to Derby County in 1980 and 59 League appearances for the Rams before his free-transfer move to Bootham Crescent in August 1982. Jones' command of the goal-area and his positional play, plus his powers of concentration, made him an outstanding 'keeper and he gave three seasons' excellent service to the club. He retired in May 1985 and went into business renovating and selling houses in the Stoke area. A keen golfer, he kept himself fit and at the age of 42 he played in Derek Hood's testimonial match at Bootham Crescent and gave a magnificent display which showed he had lost none of his skill. In an illustrious career, Roger Jones made a total of 693 League appearances and, including Cup ties, played in almost 800 games. He later assisted Sunderland in a coaching capacity.
League debut for City v Torquay United (h) 28 August 1982, Fourth Division.

	LEAGUE		*FA CUP*		*FL CUP*		*OTHERS*		*TOTAL*	
	App	*Gls*	*App*	*Gls*	*App*	*Gls*	*App*	*Gls*	*App*	*Gls*
1982-83	42	0	3	0	2	0	0	0	47	0
1983-84	41	0	3	0	1	0	1	0	46	0
1984-85	39	0	2	0	4	0	3	0	48	0
	122	0	8	0	7	0	4	0	141	0

ROGER JONES

Born in Edinburgh in October 1949, Rob Kay was City's regular left-back and captain from 1978 to 1982. He did occasionally play in the centre of the defence and midfield and served the club well. Kay captained the Scottish Junior international team whilst playing for Cross Roads FC. He signed for Hearts when he was 17 and, whilst at Tynecastle, won a Scottish FA Cup runners-up medal and played in the European Cup-winners' Cup. He then spent one season with Celtic, appearing for them in the European Cup before joining City in July 1978. A very consistent and reliable performer, his positional play was excellent and he was a virtual ever-present in his four seasons with York.
League debut for City v Rochdale (a) 19 August 1978, Fourth Division.

	LEAGUE		*FA CUP*		*FL CUP*		*TOTAL*	
	App	*Gls*	*App*	*Gls*	*App*	*Gls*	*App*	*Gls*
1978-79	46	0	5	0	2	0	53	0
1979-80	41	3	3	0	2	0	46	3
1980-81	36	1	2	0	4	0	42	1
1981-82	37	4	3	0	2	0	42	4
	160	8	13	0	10	0	183	8

ROB KAY

A skilful and exciting midfield player, Pat Lally spent two successful years at Bootham Crescent from 1971 to 1973. Paddington-born in 1952, he served his apprenticeship with Millwall, making one League appearance for the Lions in 1969-70. Lally was signed by Tom Johnston in July 1971 and soon created a big impression at the club. His strong surging runs from midfield were a feature of his play and he was very popular as City successfully avoided relegation in the two seasons he was at York. Lally was transferred to Swansea in July 1973 and made 162 League appearances for them. In 1978 he moved to Doncaster and played in 122 League games before completing a long and successful career. Upon retiring he took up a football administrative job.
League debut for City v Oldham Athletic (a) 31 August 1971, Third Division.

PAT LALLY

	LEAGUE		FA CUP		FL CUP		TOTAL	
	App	Gls	App	Gls	App	Gls	App	Gls
1971-72	33/4	2	3	0	3	0	39/4	2
1972-73	31/3	3	3	0	0/1	0	34/4	3
	64/7	5	6	0	3/1	0	73/8	5

Andy Leaning was a young local goalkeeper when he sprang to prominence in the mid-1980s. Born in 1962, Leaning had trials with City as a 16-year-old, but he decided to take up employment with British Rail as a joiner. He played for Rowntree Mackintosh in the Northern-Counties East League and in 1984-5 made a number of appearances for City Reserves. He so impressed manager Denis Smith that in the summer of 1985, he was offered a professional contract. In November that year, first-choice 'keeper Mike Astbury was badly injured and Leaning got his chance, which he literally took with both hands. He figured in the FA Cup run which took City (for the second successive season) to the fifth round and he gave a magnificent display in the replay at Anfield. City lost 3-1 after extra-time and Leaning's performance at Liverpool earned rave notices. He remained the regular first-team 'keeper until surprisingly given a free transfer at the end of 1986-7. In May 1987 he moved to Sheffield United, with whom he made 21 League appearances before a further transfer to Bristol City in November 1988.
League debut for City v Newport County (a) 6 November 1985, Third Division.

ANDY LEANING

	LEAGUE		FA CUP		FL CUP		OTHERS		TOTAL	
	App	Gls	App	Gls	App	Gls	App	Gls	App	Gls
1985-86	30	0	7	0	0	0	2	0	39	0
1986-87	39	0	1	0	4	0	3	0	47	0
	69	0	8	0	4	0	5	0	86	0

Although George Lee only made 37 Football League appearances, he was one of the outstanding players to wear City colours. His most prominent seasons at Bootham Crescent were during the war and he became the first player to score 100 goals for the club. Born in York in June 1919, Lee was spotted playing on the left wing for Acomb and impressed greatly with his accuracy in crosses and ball-control. He had trials with Tottenham Hotspur early in 1936 and played as an amateur for Scarborough, but a player cannot be signed as a professional until he is 17. In view of the interest in the young local lad, City were so keen to obtain his services that secretary Mr Sherrington went to the player's house and sat with his parents until after midnight when George became 17, signing him one minute after the hour. For a couple of seasons, Lee played chiefly in the Reserves and was selected for a Yorkshire League XI against The Corinthians in 1937-8. He established himself in the first team in 1938-9, at the age of 19. It was to be during the early war years that he made tremendous progress. During this time City had the services of England and Charlton Athletic star inside-forward, Bert 'Sailor' Brown, and he and the young Lee became the finest club wing-partnership in North-East wartime football. Lee was a natural player, relying on craft, ball control and deadly accuracy in shooting and passing. He scored his 100th goal for City when he netted a penalty in the second leg of a Football League War Cup semi-final match against Sheffield Wednesday at Bootham Crescent in April 1943. That season he scored a total of 32 goals. During the latter part of the war, military service took him abroad and he was not demobbed until 1947. On 14 August that year, Lee was transferred to Nottingham Forest, for a then club record fee received of £7,500. At the City Ground he teamed up again with his wartime partner 'Sailor' Brown. He made 76 League appearances for Forest before moving to West Brom in July 1949. He played in 271 League matches for the Throstles and won an FA Cup-winners' medal in 1953-4. Lee finished his League days with Albion in 1957-8 and went on to play for Lockheed Leamington.

GEORGE LEE

League debut for City v Oldham Athletic (h) 24 April 1937, Third Division North.

	LEAGUE		*FA CUP*		*TOTAL*	
	App	*Gls*	*App*	*Gls*	*App*	*Gls*
1936-37	2	0	0	0	2	0
1937-38	4	3	0	0	4	3
1938-39	30	8	1	0	31	8
1945-46	-	-	1	1	1	1
1946-47	1	0	0	0	1	0
	37	11	2	1	39	12

Left-back 'Eddie' Legge joined York from Carlisle in November 1935 and spent three seasons at the club. Born in Aberdeen, he played for Balmoral Cecil, Aberdeen Park Vale and Aberdeen before he moved south to Brunton Park in 1932. He was appointed captain at the start of the 1936-7 campaign and figured in the FA Cup run which took City to a fourth-round replay. He led the side the following season and played in the first two rounds of the FA Cup. Unfortunately, he suffered a serious injury on the eve of the third-round match against Coventry City and this effectively ended his career. He died in Aberdeen in December 1947.

League debut for City v Rotherham United (a) 9 November 1935, Third Division North.

	LEAGUE		*FA CUP*		*TOTAL*	
	App	*Gls*	*App*	*Gls*	*App*	*Gls*
1935-36	26	0	0	0	26	0
1936-37	36	2	7	0	43	2
1937-38	20	0	4	0	24	0
	82	2	11	0	93	2

EDWARD LEGGE

A fast and clever right winger, John Linaker had two spells with York in the 1950s. Born in Southport in January 1927, he came to prominence in wartime football and had spells with Everton and Manchester City. Linaker signed for Southport in November 1946 and, one year later, moved to Nottingham Forest. In June 1950 he joined City and in his first season was an ever-present and top scorer. His form attracted attention and in October 1951 he was transferred to Hull City. Linaker returned to Bootham Crescent in May 1953 and spent a further three seasons with the club before moving to Scarborough. He ended his career back in the League with Crewe Alexandra in 1957-8. A keen and very good golfer, he became a club professional when his footballing days finished.
League debut for City v Tranmere Rovers (a) 19 August 1950, Third Division North.

	LEAGUE		*FA CUP*		*TOTAL*	
	App	*Gls*	*App*	*Gls*	*App*	*Gls*
1950-51	46	13	4	0	50	13
1951-52	13	3	0	0	13	3
1953-54	34	4	1	0	35	4
1954-55	4	0	0	0	4	0
1955-56	1	0	0	0	1	0
	98	20	5	0	103	20

JOHN LINAKER

One of the most famous players to wear a York City shirt was Peter Lorimer, who made 32 appearances for the club in 1979-80. Born in Dundee in 1946, Lorimer joined Leeds from school and had an illustrious career with United. One of the famous Revie team in 16 years at Elland Road, he made 605 League and Cup appearances, winning Championship and FA Cup winners' medals and 21 caps for Scotland. He left Leeds in March 1979 and went to North America to play for Toronto Blizzards. When he returned to England the following autumn a number of clubs tried to obtain his services. It was City who won that race and in September 1979, 'Hot Shot' Lorimer signed for the club. His class and powerful shooting thrilled City fans during his all-too-short stay at Bootham Crescent and he scored a number of spectacular goals. Sadly, he was sent-off in his last game for the club in March 1980, against Tranmere Rovers. In the spring of 1980, he returned to Toronto and later that year City decided not to renew his contract for the forthcoming season. He returned to Leeds in 1983 and went on to break United's individual scoring record with a career total of 169 League goals.
League debut for City v Peterborough United (h) 8 September 1979, Fourth Division.

	LEAGUE		*FA CUP*		*TOTAL*	
	App	*Gls*	*App*	*Gls*	*App*	*Gls*
1979-80	29	8	3	1	32	9
	29	8	3	1	32	9

PETER LORIMER

One of City's stars in the mid-1970s, Barry Lyons was signed after a period on loan from Nottingham Forest for £12,000 in October 1973. His cultured play on the right side of midfield made an immediate impact and he played a considerable part in York City's promotion to the Second Division that season. He also had the distinction of scoring City's first-ever goal in the Second Division, in a 1-1 home draw against Aston Villa. Born in Shirebrook in 1946, Lyons joined Rotherham United from school and made 125 League appearances (24 goals) before signing for Nottingham Forest in November 1966. He went on to play 203 League games (nearly all in the First Division) and scored 28 goals for Forest. He left York City in July 1976 and joined Darlington, with whom he finished his playing days. In June 1979 he returned to Bootham Crescent as Youth-team coach and took over as manager from Charlie Wright in March 1980. Dismissed from that post in December the following year he resumed Youth-team duties but finally left the club in July 1982 (see *York City Managers*).

League debut for City v Port Vale (h) 15 September 1973, Third Division.

	LEAGUE		*FA CUP*		*FL CUP*		*TOTAL*	
	App	*Gls*	*App*	*Gls*	*App*	*Gls*	*App*	*Gls*
1973-74	40	5	2	0	5	0	47	5
1974-75	30/5	4	2	1	1	0	33/5	5
1975-76	10	1	0	0	3	0	13	1
	80/5	10	4	1	9	0	93/5	11

BARRY LYONS

A very talented left-sided midfield player, Ian McDonald was a regular in the first team during his four years at Bootham Crescent (1977-81). Born in 1953, he started as an apprentice with his home-town club Barrow, making his League debut in 1970-71. He moved to Workington in January 1973 and, showing much potential, was signed by Bill Shankly a year later for £33,000. Unfortunately, in his first game for Liverpool Reserves he broke a bone in his foot and was out of the game for several weeks. McDonald never settled at Anfield and in the summer of 1975 moved to Mansfield Town. He helped the Stags gain promotion to the Second Division and then joined City in November 1977. A skilful and gifted player, he was a penalty-kick expert and was 'Clubman of the Year' in 1979-80. In November 1981, he was transferred to Aldershot, in a player exchange deal with Malcolm Crosby, and went on to give the Hampshire club several years' service.

League debut for City v Southport (h) 12 November 1977, Fourth Division.

	LEAGUE		*FA CUP*		*FL CUP*		*TOTAL*	
	App	*Gls*	*App*	*Gls*	*App*	*Gls*	*App*	*Gls*
1977-78	30	2	1	0	0	0	31	2
1978-79	43	6	5	0	1	0	49	6
1979-80	46	8	3	1	2	0	51	9
1980-81	46	11	2	0	4	1	52	12
1981-82	10	2	0	0	2	0	12	2
	175	29	11	1	9	1	195	31

IAN McDONALD

One of the most famous goalscorers to appear for York City, Ted MacDougall netted over 250 League goals in a long and much travelled career. Born in Inverness in 1947, he joined Liverpool in 1966, but in 18 months at Anfield failed to win a first-team place. In July 1967 he was signed by Tom Lockie for £5,000 and scored on his Football League debut in August 1967. He was leading scorer in each of his two seasons at Bootham Crescent and in the summer of 1969 was transferred to Bournemouth for £8,000. He was a prolific scorer for the Cherries and netted over 100 League goals in three years. In 1971 he scored nine goals in an FA Cup match against Margate. He was transferred to Manchester United for £195,000 in September 1972. His stay at Old Trafford was for only six months and then, after another short period with West Ham, he joined Norwich. Whilst at Carrow Road he won seven Scottish caps and helped the Canaries back to the First Division. He later went on to play for Southampton, Bournemouth again and Blackpool.
League debut for City v Workington (h) 19 August 1967, Fourth Division.

	LEAGUE		*FA CUP*		*FL CUP*		*TOTAL*	
	App	*Gls*	*App*	*Gls*	*App*	*Gls*	*App*	*Gls*
1967-68	38	15	1	0	1	0	40	15
1968-69	46	19	3	4	1	2	50	25
	84	34	4	4	2	2	90	40

TED MacDOUGALL

A Glaswegian, born in 1943, John Mackin gave the club excellent service at right-back for four seasons (1969-73). He joined Northampton Town in November 1963 and made his League debut in the Cobblers' First Division side in 1965-6. He made over 100 League appearances for Town and then, after a short period with Lincoln, joined York City in September 1969. He immediately established himself in the defence and was a very sound full-back. In the promotion season of 1970-71, Mackin was an ever-present and he went on to make 184 League and Cup appearances for the club. In July 1973 he moved to Corby Town.
League debut for City v Workington (a) 20 September 1969, Fourth Division.

	LEAGUE		*FA CUP*		*FL CUP*		*TOTAL*	
	App	*Gls*	*App*	*Gls*	*App*	*Gls*	*App*	*Gls*
1969-70	36/1	0	5	0	0	0	41/1	0
1970-71	46	2	6	1	4	0	56	3
1971-72	46	4	3	0	4	0	53	4
1972-73	29/2	0	1	0	1	0	31/2	0
	157/3	6	15	1	9	0	181/3	7

JOHN MACKIN

A lively and energetic forward, Kevin McMahon was a useful goalscorer during his period with York City. Born in Tantobie in 1946, he was discovered by Newcastle whilst playing with Consett and signed for the Magpies in August 1967. McMahon did not get a first-team opportunity with United and joined City in May 1969. He was joint top-scorer in his first season at Bootham Crescent and was second-leading marksman in the promotion season of 1970-71. In the summer of 1972, he went to Barnsley in an exchange deal with Jimmy Seal and later played for Hartlepool (1973-6).
League debut for City v Newport County (a) 9 August 1969, Fourth Division.

	LEAGUE		FA CUP		FL CUP		TOTAL	
	App	Gls	App	Gls	App	Gls	App	Gls
1969-70	32/2	10	3	0	1	0	36/2	10
1970-71	27/4	13	3	1	3	0	33/4	14
1971-72	26/2	7	3	2	4	1	33/2	10
	85/8	30	9	3	8	1	102/8	34

KEVIN McMAHON

Northern Ireland international Eric McMordie joined City prior to the start of their second season in the Second Division. Born in Belfast in 1946, he played for Dundela and was a contemporary of George Best. McMordie had his first taste of English soccer when he signed for Middlesbrough in September 1964. In ten years at Ayresome Park he made 241 League appearances (23 goals) and was capped for his country 21 times. He had a spell on loan with Sheffield Wednesday in 1974-5 and moved to Bootham Crescent in May 1975. McMordie scored a spectacular goal on his debut, in a win over Portsmouth, but the clever, hard-working inside-forward never really fulfilled his potential whilst with the club. Midway through his second season (December 1976) he was transferred to Hartlepool, with whom he finished his League career in 1978.
League debut for City v Portsmouth (h) 16 August 1975, Second Division.

	LEAGUE		FA CUP		FL CUP		TOTAL	
	App	Gls	App	Gls	App	Gls	App	Gls
1975-76	37	2	1	0	3	0	41	2
1976-77	5	0	2	0	1	0	8	0
	42	2	3	0	4	0	49	2

ERIC McMORDIE

Born in Glasgow in 1926, Sam McNab played in Scottish junior football with Dalry Thistle before signing for Sheffield United in January 1952. He made 11 League appearances for the Blades and then became one of Jimmy McCormick's signings in the big recruiting drive in the summer of 1954. A clever ball-playing inside-forward, McNab scored on his debut in the memorable 6-2 win at Wrexham, on the opening day of the 1954-5 campaign. After a few weeks, he was to lose his place to Sid Storey and never really established himself with the club. He played in the FA Cup semi-final against Newcastle at Hillsborough when Storey was injured. In 1955-6 his appearances were restricted to the Midland League side and he departed in the summer of 1956.
League debut for City v Wrexham (a) 21 August 1954, Third Division North.

	LEAGUE		*FA CUP*		*TOTAL*	
	App	*Gls*	*App*	*Gls*	*App*	*Gls*
1954-55	19	3	1	0	20	3
	19	3	1	0	20	3

SAM McNAB

One of the best centre-halves to play for York City, John MacPhail was a kingpin in the record-breaking season of 1983-4. Born in Dundee in 1955, MacPhail started his career with his home-town club before joining Sheffield United in January 1979. He made 98 League appearances for the Blades before being transferred to York City in March 1983, after a period on loan. He was a commanding figure at the heart of the defence for the next three seasons and also scored a number of important goals. A dispute over terms caused him to leave Bootham Crescent in July 1986 and he was transferred to Bristol City for £14,000. He later teamed up again with Denis Smith and won a Third Division championship medal in 1987-8. A most popular player with the fans, he was twice voted 'Clubman of the Year' in 1983-4 and 1984-5.
League debut for City v Peterborough United (a) 5 February 1983, Fourth Division.

	LEAGUE		*FACUP*		*FLCUP*		*OTHERS*		*TOTAL*	
	App	*Gls*	*App*	*Gls*	*App*	*Gls*	*App*	*Gls*	*App*	*Gls*
1982-83	11/1	2	0	0	0	0	0	0	11/1	2
1983-84	46	10	3	0	2	0	1	0	52	10
1984-85	42	5	6	1	4	2	3	1	55	9
1985-86	42	7	7	0	4	1	1	0	54	8
	141/1	24	16	1	10	3	5	1	172/1	29

JOHN MacPHAIL

Born in Chesterfield in 1964, goalkeeper Chris Marples started his professional career with his home-town club. He won a Fourth Division championship medal whilst with the Spireites in 1984-5. Altogether, Marples made 97 appearances in goal for Chesterfield and was then transferred to Stockport County in March 1987. Regular first-choice 'keeper whilst at Edgeley Park, he played in 57 League games and was signed by Bobby Saxton in June 1988 for a fee of £28,000. A very sound goalkeeper and a safe handler of the ball, Marples missed only one game in his first season at Bootham Crescent. A talented cricketer, he kept wicket for Derbyshire in the County Championship in 1985 and 1986. An ever-present in 1989-90 he was elected 'Clubman of the Year' and was voted best Fourth Division goalkeeper by his fellow professionals.
League debut for City v Colchester United (a) 27 August 1988, Fourth Division.

	LEAGUE		*FA CUP*		*FL CUP*		*OTHERS*		*TOTAL*	
	App	*Gls*	*App*	*Gls*	*App*	*Gls*	*App*	*Gls*	*App*	*Gls*
1988-89	45	0	1	0	2	0	3	0	51	0
1989-90	46	0	1	0	4	0	3	0	54	0
	91	0	2	0	6	0	6	0	105	0

CHRIS MARPLES

Born in Jarrow in October 1907, Matt Middleton was a goalkeeper of great experience who played for City when he was in his 40s. He began his career with Bolden Colliery Welfare and made his Football League debut in 1931, when he signed for Southport. Middleton returned to the North-East, when he joined Sunderland in August 1933, and in six years at Roker Park he made 58 First Division appearances. He moved to Plymouth, but at the outbreak of war returned to guest for Sunderland and Middlesbrough. In August 1946, Middleton joined Bradford City and made 94 League appearances before moving to Bootham Crescent in February 1949. Although City finished bottom of the Northern Section in 1949-50, Matt served the club well and was a very popular character. He played his last game for York on 6 May 1950 at New Brighton, at the age of 42 years and 194 days — the oldest player to appear for City. His younger brother, Ray, played in goal for Chesterfield and Derby and was an England 'B' international. Matt died in 1979.
League debut for City v Bradford City (a) 12 February 1949, Third Division North.

	LEAGUE		*FA CUP*		*TOTAL*	
	App	*Gls*	*App*	*Gls*	*App*	*Gls*
1948-49	16	0	0	0	16	0
1949-50	39	0	1	0	40	0
	55	0	1	0	56	0

MATT MIDDLETON

Born in Sheffield in 1964, Simon Mills joined Sheffield Wednesday from school in 1980 and signed full-time professional forms in the summer of 1982. He played twice for England Juniors early in 1983 and was then capped five times for England Youth, playing in the European Youth Championships that were held in this country in May 1983. France won the competition and Mills was in the England team that beat Italy for third place. He made a total of five League appearances for the Owls and was then signed by City in June 1985, for a fee of £21,000. A virtual ever-present whilst at Bootham Crescent, he was 'Clubman of the Year' in 1985-6. A very skilful midfield player, he was an accurate passer of the ball. In December 1987, Mills was transferred to Port Vale for £35,000 and, by now converted to full-back, he helped Vale to win promotion to the Second Division in 1988-9.
League debut for City (sub) v Plymouth Argyle (h) 17 August 1985, Third Division.

	LEAGUE		*FA CUP*		*FL CUP*		*OTHERS*		*TOTAL*	
	App	*Gls*	*App*	*Gls*	*App*	*Gls*	*App*	*Gls*	*App*	*Gls*
1985-86	35/1	1	6	0	2	0	2	0	45/1	1
1986-87	45	1	3	1	4	1	2	0	54	3
1987-88	17	2	4	1	2	0	2	1	25	4
	97/1	4	13	2	8	1	6	1	124/1	8

SIMON MILLS

Born in Edwinstowe, Nottinghamshire, in 1932, Ron Mollatt was signed from Leeds United in July 1955. He joined Leeds as a junior and became a professional in 1950. Mollatt made his League debut in 1951-2 and played in 17 League games for United. Whilst he was at Elland Road, he was a very close friend of the legendary John Charles and was best man at John's wedding. A popular figure in his five seasons at Bootham Crescent, he had an aggressive and enthusiastic style of play at wing-half and played an important part in the 1958-9 promotion season. In the summer of 1960 he was transferred to Bradford City and in three seasons at Valley Parade made 88 League appearances. Like many others, Mollatt made his home in York and for a number of years was involved in local soccer. He was manager of Railway Institute FC in the Northern Counties East League for several seasons.
League debut for City v Gateshead (h) 3 December 1955, Third Division North.

	LEAGUE		*FA CUP*		*TOTAL*	
	App	*Gls*	*App*	*Gls*	*App*	*Gls*
1955-56	13	0	0	0	13	0
1956-57	36	0	0	0	36	0
1957-58	21	0	0	0	21	0
1958-59	33	1	0	0	33	1
1959-60	21	0	1	0	22	0
	124	1	1	0	125	1

RON MOLLATT

Alan Monkhouse was one of Sam Bartram's big-money signings (£4,000) in the summer of 1956 and much was expected of the former Millwall and Newcastle centre-forward. In the event, Monkhouse never settled with York and perhaps will go down as the most disappointing signing made by City. Born in Stockton in 1930, he played for Thornaby and was snapped up by Millwall in 1950. In four seasons at The Den, he made 65 League appearances (20 goals) and in October 1953 was transferred, for a sizeable fee, to Newcastle United. He made 21 First Division appearances for the Magpies and netted nine goals before joining York in June 1956. He played only a dozen games for City, the last being on 20 October, and in July 1957 he was transferred to South Shields. It remains a mystery why a player with a good pedigree and goalscoring reputation was such a failure at Bootham Crescent.
League debut for City v Accrington Stanley (a) 18 August 1956, Third Division North.

	LEAGUE		*FA CUP*		*TOTAL*	
	App	*Gls*	*App*	*Gls*	*App*	*Gls*
1956-57	12	1	0	0	12	1
	12	1	0	0	12	1

ALAN MONKHOUSE

Born in Scarborough in 1940, Tony Moor played in goal for York City as an amateur in the early 1960s, in the third team and the Reserves. Upon the departure of Mick Granger, he signed professional forms in the summer of 1962. Moor soon made his senior debut and for three seasons was to contest the goalkeeping berth with veteran Tommy Forgan. He was to pay the penalty, however, for a bad mistake in an FA Cup defeat at Chesterfield in December 1964 and never regained his first-team place. In the summer of 1965, Moor moved to Darlington and proved a good signing for the Quakers, making 239 League appearances in seven seasons. He was a very good cricketer and played in the Yorkshire League for Scarborough for many years.
League debut for City v Crewe Alexandra (h) 20 August 1962, Fourth Division.

	LEAGUE		*FA CUP*		*FL CUP*		*TOTAL*	
	App	*Gls*	*App*	*Gls*	*App*	*Gls*	*App*	*Gls*
1962-63	16	0	0	0	2	0	18	0
1963-64	24	0	0	0	2	0	26	0
1964-65	17	0	2	0	1	0	20	0
	57	0	2	0	5	0	64	0

TONY MOOR

BOB MORTIMER

Born in Bolton in 1909, Bob Mortimer was a much-travelled centre-forward, who played for ten clubs before joining City in the summer of 1938. He started with non-League sides Connahs Quay and Darwen and his League clubs in the 1930s were Bolton, Barrow, Northampton, Brentford, Bournemouth, Portsmouth, Accrington and Blackburn. His transfer from Accrington to Blackburn was for a four-figure sum and City paid their reported biggest fee when they signed him from Rovers. He was bought as a replacement for Reg Baines and proved a consistent marksman in his one season for the club, finishing top scorer in the 1938-9 campaign.

League debut for City v Doncaster Rovers (a) 27 August 1938, Third Division North.

	LEAGUE		*FA CUP*		*TOTAL*	
	App	*Gls*	*App*	*Gls*	*App*	*Gls*
1938-39	35	22	1	0	36	22
	35	22	1	0	36	22

Born in Manchester in 1959, Joe Neenan was a talented goalkeeper who played for York City in the late 1970s. He was on Manchester United's books as a junior and in 1975-6 played several trial games for York's intermediate side before signing as an apprentice. He won an England Youth cap in 1976-7 and made his League debut that season. Neenan went on to make over 60 senior appearances for the club, but never fully established himself in the first team. In January 1980 he was involved in a player-exchange deal which took him to Scunthorpe and brought Graeme Crawford back to York. Joe Neenan made 191 League appearances in goal for the Iron and then went on to Burnley and Peterborough United.

League debut for City v Swindon Town (h) 19 April 1977, Third Division.

	LEAGUE		*FA CUP*		*FL CUP*		*TOTAL*	
	App	*Gls*	*App*	*Gls*	*App*	*Gls*	*App*	*Gls*
1976-77	6	0	0	0	0	0	6	0
1977-78	13	0	0	0	3	0	16	0
1978-79	22	0	0	0	0	0	22	0
1979-80	15	0	3	0	0	0	18	0
	56	0	3	0	3	0	62	0

JOE NEENAN

Fourth in York City's goalscoring roll of honour is local lad Alf Patrick, who led the forward line with considerable success for seven seasons in the immediate post-war era. Born in 1921, the war years delayed his League debut until 1946-7. After some high-scoring performances in the Reserves, his first League game was in November 1946, against Stockport County, and appropriately he scored on his debut. He finished top scorer in each of his first four seasons. Patrick's best campaign was in 1948-9, when he netted 26 League goals, including five in a memorable performance against Rotherham in November 1948, which remains a club individual scoring feat. He scored four times in a match against Halifax in August 1947 and hit a hat-trick on four other occasions. Patrick thus equalled Reg Baines' pre-war record of hat-trick feats for the club and became the first player in City's history to score 100 League goals in peacetime football. At the end of the 1953-4 season he left the club and spent a year on Scarborough's books, but returned to Bootham Crescent and for some time assisted with the training and coaching of the third team. He will be remembered for his whole-hearted enthusiasm for the game. Without doubt he was one of the most popular wearers of the number-nine jersey for City. A precision machine-tool miller by trade, he worked for Cooke, Troughton and Sims for many years. A very good local cricketer, he played many seasons for Dringhouses.

League debut for City v Stockport County (h) 2 November 1946, Third Division North.

	LEAGUE		*FA CUP*		*TOTAL*	
	App	*Gls*	*App*	*Gls*	*App*	*Gls*
1946-47	23	17	1	0	24	17
1947-48	27	19	0	0	27	19
1948-49	41	26	3	1	44	27
1949-50	37	14	1	0	38	14
1950-51	33	9	4	4	37	13
1951-52	36	15	3	2	39	17
1952-53	31	9	1	1	32	10
	228	109	13	8	241	117

ALF PATRICK

No relation to Alf Patrick, this popular utility player was born in Slamanan, Scotland, in 1919. Matt Patrick played for Cowdenbeath and guested for York City during the war years. At the end of hostilities he signed for the club and was to prove a most versatile player, equally at home in defence, midfield or attack. In 1950-51 he was joint top scorer with John Linaker. He gave the club 11 years' stalwart service, the last three seasons of which he played in the Reserves and third team, helping with the development of the young players. A loyal club servant, he made his home in York after retiring from the game.

League debut for City v Chester (h) 31 August 1946, Third Division North.

	LEAGUE		*FA CUP*		*TOTAL*	
	App	*Gls*	*App*	*Gls*	*App*	*Gls*
1946-47	31	1	1	0	32	1
1947-48	42	8	1	0	43	8
1948-49	35	14	3	0	38	14
1949-50	38	9	1	0	39	9
1950-51	45	13	4	1	49	14
1951-52	11	2	2	0	13	2
1952-53	18	0	0	0	18	0
1953-54	29	0	1	0	30	0
	249	47	13	1	262	48

MATT PATRICK

Born in Dublin in 1935, Noel Peyton played with Shamrock Rovers before joining Leeds United in January 1958. In five and a half years at Elland Road, he made 104 League appearances and was capped for the Republic of Ireland six times. He moved to Bootham Crescent in July 1963. An industrious and skilful inside-forward, a series of injuries severely limited his appearances for the club and in the summer of 1965 he moved to Barnstaple Town as player-manager.
League debut for City v Rochdale (h) 24 August 1963, Fourth Division.

NOEL PEYTON

	LEAGUE		FA CUP		FL CUP		TOTAL	
	App	Gls	App	Gls	App	Gls	App	Gls
1963-64	35	4	1	0	2	1	38	5
1964-65	2	0	0	0	1	0	3	0
	37	4	1	0	3	1	41	5

Signed from Hull City in the summer of 1954, Ernie Phillips was right-back and captain of the successful City team of the mid-1950s. Born in North Shields in 1923, Phillips joined Manchester City in 1947 and made 80 First Division appearances before moving to Hull City in 1951. He played in 42 Second Division games for the Tigers and was then transferred to York City in June 1954. A fine tackler, he was an excellent defender and an outstanding captain who led City to their magnificent FA Cup exploits. Upon leaving the club, he played for Ashington and was then player-manager at Bridlington. He remained in York and worked as a representative for a sweet firm and then for British Rail in the repairs shop. One of the outstanding figures in City's history, Ernie Phillips was a model professional and a virtual ever-present in his four years at Bootham Crescent. By coincidence his last game was at the Racecourse Ground on 16 April 1958.
League debut for City v Wrexham (a) 21 August 1954, Third Division North.

ERNIE PHILLIPS

	LEAGUE		FA CUP		TOTAL	
	App	Gls	App	Gls	App	Gls
1954-55	46	1	8	0	54	1
1955-56	46	0	5	0	51	0
1956-57	36	0	1	0	37	0
1957-58	36	1	5	0	41	1
	164	2	19	0	183	2

Born in the village of New Earswick, near York, in 1926, Peter Pickering joined the club during the war years from local junior football. After completing his military service, he made his League debut in goal in May 1947. He soon attracted the attention of senior clubs with some outstanding displays and in a three-month period of the 1947-8 season he saved no less than seven penalties. Chelsea eventually prised Pickering away from Bootham Crescent in May 1948 and in three seasons at Stamford Bridge, he made 27 League appearances before joining non-League Kettering Town. He returned to the Football League with Northampton Town in 1955 and in three years played in 86 League games for the Cobblers. A very good cricketer he played for Northamptonshire in the County Championship. He later emigrated to South Africa.
League debut for City v Accrington Stanley (a) 14 May 1947, Third Division North.

	LEAGUE		*FA CUP*		*TOTAL*	
	App	*Gls*	*App*	*Gls*	*App*	*Gls*
1946-47	1	0	0	0	1	0
1947-48	41	0	1	0	42	0
	42	0	1	0	43	0

PETER PICKERING

One of York City's all-time stalwarts, Jack Pinder's playing career spanned 19 years. Pinder was born in York in December 1912 and was an England Schoolboy international in 1927 when one of his teammates was future England and Sunderland star, Raich Carter. He joined York City in the Fulfordgate days of 1929 and signed as a professional in February 1930. A hard-tackling, no-nonsense right-back, he made his League debut in September 1932. Two years later he established himself in the first team and was a regular in the defence until the outbreak of war. Pinder figured in the FA Cup runs of 1936-7 and 1937-8 and in May 1938 he received the first of two benefits, in a match against Grimsby Town. He played for City during the war years and made his last League appearance for the club in March 1948. A part-timer during his playing career, he worked for the railway as a telegraphist.
League debut for City v Stockport County (a) 5 September 1932, Third Division North.

	LEAGUE		*FA CUP*		*TOTAL*	
	App	*Gls*	*App*	*Gls*	*App*	*Gls*
1932-33	19	0	0	0	19	0
1933-34	4	0	0	0	4	0
1934-35	33	0	3	0	36	0
1935-36	20	0	1	0	21	0
1936-37	19	0	7	0	26	0
1937-38	31	0	5	0	36	0
1938-39	23	0	1	0	24	0
1945-46	0	0	8	0	8	0
1946-47	40	4	1	0	41	4
1947-48	10	0	0	0	10	0
	199	4	26	0	225	4

JACK PINDER

Born in York in 1954, Brian Pollard had two successful periods with the club. He first joined City as an amateur in the early 1970s, playing for the intermediates, and he was capped for England at Youth international level. He signed professional terms in March 1972, making his League debut in the same month. A fast and direct winger who could operate on either flank, Pollard soon established himself and played his part in the promotion season of 1973-4. He made 40 Second Division appearances for the club and then had an outstanding 1976-7 season, in which he was elected 'Clubman of the Year'. In November 1977 he was transferred to Watford, for a then record fee received of £33,000. Whilst at Vicarage Road he helped the Hertfordshire club, then under the control of new chairman Elton John and new manager Graham Taylor, gain promotion from the Fourth to the Second Division. After 71 League appearances for Watford, Pollard signed for Mansfield Town in January 1980, for a fee of £45,000. He spent 18 months with Town and then had a short trial period with Blackpool before returning to Bootham Crescent in September 1981. He was second top scorer in 1982-3 and the following season made 30 League appearances in the championship triumph. He finally left the club in the summer of 1984 and went on to play for Scarborough and North Ferriby. Upon hanging up his boots, he became a publican.

League debut for City v Rotherham United (h) 31 March 1972, Third Division.

	LEAGUE		*FA CUP*		*FL CUP*		*OTHERS*		*TOTAL*	
	App	*Gls*	*App*	*Gls*	*App*	*Gls*	*App*	*Gls*	*App*	*Gls*
1971-72	4	0	0	0	0	0	0	0	4	0
1972-73	30	7	3	1	0	0	0	0	33	8
1973-74	21/6	4	2	0	5	1	0	0	28/6	5
1974-75	11/1	1	0	0	0	0	0	0	11/1	1
1975-76	27/1	5	1	0	0	0	0	0	28/1	5
1976-77	41/3	12	4/1	1	3	0	0	0	48/4	13
1977-78	17	5	0	0	3	0	0	0	20	5
1981-82	25/1	3	3	2	0	0	0	0	28/1	5
1982-83	44/2	17	4	2	2	0	0	0	50/2	19
1983-84	29/1	6	3	0	2	1	1	0	35/1	7
	249/15	60	20/1	6	15	2	1	0	285/16	68

BRIAN POLLARD

Born in Greenock on New Year's Day 1944, Andy Provan played an important part in the promotion success of 1964-5 and gave York City four seasons' excellent service. Provan started his career with Morton and then joined Barnsley in 1963. He came to Bootham Crescent on trial in the summer of 1964 and, after an impressive start with a goal on his debut against Rochdale, he signed a contract. A lively and opportunist winger, he could play on either flank, but chiefly wore the number-11 shirt. He was an ever-present in his first season and was second leading scorer with 18 goals. He became the most prolific scoring winger for the club since Billy Fenton in the 1950s. A cheeky little player, he was a firm favourite with the fans. In a win over Bradford in September 1966, he scored an unorthodox goal which was typical of the player. He sprinted on to a through-ball, dribbled around the advancing goalkeeper and then, dropping on all fours, he lay on the ground at full-stretch and headed the ball into the net. It took the crowd a few moments to realize that it was a goal. Provan was transferred to Chester for £4,000 in August 1968 and later played for Wrexham, Southport and Torquay United.

League debut for City v Rochdale (h) 22 August 1964, Fourth Division.

	LEAGUE		*FA CUP*		*FL CUP*		*TOTAL*	
	App	*Gls*	*App*	*Gls*	*App*	*Gls*	*App*	*Gls*
1964-65	46	18	2	1	1	0	49	19
1965-66	26	2	1	0	3	1	30	3
1966-67	40/1	15	6	1	3	2	49/1	18
1967-68	44	13	1	0	1	0	46	13
1968-69	3	1	0	0	1	0	4	1
	159/1	49	10	2	9	3	178/1	54

ANDY PROVAN

A vastly experienced midfield player and former Welsh Under-23 international, David Pugh was with the club from 1978 to 1981. Born in Markham, near Newport, in 1947, he was a Welsh Schoolboy international and his first professional club was Newport County. After 77 League games, he was transferred to Chesterfield and spent six seasons with the Derbyshire club, helping them to win the Fourth Division championship in 1969-70. He played in 213 League games for the Spireites and then it was on to Halifax and 96 League appearances in three seasons. His next port of call was Rotherham and another 58 League matches before he moved to Bootham Crescent, for a £4,000 fee, in October 1978. Pugh did a good job in his time at York, with his determined tackling and hard work in midfield. He was appointed player-coach under Barry Lyons in May 1980 and was recalled to first-team duty in the latter part of the 1980-81 season, when he gave a number of typically battling displays. He left the club in 1981.
League debut for City v Huddersfield Town (a) 4 November 1978, Fourth Division.

	LEAGUE		*FA CUP*		*FL CUP*		*TOTAL*	
	App	*Gls*	*App*	*Gls*	*App*	*Gls*	*App*	*Gls*
1978-79	31	0	5	1	0	0	36	1
1979-80	31/4	1	0	0	2	0	33/4	1
1980-81	11	1	0	0	0	0	11	1
	73/4	2	5	1	2	0	80/4	3

DAVID PUGH

Born in Aston-under-Lyne in 1945, Kevin Randall was, for a number of seasons, one of the most consistent scorers in the Football League. He made his debut with Bury in 1965-6 and the following season moved to Chesterfield. Randall spent five seasons at Saltergate (258 League games, 97 goals) and helped them gain promotion to the Third Division in 1970. He then moved to Notts County (121 games, 38 goals) and figured in their promotion to the Second Division in 1973. He played for Mansfield (66 games, 20 goals) and helped the Stags to win the Third Division championship in 1977. City signed him from Mansfield, for £8,000, in October 1977 and he scored twice on his debut, in a home win over Doncaster Rovers. A very skilful player, Randall proved popular at Bootham Crescent and in 1980 he was appointed youth coach and assistant manager. Upon the departure of Barry Lyons in December 1981 he took over as caretaker manager, but three months later he was relieved of his duties and left the club. After a spell as manager of Goole Town, he was appointed coach and then manager of Chesterfield. He was dismissed from that post in November 1988 and joined the coaching staff at Mansfield.
League debut for City v Doncaster Rovers (h) 28 October 1977, Fourth Division.

	LEAGUE		*FA CUP*		*FL CUP*		*TOTAL*	
	App	*Gls*	*App*	*Gls*	*App*	*Gls*	*App*	*Gls*
1977-78	29/1	8	1	0	0	0	30/1	8
1978-79	37/5	10	5	1	0	0	42/5	11
1979-80	21/5	7	3	1	2	1	26/5	9
1980-81	9	2	0	0	0	0	9	2
	96/11	27	9	2	2	1	107/11	30

KEVIN RANDALL

Born in Tain, Scotland, in 1947, Tommy Ross appropriately started his career with Ross County in the Highland League and was a prolific scorer. He joined Peterborough United in the summer of 1965 and spent two years at the London Road club. In June 1967, Ross was signed by York City and had a good first season with the club, finishing second top scorer. He was a lively little inside-forward and a good opportunist in front of goal. In 1968-9 he was not quite able to fulfil the earlier promise he had shown, but did score a hat-trick in a 6-0 FA Cup first-round win at South Shields in November 1968. He was released at the end of that season.
League debut for City v Workington (h) 19 August 1967, Fourth Division.

	LEAGUE		FA CUP		FL CUP		TOTAL	
	App	Gls	App	Gls	App	Gls	App	Gls
1967-68	37/1	14	1	0	1	0	39/1	14
1968-69	19/4	6	3	3	1	0	23/4	9
	56/5	20	4	3	2	0	62/5	23

TOMMY ROSS

One of the finest ball players and entertainers to appear for York City, Jimmy Rudd thrilled Bootham Crescent crowds in the early post-war period. He was born in Dublin in 1919 and joined Manchester City before the war. Rudd was signed by York in March 1947 and immediately struck up a brilliant left-wing partnership with Sid Storey. Jimmy's ball skills and wizardry made him an exciting and outstanding personality. In February 1949, he was transferred to Leeds United and later moved to Rotherham, Scunthorpe and Workington, with whom he finished his League career in 1952-3. His playing days were ended with Northwich Victoria and, upon retiring, he made his home at Manchester. He died in December 1985.
League debut for City v Bradford City (a) 22 March 1947, Third Division North.

	LEAGUE		FA CUP		TOTAL	
	App	Gls	App	Gls	App	Gls
1946-47	17	9	0	0	17	9
1947-48	41	8	1	0	42	8
1948-49	25	6	3	1	28	7
	83	23	4	1	87	24

JIMMY RUDD

Nephew of Jimmy, Billy Rudd without doubt inherited a lot of his uncle's footballing skills. Born in Manchester in 1941, he played for Manchester Boys and Lancashire Boys alongside Nobby Stiles, the future Manchester United and England World Cup star. After trials at Old Trafford and Arsenal, Rudd joined Stalybridge Celtic in 1958 and then signed for Birmingham City the following year. He made 24 First Division appearances for the Blues before moving to Bootham Crescent in November 1961. In four seasons (1962-6) he missed only three League games and captained the side in the promotion campaign of 1964-5. A very skilful inside-forward, Rudd proved a fine leader and was an outstanding player during his time at York. He was transferred to Grimsby Town in the summer of 1966 and went on to play for Rochdale and Bury, ending his League days in 1976-7. In a long and excellent career, he made a total of 574 League appearances and netted 68 goals.
League debut for City v Gillingham (h) 13 January 1962, Fourth Division.

	LEAGUE		FA CUP		FL CUP		TOTAL	
	App	Gls	App	Gls	App	Gls	App	Gls
1961-62	12	3	0	0	1	0	13	3
1962-63	44	8	4	0	2	0	50	8
1963-64	46	7	1	0	4	1	51	8
1964-65	46	9	2	0	1	0	49	9
1965-66	45	3	1	0	3	0	49	3
	193	30	8	0	11	1	212	31

BILLY RUDD

Born in Lennoxtown in 1956, Ricky Sbragia served his apprenticeship with Birmingham City and signed professional forms in June 1974. He made his League debut in 1974-5 and then moved to Walsall in October 1978, for a fee of £15,000. Sbragia helped the Saddlers gain promotion to the Third Division in 1979-80 and in the summer of 1980 was transferred to Blackpool, who were then in the Second Division, for £35,000. After two years at Bloomfield Road, he was signed for York City by Denis Smith in the summer of 1982. Sbragia soon established himself at the heart of the defence and struck up a magnificent partnership with John MacPhail in the championship season of 1983-4. He did not score many goals, but one of the highlights of his career was when he netted an equalizer against Liverpool in the FA Cup fifth round in 1984-5. Injuries cut short his appearances and in 1987 he retired to concentrate on coaching duties and was given the responsibility of looking after the junior and intermediate players at Bootham Crescent.
League debut for City v Torquay United (h) 28 August 1982, Fourth Division.

	LEAGUE		FACUP		FLCUP		OTHERS		TOTAL	
	App	Gls	App	Gls	App	Gls	App	Gls	App	Gls
1982-83	46	1	4	0	2	0	0	0	52	1
1983-84	45	4	3	1	2	0	1	0	51	5
1984-85	25	2	6	1	3	0	0	0	34	3
1985-86	7	0	2	1	0	0	0	0	9	1
1986-87	26	0	2	0	4	0	1	0	33	0
	149	7	17	3	11	0	2	0	179	10

RICKY SBRAGIA

Born in Durham in 1916, Fred Scott was an England Schoolboy international. He was with Bolton Wanderers and Bradford before joining City from the Park Avenue club in February 1937. A speedy and clever outside-right, Scott played in the first two rounds of the 1937-8 FA Cup run and the following season established himself in the first team. He served in the RAF during the war and played several times for the club in wartime football. In September 1946, Scott was transferred to Nottingham Forest, for a then club record fee received of £3,000. He spent ten years at the City Ground and made 304 League appearances, playing until he was 40. He then had spells as chief scout with Sunderland, Sheffield Wednesday, Southampton and Blackpool and he was connected with football until 1983.

League debut for City v Port Vale (h) 13 February 1937, Third Division North.

	LEAGUE		*FA CUP*		*TOTAL*	
	App	*Gls*	*App*	*Gls*	*App*	*Gls*
1936-37	16	3	0	0	16	3
1937-38	22	7	4	1	26	8
1938-39	34	6	0	0	34	6
1945-46	0	0	8	3	8	3
1946-47	2	0	0	0	2	0
	74	16	12	4	86	20

FRED SCOTT

Full-back Peter Scott became the second York City player to receive international honours whilst with the club. Born in Liverpool in 1952, he served his apprenticeship with Everton and signed full-time professional forms at Goodison Park in July 1970. Scott made his First Division debut in 1971-2 and went on to make 44 League appearances for the Toffeemen. In December 1975, Wilf McGuinness signed him for York for a fee in the region of £11,000. A strong, hard-tackling defender, he was an England Youth international, but was capped for Northern Ireland at full international level ten times. Seven of these caps were won whilst he was at Bootham Crescent. In March 1979 he was transferred to Aldershot for £3,000 and went on to make 121 League appearances for the Hampshire club.

League debut for City v Hull City (h) 6 December 1975. Second Division.

	LEAGUE		*FA CUP*		*FL CUP*		*TOTAL*	
	App	*Gls*	*App*	*Gls*	*App*	*Gls*	*App*	*Gls*
1975-76	19	0	2	0	0	0	21	0
1976-77	24/1	0	3	0	3	0	30/1	0
1977-78	45	3	1	0	3	0	49	3
1978-79	11	0	0	0	2	0	13	0
	99/1	3	6	0	8	0	113/1	3

PETER SCOTT

Born in Pontefract in 1950, Jimmy Seal joined Wolves as a junior and signed professional forms in March 1968. He made one First Division appearance whilst at Molineux before moving to Walsall during the 1969-70 campaign. After 40 League games and 14 goals for the Saddlers, he was transferred to Barnsley in the summer of 1971. Seal spent one season at Oakwell and scored 12 goals in 43 League matches. In July 1972, he moved to Bootham Crescent for a fee of £6,000 plus Kevin McMahon. Seal had a difficult first season with the club and managed only three goals in 31 League appearances. The following season, however, he formed a fine striking partnership with Chris Jones and netted 17 League goals as City marched to the Second Division. In 1974-5 he was top scorer in the Second Division side, again with 17 goals, and scored a magnificent goal in a 1-1 FA Cup third-round draw at Arsenal. In November 1976, Seal was transferred to Darlington and spent three seasons at Feethams (122 League games). He finished his League career with Rochdale 1979-81 (53 League matches). He made his home in York and played in local football for a number of years, working as a self-employed painter and decorator and later as a milkman.

League debut for City v Grimsby Town (h) 12 August 1972, Third Division.

	LEAGUE		*FA CUP*		*FL CUP*		*TOTAL*	
	App	*Gls*	*App*	*Gls*	*App*	*Gls*	*App*	*Gls*
1972-73	29/2	3	3	1	1	0	33/2	4
1973-74	43/1	17	2	0	5	0	50/1	17
1974-75	41	17	2	1	1	0	44	18
1975-76	34/5	5	2	1	3	2	39/5	8
1976-77	5/1	1	0	0	3	0	8/1	1
	152/9	43	9	3	13	2	174/9	48

JIMMY SEAL

Born in Mansfield in June 1924, goalkeeper Harold Searson started his professional career with Sheffield Wednesday in August 1946, after returning from wartime service in the Fleet Air Arm in India. However, he did not make his League debut until joining Mansfield Town in 1947. After making 42 League appearances for the Stags he moved to Leeds United in January 1949. In nearly four years at Elland Road, Searson played in 104 League games. He was signed by City in November 1952, as replacement for Des Thompson, who had been transferred to Burnley. For one and a half seasons at Bootham Crescent, Searson proved a sound and capable 'keeper. He is one of the few players in post-war football to have played League football on his wedding day.

League debut for City v Carlisle United (h) 29 November 1952, Third Division North.

	LEAGUE		*FA CUP*		*TOTAL*	
	App	*Gls*	*App*	*Gls*	*App*	*Gls*
1952-53	27	0	0	0	27	0
1953-54	35	0	1	0	36	0
	62	0	1	0	63	0

HAROLD SEARSON

Born in Sheffield in 1963, Steve Senior joined York as an apprentice in 1979. After making good progress with the intermediates and reserves, he signed professional terms on his 18th birthday, shortly after making his first-team debut. He was nursed along gently and then, in 1983-4, established himself at right-back and was an ever-present in the championship-winning side until breaking a leg at Aldershot in April 1984. He made a full recovery and regained his place in the first team the following season, playing his part in the FA Cup runs of 1984-5 and 1985-6. He was a very talented defender and, in his last four seasons at Bootham Crescent, a vital cog in the back-four. In May 1987, Senior was transferred to Northampton Town for £15,000 and a few months later moved on to Wigan Athletic.
League debut for City (sub) v Aldershot (a) 25 April 1981, Fourth Division.

	LEAGUE		*FA CUP*		*FL CUP*		*OTHERS*		*TOTAL*	
	App	*Gls*	*App*	*Gls*	*App*	*Gls*	*App*	*Gls*	*App*	*Gls*
1980-81	1/2	0	0	0	0	0	0	0	1/2	0
1981-82	14/3	1	3	0	0	0	0	0	17/3	1
1982-83	6/4	1	0	0	0	0	0	0	6/4	1
1983-84	39	1	3	0	2	0	1	1	45	2
1984-85	28	0	5	0	0/1	0	4	0	37/1	0
1985-86	33/1	3	6	0	2	0	2	0	43/1	3
1986-87	37	0	3	0	3	0	3	0	46	0
	158/10	6	20	0	7/1	0	10	1	195/11	7

STEVE SENIOR

Right-back Bob Sibbald was born in Hebburn, County Durham, in January 1948 and started his footballing career north of the border with Airdrie. He then joined Leeds United and signed professional forms in January 1965. Whilst at Elland Road he was a regular in the Central League side but only made two First Division appearances for Don Revie's all-conquering team. He moved to Bootham Crescent in February 1969 and quickly settled down in City's defence. Sibbald captained the side in 1969-70, missing only one match that season. In the promotion campaign of 1970-71, however, he made only 14 League appearances and in the summer of 1971 was transferred to Southport. In six good seasons at Haigh Avenue he played in 340 League matches. Later in the 1970s, Sibbald played alongside George Best and Johann Cruyff for Los Angeles Aztecs in the NASL and in 1980 was appointed assistant coach to that club.
League debut for City (sub) v Wrexham (h) 24 February 1969, Fourth Division.

	LEAGUE		*FA CUP*		*FL CUP*		*TOTAL*	
	App	*Gls*	*App*	*Gls*	*App*	*Gls*	*App*	*Gls*
1968-69	18/2	2	0	0	0	0	18/2	0
1969-70	45	4	7	1	1	0	53	5
1970-71	11/3	1	0	0	4	0	15/3	1
	74/5	7	7	1	5	0	86/5	6

BOB SIBBALD

John Simpson served York City splendidly, first as a player (1948-54) and then as physiotherapist (1977-83). Born in Hull in 1918, he spent a lifetime in football. He played for Hull City Boys whilst at school and then joined Hull City as an amateur, playing a number of times for the Tigers' reserve team. After trials with Huddersfield Town, he signed professional terms in 1936 and made a number of First Division appearances for the Leeds Road club. During the war, Simpson was in the Army Physical Training Corps and guested for several clubs. He also captained the Southern Command side. After the war he rejoined Huddersfield and in March 1948 was signed by City for a then record fee paid of £1,000. For the next six seasons, he gave the club excellent service at left-back. A hard-tackling, no-nonsense player, his chief attributes were his great fitness and speed. His playing days ended in 1954 and he then spent nine years as coach with Hull City. Simpson moved to Hartlepool, first as coach and then manager. In 1971 he joined Cambridge United as coach and physiotherapist and in the summer of 1977 was appointed trainer and physiotherapist at Bootham Crescent. For six years he carried out these duties in meticulous and dedicated fashion and was rewarded with a testimonial match against Leeds United in May 1983, which attracted a crowd of over 3,000. Shortly afterwards he retired and moved with his wife to Market Weighton.

League debut for City v Southport (h) 13 March 1948, Third Division North.

	LEAGUE		*FA CUP*		*TOTAL*	
	App	*Gls*	*App*	*Gls*	*App*	*Gls*
1947-48	10	0	0	0	10	0
1948-49	39	0	3	0	42	0
1949-50	22	0	1	0	23	0
1950-51	41	0	4	0	45	0
1951-52	44	0	3	0	47	0
1952-53	29	0	1	0	30	0
1953-54	22	0	1	0	23	0
	207	0	13	0	220	0

JOHN SIMPSON

Son of a famous England and Manchester United player, Joe Spence was born in Salford in 1925. He began his footballing days with Buxton and then signed for Chesterfield in 1948. He did not appear in the first team whilst at Saltergate and moved to York in July 1950. A polished and cool defender, Spence played at either right-back or centre-half and was virtually an ever-present in seasons 1951-2 and 1952-3. He left the club in the summer of 1954 and moved to Gainsborough Trinity in the Midland League.

League debut for City v New Brighton (a) 21 October 1950, Third Division North.

	LEAGUE		*FA CUP*		*TOTAL*	
	App	*Gls*	*App*	*Gls*	*App*	*Gls*
1950-51	10	0	1	0	11	0
1951-52	43	0	3	0	46	0
1952-53	45	0	1	0	46	0
1953-54	12	0	0	0	12	0
	110	0	5	0	115	0

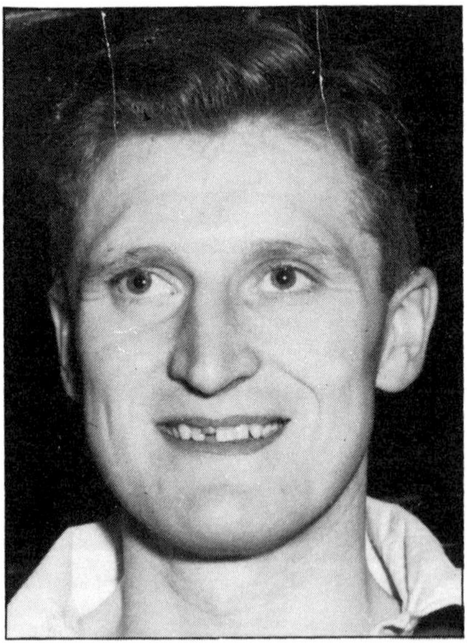

JOE SPENCE

Apart from a three-year break in the early 1960s, Ron Spence served York City from 1948 to 1975, first as an outstanding wing-half and then as trainer and physiotherapist. Born in Spennymoor in 1927, Spence was playing for Rossington Colliery in South Yorkshire when spotted by City and he joined the club in March 1948. He proved to be one of York's finest signings. Once established in the first team in 1950, he was a fixture in the side for six seasons. A fine attacking half-back and tireless worker, Spence was an integral part of the great 1954-5 side. A serious knee injury, sustained in a match against Barrow in March 1956, was to sideline him for 18 months. In typical fashion he fought his way back to fitness and was in the side that played Birmingham and Bolton in the FA Cup in 1957-8. He made his last League appearance in November 1958 and ended his playing days with the club in May 1960. After a spell with Scarborough, Spence returned to Bootham Crescent in the summer of 1963 and for 12 years served the club as trainer, coach and physiotherapist. In September 1975, he retired from football and went into the licensing trade. One of the finest servants in the club's history, he received a benefit in May 1955.

League debut for City v Barrow (h) 24 April 1948, Third Division North.

	LEAGUE		*FA CUP*		*TOTAL*	
	App	*Gls*	*App*	*Gls*	*App*	*Gls*
1947-48	1	0	0	0	1	0
1948-49	15	0	0	0	15	0
1949-50	6	4	0	0	6	4
1950-51	32	6	4	0	36	6
1951-52	44	2	3	0	47	2
1952-53	46	2	1	0	47	2
1953-54	34	7	1	0	35	7
1954-55	46	2	8	1	54	3
1955-56	36	2	5	0	41	2
1956-57	0	0	0	0	0	0
1957-58	9	0	3	0	12	0
1958-59	11	0	1	0	12	0
	280	25	26	1	306	26

RON SPENCE

A well-built, hard-working centre-forward, Tom Spencer joined City in June 1966 from Southampton and in his season at Bootham Crescent topped the scoring list with 23 League and Cup goals. Born in Glasgow in 1945, Spencer played junior football in that city for Pollok United before signing amateur forms for Celtic. Whilst at Parkhead, he made a number of appearances in their reserve side and then moved to Southampton in June 1965. He made three Second Division appearances for the Saints before signing for York. Spencer was unable to find his scoring touch in his second season with City and in March 1968 he was involved in a player-exchange deal with Workington which brought Tommy Spratt to York. He went on to play for Lincoln and Rotherham and his League career lasted until 1977-8. He made a total of 439 League appearances and scored 50 goals. Very strong in the air, Spencer spent most of his time as a central defender after leaving City.

League debut for City v Chesterfield (h) 20 August 1966, Fourth Division.

	LEAGUE		*FA CUP*		*FL CUP*		*TOTAL*	
	App	*Gls*	*App*	*Gls*	*App*	*Gls*	*App*	*Gls*
1966-67	40/2	18	3	2	4	3	47/2	23
1967-68	14/1	3	0	0	1	0	15/1	3
	54/3	21	3	2	5	3	62/3	26

TOM SPENCER

One of the heroes of the 1937-8 FA Cup run, Peter Spooner had two spells with York City in the 1930s. Born at Hepscott in the North-East in 1910, he played for Newbiggin United and Ashington and had trials with Newcastle United before signing for Bradford in 1930. Spooner joined City from Park Avenue in the summer of 1931 and the talented outside-left quickly impressed. In May 1933 he was transferred to Sheffield United for a fee of £500 and joined former teammate Reg Baines at Bramall Lane. He returned to Bootham Crescent two years later and for the next three seasons was City's regular number-11. In the 1937-8 FA Cup run he scored one of the goals that beat Coventry in the third round and netted the winner in the fifth-round victory over Middlesbrough. He was almost the match winner in the quarter-final tie against Huddersfield, when he came nearest to scoring, seeing his header kicked off the line. In May 1939, he finally left the York club.
League debut for City v Rotherham United (a) 5 September 1931, Third Division North.

	LEAGUE		*FA CUP*		*TOTAL*	
	App	*Gls*	*App*	*Gls*	*App*	*Gls*
1931-32	22	2	0	0	22	2
1932-33	35	11	1	1	36	12
1935-36	42	7	1	0	43	7
1936-37	41	12	7	3	48	15
1937-38	37	10	9	2	46	12
1938-39	12	0	0	0	12	0
	189	42	18	6	207	48

PETER SPOONER

Born in Sutton, Surrey, in 1961, Steve Spooner began his footballing career as an apprentice with Derby County and signed professional terms in December 1978. He made his Football League debut as an 18-year-old for the Rams against Tottenham Hotspur in March 1979. Spooner joined Halifax Town in 1981 and then moved to Chesterfield during the summer of 1983. He was a key figure in the Blues' Fourth Division championship-winning side of 1984-5 and a teammate at The Recreation Ground was Chris Marples. After two seasons at Hereford, where he was a virtual ever-present, he moved to Bootham Crescent for a fee of £29,000 in June 1988. A troublesome foot injury caused him to miss the first half of the 1988-9 season, but the hardworking, talented midfielder played a vital role as City finished the campaign strongly. He was appointed captain for the 1989-90 season. In a Littlewoods Cup tie against Hartlepool United in August 1989, Steve Spooner hit an eight-minute hat-trick — the second fastest recorded in the club's history. He was voted into the PFA Fourth Division team of 1989-90 by his fellow professionals. He was transferred to Rotherham United in July 1990.
League debut for City v Colchester United (a) 27 August 1988, Fourth Division.

	LEAGUE		*FA CUP*		*FL CUP*		*OTHERS*		*TOTAL*	
	App	*Gls*	*App*	*Gls*	*App*	*Gls*	*App*	*Gls*	*App*	*Gls*
1988-89	31	5	0	0	2	0	2	0	35	5
1989-90	41	6	1	0	4	3	2	1	48	10
	72	11	1	0	6	3	4	1	83	15

STEVE SPOONER

JOHN STAINSBY

A strong, bustling centre-forward of the old-school type, John Stainsby spent two seasons with the City club (1961-3). Born in Stainfoot, South Yorkshire, in 1936, he was an amateur on the books of Wolves, playing with the juniors at Molineux. He signed professional terms with Barnsley in 1955 and scored 12 goals in 34 League appearances for the Oakwell club. In July 1961, he moved to Bootham Crescent and had a very good first season with York. He finished second top scorer with 19 League and Cup goals and played an important part in the side's Football League Cup run to the quarter-finals. Not so successful in 1962-3, he was transferred to Stockport County in July 1963, but spent only one season at Edgeley Park.

League debut for City v Bradford City (a) 19 August 1961, Fourth Division.

	LEAGUE		*FA CUP*		*FL CUP*		*TOTAL*	
	App	*Gls*	*App*	*Gls*	*App*	*Gls*	*App*	*Gls*
1961-62	38	15	0	0	7	4	45	19
1962-63	31	6	1	0	1	0	33	6
	69	21	1	0	8	4	78	25

Hull-born in 1957, Gordon Stainforth was an England Schoolboy international and also represented Hull and Yorkshire Schoolboys. He joined his home-town club as an apprentice and signed professional terms in 1974. Having made a number of Second Division appearances for the Tigers, Staniforth joined York on loan midway through the 1976-7 season and, a month later in January 1977, he was signed for a fee of £7,500. Gordon was an instant success and was a fine attacking player, chiefly down the left. He had considerable flair and skill and was leading scorer in 1977-8 and 1978-9, winning the 'Clubman of the Year' award in each of these seasons. In October 1979 he was transferred to Carlisle United, then in the Third Division, for a club record fee received of £120,000. Staniforth made 126 League appearances for the Cumbrians and scored 33 goals before moving to Plymouth Argyle in March 1983. The following season he helped the Devon club reach the FA Cup semi-finals. After 91 League games and 19 goals, his next port of call was Newport County and in two seasons at Somerton Park he played in 87 League matches and scored 13 goals. He returned to Bootham Crescent in October 1987 and played on a non-contract basis for the rest of that season. In 1988-89 he played for North Ferriby and, for the second time in his career, came close to a Wembley appearance. The Humberside club narrowly lost to Tamworth in the FA Vase semi-finals. Gordon Staniforth finally hung up his books and in the summer of 1989 he was appointed community officer at York City FC and steward at the social club at Bootham Crescent.

League debut for City v Sheffield Wednesday (a) 27 December 1976, Third Division.

	LEAGUE		*FA CUP*		*FL CUP*		*TOTAL*	
	App	*Gls*	*App*	*Gls*	*App*	*Gls*	*App*	*Gls*
1976-77	28	3	0	0	0	0	28	3
1977-78	46	12	1	0	3	1	50	13
1978-79	45	15	5	4	2	0	52	19
1979-80	9	3	0	0	2	1	11	4
1987-88	15/4	1	4	0	0	0	19/4	1
	143/4	34	10	4	7	2	160/4	40

GORDON STANIFORTH

Signed from Huddersfield Town in August 1949 for what was then the second highest fee paid in York City's history, Alan Stewart was a tall, commanding figure at the heart of City's defence in the 1950s. Born in Newcastle in 1922, he joined Huddersfield during the war and made a number of First Division appearances whilst at Leeds Road. He overcame a series of bad injuries — he missed the whole of the 1952-3 campaign — and played an important role in the season that York reached the FA Cup semi-final. Without doubt one of the best 'stoppers' and headers of the ball to wear City's colours, he received a benefit from the club in 1955. Upon retiring from the game two years later, he worked as a representative for a York brewery.
League debut for City v Barrow (a) 20 August 1949, Third Division North.

ALAN STEWART

	LEAGUE		*FA CUP*		*TOTAL*	
	App	*Gls*	*App*	*Gls*	*App*	*Gls*
1949-50	29	0	1	0	30	0
1950-51	30	0	4	0	34	0
1951-52	20	0	2	0	22	0
1952-53	0	0	0	0	0	0
1953-54	28	1	0	0	28	1
1954-55	35	0	8	0	43	0
1955-56	46	0	5	0	51	0
1956-57	20	0	3	0	23	0
	208	1	23	0	231	1

Born in Saltburn in 1953, John Stone joined Middlesbrough from South Bank in the summer of 1970. He made a couple of Second Division appearances for the 'Boro before signing for City in July 1972. A sound and constructive right-back, Stone immediately established himself in the defence. He did have a few games at centre-forward, however, in his first season at York and scored some vital goals. He had an outstanding season in the promotion campaign of 1973-4. Alas, in September 1974, in a Second Division game against Sunderland, he sustained a serious injury which effectively ended his City career. He was transferred to Darlington in the summer of 1976 and later played for Grimsby and Rotherham.
League debut for City v Tranmere Rovers (a) 15 September 1972, Third Division.

JOHN STONE

	LEAGUE		*FA CUP*		*FL CUP*		*TOTAL*	
	App	*Gls*	*App*	*Gls*	*App*	*Gls*	*App*	*Gls*
1972-73	31	5	3	0	0	0	34	5
1973-74	43	0	2	0	6	0	51	0
1974-75	6	0	0	0	1	0	7	0
1975-76	6	0	0	0	0	0	6	0
	86	5	5	0	7	0	98	5

Sid Storey was perhaps the best bargain buy York City ever made. He joined them from Wombwell in May 1947, for £100, and in nine splendid seasons made over 350 League and Cup appearances for City. Born at Darfield, South Yorkshire, on Christmas Day 1919, Storey was a coalminer and played his early football with mining sides, Ardsley Welfare and Grimethorpe Athletic. He played some wartime games for Huddersfield Town and then joined Wombwell Athletic. A little inside-forward with tremendous talent and skills, he was regarded at one time as the best ball-player in the Northern Section. For nine seasons he was a first-team regular and was a key man in City's attack in 1954-5. It was a big blow when injury caused him to miss the semi-final match against Newcastle at Hillsborough. He did play in the replay, but missed several games at the end of that season, which upset promotion hopes. Storey received a benefit in 1955 but at the end of the following campaign he was rather surprisingly given a free transfer. The club sent him a letter thanking him for his 'fine football' and recorded in the club minute book his 'outstanding service and loyalty'. He joined Second Division Barnsley and made 29 League appearances for the Oakwell club before moving on to Accrington Stanley and Bradford — ending his playing days at Park Avenue when he was 40. He returned to Bootham Crescent in 1960 in the capacity of trainer-coach and served in this position for three years. Throughout his playing days, Sid had remained a coal miner. In his later years he worked for the West Yorkshire Bus Company as a driver.

League debut for City v Wrexham (h) 27 May 1947, Third Division North.

SID STOREY

	LEAGUE		*FA CUP*		*TOTAL*	
	App	*Gls*	*App*	*Gls*	*App*	*Gls*
1946-47	3	0	0	0	3	0
1947-48	41	12	1	0	42	12
1948-49	35	6	3	0	38	6
1949-50	28	1	1	0	29	1
1950-51	39	8	2	0	41	8
1951-52	38	1	3	0	41	1
1952-53	44	3	1	0	45	3
1953-54	36	3	1	0	37	3
1954-55	27	4	7	2	34	6
1955-56	37	2	5	0	42	2
	328	40	24	2	352	42

An outstanding centre-half and captain, Barry Swallow led City from the Fourth to the Second Division in the 1970s. Son of Ernie Swallow, who had played in the Doncaster Rovers Third Division North championship side in 1946-7, Barry was born in Doncaster in 1942 and played for Doncaster Boys and Yorkshire Boys. Peter Docherty, the Doncaster manager, invited him to join the groundstaff at Belle Vue when he left school and at the age of 17 he signed professional forms. He was given his Football League debut in October 1960 and made 51 League appearances for Rovers before joining Crewe Alexandra for a small fee in August 1962. It was to be the only club outside Yorkshire that Swallow played for and after only one season at Gresty Road, in which he played in 14 League games as Alexandra won promotion to the Third Division, he was transferred to Barnsley. Swallow captained the Oakwell club and made 97 League appearances before his next move, to Bradford City in February 1967. He helped them to promotion in 1968-9 and on 29 October 1969 was signed for York by Tom Johnston for £3,000. In seven seasons he was to make over 300 League and Cup appearances and proved one of City's best-ever signings. He led the side to promotion to the Third Division in 1970-71 and then to the Second Division for the first time in their history in 1973-4. Upon retiring in 1976, he stayed in York and, with his wife Elisabeth, went into the licensing trade and then hotel ownership. In August 1981 he became a City director and had a spell as caretaker manager from March to May 1982, during which time he was instrumental in bringing Denis Smith to York. In September and October 1988, he again filled that capacity prior to the appointment of John Bird. Without doubt Barry Swallow will go down as one of the most important figures in the history of York City.

BARRY SWALLOW

League debut for City v Southend United (h) 22 November 1969, Fourth Division.

	LEAGUE		*FA CUP*		*FL CUP*		*TOTAL*	
	App	*Gls*	*App*	*Gls*	*App*	*Gls*	*App*	*Gls*
1969-70	28	3	7	2	0	0	35	5
1970-71	44	5	5	0	4	0	53	5
1971-72	46	5	3	1	4	1	53	7
1972-73	43/1	2	3	0	1	0	47/1	2
1973-74	46	3	2	1	6	1	54	5
1974-75	37	2	2	0	1	0	40	2
1975-76	24	1	2	0	3	0	29	1
	268/1	21	24	4	19	2	311/1	27

Born in Doncaster in 1939, Archie Taylor played for his home-town club as an amateur before signing professional forms with Bristol City in 1958. He made his League debut in 1959-60 and went on to play for Barnsley, Mansfield Town, Goole Town and Hull City before joining Halifax Town in 1963. In four and a half years at The Shay he made 173 League appearances and scored 18 goals. He had a short spell with Bradford City before moving to Bootham Crescent in October 1968. He scored on his debut and soon became very popular with the fans. He had tremendous pace, coupled with a fierce shot, and could play on either wing. He played an important part in the 1970-71 promotion season, making 39 appearances, but was not retained at the end of the campaign and moved on to non-League football with Gainsborough Trinity. As a schoolboy he played for Doncaster and Yorkshire Boys.
League debut for City v Bradford Park Avenue (h) 5 October 1968, Fourth Division.

	LEAGUE		*FA CUP*		*FL CUP*		*TOTAL*	
	App	*Gls*	*App*	*Gls*	*App*	*Gls*	*App*	*Gls*
1968-69	30	3	3	0	0	0	33	3
1969-70	27	1	5	1	0	0	32	2
1970-71	36/3	5	4	0	4	0	44/3	5
	93/3	9	12	1	4	0	109/3	10

ARCHIE TAYLOR

Son of a former City goalkeeper George Thompson, who played for the club in the Midland League in 1926-7, Des Thompson was born in Southampton in 1928. He had been on the books of Scunthorpe and Gainsborough before City signed him from South Yorkshire club, Dinnington, in January 1951. After only three games in the Reserves, he won a place in the senior side and in his one and a half years at Bootham Crescent was to be the regular first-choice 'keeper. Very agile and a sound handler of the ball, Thompson was an outstanding goalkeeper and soon attracted the attention of leading clubs. In November 1952 he was transferred to First Division Burnley, for the then sizeable fee of £7,350. He spent seven and a half years at Turf Moor and made 62 League appearances before joining Sheffield United in 1955. He was nine years with the Blades, which he spent mostly as understudy to England international Alan Hodgkinson, before retiring from the League scene in 1964. He finished his playing days with Buxton. His brother George was also a goalkeeper of note, in the 1950s and '60s, with Scunthorpe. Preston North End and Carlisle United.
League debut for City v Halifax Town (a) 10 February 1951, Third Division North.

	LEAGUE		*FA CUP*		*TOTAL*	
	App	*Gls*	*App*	*Gls*	*App*	*Gls*
1950-51	19	0	0	0	19	0
1951-52	42	0	3	0	45	0
1952-53	19	0	0	0	19	0
	80	0	3	0	83	0

DES THOMPSON

Oliver Thompson joined York in June 1929 from Queen's Park Rangers and captained the side in their first three seasons of League football. A very constructive left-half, he was an able skipper and his experience was invaluable in those important early days in the Football League. He also figured in the FA Cup triumphs of 1929-30 and 1930-31. Born in Gateshead in 1902, Thompson played for Spennymoor before entering League football with Chesterfield in 1922. He then spent two seasons with QPR before moving to Fulfordgate. After leaving City, he joined Halifax Town and then returned to Chesterfield in 1933. He was to stay at Saltergate as trainer until the 1960s.

League debut for City v Wigan Borough 31 August 1929, Third Division North.

	LEAGUE		*FA CUP*		*TOTAL*	
	App	*Gls*	*App*	*Gls*	*App*	*Gls*
1929-30	42	0	6	0	48	0
1930-31	39	0	5	0	44	0
1931-32	40	2	1	0	41	2
	121	2	12	0	133	2

OLIVER THOMPSON

Born at Bubwith, near Selby, in 1951, Chris Topping joined City in 1967 and became the club's first-ever apprentice professional. He made his League debut as a 17-year-old in December 1968 and quickly established himself in the side. An outstanding defender, he was very good in the air and a keen tackler and was a most consistent performer. He played alongside Barry Swallow in the promotion seasons of 1970-71 and 1973-4, in the centre of the defence, and was an ever-present from September 1970 until April 1978 — an amazing run of 355 consecutive League games, easily a record for the club. He made a total of 463 League and Cup appearances for City, which has been bettered only by Barry Jackson. In 1974-5, City's first season in the Second Division, Chris Topping was voted 'Clubman of the Year'. In May 1978 he was transferred to Huddersfield Town, for £20,000, where he teamed up again with former City boss, Tom Johnston. He spent three years at Leeds Road (43 League appearances) and then, after a spell with Scarborough, became player-manager of Northern League side Northallerton Town. Upon retiring from football he was a manager at a mushroom farm near his home at Cliffe, Selby.

League debut for City v Newport County (h) 28 December 1968, Fourth Division.

	LEAGUE		*FA CUP*		*FL CUP*		*TOTAL*	
	App	*Gls*	*App*	*Gls*	*App*	*Gls*	*App*	*Gls*
1968-69	22	1	1	0	0	0	23	1
1969-70	32/2	1	1	0	0	0	33/2	1
1970-71	42	3	6	0	4	0	52	3
1971-72	46	0	3	0	4	1	53	1
1972-73	46	0	3	0	1	0	50	0
1973-74	46	1	2	0	6	0	54	1
1974-75	42	2	2	0	1	0	45	2
1975-76	42	0	2	0	3	0	47	0
1976-77	46	0	5	0	3	0	54	0
1977-78	46	3	1	0	3	1	50	4
	410/2	11	26	0	25	2	461/2	13

CHRIS TOPPING

Local lad Steve Tutill, born in 1969, attended Joseph Rowntree School, New Earswick, played for York City Boys and Yorkshire Boys and was capped eight times for England Schoolboys. He joined City as an associate schoolboy before signing for the club on the Youth Training Scheme in the summer of 1986. After a number of fine displays for the intermediates and reserves, he made his first-team debut in January 1987. A broken ankle was a set-back in 1987-8, but the strong-tackling and determined central defender made a good recovery. By 1989-90 he had established himself in the senior side at the heart of the defence and by the end of the campaign he had made 100 senior appearances for the club. He shows signs of following in the footsteps of the two other local central defenders, Barry Jackson and Chris Topping, who gave York City such outstanding service.
League debut for City v Doncaster Rovers (h) 26 September 1987, Fourth Division.

	LEAGUE		*FA CUP*		*FL CUP*		*OTHERS*		*TOTAL*	
	App	*Gls*	*App*	*Gls*	*App*	*Gls*	*App*	*Gls*	*App*	*Gls*
1986-87	0	0	0	0	0	0	0/1	0	0/1	0
1987-88	20/1	0	4	0	2	0	1/1	0	27/2	0
1988-89	21/1	1	1	0	1	0	1	0	24/1	1
1989-90	42	0	1	0	3	0	3	1	49	1
	83/2	1	6	0	6	0	5/2	1	100/4	2

STEVE TUTILL

Born in Singapore in 1932, Charlie Twissell served in the Royal Navy for a number of years. He was a noted amateur player, gaining several England caps and also playing in the Great Britain team in the Melbourne Olympics of 1956. He joined Plymouth Argyle and made his League debut in 1955-56, turning professional in April 1957. He made 41 League appearances for the Devon club, scoring nine goals, and joined City in November 1958. A fast and direct left winger with a strong shot, he scored five goals in 19 League games as City won promotion that term. He left the club in May 1961 and played in local football for many seasons when he was employed in the insurance business.
League debut for City v Walsall (h) 22 November 1958, Fourth Division.

	LEAGUE		*FA CUP*		*TOTAL*	
	App	*Gls*	*App*	*Gls*	*App*	*Gls*
1958-59	19	5	0	0	19	5
1959-60	28	3	3	0	31	3
1960-61	6	0	0	0	6	0
	53	8	3	0	56	8

CHARLIE TWISSELL

Born in Northwich in 1944, Dennis Walker joined Manchester United from school and played several times in their Central League side. He signed for City in April 1964 and made his debut at the start of the 1964-5 campaign. Walker started at inside-right and made an explosive beginning to his career at Bootham Crescent, topping the scoring charts in early October with 12 goals. He then switched to his customary left-half position and his skilful, constructive midfield play was an important factor as City swept to promotion to the Third Division that season. Walker spent a further three years at York, with variable success, but he was never quite able to maintain his form and promise of his first season. In the summer of 1968 he moved to Cambridge United, then in the Southern League, and he was with them when they were elected to the Football League in 1970. He later played for Poole Town.

League debut for City v Rochdale (h) 22 August 1964, Fourth Division.

	LEAGUE		*FA CUP*		*FL CUP*		*TOTAL*	
	App	*Gls*	*App*	*Gls*	*App*	*Gls*	*App*	*Gls*
1964-65	44	15	1	0	0	0	45	15
1965-66	41	2	1	0	3	0	45	2
1966-67	32	0	6	0	3	0	41	0
1967-68	32/5	2	1	0	0	0	33/5	2
	149/5	19	9	0	6	0	164/5	19

DENNIS WALKER

Goalkeeper Mike Walker was born in Colwyn Bay in 1945 and joined Reading as a junior in January 1963. He signed for Shrewsbury Town in the summer of 1964 and made his League debut in 1964-5. Walker moved to Bootham Crescent in May 1966 and, in his first season at York, contested the goalkeeping berth with Harry Fallon. The following campaign he was first-choice 'keeper and was capped for Wales at Under-23 level. In September 1968 he was transferred to Watford and made a total of 137 appearances in goal for that club. After a spell on loan to Charlton, Walker moved to Colchester United in June 1973 and, in a long and splendid career, made 451 League appearances for United in a stay of over ten years at Layer Road.

League debut for City v Barrow (a) 17 October 1966, Fourth Division.

	LEAGUE		*FA CUP*		*TOTAL*	
	App	*Gls*	*App*	*Gls*	*App*	*Gls*
1966-67	20	0	6	0	26	0
1967-68	37	0	1	0	38	0
1968-69	3	0	0	0	3	0
	60	0	7	0	67	0

MIKE WALKER

Born in London in 1954, Jimmy Walsh joined Watford as an apprentice and signed professional forms in July 1973. He made his League debut in 1973-4 and went on to make 65 League appearances for the Vicarage Road club. He moved to Bootham Crescent in June 1978 and quickly settled down in the defence at left-back. A very fit and fast defender, he was a dedicated and enthusiastic professional, who was very popular during his time at Bootham Crescent. In his career, he scored only two goals and they came in the same match, against Hartlepool in April 1980 when he came on as a substitute and netted twice in a 2-1 City win. He left York in May 1981 and later played for Slough Town.
League debut for City v Hereford United (h) 26 September 1978, Fourth Division.

	LEAGUE		*FA CUP*		*FL CUP*		*TOTAL*	
	App	*Gls*	*App*	*Gls*	*App*	*Gls*	*App*	*Gls*
1978-79	38/1	0	5	0	2	0	45/1	0
1979-80	19/1	2	0	0	2	0	21/1	2
1980-81	34/6	0	2	0	4	0	40/6	0
	91/8	2	7	0	8	0	106/8	2

JIMMY WALSH

Born in Nevis in the West Indies in 1956, Keith Walwyn was a bargain £4,000 signing from Chesterfield in June 1981. He played for Winterton before joining the Saltergate club in November 1979. Walwyn's opportunities were limited with the Spireites and he made only three League appearances, scoring two goals. He was an instant success with York, however, scoring on his debut in the opening game of the 1981-2 campaign. For six seasons he led the City attack with great success and was one of the most feared and respected strikers in the lower leagues. Apart from 1984-5, when he missed a number of games through injury, he notched over 20 League and Cup goals each season and twice (1981-2 and 1986-7) was voted 'Clubman of the Year'. He netted 25 goals in the championship season of 1983-4 and when he left the club in June 1987, he had become the second leading City marksman of all time with 140 League and Cup goals in six magnificent seasons. He was transferred to Blackpool for £35,000 and later moved to Carlisle United.
League debut for City v Tranmere Rovers (a) 29 August 1981, Fourth Division.

	LEAGUE		*FACUP*		*FLCUP*		*OTHERS*		*TOTAL*	
	App	*Gls*	*App*	*Gls*	*App*	*Gls*	*App*	*Gls*	*App*	*Gls*
1981-82	44	23	3	2	2	0	0	0	49	25
1982-83	41	21	4	2	2	1	0	0	47	24
1983-84	45	25	1	0	2	0	1	0	49	25
1984-85	27	9	6	2	4	1	0	0	37	12
1985-86	46	22	7	4	4	3	0	0	57	29
1986-87	42	19	3	1	4	4	3	1	52	25
	245	119	24	11	18	9	4	1	291	140

KEITH WALWYN

Born in Blackpool in 1950, Dennis Wann started his career with his home-town club in 1967 and made a number of League appearances before joining City for a £7,000 fee in January 1972. A talented and pacy left-sided midfield player, he played a vital role as City staved off the relegation threat that season and he continued his good form the following campaign. Sadly, he sustained a broken leg in a Christmas holiday fixture at Chesterfield in 1972 and this badly affected his career with the club. He did not get back into the first team until the closing weeks of the 1973-4 promotion season and was to make only a handful of Second Division appearances for York. He had spells on loan to Southend, Chesterfield and Hartlepool whilst with City and then, in July 1976, was transferred to Darlington. He made 121 League appearances for the Quakers before playing for Rochdale, Blackpool again, Workington and Chester.
League debut for City v Torquay United (a) 29 January 1972, Third Division.

	LEAGUE		*FA CUP*		*FL CUP*		*TOTAL*	
	App	*Gls*	*App*	*Gls*	*App*	*Gls*	*App*	*Gls*
1971-72	19	1	0	0	0	0	19	1
1972-73	23	4	2	0	1	0	26	4
1973-74	5	0	0	0	0	0	5	0
1974-75	10/1	1	0	0	0	0	10/1	1
1975-76	8	1	0	0	0	0	8	1
	65/1	7	2	0	1	0	68/1	7

DENNIS WANN

Born in Consett in 1930, Ernie Wardle was a useful utility player, who could fill a number of defensive positions and served York City well from 1955 to 1960. He played for Billingham Synthonia before signing for Middlesbrough in May 1948, but in six and a half seasons at Ayresome Park, he was unable to break into the First Division side and in January 1955 was transferred to City. Whether at full-back, half-back or in the centre of the defence, Wardle could always be relied upon and was an invaluable member of the first-team squad. In the promotion season of 1958-9, he made 29 League appearances.
League debut for City v Oldham Athletic (h) 5 February 1955, Third Division North.

	LEAGUE		*FA CUP*		*TOTAL*	
	App	*Gls*	*App*	*Gls*	*App*	*Gls*
1954-55	6	0	0	0	6	0
1955-56	4	0	0	0	4	0
1956-57	10	0	3	0	13	0
1957-58	11	1	0	0	11	1
1958-59	29	1	0	0	29	1
	60	2	3	0	63	2

ERNIE WARDLE

Ted Wass gave York City splendid and dedicated service throughout the 1930s. He played at full-back in the early part of his footballing career but, by the time of the great FA Cup runs (1936-8), he had been converted to centre-half and developed into a great 'stopper'. Born near Chesterfield, he was the younger brother of Horace, who for many years played with great distinction for the Spires. Ted Wass was also on Chesterfield's books before moving to York in September 1931. Within two years he had established himself in the first team and for five seasons was a regular in City's defence. He was granted a benefit match in May 1939, when Newcastle United provided the opposition. Throughout his City days, Wass was a part-time professional and lived and worked at Chesterfield as an engineer. During the war he served in the Royal Navy and suffered serious wounds when his minesweeper was sunk off Crete. He died in 1955.
League debut for City v Tranmere Rovers (a) 2 January 1932, Third Division North.

	LEAGUE		*FA CUP*		*TOTAL*	
	App	*Gls*	*App*	*Gls*	*App*	*Gls*
1931-32	1	0	0	0	1	0
1932-33	10	0	0	0	10	0
1933-34	39	0	1	0	40	0
1934-35	33	0	3	0	36	0
1935-36	40	0	1	0	41	0
1936-37	39	0	7	0	46	0
1937-38	41	0	9	0	50	0
1938-39	19	0	1	0	20	0
	222	0	22	0	244	0

TED WASS

Before joining City in June 1964, Derek Weddle had a varied and much-travelled career. Born in Newcastle in 1935, he began his footballing life as a junior with Sunderland, signing professional terms for the Wearsiders in 1953. He moved to Portsmouth in 1956 and made a number of First Division appearances in his three seasons at Fratton Park before having a spell with non-League Cambridge City. He returned to League football with Middlesbrough and then Darlington before coming to York. Weddle, a tall, well-built right winger, made 30 League appearances in the promotion season of 1964-5 and scored 11 goals. His most memorable performance was in March 1965, when he scored a hat-trick in a top-of-the-table clash against Tranmere Rovers at Bootham Crescent, which City won 4-0. He made only 14 Third Division appearances the following season and left the club at the end of that term. A part-time player whilst with City, he lived in Newcastle and was a chiropodist by profession.
League debut for City v Rochdale (h) 22 August 1964, Fourth Division.

	LEAGUE		*FA CUP*		*FL CUP*		*TOTAL*	
	App	*Gls*	*App*	*Gls*	*App*	*Gls*	*App*	*Gls*
1964-65	30	11	2	1	1	0	33	12
1965-66	14	2	1	0	1	0	16	2
	44	13	3	1	2	0	49	14

DEREK WEDDLE

A Glaswegian, born in 1939, Jimmy Weir joined Fulham from Clydebank Juniors in 1957. He made only a handful of League appearances whilst at Craven Cottage and moved to York in June 1960, making his City debut on the opening day of the 1960-61 campaign. A very skilful ball-player, he could operate on either wing, although he chiefly played on the left. He was a fine opportunist and had an outstanding second season when he netted 28 goals in 41 League outings. Weir hit two hat-tricks that term, as City just failed to gain promotion. At times a controversial character, he was, none the less, very popular with the fans and on his day could be a match-winner. He was transferred to Mansfield Town in September 1962 and later moved to Luton Town, Tranmere Rovers and Scarborough.

League debut for City v Millwall (h) 20 August 1960, Fourth Division.

	LEAGUE		FA CUP		FL CUP		TOTAL	
	App	Gls	App	Gls	App	Gls	App	Gls
1960-61	36	10	6	0	0	0	42	10
1961-62	41	28	1	0	6	1	48	29
1962-63	5	0	0	0	0	0	5	0
	82	38	7	0	6	1	95	39

JIMMY WEIR

Born at Askham, near Barrow, in 1903, Norman Wharton was City's first-choice goalkeeper for the last three seasons before the war. A very experienced 'keeper, he had been with a number of clubs before moving to York. He started his playing career with his home town club in 1920, then moved to Preston before returning to Holker Street in 1923. He was transferred to Sheffield United in 1928, for a fee of £250, and from there he joined Norwich City three years later. Wharton won a Third Division South championship medal with the Canaries in 1933-4 and in May 1935, teamed up with Doncaster Rovers. A year later he was signed by City and immediately established himself in the senior side. Arguably the best goalkeeper to play for the club before the war, he figured in all 16 FA Cup ties played in 1936-7 and 1937-8. His finest display was in a fourth-round tie at Swansea in January in 1937, when he gave a magnificent exhibition of goalkeeping in a goalless draw. He moved to Leeds United in August 1939. An electrician by trade, Wharton was quite a character. He took life very seriously and in the dressing-room would talk on every subject under the sun switching from politics to religion, and so on, in a flash and he was the victim of many a leg pull. He died in July 1961, shortly before his 58th birthday.

League debut for City v Halifax Town (a) 29 August 1936, Third Division North.

	LEAGUE		FA CUP		TOTAL	
	App	Gls	App	Gls	App	Gls
1936-37	42	0	7	0	49	0
1937-38	41	0	9	0	50	0
1938-39	34	0	1	0	35	0
	117	0	17	0	134	0

NORMAN WHARTON

Without a doubt one of the most loyal and outstanding players to appear for York City, Norman Wilkinson gave 12 years' fine service to the club. Born in Alnwick in 1931, he played for Hull City as an amateur whilst in the RAF and scored three goals in eight Second Division appearances for the Tigers in 1953-4. Wilkinson joined York City in May 1954 and scored twice on his debut in the famous 6-2 victory at Wrexham on the opening day of the 1954-5 season. The youngest member of the semi-final team, his finest hour was when he netted twice in the 3-1 victory over Tottenham Hotspur in the fifth round. He figured in two promotion-winning campaigns — 1958-9 and 1964-5 — and netted three League hat-tricks in his City career. His total of 127 League goals and, including Cup ties, an overall aggregate of 143 goals are club records which make him the leading scorer in City's history. His chief attributes were his skill in the air, his outstanding positional play and ability to create space and openings. Particularly, however, he will be remembered for his fine sportsmanship and club loyalty. After leaving Bootham Crescent, he played for Annfield Plain in the Wearside League but retained his links with York, acting as a scout in the North-East. Throughout his playing career he was a part-time professional, having a boot-and-shoe repair business. No other York City player has matched his record of 39 FA Cup appearances for the club.

League debut for City v Wrexham (h) 21 August 1954, Third Division North.

	LEAGUE		*FA CUP*		*FL CUP*		*TOTAL*	
	App	*Gls*	*App*	*Gls*	*App*	*Gls*	*App*	*Gls*
1954-55	39	19	8	4	0	0	47	23
1955-56	27	10	5	1	0	0	32	11
1956-57	38	17	3	1	0	0	41	18
1957-58	41	10	5	2	0	0	46	12
1958-59	27	9	1	0	0	0	28	9
1959-60	37	14	3	0	0	0	40	14
1960-61	35	11	6	4	1	0	42	15
1961-62	18	3	1	0	5	0	24	3
1962-63	38	15	4	2	0	0	42	17
1963-64	27	10	1	2	3	0	31	12
1964-65	23	9	2	0	0	0	25	9
1965-66	4	0	0	0	0	0	4	0
	354	127	39	16	9	0	402	143

NORMAN WILKINSON

A most popular, talented and very industrious midfield player, Alan Woods spent six seasons at Bootham Crescent in the 1960s. Born in Doncaster in 1937, Woods was capped for England Schoolboys and England Youth and a teammate at both these levels was Duncan Edwards. Woods joined Tottenham Hotspur as a junior and signed professional forms on his 17th birthday. He played in six First Division games for Spurs before being transferred to Swansea Town in December 1956. After three and a half years at Vetch Field (30 League games) he moved to York in June 1960. A most consistent player, Woods missed only 21 League games in his first five seasons with City and was a key man at wing-half in the promotion season of 1964-5. He left Bootham Crescent at the end of the following season, but remained in York and worked as a dairyman. His son, Neil, who was on City's books as a schoolboy, went on to play for Doncaster Rovers, Glasgow Rangers and Ipswich Town.

League debut for City v Millwall (h) 20 August 1960, Fourth Division.

	LEAGUE		*FA CUP*		*FL CUP*		*TOTAL*	
	App	*Gls*	*App*	*Gls*	*App*	*Gls*	*App*	*Gls*
1960-61	46	1	6	0	1	0	53	1
1961-62	42	1	1	0	7	0	50	1
1962-63	38	0	4	0	2	0	44	0
1963-64	37	2	1	0	3	0	41	2
1964-65	44	0	2	0	1	0	47	0
1965-66	20/1	0	1	0	2	0	23/1	0
	227/1	4	15	0	16	0	258/1	4

ALAN WOODS

Born in Glasgow in 1949, John Woodward was a Scottish Youth international. He was spotted by Arsenal whilst playing for Glasgow junior side, Possilpark, and joined the Gunners in January 1966. He was to make only three League appearances in a five-and-a-half-year stay at Highbury and he was signed by City in July 1971. A versatile utility player, who could operate in either defence or midfield, Woodward took a little while to settle down at Bootham Crescent. He established himself in the senior side in 1972-3 and the following season made 40 League appearances in the promotion campaign. He went on to complete seven seasons with the club and made nearly 200 League and Cup appearances. A somewhat underrated performer, he served the club well. Woodward left City in 1978, but continued to live and work in York and for many years played in local soccer.
League debut for City v Torquay United (h) 18 October 1971, Third Division.

	LEAGUE		FA CUP		FL CUP		TOTAL	
	App	Gls	App	Gls	App	Gls	App	Gls
1971-72	10/4	1	0/1	0	0/1	0	10/6	1
1972-73	35/3	2	3	0	0	0	38/3	2
1973-74	38/2	4	2	0	6	0	46/2	4
1974-75	12/5	0	2	0	0	0	14/5	0
1975-76	33/1	0	2	0	1	0	36/1	0
1976-77	17	0	0	0	3	0	20	0
1977-78	7	0	0	0	3	0	10	0
	152/15	7	9/1	0	13/1	0	174/17	7

JOHN WOODWARD

Born in Rotherham in 1931, Peter Wragg was an England Schoolboy international and joined his home-town club as a junior. He signed professional terms in April 1948 and, in four and a half years at Millmoor, made 31 League appearances and scored four goals. He was transferred to Sheffield United in January 1953 and went on to play 56 League games for the Blades, most of them in the First Division, and scored 17 goals. Just prior to the start of the 1956-7 campaign he was signed by Sam Bartram for a fee of £4,000. Wragg gave City seven seasons' outstanding service and was a most versatile player, equally at home at centre-forward, inside-forward and half-back. Twice (1958-9 and 1960-61) he was leading scorer and he netted three League hat-tricks, plus four goals in a 5-1 win at Crewe in January 1961. A fully-qualified FA coach, he captained the side in the 1958-9 promotion season. He was transferred to Bradford City in July 1963 and spent two seasons at Valley Parade, making 73 League appearances (five goals). Wragg continued to live in York and for some time helped with the running of Haxby in the York & District Football League.
League debut for City v Accrington Stanley (a) 18 August 1956, Third Division North.

	LEAGUE		FA CUP		FL CUP		TOTAL	
	App	Gls	App	Gls	App	Gls	App	Gls
1956-57	46	8	3	1	0	0	49	9
1957-58	42	11	5	1	0	0	47	12
1958-59	41	14	1	0	0	0	42	14
1959-60	39	3	3	0	0	0	42	3
1960-61	32	22	6	0	1	0	39	22
1961-62	42	15	1	0	7	5	50	20
1962-63	22	5	4	2	2	0	28	7
	264	78	23	4	10	5	297	87

PETER WRAGG

Tom Lockie supervising a training session during the 1937-8 season.

Glory Days in the FA Cup

So near to the semi-finals – 1937-8

THIS was the first of York City's two great FA Cup runs which captured the imagination and attention of the whole country. They had to battle through a couple of replays in the first two rounds but, favoured with home draws, it was then a case of records being broken all along the way as City progressed to the quarter-finals. New attendance figures and gate receipts were established at each stage, culminating in the all-time record Bootham crowd in the sixth round.

City played a total of nine Cup ties and used only 13 players, whose names go down in the club's Hall of Fame. They were: Norman Wharton (goalkeeper); Jack Pinder, Eddie Legge and Claude Barrett (full-backs); Dick Duckworth, Ted Wass and Ted Hathway (half-backs); Fred Scott, Sam Earl, Reg Baines, Malcolm Comrie, Jimmy Hughes and Peter Spooner (forwards).

The start of this memorable pre-war FA Cup run began on a rather low key. On 27 November 1937, City entertained Yorkshire rivals Halifax Town and, after a hard, competitive game, they were held to a 1-1 draw. Conditions were good on a bright sunny day and there was the usual Cup-tie atmosphere with Town having a good following of fans.

City made a lively start and visiting goalkeeper Owen made a magnificent save to keep out a close-range Duckworth header. In their first attack, Town gained a shock lead with a well-taken goal by Barkas in the seventh minute. City stormed back and Spooner missed a good chance when he shot over the bar. Town had to defend stoutly and their goalkeeper was constantly in action. Halifax did make one or two counter-attacks but Wass, at the centre of defence, and his colleagues were rarely troubled.

After the interval City forced a number of corners and from one of these they equalized in the 52nd minute. Spooner's cross was headed on by Baines and Hughes nipped in to head home. Play now switched from end to end and the game became very exciting. City got the ball into the net when, in a goalmouth scramble, Spooner shot past Owen. The referee awarded the goal but, upon the intervention of a linesman, disallowed it because of a handling offence.

City continued to press but Town's defence held firm and at the other end Wharton had to make one fine save to thwart Barkas. With the home attack generally lacking sharpness, Halifax held on to earn a replay. For City, Duckworth and Wass took the honours, whilst Owen was outstanding for Town. At inside-right for the visitors was Steve Griffiths, who was to captain City some 14 years later.

York City: Wharton; Barrett, Legge, Duckworth, Wass, Hathway, Scott, Hughes, Baines, Comrie, Spooner.

Halifax Town: Owen; Allsop, Jackson, Green, Craig, Brook, Pritchard, Griffiths, Copeland, Barkas, Hoyland.

Attendance: 7,063 (Receipts £372) *Referee: J.H. Wilkinson (Hull)*

The replay was held at The Shay on Wednesday afternoon, 1 December. Both teams were unchanged but there was a change of referee with L.Dale of Sheffield taking charge. The pitch was in good condition but the weather was rather foggy. Defences were well on top in the early stages and the tackling was keen and hard. Halifax then had a period when they were in command and on a number of occasions City were indebted to goalkeeper Wharton, who made some outstanding saves.

Town almost opened the scoring when Hoyland's fierce shot was deflected on to the crossbar by Wharton but City celebrated this narrow escape by taking a 35th-minute lead. Comrie's pass was taken in his stride by Baines and from 20 yards he cracked a fine shot past Owen.

In the second half, City were generally on top and Baines proved a constant handful for the home defence. Halifax, after their period of supremacy in the first half-hour, faded away and City finished worthy winners. In a good team effort Wharton took the early honours, whilst Wass and Legge were good defenders. Hughes and Comrie worked hard at inside-forward and a crowd of 6,244, paying receipts of £307, saw City earn the right to visit Clapton Orient of Division Three South at the next stage.

On 11 December, City travelled down to Leytonstone to play their first-ever game in London. They were given an enthusiastic reception by their supporters when they took the field on a fine afternoon. The pitch was soft after morning rain.

Orient made a determined start and City had to defend strongly, but Baines headed just wide in a counter-attack and then Spooner shot over the bar. The home side kept up the pressure, however, and scored twice in a two-minute spell. In the 35th minute, Wharton parried a shot from Crawford and Lane tapped the ball into the net. Smith then scored after a fine solo dribble. This quick double blow shook City but in a tremendous second-half rally they fought back in great style. York threw everything into attack but the Clapton defence somehow held on and with 15 minutes left, they were still 2-0 ahead. City looked to be on their way out of the Cup but in the 75th minute they finally broke through and, following a goalmouth tussle, Scott tapped the ball into the net from close range.

This set up a tremendous finish and with only four minutes remaining, to the great delight of the York fans, Comrie equalized after good work by Spooner on the left wing. It had been a magnificent fight-back. Singled out for praise was full-back Legge for his fine captaincy and leadership. He helped rally his team when, at one stage, all appeared lost. Wass was again outstanding at centre-half and Comrie and Hughes had fine games. The line ups were:

Clapton Orient: Hillam; Searle, Hearty, Allan, Taylor, Lawrence, Tully, Lane, Crawford, Smith, Dodds.

York City: Wharton; Barrett, Legge, Duckworth, Wass, Hathway, Scott, Hughes, Baines, Comrie, Spooner.

Attendance: 7,713 (Receipts £430) *Referee: J.McCall (Leicester)*

A lot of work had to be done to make the Bootham Crescent pitch playable for the replay on Wednesday afternoon, 15 December. Several inches of snow had to be cleared and ten tons of sand were applied to the pitch and then rolled level. City were unchanged but Orient made a number of alterations and their team was: Iceton; Searle, Hearty, Allan, Taylor, Heinemann, Tully, Fletcher, Lane, Smith, Dodds.

Mr McCall was again the official in charge and on the difficult pitch City immediately took control, twice hitting the woodwork in the first 15 minutes. Orient weathered the storm, however, and playing some neat controlled football they had a period on top without seriously worrying Wharton and his colleagues.

City pressed strongly in the second half but the Londoners' defended grimly and once or twice made sharp counter-attacks. In the 78th minute the home side got the goal they fully deserved. Scott took a free-kick just outside the penalty area and Baines deflected the ball to Hughes, who scored from close range. In the last minute, Spooner's shot hit a post and then the crowd of 7,599 (£405) greeted City's win. It had been an excellent Cup tie. As reported in the *Northern Echo*: 'Both sides gave a clean, clever and exhilarating display that will go down in the annals of Bootham Crescent as one of the best of Cup matches'.

After four hard-fought Cup ties, City had won their way into the third round of the competition for the fifth time in their history.

Their opponents at the next hurdle were Coventry City, who at the time were joint leaders of the Second Division having lost only two of their 22 League games. The week before the game City had a jolt to their morale when they crashed to a 5-0 home defeat at the hands of Rochdale. Perhaps the visitors were inspired by the fact that Gracie Fields had been made a CBE that day in the New Year's Honours List.

Despite this rude shock inflicted by Rochdale, City approached the Cup tie with quiet optimism. Officials and players of both clubs attended the second performance at the Theatre Royal on the Friday night. City had to make two changes from the side that had done duty in the four previous FA Cup games. Skipper Legge was ruled out through injury. Barrett moved over to left-back and Pinder came into the side. Captain of the Coventry side was Mason, who had played alongside Pinder for England Schoolboys in 1927. At outside-right Earl was preferred to Scott. The York team was captained by Dick Duckworth. Following a keen overnight frost, the sun softened the surface and the pitch was rather sticky. For what was to be an afternoon of drama and excitement the teams lined up as follows.

York City: Wharton; Pinder, Barrett, Duckworth, Wass, Hathway, Earl, Hughes, Baines, Comrie, Spooner.

Coventry City: Morgan; Astley, Metcalfe, MacDonald, Mason, Archer, Taylor, Roberts, McPhee, Davidson, Brown.

Attendance: 13,917 (Receipts £838) *Referee: G.Jones (Nottingham)*

After only five minutes, the large crowd greeted a York goal. Good play by Pinder, Baines and Comrie set up a chance for Spooner, who placed a hard shot wide of goalkeeper Morgan. Within a couple of minutes, however, the Second Division

The 1937-8 FA Cup heroes. Back row (left to right): R.Baines, E.Wass, N.Wharton, C.Barrett, P.Spooner, T.Hathway, T.Lockie (trainer). Front row: S.Earl, M.Comrie, R.Duckworth (captain), J.Pinder, J.Hughes

side equalized. Wharton misjudged a left-wing corner from Brown and the ball spun into the net off the goalkeeper. The lively start continued as both sides attacked in turn but York began to get on top and in the 23rd minute they regained the lead. Comrie crossed the ball from the left and Hughes took the pass in his stride before cracking a fine shot into the net.

York kept up the pressure and Coventry were forced back on defence and had to concede a number of corners. It was no surprise when they went further ahead in the 33rd minute. Duckworth's long cross-field pass was collected by Earl for the right winger to score. The visitors fought back towards the interval but York fully deserved their two-goal half-time advantage.

For 20 minutes after the resumption, Coventry played some fine football. They had the York defence at full stretch and after 62 minutes reduced their arrears when Brown scored. In the last quarter, York defended their lead resolutely and also launched a number of sharp attacks which worried Coventry. In a dramatic last five minutes, Earl was injured and carried off the field unconscious, whilst Wass had blood streaming from a cut head. The crowd urged on the depleted side to a famous victory and at the end they gave an ovation to the York team. The attendance of 13,917 set a new record for Bootham Crescent and, indeed, for any game in York.

In the fourth round City were drawn at home to First Division West Bromwich Albion, a club with fine FA Cup traditions. Albion had won the Cup three times, the most recent time in 1931, and had been beaten Finalists as recently as 1935.

There was great enthusiasm in the city of York and tremendous anticipation. Prices for the game were 5s (25p) for reserved stand seats, 2s 6d (13p) for the enclosure, 2s (10p) for the popular stand and 1s (5p) for the rest of the ground. Juniors paid 6d (3p).

The First Division side arrived in York on the Friday afternoon and both teams visited the Empire theatre that evening. On the day of the match there was a tremendous Cup-tie atmosphere. Queues formed two hours before the start and there was the usual banter as each club paraded a mascot around the ground. Conditions were excellent and the pitch was in good trim, apart from some muddy patches in the centre.

Saturday, 22 January 1938, will go down as one of the truly great days in York City's history. In a sensational finish they knocked out Albion, 3-2, and so reached the last 16 of the competition. It was a match full of thrills with a story-book ending for the local club.

The teams lined up on this unforgettable day as follows:

York City: Wharton; Pinder, Barrett, Duckworth, Wass, Hathway, Earl, Hughes, Baines, Comrie, Spooner.

West Bromwich Albion: Adams; Finch, Shaw, Murphy, Robbins, Sankey, Jones, Clarke, Richardson, Boyes, Johnson.

Attendance: 18,795 (Receipts £1,426) Referee: A.A.Horwood (Walton-on-Thames)

Amongst the new record crowd were the civic heads of both York and West Bromwich and the MP for York, the Hon Charles Wood.

City made a lively start and the visitors were forced on the defensive in the early stages. Adams saved a Baines header and Spooner was only just wide with a fierce cross-shot. It was somewhat against the run of play, then, when Albion took a 23rd-minute lead with a very fortunate goal. Richardson's shot was going wide but struck Pinder and was deflected into the net past the despairing dive of Wharton.

City fought back and twice Baines was brought down in the penalty area but the referee waved play on. Comrie shot inches wide as the home side strove to get on level terms and Wharton made a fine save just before the interval to thwart Jones. City had given a fine first-half display and scarcely deserved to be in arrears.

Upon the resumption Albion came near to increasing their lead when Jones hit the post and, from the rebound, Wharton made a tremendous save. City battled away and in the 55th minute equalized. Baines was tripped in the penalty area and from the resultant spot-kick he beat Adams. With the crowd roaring them on, City had Albion pinned back on defence. Pinder was injured and whilst he was off the field, the visitors regained the lead in the 68th minute. Johnson crossed the ball from the left and Richardson netted from close range. Pinder returned to the fray but Albion were now in the driving seat and with only six minutes left City's gallant Cup run looked to be over.

Then came the dramatic finale. In the 84th minute, Pinder's free-kick from the right was headed into goal by Baines. The crowd went wild with delight and then, with only three minutes remaining, the home centre-forward forced an Earl right-wing cross into the net. Albion protested that Baines had handled but the referee had no doubts and City were ahead. The closing seconds were played amidst scenes of incredible excitement and at the end, thousands spilled on to the field to mob the City team.

The hero of the day was the hat-trick man, Reg Baines, but this was a tremendous team effort. All 11 players rose to the occasion in a magnificent fighting display and York City had written the most glorious chapter in their Cup history to date.

For the first time ever they had beaten First Division opposition. The *Yorkshire Evening Press* described it as 'York's Biggest Football Thrill' and as 'Citizen' wrote: 'It was a stirring sight to see those red-shirted players simply refuse to be beaten'. City had now beaten a club in each section of the League — Halifax Town (Third Division North), Clapton Orient (Third Division South), Coventry City (Division Two) and West Brom (Division One).

'Who is next?' asked the *Northern Echo* as York City looked ahead to the fifth round. The answer was Middlesbrough, who were enjoying a successful season in the First Division (they finished fifth) and who were fancied in a number of quarters to win the Cup that season.

The tie attracted the attention of the whole of North Yorkshire and the Middlesbrough directors inquired about the possibility of the match being switched to Ayresome Park. The York club gave not the slightest thought to doing this and they also turned down the request of Middlesbrough that ground prices be doubled for the game. Main stand seats were increased, however, to 7s 6d (38p), enclosure prices were to be 3s 6d (18p) and the popular stand 2s 6d (13p). The stand tickets at York were disposed of in an hour and a half and, so great was the demand, they could have been sold three or four times over.

To increase the accommodation, over 1,000 tons of material was deposited to improve the banking behind the goals. On the day of the game, Saturday, 12 February, the city of York was stirred to new heights of great enthusiasm. With the influx of thousands of 'Boro fans, all the approaches to the ground were packed with cars and people. Mounted police helped to control the crowds and police were stationed on top of the popular stand to prevent people climbing on to the roof, as had happened in the West Brom match. Several thousand were outside the ground when the gates were opened at 12 noon. The weather was fine and the pitch very firm, but there was a very strong, blustery wind.

City were again unchanged whilst in a strong visitors' attack was the highly-rated young inside-forward, Wilf Mannion.

York City: Wharton; Pinder, Barrett, Duckworth, Wass, Hathway, Earl, Hughes, Baines, Comrie, Spooner.

Middlesbrough: Cumming; Laking, Stuart, Martin, Baxter, Forrest, Birkett, Fenton, Camsell, Mannion, Milne.

Attendance: 23,860 (Receipts £2,193) – both new records

Referee: J.E. Williams (Bolton)

'Boro won the toss and elected to play with the wind, which was blowing directly down the pitch towards the Bootham Crescent end. City had to do a good deal of defending in the first quarter as they struggled somewhat against the strong wind. Wass and his colleagues did their job well, however, and it was 20 minutes before Wharton was called into action, when he made a fine diving save to thwart Camsell.

City gradually settled down and, putting on a fine show, they began to give the visitors' defence a few problems with Baines and Earl both going close. Hughes shot just wide and then Mannion brought the best out of Wharton. It was a good first half for City, who had matched their First Division opponents in every department.

With the wind now in their favour, City resumed strongly and in the 53rd minute came the match-winning goal. Comrie, who was having a fine match, slipped the ball through to Spooner who, with a magnificent left-foot drive, beat Cumming all the way. The York crowd went wild with excitement and in the next minute City almost scored again. A fierce shot by Baines was parried by the 'keeper and Spooner headed the rebound just over the bar.

There was no question of City hanging on to their lead and 'Boro were penned in their own half for long periods. Middlesbrough desperately tried to save the

Above: *City's winning goal against Middlesbrough, scored by Peter Spooner who is hidden by the 'Boro defender on the left of the picture.*
Below: *Action from the fifth-round tie as Middlesbrough are forced back on defence.*

game in the closing stages but the Third Division side deservedly held on to record another famous giantkilling act.

The scenes at the end were even more enthusiastic than those that greeted the West Brom result as fully 5,000 supporters dashed on the pitch to mob their heroes. York City FC, less than 16 years old and in the League for only nine seasons, had reached the quarter-finals of the FA Cup.

Newspaper headline writers revelled in it:

Sports Press: CITY MARCH ON — AMAZING ODD GOAL VICTORY.
EVERY PLAYER A HERO IN A MERITED WIN.
Northern Echo: YORK CITY'S £50 TEAM STILL MAKING HISTORY.
Sunday Express: YORK GOES WILD AS CITY TRIUMPH AGAIN.

The '£50 team' referred to the fact that that was the fee paid to Sheffield United for match-winner Peter Spooner. None of the other players cost any money. It had been another great team effort, with the defence superb. They held the much-vaunted Middlesbrough attack and tackled in masterly fashion.

The draw for the sixth round resulted in another all-Yorkshire clash at Bootham Crescent — York City against Huddersfield Town of the First Division.

As preparation for the game the City players spent a few days at Scarborough. The club were now the football talk of the country and the quarter-final tie was already being described as one which was going to be an epic game in the club's

City players relax in a Scarborough Hotel before the quarter-final match. Norman Wharton, at the piano, leads the sing-song.

history. Hopes were high that York could emulate Millwall who, as a Third Division South club, had reached the semi-final the previous year. No Northern Section club had ever achieved such a feat.

The great day — Saturday, 5 March 1938 — dawned and in spring-like weather the crowds began to assemble several hours before the start. It was reported that spectators from many parts of Britain were present at the match and that the 'eyes of the country were on York City'.

York's MP and Viscount Halifax, the Foreign Secretary, were in attendance, along with the Lord Mayor and Lady Mayoress. The turnstiles had to be closed shortly before the start and every vantage point was taken. The all-time record crowd of 28,123 (paying receipts of £2,735 17s 6d) gave both teams a tremendous reception.

For the fourth successive Cup tie City were unchanged, whilst Town, who were mid-table in the First Division, had to make late alterations. Left-half Boot was unfit and Chivers switched from inside-left to take his place, whilst Watson was brought into the side.

The teams lined up:

York City: Wharton; Pinder, Barrett, Duckworth, Wass, Hathway, Earl, Hughes, Baines, Comrie, Spooner.

Huddersfield Town: Hesford; Craig, Mountford, Willingham, Young, Chivers, Wienand, Barclay, McFadyen, Watson, Beasley.

Attendance: 28,123 (Receipts £2,736) *Referee: L.Brown (London)*

The match proved a typical Cup tie — fast and furious. City made the early running and in the opening 15 minutes Town had to defend resolutely. The ground was absolutely jammed full and spectators in some parts spilled over the barriers and lined the touch-line. The visitors gradually settled down, but the first half certainly belonged to City. Huddersfield had been unsettled by the strong York tackling and also the pace set by the home side.

Town resumed strongly and it was City's turn to defend. Wharton made one magnificent save to stop an effort from Watson and a Beasley shot was deflected against the crossbar. Thrills were coming thick and fast now and in the 71st minute, City were so near to breaking the deadlock. Earl centred the ball from the right and, as Hesford advanced, Spooner headed the ball over the 'keeper. With the crowd about to greet a goal, Mountford made a spectacular clearance on the line and hooked the ball away. City could not have been nearer to scoring.

Huddersfield stormed back and Watson's lobbed shot struck the York crossbar with Wharton beaten. In a tense and dramatic last few minutes, with the crowd in a ferment of excitement, City forced four corners and then at the other end, Wass kicked the ball off the goal-line. In the end, honours were even with both defences coming out on top. All City's rearguard had fine games, none more so than Jack Pinder. For Huddersfield, centre-half Alf Young was outstanding and he kept a tight grip on Reg Baines. (Young was to play for York in 1945-6).

York City, therefore, went into the draw for the semi-finals which resulted as follows:

Aston Villa v Preston North End.

York City or Huddersfield Town v Sunderland.

Interest in the replay at Leeds Road on the Wednesday afternoon of 9 March was immense and the attendance was 58,066 (receipts £4,159). There were remarkable scenes of traffic congestion on the Leeds-Huddersfield road. Some of the fans abandoned their vehicles and walked several miles to the ground.

For what was their 16th FA Cup tie in two seasons, City again fielded the same side, whilst Boot returned for Town. Chivers reverted to inside-forward and McFadyen was omitted.

It was another full-blooded encounter with thrills and spills throughout. City

OUT OF THE MOUTHS OF EVERY FOOTBALL FAN
N THIS COUNTRY, MUST COME A WONDERFUL
ESCRIPTION OF A GREAT LITTLE TEAM
YORK CITY !!

weathered a first-half bombardment by Huddersfield and fought every inch of the way as they faced a strong wind. In the 58th minute, Town took the lead when Watson hit a Weinand cross into the net from close range. Within a couple of minutes, the gallant City team were level when Baines escaped the clutches of Young and, collecting a Hathway pass, beat Hesford.

In the 68th minute came the decisive goal when, following a Beasley corner, Chivers netted in a goalmouth scramble. City battled right until the end and Comrie almost grabbed an equalizer with a backward header. In the end, however, Huddersfield earned their victory but for City there was no disgrace — only honour and added prestige in defeat.

As the *Northern Echo's* headlines proclaimed: 'York City's Run Ended — But No Regrets. Team Have Shed Limelight on the Northern Section.'

Huddersfield Town went on to reach Wembley, where they lost to Preston North End. In the nine Cup ties played, a total of 171,336 people had watched City in action and the receipts amounted to £12,865. Along with the players great praise was due to manager Tom Mitchell and trainer Tom Lockie.

A remarkable and perhaps unique fact was that City played in six rounds at home and were unbeaten. Five times they had been drawn at home and in the second round they figured in a replay at Bootham Crescent. It had been, as the *Football Press* described: 'A glorious chapter in York City's history — the victories against teams from every section of the Football League — the crowds — the receipts — the almost world-wide publicity.

'City supporters will never forget 1937-8. It may be years and years before a York City team equals the Cup performances of the present side.'

In fact, it was to be 17 years before the club once again hit the national headlines as Cup fighters.

One step from Wembley - 1954-5

THIS was arguably York City's finest season. They equalled their best-ever League campaign by finishing fourth in Division Three North, but it was in the FA Cup that they gained everlasting glory by becoming the first Third Division club to play in a semi-final replay.

As in the 1937-8 run, only 13 players were used and their names will live forever in the annals of the club's history. They were: Tommy Forgan and Mick Granger (goalkeepers); Ernie Phillips and George Howe (full-backs); Gordon Brown, Alan Stewart and Ron Spence (half-backs); Billy Hughes, Arthur Bottom, Norman Wilkinson, Sid Storey, Sam McNab and Billy Fenton (forwards).

Billed as 'The Happy Wanderers' — from the title of a popular song of the period — these players reached the very threshold of Wembley and so eclipsed the great feats of the pre-war team. And they achieved all this without a manager because Jimmy McCormick had resigned early in the season. Chief trainer Tom Lockie, who provided the link with the 1937-8 days, was in charge of playing matters.

The draw for the first round provided a lot of local North Yorkshire interest as Midland League club, Scarborough, were paired against City at Bootham Crescent. The Seasiders had a strong contingent of former York players in their line-up — Bert Brenen, Don Barber and Charlie Ware. Another former York player, Alf Patrick, missed the game through injury. The teams lined up:

York City: Granger; Phillips, Howe, Brown, Stewart, Spence, Hughes, Bottom, Wilkinson, Storey, Fenton.

Scarborough: Hyde; Fowler, Myers, Brenen, Lee, Mackenzie, Barber, Mitchell, Pickard, Redhead, Ware.
Attendance: 10,155 (Receipts £971) *Referee: R. Wood (Sunderland)*

On a grey, foggy, 20 November, City so nearly fell at the first hurdle. In retrospect, it proved to be the toughest fight they had on the way to the semi-finals. York went into the game with a run of ten unbeaten League matches under their belt and five successive wins. They were shaken, however, by an enthusiastic 'Boro side, who, encouraged by a large following of fans, put up a tremendous display. Outside-left Ware had a fine match and, especially in the first half, proved a real handful for Ernie Phillips.

City nearly opened the scoring when Brown hit the crossbar but Scarborough celebrated this escape by taking a 24th-minute lead. Ware beat Phillips and his perfect cross was headed into the net by Barber. Although Wilkinson had a header cleared off the line by full-back Myers, the visitors always threatened with some lively attacks and they deserved their interval lead.

City equalized early in the second half, when Hughes crossed the ball for Wilkinson to head firmly into goal. There were thrills at both ends as Hughes went close for City and then Barber for the visitors. In the 70th minute, the non-Leaguers regained the lead when, in a goalmouth scramble, Mitchell drove the ball past Granger. With only ten minutes remaining, it appeared that City were going to be the victims of a Cup shock. But then, after good work by Storey and Hughes, they equalized when Bottom put a low shot into the net from 15 yards. In the 85th minute, City took the lead for the first time when, following a corner, Spence collected a loose ball from just outside the penalty area and sent a lobbed centre-cum-shot high into the net past the despairing goalkeeper.

It had been a close call and the historic events that lay ahead had almost been nipped in the bud. Said the *Sports Press*: 'City through — but left it so late'.

To Scarborough went the honour and glory but for City it was on to the second round and a trip to Dorchester Town of the Western League. The Dorset club were very much an unknown quantity as far as City were concerned and they travelled down south two days before the game and made their headquarters at Bournemouth.

Saturday, 11 December 1954 was a big day for Dorchester Town as, for the first time in their 75-year history, they entertained a League club. City players and officials were given a very hospitable welcome and a special marquee was erected for the use of the directors. With Tommy Forgan still ruled out through injury City were unchanged and the teams lined up as follows:
Dorchester Town: Bird; Gale, Symes, Presley, Cox, West, Curtis, Dobson, Spink, Dare, Moscrop.
York City: Granger; Phillips, Howe, Brown, Stewart, Spence, Hughes, Bottom, Wilkinson, Storey, Fenton.
Attendance: 5,191 (Receipts £445) *Referee: B.M. Griffiths (Newport)*

The band of the Dorset Regiment, included *On Ilkla Moor Baht 'At* in the selection of music and both teams were greeted enthusiastically as they took the field on a fine, sunny day. About 150 City fans had made the long journey and they saw the home side put up a tremendous first-half display. Town defended strongly and then shook City by taking the lead after half an hour, when Curtis shot a fine goal. For a few minutes the visitors were knocked out of their stride but shortly before the interval, Wilkinson and Hughes set up a chance for Bottom to equalize.

Early in the second half, Dorchester's centre-half, Cox, was injured and after treatment he returned to play on the right wing. Playing some fine football, City now took command and scored three times in ten minutes. Bottom completed his hat-trick by netting twice and a characteristic Wilkinson header put the York side well on top. Gale pulled one back from the penalty-spot for the non-Leaguers and the scoring was completed by Fenton, who sealed a 5-2 win for York.

The Dorchester secretary made a prophetic statement when he said: "I pity any First Division team who meet these continental Yorkshiremen." Former England international star David Jack, who was at the game, said: "York played some really brilliant football and performed like world-beaters in a devastating spell."

The draw for the third round resulted in a glamour tie at Blackpool, then a well-established First Division club who, only 18 months earlier, had won the Cup in the memorable 'Matthews Final', when they beat Bolton 4-3.

The match attracted a lot of excitement and interest and no less than 5,000 fans made the journey over the Pennines to Blackpool on that fine but cold day, 8 January 1955. The City party spent two days at Southport before the game and had Tommy Forgan back after injury.

Apart from the legendary Stanley Matthews on the right wing, the Seasiders also fielded such international stars as Stan Mortensen, Ernie Taylor, Harry Johnston and George Farm. On what was to be a famous afternoon, the teams lined up as follows:

Blackpool: Farm; Gratrix, Garrett, J.Kelly, Johnston, H.Kelly, Matthews, Mudie, Mortensen, Taylor, Perry.

York City: Forgan; Phillips, Howe, Brown, Stewart, Spence, Hughes, Bottom, Wilkinson, Storey, Fenton.

Attendance: 26,030 (Receipts £4,364) *Referee: G.F.Sawyer (Weston-super-Mare)*

Billy Fenton (left) and Sid Storey – City's goalscorers at Bloomfield Road – putting pressure on Blackpool's defence.

City gave a magnificent performance and fully deserved their 2-0 success. It marked the first and, indeed remains, the only occasion that they have beaten First Division opposition away from home.

After weathering early pressure at Bloomfield Road, City, wearing their change strip of blue shirts, settled into their now familiar skilful close-passing push-and-run game. With the half-back line in outstanding form and George Howe, with intelligent positional play, keeping Matthews quiet, City gradually began to dictate proceedings. In the 37th minute they took the lead when Storey, out on the left, sent in a swerving centre-cum-shot which Farm misjudged and allowed to cross the line. Greatly encouraged by this, City finished the first half strongly with a number of menacing attacks.

Blackpool resumed in determined fashion but City held firm, even though they were handicapped early in the second period by an injury to Billy Hughes which left him limping rather badly on the wing.

There was no question, however, of City hanging on to their lead and Farm was kept busy in the home goal. Then, in the 70th minute, came a classic second goal for the Third Division side.

Wilkinson placed a perfect through-ball to Fenton, who ran on to score from 12 yards with a fine shot.

With 12 minutes remaining, Blackpool were awarded a rather controversial penalty but Forgan rose to the occasion by punching Jim Kelly's spot-kick over the bar.

At the final whistle, City fans mobbed their team and that evening the *Sports Press* spelled it out: '5,000 did like to be beside the seaside'.

Other headlines included:

Sunday Express: OH BLACKPOOL, WHAT A YORKER!

Northern Echo: GIANTKILLING ACT WAS A TRIUMPH OF SKILL.

It had been a tremendous team effort, with particular praise due to George Howe, Alan Stewart and Gordon Brown. The Cup giants Blackpool, with their star-studded international line-up, had been eclipsed.

The City players and officials held a celebration dinner at Clitheroe after the match and a champagne toast was made to the team and trainer by chairman Hugh Kitchin. It had been been a memorable day and one which thousands of York City enthusiasts would never forget. The club received many telegrams of congratulations from far and near and *Pathe News* presented Ernie Phillips with a copy of a film showing highlights of the win.

City had to travel again in the next round, either to Ipswich Town or Bishop Auckland. These teams had drawn 2-2 at Portman Road but in the replay the amateur club comprehensively defeated the Second Division side 3-0 at home.

Bishop Auckland were the top amateur club in the country. They had won the FA Amateur Cup a record number of times and were destined to win it again that season. They operated in the Northern League and had several amateur internationals in their side, most notable of whom was captain Bob Hardisty, who led Great Britain's soccer team in the 1948 Olympics.

It was to be a battle of the giantkillers, on 29 January 1955, to decide who would go forward to the last 16 of the competition. Billed as 'The Bishops v The Minstermen', the match was an all-ticket affair of 15,000, of whom 3,700 were York supporters. City were unchanged from the Blackpool tie and the teams were:

Bishop Auckland: Sharratt; Marshall, Stewart, Hardisty, Cresswell, Nimmins, McKenna, Lewin, Oliver, Major, Edwards.

York City: Forgan; Phillips, Howe, Brown, Stewart, Spence, Hughes, Bottom, Wilkinson, Storey, Fenton.

Attendance: 15,000 (Receipts £1,727) *Referee: T.Jepson (Mansfield)*

The game was a hard-fought affair and City had to overcome spirited opposition

Sid Storey (right) opens the scoring at Bishop Auckland. Other City players are Norman Wilkinson (left) and Billy Hughes (centre).

before winning 3-1. The first half was very even. Storey opened the scoring in the sixth minute with a well-placed left-foot shot, but the home side equalized immediately when Edwards swept the ball past Forgan. These quick goals had the capacity crowd on their toes and play switched from end to end in thrilling fashion. Sharratt made some fine saves as City pressed forward, but Auckland also brought the best out of Phillips and his colleagues.

The early part of the second half followed a similar pattern but gradually City began to get on top and their clever approach work had the home side at full stretch. Auckland were still dangerous on the break but eventually City broke through and a couple of late Bottom goals settled the tie. In the 79th minute, the inside-forward collected a pass from Fenton, side-stepped a defender and then coolly placed the ball into the net. In the 84th minute, Hughes was tripped in the penalty area and Bottom made it 3-1 from the spot. In the end it was a deserved success and City had reached the fifth round for only the second time in their history.

The *Sports Press* headline read: 'Amateurs eclipsed by Methodical Football'.

City were at last rewarded with a home draw at the next stage and the very

Bishop Auckland's defence is in a tangle as Billy Fenton and Arthur Bottom are ready to pounce.

attractive opposition was to be Tottenham Hotspur. With City now gaining a reputation for the close-passing game, similar to that of the skilful Spurs side, the match was awaited with eager anticipation and was billed as a possible classic. An all-ticket crowd of 21,000 was fixed after consultations with the police authorities and this was some 7,000 below the ground record. The season before, Dave Dunmore had been transferred to the London club and with the money received, City had signed a number of their very successful side. Although Dunmore was out of the Spurs side and was not destined to play in the Cup tie, this added further spice to the match.

It was the first time since 1938 that City had entertained First Division opposition and tickets sold out quickly. The only problem was the weather and a major operation was engaged upon to clear the pitch of snow and ice. The Tottenham party stayed overnight at Harrogate and included amongst their reserves was Alan Woods, later to play for City in the 1960s. Although they were having, by their standards, a moderate First Division season, the White Hart Lane club had a star-studded line up and were parading their new £30,000 capture, Danny Blanchflower from Aston Villa. Other household names were Alf Ramsey, later to manage England's World Cup-winning team of 1966, Mel Hopkins, Tony Marchi, Eddie Baily, Len Duquemin and George Robb. When the gates of Bootham Crescent were opened, two hours before the start on that wintry day of 19 February, the sell-out crowd, who paid a total of £3,845, soon began to pour through them. The groundstaff had done

Norman Wilkinson (second left) coolly slots home goal York's third goal against Spurs.

a good job to get the pitch playable, but conditions were difficult and snow flurries were falling at the kick-off. City were again unchanged and the teams lined up:
York City: Forgan; Phillips, Howe, Brown, Stewart, Spence, Hughes, Bottom, Wilkinson, Storey, Fenton.
Tottenham Hotspur: Reynolds; Ramsey, Hopkins, Blanchflower, Clarke, Marchi, Walters, Baily, Duquemin, Brooks Robb.
Attendance: 21,000 (Receipts £3,845) *Referee: G. Gibson (Manchester)*

It was to be an unforgettable afternoon and, as City swept to a magnificent 3-1 victory, their display was arguably the finest in the club's history.

Although Spurs opened the scoring in the 11th minute, when Robb netted from close range, City, playing some magnificent football, went on to outplay their famous opponents.

Stung by the early reverse, York stormed into attack and the visitors were forced to defend desperately and conceded a number of corners. Then, in the space of two breathtaking minutes, City scored twice. In the 29th minute, Fenton went on a crossfield run pursued by Ramsey. The left winger then back-heeled the ball to Hughes, who crossed perfectly for Wilkinson to head a glorious goal. In the next attack, Bottom beat two defenders and then passed to Wilkinson, whose fierce shot was parried by Reynolds. The ball ran loose and Fenton dashed up to slam it into the net. Pandemonium broke out as the crowd roared their approval and there was no doubt that City deserved the lead. They kept up the pressure and the First Division side were sorely pressed, with Fenton's speed causing a lot of problems.

The Spurs forwards at times played some clever football, but the home defence covered very well. The York team left the field at half-time to a great ovation and then resumed where they had left off, playing Spurs at their own traditional game. The crowd constantly roared approval.

Sid Storey, shadowed by Danny Blanchflower, is too late to prevent Tony Marchi clearing the Tottenham Hotspur lines.

The Londoners desperately tried to get back into the game and came near to equalizing when Baily's header, following a Robb corner, was cleared off the line by Howe. Playing some dazzling football, City twice tore through the visitors defence.

First Fenton shot inches too high and then a Bottom shot was luckily saved by Reynolds with his feet. Forgan had to make one fine save to keep out a Duquemin header, but with ten minutes to go City were still well in command. Then, in the 80th minute, the seal was set on a famous victory. Fenton beat Ramsey on the left and his cross was steered into the net by Wilkinson. Only a magnificent diving save by Reynolds prevented a hat-trick by the centre-forward, when he shot powerfully from 20 yards. At the final whistle, City fans swarmed on to the pitch to acclaim the team that had equalled the 1938 record by reaching the quarter-finals. They had also become the first Northern Section club to reach the last eight of the competition twice. York City had given a display of outstanding football skill and it earned unstinted and widespread praise nation-wide. Many tributes were paid and some of the headlines spelled out City's triumph.

Sports Press: CITY GIANTKILLERS DO IT AGAIN.
SPURS OUTPLAYED FROM START TO FINISH OF THRILLER.
Sunday Express: SPURS' RIDE ENDS AT YORK.
News Chronicle: YORK CITY LOOKED LIKE 1950 SPURS SIDE.
Daily Express: NO FLUKE: IT MIGHT HAVE BEEN SIX!
Yorkshire Post: A FOOTBALLING TRIUMPH.

The following quotes were made after the game:

Danny Blanchflower: "York's standard of play left us speechless. They were better in all departments. They played so well we could not blame the state of the pitch. I think they would have won whatever the conditions."

Alf Ramsey: "York were the better team and deserved to win. They showed they could play good football on the difficult pitch."
Henry Rose (*Daily Express* chief soccer correspondent): "The humiliation, the unmistakable Cup blitz of London's soccer aristocrats was achieved by a team who played the Spurs' own immaculate stylish soccer but played it more quickly, more accurately and played it with more sense of urgency, more spirit."

The game had been billed as a classic and it had certainly been a classical display by the Third Division side. Although Norman Wilkinson was the two-goal hero, it had been another marvellous team display.

Skipper Ernie Phillips said: "Once again it was a triumph for our team work."

Trainer Tom Lockie: "We have no special plan. We try to play correct football and depend a lot on defensive cover. If one man is beaten a teammate doubles back to cover him. There is only one ball on the field. One side cannot have it all the time. We make sure we get most of it."

A few days later, the City chairman received a letter from Arthur Rowe, the Tottenham manager, expressing appreciation, on behalf of his chairman and directors, of the cordial reception and hospitality extended to the Spurs party. He wished City success in the next round and continued success in the League programme.

Amongst a big batch of congratulatory messages were several from former players, including Joe Harron, Jack Middlemiss and Jimmy Cowie of the Midland League days. Once again *Pathe News* presented a copy of the filmed highlights of the game and a week later the directors entertained the players to a dinner at the Ainsty Hotel in York.

City's share of the Tottenham receipts was £906, whilst the entertainment tax of £933 was more than either club received.

The nation was now sitting up and taking notice of this City team which included four part-time players: Sid Storey worked in the mines near Barnsley; Billy Fenton was a draughtsman in York; Gordon Brown was a storeman in Mansfield; Norman Wilkinson worked as a cobbler at his native West Stanley. The team were featured on BBC TV's *Sportsnight* programme and a special filmed profile of Wilkinson was shown.

City had to travel in the sixth round to Notts County, who at the time were well placed in the Second Division. York's initial reaction as they heard the draw, *en route* to a rearranged League game at Stockport, was one of confidence that they could make further progress.

County did represent a stiff hurdle, however, and to reach this stage they had knocked out Middlesbrough, Sheffield Wednesday and Chelsea, who were destined to be First Division champions that season. Included in their side were goalkeeper Gordon Bradley, who had played for Leicester City in the 1949 Cup Final, and centre-half Leon Leuty, who had appeared in Derby County's 1946 Cup-winning team and had England representative honours to his name. At left-half was a Scot by the name of Tom Johnston, who was to play a big part in York City's history in the years ahead.

An all-ticket crowd of 47,301 (receipts £6,425) saw the match and this created a new Meadow Lane record which still stands. City's share of the tickets was 11,225 and this represented, at the time, the biggest exodus of York fans to an away match. The players stayed overnight at Matlock before Saturday, 12 March 1955 dawned bright and sunny. It was a day that will live for ever in the history of York City.

Once again City were unchanged and the players on duty were.

Notts County: Bradley; Southwell, Deans, Adamson, Leuty, Johnston, Wills, Wylie, Jackson, Leverton, Broadbent.

York City: Forgan; Phillips, Howe, Brown, Stewart, Spence, Hughes, Bottom, Wilkinson, Storey, Fenton.

Attendance: 47,301 (Receipts £6,425) *Referee: H.Haworth (Blackburn)*

Pre-match scenes at Meadow Lane with York City fans in confident mood.

Arthur Bottom challenges Notts County's goalkeeper Gordon Bradley. Number-six for Notts is Tom Johnston, later to become arguably City's most successful manager.

A tense and keenly contested Cup tie never reached the standards of the matches against Blackpool, Bishop Auckland and Spurs. On this occasion it was City's resolute and solid defence which carried the day, especially in the second half when County hurled everything into attack.

There were few scoring opportunities in the first period with both defences on top. Bottom put the ball in the net in the tenth minute but was ruled offside, as was Leverton when he shot past Forgan soon after the interval. County had their best spell during this time but Phillips, having an outstanding game, generalled his defence in true captain's style and the home side were held at bay. When County did get through the defence, they found 'keeper Forgan in masterly form. As the game entered its last quarter, City began to be more active in attack and Bradley had to make one fine save to thwart Storey. It was now touch and go as each team attacked in turn and then in the 78th minute came the historic moment, when City scored the all-important goal. Leuty fouled Wilkinson just outside the penalty area to the right of the goal. Hughes took the free-kick and Storey's shot was deflected by Leuty into the path of Bottom, who scored from close range. With this goal the inside-forward equalled the club's scoring record of 31 for the season.

City nearly increased their lead, but Fenton shot wide when well placed. The closing minutes were unbearably tense as County desperately tried to save the game, but City held on to gain an historic victory.

In that night's issue of the *Sports Press*, Wilf Meek wrote: 'Amidst scenes which I have never seen equalled before on a football ground this amazing York City

Goalkeeper Bradley is too late to prevent Arthur Bottom scoring the goal that put York City into the 1955 FA Cup semi-final. Norman Wilkinson and Billy Fenton prepare to celebrate.

team could hardly fight its way to the dressing room after their 1-0 victory over Notts County'.

There was great excitement in York as news came through of the result. Progress of the match had been relayed to Clarence Street, where York RL were in action, and the biggest cheer of the afternoon followed the announcement of City's win. There was cheering in local cinemas as the result was flashed on the screens. Telegrams of congratulations poured into Meadow Lane and the Victoria Hotel in Nottingham where City had based themselves. Amongst these were messages from York's MP, Sir Harry Hylton-Foster, York Rugby League club and Brighton & Hove Albion, who congratulated City on upholding the prestige of the Third Division.

'York City's famous Cup victory was well deserved' read the *Yorkshire Post* headlines. 'This was York City's Finest Hour' spelled out the *Yorkshire Evening Press*.

The scenes in the city of York on that Saturday night were quite incredible. The first of 14 special trains arrived back at 8.10pm and many people assembled at the station to greet those who 'had been there'. To the roar of rattles, bells and wild cheering, the supporters arrived back in triumph. Red and white favours, top-hats, umbrellas, even suits in red and white were everywhere and the station remained a cauldron of noise and excitement until midnight, when the last train arrived. By 9.30pm a crowd of several hundred had congregated in Blossom Street, waiting for the arrival of the City team by coach as they arrived along Tadcaster Road. They had a celebration dinner at the Victoria Hotel. A police car escorted the coach into York and the team were given a heroes' welcome.

The 1938 record had been beaten and City had become only the third Third Division side to reach the semi-finals — Millwall (1936-7) and Port Vale (1953-4) being the others. Present at Meadow Lane were two men who had played such a big part in the pre-war Cup triumphs: Tom Mitchell, who in 1937-8 was the manager, and Reg Baines, the scoring hero of that side. Another of that side, Freddie Scott, had been on duty with Nottingham Forest that day but he was invited to be a guest at City's celebration dinner in the evening.

It had been York's biggest-ever soccer day and as Wilf Meek described it: 'The sort of day you dream about but seldom experience'.

The draw for the semi-finals resulted as follows:
Manchester City v Sunderland at Villa Park.
York City v Huddersfield Town or Newcastle United at Hillsborough.

The Magpies subsequently won the replay and all-ticket crowd of 65,000 was fixed for the Hillsborough tie. York City issued a souvenir brochure to commemorate their history-making feats. Entitled 'Those Happy Wanderers', it provided a pictorial record of the Cup ties. Compiled by Wilf Meek, sports editor of the *Yorkshire Evening Press*, it is now a collectors' item and a prized possession of many a City fan of those now long ago days.

The build-up to the semi-final was naturally one of great excitement and anticipation and there was only one topic of conversation in pubs, clubs and work places.

Letters were received from York exiles from all over the world, especially from servicemen stationed abroad. One letter received was from Vic Wilson, the Yorkshire cricketer who was on tour with the MCC party in Australia and New Zealand. The England side, who had retained the Ashes, had kept a close interest in City's fortunes.

The City team again made their headquarters at the Lilybank Hydro Hotel, Matlock. A special dinner was organized on the eve of the match by the hotel manager, Stanley Connor, and the table was set out as a football pitch with cardboard caricatures of each City player. After dinner, the players watched television on a giant-sized screen.

Some 21,000 York supporters — one fifth of the city's population — made the journey by road and rail to Sheffield on Saturday, 26 March 1955. Twenty special trains were organized, along with many buses and coaches and hundreds more went by private car. West Yorkshire Road Car Company organized 43 coaches and Pullman Coaches sent 26 excursions, whilst several small coach firms arranged special trips.

Heavy and persistent rain did not dampen the fans' spirits as they started to arrive in Sheffield before 10am. The bad news from the City camp that morning was that Sid Storey, who had been injured in training during the week, had failed a fitness test. He had strained back muscles and his place was taken by Sammy McNab. It was the first team change City had been forced to make in the Cup since the second round at Dorchester.

Before the match, the directors of York and Newcastle were entertained to lunch by Sheffield Wednesday at the Grand Hotel. Guests included the Lord Mayor of York (Ald Frank Wright), the City Sheriff (Ald G.J.Bellerby), the Archbishop of York (Dr Cyril Garbett) and Sir Harry Hylton-Foster MP, all of whom later attended the match.

The Hillsborough pitch, although very heavy, had stood up reasonably well to 12 hours of incessant rain and the sides lined up as follows.

York City: Forgan; Phillips, Howe, Brown, Stewart, Spence, Hughes, Bottom, Wilkinson, McNab, Fenton.

Newcastle United: Simpson; Cowell, Batty, Scoular, Stokoe, Casey, White, Davies, Keeble, Milburn, Mitchell.

Attendance: 65,000 (Receipts £16,000) *Referee: J.Kelly (Chorley)*

The band of the 5th West Yorkshire Regiment entertained the crowd before the start. The Dagenham Girl Pipers' Band formed a tunnel as the teams took the field and City's reception was thunderous. Experienced *Yorkshire Post* sportswriter, Richard Ulyatt, described the roar as the most deafening he had ever heard at a sporting occasion and he had reported many a game at Wembley and Hampden Park. Unfortunately, at the time there was a national newspaper strike and City's latest stirring deed went largely unreported. *The Northern Echo* said: 'York City Merited Second Chance after a Great Struggle' and the *Sports Press,* which sold a record number of copies that night, spelled out: 'City Live to Fight Again'.

It was still raining as the teams kicked-off and both sides made early attacks. After settling down quite well, City fell behind in the 14th minute, when Cowell and Davies set up Keeble who, from the left of goal, shot past Forgan. Undismayed, the Third Division side fought back and only a last-ditch tackle by Scoular thwarted Fenton. United went close through Keeble and then after half an hour, City equalized amidst scenes of terrific enthusiasm. Bottom took the ball off Stokoe in midfield and ran 30 yards before drawing Simpson out of goal. He placed his shot into the empty net and then did a jig back to the half-way line, pursued by his delighted teammates. Newcastle were clearly knocked out of their stride and for a time had to defend desperately. Half-time came with honours even.

With conditions deteriorating, both sides found the going hard on the resumption. For the first 25 minutes of the second half, Newcastle did most of the attacking but City defended soundly. Ernie Phillips again played a captain's part and he

City would have achieved even greater success if Arthur Bottom (8) had been able to reach this ball in the Newcastle goalmouth at Hillsborough. If he had scored, York would surely have become the first Third Division side to reach the Final. The other City player is Sam McNab.

The controversial semi-final incident as Arthur Bottom challenges Newcastle goalkeeper Ronnie Simpson.

completely subdued United's talented forward, Bobby Mitchell. In the later stages, City came back well and undoubtedly finished the stronger side. In the 80th minute came an incident which is still often talked about. A tremendous scramble in United's penalty area saw Bottom's header scooped off the line by Simpson's despairing one-handed save. Many thought that the ball had crossed the line but the referee, amidst controversial scenes, awarded a free-kick against Bottom. At the other end, Jackie Milburn shot over from point-blank range and then Fenton shot straight at Simpson when well placed. In a thrilling finish, Forgan made a brave save at Keeble's feet and then Brown headed just wide when City got a last-minute corner.

In the end, a draw was a just result after a gruelling Cup tie played in terrible conditions. City had made history by becoming the first Third Division side to force a semi-final replay and their supporters went home, wet but happy. Because of the heavy rain, resulting in flooding in South Yorkshire, many trains were diverted on the way home. Once again, however, there were great scenes of excitement that evening at York station.

For the replay at Roker Park, City were allocated 12,000 tickets and these were quickly snapped up. The day before the Wednesday afternoon replay, City made their headquarters at Whitley Bay.

The Magpies' defence again under pressure at Hillsborough.

Simpson punches clears a City corner in the semi-final replay at Roker Park. York players are (from left to right) Norman Wilkinson, Billy Fenton and Arthur Bottom.

In direct contrast to the day of the first match, 30 March 1955 was a fine spring-like day and the pitch was firm. City welcomed back Sid Storey, whilst Newcastle also made one change with Crowe taking Casey's place at left-half.

City's Wembley dreams were extinguished that afternoon but only after a gallant fight. They fell behind to a third-minute goal when White netted a close-range shot, following a Milburn pass. City fought back with great spirit and in the first half were the better footballing side, but their attacks broke down on the edge of the Newcastle penalty area. Just before the interval, Fenton hit a great chance into the side netting.

City's hopes received a big blow in the first minute of the second half, when Stewart collided with Keeble and sustained a severe cut over his right eye. He had five stitches inserted and after 12 minutes returned to play on the right wing. Spence took over the cente-half role and did a fine job. The handicapped team put up a tremendous fight, however, and searched gallantly for the equalizer. The result was in doubt right until the last minute, when Keeble headed United's second goal. During the game the whole of York almost came to a standstill as people listened to the radio commentary. At a number of schools and factories, the broadcast was relayed. In York market-place, a loudspeaker was installed and a large crowd congregated to listen.

The great Cup run was over but the team had gained great prestige in defeat and many tributes were paid after the game.

Stan Seymour, the Newcastle chairman, praised the efforts of the City team: "You ought to go and win promotion to the Second Division and you would be a credit to it from what we have seen." E.W.Ditchburn, the Sunderland chairman, said: "York City's football would not only be a credit to the Second Division but also the First and the club had given the Northern Section enhanced prestige."

Sir Stanley Rous, secretary of the Football Association, who was at the game, said that he was most impressed by the wonderful way the York team had fought when a player short.

Later at a dinner at the Metropole Hotel, Stockton, the Lord Mayor of York said: 'The team went out in a blaze of glory'. Hugh Kitchin, the City chairman, reflected that the club was naturally disappointed that they had failed to get to Wembley but felt the team had acquitted themselves well. Most of the 58,239 crowd (receipts £12,000) would have agreed with those sentiments. After the game, the York City supporters remained in good voice — disappointed but not despondent — as they made the trek home.

Newcastle had reached the FA Cup Final for a record tenth time and in May they beat Manchester City 3-1 at Wembley. It was the Geordies' third Cup win in five years.

A total of 247,916 had watched York's eight FA Cup games and receipts amounted to £45,776. After tax and shares to other clubs etc, the surplus to City amounted to approximately £8,000.

A civic reception was held later at the Mansion House and the team went on an Irish tour at the end of the season.

This magnificent City team had been so near to Wembley and those marvellous feats will live for evermore. Certainly supporters who experienced them will always remember those magical days of 1954-5.

For the City players who figured in those triumphs, for Tom Lockie, in charge of the training, for Billy Sherrington, who did the administrative work, and for the directors, it was a case of thanks for the memories.

Postscript

IN October 1969, the famous team assembled for the last time when they played the then present City side in a testimonial match for Gerry Baker. Only Arthur Bottom did not play and seven of the players still lived in York.

The 1954-5 side, 15 years after their hour of glory, was:
Tommy Forgan (bricklayer); Ernie Phillips (tobacco salesman), George Howe (joiner's mate in Wakefield), Gordon Brown (miner at Warsop, near Mansfield), Alan Stewart (brewery representative), Ron Spence (still connected with City as trainer), Billy Hughes (DIY shop owner in Huntington, near York), Norman Wilkinson (shoe machinist at Annfield Plain), Sid Storey (York bus driver), Billy Fenton (draughtsman).

Colin Addison played in Bottom's place. The City top scorer of 1954-5 worked in a Sheffield cutlery factory. Two of the players, Howe and Fenton, have since died.

The Promotion Years

1958-59

THE first season of Fourth Division football saw York City achieve their objective by winning promotion and immediately restoring their Third Division status which they had lost, rather unluckily on goal-average, a year earlier.

The campaign started well and the first three games were won without a goal being conceded. Local centre-half Barry Jackson made his debut on the opening day of the season at Oldham, deputizing for the injured Howard Johnson, and he immediately made a big impact. A four-goal home victory over Crewe Alexandra on 22 September sent York to the top of the table and they occupied that position for six weeks.

Three successive away wins at the beginning of October yielded 11 goals, six of which were netted by Peter Wragg. The highlight was a 5-1 triumph at Hartlepool when the captain hit a hat-trick. A 2-2 draw at Gillingham on 18 October kept York firmly at the top with the following record.
P16 W8 D7 L1 F32 A14 Pts 23.

The following week Exeter won at Bootham Crescent, the only home defeat suffered by York that season. The following Saturday (1 November) City were knocked off their perch at the top when they lost to Coventry City, 2-0 at Highfield Road in front of 24,462 fans. This was a rather unlucky defeat in which Colin Addison missed a penalty and Ken Boyes put through his own goal. Four defeats in six matches proved a set-back and to strengthen the squad, new signings Tommy Brownlee, a centre-forward from Walsall, and Charlie Twissell, an outside-left from Plymouth Argyle, were acquired. A holiday double over Barrow was achieved and the fixture at Bootham Crescent on Boxing Day drew the season's biggest home crowd — 10,382.

A 2-1 defeat at Bradford's Park Avenue ground at the turn of the year, when the home side scored twice in the last three minutes, heralded a run of seven games which yielded only one victory, and at the beginning of February, York lost their place in the top four for the first and only time. It was an exciting win at Watford on 14 February that put them back in the promotion frame. City were two down after only 11 minutes at Vicarage Road, but in a storming fight-back they won in fine style, 3-2.

York lost only one of their last 20 League fixtures and that was a remarkable

Division Four 1958-9

	P	W	D	L	F	A	Pts
Port Vale	46	26	12	8	110	58	64
Coventry C	46	24	12	10	84	47	60
YORK C	46	21	18	7	73	52	60
Shrewsbury T	46	24	10	12	101	63	58
Exeter C	46	23	11	12	87	61	57
Walsall	46	21	10	15	95	64	52
Crystal P	46	20	12	14	90	71	52
Northampton T	46	21	9	16	85	78	51
Millwall	46	20	10	16	76	69	50
Carlisle U	46	19	12	15	62	65	50
Gillingham	46	20	9	17	82	77	49
Torquay U	46	16	12	18	78	77	44
Chester	46	16	12	18	72	84	44
Bradford	46	18	7	21	75	77	43
Watford	46	16	10	20	81	79	42
Darlington	46	13	16	17	66	68	42
Workington	46	12	17	17	63	78	41
Crewe A	16	15	10	21	70	82	40
Hartlepools U	46	15	10	21	74	88	40
Gateshead	46	16	8	22	56	85	40
Oldham A	46	16	4	26	59	84	36
Aldershot	46	14	7	25	63	97	35
Barrow	46	9	10	27	51	104	28
Southport	46	7	12	27	41	86	26

Skipper Peter Wragg, a key figure in York's promotion to Division Three. Wragg was top scorer with 14 goals from 41 League games.

five-goal drubbing at Walsall on 11 April. An important victory was at Exeter in early March when City avenged their home defeat. Promotion was clinched in the penultimate game with a win at Aldershot.

It had been a season of unspectacular success and York owed much to a strong defence. Only Coventry City conceded fewer goals than City. Outstanding were ever-present Tommy Forgan in goal and the always reliable George Howe at left-back. Ernie Wardle and Bob Ramsey also did well, whilst the discovery of the campaign was Barry Jackson. Although his opportunities were limited, Ken Boyes was also a pillar of strength. In midfield Ron Mollatt was an enthusiastic and tireless worker. Billy Hughes, especially in the closing weeks, was at his brilliant best, showing all his outstanding ball skills on the right wing. At the end of the season, along with reserve 'keeper Mick Granger, he was awarded a benefit cheque by the club. Skipper Peter Wragg proved a fine leader and was top scorer with 14 goals. Youngster Colin Addison continued to make good progress and had started to attract the attention of a number of senior clubs.

The reserve team did well in their first season in the North Regional League, finishing fifth out of 19 clubs. Top scorer was Barry Tait with 24 goals.

Average League attendances were 8,124 and in the annual report, a loss of £1,114 was reported. Lack of Cup revenue was partly the reason as, for the first time since 1953-4, City fell at the first hurdle when they lost away to Third Division Bury.

1964-65

THIS was an outstanding season which provided some splendid football as York City narrowly missed winning the Fourth Division title. They finished third, only one point behind champions Brighton & Hove Albion.

The previous season, York had to apply for re-election and, although relying on virtually the same defence, they paraded a number of newcomers in the attack. Centre-forward Paul Aimson was signed from Manchester City and new wingers were Derek Weddle, from Darlington, and Andy Provan, formerly of Barnsley. Inside-forward or wing half Dennis Walker had been signed from Manchester United in April 1964.

A good start was made with three wins and three draws in the opening six games and with the side playing attractive, attacking football, the crowds started to flock back to Bootham Crescent. Just under 9,000 saw an exciting victory over Brighton in late September and the following month, 11,898 saw a thrilling win against Doncaster. In both these matches, Dennis Walker scored twice and, with 12 goals in his first 13 matches, he was being likened to the 1950s scoring hero, Arthur Bottom. The first 15 games yielded 19 points but then in mid-October came a 'mini-slump' with three successive defeats, during which York failed to score. The side slipped to seventh position, which was to be the lowest point of the season. On 27 October, a 1-1 draw was scrambled at Halifax and then followed a magnificent sequence which saw the side win ten of their next 11 League games. A new club record was set with seven straight wins, culminating in a 7-1 thrashing of Chesterfield at Bootham Crescent on Boxing Day.

By now veteran Norman Wilkinson had been recalled to the attack and Walker had switched to midfield. With Billy Rudd scheming at his brilliant best, City produced some magnificent football — the finest seen at York since the great days of the mid-1950s. The sequence of wins was halted with a 1-1 draw in the return game at Saltergate and then followed three more victories, including a thrilling 3-2 success over Chester. Two goals down after half an hour, City staged a magnificent revival to win the points. By now York had moved up to second place behind Tranmere Rovers. On 29 January the teams met at Prenton Park and a crowd of 13,035 saw the Birkenhead club end City's run with a 2-1 victory. Starting with the draw

at Halifax back in October, City had gone 12 matches without defeat. That record was:
P 12 W 10 D 2 F 30 A 13 Pts 22.

In February, York figured in another remarkable game against Doncaster. Incredibly, City found themselves four goals down at Belle Vue after only 25 minutes, but in what proved a wonderful game, they pulled three goals back and also missed a penalty. A vital point was earned at Park Avenue against fellow promotion rivals Bradford in front of 13,745, whilst a week earlier, Newport County were beaten 5-1 at Bootham Crescent. A 3-2 victory over Southport on 12 March sent City to the top of the League. Defeat followed at Wrexham in the next match and Tranmere regained top spot.

York City 1964-5. Back row (left to right): Tom Lockie (manager), Gerry Baker, Barry Jackson, Tommy Forgan, Alan Woods, Dennis Walker, Tommy Heron. Front row: Derek Weddle, Norman Wilkinson, Billy Rudd, Paul Aimson, Andy Provan.

Division Four 1964-5

	P	W	D	L	F	A	Pts
Brighton & HA	46	26	11	9	102	57	63
Millwall	46	23	16	7	78	45	62
YORK C	46	28	6	12	91	56	62
Oxford U	46	23	15	8	87	44	61
Tranmere R	46	27	6	13	99	56	60
Rochdale	46	22	14	10	74	53	58
Bradford	46	20	17	9	86	62	57
Chester	46	25	6	15	119	81	56
Doncaster R	46	20	11	15	84	72	51
Crewe A	46	18	13	15	90	81	49
Torquay U	46	21	7	18	70	70	49
Chesterfield	46	20	8	18	58	70	48
Notts C	46	15	14	17	61	73	44
Wrexham	46	17	9	20	84	92	43
Hartlepools U	46	15	13	18	61	85	43
Newport C	46	17	8	21	85	81	42
Darlington	46	18	6	22	84	87	42
Aldershot	46	15	7	24	64	84	37
Bradford C	46	12	8	26	70	88	32
Southport	46	8	16	22	58	89	32
Barrow	46	12	6	28	59	105	30
Lincoln C	46	11	6	29	58	99	28
Halifax T	46	11	6	29	54	103	28
Stockport C	46	10	7	29	44	87	27

Rovers' visit to York for the big promotion clash on 26 March attracted Bootham Crescent's biggest crowd for four years and with a sensational four-goal victory, City leap-frogged over their rivals to take over the leadership once again. Hero of this victory was Derek Weddle, with a spectacular hat-trick. The other goal was netted by Gerry Baker, deputizing at centre-forward for the injured Paul Aimson.

Championship hopes were high following this success but disappointing defeats at Darlington and Newport in the closing weeks proved crucial. Promotion was clinched in a grand manner with a 4-0 home victory in the final match against Halifax Town, a game watched by 12,719. This win put York back on top, but with games in hand Brighton and Millwall overtook them in the closest finish for years in the Fourth Division. Tranmere, who had led virtually all the way, finished fifth.

It had been a marvellous season and York's 91 League goals has only twice been bettered in the club's history (1954-5 with 92 and 1983-4 with 96). Top marksman was Paul Aimson with 26 League goals and the average League attendance of 7,185 was almost double the previous season. Three of the 1958-9 promotion side — Jackson, Forgan and Wilkinson — played their part in this success. Ever-presents were Tommy Heron, Andy Provan and Billy Rudd, the latter proving to be an inspirational skipper.

The home record was the best in the club's history.
P 23 W 20 D 1 L 2 F 63 A 21.

To celebrate the promotion success, the players, staff and directors were guests at a civic reception at the Mansion House. The Lord Mayor, Councillor S.Palphramand, said that the City team had brought honour to York. In replying, chairman Hugh Kitchin said: "It was a side of which we are proud. We feel that York City FC is a respected club in soccer circles and we treasure a comment from the late Tom Whittaker, when Arsenal manager, that he regarded York City as the Arsenal of the smaller clubs."

The Lord Mayor presented a coloured photograph of the City team to the club management to hang in the boardroom as a permanent reminder of a successful season.

1970-71

CITY'S third promotion success was perhaps their most remarkable. At the end of January their prospects looked slim. A defeat at Southend left them tenth in the table with the following record:
P 26 W 12 D 4 L 10 F 39 A 33 Pts 28

Three successive draws followed and with 17 games remaining, York were ten points behind fourth-placed Northampton.

The season had opened quite brightly and in the early weeks, City were amongst the front runners. Two exciting 4-3 victories were recorded at Crewe and at home to Barrow. In both these games, York came from 3-1 down to take the points. In the latter match, City scored twice in the last two minutes to gain a sensational win.

On 9 November they figured in a remarkable ten-goal affair at Brentford. City were 5-1 down after 65 minutes and heading for a heavy defeat when, in a dramatic

Division Four 1970-71

	P	W	D	L	F	A	Pts
Notts C	46	30	9	7	89	36	69
Bournemouth & BA	46	24	12	10	81	46	60
Oldham A	46	24	11	11	88	63	59
YORK C	46	23	10	13	78	54	56
Chester	46	24	7	15	69	55	55
Colchester U	46	21	12	13	70	54	54
Northampton T	46	19	13	14	63	59	51
Southport	46	21	6	19	63	57	48
Exeter C	46	17	14	15	67	68	48
Workington	46	18	12	16	48	49	48
Stockport C	46	16	14	16	49	65	46
Darlington	46	17	11	18	58	57	45
Aldershot	46	14	17	15	66	71	45
Brentford	46	18	8	20	66	62	44
Crewe A	46	18	8	20	75	76	44
Peterborough U	46	18	7	21	70	71	43
Scunthorpe U	46	15	13	18	56	61	43
Southend U	46	14	15	17	53	66	43
Grimsby T	46	18	7	21	57	71	43
Cambridge U	46	15	13	18	51	66	43
Lincoln C	46	13	13	20	70	71	39
Newport C	46	10	8	28	55	85	28
Hartlepool	46	8	12	26	34	74	28
Barrow	46	7	8	31	51	90	22

One of the teams that helped York gain promotion in 1970-71. Back row (left to right): R.Spence (physiotherapist), Swallow, Topping, Hillyard, Aimson, McMahon, Burrows, Sibbald. Front row: Henderson, Davidson, Taylor, Hewitt, Mackin.

100 seconds, they scored three times to pull the score back to 5-4. The home side notched a sixth goal near the end. This defeat at Griffin Park was City's seventh successive away League reverse and, having lost five games out of six, they dropped below mid-table.

Just before Christmas, talented inside-forward Phil Boyer was transferred to Bournemouth for a club record fee received of £20,000 and the following month the exciting FA Cup ties against Bolton Wanderers and Southampton were staged.

A three-goal victory at Newport on 26 February heralded the start of the tremendous promotion surge as a sequence of ten wins and one draw in 11 games emulated the run of the 1964-5 promotion campaign.

A 4-1 victory over promotion rivals Northampton Town at Bootham Crescent at the end of March put City into the top four and they were not to be displaced.

They were involved in another high-scoring game when they won 5-4 at Lincoln. The half-time score at Sincil Bank was 4-4 and the decisive goal was netted by Paul Aimson near the end.

The unbeaten League run was extended to 16 games which set, at the time, a new club record:

P 16 W 10 D 6 F 37 A 15 Pts 26

The sequence came to an end on 19 April when, in front of Bootham Crescent's biggest crowd for over five years — 14,321 — Oldham Athletic won a vital promotion clash by the only goal. It was City's first home defeat since 31 January, 1970, and so ended a club record run of 36 consecutive unbeaten League and Cup games at Bootham Crescent.

Although they were to lose three of their last four games, City held on to fourth place.

Throughout the campaign, their home form (average League crowds 4,962) had been good. And their record of seven away League victories equalled the number of the previous four seasons totalled together.

The back four of John Mackin, Phil Burrows, Barry Swallow and Chris Topping were outstanding and missed only six games between them. Young goalkeeper Ron Hillyard also did well and in midfield, Dick Hewitt and Ian Davidson had good seasons. As in the promotion season of six years earlier, Paul Aimson again headed

Manager Tom Johnston and players toast the promotion success.

the scoring charts with an identical number of League goals — 26. He had good support from Kevin McMahon, who re-established himself in the side after the departure of Phil Boyer.

Under the inspired and fine leadership of Barry Swallow, York City's storming rally in the second half of the season had won the day.

1973-74

THIS was an historic campaign which saw York City win promotion and so achieve Second Division status for the first time. Having escaped relegation by winning the last game of the 1972-3 season, this was indeed a remarkable and astounding achievement.

York started with an impressive 4-2 victory on the opening day at Charlton but on the third Saturday of the season crashed to a four-goal defeat at Blackburn. Incredibly, however, City were not to lose again in the League until 19 January, when Charlton gained revenge with a 1-0 victory at Bootham Crescent. This four-month period saw a new club record of 21 League games without defeat established. The record was:

P 21 W 10 D 11 F 28 A 10 Pts 31

This was the first season of three-up-three-down in the higher divisions and following a home victory over Southend on 10 November, City were never out of the top three. A week earlier, their game at Brighton had attracted national attention. It was Brian Clough's first match in charge of Albion and 16,017 were at the Goldstone Ground.

During the first half of the campaign, City equalled a Football League record, set by Millwall in 1926, by going 11 matches without conceding a goal. On 29 September they beat Aldershot 3-1 at Bootham Crescent and Jack Howarth headed the visitor's goal. It was 22 December before City let in another League goal and that was in the return game at Aldershot when, by an amazing coincidence, it was Howarth who ended the sequence (17 hours 19 minutes) with another header.

March was a crucial month and City firmly established themselves as promotion favourites with excellent wins at Grimsby and Bournemouth. They completed the double over the Cherries that month with a fine 4-1 win at Bootham Crescent. By now, City were in second place behind Bristol Rovers and when the West Country club visited York on 16 March there was a match of high drama which City won in dramatic style. A few days earlier, City had lost 2-1 in controversial fashion away to Oldham Athletic in front of 15,806.

Although suffering a shock home defeat to lowly Shrewsbury Town at Easter, a holiday double over Huddersfield kept them firmly on course.

Promotion was finally clinched on Saturday, 27 April 1974. Oldham Athletic, whose progress and fortunes had been so interwoven with City in the early 1970s, were the visitors on that historic day. The biggest home crowd of the season — 15,583 (average League attendance 6,660) — saw a tense 1-1 draw. The Latics, with a storming finish, snatched the championship and City finished third behind Bristol Rovers with one point separating the three promoted clubs.

It had been a memorable season and only six League games were lost and 38 goals conceded — both club records.

The players who formed the magnificent defence missed only six games between

Division Three 1973-4

	P	W	D	L	F	A	Pts
Oldham A	46	25	12	9	83	47	62
Bristol R	46	22	17	7	65	33	61
YORK C	46	21	19	6	67	38	61
Wrexham	46	22	12	12	63	43	56
Chesterfield	46	21	14	11	55	42	56
Grimsby T	46	18	15	13	67	50	51
Watford	46	19	12	15	64	56	50
Aldershot	46	19	11	16	65	52	49
Halifax T	46	14	21	11	48	51	49
Huddersfield T	46	17	13	16	56	55	47
AFC Bournemouth	46	16	15	15	54	58	47
Southend U	46	16	14	16	62	62	46
Blackburn R	46	18	10	18	62	64	46
Charlton A	46	19	8	19	66	73	46
Walsall	46	16	13	17	57	48	45
Tranmere R	46	15	15	16	50	44	45
Plymouth A	46	17	10	19	59	54	44
Hereford U	46	14	15	17	53	57	43
Brighton & HA	46	16	11	19	52	58	43
Port Vale	46	14	14	18	52	58	42
Cambridge U	46	13	9	24	48	81	35
Shrewsbury T	46	10	11	25	41	62	31
Southport	46	6	16	24	35	82	28
Rochdale	46	2	17	27	38	94	21

Below: *Barry Swallow (extreme right) beats the Port Vale goalkeeper with a glancing header in September 1973.*

Above: *Phil Burrows shows his delight as he scored against Brighton in March 1974.*
Below: *Jimmy Seal (out of picture) opens the scoring against Cambridge United in February 1974.*

them — Graeme Crawford, John Stone, Barry Swallow, Chris Topping and Phil Burrows. The latter player, who was voted City's first-ever 'Clubman of the Year', was an ever-present for the fourth successive season. Newcomers Barry Lyons and Ian Holmes exercised a big influence in midfield, whilst Chris Jones and Jimmy Seal formed a fine striking partnership. Utility players John Woodward and local lad Cliff Calvert played a big part and youngster Brian Pollard showed much promise on the wing. Although missing a good part of the season owing to a broken leg, Ian Butler's experience was invaluable, especially in the closing weeks. Last but not least, immense credit was due to Barry Swallow for his outstanding leadership in this second promotion success in four years.

Having beaten Second Division clubs Aston Villa and Orient in a successful Football League Cup run, City could look ahead with confidence to the challenges ahead.

The champagne flows again as vice-chairman Gordon Winters tops up the glasses.

1983-84

THIS was a marvellous season as City finished runaway Fourth Division champions and so won the first major honour in their history. It was a record-breaking campaign as York became the first club in the Football League to reach 100 points.

New clubs records set were:

Most wins 31. Most away wins 13. Most goals 96.

Division Four 1983-84

	P	W	D	L	F	A	Pts
YORK C	46	31	8	7	96	39	101
Doncaster R	46	24	14	8	82	53	86
Reading	46	22	16	8	84	56	82
Bristol C	46	24	10	12	70	44	82
Aldershot	46	22	9	15	76	69	75
Blackpool	46	21	9	16	70	52	72
Peterborough U	46	18	14	14	72	48	68
Colchester U	46	17	16	13	69	53	67
Torquay U	46	18	13	15	59	64	67
Tranmere R	46	17	15	14	53	53	66
Hereford U	46	16	15	15	54	53	63
Stockport C	46	17	11	18	60	64	62
Chesterfield	46	15	15	16	59	61	60
Darlington	46	17	8	21	49	50	59
Bury	46	15	14	17	61	64	59
Crewe A	46	16	11	19	56	67	59
Swindon T	46	15	13	18	58	56	58
Northampton T	46	13	14	19	53	78	53
Mansfield T	46	13	13	20	66	70	52
Wrexham	46	11	15	20	59	74	48
Halifax T	46	12	12	22	55	89	48
Rochdale	46	11	13	22	52	80	46
Hartlepool U	46	9	11	26	46	85	38
Chester C	46	7	13	26	45	82	34

John Byrne's penalty is saved in the top-of-the-table clash against Doncaster Rovers in April 1984.

They scored in every home League game for the first time and they finished 15 points clear of runners-up Doncaster Rovers — the biggest margin in League history. They also completed no less than 11 League doubles.

The season opened with three successive 2-0 victories and not once were York out of the top two. After a slight hiccup with successive defeats against Swindon and Bristol City, they regained top spot on 29 October with a win at Northampton and they were never again headed.

Only one home defeat was suffered when Torquay United won 3-2 in November. This reverse ended a tremendous sequence at Bootham Crescent. Since losing to

City players on a triumphant drive through the centre of York. John Byrne holds the Fourth Division championship trophy aloft.

Wimbledon on 16 October 1982, York had played 28 League and Cup games at home and could boast the following magnificent record:
P28 W25 D3 F80 A17

Twice City won five successive away League games as they marched on in fine style. Outstanding performances on their travels included wins at Bury 3-1, Torquay 3-1, Peterborough 2-0 and Aldershot 4-1. The one blot was a three-goal defeat at Blackpool on 4 February, in a game which was featured on BBC TV's *Match of the Day*.

The top-of-the-table clash with Doncaster Rovers attracted 11,297, the biggest Bootham Crescent crowd for eight years (average League attendances were 5,008). Promotion was clinched on 18 April with a 1-1 draw at Chester and the championship was assured ten days later when Hartlepool were beaten.

A 3-0 success in the last home match against Bury lifted York's points tally to 101 and earned them the *Yorkshire Evening Press* headline of 'Team of the Century'.

There were unprecedented scenes of enthusiasm at the end of this game and the crowd swarmed on the pitch to greet their heroes.

The Fourth Division Canon Trophy was presented to captain Roger Jones by Ian Jones, a member of the Football League Management Committee. Later, the team travelled on an open-top bus, driven by former City 1950s hero Sid Storey, to the Mansion House for a civic reception. Over 2,000 fans greeted them on arrival at St Helens Square.

City used only 16 players. There were three ever-presents — John MacPhail, central defender and 'Clubman of the Year', John Byrne, top scorer with 27 League goals, and the ever-reliable Gary Ford, who during the season completed his 250th senior game for the club. Keith Walwyn (25 League goals) and Ricky Sbragia missed only one game each. Left-back Alan Hay made 42 appearances and goalkeeper and skipper Roger Jones played in 41 games. Steve Senior was an ever-present until breaking his leg in the game at Aldershot in April. Other players who played an important part were midfielders Derek Hood (33 games), Malcolm Crosby (31) and Sean Haslegrave (24) and wingmen Brian Pollard (29) and Alan Pearce (17). Chris Evans made 16 appearances.

Other appearances were made by Viv Busby (coach), Mike Astbury, Brian Chippendale and newcomer Keith Houchen.

As Fourth Division champions, York City won £8,000 plus £2,000 for finishing highest scorers. To mark the achievement of 100 points, the sponsors of the League, Canon, awarded an additional £1,000 to City. It was, truly, an unforgettable season.

Second Division Days 1974-76

THE peak of York City's Football League career to date was in the mid 1970s, when they spent two seasons in the Second Division and during that time they were, of course, full members of the League.

The date 17 August 1974 was the red-letter day when York played their first-ever game in Division Two. Aston Villa were the visitors to Bootham Crescent and the 1-1 draw was watched by a slightly disappointing crowd of 9,396.

The season proved a memorable one and City finished a creditable 15th. Highlights were doubles over Norwich City, who won promotion, and Fulham, who were the beaten FA Cup Finalists that season. City also beat Millwall and Bristol Rovers twice.

It was a season of many firsts for York and during the campaign they met no less than 11 clubs in League football for the first time. Most notably they were competing at the same level with Manchester United, Sunderland, Nottingham Forest, Sheffield Wednesday and West Bromwich Albion.

Barry Lyons went down in the record books as the scorer of the club's first Second Division goal in the Villa game, whilst in the next home match, Chris Jones netted the winner as City recorded their first win in the higher grade, against Cardiff City. Jones scored both goals in an away success at Fulham. The visit of Sunderland on 14 September saw the occasion of the first all-ticket League match at Bootham Crescent since April 1949, when Hull City provided the opposition in a Northern Section game. Just under 15,000 (about 1,500 tickets were unsold) saw Sunderland take the points with an 87th-minute goal scored by Vic Halom. John Stone received a serious injury in this match and the right-back did not play again that season.

Three-goal victories in successive home matches against Portsmouth and Bristol Rovers maintained an encouraging start to the season, whilst useful away points were collected at Blackpool and Bristol City.

On 19 October, York travelled to Boundary Park and gained a tremendous 3-2 victory over Oldham. Barry Lyons, Ian Holmes and Jimmy Seal scored the goals and that Saturday evening, City were fifth in the Second Division, their highest-ever placing in the League.

Above: *Chris Jones just fails with this header in the opening game against Villa.*
Below: *Graeme Crawford makes a fine save against Manchester United in December 1974.*

The top of the table read as follows:

	P	W	D	L	F	A	Pts
Manchester United	14	10	3	1	24	7	23
Sunderland	13	7	5	1	22	6	19
Norwich City	13	7	5	1	18	9	19
Aston Villa	13	6	5	2	21	8	17
CITY	14	5	5	4	20	16	15
West Bromwich Albion	12	5	4	3	14	7	14
Hull City	14	4	6	4	16	24	14

This was to prove the high point of the campaign. In the next ten games, York won two and lost eight and slipped to 17th, which was to be their lowest position that term. One bright spot during this period was a home victory over high-flying Norwich City. The low point came in December when four successive defeats were suffered. The heaviest reverse was at Villa Park, where York went down 4-0, and the following week came the eagerly awaited match against Manchester United. Bootham Crescent's biggest League crowd of the season saw the Reds win by the only goal, scored by Stuart Pearson. United were much the better side, however, and as described it was an 'easily forgotten game'.

Over 35,000 at Roker Park on Boxing Day saw Sunderland win 2-0, but City finished 1974 on a high note with a three-goal victory at Bootham Crescent over old rivals, Hull City.

January saw the departure of manager Tom Johnston, but it proved a very profitable month. A home draw against Southampton was followed by a sensational win at Norwich and then a convincing victory at Bootham Crescent against bottom club Sheffield Wednesday was chalked up.

New boss Wilf McGuinness took over the reins and had the best possible start with a vital 3-1 win at Millwall. March was notable for home victories against Bristol City and Fulham. The latter game was a thrilling affair. Easter Saturday saw the big occasion of the trip to Old Trafford. City put on a gallant display but went down 2-1 in front of nearly 47,000 spectators. A run of seven successive home games without defeat ended when West Brom won 3-1 on 12 April. Making

Brave header by Chris Topping (right, partly hidden) in a match against Southampton in January 1975. He later scored the equalizing goal.

his Football League debut that day for Albion was an 18-year-old youngster by the name of Bryan Robson.

A 3-1 victory at Bristol Rovers in the penultimate game ended any fears about relegation and City rounded off their season with a home draw against Oldham Athletic.

Average League crowds of 8,828 were the highest since 1956-7. 'Clubman of the Year' was Chris Topping, an ever-present for the fourth successive season.

Two other players who did not miss a game in 1974-5 were Graeme Crawford and Ian Holmes. Jimmy Seal top scorer with 17 goals, missed only one match. Two of the newcomers, Micky Cave from Bournemouth, and left-back Peter Oliver, from Hearts, who took over from Phil Burrows, also did well. Barry Swallow again led the side with distinction and others to top 30 appearances were Chris Jones and Barry Lyons.

The second season of Second Division football was to prove very disappointing and culminated in relegation. On the opening day, City beat Portsmouth and early results were reasonably satisfactory.

Away matches at West Bromwich and Plymouth were drawn and Oxford were beaten at Bootham Crescent. On their first-ever visit to Stamford Bridge, York gained a useful draw and with two wins and three draws in their opening nine games they were 16th.

Alas, it was all downhill after that and nine of the next ten games were lost.

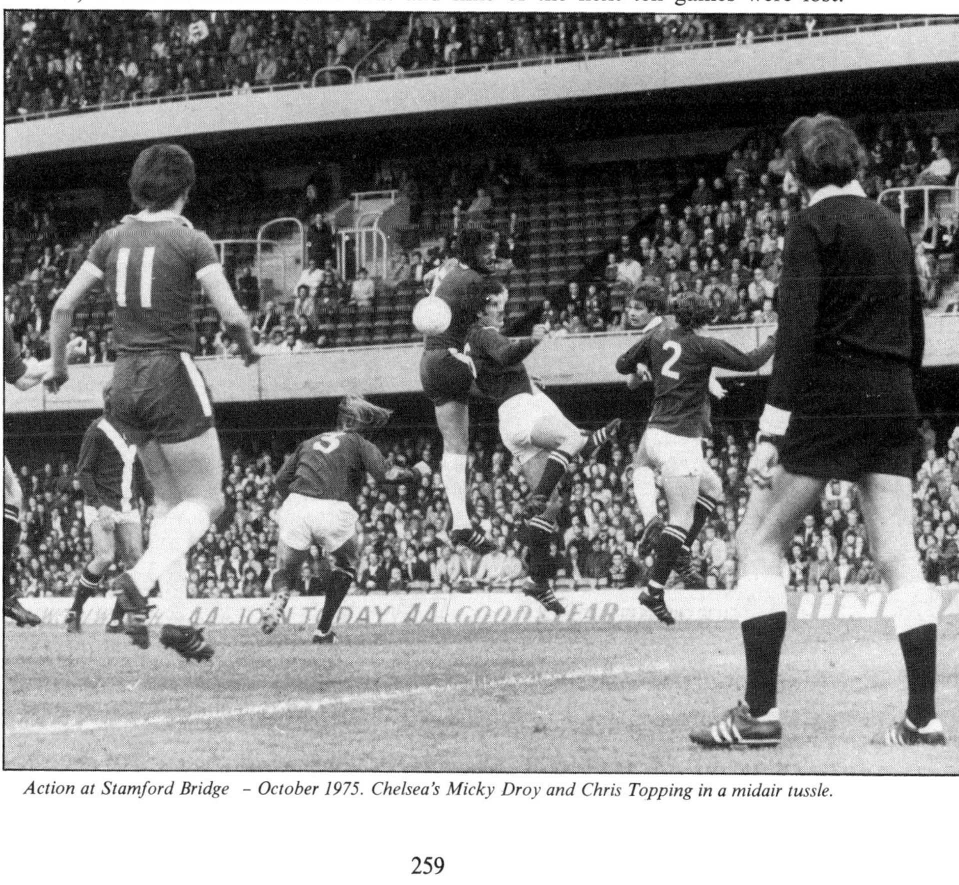

Action at Stamford Bridge – October 1975. Chelsea's Micky Droy and Chris Topping in a midair tussle.

Micky Cave (right) scoring at The Valley against Charlton in January 1976.

The solitary success during this period was a 1-0 home victory over Fulham as York alternated at the bottom of the table with fellow strugglers, Portsmouth.

They staged a 'mini-revival' in December, when they went four games unbeaten, but a run of seven successive defeats in the New Year quashed any hopes of the club escaping the relegation zone. By the end of February they were detached at the foot of the League and practically doomed.

Ironically, the side then produced their best football of the season and won three successive games in fine style. Southampton, who went on to win the FA Cup in May, were beaten 2-1 in a thrilling match. A Micky Cave goal was cancelled out by a Mick Channon effort and then in a storming finish, Jim Hinch scored the winner. Oldham Athletic were beaten and the hat-trick of victories was completed with an exciting 3-2 success over Nottingham Forest at Bootham Crescent. City led 2-0 with 13 minutes to go and then Forest hit back to draw level with two quick goals. In the 86th minute, however, Brian Pollard smashed in the winning goal and for the first time that season, City had scored three goals in a League match. (Two seasons later, Nottingham Forest were League Champions whilst City were having to apply for re-election).

A draw at Hull followed and then at the end of March, York suffered a very unlucky defeat away to promotion-seeking Sunderland. In front of 33,000 spectators, City outplayed the home team in the first half. Twice they hit the woodwork and twice Jim Montgomery made fine saves in the Sunderland goal. First he brilliantly saved an Ian Holmes penalty and then he thwarted Eric McMordie. Very much against the run of play the Rokermen scored in first-half injury-time.

The Roker crowd applauded the City team back on to the field in the second half. Play was more even on the resumption but City still had their chances and at the end, the Sunderland boss, Bob Stokoe, described his teams 1-0 victory as "the luckiest result since I joined the club in 1973."

York's relegation fate was settled on 10 April when, although they gained their fourth successive home victory by beating Plymouth, their rivals in distress also won. City were going down with a flourish, however, as they dented Bolton Wanderers' promotion hopes with a 2-1 victory at Burnden Park.

The Second Division curtain was rung down at Bootham Crescent with a 2-2 draw against Chelsea.

Of their last 11 games, York had won five and drawn three and this enabled them to vacate the bottom position.

The biggest crowd of the season was 15,225 to see the visit of Sunderland in November and average crowds dropped to 5,189.

Micky Cave was 'Clubman of the Year' and top scorer with only eight League goals. The total number of goals scored — 39 — was the lowest in the club's history.

Graeme Crawford and Chris Topping were again ever-presents, the latter for the fifth successive campaign.

So ended York City's Second Division days — two heady seasons of triumph, drama, big occasions and finally disappointment. It had been an unforgettable chapter in the club's history.

Eric McMordie (second right) drives the ball into the net but the 'goal' was disallowed in the match against Nottingham Forest in March 1976.

Division Two 1974-5

	P	W	D	L	F	A	Pts
Manchester U	42	26	9	7	66	30	61
Aston Villa	42	25	8	9	69	32	58
Norwich C	42	20	13	9	58	37	53
Sunderland	42	19	13	10	65	35	51
Bristol C	42	21	8	13	47	33	50
West Brom A	42	18	8	15	54	42	45
Blackpool	42	14	17	11	38	33	45
Hull C	42	15	14	13	40	53	44
Fulham	42	13	16	13	44	39	42
Bolton W	42	15	12	15	45	41	42
Oxford U	42	15	12	15	41	51	42
Orient	42	11	20	11	28	39	42
Southampton	42	15	11	16	53	54	41
Notts C	42	12	16	14	49	59	40
YORK C	42	14	10	18	51	55	38
Nottm F	42	12	14	16	43	55	38
Portsmouth	42	12	13	17	44	54	37
Oldham A	42	10	15	17	40	48	35
Bristol R	42	12	11	19	42	64	35
Millwall	42	10	12	20	44	56	32
Cardiff C	42	9	14	19	36	62	32
Sheffield W	42	5	11	26	29	64	21

Division Two 1975-6

	P	W	D	L	F	A	Pts
Sunderland	42	24	8	10	67	36	56
Bristol C	42	19	15	8	60	35	53
West Brom A	42	20	13	9	50	33	53
Bolton W	42	20	12	10	64	38	52
Notts C	42	19	11	12	60	41	49
Southampton	42	21	7	14	66	50	49
Luton T	42	10	10	13	61	51	48
Nottingham F	42	17	12	13	55	40	46
Charlton A	42	15	8	15	61	72	42
Blackpool	42	14	14	14	40	49	42
Chelsea	42	12	16	14	53	54	40
Fulham	42	13	14	15	45	47	40
Orient	42	13	14	15	37	39	40
Hull C	42	14	11	17	45	49	39
Blackburn R	42	12	14	16	45	50	38
Plymouth A	42	13	12	17	48	54	38
Oldham A	42	13	12	17	57	68	38
Bristol R	42	11	16	15	38	50	38
Carlisle U	42	12	13	17	45	59	37
Oxford U	42	11	11	20	39	59	33
YORK C	42	10	8	24	39	71	28
Portsmouth	42	9	7	26	33	61	25

Although surrounded by Plymouth players, Brian Pollard still managed to crack home a fine goal in April 1976.

Action from York City's last season in the Second Division. Above: Jimmy Seal volleys home against Bristol City at Ashton Gate in November 1975, but York lost 4-1. Below: Micky Cave cracks in the equalizer as York, after three consecutive wins, draw at Hull City in March 1976.

Tom Lockie who played at centre-half for Mansfield Town in this 12-goal epic.

Match to Remember 1 — 16 November 1935

York City 7 Mansfield Town 5

THIS was a remarkable 12-goal affair which produced thrills and spills aplenty. City went into the game fourth from the bottom of Division Three North and had scored only 18 goals in 14 outings. Mansfield were in 14th position.

Making his first appearance of the season was Scottish inside-forward Jimmy Hughes and also drafted into the side was recent signing Duncan Lindsay. They were to play a big part in City's success that afternoon. In the visitors' line-up were former York players, Desmond Fawcett and Tom Lockie, the latter of whom was soon to return to Bootham Crescent as trainer.

The pitch was greasy as the teams kicked-off and the catalogue of goals and incidents unfolded as follows:

Third minute, 0-1. Town took the lead when Johnson back-heeled an Atkinson pass into the net. Mansfield were smart in early attacks.

12th minute, 1-1. Lindsay equalized after good work by Hughes.

18th minute, 2-1. After Bytheway had missed an easy chance for the visitors, a left-foot shot from Hughes put City ahead.

24th minute, 3-1. Hughes put the home team further ahead with a shot into the roof of the net.

City were handicapped by an injury to Albert Banfield which left him limping rather badly. Play switched from end to end with both sides going close, but at half-time the score was still 3-1.

The pitch began to cut up rather badly as the game resumed, but within eight minutes City netted a further two goals to put them well in command.

49th minute, 4-1. Peter Spooner scored after receiving a pass from Hughes.

53rd minute, 5-1. The left winger grabbed his second goal after an opening was provided by Banfield and Green. Town then staged a magnificent fight-back and within 15 minutes scored three times to reduce City's lead to one goal.

55th minute, 5-2. Following a mistake by full-back Legge, Town's winger Bytheway scored.

60th minute, 5-3. After Green had headed against a Mansfield upright Johnson lobbed the ball past Wilson.

68th minute, 5-4. The visitors shook City with a fourth goal when, after another weak clearance by Legge, Clenshaw ran through to easily beat Wilson.

77th minute, 6-4. Banfield headed home a cross by Lindsay but then finally limped off to leave the home side down to ten men.

80th minute, 6-5. Whittam's low shot was deflected by Wass into his own goal.

89th minute, 7-5. City made sure of the points when Green drove a Lindsay centre past Fawcett.

Splendid entertainment had been served up by both teams and the crowd gave them a rousing ovation at the end especially the City side, for whom Lindsay had an outstanding match.

York City: Wilson; Wass, Legge, Hathway, Routledge, Speed, Green, Banfield, Hughes, Lindsay, Spooner.
Mansfield Town; Fawcett; Dronsfield, Darville, Gilmore, Lockie, Slack, Bytheway, Atkinson, Johnson, Whittam, Clenshaw.

Attendance: 3,643 *Referee: R.S. Warr (Bolton)*

Match to Remember 2 1 February 1936

Chester 12 York City 0

ONLY ten weeks after their 12-goal thriller against Mansfield Town, City were involved in another 12-goal match, but this time all the scoring was done by the opponents in what should perhaps be billed as a 'match to forget'.

Three days before the game the Sealand Road ground was under a foot of water after the River Dee overflowed its banks. The local fire brigade spent several hours pumping water off the pitch and the groundstaff worked round the clock, but it was only after great deliberation that the referee decided the game could go ahead. In view of what was to happen York City would wish that it had not taken place!

The pitch was an absolute quagmire with a six-inch coating of mud, but on this surface the home side produced some of the best football of the season and most of their goals were brilliantly taken efforts. They used the flanks to devastating effect with wingmen Horsman and Sargeant in magnificent form and these two players had a hand in all 12 goals.

Sargeant netted four times, Horsman twice and each winger supplied three passes for the other goals. Goalkeeper Wilson could not at all be blamed. He was beaten by first-class shooting and his side were 4-0 down before he actually fielded the ball.

At half-time Chester led by eight goals and a new Football League high-scoring record was in their sights (Stockport 13 Halifax 0 — January 1934 and Tranmere 13 Oldham 4 — December 1935 were the targets to beat). The score was to remain at 9-0, however, for a period of 27 minutes in the second half, during which time City held their own and, indeed, missed a number of chances.

Their best opening came early in the game when Chester led 1-0. In that instance, Speed failed with an easy opportunity. With late goals, the home side took their total to 12 and came near to the record when Wrightson twice hit the crossbar.

It was a great performance by Chester in the mud. City had been outplayed and 'out-generalled' and it was to be a long time before they were to forget that February afternoon in Cheshire.

Chester: Middleton; Common, Hall, Wharton, Wilson, Howarth, Horsman, Hughes, Wrightson, Cresswell, Sargeant.
York City: Wilson; Fox, Legge, Lawie, Wass, Hathway, Green, Routledge, Speed, Lindsay, Spooner.

Attendance: 3,775

York City 6 Rotherham United 1

THIS was arguably City's most sensational League victory and an afternoon of triumph for local centre-forward Alf Patrick. Rotherham travelled to Bootham Crescent Third Division North leaders with the following record: P17 W15 D1 L1 F49 A15 Pts31. City were in fifth position with 19 points from 17 games and in the midst of a good home run which had seen them win six successive matches, scoring 23 goals with two against in the process. The stage was set for a tremendous tussle and with a big following from Rotherham, a huge crowd welcomed the teams in what was a very exciting atmosphere.

Honours were even in the early stages. United threatened through Guest and City full-back, Harry Brigham, had to clear the danger. Then Matt Patrick had a shot well saved by Bolton. With Jimmy Rudd showing fine footwork, City began to get on top and in the 28th minute they took the lead. City's outside-left set up the attack and his neat pass sent Sid Storey down the left unchallenged. His cross to the far post eluded United's 'keeper and Alf Patrick turned the ball into the net. The visitors immediately hit back and the two danger men up front — Guest and Ardron — put pressure on the City defence, but they found Jack Frost and his colleagues in resolute form. Alf Patrick almost increased the lead with a fine shot which just cleared the crossbar and then, on the stroke of half-time, Frost thwarted Ardron by making a tremendous save.

Three minutes after the interval City scored a picture-book second goal. Matt Patrick sent George Ivey racing down the right wing. The diminutive number-seven beat Radford and crossed perfectly for Alf Patrick to crack a tremendous right-foot shot into the roof of the net.

The League leaders retaliated by producing some very smart, fast football but they were shaken when City were awarded a debatable penalty in the 57th minute, for hands against Radford. The referee overruled their protests and Brigham scored from the spot with a low drive. United continued to fight and only a magnificent save by Frost prevented a Shaw goal. This was to be City's day, however, and the crowd roared their approval when Alf Patrick completed his hat trick in the 62nd minute. Storey did the spadework and a fine move ended with the centre-forward placing a right-foot shot into the net as he was challenged by two opponents.

Alf Patrick, who set a new club individual scoring record of five goals, is pictured here in action earlier that season against Mansfield Town. The goalkeeper is Harold Searson later to play for City.

United finally got on the score-sheet after 70 minutes when the Northern Section's leading scorer, Wally Ardron, netted a spectacular goal — his 20th of the season. City were, however, to set the seal on a famous victory with two more goals from Alf Patrick. In the 83rd minute he scored a fine individual goal when he outpaced United's centre-half and then slipped the ball past the advancing 'keeper. Four minutes from the end he netted again in a goalmouth scramble. The local lad received a tremendous ovation and in the closing moments the crowd chanted the goals in sequence: 'One, two, three, four, five, six'.

On the day City had outplayed the League leaders, who had no answer to York's quick moving, short-passing attack. The defence also played their part in keeping United at bay and it was a superb City team effort on what was a record-breaking day. The attendance of 19,216 (receipts £1,271) was a League record for the club, the previous best having been 15,485 (£951) in October 1946 when Doncaster were the visitors. At the time the crowd figure had only been exceeded twice at Bootham Crescent and that was during the 1937-8 FA Cup run, for the matches against Middlesbrough and Huddersfield Town. Alf Patrick's five-goal feat also set a new individual City record in League football. Following this match he was the Northern Section's second-leading scorer with 14 goals behind Ardron. It truly was a day to remember.

York City: Frost; Brigham, Simpson, Brenen, Gale, Allen, Ivey, M.Patrick, A.Patrick, Storey, Rudd.
Rotherham United: Bolton; Selkirk, Radford, Edwards, H.Williams, D.Williams, Grainger, Guest, Ardron, Shaw, McMahon.

Attendance: 19,216 *Referee: F. Walton (Goole)*

Match to Remember 4 — 6 April 1949

Hull City 2 York City 3

A CROWD of over 40,000 — the second-largest ever to watch York in a League match (the highest was the 46,802 at Old Trafford in March 1975) were stunned as Hull saw a two-goal lead swept away in the closing stages of a remarkable match.

The Tigers were top of the Northern Section and heading for the Second Division. Under the player-managership of former England star Raich Carter, soccer on Humberside was having a boom time with record crowds and record results to match. In the first half, on a heavy pitch, Hull were much the better side and they dominated proceedings.

With Carter in fine form the home side were swiftly into their stride and took the lead in the 15th minute. Burbanks and Jensen combined well down the right and Moore finished the move with a well-placed shot. The Hull player-manager increased his side's lead just before the interval, with a neat shot following a Taylor free-kick, and the visitors were glad to reach half-time only two goals in arrears.

In the second half, York came more into the picture, but for a long time it looked as if Hull's lead was going to prove decisive. With 18 minutes remaining, the score remained 2-0 but then came a sensational turnabout as York netted three times to shake the League leaders.

In the 72nd minute Bert Brenen's free-kick was headed across goal by George

Ivey and Alf Patrick turned the ball into the net. With Ivey and Tom Hindle showing speedy and direct play down the wings, the home defence started to creak.

With ten minutes remaining, Alf Patrick shot the equalizer from Hindle's cross and then, in the 84th minute, the York left winger put across a corner and Ivey cracked in goal number-three.

Outstanding for City were Brenen, who in the end got the better of Carter, and centre-half Tom Gale. It was a tremendous fight-back by York and the crowd, who paid receipts of £3,625, were quite dazed at the end. It was only Hull's second home defeat of the season and the match, which was played on a Wednesday evening, produced a then record midweek crowd for the Boothferry Park club.

Hull City: Robinson; Taylor, Fowler, Greenhalgh, Meens, Mellor, Harrison, Jensen, Moore, Carter, Burbanks.
York City: Middleton; Brown, Simpson, Brenen, Gale, Allen, Ivey, M.Patrick, A.Patrick, Storey, Hindle.
Attendance: 40,002

Less than three weeks later, the teams met in the return game at Bootham Crescent (23 April 1949) and Hull gained revenge by winning 3-1. Alf Patrick gave York a first-half lead, but the visitors took the initiative and scored through Jensen, Carter and Moore. The all-ticket crowd of 21,010 set a new League attendance record for York and the receipts were £1,451.

Match to Remember 5 — 21 August 1954

Wrexham 2 York City 6

THE opening day of the season saw a truly remarkable performance by a York City team fielding no less than seven newcomers. Tommy Forgan, Ernie Phillips, George Howe, Les Slatter, Arthur Bottom, Norman Wilkinson and Sam McNab were all making their debuts in what was a sensational start to the campaign.

It was a great team effort, but the hero was Bottom, who netted a hat-trick. The banner headline in the *Sports Press* that evening read:

BOTTOM LOOKS LIKE PUTTING CITY ON TOP

The former Sheffield United forward opened the scoring after only 90 seconds when, following a Gordon Brown free-kick, he shot home from 20 yards. Forgan made one fine save but, City produced some classy football and it was no surprise when they went further ahead in the 27th minute.

Again Bottom was the marksman as he collected a Billy Fenton pass and cracked the ball into the roof of the net from eight yards. Wrexham immediately hit back, however, and reduced their arrears through a fine goal by Bannen.

City swept back and in the 40th minute, Wilkinson ran on to a Bottom pass and drove the ball past Egglestone. On the stroke of half-time the City number-eight completed a memorable debut hat-trick when, following a fine four-man passing movement, he slammed in goal number-four. Within a minute of the restart, City increased their lead. Bottom hit the post with a fine drive and McNab, following up, shot the rebound into the net.

In the 48th minute Tapscott headed past Forgan from close range to make the score 5-2 and, for a time, the home side desperately fought to get back into the game.

But City swung back to take full command and they completed the scoring in the 73rd minute when McNab pin-pointed a pass to Wilkinson, who made no mistake with a shot from near the penalty-spot.

A quote from the local match report read: 'A magnificent 6-2 win at Wrexham with an exhibition of classy, attacking football, the like of which has seldom been seen in the Northern Section'.

The Wrexham reporter summed it up as follows: 'If there is one thing Wrexham FC will want to forget, it will be this first match of the season and the hammering they took at the hands of York City. Six goals from the visitors and no less than they deserved. Wrexham can be grateful the total did not rise higher. York's football was such a delight to watch and they played with understanding and precision. The sheer speed and brilliance of some of the York moves left Wrexham floundering.'

Wrexham: Egglestone; Speed, McGowan, Griffiths, Wynn, Tapscott, Hughes, Hewitt, Bannen, Samuels, Richards.
York City: Forgan; Phillips, Howe, Brown, Stewart, Spence, Slatter, Bottom, Wilkinson, McNab, Fenton.

Attendance: 11,695 *Referee: S.J.Bostock (Manchester)*

Match to Remember 6 — 6 November 1954

Carlisle United 4 York City 5

THIS nine-goal thriller in the mud at Brunton Park saw City lose a three-goal lead and then net the winner in the last minute.

City went into this match unbeaten in eight League games (won five, drawn three) but were forced to make one change. Tommy Forgan had broken a thumb in a practice session and making his Football League debut in goal was Micky Granger, who had just completed his National Service. The local 'keeper had only one senior game to his credit — an FA Cup appearance in a first-round home tie against Barrow in November 1952.

After recent heavy rain, the ground was on the heavy side. In their first attack, City opened the scoring in the fourth minute. Norman Wilkinson put Billy Fenton clear down the left and the winger ran into the penalty area to shoot past goalkeeper McLaren. In the tenth minute, the City left winger netted again after Sid Storey and Wilkinson had spread-eagled the home defence with a fine passing movement.

Granger made one fine save to thwart Ashman and then Arthur Bottom, with a typical effort, smashed home goal number-three from 15 yards. With Storey at his scheming best, City played some fine, constructive football and had the United defence constantly at full stretch. Just before the interval Bottom cracked a fierce drive against the crossbar.

The game took a dramatic turn shortly after the resumption, when the home side scored twice within a minute through Whitehouse. Granger was called into constant action as United staged a tremendous fight-back which culminated in an equalizer in the 68th minute when Whitehouse completed a fine hat-trick.

Play now switched from end to end in the gruelling conditions and the crowd were in a state of high excitement. McLaren pulled off one magnificent save to

Arthur Bottom (right) netting the equalizer against Accrington.

thwart Ron Spence and then in the 80th minute, Brown passed to Fenton, who completed his hat-trick with a fine left-foot shot from 15 yards. Two minutes from the end, Moran beat Granger with a fierce cross-shot, but in a dramatic finish, Fenton raced on to a Wilkinson through-pass to drive the ball past the Carlisle goalkeeper and win the match for City.

It had proved a magnificent game of football which was eventually won by tremendous team spirit and craft. Even in the muddy conditions, City continued to play their close-passing style which, in the end, brought its reward.

Storey and Hughes dribbled in elusive style, whilst Bottom ploughed his way constantly through the home defence. The scoring hero was, of course, Fenton and his four goals were to be his best scoring feat for the club. Granger had a very lively debut and at times was subjected to some heavy challenges. Two or three times he had to have treatment from the trainer and suffered a cut nose and a damaged shoulder, but he pluckily battled on. City, therefore, extended their unbeaten run to nine games after this thrilling victory.

Carlisle United: McLaren; Hill, Mackintosh, Kinloch, Waters, Thompson, Harrison, Whitehouse, Ashman, Atkinson, Moran.
York City: Granger; Phillips, Howe, Brown, Stewart, Spence, Hughes, Bottom, Wilkinson, Storey, Fenton

Attendance: 5,616 *Referee: W.J.Geiger (Manchester)*

Match to Remember 7 — 8 April 1955

York City 1 Accrington Stanley 1

THE 1954-5 season was one of FA Cup glory for York City, but on Good Friday 1955 it was promotion fever that was in the air as thousands made their way to Bootham Crescent. The Third Division North leaders, Accrington Stanley, were the visitors, whilst City, with games in hand, were on the fringe of the pack of clubs chasing for the promotion prize.

A crowd of 19,843 had gained admittance — the second-biggest League attendance in York City's history — when the police ordered the gates to be closed with some 2,000 to 3,000 still outside.

With so much at stake the game was played in a tense and strained atmosphere and, unfortunately, it did not live up to expectations. It was exciting at times, true, but was too fiercely fought with some very heavy tackling, especially by the visitors.

In only the fifth minute, Sid Storey was badly fouled by Hunter. The little inside-forward was off the field receiving treatment for over 15 minutes and when he did return, he was unable to play an effective part in the game. Indeed, the injury proved so serious that he did not play again that season and certainly that was to prove a decisive factor in the closing weeks as City bid for promotion.

On the day, the scheming and creative ability of a fit Storey was missed and it greatly reduced the effectiveness of the City attack, which never quite came to terms with their hard-tackling opponents.

There were occasional flashes of City's capabilities, once when Billy Fenton forced a fine save from McQueen and then when the goalkeeper did well to keep out an effort by Norman Wilkinson.

At times Stanley showed some clever approach play and they took the lead in the 35th minute when Gordon Stewart outwitted his namesake and beat Tommy Forgan from close range.

Accrington had slightly the better of the first half but, as the game progressed after the interval, City gradually improved with Storey able to play a slightly more active part. They deservedly equalized in the 75th minute when, following a free-kick, Wilkinson knocked the ball down to Arthur Bottom, who placed the ball past McQueen from close range.

In a rather frenetic finish, City almost snatched a vital winner but the resolute visitors defence held on.

Skipper Ernie Phillips emerged from the game as the pick of the City side and Accrington defender Harrower was his side's best player.

Tension and drama there were aplenty, but the game was not a worthy spectacle for the huge crowd. It was still, though, an afternoon to remember.

York City: Forgan; Phillips, Howe, Brown, Stewart, Spence, Hughes, Bottom, Wilkinson, Storey, Fenton.
Accrington Stanley: McQueen; Ashe, Harrower, Hunter, Ryden, Bodle, Devlin, Cocker, Stewart, Wright, Scott.

Attendance: 19,843 *Referee: T.Seymour (Wakefield)*

Three days later, the teams met in the return game at Peel Park where the attendance of 15,598 was a League record for Accrington. Bottom and Wilkinson gave City a two-goal lead after half an hour. York then suffered serious injuries to Bottom and Forgan and were effectively reduced to nine men. The home side scored just before and just after half-time to equalize and in the end, badly handicapped City had to stage a rearguard action to salvage a point. Bottom was to miss the last games of the season and, coupled with Storey's absence, the two Accrington games certainly had serious repercussions for City's promotion hopes.

Match to Remember 8 — 17 December 1955

Wrexham 4 York City 5

FOR the second season in succession, City were involved in a remarkable game at The Racecourse. The previous year they dominated throughout in a spectacular 6-2 success, but this time they had to stage a sensational fight-back to win after trailing 4-1 with 25 minutes to go.

It was a grey, murky day in North Wales as City made the early running with Bottom going close in the fifth minute. A remarkable spell of scoring then followed, with three goals in four minutes. Jones opened the scoring in the 11th minute for the home side and, almost immediately, Richards headed goal number-two.

City hit back straight away when Norman Wilkinson netted with a low shot. Both teams provided some fast, entertaining football but it was Wrexham who were calling the tune and in the 19th minute they scored a fine third goal when Evans cracked a tremendous shot past Tommy Forgan. Johnny Linaker, making his only appearance of the season on the right wing, was prominent as City tried to get back into the game.

As half-time approached there were near misses at both ends. Wilkinson headed inches wide and then Forgan scrambled the ball against the post and managed to collect the rebound.

After early second-half pressure, City fell further into arrears in the 56th minute when Evans headed a neat goal following a Richards cross. It appeared that Wrexham had gained revenge for the previous season's defeat, but then came a quite unbelievable transformation as City scored four goals in an amazing ten-minute spell.

In the fading light, the Wrexham defenders were mesmerized as City hit top gear. Billy Fenton started the dramatic rally in the 65th minute, using his speed to beat the defence. Four minutes later he crashed in City's third goal and after 73 minutes he supplied the pass from which Wilkinson tapped in the equalizer. Two minutes later, in a goalmouth scramble, the centre-forward completed his hat-trick to set the seal on a fantastic City rally.

The game was summed up in the *Sports Press* as follows: 'There are some games which linger in the memory and which one never forgets as the years roll by. There is no hesitation that such a one will be City's wonderful feat at Wrexham which thrilled the few York fans present but also surprised and stunned the Welsh crowd. This was soccer at its best.'

At the end, the Wrexham chairman declared it to be the best match and the most brilliant football ever seen on the ground. It was City's seventh successive League and Cup victory.

Wrexham: Waters; Parker, McGowan, Griffiths, Wynn, Tapscott, Jones, Rowley, Evans, Hewitt, Richards.
York City: Forgan; Phillips, Howe, Brown, Stewart, Spence, Linaker, Bottom, Wilkinson, Storey, Fenton.

Attendance: 5,685 *Referee: R.H. Windle (Chesterfield)*

Match to Remember 9 2 February 1957

York City 9 Southport 1

THIS was the day when City went one over the eight to record their biggest victory in the Football League. At the time, York were on the fringe of the promotion race in the Third Division North, whilst Southport were second from the foot of the table. But no one could have anticipated the goal rush and the rout which was to ensue.

The pitch was greasy and it was the visitors who got the ball in the net first, through Miles, but the effort was ruled offside.

Southport, indeed, made quite a lively start, but it was City who opened the scoring in the 14th minute with an Arthur Bottom special. Norman Wilkinson crossed from the left and the inside-right hit the ball first time from outside the penalty area and if flew into the net with tremendous force.

Arthur Bottom, scorer of four goals in the win over Southport.

Billy Fenton went close and then Southport's right-back, Peter Lomas, was badly injured and was unable to take any further part in the game.

City now began to take command and increased their lead in the 27th minute, thanks to a penalty. Bottom was brought down in the area and, from the subsequent spot-kick, he beat goalkeeper Richardson.

Ron Mollatt shot just wide and then Bottom was thwarted by a fine save. The City number-eight was not to be denied, however, and he completed his hat-trick in the 41st minute when he collected a Peter Wragg pass and netted with a low shot via the inside of a post.

On the stroke of half-time he almost scored a fourth, only this time his shot rebounded from the woodwork and went out of play. Right winger Billy Hill made two good attempts soon after the resumption and then City got back on the goal trail in the 59th minute when Wilkinson headed a perfect cross from Fenton wide of the 'keeper.

City's pressure became irresistible and Richardson was simply bombarded, making two particularly fine saves from Bottom and Wilkinson. The hard-pressed Seasiders' defence simply had to crack and crack it did with a dazzling City spell which produced five goals between the 75th and 83rd minutes.

First Bottom scored his fourth goal when he converted a Hill centre and straight from the kick-off, Fenton dribbled through for number-six. Gordon Brown was the next man to get on the score-sheet when he cracked the ball home after a Bottom shot had rebounded to him.

Wilkinson made it eight, after a good work by Bottom, and then Wragg headed a right-wing cross past the bemused Southport 'keeper. The last goal of the game, however, was scored by the visitors when, in the 89th minute, George Howe handled in the penalty area and Charlton netted from the spot.

Even allowing for the fact that Southport played with only ten men for three quarters of the game, they seldom looked like holding a City team which, on the day, fired on all cylinders. The forwards played some devastating football and their positional play and accurate passing was of the highest standard. Bottom had an outstanding game and his tally of four goals was to be his best return for the club.

York City: Forgan; Phillips, Howe, Brown, Cairney, Mollatt, Hill, Bottom, Wilkinson, Wragg, Fenton.

Southport: Richardson; Lomas, Forsyth, Gryba, Taylor, Charlton, Miles, Evans, Bromilow, McIlvenny, McDermott.

Attendance: 8,801 *Referee: A.E.Ellis (Halifax)*

York City team group pictured in 1957-8 which fielded eight of the players trounced by Chester. Back row (left to right): Greensmith, Brown, Spence, Granger, Wilkinson, Johnson. Front row: Hughes, Bottom, Phillips, Wragg, Howe.

Match to Remember 10 — 8 February 1958

Chester 9 York City 2

ALMOST 22 years to the day when City lost 12-0 at Chester, they suffered their heaviest post war defeat in the mud and slush at Sealand Road.

Both teams went into this match in the bottom four of the Northern Section. Before the start, a two-minutes silence was observed in memory of those who had lost their lives in the Munich air disaster two days earlier.

Honours were even in the early stages, but after 18 minutes Jepson beat Mick Granger with a header. Farmer and Bottom went close for City, but the home side increased their lead in the 25th minute, thanks to a fine left-foot volley by Evans.

Then came a crucial incident after half an hour, when Granger was injured in a collision with Jepson. He went off and Gordon Brown donned the green jersey, only to almost immediately punch the ball into his own net following a centre from Evans.

As York counter-attacked, Hughes hit the post and in a good spell for the visitors, Bottom had a shot well saved and Ernie Phillips rattled the crossbar. Granger resumed in goal but, on the stroke of half-time, a bad back-pass by Wragg was intercepted by Jepson, who scored easily to make the interval score 4-0.

For the second half Brown went back in goal and Granger played out for a while. City reduced their arrears in the 53rd minute, when Farmer turned a Bottom shot into the net. Brown made one good save to thwart Pearson, but after an hour he lost the ball in a goalmouth scramble and Richards scored. In the 64th minute Phillips shot a good goal following a corner.

It was only the City captain's second goal for the club in his four years at Bootham Crescent. Two minutes later, a close-range Jepson header made the score 6-2 and in the 69th minute there was further despair for City when Brown fisted out a header from the Chester centre-forward and Ireland, following up, easily scored.

After 75 minutes, a Jepson shot slithered through the hapless City goalkeeper's arms and the scoring was completed five minutes later when Jepson netted his fifth goal.

Even allowing for the unfortunate mishap to Granger, this had been a poor defensive performance by City and, in retrospect, it was to cost them dear. At the end of the season they failed on goal-average to qualify for the new national Third Division and the nine goals conceded that day at Sealand Road were indeed crucial.

Chester: Griffiths; Hughes, Gill, Williams, Handscombe, Anderson, Evans, Ireland, Jepson, Pearson, Richards.
York City: Granger; Phillips, Howe, Brown, Cairney, Wragg, Hughes, Bottom, Robertson, Farmer, Greensmith.
Attendance: 4,812 *Referee: K.Dagnall (Bolton)*

Match to Remember 11 25 April 1959

Aldershot 0 York City 1

THIS was the day when, for the first time in their history, York City clinched a promotion prize. Throughout the season City had been in the top four and they went into their last away match needing two points to be absolutely certain of going up to the Third Division. Aldershot, meanwhile, desperately required the points to escape the re-election zone and the stage was obviously set for a keen contest.

Heavy rain and a strong wind made conditions difficult and Aldershot, with the advantage of the elements in the first half, made the early running.

City defended soundly, however, and Tommy Forgan was rarely troubled. Gradually they settled and George Patterson shot just wide after good work by Ron Mollatt. Further Aldershot pressure followed, but City were looking the more competent side and Terry Farmer forced Brodie to make a fine save. The centre-forward also saw another shot charged down and then Johnny Powell hit a swerving left-wing centre which caused the Aldershot defence problems.

The home side hit back. First Forgan had to save well against Pearson, then Ken Boyes put in a timely tackle to thwart Norris, who was bearing down on goal. City's narrowest escape was when George Howe had to clear the ball off the line with Forgan beaten. Indeed, they did well to survive a lively spell of Aldershot attacking.

Within a minute of the resumption and with the wind and rain now at their backs, City scored the vital goal. Billy Hughes did the spadework down the right wing and his perfect centre was headed firmly past Brodie by Terry Farmer.

In the next minute, Wilkinson got the ball into the net, only for the effort to be disallowed for offside. Hughes was showing fine form as City kept up the pressure, but Aldershot should have equalized when Humphries missed with a good chance. In the closing stages play switched from end to end and both goals had narrow escapes, but City held on to the precious points and were assured of promotion.

The last game of the season, at home to Gateshead, was won and City finished third behind Port Vale and Coventry. A year after losing their Third Division status by virtue of an inferior goal-average, City had therefore made a speedy return and had enjoyed the shortest possible stay in the newly-formed Fourth Division.

Aldershot: Brodie; Price, Jackson, Mundy, McMahon, Pearson, Walters, Stepney, Norris, Humphries, Tyrer.
York City: Forgan; Ramsey, Howe, Patterson, Boyes, Mollatt, Hughes, Wilkinson, Farmer, Wragg, Powell.

Attendance: 2,862 *Referee: W. Clements (West Bromwich)*

Match to Remember 12 7 October 1961

York City 5 Colchester United 0

YORK CITY gave a sparkling display as they outplayed a Colchester United side who, at the time, were clear leaders of the Fourth Division. United came to Bootham Crescent on what was a very wet October day with the following impressive record. P14 W10 D2 L2 F39 A14 Pts22.

The heavy rain affected the attendance and left the pitch in a very greasy condition. The game opened quietly, although City nearly took an early lead when Wally Gould burst through the visitor's defence, only to shoot just wide.

Gradually City took command with Jimmy Weir in fine form and the right winger glanced a header inches wide of an upright. Then John Stainsby cracked in a great shot which was brilliantly saved by Ames.

In isolated United attacks, Barry Jackson was in commanding form and after 28 minutes City took a deserved lead. Alan Woods took a free-kick on the right which Norman Wilkinson headed into the goalmouth and Weir darted in to score with a close-range header.

Encouraged by this, the home side now started to play some brilliant, attacking football which had the League leaders' defence in disarray. Ames was kept busy and had to make a succession of saves as City piled on the pressure, with Stainsby and Weir both going close.

It was no surprise when the lead was increased in the 38th minute, with what was a magnificent goal. City were under pressure in their own penalty area but played their way out of trouble with man-to-man passing down the field. Stainsby collected the ball, shook off a defender and then pin-pointed a pass to Gould who shot first-time into the net.

The crowd rose to the goal and within a couple of minutes they were celebrating a third when the irrepressible Weir dribbled through for his 14th goal of the season, which made him joint top-scorer in the whole of the Football League.

He could have had another just before the interval but, although well-placed, he shot straight at Ames. City resumed where they left off and within a minute were 4-0 in front when Stainsby converted a Wilkinson pass with a fierce shot. Colchester were now completely overrun and it was one-way traffic as shots literally rained in on their goal. In the 57th minute, Gould was tripped in the penalty area and from the resultant spot-kick Peter Wragg notched number-five. After Tommy Forgan was called upon to make a rare save, Gould rattled in a tremendous shot which thudded against the crossbar and then Weir's shot hit the 'keeper and was scrambled clear. It was not until the closing minutes that the visitors had a clear chance and then Wright delayed his shot which was blocked by Forgan.

It was an outstanding team display with the half-backs dictating the pace of the game and not allowing United to settle. The League leaders had been totally eclipsed and outplayed in all departments by a City side who, as a result of this victory, moved up to fourth position. Two days later, City, in confident mood, defeated First Division Leicester City 2-1 at Bootham Crescent in the second round of the Football League Cup.

York City: Forgan; Bingley, Heron, Woods, Jackson, Fountain, Weir, Wragg, Stainsby, Wilkinson, Gould.
Colchester United: Ames; Miller, Fowler, Harris, Abrey, R.M.Hunt, Hill, R.R.Hunt, King, McLeod, Wright.

Attendance: 5,714 *Referee: F.V.Stringer (Liverpool)*

Match to Remember 13 9 October 1964

York City 4 Doncaster Rovers 2

THE 1964-5 season was an outstanding one for York City, who produced some of their best football since the glory days of ten years earlier. They gained promotion in style and one of their best, and most exciting games, of that campaign was a Friday night thriller at Bootham Crescent in early October.

City had made a good start to the season with six wins and three draws in their opening 13 fixtures, whilst Doncaster Rovers had done even better, with seven victories and three draws. A big Doncaster travelling contingent, therefore, made the short journey to York that evening and the game was played in a tense, electrifying atmosphere.

The match got off to a dramatic start when Alfie Hale hit a tremendous goal with a fierce shot from just outside the penalty area in the fifth minute. The Doncaster supporters greeted the goal by hurling so many paper rolls into the goalmouth that the referee had to stop the game for almost four minutes whilst groundstaff cleared the pitch.

Straight from the restart, City equalized when Billy Rudd centred beyond the goalkeeper and Paul Aimson turned the ball into the net. Playing some fine attacking football, City took the lead after 24 minutes when Aimson set up Dennis Walker, who chipped a curling shot over Ken Oxford.

Play ebbed and flowed in a fast, fluctuating game and Tommy Forgan made magnificent saves to thwart Jeffrey, Hale and Broadbent. In the 41st minute, however, George Hamstead's neat inside pass found Walker, who slipped the ball wide of the goalkeeper to score his 12th goal of the season.

For 25 minutes of the second half, City played some outstanding football and twice Walker had shots cleared off the line with the goalkeeper well beaten. The visitors struck back in the 70th minute when Alick Jeffrey cracked in a first-timer from 18 yards and so set up a nail-biting finish. The result was in the balance until three minutes from time when Andy Provan hit a fine drive into the net after a good work by Hamstead.

It had been a truly magnificent match with both teams putting on a superb show. City's wing-halves had fine games, whilst Forgan and Baker were outstanding in defence. The 'man of the match' was skipper Rudd, who worked tirelessly throughout and stamped his authority on the play.

The referee, the experienced Mr Hamer, had handled many First Division games and he said afterwards that this was the best soccer match he had refereed in recent years. Certainly it was the most exciting game seen at Bootham Crescent for some seasons and the biggest League crowd for three and a half years — 11,898 — gave both sides an ovation at the end.

York City: Forgan; Baker, Heron, Wood, Jackson, Ashworth, Provan, Walker, Aimson, Rudd, Hamstead.
Doncaster Rovers: Oxford; Raine, Watton, Wylie, Ripley, Ricketts, Robinson, Jeffrey, Hale, Broadbent, Granger.

Attendance: 11,898 *Referee: L.J.Hamer (Horwich)*

In the return game at Belle Vue later in the season the clubs were involved in another thriller. After 25 minutes Rovers led 4-0, but City fought back with goals from Aimson, Rudd and Wilkinson and in the end a missed penalty by Walker cost them a point after a marvellous fight-back.

Match to Remember 14 18 September 1965

Hull City 1 York City 4

THE 1965-6 campaign was disastrous for York City as they finished bottom of the Third Division. By contrast, neighbours Hull City had a season of triumph and ran away with the championship. What happened, therefore, on a sunny Saturday afternoon in September at Boothferry Park was quite remarkable, to say the least.

Although York had still to record a home victory in the League, they had won at Brentford and Southend and were reasonably happy with their start to their first season back in Division Three since 1960. The Tigers, who had spent heavily in the transfer market, were the bookies' favourites for promotion and had made a good start with four wins and a draw in their opening six games.

It was York's first visit to Humberside for eight years and, after early skirmishes at both ends, they missed a glorious chance to take the lead. Dave Dunmore crossed from the left and Andy Provan, in front of goal, put his shot wide from close range.

In the 22nd minute, however, York shook the home supporters when Paul Aimson headed a Provan centre past goalkeeper Williams. Hull hit back and Harry Fallon, playing only his second game in goal for the club following his transfer from St Johnstone, made a brilliant save to keep out a Ken Wagstaff header.

There was plenty of excitement and incident as each team attacked in turn. Ian Butler, later to play for York, shot across goal and then Aimson went close with another header. Playing some clever and skilful football, York got on top and fully deserved their interval lead.

For 20 minutes after the resumption, Hull had their best period and after Butler skimmed the crossbar with a fine shot, the outside-left equalized from close range in the 57th minute, following good work by Chris Chilton.

Spurred on by their fans, the Tigers put pressure on the visitor's defence but, with Barry Jackson on top form, York held firm and went away to regain the lead in the 67th minute. Provan split the Hull defence with a through-ball for Aimson and the centre-forward finished in fine style.

Three minutes later, a 25-yard John Pearson shot was deflected into the path of Dunmore, who made no mistake with a low drive into the net. York were now completely in charge and sent their supporters wild with delight when Aimson set the seal on the victory with a great volley from the edge of the penalty area in the 77th minute.

Aimson was the hero with a truly magnificent hat-trick — a header, a right-foot shot and a left-footer — and with 11 goals he was top marksman in the Third Division. York's win was not a one-man effort, though, and in a fine team effort, Eamonn Dunphy, Dennis Walker, together with Jackson and Pearson, took the eye.

Contemporary newspapers bear witness to York's achievement:

Evening Press: 'Hull were beaten by an immaculate and brilliant display of football'.

Hull Daily Mail: 'A generally livelier and nippier York City had the edge all-round over Hull City in the derby clash at Boothferry Park'.

Daily Express: 'The team that Tom Lockie has built with a few thousand here and a few thousand there, is a credit to the Third Division'.

Sunday Telegraph: 'Nimble York City coasted home to a remarkable victory'.

It was indeed a remarkable victory but, sadly, York were not able to maintain the high standards that they achieved that glorious afternoon. Later in the season Hull gained revenge with a 2-1 victory at Bootham Crescent in front of 19,372 spectators.

Hull City: Williams; Davidson, D.Butler, Collinson, Milner, Simpkin, Heath, Wagstaff, Chilton, Houghton, I.Butler.
York City: Fallon; Baker, Walker, Woods, Jackson, Dunphy, Pearson, Dunmore, Aimson, Rudd, Provan.

Attendance: 20,554 *Referee: P.Baldwin (Middlesbrough)*

Match to Remember 15 16 March 1974

York City 2 Bristol Rovers 1

THIS was a top-of-the-table Third Division clash, an incident-packed affair with Rovers having two players sent off and the match decided by an injury-time penalty.

The Eastville club were leaders of the table with City in second place as the teams kicked off on a rather blustery day in front of the biggest crowd of the season to date at Bootham Crescent.

The wind proved troublesome and play was a little scrappy in the early stages. Two early chances fell to City, with first Chris Jones shooting wide from a good position and then Jimmy Seal heading inches over the bar from close range.

With the wind behind them, City continued to put Rovers under pressure and goalkeeper Eadie was kept busy, making one particularly good save to thwart Jones. Towards the interval, the leaders came more into the picture with right winger Stephens causing a few problems, but the first half ended goalless after a rather tense struggle.

Early in the second period, John Stone came to the rescue when he headed a Dobson shot off the line, with Graeme Crawford beaten, and within a couple of minutes City celebrated this escape by taking the lead.

Ian Holmes created the goal by dribbling past three defenders down the left and his low cross was crashed into the roof of the net from point-blank range by Jones.

This goal came in the 52nd minute and Rovers immediately hit back when Prince

'Man of the match' Ian Holmes bursts through the Bristol Rovers defence to set up the opening goal netted by Chris Jones.

fired in a 25-yard shot which was well saved by Crawford. The visitors nearly equalized when Staniforth raced clear with the goal at his mercy, but Phil Burrows came to the rescue with a fine last-ditch tackle.

As Rovers staged a strong rally, Stone blocked Staniforth's shot and City did well to survive this period of pressure. The storm was weathered and 'man of the match' Holmes again darted through the defence, only to see his shot hit the woodwork.

City survived a penalty appeal and then in the 81st minute, the game erupted when Bannister was sent off for retaliation after being fouled by Chris Topping.

Yet ten-men Rovers equalized with five minutes remaining, when Stephens sent in a low shot which, aided by the wind, crept just inside the far post. Eadie made a fine save from Barry Lyons and then, in the fifth minute of injury time, came the dramatic and sensational finish.

Following a right-wing corner, John Woodward was barged to the ground and the referee awarded a penalty. Rovers protested bitterly and Stephens, who had earlier been booked, argued so strongly that he was dismissed.

When order was eventually restored, Ian Holmes scored from the spot with what was the last kick of this remarkable game. At the end of the day there had been six cautions (Seal and Topping for City) as well as the sending-offs, but although it was obviously a hard-fought affair, the game could not have been described as 'dirty'.

It was hardly a classic, either, but certainly one that remained in the memory and it was a vital win for City, who closed the gap at the top of the table. They now stood three points behind Rovers, but with a game in hand.

York City: Crawford; Stone, Burrows, Holmes, Swallow, Topping, Lyons, Calvert, Seal, Jones, Woodward.

Bristol Rovers: Eadie; Jacobs, Aitken, Green, Taylor, Prince, Stephens, Stanton, Staniforth, Bannister, Dobson.

Attendance: 11,066 *Referee: J. Whalley (Southport)*

Jimmy Seal (second right) shoots past Oldham 'keeper Ogden but is ruled offside.

Match to Remember 16 — 27 April 1974

York City 1 Oldham Athletic 1

THIS was an historic day in York City's history as they clinched promotion to the Second Division for the first time, after 38 seasons in the Football League.

On a bright, sunny afternoon, a very big crowd greeted the teams for this top-of-the-table encounter. Bristol Rovers still led the table and Oldham were second, only two points ahead of City. Including this match there were only three games remaining.

There was a dramatic start when, almost immediately, Athletic defender Ian Wood fell awkwardly, injuring his shoulder, and was carried off on a stretcher.

City put on a lot of early pressure, forcing a succession of corners, but Oldham defended stoutly and were dangerous in counter-attacks. Indeed, Graeme Crawford had to make an outstanding save in the 24th minute to keep out a fierce shot by McVitie.

Tempers became a little frayed and the referee was kept busy as tension mounted. Ian Butler was prominent in a number of City attacks and Chris Jones shot inches wide. City certainly had the better of the first half but at the interval the score-sheet remained blank.

Oldham began the second half brightly, but it was City who went close when Jones fired in a close-range shot which hit Ogden in the face. John Woodward put the rebound wide and the visitor's goalkeeper had to receive prolonged attention before he could resume.

After 56 minutes the deadlock was broken and it was City who opened the scoring. Barry Lyons took an indirect free-kick and Jones headed high into the net from six yards. Two minutes later, City were within an ace of increasing their lead when Butler smashed a tremendous shot against the post with Ogden well beaten. Jones headed the rebound over the bar.

Lyons went close after good work by Ian Holmes and then in the 65th minute came a shock equalizer. Athletic were awarded a free-kick just outside the penalty area and full-back Whittle curled a shot over the defensive wall and into the net via the inside of a post.

City retaliated and Holmes had a shot well saved, but the visitors, encouraged by their equalizer, now began to get on top and Crawford had to make a brilliant save to stop a 25-yard McVitie effort. Oldham attacked strongly in the closing stages, encouraged by their large following, but the final whistle went with the scores level and at the end of the day, honours were even and a draw was a fair result.

The point was sufficient to earn City promotion and, as for Oldham, they were almost assured of the Third Division title. There were remarkable scenes at the end of the game and the City players did a lap of honour as the crowd rose to them. Captain Barry Swallow described the day as the greatest in his 13-year career. Only 12 months earlier, City had narrowly avoided relegation to the Fourth Division on goal-average. Now they could look forward to meeting the likes of Manchester United, Aston Villa, Sunderland and West Brom. It truly was a dream come true.

York City: Crawford; Calvert, Burrows, Holmes, Swallow, Topping, Lyons, Woodward, Seal, C.Jones, Butler.
Oldham Athletic: Ogden; Wood(Edwards), Whittle, Blair, Hicks, Bailey, McVitie, G.Jones, Lochhead, Robins, Groves.

Attendance: 15,583 *Referee: T.Bosi (Wolverhampton)*

Match to Remember 17 17 August 1974

York City 1 Aston Villa 1

THIS was a famous day in York City's history — the occasion of their first-ever match in Division Two. Ever since promotion had been clinched from Division Three, the opening of the 1974-5 campaign had been eagerly awaited and when skipper Barry Swallow led his side on to the Bootham Crescent turf for this historic first match, the home crowd gave them a huge ovation.

With new signings Micky Cave and Peter Oliver in their line-up City, urged on by the excited crowd, roared into action and almost made a sensational start. In the first minute, Ian Butler's free-kick from the left was headed just over the bar by Swallow.

Playing some very entertaining football in the early stages, City put the Villa defence under considerable pressure and goalkeeper Jim Cumbes was kept very busy. Ray Graydon put one shot wide for Villa and then, in the eighth minute and to the great delight of their supporters, City opened the scoring. Cumbes was penalized for carrying the ball too many paces and from the resultant indirect free-kick, Ian Holmes placed a short pass to Barry Lyons, who cracked a low shot through the defensive wall and just inside the goalkeeper's right hand post.

City's first-ever goal in Division Two. Barry Lyons (out of picture) beats Villa 'keeper Jim Cumbes.

Villa hit back and twice Graeme Crawford made magnificent saves to thwart Gidman. In the 27th minute, City were within an ace of increasing their lead, when Jimmy Seal rounded Cumbes and then saw his shot kicked off the line by Aitken. After half an hour, and rather against the run of play, the visitors equalized when Graydon headed a cross from Hamilton past Crawford from point-blank range.

Encouraged by this goal, Villa began to get on top and City were kept at full stretch in the closing stages of the first half.

On the resumption, Villa again began to dominate proceedings and City were finding it difficult to adapt to the pace of the game. During this difficult period they were indebted to strong work by Swallow and Crawford.

Gradually, City shook off the persistent Villa attack and in the last quarter, Chris Jones and Seal went close. As play now switched from end to end, Nicholl headed a corner past Crawford but the goal was disallowed for an infringement.

Chris Topping cleared two dangerous crosses and then, when Jones went down in the penalty area, the referee waved aside City's appeals for a spot-kick.

In the end, City were pleased to collect a point. They had played very well in the early stages but then had to withstand a long period of Villa pressure. In retrospect, it was indeed a useful performance, for at the end of the season Villa finished runners-up to Manchester United and so returned to Division One.

York City: Crawford; Stone, Oliver, Holmes, Swallow, Topping, Lyons, Cave, Seal(Hinch), Jones, Butler.
Aston Villa: Cumbes; Gidman, Aitken, Ross, Nicholl, Robson, Graydon, Little, Morgan, Hamilton(Betts), Carrodus.
Attendance: 9,396 *Referee: G.M.Trevett (Manchester)*

Match to Remember 18 — 18 January 1975

Norwich City 2 York City 3

THIS was a quite fantastic match and was arguably York City's best performance in their first season of Second Division football. The Canaries were third in the table and on the point of reaching the Football League Cup Final, whilst York went into the match with only two wins and one draw in their previous eight games.

This sequence had dropped them to their lowest position of the season — 17th — and they were also without a manager. The previous week Tom Johnston had departed for Huddersfield Town and the team were under the caretaker managership of trainer-coach Clive Baker.

York made a truly remarkable start and unbelievably scored twice with the game less than two minutes old. Straight from the kick-off they attacked down the right and after Barry Lyons' shot was blocked, there was a tremendous scramble in the goalmouth before Jimmy Seal forced the ball into the net after only 83 seconds.

Immediately on the restart, York again attacked strongly down the right and when Ian Holmes put in a low centre, Chris Jones cracked a fierce shot into goal from eight yards to make it 2-0 after 125 seconds.

It was a dream start for Baker and his men and Norwich were well and truly shaken. Former York players, Ted MacDougall and Phil Boyer, were prominent as the home side desperately fought back, but Keelan had to make an outstanding save after 15 minutes to thwart Seal.

Gradually Norwich began to exert more pressure and, as half-time approached, they began to gain territorial advantage. But York defended strongly and fully deserved their interval lead of two goals.

Chris Jones (extreme right) scores City's second goal in the dramatic start at Carrow Road.

After the break, York were thrust completely on defence and it was no surprise when Norwich reduced their arrears in the 63rd minute. Colin Suggett collected the ball 35 yards out and ran on unchallenged to the edge of the penalty area, firing in a shot that was deflected past Graeme Crawford's left hand and into the net.

Norwich continued to pile on the pressure and York were having to hang on, but in the 75th minute they stunned the home crowd by scoring a third goal. Jones picked up a pass out on the right touch-line and, with the Norwich defence back-pedalling, he cut in for goal. From just inside the penalty area he cracked a tremendous rising shot from a narrow angle past Keelan into the roof of the net.

MacDougall headed narrowly over the bar as Norwich counter-attacked and with six minutes to go Dave Stringer glanced a right-wing cross into goal to make the scoreline 3-2.

In a hectic finish, York had to withstand tremendous pressure and Crawford had to make one remarkable save to foil MacDougall. York City held on, however, to record an outstanding victory and also complete a League double, having beaten Norwich 1-0 at Bootham Crescent earlier in the campaign. Just over a month later, the Canaries lost to Aston Villa in the League Cup Final at Wembley, but finished the season third in the League and so returned to Division One.

Norwich City: Keelan; Machin, Sullivan, Morris, Forbes, Stringer, McGuire, MacDougall, Boyer, Suggett, Powell.
York City: Crawford; Calvert, Oliver, Holmes, Swallow, Topping, Lyons, Cave, Seal, Jones, Butler.

Attendance: 23,382 *Referee: M.J.Taylor (Walmer)*

Jimmy Seal and Ian Butler greet Chris Jones' (out of picture) opening goal against Fulham.

Match to Remember 19 — 22 March 1975

York City 3 Fulham 2

THIS match was a thrilling, all-action Second Division game. It was the Cottagers' first-ever visit to York and they were in the midst of a very good run — 13 League and Cup games without a defeat. The Londoners went on to reach Wembley that season, finishing FA Cup runners-up to West Ham United. At the time of their visit to Bootham Crescent they occupied a comfortable mid-table position, whilst City were just above the relegation zone.

In Fulham's line-up were former England stars Bobby Moore and Alan Mullery and at centre-forward was Viv Busby, who in a few years time would play an important part in York City's fortunes.

The game had an electrifying start and after only 20 minutes the scoreline read 2-2. It was City who struck first, in the seventh minute. Chris Jones, who had scored twice in a 2-0 victory at Craven Cottage in September, collected a pass from Brian Pollard and chipped a curling shot over Cottagers' goalkeeper Mellor and into the net via the inside of a post.

The visitors hit back and equalized after 11 minutes when Slough beat two defenders and then cracked a low shot past Graeme Crawford. In the 19th minute, Busby hit a spectacular goal from outside the penalty area, but straight from the kick-off, City equalized when Jones glanced a header wide of Mellor following a Pollard centre.

A couple of minutes later, Busby shot over from a good position and then Mitchell fired wide. Jimmy Seal and Micky Cave both went close for City and both defences struggled — all of which added to plenty of goalmouth incident.

City resumed strongly and brilliant footwork by Butler and a fine pass down the middle sent Jones racing clear. As he was about to shoot, he was challenged by Moore and the referee awarded a penalty. From the spot Ian Holmes restored City's lead in the 51st minute.

Thrills continued to abound as Fulham strove to get back on level terms and Dowie shot just too high from ten yards. Play switched from end to end and chances went begging. Busby and Mitchell went close for Fulham and Butler twice failed with clear-cut openings for City.

Crawford made a couple of brilliant saves in the closing stages as the visitors went all out for the equalizer, but City held on and just deserved the points after a fine contest which might have produced a dozen goals. The home side had the edge in midfield where Butler, Holmes and Cave had outstanding games. City therefore ended Fulham's long unbeaten run and completed a double over their London opponents.

It was a tremendous game and the crowd gave both teams a standing ovation at half-time and at the final whistle.

York City: Crawford; Calvert, Oliver, Holmes, Swallow, Topping, Pollard, Cave, Seal, Jones, Butler.
Fulham: Mellor; Fraser, Strong, Mullery, Lacy, Moore, Dowie, Mitchell, Busby, Slough, Barrett.
Attendance: 7,495 *Referee: K. Walmsley (Fleetwood)*

Barry Swallow in action at Old Trafford. United's players are Pearson and Houston.

Match to Remember 20 — 29 March 1975

Manchester United 2 York City 1

ALTHOUGH this game was a rather ordinary affair, it has to be remembered in the club's history. It was the day that City crossed swords at Old Trafford with one of the great names in world soccer.

Seven years earlier, Manchester United had won the European Cup by beating Benfica 4-1 at Wembley in one of the great nights in British soccer. That season

City had to apply for re-election to the Football League, having finished in the bottom four of the Fourth Division. Few could have imagined that, just a few seasons later, these clubs would be competing at the same level.

It was truly *Roy of the Rovers* material but, sure enough, on a bright, breezy afternoon City trotted out at the famous Old Trafford stadium. To add even more spice, they had recently appointed former United boss, Wilf McGuinness, as their new manager and it was obviously a poignant day for him.

By this Easter Saturday, United had just about clinched immediate promotion back to the First Division and a big crowd roared them into action. In the fifth minute Graeme Crawford made a magnificent save to keep out a shot by Daly and, almost immediately, the City goalkeeper had to beat away a thunderous drive by McIlroy.

In City's first attack, Brian Pollard shot past Stepney's left-hand post and a Chris Jones header gave United's defence a few problems. Crawford was kept busy as he dived to save a McIlroy header, but City went close in the 20th minute when Stepney had to go down at full stretch to hold on to a shot from Ian Holmes.

Full-back Houston almost opened the scoring midway through the first half, when his first-time shot shaved a post as United kept up the pressure. City defended well and mounted some lively counter attacks, from one of which Jimmy Seal shot just wide.

At the start of the second half Barry Lyons replaced Jones, who had suffered a leg injury. Facing a strong sun and a breeze, City were forced to defend for long periods but, with Crawford in fine form, they continued to frustrate the League leaders.

Eventually the deadlock was broken in the 74th minute. A free-kick from the right was headed into the goalmouth by Houston and Willie Morgan headed in from close range. Shortly afterwards, a fierce Macari shot was brilliantly turned away by City's goalkeeper and then Pollard, with a fine solo effort, nearly equalized.

With four minutes remaining, United clinched the points when Morgan crossed from the right and Macari hammered a tremendous shot into the roof of the net. Seal reduced the arrears in the 88th minute, following a goalmouth scramble, but the final whistle went with the Reds deserved winners.

It was far from a classic, but a day indeed to remember for the City club and their fans. It was a brave, defensive effort and they were far from disgraced. The attendance of 46,802 was the largest ever to watch York City in a League game, the previous biggest being the 40,002 at Hull in April 1949.

Manchester United: Stepney; Forsyth, Houston, Morgan, Greenhoff, Buchan, Coppell, McIlroy, Pearson, Macari, Daly.

York City: Crawford; Calvert, Oliver, Holmes, Swallow, Topping, Pollard, Cave, Seal, Jones(Lyons), Butler.

Attendance: 46,802 *Referee: P.Partridge (County Durham)*

Match to Remember 21 28 April 1984

York City 2 Hartlepool United 0

THIS was a red-letter day for City. With this victory over Hartlepool they clinched the Fourth Division championship and thus collected the first major honour in the club's history.

Promotion to the Third Division had long since been assured in that memorable 1983-4 campaign and the title race had become a one-horse race as City went into this match at Bootham Crescent on a glorious spring afternoon.

They required three points to lift the title and the opposition was Hartlepool United, who were second from bottom of the table and almost certain to have to apply for re-election.

In the visitors' line-up were former City goalkeeper, Eddie Blackburn, and at centre-half was John Bird who, four and a half years later, was to become manager at Bootham Crescent.

In front of a big crowd and with the atmosphere tense with excitement, City gave a nervous display in the first half. In the fifth minute United should have scored when Dobson broke down the middle and his pass put Lowe clear, but from a good position the visitors' striker shot inches wide.

After a very slow start, City began to improve and were unlucky not to take the lead when John MacPhail headed a Brian Pollard corner against the underside of the crossbar. 'Pool hit back, however, and Taylor glanced a header just past the post.

MacPhail once had to clear over his own bar as further pressure was put on the home defence but, as the interval approached, City showed signs of getting on top. Within a minute of the resumption the crowd went wild with delight when Keith Walwyn smashed the ball into the roof of the net after fine work by John Byrne down the right.

City piled on the pressure and in the 56th minute, Walwyn increased the lead with a close-range header after MacPhail had put an overhead kick into the goalmouth. City were inches away from a third goal when Blackburn turned a Byrne shot on to the crossbar and then Sean Haslegrave cracked a fierce shot just wide.

When the final whistle sounded, many of the crowd invaded the pitch and mobbed the players. Later they chanted for the team and Denis Smith and Viv Busby appeared in the directors' box to acknowledge the cheers. The champagne corks popped and there were memorable scenes as everyone celebrated and savoured the historic occasion.

Another club record was created that day as York completed their 29th League victory of the season, beating the 28 in the promotion season of 1964-5.

York City: Jones; Evans, Hay, Sbragia, MacPhail, Hood, Ford, Haslegrave, Walwyn, Byrne, Pollard(Houchen).

Hartlepool United: Blackburn; Smithies, Barker, Hogan, Linighan, Bird, Brown, Lowe, Linacre, Dobson, Taylor(Borthwick).

Attendance: 6,063 *Referee: L.R.Dilkes (Mossley)*

Keith Walwyn (9) opens the scoring against Pool. The beaten goalkeeper is Eddie Blackburn, formerly with City.

Alan Pearce (left) cracks home the second goal against Gillingham.

Match to Remember 22 — 3 November 1984

York City 7 Gillingham 1

THIS was a thrill-packed afternoon for City fans as the club hit their biggest score for 20 years — the first time they had scored more than six since Boxing Day 1964 and a 7-1 victory over Chesterfield at Bootham Cresent.

City went into this game with only one point from five games and had dropped from the top of the Third Division to eighth place. This mini-slump, plus a wretched cold and wet afternoon, resulted in the smallest attendance of the season, but what a treat those fans who braved the elements were served up.

Several hours of rain had left the pitch in a very heavy, and in places waterlogged, condition. City made a flying start and within six minutes were two goals ahead. Keith Houchen opened the scoring when he headed a right-wing Keith Walwyn cross powerfully past the visitors' goalkeeper after good work by Sean Haslegrave.

Alan Pearce fired home the second goal after Derek Hood's pass sent Walwyn racing down the left wing. The City number-nine centred the ball, which rebounded to Pearce, who right-footed a shot into the net. Goalkeeper Fry was kept busy as Gillingham tried to stem the tide and he made fine saves to thwart Hood and then Walwyn.

The visitors almost reduced their arrears when, following a corner, Oakes hit the crossbar with Roger Jones beaten, but City swarmed back, only for Walwyn to miss an open goal. After half an hour they increased their lead, however, when Walwyn, who was revelling in the conditions, ploughed down the right and his cross was turned into the net by Houchen.

In isolated Gillingham attacks Jones made a fine save to keep out a Shearer header and then Cascarino shot just wide. After further City pressure, Walwyn made it 4-0 in the 41st minute. Gary Ford's corner was touched on by Ricky Sbragia and the centre-forward blasted in from close range. Only a spectacular save by Fry foiled Houchen on the stroke of half-time and City left the field to a standing ovation.

City resumed where they left off and in the 51st minute scored the best goal of the game. Houchen won the ball in midfield and found Ford with a neat pass. The right winger centred to the far post and Pearce, running in from the left, volleyed a tremendous first-time shot past the hapless Fry. Within a couple of minutes Gillingham reduced their vast arrears when Shearer netted with a low shot from just outside the area.

Walwyn missed a sitter as City continued to pull the visitors' defence apart and then, after a fine run down the left by Pearce, the ball was turned into his own goal by Oakes. The referee disallowed a Walwyn 'goal' but the scoring was completed in the 82nd minute. Hood's pass put Houchen clear on the right and the striker ran through to calmly shoot into the net to record his hat-trick.

It had been a magnificent display of attacking football and Gillingham had been outplayed from start to finish. Considering the quagmire conditions, it was a remarkable show and an outstanding team performance on an afternoon to remember.

York City: Jones; Evans, Hay, Sbragia, MacPhail, Hood, Ford, Haslegrave, Walwyn, Houchen, Pearce.

Gillingham: Fry; Leslie, Sage, Oakes, Weatherly, Shaw, Shearer, Johnson, Robinson, Mehmet, Cascarino.

Attendance: 2,921 *Referee: K. Walmsley (Blackpool)*

Match to Remember 23 5 October 1985

York City 7 Darlington 0

THIS goal-feast for City fans saw York record their biggest victory since the 9-1 rout of Southport back in 1957. City went into the game in fourth position in the Third Division, whilst the newly-promoted Quakers were 23rd with only one win to their credit.

Within five minutes City had the ball in the net, only for Tony Canham's cross-shot to be ruled out because of offside. The visitors were pinned back on defence and it was no surprise when City took the lead in the 14th minute. Keith Walwyn started the move and a pass from Gary Ford was collected by Canham who fired a low shot past Barber.

Three minutes later, Walwyn powered his way through the Darlington defence and scored a brilliant solo goal. The visitors' task became even harder when, midway through the first half, full-back Paul Ward was sent off for a second bookable offence.

Gary Ford had a goal disallowed and Barber was constantly in action as the eager City forwards piled on the pressure. In the early part of the second half, City's play became rather lethargic and the ten-man visitors began to show signs of getting back into the game.

The crowd became a little restless but, in the 63rd minute, Canham headed a Walwyn cross into the net for goal number-three and the floodgates were opened. Four minutes later the City centre-forward got his second goal, when Dale Banton set up an easy chance, and in the 75th minute the crowd greeted a Canham hat-trick. Walwyn was fouled in the penalty area and regular penalty-taker John MacPhail handed the ball to the little left winger, who gleefully thumped it into the net for City's fifth goal.

Luckless Darlington were now completely outplayed and overrun as the home team tore them to shreds and further spectacular goals were scored by Steve Senior (81 minutes) and Keith Houchen (84).

The game was a personal triumph for Canham, who was in his first season as

Keith Walwyn hits an angled drive past Barber for City's second goal in the 7-0 rout over the Quakers.

a professional, but overall it was a devastating team display, especially the 22-minute spell in the second half when City rattled in five goals.

York City: Astbury; Senior, Hay, McAughtrie(Hood), MacPhail, Haslegrave, Ford, Banton, Walwyn, Houchen, Canham.
Darlington: Barber; Aldred, Ward, Tupling, Huntley(Haire), Carney, Roberts, Poskett, Airey, MacDonald, McLean.
Attendance: 5,039 *Referee: R.A.Banks (Manchester)*

Match to Remember 24 1 January 1987

York City 3 Middlesbrough 1

THIS match marked the first-ever League meeting between the clubs and produced a surprise and very welcome victory for City, who went into the game without a win in nine outings (four draws and five defeats). Middlesbrough were the Third Division leaders and a large following of their fans ensured the biggest crowd of the season at Bootham Crescent.

On a heavy pitch the match started in lively style and after early 'Boro pressure, Tony Canham shot inches wide after beating two defenders.

Stephens went close, with only Andy Leaning to beat, and then came great excitement as City scored twice in three minutes. Keith Walwyn's pass set up Martin Butler, whose fierce 15-yard shot was deflected by Gary Hamilton into the net in

Martin Butler's opening goal against 'Boro.

the 31st minute. In the next attack, goalkeeper Pears got into a tangle at the edge of the area and Walwyn gratefully accepted the gift as the ball ran loose. Stung by these reverses, the visitors fought back strongly but City held on and led 2-0 at the interval.

Within a couple of minutes after the break, 'Boro had reduced the arrears. They were awarded an indirect free-kick in the penalty area and, as the ball bounced off the defensive wall in a crowded goalmouth, it was forced into the net by Mowbray.

City were forced back on defence, but Walwyn nearly restored their two-goal lead with a spectacular diving header.

The leaders fought desperately to get on level terms and Andy Leaning had to make a couple of fine saves before receiving attention after a collision with Stephens.

The points were clinched in the 85th minute with a rather fortunate goal. Gary Ford and Butler linked up and supplied an opening for Canham, whose shot hit Walwyn and, as Pears dived, the ball was diverted into the opposite corner of the net.

City, therefore, ended a long run without a victory and had started the New Year in fine style. Outstanding in midfield in the muddy conditions were Sean Haslegrave and Simon Mills. It was the 100th League success under manager Denis Smith.

York City: Leaning; Senior(Hood), Pearce, Sbragia, Pickering, Haslegrave, Ford, Butler, Walwyn, Mills, Canham.
Middlesbrough: Pears; Laws, Cooper, Mowbray, Parkinson, Pallister, Slaven, Stephens, Hamilton, Gill, Ripley.
Attendance: 8,611 *Referee: C.Seel (Carlisle)*

Match to Remember 25 — 26 March 1988

York City 2 Sunderland 1

THIS was one of the surprise League results of the 1987-8 season. City were at the foot of Division Three, with only four wins and 20 points in 37 games, whilst Sunderland were second in the table with 20 victories and 72 points from the same number of matches. On paper it was one of the day's away bankers.

The game had been eagerly awaited. Sunderland were managed by the former City duo of Denis Smith and Viv Busby and this was their first visit to Bootham Crescent since their dramatic departure in May 1987.

In the visitors' line-up were former City favourites, John MacPhail and Marco

Dale Banton's (left) spectacular header put City 2-0 ahead against the Third Division leaders.

Gabbiadini. City recalled Steve Tutill to first-team duty after a three-month absence owing to a broken ankle.

Sunderland should have opened the scoring in the first minute. Gordon Armstrong ran on to a through ball from Steve Doyle, but shot straight at Scott Endersby and then hit the rebound wide.

The visitors kept City at full stretch in the early stages but, with Tutill and Endersby in fine form, the defence held firm and gradually the home side gained in confidence.

In the 34th minute City stunned Sunderland by taking the lead. Gary Howlett placed a fine pass out to Ian Helliwell on the left. The centre-forward took the ball in his stride, cut inside Gary Bennett and then saw his low, angled shot hit both posts before crossing the line.

Endersby made a magnificent save to thwart Bennett just before the interval and, as Sunderland piled on the pressure, MacPhail headed inches over the bar.

Upon the restart, City continued to defend for long periods and Endersby was constantly in action, making another great save to keep out a shot from Armstrong.

City held on and in the 75th minute scored perhaps their 'goal of the season'. Helliwell's pass set Gary Himsworth free down the left. The young winger put across a perfect centre and Dale Banton, running in, rocketed a magnificent header into the roof of the net.

Sunderland roared back and, with eight minutes to go, pulled a goal back. Doyle crossed from the right and Eric Gates back-heeled the ball to Colin Pascoe, who cracked a low shot just inside Endersby's right-hand post.

The goal set up a dramatic and frantic finale as Sunderland swarmed on attack. Frank Gray shot just wide, Gabbiadini tangled with Tutill in the area but Sunderland's claims for a penalty were turned down, and then, in injury time, Armstrong had a goal disallowed for a foul on City's goalkeeper.

It was remarkable win for City after a battling and determined display. Their defence was outstanding with the men of the match being Tutill — who kept such a tight grip on his former teammate and close friend, Gabbiadini — and Endersby, who performed heroics in goal. Unfortunately the afternoon was marred at the end when a number of visiting fans invaded the pitch and smashed the goal-posts.

York City: Endersby; McMillan, Johnson, Clegg, Tutill, Branagan, Howlett, Bradshaw, Helliwell, Banton, Himsworth.

Sunderland: Hesford; Kay, Bennett, MacPhail, Agboola, McGuire(Pascoe), Owers(Gray), Doyle, Armstrong, Gabbiadini, Gates.

Attendance: 9,183 *Referee: P.Danson (Leicester)*

(Receipts £31,612, a record for a League game at Bootham Crescent.)

City's Internationals

The following players have gained representative honours whilst with York City.

Eamonn Dunphy

Republic of Ireland — 1 Full International Cap
10 November 1965 v Spain (World Cup Qualifying match in Paris)

Peter Scott

Northern Ireland — 7 Full International Caps
24 March 1976 v Israel (Tel Aviv)
8 May 1976 v Scotland (Hampden Park)
11 May 1976 v England (sub) (Wembley)
14 May 1976 v Wales (Swansea)
13 May 1978 v Scotland (Hampden Park)
16 May 1978 v England (Wembley)
19 May 1978 v Wales (Wrexham)

Mike Walker

Wales — 3 Under-23 Caps
22 February 1967 v Northern Ireland (Belfast)
1 November 1967 v England (Swansea)
20 March 1968 v Northern Ireland (Cardiff)

The following three players gained England Youth International caps.
Brian Pollard 1971 and 1972
Cliff Calvert 1972
Mike De Placido 1972

Whilst with the club as an associate schoolboy, Steve Tutill was capped for England Schoolboys in 1975 and 1976

Gordon Jones played for a Football League XI in a wartime representative match against the Northern Command. This game was staged at Bootham Crescent in October 1942.

York City in the Football League 1929-30 to 1989-90

		HOME					AWAY						
	P	W	D	L	F	A	W	D	L	F	A	Pts	Pos
DIVISION THREE NORTH													
1929-30	42	11	7	3	43	20	4	9	8	34	44	46	6th
1930-31	42	15	3	3	59	30	3	3	15	26	52	42	12th
1931-32	40	14	3	3	49	24	4	4	12	27	57	43	9th
1932-33	42	10	4	7	51	38	3	2	16	21	54	32	20th
1933-34	42	11	5	5	44	28	4	3	14	27	46	38	12th
1934-35	42	12	5	4	50	20	3	1	17	26	62	36	15th
1935-36	42	10	8	3	41	28	3	4	14	21	67	38	16th
1936-37	42	13	3	5	54	27	3	8	10	25	43	43	12th
1937-38	42	11	4	6	40	25	5	6	10	30	43	42	11th
1938-39	42	8	5	8	37	34	4	3	14	27	58	32	20th
Suspended due to war													
1946-47	42	6	4	11	35	42	8	5	8	32	39	37	15th
1947-48	42	8	7	6	38	25	5	7	9	27	35	40	13th
1948-49	42	11	3	7	49	28	4	6	11	25	46	39	14th
1949-50	42	6	7	8	29	33	3	6	12	23	37	31	22nd
1950-51	46	7	12	4	37	24	5	3	15	29	53	39	17th
1951-52	46	16	4	3	53	19	2	9	12	20	33	49	10th
1952-53	46	14	5	4	35	16	6	8	9	25	29	53	4th
1953-54	46	8	7	8	39	32	4	6	13	25	54	37	22nd
1954-55	46	13	5	5	43	27	11	5	7	49	36	58	4th
1955-56	46	12	4	7	44	24	7	5	11	41	48	47	11th
1956-57	46	14	4	5	43	21	7	6	10	32	40	52	7th
1957-58	46	11	8	4	40	26	6	4	13	28	50	46	13th
DIVISION FOUR													
1958-59	46	12	10	1	37	17	9	8	6	36	35	60	3rd
DIVISION THREE													
1959-60	46	11	5	7	38	26	2	7	14	19	47	38	21st
DIVISION FOUR													
1960-61	46	17	3	3	50	14	4	6	13	30	46	51	5th
1961-62	44	17	2	3	62	19	3	8	11	22	34	50	6th
1962-63	46	12	6	5	42	25	4	5	14	25	37	43	14th
1963-64	46	9	3	11	29	26	5	4	14	23	40	35	22nd
1964-65	46	20	1	2	63	21	8	5	10	28	35	62	3rd
DIVISION THREE													
1965-66	46	5	7	11	30	44	4	2	17	23	62	27	24th
DIVISION FOUR													
1966-67	46	11	5	7	45	31	1	6	16	20	48	35	22nd
1967-68	46	9	6	8	44	30	2	8	13	21	38	36	21st
1968-69	46	12	8	3	36	25	2	3	18	17	50	39	21st
1969-70	46	14	7	2	38	16	2	7	14	17	46	46	13th
1970-71	46	16	6	1	45	14	7	4	12	33	40	56	4th

		HOME					*AWAY*						
	P	W	D	L	F	A	W	D	L	F	A	Pts	Pos
				DIVISION THREE									
1971-72	46	8	8	7	32	22	4	4	15	25	44	36	19th
1972-73	46	8	10	5	24	14	5	5	13	18	32	41	18th
1973-74	46	13	8	2	37	15	8	11	4	30	23	61	3rd
				DIVISION TWO									
1974-75	42	9	7	5	28	17	5	3	13	23	38	38	15th
1975-76	42	8	3	10	28	34	2	5	14	11	37	28	21st
				DIVISION THREE									
1976-77	46	7	8	8	24	34	3	4	16	26	55	32	24th
				DIVISION FOUR									
1977-78	46	8	7	8	27	31	4	5	14	23	38	36	22nd
1978-79	46	11	6	6	33	24	7	5	11	18	31	47	10th
1979-80	46	9	6	8	35	34	5	5	13	30	48	39	17th
1980-81	46	10	2	11	31	23	2	7	14	16	43	33	24th
1981-82	46	9	5	9	45	37	5	3	15	24	54	50	17th
1982-83	46	18	4	1	59	19	4	9	10	29	39	79	7th
1983-84	46	18	4	1	58	16	13	4	6	38	23	101	1st
				DIVISION THREE									
1984-85	46	13	5	5	42	22	7	4	12	28	35	69	8th
1985-86	46	16	4	3	49	17	4	7	12	28	41	71	7th
1986-87	46	11	8	4	34	29	1	5	17	21	50	49	20th
1987-88	46	4	7	12	27	45	4	2	17	21	46	33	23rd
				DIVISION FOUR									
1988-89	46	10	8	5	43	27	7	5	11	19	36	64	11th
1989-90	46	10	5	8	29	24	6	11	6	26	29	64	13th

1929-30

Manager: John Collier

1	Aug	31	(a)	Wigan Borough	W 2-0	Cowie, Stockill	8,880
2	Sep	4	(h)	Wrexham	D 0-0		8,726
3		7	(h)	Carlisle U	D 2-2	Gardner 2	7,462
4		11	(a)	Wrexham	D 1-1	Davis	6,235
5		14	(a)	Nelson	L 1-3	Cowie	4,483
6		18	(h)	New Brighton	W 3-0	Bottrill 2, Evans	5,422
7		21	(h)	Southport	L 0-4		5,852
8		28	(a)	Crewe A	D 2-2	Beck, Gardner	5,373
9	Oct	5	(h)	Chesterfield	D 1-1	Cowie	4,773
10		12	(h)	Stockport C	L 1-2	Bottrill	6,189
11		19	(a)	Lincoln C	L 0-3		5,310
12		26	(h)	Tranmere R	D 0-0		3,835
13	Nov	2	(a)	Halifax T	D 2-2	Bottrill 2 (1 pen)	4,656
14		9	(h)	Rotherham U	W 3-0	Fenoughty, Cowie, Millar	3,715
15		23	(h)	South Shields	D 2-2	Gardner 2	3,608
16	Dec	7	(h)	Darlington	D 1-1	Millar	4,892
17		21	(h)	Doncaster R	D 2-2	Gardner, Opp own-goal	2,654
18		25	(a)	Barrow	D 0-0		2,229
19		26	(h)	Barrow	W 3-1	Evans, Fenoughty, Bottrill	7,834
20		28	(h)	Wigan Borough	W 4-0	Bottrill 3, Gardner	4,395
21	Jan	1	(a)	New Brighton	D 1-1	Fenoughty	5,440
22		4	(a)	Carlisle U	D 2-2	Fenoughty, Bottrill	7,149
23		18	(h)	Nelson	W 1-0	Bottrill	5,289
24		25	(a)	Southport	L 0-1		3,375
25	Feb	1	(h)	Crewe A	W 4-2	Millar 3, Bottrill	4,631
26		8	(a)	Chesterfield	L 0-3		4,830
27		15	(a)	Stockport C	W 3-2	Beck, Gardner, Fenoughty	9,434
28		22	(h)	Lincoln C	W 1-0	Gardner	5,298
29	Mar	1	(a)	Tranmere R	D 4-4	Gardner, Fenoughty, Millar, Bottrill	4,079
30		5	(a)	Accrington S	D 1-1	Evans	2,017
31		8	(h)	Halifax T	W 3-0	Evans, Fenoughty, Millar	4,355
32		15	(a)	Rotherham U	W 5-2	Fenoughty 2, Bottrill 2, Gardner	2,259
33		22	(h)	Rochdale	W 6-0	Gardner 2, Fenoughty 2, Millar, Bottrill	4,720
34		29	(a)	South Shields	L 1-4	Fenoughty	2,234
35	Apr	2	(a)	Hartlepools U	L 1-3	Aitken	4,390
36		5	(h)	Accrington S	W 2-0	Sharpe, Fenoughty	4,529
37		12	(a)	Darlington	L 2-5	Beck (pen), Millar	6,028
38		18	(a)	Port Vale	D 1-1	Gardner	15,346
39		19	(h)	Hartlepools U	W 4-1	Evans 2, Gardner, Bottrill	2,563
40		21	(h)	Port Vale	L 0-2		10,120
41		26	(a)	Doncaster R	W 3-0	Fenoughty 2, Evans	4,322
42	May	3	(a)	Rochdale	L 2-4	Gardner, Bottrill	1,564

FINAL LEAGUE POSITION: 6th in Division Three North

Appearances
Goals

FA Cup

4Q	Nov	16	(a)	Scarborough	W 3-1	Bottrill 2, Cowie	8,089
1	Nov	30	(h)	Tranmere R	D 2-2	Fenoughty 2	5,580
R	Dec	5	(a)	Tranmere R	W 1-0	Fenoughty	4,882
2	Dec	14	(a)	Southend U	W 4-1	Davis, Gardner, Fenoughty 2	11,000
3	Jan	11	(a)	Newcastle U	D 1-1	Gardner	38,674
R		15	(h)	Newcastle U	L 1-2	Evans	12,583

Appearances
Goals

Farmery J	Archibald D	Johnson S	Beck H	Davis C	Thompson O	Evans S	Gardner W	Cowie J	Smiles T	Stockill R	Millar W	Bottrill W	Fenoughty T	Glidden S	Gallacher S	Brooks J	Sharpe G	Aitken J	Ridley R	
1	2	3	4	5	6	7	8	9	10	11										1
1	2	3	4	5	6	7	8	9	10		11									2
1	2	3	4	5	6	7	8	9			11	10								3
1	2	3	4	5	6	7	8				11	9	10							4
1	2	3	4	5	6	7	8	9			11	10								5
1	2	3	4	5	6	7					11	10		8	9					6
1	2	3	4	5	6	7		9			11	10		8						7
1	2	3	4	5	6	7	8	9	11			10								8
1	2	3	4	5	6	7	8	9	11			10								9
1	2	3	4	5	6	7	8		10		11	9								10
1	2	3	4	5	6	7	8		10		11	9								11
1		3	4	5	6	7			10		11	9			8	2				12
1		3	4	5	6	7		9			11	10	8			2				13
1	2	3	4	5	6	7		9			11	10	8							14
1		3	4	5	6	7	8	9			11		10			2				15
1		3		5	6	7		9			11	10	4		8	2				16
1		3	4	5	6	7	9					8	10			2	11			17
1		3	4	5	6	7	9				11	8	10			2				18
1		3	4	5	6	7	9				11	8	10			2				19
1		3	4	5	6	7	9				11	8	10			2				20
1		3	4	5	6	7	9				11	8	10			2				21
1		3	4	5	6	7		9			11	8	10			2				22
1		3	4	5	6	7	9				11	8	10			2				23
1		3	4	5	6	7	9				11	8	10			2				24
1		3	4	5	6						11	8	10			2	7	9		25
1		3	4	5	6						11	8	10			2	7	9		26
1		3	4	5	6	7	9				11	8	10			2				27
1		3	4	5	6	7	9				11	8	10			2				28
1		3	4	5	6	7	9				11	8	10			2				29
		3	4	5	6	7	9				11	8	10			2			1	30
1		3	4	5	6	7	9				11	8	10			2				31
1		3	4	5	6	7	9				11	8	10			2				32
1		3	4	5	6	7	9				11	8	10			2				33
1		3	4	5	6	7	9				11	8	10			2				34
1		3	4	5	6			9	7		11	8				2		10		35
1		3	4	5	6		9				11	8	10			2	7			36
1		3	4	5	6		9				11	8	10			2	7			37
1	3		4	5	6	7	9				11	8	10			2				38
1	3		4		5	7	10	9				8	6			2	11			39
	3		4	5	6	7					11	8				2	10	9	1	40
	3		4	5	6	7	9				11	8	10			2			1	41
	3		4	5	6	7	9				11	8	10			2			1	42
38	17	37	41	41	42	37	31	14	8	1	37	39	29	2	3	30	7	4	4	
			3	1		7	16	4		1	9	18	15				1	1		

1 own-goal

Farmery J	Archibald D	Johnson S	Beck H	Davis C	Thompson O	Evans S	Gardner W	Cowie J	Smiles T	Stockill R	Millar W	Bottrill W	Fenoughty T	Glidden S	Gallacher S	Brooks J	Sharpe G	Aitken J	Ridley R	
1		3	4	5	6	7		9		11		8	10			2				4Q
1		3	4	5	6	7		9			11	8	10			2				1
1		3	4	5	6	7		9			11	8	10			2				R
1		3	4	5	6	7	9				11	8	10			2				2
1		3	4	5	6	7	9				11	8	10			2				3
1		3	4	5	6	7	9				11	8	10			2				R
6		6	6	6	6	6	3	3		1	5	6	6			6				
				1		1	2	1				2	5							

1930-31

Secretary-Manager: Mr G.W.Sherrington

No	Month	Day	Venue	Opponent	Res	Score	Scorers	Att
1	Aug	30	(a)	Rotherham U	L	1-2	Beck (pen)	6,354
2	Sep	3	(a)	Wrexham	L	2-3	Gardner, Laycock	6,925
3		6	(h)	Chesterfield	D	2-2	Beck (pen), Fenoughty	5,373
4		10	(h)	Tranmere R	W	3-1	Fenoughty, Gardner, D.Kelly	3,975
5		13	(a)	Barrow	W	2-1	Fenoughty, Gardner	7,127
6		18	(a)	Tranmere R	L	1-4	Evans	3,758
7		20	(h)	Southport	W	3-1	Beck (pen), Fenoughty, Gardner	4,063
8		27	(a)	Accrington S	L	2-4	Gardner 2	4,295
9	Oct	4	(h)	Rochdale	W	3-0	Fenoughty, Sharpe, Laycock	4,308
10		11	(a)	Crewe A	L	1-5	Fenoughty	3,506
11		18	(h)	Stockport C	L	1-2	Jenkinson	4,676
12		25	(a)	Doncaster R	W	2-0	Evans, Fenoughty	4,331
13	Nov	1	(h)	Halifax T	W	4-1	Beck 2, Fenoughty, D.Kelly	3,830
14		8	(a)	Darlington	L	0-3		4,832
15		15	(h)	Nelson	W	3-0	Ellis, J.Kelly, D.Kelly	3,874
16		22	(a)	Wigan Borough	L	1-3	J.Kelly	4,671
17	Dec	6	(a)	Lincoln C	L	1-4	J.Kelly	5,679
18		20	(a)	New Brighton	L	3-5	Gardner, Laycock, D.Kelly	2,223
19		25	(h)	Carlisle U	W	4-0	Gardner 2, Beck, Laycock	4,663
20		26	(a)	Carlisle U	L	0-2		7,772
21		27	(h)	Rotherham U	D	1-1	Tomlinson	4,352
22	Jan	1	(a)	Gateshead	L	1-2	Gardner	4,004
23		3	(a)	Chesterfield	L	1-3	Laycock	4,760
24		17	(h)	Barrow	W	4-2	Evans 2, Fenoughty, J.Kelly	3,534
25	Feb	4	(h)	Hartlepools U	W	4-2	Cowie 3, Millar	1,793
26		7	(a)	Rochdale	D	2-2	Evans, Cowie	2,577
27		14	(h)	Crewe A	W	4-3	Laycock 2, Cowie, Millar	3,445
28		17	(a)	Southport	L	0-1		2,400
29		21	(a)	Stockport C	D	0-0		4,982
30		28	(h)	Doncaster R	W	4-2	D.Kelly 2, Fenoughty, McCabe	3,921
31	Mar	7	(a)	Halifax T	D	0-0		2,429
32		14	(h)	Darlington	W	2-1	Fenoughty 2	4,439
33		18	(h)	Hull C	W	3-2	Beck (pen), McCabe, Laycock	3,548
34		21	(a)	Nelson	W	5-2	Fenoughty 2, McCabe, Laycock, D.Kelly	1,645
35		28	(h)	Wigan Borough	L	2-3	Beck, Laycock	2,678
36	Apr	3	(h)	Gateshead	W	4-3	Beck, Fenoughty, McCabe, Laycock	4,352
37		4	(a)	Hartlepools U	L	0-3		3,329
38		6	(h)	Accrington S	W	3-1	Fenoughty, McCabe, Laycock	4,933
39		11	(h)	Lincoln C	D	1-1	Fenoughty	6,004
40		18	(a)	Hull C	L	1-3	Brewis	4,432
41		25	(h)	New Brighton	W	4-1	McCabe 2, Brewis, Millar	1,735
42	May	2	(h)	Wrexham	L	0-1		2,533
	FINAL LEAGUE POSITION: 12th in Division Three North							Appearances
								Goals

FA Cup

Rd	Month	Day	Venue	Opponent	Res	Score	Scorers	Att
1	Nov	29	(h)	Gresley R	W	3-1	Evans, Laycock, J.Kelly	4,236
2	Dec	13	(a)	Nelson	D	1-1	Brewis	3,000
R		18	(h)	Nelson	W	3-2	Laycock 2, Sharpe	2,206
3	Jan	10	(a)	Sheffield U	D	1-1	Laycock	31,821
R		14	(h)	Sheffield U	L	0-2		12,721
								Appearances
								Goals

Farmery J	Brooks J	Johnson S	Beck H	Davis C	Thompson O	Evans S	Fenoughty T	Gardner W	Laycock F	Stockill R	Kelly D	Kelly J	Brewis T	Sharpe G	Archibald D	Ridley R	Jenkinson M	Duthie J	Ellis T	Cowie J	Tomlinson R	Millar W	McCabe B	Loughran J	
1	2	3	4	5	6	7	8	9	10	11															1
1	2	3	4	5	6	7	8	9	10		11														2
1	2	3	4	5	6	7	8				11	10	9												3
1	2	3	4	5		7	8	9			11			10	6										4
1	2	3	4	5		7	8	9			11			10	6										5
1	2	3	4	5		7	8	9			11			10	6										6
1	2	3	4	5	6	7	8	9			11			10											7
1	2	3	4	5	6	7	8	9			11			10											8
1	2	3	4	5	6	7	8	9	10					11											9
1	2	3	4	5	6	7	8	9	10					11											10
	2	3	5		6		10	9					8	11		1	7	4							11
1	2	3	4	5	6	7	8	9			11			10											12
1	2	3	4	5	6	7	8	9			11			10											13
1	2	3	4	5	6	7	8	9			11			10											14
1	2	3	4	5	6	7	8				11	10							9						15
1	2	3	4	5	6	7	8					11							9	10					16
1	2	3	4	5	6		8		10			11		9			7								17
1	2	3	4	5	6			9	10		11			8					7		•				18
	2	3	5		6	7		9	8					10		1		4			11				19
	2	3	5		6	7		9	8					10		1		4			11				20
	2		5		6	7		9	8					10	3	1		4			11				21
	2	3	5		6	7	10	9	8							1		4				11			22
	2	3	5		6		10	9	8		7					1		4				11			23
1	2	3	4	5	6	7	10		8			9										11			24
1	2	3	4	5	6	7	10		8											9		11			25
1	2	3	5		6	7	10		8									4		9		11			26
1	2	3	5		6	7	10		8									4		9		11			27
1	2		5		6	7	10	9	8						3			4				11			28
1	2	3	5		6		10		8		7	9						4				11			29
1	2	3	5		6		10		8		7							4				11	9		30
1	2	3	5		6		10		8		7							4				11	9		31
1	2	3	5		6		10		8		7							4				11	9		32
1	2	3	5		6		10		8		7							4				11	9		33
1	2	3	5		6		10		8		7							4				11	9		34
1	2	3	5		6		10		8		7							4				11	9		35
	2	3	5		6	7	10		8							1		4				11	9		36
	2	3			6	7	10		8							1		4				11	9	5	37
	2	3	5		6	7	10		8							1		4				11	9		38
	2		5		6	7	10		8						3	1		4				11	9		39
	2		5		6	7	10						8		3	1		4				11	9		40
	2		5		6		10				7		8		3	1		4				11	9		41
	2		4	5	6		10				7		8		3	1						11	9		42
29	42	36	41	20	39	29	38	20	27	1	22	6	5	16	9	13	2	22	3	4	3	21	13	1	
			9			5	17	10	12		7	4	2	1			1		1	5	1	3	7		

Farmery J	Brooks J	Johnson S	Beck H	Davis C	Thompson O	Evans S	Fenoughty T	Gardner W	Laycock F	Stockill R	Kelly D	Kelly J	Brewis T	Sharpe G	Archibald D	Ridley R	Jenkinson M	Duthie J	Ellis T	Cowie J	Tomlinson R	Millar W	McCabe B	Loughran J	
1	2	3	4	5	6	7	10		8			9							11						1
1	2	3	4	5	6				10		7	9	8					11							2
1	2	3	4	5	6			9	10		7		8	11											R
1	2	3	4	5	6	7	10	9	8													11			3
1	2	3	4	5	6	7	10	9	8													11			R
5	5	5	5	5	5	3	3	3	5		2	2	2	1				1	1			2			
						1			4			1	1	1											

1931-32

Secretary-Manager: Mr G.W.Sherrington

1	Aug	29	(h)	Tranmere R	W 3-2	Brewis, McCabe, Fenoughty	5,203
2	Sep	2	(h)	Southport	L 1-2	Brewis	2,574
3		5	(a)	Rotherham U	W 1-0	McCabe	6,685
4		9	(a)	Gateshead	L 0-6		14,100
5		12	(h)	Stockport C	W 1-0	Fenoughty	4,130
6		16	(h)	Gateshead	W 3-2	Brewis 2, McDonald	6,199
7		19	(a)	Accrington S	L 1-2	McCabe	4,468
8		26	(h)	Wrexham	W 3-2	Kelly 2, Thompson	4,855
9	Oct	3	(a)	Carlisle U	D 1-1	Baines	5,809
10		10	(h)	Crewe A	D 3-3	Fenoughty 2, Kelly	3,998
11		17	(a)	New Brighton	W 2-0	Baines 2 (1 pen)	2,836
12		24	(h)	Barrow	W 1-0	McDonald	3,895
13		31	(a)	Hull C	W 3-2	Baines 2, Mitchell	7,155
14	Nov	7	(h)	Lincoln C	D 1-1	Baines	4,626
15		14	(a)	Chester	L 0-3		7,207
16		21	(h)	Hartlepools U	W 3-1	Baines 2 (1 pen), Brewis	4,113
17	Dec	5	(h)	Darlington	W 3-0	Brewis 2, McDonald	4,146
18		12	(a)	Walsall	D 2-2	Brewis, Baines	3,181
19		19	(h)	Walsall	W 2-0	Kelly 2	3,664
20		25	(a)	Doncaster R	L 0-1		4,896
21		26	(h)	Doncaster R	L 1-2	McDonald	8,183
22	Jan	1	(a)	Southport	L 0-3		6,378
23		2	(a)	Tranmere R	D 2-2	Baines 2	5,037
24		16	(h)	Rotherham U	W 2-0	Baines, Fenoughty	3,692
25		23	(a)	Stockport C	L 2-3	Baines, Fenoughty	5,499
26		30	(h)	Accrington S	W 1-0	Fenoughty	3,860
27	Feb	6	(a)	Wrexham	L 1-2	Brewis	3,829
28		13	(h)	Carlisle U	L 2-4	Baines, Fenoughty	2,475
29		20	(a)	Crewe A	L 1-8	Baines	6,220
30		27	(h)	New Brighton	W 4-0	Baines 3, Jenkinson	3,169
31	Mar	5	(a)	Barrow	L 1-3	Fenoughty	4,885
32		12	(h)	Hull C	D 0-0		5,012
33		19	(a)	Lincoln C	D 1-1	Opp own-goal	7,327
34		25	(h)	Rochdale	W 5-2	Jenkinson 2, Baines 2, Thompson	5,285
35		26	(h)	Chester	W 3-1	Spooner, Jenkinson, Baines	5,368
36		28	(a)	Rochdale	W 5-3	Baines 3, Spooner, Fenoughty	1,387
37	Apr	2	(a)	Hartlepools U	L 2-7	Baines, Fenoughty	2,590
38		16	(a)	Darlington	L 1-4	Baines	2,478
39		23	(h)	Halifax T	W 7-2	Baines 3, McDonald 2, Jenkinson, Fenoughty	2,154
40		28	(a)	Halifax T	L 1-4	Fenoughty	1,618

FINAL LEAGUE POSITION: 9th in Division Three North

Appearances
Goals

FA Cup

1	Nov	28	(a)	New Brighton	L 1-3	McDonald	3,371

Appearances
Goals

Ridley R	Archibald D	Johnson S	Jones W	Beck H	Thompson O	Kelly D	Brewis T	McCabe B	Fenoughty T	McDonald T	Brooks J	Spooner P	Mitchell T	Baines R	Harris J	Blackburn S	Wass E	Jenkinson M	Thornton R	Fox S	
1	2	3	4	5	6	7	8	9	10	11											1
1	2	3	4	5	6	7	8	9	10	11											2
1			4	5	6	7	8	9	3	10	2	11									3
1		3	4	5	6	7	8	9		10	2	11									4
1		3	4	5	6	7	8	9	10	11	2										5
1		3	4	5	6	7	8	9	10	11	2										6
1		3	4	5	6	7		9	8	10	2		11								7
1		3	4	5	6	7		9	8	10	2		11								8
1		3	4	5	6	7	8			10	2		11	9							9
1		3	4	5	6	7			8	10	2		11	9							10
1		3	4	5	6	7			8	10	2		11	9							11
1	2	3		5	6	7			8	10			11	9	4						12
1	2	3		5	6	7			8	10			11	9	4						13
1	2	3		5	6	7			8	10		11		9	4						14
1	2	3		5	6	7			8	10			11	9	4						15
1	2	3		5	6	7	8			11				9	4	10					16
1	2	3		5	6	7	8			10			11	9	4						17
1	2	3		5	6	7	8			10		11		9	4						18
1	2	3		5	6	7	8			10			11	9	4						19
1	2	3		5	6	7	8			10			11	9	4						20
1	2	3		5	6	7	8			10			11	9	4						21
1	2	3	4	5	6	7	8		10			11		9							22
1	2			5	6	7	8		4	10		11		9			3				23
1	2	3		5	6	7	8		10			11		9	4						24
1	2	3		5	6		8		10			11		9	4			7			25
1	2	3		5	6		8		10			11		9	4			7			26
1	2	3		5	6		8		10			11		9	4			7			27
1	2	3		5	6		8		10			11		9	4			7			28
1		3			6		8		5	10	2	11		9	4			7			29
	2	3			6	8				10		11		9	5			7	1	4	30
	2	3			6				8	10		11		9	5			7	1	4	31
	2	3		4	6				8	10		11		9	5			7	1		32
	2	3		4	6				8	10		11		9	5			7	1		33
	2	3		4	6	8				10		11		9	5			7	1		34
	2	3		5	6				8	10		11		9				7	1	4	35
	2	3		5	6				8	10		11		9				7	1	4	36
	2	3		4	6				8	10		11		9	5			7	1		37
	2	3		4	6				8	10				9	5			7	1	11	38
	2	3		4	6				8	10		11		9	5			7	1		39
	2	3		4	6				8	10		11		9	5			7	1		40
29	30	38	12	37	40	26	21	8	30	34	10	22	12	32	25	1	1	16	11	5	
					2	5	9	3	13	6		2	1	29				5			

1 own-goal

1	2	3		5	6	7			8	10			11	9	4						1
1	1	1		1	1	1			1	1			1	1	1						
										1											

1932-33

Secretary-Manager: Mr G.W.Sherrington

1	Aug	27	(a)	Crewe A	L 0-1		6,086
2		31	(h)	Stockport C	D 2-2	Baines (pen), Mitchell	8,106
3	Sep	3	(h)	Rochdale	L 2-6	Fenoughty, Mitchell	4,363
4		5	(a)	Stockport C	L 0-2		6,157
5		10	(a)	Southport	L 1-5	Baines	5,381
6		17	(h)	Mansfield T	W 4-3	Baines 3 (1 pen), Fenoughty	4,313
7		24	(a)	Rotherham U	L 0-1		4,130
8	Oct	1	(h)	Accrington S	D 0-0		4,553
9		8	(a)	New Brighton	W 1-0	Baines	2,840
10		15	(h)	Chester	W 3-1	McDonald 2, Baines	5,689
11		22	(h)	Gateshead	D 2-2	Baines, Spooner	6,150
12		29	(a)	Walsall	L 2-4	Baines, Spooner	3,623
13	Nov	5	(h)	Wrexham	L 2-3	T.Maskill, Baines	5,130
14		12	(a)	Tranmere R	W 3-2	Baines 2, Spooner	3,230
15		19	(h)	Halifax T	W 5-3	Fenoughty 2, Spooner 2, McDonald	3,624
16	Dec	3	(h)	Barnsley	W 3-2	Baines, McDonald, Spooner	3,480
17		17	(h)	Doncaster R	L 2-3	Fox, Baines	3,234
18		24	(a)	Darlington	L 0-3		4,524
19		27	(a)	Barrow	L 0-1		3,830
20		31	(h)	Crewe A	W 4-0	Baines 2, McDonald, T.Maskill	3,058
21	Jan	7	(a)	Rochdale	W 4-1	Baines 2, Fenoughty, Spooner	3,968
22		14	(a)	Hartlepools U	L 2-4	Donaldson, Baines	3,105
23		28	(a)	Mansfield T	L 0-2		4,127
24	Feb	4	(h)	Rotherham U	W 4-3	Spooner 2, Baines, T.Maskill	3,237
25		11	(a)	Accrington S	L 0-5		2,199
26		18	(h)	New Brighton	W 3-0	Spooner 2, Jenkinson	2,683
27	Mar	4	(a)	Gateshead	D 2-2	Jenkinson, Fenoughty	3,651
28		11	(h)	Walsall	W 4-2	Baines 2, Fenoughty, Jenkinson	4,992
29		18	(a)	Wrexham	L 1-3	Baines	7,487
30		25	(h)	Tranmere R	L 0-1		3,847
31		29	(a)	Chester	L 0-5		7,927
32	Apr	1	(a)	Halifax T	L 0-2		2,845
33		5	(h)	Barrow	W 3-1	Baines 3	2,332
34		8	(h)	Hartlepools U	D 1-1	Baines	3,720
35		14	(a)	Carlisle U	L 1-5	Fenoughty	6,256
36		15	(a)	Barnsley	D 1-1	Jenkinson	4,667
37		17	(h)	Carlisle U	L 0-1		4,250
38		22	(h)	Hull C	L 1-2	Baines	8,673
39		26	(h)	Southport	L 0-1		2,904
40		29	(a)	Doncaster R	L 2-3	Jenkinson, Baines	4,275
41	May	1	(a)	Hull C	L 1-2	Jenkinson	19,233
42		6	(h)	Darlington	W 6-1	Fox, Jenkinson 2, Mitchell 2, Fenoughty	3,432

FINAL LEAGUE POSITION: 20th in Division Three North

Appearances
Goals

FA Cup

1	Nov	26	(h)	Scarborough	L 1-3	Spooner	8,958

Appearances
Goals

Duckworth J	Archibald D	Johnson S	Maskill G	Harris J	Bolton J	Williams L	Fenoughty T	Baines R	McDonald T	Mitchell T	Fox S	Pinder J	Turnbull J	Spooner P	Spargo S	Wass E	Donaldson T	Fawcett D	Greener R	Camidge W	Jenkinson M	Moore W	Maskill T	
1	2	3	4	5	6	7	8	9	10	11														1
1	2	3	4	5	6	7	8	9	10	11														2
1	2		4	5	6		8	9	10	11	7					3								3
1				4	6				10	11	8	2	9	7	5	3								4
1				4	6	7		9	10	11		2		7	5	3								5
1	2	3		4	6	7	8	9	10					11	5									6
1	2	3			6	7	8	9	10					11	5								4	7
	2	3		4			8	9	10					11	5		7	1					6	8
	2	3		4			8	9	10					11	5		7	1					6	9
	2			4			8	9	10		3			11	5		7	1					6	10
	2	3		4			8	9	10					11	5		7	1					6	11
	2			4			8	9	10		3			11	5		7	1					6	12
	2	3		4			8	9	10					11	5		7	1					6	13
		3		4			8	9	10					11	5		7	1	6				2	14
		3		4			8	9	10					11	5		7	1	6				2	15
		3		4			8	9	10					11	5		7	1	6				2	16
		3		4				9	10		8			11	5		7	1	6				2	17
	2			4		7		9	10			3		11	5			1		8			6	18
	2			4				9	10			3		11	5		7	1	8				6	19
	2			4				9	10			3		11	5		7	1	8				6	20
	2			4			6	9	10			3		11	5		7	1	8					21
	2			4			6	9	10			3		11	5		7	1	8					22
	2			4				9	10			3		11	5		7	1	8				6	23
	2			4				9	10			3		11	5		7	1	8				6	24
	2			4		7	6	9	10			3		11	5			1	8					25
	2			4			6	9	10			3		11	5			1	8		7			26
	2			4			8	9	10			3		11	5			1			7		6	27
	2			4			8	9	10			3		11	5			1			7		6	28
	2			4			8	9	10			3		11	5			1			7		6	29
	2			4			8	9	10			3		11	5			1			7		6	30
	2			4				9	10					11	5			1	8	3	7		6	31
	2			4				9	10	6				11	5	3		1	8		7			32
	2			4				9	10	6		3		11	5			1	8		7			33
	2			4				9	10	6		3		11	5			1	8		7			34
				4			3	9	10	11		2			5			1	8		7		6	35
				5			10	9			4					3	2	1	8		7	11	6	36
				5			10	9			4					3	2	1	8		7	11	6	37
	2			5			8	9	10		4	11						1	6		7		3	38
		2					8	9	10		4			11		5		1	6		7		3	39
							8	9	10		4			11	5	2		1	6		7		3	40
							8		10	9	4			11	5	2		1	6		7		3	41
							8		10	9	4			11	5	2		1	6		7		3	42
7	29	13	3	37	7	7	30	39	40	11	12	19	1	35	35	10	18	35	24	2	17	2	29	
							9	29	5	4	2			11			1				8		3	

Duckworth J	Archibald D	Johnson S	Maskill G	Harris J	Bolton J	Williams L	Fenoughty T	Baines R	McDonald T	Mitchell T	Fox S	Pinder J	Turnbull J	Spooner P	Spargo S	Wass E	Donaldson T	Fawcett D	Greener R	Camidge W	Jenkinson M	Moore W	Maskill T	
		3		4			8	9	10					11	5		7	1	6				2	1
		1		1			1	1	1					1	1		1	1	1				1	
														1										

1933-34

Manager: John Collier

1	Aug	26	(h)	Walsall	D 2-2	Wilcockson, Ivory	5,475
2		30	(a)	Crewe A	L 3-5	Dando 2, Lockie	4,899
3	Sep	2	(a)	Hartlepools U	L 0-2		5,310
4		6	(h)	Crewe A	W 4-1	Wilcockson, Fenoughty, Dando, Opp own-goal	5,632
5		9	(a)	Chester	D 1-1	Jenkinson	7,942
6		16	(h)	Doncaster R	L 1-2	Ivory (pen)	6,708
7		23	(a)	Barrow	D 2-2	Dawson, Dando	5,305
8		30	(h)	Carlisle U	W 4-1	Dando 2, Fenoughty, Ivory	5,179
9	Oct	7	(a)	Stockport C	L 1-2	Fox	5,137
10		14	(h)	Halifax T	W 1-0	Jenkinson	5,555
11		21	(h)	Mansfield T	W 1-0	Hathway	5,261
12		28	(a)	Barnsley	L 0-1		5,300
13	Nov	4	(h)	Tranmere R	W 1-0	Jenkinson	4,434
14		18	(h)	Chesterfield	L 1-2	Dando	6,103
15	Dec	2	(h)	Gateshead	D 1-1	Hathway	3,569
16		9	(a)	Darlington	L 0-4		2,577
17		16	(h)	Southport	W 1-0	Dando	2,919
18		23	(a)	Wrexham	W 3-2	Dando 2, Lax	3,719
19		25	(h)	Rotherham U	L 0-1		3,641
20		26	(a)	Rotherham U	L 2-3	Lax 2	6,783
21		30	(a)	Walsall	L 0-1		5,839
22	Jan	1	(a)	Southport	D 0-0		3,537
23		6	(h)	Hartlepools U	L 1-3	Dando	4,118
24		20	(h)	Chester	W 3-2	Hathway 2 (2 pens), Ivory	4,171
25		24	(a)	Accrington S	L 1-4	Hathway	1,306
26		27	(a)	Doncaster R	L 1-3	Ivory	4,878
27	Feb	3	(h)	Barrow	W 6-1	Hathway 3, Dando 2, Jenkinson	2,857
28		10	(a)	Carlisle U	L 2-3	Wilcockson, Ivory	3,319
29		17	(h)	Stockport C	D 2-2	Scott, Ivory	5,030
30		20	(a)	Rochdale	W 6-3	Wilcockson 2, Dando 2, Ivory, Hathway	800
31		24	(a)	Halifax T	L 0-3		5,400
32	Mar	3	(a)	Mansfield T	W 2-0	Jenkinson, Hathway	4,843
33		10	(h)	Barnsley	D 1-1	Jenkinson	2,851
34		17	(a)	Tranmere R	L 0-3		2,610
35		24	(h)	Rochdale	W 6-1	Dando 3, Hathway 2, Lax	3,382
36		30	(h)	New Brighton	W 2-1	Dando 2	5,026
37		31	(a)	Chesterfield	L 0-2		10,163
38	Apr	2	(a)	New Brighton	L 1-2	Dando	3,441
39		7	(h)	Accrington S	W 3-2	Dando 2, Lax	3,928
40		14	(a)	Gateshead	W 2-0	Hathway, Dando	1,482
41		21	(h)	Darlington	D 1-1	Ivory	3,455
42	May	5	(h)	Wrexham	L 2-4	Hathway, Dando	2,286

FINAL LEAGUE POSITION: 12th in Division Three North

Appearances
Goals

FA Cup

1	Nov	25	(h)	Hartlepools U	L 2-3	Lax, Jenkinson	6,734

Appearances
Goals

Fawcett D	Pinder J	Dawson W	Scott J	Lockie T	Wilcockson S	Jenkinson M	Ivory G	Clayson W	Fenoughty T	King H	Dando M	Fox S	Wass E	Bonass A	Wightman J	Slicer J	Hathway T	Lax W	Burrows W	Whitelaw W	Strain D	
1	2	3	4	5	6	7	8	9	10	11												1
1	2	3	4	5	6	7	8	11	10		9											2
1	2			5	6	7	8		10		9	4	3	11								3
1		3	5		6	7	8		10		9	4	2	11								4
1		3	5		6	7	8		10		9	4	2	11								5
1		3	5			7	8		10		9	4	2	11	6							6
1		3	5		6	7	8		10		9	4	2	11								7
1		3	5		6	7	8		10		9	4	2			11						8
1		3	5		6	7	8		10		9	4	2			11						9
1		3	5		6	7	8		10		9		2			11	4					10
1		3	5		6	7	8		10		9		2			11	4					11
1		3	5		6	7		8	10		9	4	2			11						12
1		3	5		6	7		8	10		9		2		4	11						13
1		3	5		6	7		8			9		2		10		4	11				14
1		3	5		6	7			10		9	4	2				8	11				15
1		3	5		6	7		8			9	4	2				10	11				16
1		3		5	6	7			10		9	4	2				8	11				17
1		3		5	6	7			10		9	4	2				8	11				18
		3		5	6	7			10		9	4	2				8	11	1			19
	2	3	4	5	6				10		9	7					8	11	1			20
1		3		5	6	7			10		9	4	2				8	11				21
1		3		5	6	7			10		9	4	2				8	11				22
1		3	4	5	6		8				9	7	2				10	11				23
1		3	4	5	6	7	8				9		2				10	11				24
1		3	4	5	6	7	8				9		2				10	11				25
1		3	4	5	6		8	7			9		2				10	11				26
1		3	4	5	6	7	8				9		2				10	11				27
1		3	4	5	6	7	8				9		2				10	11				28
1		3	4	5	6	7	8				9		2				10	11				29
1			4	5	6	7	8				9		2				10	11			3	30
1			4	5	6	7	8				9		2				10	11			3	31
1				5	6	7	8				9	4	2				10	11			3	32
1			4	5	6	7	8				9		2				10	11			3	33
1			4	5	6	7	8				9		2				10	11			3	34
1			4	5	6	7	8				9		2				10	11			3	35
1			4	5	6	7	8				9		2				10	11			3	36
1			4	5		7	8				9		2		6		10	11			3	37
1			4	5		7	8				9		2		6		10	11			3	38
1			4	5	6	7	8				9		2				10	11			3	39
1			4	5	6		8				9		2				10	11		7	3	40
1			4	5	6		8				9		2				10	11		7	3	41
				5	6	7	8				9	4	2	11			10		1		3	42
39	4	28	34	29	39	37	31	7	20	1	41	19	39	6	5	6	31	28	3	2	13	
		1	1	1	5	6	9		2		25	1					14	5				

1 own-goal

Fawcett D	Pinder J	Dawson W	Scott J	Lockie T	Wilcockson S	Jenkinson M	Ivory G	Clayson W	Fenoughty T	King H	Dando M	Fox S	Wass E	Bonass A	Wightman J	Slicer J	Hathway T	Lax W	Burrows W	Whitelaw W	Strain D	
1		3	5			7	8		10		9		2		6		4	11				1
1		1	1			1	1		1		1		1		1		1	1				
						1												1				

1934-35

Manager: John Collier

1	Aug	25	(a)	Darlington	L 0-2		5,763
2		29	(h)	Stockport C	W 3-1	Bowater 2, Dando	5,177
3	Sep	1	(h)	Lincoln C	L 1-2	Dando	5,977
4		3	(a)	Stockport C	D 0-0		10,519
5		8	(h)	New Brighton	W 1-0	Bowater	4,217
6		15	(a)	Chester	L 1-5	Dando	8,592
7		22	(h)	Southport	W 3-1	Jenkins, Eyres, Dando	3,923
8		29	(a)	Doncaster R	L 1-4	Fox	5,041
9	Oct	6	(h)	Hartlepools U	W 3-1	Speed, Eyres, Dando	4,387
10		13	(a)	Crewe A	L 2-3	Barnes, Eyres	3,405
11		20	(a)	Tranmere R	L 0-4		7,362
12		27	(h)	Wrexham	D 0-0		4,035
13	Nov	3	(a)	Halifax T	L 3-5	Jenkins 2, Dando	9,013
14		10	(h)	Rotherham U	W 5-0	Dando 3, Eyres, Bowater	3,992
15		17	(a)	Walsall	W 3-2	Jenkins 2, Eyres	6,239
16	Dec	1	(a)	Mansfield T	L 1-5	Bowater	5,227
17		15	(a)	Carlisle U	L 0-4		2,629
18		22	(h)	Rochdale	L 0-1		3,003
19		25	(h)	Accrington S	W 5-2	Jenkins 2, Dando, Hathway, Bowater	3,867
20		26	(a)	Accrington S	L 2-5	Dando, Bowater	3,877
21		29	(h)	Darlington	W 2-1	Dando, Hathway	4,223
22	Jan	5	(a)	Lincoln C	L 1-3	Hathway (pen)	3,900
23		19	(a)	New Brighton	L 2-4	Dando 2	2,948
24		26	(h)	Chester	D 1-1	Bowater	2,456
25	Feb	2	(a)	Southport	W 3-0	Speed, Eyres, Dando	2,112
26		9	(h)	Doncaster R	L 1-2	Dando	6,517
27		16	(a)	Hartlepools U	L 1-3	Opp own-goal	2,014
28		23	(h)	Crewe A	W 7-3	Johnson 2, Dando 2, Hathway 2, Eyres	3,023
29	Mar	2	(h)	Tranmere R	D 0-0		5,606
30		9	(a)	Wrexham	L 0-2		3,102
31		16	(h)	Halifax T	L 0-1		4,322
32		23	(a)	Rotherham U	L 1-4	Jenkins	5,302
33		27	(h)	Chesterfield	D 1-1	Tucker	1,862
34		30	(h)	Walsall	W 4-1	Hughes 3, Bowater	2,485
35	Apr	3	(h)	Barrow	D 1-1	Bowater	2,183
36		6	(a)	Chesterfield	L 1-3	Bowater	2,781
37		13	(h)	Mansfield T	W 2-1	Hughes, Eyres	3,504
38		19	(a)	Gateshead	L 1-2	Eyres	3,424
39		20	(a)	Barrow	W 3-0	Jenkins 2, Hughes	3,979
40		22	(h)	Gateshead	W 3-0	Eyres 2, Hathway (pen)	4,312
41		27	(h)	Carlisle U	W 7-0	Dando 3, Eyres 2, Pawson, Opp own-goal	2,864
42	May	4	(a)	Rochdale	L 0-2		5,212

FINAL LEAGUE POSITION: 15th in Division Three North

Appearances
Goals

FA Cup

1	Nov	24	(a)	Burton T	W 3-2	Hathway, Jenkins, Bowater	6,067
2	Dec	8	(h)	New Brighton	W 1-0	Speed	6,039
3	Jan	12	(h)	Derby C	L 0-1		13,612

Appearances
Goals

Cunningham J	Wass E	Turner A	Turner R	Routledge W	Speed F	Jenkins E	Eyres J	Dando M	Hathway T	Bowater G	Fox S	Pinder J	Barnes J	Hughes J	Bullock A	Johnson C	McDonald T	Tucker W	Pawson T	
1	2	3	4	5	6	7	8	9	10	11										1
1	3			5	6		8	9	10	11	4	2	7							2
1	3			5	6		8	9	10	11	4	2		7						3
1	3			5	6		8	9	10	11	4	2	7							4
1	3			5	6		8		10	11	4	2	7	9						5
1	3			5	6		8	9	10	11	4	2	7							6
1				5	6	7	8	9	3	11	4	2		10						7
1		3		5	6	7	8	9	10	11	4	2								8
1	3			5	6		8	9	10	11	4	2	7							9
1	3		4	5			8	9	10	11	6	2	7							10
1	3		4	5		7	8	9	10	11	6		2							11
1	3		4	5	6	7	8	9	10	11	2									12
1	3			5	6	7	8	9	10	11	2		4							13
1	3			5	6	7	8	9	10	11	4	2								14
1	3			5	6	7	8	9	10	11	4	2								15
1	3			5	6	7	8	9	10	11		2	4							16
1	3			5	6	7	8	9	10	11		2		4						17
1			4	5	6	7	8	9		10	3	2			11					18
1	3			5	6	7	8	9	10	11	4	2								19
1	3			5	6	7	8	9	10	11	4	2								20
1	3			5	6	7	8	9	10		4	2			11					21
1	2	3		5	6	7	8	9	10	11	4									22
1	3			5	6	7	8	9	10		4	2			11					23
1	3			5	6	7	8	9	10	11	4	2								24
1	3			5	6	7	8	9	10	11	4	2								25
1	3			5	6	7	8	9	10	11	4	2								26
1	3			5	6	7	8	9	10		4	2	11							27
1	3			5	6		8	9	10		4	2			11	7				28
1	3			5	6		8	9	10		4	2		11		7				29
1	3			5	6			9	10		4	2		8	11	7				30
1	3			5	6			9	10		4	2		8	11	7				31
1	3		5		6	7		9	10		4	2	8				11			32
1	2	3			5	8		9	6	11	4			10				7		33
1	2	3			5			9	6	11	4		8	10				7		34
1		3		5	6		8	9	2	11	4		7	10						35
1	2	3			5	7	8	9	10	11	4			6						36
1	3				5	7	8	9	10	11	4	2		6						37
1		3		5	6	7	8	9	10	11		2		4						38
1		3	4	5	6	7	8	9	10			2		11						39
1		3	4	5	6	7	8	9	10			2		11						40
1		3	4	5	6		8	9	10			2	7						11	41
1		3		5	6	7	8	9	10		4	2	11							42
42	33	12	9	37	40	28	37	41	41	30	35	33	15	15	6	4	1	2	1	
					2	10	13	21	6	11	1		1	5		2		1	1	

2 own-goals

Cunningham J	Wass E	Turner A	Turner R	Routledge W	Speed F	Jenkins E	Eyres J	Dando M	Hathway T	Bowater G	Fox S	Pinder J	Barnes J	Hughes J	Bullock A	Johnson C	McDonald T	Tucker W	Pawson T	
1	3			5	6	7	8	9	10	11	4	2								1
1	3			5	6	7	8	9	4	11		2		10						2
1	3			5	6	7	8	9	10		4	2			11					3
3	3			3	3	3	3	3	3	2	2	3		1	1					
					1	1			1	1										

1935-36

Manager: Mr J.Collier

1	Aug	31	(h)	Stockport C	L 0-4		6,605
2	Sep	2	(a)	Chesterfield	D 2-2	Banfield, Hathway	6,485
3		7	(a)	Crewe A	L 1-2	Speed	4,997
4		11	(h)	Chesterfield	D 1-1	Hathway	5,279
5		14	(h)	Accrington S	D 1-1	Speed	3,430
6		18	(h)	New Brighton	W 2-0	Speed, Green	3,271
7		21	(a)	Southport	W 1-0	Green	2,549
8		28	(h)	Chester	L 1-2	Hathway	4,917
9	Oct	5	(a)	Lincoln C	L 2-3	Lawie, Banfield	5,885
10		12	(h)	Rochdale	W 2-1	Speed, Green	4,487
11		19	(h)	Halifax T	D 2-2	Green 2	3,213
12		26	(a)	Oldham A	L 2-6	Banfield 2	4,880
13	Nov	2	(h)	Wrexham	D 1-1	Lindsay	4,047
14		9	(a)	Rotherham U	L 0-5		7,153
15		16	(h)	Mansfield T	W 7-5	Banfield, Hughes 2, Spooner 2, Lindsay, Green	3,643
16		23	(a)	Hartlepools U	L 2-4	Speed, Hathway	4,247
17	Dec	7	(a)	Walsall	L 0-6		6,182
18		21	(a)	Gateshead	D 0-0		2,417
19		26	(h)	Darlington	W 4-1	Speed 2, Lindsay, Spooner	3,290
20		28	(a)	Stockport C	L 2-3	Speed 2	6,394
21	Jan	2	(a)	Darlington	L 0-3		4,024
22		4	(h)	Crewe A	W 4-1	Green 2, Speed (pen), Routledge	3,883
23		11	(h)	Carlisle U	W 2-0	Hughes, Hathway	4,134
24		18	(a)	Accrington S	L 2-7	Speed, Spooner	2,345
25	Feb	1	(a)	Chester	L 0-12		3,775
26		8	(h)	Lincoln C	W 2-1	Hughes, Spooner	3,485
27		15	(a)	Rochdale	W 3-2	Speed, Hughes, Spooner	4,670
28		22	(a)	Halifax T	L 0-2		3,690
29		29	(h)	Rotherham U	W 2-1	Hughes 2	1,811
30	Mar	7	(a)	Wrexham	L 0-1		1,522
31		14	(h)	Oldham A	W 3-1	Speed (pen), Banfield, Spooner	3,604
32		18	(h)	Southport	D 0-0		2,039
33		21	(a)	Mansfield T	L 0-5		4,367
34		28	(h)	Hartlepools U	D 2-2	Gray, Banfield	2,686
35	Apr	4	(a)	Carlisle U	D 0-0		4,537
36		10	(h)	Barrow	L 1-2	Banfield	5,589
37		11	(h)	Walsall	D 0-0		2,762
38		13	(a)	Barrow	D 1-1	Banfield	3,486
39		18	(a)	Tranmere R	L 1-3	Lindsay	5,215
40		22	(h)	Tranmere R	W 2-0	Banfield, Hathway	3,694
41		25	(h)	Gateshead	D 2-2	Lindsay 2	2,264
42	May	2	(a)	New Brighton	W 2-0	Lindsay 2	1,675

FINAL LEAGUE POSITION: 16th in Division Three North

Appearances
Goals

FA Cup

1	Nov	30	(h)	Burton T	L 1-5	Lindsay (pen)	6,182

Appearances
Goals

Wilson G	Pinder J	Young H	Fox S	Routledge W	Speed F	Green H	Banfield A	Graham J	Lawie C	Spooner P	Hathway T	Wass E	Lindsay D	Gray R	Legge E	Hughes J	Robinson A	Craven G	
1	2	3	4	5	6	7	8	9	10	11									1
1	2	3	4	5	6	7	8	9		11	10								2
1	2		4	5	6	7	8	9		11	10	3							3
1	2		4	5	6	7	8		9	11	10	3							4
1	2		4	5	6	7	8		9	11	10	3							5
1	2		4	5	6	7	8	9		11	10	3							6
1	2		4	5	6	7	8	9		11	10	3							7
1	2		4	5	6	7	8	9		11	10	3							8
1	2		4	5		7	8	9	10	11	6	3							9
1	2			5	6	7	8		10	11	4	3	9						10
1	2		4	5	6	7	8			11	10	3	9						11
1	2		4	5	6	7	8			11	10	3	9						12
1	2			5	6	7	8			11	10	3	9	4					13
1				5	6	7	8		10	11	4	2	9		3				14
1				5	6	7	8			11	4	2	9		3	10			15
1	2			5	6	7			10	11	4	3	9			8			16
1	2		4		5	7				11	6	3	9	8		10			17
1	2		4	5	8	7				11	10	3	9		6				18
1	2		4	5	6	7				11	8	3	9		6				19
1	2		4	5	6	7				11	8	3	9		6				20
1	2		4	5		7				11	8	3	9		6	10			21
1			4	5	6	7				11	8	2	9		3		10		22
1			4	5	6	7				11	8	2			3	9	10		23
1			4	5	6	7				11	8	2	9		3		10		24
1			2	8	6	7			4	11	8	5	9		3				25
1			4	5	6	7				11	8	2	9		3	10			26
1			4	5	6	7	8			11	10	2			3	9			27
1			4	5	6	7	8			11	10	2	9		3				28
1			4	5		7	8			11	10	2	9		3	6			29
1			4	5	6	7	8			11		2	9		3	10			30
1			4	5	6	7	8			11		2	9		3	10			31
1			4	5	6	7	8			11	10	2			3	9			32
1			4	5	6	7	8			11	2	3	9			10			33
			4	5	6	7	8			11	10	2		9	3			1	34
			4	5	6	7	8		10	11	9	2			3			1	35
			4	5	6	7	8		10	11	9	2			3			1	36
1			4	5	6	7				11	9	2		8	3	10			37
1			4	5	6	7	8			11	10	2			3	9			38
1			4	5	6	7	8			11	10	2	9		3				39
1			4	5	6	7	8			11	10	2	9		3				40
1			4	5	6	7	8			11	10	2	9		3				41
1	2			8	6	7	10			11	4	5	9		3				42
39	20	2	36	41	39	42	30	7	10	42	39	40	25	4	26	14	3	3	
				1	13	8	10		1	7	6		8	1		7			

Wilson G	Pinder J	Young H	Fox S	Routledge W	Speed F	Green H	Banfield A	Graham J	Lawie C	Spooner P	Hathway T	Wass E	Lindsay D	Gray R	Legge E	Hughes J	Robinson A	Craven G	
1	2			5	6	7			8	11	4	3	10			9			1
1	1			1	1	1			1	1	1	1	1			1			
													1						

1936-37

Manager: John Collier

1	Aug	29	(a)	Halifax T	W 2-1	Hathway (pen), Hughes	8,955
2	Sep	2	(h)	Tranmere R	W 4-0	Spooner 2, Hathway, Nicol	7,118
3		5	(h)	Mansfield T	D 1-1	Agar	7,504
4		7	(a)	Tranmere R	D 0-0		5,272
5		12	(a)	Crewe A	D 2-2	Nicol, Spooner	4,090
6		19	(h)	Chester	L 0-2		10,629
7		26	(a)	Rochdale	L 0-3		4,598
8	Oct	3	(h)	Barrow	L 1-2	Hewitson	5,883
9		10	(a)	Port Vale	D 1-1	Spooner	7,627
10		17	(h)	Rotherham U	W 4-3	Spooner 2, Hughes, Comrie	3,804
11		24	(a)	Stockport C	L 0-6		9,835
12		31	(h)	Wrexham	L 3-4	Thompson 2 (1 pen), Comrie	4,660
13	Nov	7	(a)	Darlington	D 1-1	Thompson	3,739
14		14	(h)	Gateshead	W 2-0	Hathway, Thompson	5,511
15		21	(a)	Hull C	L 0-1		7,039
16	Dec	5	(a)	Lincoln C	L 1-3	Agar	4,758
17		19	(a)	Oldham A	D 2-2	Thompson 2	5,636
18		25	(h)	Hartlepools U	W 4-1	Hughes 2, Thompson 2	7,170
19		26	(h)	Halifax T	W 4-0	Agar, Hughes, Thompson, Spooner	6,418
20		28	(a)	Hartlepools U	L 0-2		2,744
21	Jan	1	(a)	Carlisle U	D 1-1	Legge (pen)	9,904
22		2	(a)	Mansfield T	W 2-1	Hathway 2	4,008
23		9	(h)	Crewe A	L 2-3	Hughes, Thompson	5,240
24		23	(a)	Chester	L 1-3	Nicol	4,235
25	Feb	6	(a)	Barrow	D 2-2	Thompson, Spooner	3,905
26		10	(h)	Rochdale	W 4-1	Comrie 2, Agar, Thompson	2,292
27		13	(h)	Port Vale	L 1-2	Comrie	4,241
28		20	(a)	Rotherham U	D 2-2	Thompson, Spooner	4,035
29		27	(h)	Stockport C	W 2-1	Legge, Spooner	3,993
30	Mar	6	(a)	Wrexham	L 0-2		2,995
31		13	(h)	Darlington	W 3-0	Thompson 3	3,805
32		20	(a)	Gateshead	L 2-3	Hathway 2	2,233
33		26	(a)	Southport	W 4-1	Whitelaw 2, Thompson 2	5,603
34		27	(h)	Hull C	D 1-1	Thompson	6,975
35		29	(h)	Southport	W 4-0	Thompson 2, Whitelaw, Comrie	6,191
36	Apr	3	(a)	New Brighton	L 1-4	Whitelaw	3,487
37		10	(h)	Lincoln C	D 0-0		5,086
38		14	(h)	Accrington S	W 4-2	Gledhill 2, Scott 2	3,065
39		17	(a)	Accrington S	L 1-2	Gledhill	2,318
40		21	(h)	New Brighton	W 2-1	Gledhill, Spooner	3,313
41		24	(h)	Oldham A	W 3-1	Comrie 2, Gledhill	4,347
42	May	1	(h)	Carlisle U	W 5-2	Thompson 3, Scott, Spooner	3,147

FINAL LEAGUE POSITION: 12th in Division Three North

Appearances
Goals

FA Cup

1	Nov	28	(h)	Hull C	W 5-2	Agar 3, Thompson 2	7,783
2	Dec	12	(a)	Southend U	D 3-3	Spooner, Thompson 2	11,200
R		16	(h)	Southend U	W 2-1*	Comrie, Spooner	6,789
3	Jan	16	(a)	Bradford C	D 2-2	Comrie, Spooner	13,291
R		20	(h)	Bradford C	W 1-0	Nicol	12,226
4		30	(a)	Swansea T	D 0-0		12,110
R	Feb	3	(h)	Swansea T	L 1-3	Hathway	11,545

* After extra-time

Appearances
Goals

Wharton N	Wass E	Legge E	Fox S	Duckworth R	Hathway T	Agar A	Hughes J	Nicol J	Comrie M	Spooner P	Hewitson W	Porritt W	Denholme G	Pinder J	Gledhill S	Young H	Thompson A	Scott J	Whitelaw J	Lee G	
1	2	3	4	5	6	7	8	9	10	11											1
1	2	3	4	5	6	7	8	9	10	11											2
1	2	3	4	5	6	7	8	9	10	11											3
1	2	3	4	5	6	7	8	9	10	11											4
1	2	3	4	5	6	7	8	9	10	11											5
1	2	3	4	5	6	7	8	9	10	11											6
1	2	3	4	5	6		8		10	11	9	7									7
1	2	3	4	5	6	7			10	11	9	7	8								8
1	5	3		4	6	7		9	10	11				2	8						9
1		3	4	5	6	7	9		10	11				2	8						10
1		3		5		7	8	9	10	11				2	4	6					11
1	3			5		7	8		10	11				2	4	6	9				12
1	5			4	6	7	8		10	11				2		3	9				13
1	5			4	6	7	8		10	11				2		3	9				14
1	5	3		4	6	7	8		10	11				2			9				15
1	5	3		4	6	7	8		10	11				2			9				16
1	5	3		4	6	7	8		10			11		2			9				17
1	5	3		4	6	7	8		10	11				2			9				18
1	5	3		4	6	7	8		10	11				2			9				19
1	5	3		4	6	7	8		10	11				2			9				20
1	5	3		4	6	7	8	9	10	11				2							21
1	5	3		4	6		8	9	10	11				2	7						22
1	5	3		4	6	7	8		10	11				2			9				23
1		3	4	5	6	7	8	9	10	11						2					24
1	5	3		4	6	7	8		10	11				2			9				25
1	5	3		4	6	7	8		10	11				2			9				26
1	5	3		4	6		8		10	11				2			9	7			27
1	5	3		4	6		8		10	11				2			9	7			28
1	5	3	2	4	6		8		10	11							9	7			29
1	5	3	2	4	6		8		10	11							9	7			30
1	5	3	2	4	6				10	11							9	7	8		31
1	5	3	2	4	6				10	11							9	7	8		32
1	5	3	2		6				10	11		4					9	7	8		33
1	5	3	2		6				10	11		4					9	7	8		34
1	5	3	2	4	6				10	11							9	7	8		35
1	5	3	2	4	6				10	11							9	7	8		36
1	5	3	2	4	6				10	11							9	7	8		37
1	5	3	2	4	6				10	11					9			7	8		38
1	5		2	4	6				10	11			3		9			7	8		39
1	5		2	4	6				10	11			3		9			7	8		40
1	5		2	4	6				8	10			3		9			7		11	41
1	5	3	2	4	6				8	10							9	7		11	42
42	39	36	24	40	40	24	28	11	42	41	2	4	4	19	9	5	24	16	10	2	
		2			7	4	6	3	8	12	1				5		24	3	4		

Wharton N	Wass E	Legge E	Fox S	Duckworth R	Hathway T	Agar A	Hughes J	Nicol J	Comrie M	Spooner P	Hewitson W	Porritt W	Denholme G	Pinder J	Gledhill S	Young H	Thompson A	Scott J	Whitelaw J	Lee G	
1	5	3		4	6	7	8		10	11				2			9				1
1	5	3		4	6	7	8		10	11				2			9				2
1	5	3		4	6	7	8		10	11				2			9				R
1	5	3	6	4	8		7	9	10	11				2							3
1	5	3		4	6		7	9	10	11				2			8				R
1	5	3	6	4	8		7	9	10	11				2							4
1	5	3	6	4	8		7		10	11				2			9				R
7	7	7	3	7	7	3	7	3	7	7				7			5				
					1	3		1	2	3							4				

1937-38

Manager: Tom Mitchell

1	Aug	28	(a)	Rochdale	D 0-0		8,448
2	Sep	1	(h)	Doncaster R	W 2-0	Comrie 2	8,633
3		4	(h)	Rotherham U	W 4-1	Hathway, Scott, Baines, Spooner	7,395
4		11	(a)	Chester	L 3-4	Baines 3	7,284
5		14	(a)	Southport	W 3-2	Spooner 2, Scott	5,601
6		18	(h)	Accrington S	D 1-1	Scott	7,033
7		25	(a)	Carlisle U	L 1-2	Comrie	6,467
8	Oct	2	(h)	Halifax T	D 1-1	Comrie	6,278
9		9	(a)	Tranmere R	W 2-1	Baines, Spooner	8,924
10		16	(a)	Oldham A	L 2-6	Comrie 2	7,967
11		23	(h)	Darlington	L 1-2	Hughes	3,178
12		30	(a)	Port Vale	L 2-3	Scott, Hughes	5,139
13	Nov	6	(h)	Crewe A	L 1-2	Spooner	3,996
14		13	(a)	Barrow	W 2-1	Baines, Hughes	4,368
15		20	(h)	Wrexham	W 2-1	Baines 2	4,719
16	Dec	4	(h)	Lincoln C	W 3-1	Scott, Hughes, Baines (pen)	3,418
17		18	(h)	New Brighton	W 3-1	Hughes, Baines, Comrie	4,235
18		25	(a)	Gateshead	D 2-2	Hughes, Spooner	10,439
19		27	(h)	Gateshead	W 5-1	Baines 2, Spooner 2, Earl	9,069
20	Jan	1	(h)	Rochdale	L 0-5		5,971
21		12	(a)	Hartlepools U	D 0-0		2,665
22		15	(a)	Rotherham U	L 0-3		6,117
23		26	(h)	Chester	W 4-0	Earl 2, Baines, Comrie	3,380
24		29	(a)	Accrington S	W 2-1	Earl, Spooner	3,067
25	Feb	5	(h)	Carlisle U	W 3-1	Baines 2, Spooner	6,284
26		14	(a)	Halifax T	D 2-2	Carr 2	1,785
27		19	(h)	Tranmere R	W 2-0	Hughes 2	6,141
28		26	(h)	Oldham A	D 0-0		8,519
29	Mar	12	(h)	Port Vale	D 2-2	Baines 2	7,319
30		16	(a)	Darlington	D 2-2	Scott 2	2,808
31		19	(a)	Crewe A	L 2-4	Baines, Comrie	4,961
32		26	(h)	Barrow	L 1-2	Baines	4,593
33	Apr	2	(a)	Wrexham	D 1-1	Comrie	3,412
34		9	(h)	Hartlepools U	W 1-0	Baines	3,565
35		15	(h)	Bradford C	W 3-1	Comrie 2, Baines	7,796
36		16	(a)	Lincoln C	L 0-2		7,088
37		19	(a)	Bradford C	W 1-0	Baines	7,296
38		23	(h)	Hull C	L 0-1		9,494
39		25	(a)	Hull C	L 1-3	Lee	15,416
40		30	(a)	New Brighton	L 1-2	Baines	2,775
41	May	2	(a)	Doncaster R	L 1-2	Lee	1,259
42		7	(h)	Southport	L 1-2	Lee	4,082

FINAL LEAGUE POSITION: 11th in Division Three North — Appearances

Goals

FA Cup

1	Nov	27	(h)	Halifax T	D 1-1	Hughes	7,063
R	Dec	1	(a)	Halifax T	W 1-0	Baines	6,244
2		11	(a)	Clapton O	D 2-2	Scott, Comrie	7,713
R		15	(h)	Clapton O	W 1-0	Hughes	7,599
3	Jan	8	(h)	Coventry C	W 3-2	Spooner, Hughes, Earl	13,917
4		22	(h)	West Brom A	W 3-2	Baines 3	18,795
5	Feb	12	(h)	Middlesbrough	W 1-0	Spooner	23,860
6	Mar	5	(h)	Huddersfield T	D 0-0		28,123
R		9	(a)	Huddersfield T	L 1-2	Baines	58,066

Appearances

Goals

Wharton N	Pinder J	Legge E	Duckworth R	Wass E	Hathway T	Scott J	Earl S	Baines R	Comrie M	Spooner P	Fox S	Gledhill S	Young H	Denholme G	Hughes J	Porritt W	Barrett C	McCartney C	Carr J	Lee G	Milton S	Milner L	
1	2	3	4	5	6	7	8	9	10	11													1
1	2	3	4	5	6	7	8	9	10	11													2
1	2	3	4	5	6	7	8	9	10	11													3
1	2	3	4	5	6	7	8	9	10	11													4
1	2	3	4	5		7	8	9	10	11	6												5
1	2	3	4	5		7	8	9	10	11	6												6
1	2	3	4	5		7	8	9	10	11		6											7
1	2	3	4	5	6	7	8	9	10	11													8
1		3		5	4	7	8	9	10	11			2	6									9
1		3		5	4	7	8	9	10	11			2	6									10
1		3	4	5	6	7	8		10	11			2		9								11
1	2	3	4	5	6	7		9	10	11					8								12
1	2		4	5	6	7		9	10	11					8		3						13
1		3		5	6		8	9		11		4			10	7	2						14
1		3	4	5	6		8	9		11					10		3	7					15
1		3	4	5	6	7		9	10	11					8		2						16
1		3	4	5	6			9	10	11					8	7	2						17
1		3	4	5	6		7	9	10	11					8		2						18
1		3	4	5	6		7	9	10	11					8		2						19
1		3	4	5	6		7	9	10	11					8		2						20
1	2		5		4		7		10	11				6	8		3		9				21
1	2		4	5	6		7	9	10	11					8		3						22
1	2		4	5	6		7	9	10	11					8		3						23
1	2			5	6		7	9	10	11		4			8		3						24
1	2		4	5	6		7	9	10	11					8		3						25
1		3	4	5		7	8			11	2	6			10				9				26
1	2		4	5	6		7	9	10	11					8		3						27
1	2		4	5	6		7	9	10	11					8		3						28
1	2		4	5			7	9	10	11		6			8		3						29
1	2		4	5		7	8	9		11		6			10		3						30
1	2		4	5	6	7	8	9	10	11							3						31
1	2		4	5			7	9	10	11		6			8		3						32
1	2		4	5			7	9	10	11		6			8		3						33
1	2		4	5			8	9	10	11		6				7	3						34
1	2		4	5			8	9	10	11		6				7	3						35
1	2			5			7	9	10	11	4	6			8		3						36
1	2		4	5			7	9	10	11		6			8		3						37
1	2		4	5		11	7	9	10			6			8		3						38
1	2		4	5		7	8	9	10			6					3			11			39
1	2		4	5		7	8	9	10			6					3			11			40
1	2		4	5		7	8	9	10			6					3			11			41
	2		4	5		7	8	9			6						3			11	1	10	42
41	31	20	37	41	25	22	38	39	37	37	5	16	3	3	25	4	29	1	2	4	1	1	
					1	7	4	23	12	10					8				2	3			

Wharton N	Pinder J	Legge E	Duckworth R	Wass E	Hathway T	Scott J	Earl S	Baines R	Comrie M	Spooner P	Fox S	Gledhill S	Young H	Denholme G	Hughes J	Porritt W	Barrett C	McCartney C	Carr J	Lee G	Milton S	Milner L	
1		3	4	5	6	7		9	10	11					8		2						1
1		3	4	5	6	7		9	10	11					8		2						R
1		3	4	5	6	7		9	10	11					8		2						2
1		3	4	5	6	7		9	10	11					8		2						R
1	2		4	5	6		7	9	10	11					8		3						3
1	2		4	5	6		7	9	10	11					8		3						4
1	2		4	5	6		7	9	10	11					8		3						5
1	2		4	5	6		7	9	10	11					8		3						6
1	2		4	5	6		7	9	10	11					8		3						R
9	5	4	9	9	9	4	5	9	9	9					9		9						
						1	1	5	1	2					3								

1938-39

Manager: Tom Mitchell

1	Aug	27	(a)	Doncaster R	L 0-1		13,337
2		31	(h)	Darlington	D 1-1	Mortimer	6,080
3	Sep	3	(h)	Rotherham U	L 0-1		5,310
4		6	(a)	Southport	D 1-1	Firth	6,340
5		10	(a)	Rochdale	D 2-2	Scott, Hughes	5,494
6		17	(h)	Halifax T	W 3-0	Mortimer 2, Earl	6,018
7		24	(h)	Wrexham	W 1-0	Mortimer	6,191
8	Oct	1	(a)	Gateshead	W 3-2	Mortimer 2, Lee	8,723
9		8	(h)	Hartlepools U	W 2-0	Mortimer, Earl	6,208
10		15	(a)	New Brighton	L 2-3	Mortimer, Lee	5,177
11		22	(h)	Barrow	L 2-3	Scott, Earl	6,484
12		29	(a)	Chester	L 1-5	Hughes	7,315
13	Nov	5	(h)	Bradford C	L 0-1		5,995
14		12	(a)	Hull C	L 0-2		8,159
15		19	(h)	Lincoln C	L 1-3	Mortimer	5,333
16		26	(a)	Barnsley	L 0-1		10,708
17	Dec	3	(h)	Accrington S	D 2-2	Hathway (pen), Lee	4,561
18		10	(a)	Bradford C	L 0-6		5,549
19		17	(h)	Oldham A	W 4-1	Mortimer 2, Milner, Lee	5,141
20		24	(h)	Doncaster R	D 2-2	Hughes, Earl	6,562
21		26	(h)	Crewe A	W 4-1	Mortimer 2, Earl, Lee	8,182
22		27	(a)	Crewe A	L 2-8	Mortimer, Lee	7,240
23		31	(a)	Rotherham U	L 0-2		6,615
24	Jan	14	(h)	Rochdale	L 0-7		3,826
25		21	(a)	Halifax T	L 1-2	Mortimer	3,393
26		28	(a)	Wrexham	W 3-1	Mortimer 2, Scott	3,565
27	Feb	4	(h)	Gateshead	D 1-1	Hughes	5,754
28		11	(a)	Hartlepools U	L 2-3	Porritt, Scott	3,105
29		18	(h)	New Brighton	W 2-0	Mortimer 2	4,935
30		25	(a)	Barrow	L 0-2		5,581
31	Mar	4	(h)	Chester	D 2-2	Mortimer, Brenen	4,106
32		18	(h)	Hull C	W 1-0	Mortimer	5,023
33		25	(a)	Lincoln C	D 3-3	Porritt, Mortimer, Brenen	4,178
34	Apr	1	(h)	Stockport C	L 1-2	Hathway	5,262
35		7	(a)	Carlisle U	W 3-1	Hathway, Scott, Brenen	5,285
36		8	(a)	Accrington S	L 1-3	Hathway	2,545
37		10	(h)	Carlisle U	W 4-1	Milner 2, Brenen (pen), Lee	5,479
38		15	(h)	Barnsley	L 2-3	Milner, Opp own-goal	6,454
39		22	(a)	Oldham A	L 0-6		3,340
40		24	(a)	Stockport C	L 1-3	Hawkins	2,160
41		29	(a)	Darlington	W 2-1	Scott, Porritt	3,462
42	May	6	(h)	Southport	L 2-3	Brenen, Lee	3,523

FINAL LEAGUE POSITION: 20th in Division Three North

Appearances
Goals

FA Cup

3	Jan	11	(h)	Millwall	L 0-5		6,950

Appearances
Goals

Wharton N	Pinder J	Barrett C	Duckworth R	Wass E	Hathway T	Reynolds W	Firth J	Mortimer R	Earl S	Spooner P	Milner L	Scott J	Hughes J	Springett F	Gledhill S	Lee G	Hamer A	Porritt W	Milton S	Kelly J	Hawkins J	Denholme G	Flatley A	Brenen A	Chappell S	
1	2	3	4	5	6	7	8	9	10	11																1
1	2	3	4	5	6	7	8	9	10	11																2
1	2	3	4	5	6		8	9		11	10	7														3
1		3		5	6		8	9		11		7	10	2	4											4
1	2	3		5	6			9	8	11		7	10		4											5
1	2			5	6			9	8			7	10		4	11	3									6
1	2			5	4			9	8			7	10		6	11	3									7
1	2			5	4			9	8			7	10		6	11	3									8
1	2			5	4			9	8			7	10		6	11	3									9
1		3	4	5	6			9	8			7	10			11	3									10
1	2			5	4			9	8			7	10		6	11	3									11
1		3		5	4			9				8	10		6	11	3	7								12
	2	3		5	4			9				8	10		6	11		7	1							13
	2	3	4	5	6	7		9				8	10			11			1							14
	2		4	5	6			9	7	11		8	10				3		1							15
1	2	3	4	5	6		8			11		7	10		9											16
1	2	3	4	5	6			9				7	10		8	11										17
1	2	3	4	5	6		8	9				7	10			11										18
1					4			9	7		10		8	2	6	11				3	5					19
					4			9	7		10		8	2	6	11			1	3	5					20
1					4			9	7		10		8	2	6	11				3	5					21
1	2				4			9	7		10		8		6	11				3	5					22
1	2		5		4			9	7		10		8		6	11				3						23
	2		4	5	6			9			10	7			8	11			1	3						24
1					4			9	8			7	10	2	6	11				3	5					25
1					4			9	8	11		7	10	2	6					3	5					26
1					4			9	8	11		7	10	2	6					3	5					27
1	2				4				10	11		7	9		6			8		3		5				28
1					4			9		11		7		2	6			8		3	5		10			29
1					4			9		11		7		2	6			8		3	5		10			30
1					4			9				7		2	6	11		10		3	5			8		31
1					4			9				7		2	6	11		10		3	5			8		32
1					4			9				7		2	6	11		10		3	5			8		33
1					4			9				7		2	6	11		10		3	5			8		34
1					4							7		2	6	11		10		3	5		9	8		35
1					4							7		2	6	11		10		3	5		9	8		36
1					4						9	7		2	6	11		10		3	5			8		37
1					4						9	7		2	6	11		10		3	5			8		38
1	2				4				7		9				6	11		10		3	5			8		39
	2				4			9				7			6	11		10	1	3	5			8		40
	2				4			9				7			6	11		10	1	3	5			8		41
	2				4			9				7				11		10	1	3	5			8	4	42
34	23	12	11	19	42	3	6	35	20	12	10	34	24	17	34	30	8	17	8	24	21	1	4	12	1	
					4		1	22	5		4	6	4			8		3			1			5		

1 own-goal

1	2		4	5	6			9	7				8		10	11				3						3
1	1		1	1	1			1	1				1		1	1				1						

1946-47

Manager: Tom Mitchell

1	Aug	31	(h)	Chester	D 4-4	Carr 2, Allen, Nettleton	7,016
2	Sep	4	(h)	Rotherham U	L 2-3	Allen 2	5,229
3		7	(a)	Rochdale	W 1-0	Allen	8,315
4		11	(h)	Lincoln C	L 2-4	Winters, Nettleton	6,930
5		14	(a)	Tranmere R	L 1-2	Allen	6,958
6		21	(h)	Darlington	W 3-0	Pinder (pen), Forster, Jackson	7,712
7		28	(a)	Hull C	D 2-2	Allen, Winters	22,249
8	Oct	5	(h)	Gateshead	W 3-1	Allen 2, Jackson	8,502
9		12	(a)	Hartlepools U	D 1-1	Brenen	9,238
10		19	(h)	Doncaster R	L 1-4	Pinder (pen)	15,485
11		26	(a)	Wrexham	L 1-3	Park	5,369
12	Nov	2	(h)	Stockport C	W 3-2	Pinder (pen), Forster, A.Patrick	6,842
13		9	(a)	Oldham A	D 2-2	Allen, A.Patrick	9,439
14		16	(h)	Bradford C	L 0-3		8,725
15		23	(a)	Barrow	W 1-0	Bradley	4,757
16	Dec	7	(a)	Carlisle U	W 2-1	Porritt 2	11,144
17		25	(a)	Southport	W 3-0	A.Patrick 2, Allen	5,435
18		26	(h)	Southport	D 1-1	Pinder (pen)	10,410
19		28	(a)	Chester	L 0-6		7,358
20	Jan	1	(a)	Rotherham U	L 1-6	Carr	14,947
21		4	(h)	Rochdale	L 2-3	Gledhill, Allen	5,363
22		11	(h)	Accrington S	L 0-1		2,273
23		18	(h)	Tranmere R	L 0-1		5,918
24		25	(a)	Darlington	L 1-3	A.Partick	7,625
25	Feb	1	(h)	Hull C	W 3-0	A.Patrick 2, Allen	7,099
26	Mar	22	(a)	Bradford C	L 2-3	Allen, A.Patrick	9,447
27		29	(h)	Barrow	L 0-2		5,731
28	Apr	4	(a)	Crewe A	L 0-2		7,267
29		7	(h)	Crewe A	L 2-3	A.Patrick 2	6,610
30		12	(h)	Carlisle U	D 2-2	Rudd 2 (1 pen)	6,090
31		19	(a)	Halifax T	W 3-0	A.Patrick 2, Rudd	3,804
32		26	(h)	New Brighton	L 1-2	Bradley	4,448
33	May	3	(a)	Lincoln C	D 2-2	A.Patrick, Rudd	6,443
34		10	(h)	Hartlepools U	L 1-4	Butt	4,514
35		14	(a)	Accrington S	W 2-1	A.Patrick 2	3,252
36		17	(a)	New Brighton	W 3-0	M.Patrick, A.Patrick, Rudd (pen)	4,223
37		21	(h)	Oldham A	W 1-0	A.Patrick	4,975
38		24	(a)	Gateshead	W 2-1	Winters 2	8,502
39		26	(h)	Halifax T	W 2-0	Rudd 2	5,745
40		27	(h)	Wrexham	D 2-2	Winters, Rudd	4,753
41		31	(a)	Stockport C	L 2-4	Winters, Rudd	5,615
42	Jun	7	(a)	Doncaster R	D 0-0		15,070

FINAL LEAGUE POSITION: 15th in Division Three North

Appearances
Goals

FA Cup

1	Dec	14	(h)	Scunthorpe U	L 0-1		7,849

Appearances
Goals

Ferguson R	Pinder J	Gledhill S	Brenen A	Roberts A	Collier A	Scott F	Carr F	Allen W	Patrick M	Nettleton E	Rodgers C	Jackson A	Porritt W	Duthoit J	Winters I	Reagan M	Jowett J	Park W	Forster L	Kubicki E	Wojtczak E	Porteous J	Patrick A	Bradley C	Lee G	Gargan J	Butt L	Rudd J	Greenwell D	Bentall E	Pickering P	Lawson J	Storey S	
1	2	3	4	5	6	7	8	9	10	11																								1
1	2	3	4		6	7	8	9	10	11	5																							2
1	2		5		6		8	9	10	11	3	4	7																					3
1	2		5		6			8	10	11	3	4		7	9																			4
1	2	6	5		4			8				10		3	9	7	11																	5
1	2	3	4		6			8		11		10			9			5	7															6
1	2	3	10		4			8	11			6			9			5	7															7
1	2	6	10		4			9				8		3				5	7	11														8
1	2	6	10		4			9				8		3				5	7	11														9
1	2	6	8		4			9	10					3				5	7	11														10
	2	3	4					9	10			8						5	7	11	1	6												11
	2		4					8	10		3							5	7	11	1	6	9											12
	2	4	5					8	11		3								7		1	6	9	10										13
	2		4					8	11		3							5	7		1	6	9	10										14
1	2		4					8	11		3		7					5				6	9	10										15
1	2		4					8	11		3		7					5				6	9	10										16
1	2		4					8	11		3		7					5				6	9	10										17
1	2		4					8	7		3							5				6	9	10	11									18
1	2		4					8	11		3		7					5				6	9	10										19
1	2		4				10	8	11		3		7					5				6	9											20
1	2	4					10	8	11				7	3	9			5				6												21
1	2						10	8				6	11	3	9			5	7							4								22
1	2	4						9	11			10	7	3				5				6					8							23
1	2	4					8		10	11			7	3				5				6	9											24
1	2	4						8		11	3		7					5				6	9				10							25
1	2	4						8			3		7					5				6	9				10	11						26
1	2	4	5					8			3		7									6	9				10	11						27
1	2		5					8			3		7									6	9				10	11	4					28
1		4	5					8	7		3			2								6	9				10	11						29
1		4	5						7		3			2								6	9	10			8	11						30
	2	4	5						7					3							1	6	9	10			8	11						31
	2		4						7					3				5			1	6	9	10			8	11						32
	2		4						7					3	10			5			1	6	9				8	11						33
	2	3	4						7						10						1	6	9				8	11		5				34
	2	4	5						7		3	6			10								9				8	11			1			35
	2	4	5						7		3	6			10								9				8	11			1			36
	2	4	5						7		3	6			10								9				8	11			1			37
	2	4	5					9	7		3	6			10												8	11			1			38
	2	4	5					9	7		3	6			10												8	11			1			39
	2	4	5					9			3	6			8													11			1	7	10	40
	2	4	5					9	7		3	6			8													11			1		10	41
	2	4	5					9			3	6	7		8													11			1		10	42
26	40	28	36	1	10	2	7	33	31	7	26	18	15	14	16	1	1	22	10	5	8	23	23	10	1	1	16	17	1	1	8	1	3	
	4	1	1				3	13	1	2		2	2		6			1	2				17	2			1	9						

Ferguson R	Pinder J	Gledhill S	Brenen A	Roberts A	Collier A	Scott F	Carr F	Allen W	Patrick M	Nettleton E	Rodgers C	Jackson A	Porritt W	Duthoit J	Winters I	Reagan M	Jowett J	Park W	Forster L	Kubicki E	Wojtczak E	Porteous J	Patrick A	Bradley C	Lee G	Gargan J	Butt L	Rudd J	Greenwell D	Bentall E	Pickering P	Lawson J	Storey S	
1	2	6	4					8	11		3	10	7					5					9											1
1	1	1	1					1	1		1	1	1					1					1											

1947-48

Manager: Tom Mitchell

1	Aug	23	(a)	Mansfield T	W 2-1	A.Patrick, Storey	9,695
2		25	(h)	Carlisle U	D 2-2	Butt, A.Patrick	8,681
3		30	(h)	Halifax T	W 6-0	A.Patrick 4, M.Patrick 2	9,515
4	Sep	4	(a)	Carlisle U	D 1-1	Jackson (pen)	17,317
5		6	(h)	Oldham A	W 1-0	Rudd	10,899
6		10	(h)	Rotherham U	W 2-0	Rudd 2	13,684
7		13	(a)	Tranmere R	L 2-4	M.Patrick, Rudd	12,166
8		20	(h)	Darlington	L 0-2		10,008
9		27	(a)	Gateshead	D 0-0		6.723
10	Oct	4	(h)	Hartlepools U	W 4-0	Allen 2, M.Patrick, Winters	9,219
11		11	(a)	Rochdale	L 0-3		8,743
12		18	(h)	New Brighton	W 3-1	Allen 2, M.Patrick	8,218
13		25	(a)	Southport	L 1-2	Storey	7,518
14	Nov	1	(h)	Lincoln C	L 0-1		9,816
15		8	(a)	Accrington S	L 0-1		6,305
16		15	(h)	Hull C	D 2-2	Pyle, Winters	14,125
17		22	(a)	Stockport C	L 2-4	Brenen, Winters	9,282
18	Dec	6	(a)	Barrow	L 0-1		6,146
19		20	(h)	Mansfield T	L 1-2	Winters	5,863
20		26	(h)	Chester	W 2-0	A.Patrick 2	10,435
21		27	(a)	Chester	W 3-2	A.Patrick 3	8,754
22	Jan	1	(a)	Rotherham U	L 2-3	Jackson 2 (1 pen)	16,973
23		3	(a)	Halifax T	W 1-0	Rudd	7,696
24		10	(h)	Bradford C	D 3-3	M.Patrick, Storey, Rudd	8,007
25		17	(a)	Oldham A	D 2-2	Storey 2	10,239
26		24	(h)	Wrexham	D 1-1	M.Patrick	6,141
27		31	(h)	Tranmere R	L 1-2	Little	8,402
28	Feb	7	(a)	Darlington	D 1-1	A.Patrick	5,875
29		14	(h)	Gateshead	W 3-1	A.Patrick, Storey, Rudd	7,611
30		21	(a)	Hartlepools U	D 2-2	A.Patrick 2	4,890
31		28	(h)	Rochdale	D 0-0		7,311
32	Mar	6	(a)	New Brighton	L 1-2	Storey	4,614
33		13	(h)	Southport	D 3-3	Little, A.Patrick, Storey	7,964
34		20	(a)	Lincoln C	D 0-0		11,703
35		26	(a)	Crewe A	W 3-1	A.Patrick 2, M.Patrick	8,038
36		27	(h)	Accrington S	L 1-2	Pyle	10,156
37		29	(h)	Crewe A	L 0-1		9,712
38	Apr	3	(a)	Hull C	D 1-1	Storey	32,466
39		10	(h)	Stockport C	W 3-2	Brenen, Storey, Rudd	7,511
40		17	(a)	Bradford C	W 3-1	Storey 2, A.Patrick	6,341
41		24	(h)	Barrow	D 0-0		5,855
42	May	1	(a)	Wrexham	L 0-3		7,655

FINAL LEAGUE POSITION: 13th in Division Three North

Appearances
Goals

FA Cup

1	Nov	29	(h)	Rochdale	L 0-1		9,830

Appearances
Goals

Pickering P	Pinder J	McDermott M	Jackson A	Brenen A	Browne R	Patrick M	Butt L	Patrick A	Storey S	Rudd J	Gale T	Andrews P	Gledhill S	Duthoit J	Allen W	Winters I	Harnby D	Pyle E	Little G	Brown J	Simpson J	Pears J	Spence R	No.
1	2	3	4	5	6	7	8	9	10	11														1
1	2	3	4	5	6	7	8	9	10	11														2
1		3	4	2	6	7	8	9	10	11	5													3
1		3	4		6	7	8	9	10	11	5	2												4
1		3	4	2	6	7	8	9	10	11	5													5
1		3	6	2		7	8	9	10	11	5		4											6
1		3	6	2		7	8	9	10	11	5		4											7
1			6	2		7	8	9	10	11	5		4				3							8
1			6	4		7	8		10	11	5		3	2	9									9
1			6	4		7			10	11	5		3	2	9	8								10
1			6	4		7			10	11	5		3	2	9	8								11
1			6	4		7			10	11	5		3	2	9	8								12
1			6	4		7			10	11	5		3	2	9	8								13
1			6	4		7			10	11	5		3	2	9	8								14
1			6	4		7		9	10	11	5		3	2		8								15
1			6	4		7			10	11	5		3	2		9		8						16
1			6	4		7			10	11	5		3	2	8	9								17
1			6	4		7			10	11	5		3	2		9		8						18
1				4		7			8	11	5		3	2	6	9		10						19
1				4		10		9		11	5		3	2	6	8			7					20
1				4		8		9	10	11	5		3	2	6				7					21
1			6	4		8		9	10	11	5		3	2					7					22
1			6	4		8		9	10	11	5		3	2					7					23
1	2			4		8		9	10	11	5		3		6				7					24
1	2		9	4		8			10	11	5		3		6				7					25
1	2		9	4		8			10	11	5		3		6				7					26
1			9	4		8			10	11	5		3	2	6				7					27
1	2			4		11		9	10		5		3		6			8	7					28
1	2			4		8		9	10	11	5		3		6				7					29
1	2			4		8		9	10	11	5		3		6				7					30
1	2		9	4		8			10	11	5		3		6				7					31
1	2			4		8		9	10	11	5		3		6				7					32
1				4		8		9	10	11	5				6				7	2	3			33
1				4		7		9	10	11	5				6			8		2	3			34
1				4		7		9	10	11	5				6			8		2	3			35
1				4		7		9	10	11	5				6			8		2	3			36
				8		7		9	10	11	5		4		6					2	3	1		37
1			9	8		7			10	11	5		4		6					2	3			38
1				8		7		9	10	11	5		4		6					2	3			39
1				8		7		9	10	11	5		4		6					2	3			40
1				8		7		9	10	11	5		2		6						3		4	41
1				4		8		9	10	11	5				6				7	2	3			42
41	10	7	25	41	5	42	9	27	41	41	40	1	32	16	29	11	1	7	15	9	10	1	1	
			3	2		8	1	19	12	8					4	4		2	2					

Pickering P	Pinder J	McDermott M	Jackson A	Brenen A	Browne R	Patrick M	Butt L	Patrick A	Storey S	Rudd J	Gale T	Andrews P	Gledhill S	Duthoit J	Allen W	Winters I	Harnby D	Pyle E	Little G	Brown J	Simpson J	Pears J	Spence R	No.
1			6	4		7			10	11	5		3	2	8	9								1
1			1	1		1			1	1	1		1	1	1	1								

1948-49

Manager: Tom Mitchell

1	Aug	21	(h)	Crewe A	L 1-3	A.Patrick	10,123
2		23	(a)	Southport	W 2-0	Brigham (pen), Pyle	10,280
3		28	(a)	Halifax T	W 2-1	Storey, M.Patrick	10,749
4		30	(h)	Southport	L 1-3	Storey	9,315
5	Sep	4	(a)	Stockport C	D 1-1	Storey	12,157
6		8	(a)	Chester	L 1-4	Storey	6,818
7		11	(h)	Carlisle U	W 6-0	Ivey 2, M.Patrick, A.Patrick, Rudd 2	8,041
8		13	(h)	Chester	W 2-0	Ivey, M.Patrick	9,511
9		18	(a)	Gateshead	D 1-1	A.Patrick	6,502
10		25	(h)	Hartlepools U	W 4-0	A.Patrick 2, M.Patrick, Allen	10,706
11	Oct	2	(a)	Darlington	L 1-3	Rudd	11,595
12		9	(h)	Wrexham	W 5-1	M.Patrick 2, A.Patrick 2, Allen	10,611
13		16	(a)	Barrow	L 0-5		9,336
14		23	(h)	Mansfield T	W 2-1	M.Patrick, Rudd	10,888
15		30	(a)	Tranmere R	D 0-0		8,019
16	Nov	6	(h)	Oldham A	W 4-0	A.Patrick 2, Brenen, Rudd	9,921
17		13	(a)	Accrington S	L 1-2	Brigham (pen)	3,617
18		20	(h)	Rotherham U	W 6-1	A.Patrick 5, Brigham (pen)	19,216
19	Dec	25	(a)	New Brighton	L 1-3	Price	4,772
20		26	(h)	New Brighton	W 2-1	A.Patrick 2	10,870
21	Jan	1	(h)	Halifax T	D 2-2	M.Patrick, Rudd	9,175
22		8	(h)	Doncaster R	L 2-3	Brigham (pen), Price	11,230
23		15	(h)	Stockport C	W 4-0	A.Patrick 3, Allen	5,487
24		22	(a)	Carlisle U	D 3-3	M.Patrick 2, Ivey	9,035
25		29	(a)	Crewe A	L 0-2		6,765
26	Feb	5	(h)	Gateshead	L 0-1		9,704
27		12	(a)	Bradford C	D 2-2	Hindle 2	9,405
28		19	(a)	Hartlepools U	W 3-2	Brigham (pen), M.Patrick, A.Patrick	8,148
29		26	(h)	Darlington	L 2-5	M.Patrick, A.Patrick	10,586
30	Mar	5	(a)	Wrexham	D 3-3	A.Patrick 2, Storey	3,062
31		12	(h)	Barrow	W 2-0	Hindle, Ivey	8,853
32		19	(a)	Mansfield T	L 0-3		8,197
33		26	(h)	Tranmere R	W 1-0	M.Patrick	6,799
34	Apr	2	(a)	Oldham A	L 0-4		16,317
35		6	(a)	Hull C	W 3-2	A.Patrick 2, Ivey	40,002
36		9	(h)	Accrington S	D 1-1	M.Patrick	8,409
37		15	(h)	Rochdale	D 1-1	Storey	12,438
38		16	(a)	Rotherham U	L 1-2	Ivey	14,229
39		18	(a)	Rochdale	L 0-2		7,759
40		23	(h)	Hull C	L 1-3	A.Patrick	21,010
41		30	(a)	Doncaster R	L 0-1		7,079
42	May	7	(h)	Bradford C	L 0-2		5,706
				FINAL LEAGUE POSITION: 14th in Division Three North			Appearances
							Goals

FA Cup

1	Nov	27	(h)	Runcorn	W 2-1	Brigham (pen), Rudd	10,858
2	Dec	11	(a)	Southport	D 2-2	Ivey, A.Patrick	10,000
R		18	(h)	Southport	L 0-2		12,837
							Appearances
							Goals

Frost J	Brigham H	Gledhill S	Peart R	Gale T	Allen W	Patrick M	Brenen A	Patrick A	Storey S	Rudd J	Spence R	Burton E	Pyle E	Simpson J	Brown J	Ivey G	Jackson A	Price J	Pears J	Middleton M	Hindle T	Duthoit J	Woollett C	Porter L	Andrews P	
1	2	5	4	5	6	7	8	9	10	11																1
1	2		3	5		8	6	9		11	4	7	10													2
1	2		6	5		7	4	9	10	11			8	3												3
1	2		6	5		7	4	9	10	11			8	3												4
1		2		5		8	6	9	10	11	4	7		3												5
1				5	6	8		9	10	11	4	7		3	2											6
1	2			5		8	6	9	10	11	4			3		7										7
1	2			5		8	6	9	10	11	4			3		7										8
1	2			5	10	8	6	9		11	4			3		7										9
1	2			5	10	8	6	9		11	4			3		7										10
1	2			5	10	8	6	9		11	4			3		7										11
1	2	6	4	5	10	8		9		11				3		7										12
1	2	6		5	10	8	4	9		11				3		7										13
1	2			5	6	8	4	9	10	11				3		7										14
1	2			5	6		4	9	10	11				3		7	8									15
1	2			5	6		8	9	10	11				3		7	4									16
1	2				6		5	9	10	11	8			3		7	4									17
1	2			5	6	8	4	9	10	11				3		7										18
1	2			5	6	8	4		10	11				3		7		9								19
	2			5	6	8	4	9	10	11				3		7			1							20
	2			5	6	8	4	9	10	11				3		7			1							21
1	2			5	6	8	4	9		11				3		7		10								22
1	2			5	8	7	6	9	10		4			3		11										23
1	2			5	6	8	4	9	10	11				3		7										24
1	2			5	6	8	4	9	10	11				3		7										25
1	2			5	8		6	9	10	11	4			3		7										26
	2			5	6		4	9	10					3		7				1	8		11			27
	2			5	6	7		9	10		4			3		11				1	8					28
	2			5	6	7	4	9	10					3		11				1	8					29
	2			5	6	7	4	9	10											1	8	3	11			30
	2			5	6	7	4	9	10					3		11				1	8					31
	2			5	6	7	4	9	10					3		11				1	8					32
				5	6	7	4	9	10					3	2	11				1	8					33
				5	6	7	4	9	10					3	2	11				1				8		34
				5	6	8	4	9	10					3	2	7				1	11					35
				5	6	8	4	9	10					3	2	7				1	11					36
					6	8	4	9	10					3	2	7				1	11				5	37
				5			6	9	10		4			3	2	7				1	8		11			38
					6		4	9	10					3	2	7				1	8		11		5	39
					6	8	4	9	10					3	2	7				1	11				5	40
						8	6	9	10		4			3	2	7				1	11				5	41
						8		9	10		4			3	2	7				1	11			6	5	42
24	30	4	5	36	33	35	38	41	35	25	15	3	3	39	11	35	3	2	2	16	15	1	4	2	5	
	5				3	14	1	26	6	6			1			7		2			3					

Frost J	Brigham H	Gledhill S	Peart R	Gale T	Allen W	Patrick M	Brenen A	Patrick A	Storey S	Rudd J	Spence R	Burton E	Pyle E	Simpson J	Brown J	Ivey G	Jackson A	Price J	Pears J	Middleton M	Hindle T	Duthoit J	Woollett C	Porter L	Andrews P	
1	2			5	6	8	4	9	10	11				3		7										1
1	2			5	6	8	4	9	10	11				3		7										2
1	2			5	6	8	4	9	10	11				3		7										R
3	3			3	3	3	3	3	3	3				3		3										
	1							1		1						1										

1949-50

Manager: Tom Mitchell

1	Aug	20	(a)	Barrow	L 2-3	M.Patrick, A.Patrick	8,136
2		24	(a)	Lincoln C	L 0-1		11,881
3		27	(h)	Crewe A	D 1-1	Coop	10,067
4		29	(h)	Lincoln C	L 1-2	Coop	9,007
5	Sep	3	(a)	Tranmere R	L 0-1		9,740
6		5	(h)	Mansfield T	D 3-3	Brenen, Ivey, Walker	8,563
7		10	(h)	Halifax T	W 3-1	M.Patrick, A.Patrick, Walker	8,776
8		12	(a)	Mansfield T	L 0-1		14,914
9		17	(h)	Oldham A	L 0-1		8,859
10		24	(a)	Wrexham	L 0-2		8,262
11	Oct	1	(h)	Accrington S	W 2-1	A.Patrick 2	7,274
12		8	(a)	Rochdale	L 1-3	M.Patrick	8,049
13		15	(h)	Bradford C	D 1-1	Allen	8,508
14		22	(a)	Chester	W 3-2	Benson, A.Patrick, Collins	6,370
15		29	(h)	Southport	L 0-1		7,919
16	Nov	5	(a)	Stockport C	L 1-3	Birch	10,626
17		12	(h)	Doncaster R	L 0-3		12,952
18		19	(a)	Gateshead	D 1-1	Walker	5,617
19	Dec	3	(a)	Darlington	D 1-1	Walker	6,472
20		17	(h)	Barrow	W 2-0	Allen, A.Patrick	4,358
21		24	(a)	Crewe A	D 3-3	A.Patrick 2, Walker	8,348
22		26	(h)	Carlisle U	D 1-1	Walker	11,648
23		27	(a)	Carlisle U	L 3-4	Walker 2, M.Patrick	14,298
24		31	(h)	Tranmere R	W 1-0	Benson	6,873
25	Jan	14	(a)	Halifax T	W 2-1	M.Patrick, Walker	6,286
26		21	(a)	Oldham A	L 0-2		13,423
27		28	(h)	Hartlepools U	L 0-2		5,913
28	Feb	4	(h)	Wrexham	W 5-0	Spence 3 (2 pens), A.Patrick 2	3,976
29		11	(h)	New Brighton	W 2-1	A.Patrick 2	5,257
30		18	(a)	Accrington S	D 0-0		6,059
31		25	(h)	Gateshead	L 1-5	Spence (pen)	5,465
32	Mar	4	(a)	Hartlepools U	L 0-2		6,134
33		11	(h)	Chester	L 2-3	Allen, Benson	5,986
34		18	(a)	Southport	D 1-1	Storey	5,851
35		25	(h)	Stockport C	D 1-1	M.Patrick	6,365
36	Apr	1	(a)	Doncaster R	D 1-1	A.Patrick	15,866
37		7	(h)	Rotherham U	L 0-3		12,382
38		8	(h)	Rochdale	D 2-2	A.Patrick, M.Patrick	6,102
39		10	(a)	Rotherham U	L 1-2	M.Patrick	6,367
40		15	(a)	Bradford C	W 2-0	M.Patrick, Coop	13,327
41		22	(h)	Darlington	D 1-1	Coop	7,055
42	May	6	(a)	New Brighton	L 1-3	Ivey	2,512

FINAL LEAGUE POSITION: 22nd in Division Three North

Appearances
Goals

FA Cup

1	Nov	26	(a)	Gateshead	L 1-3	Birch	6,144

Appearances
Goals

Middleton M	Stewart A	Simpson J	Spence R	Burgin E	Allen W	Ivey G	Patrick M	Patrick A	Hindle T	Coop J	Brenen A	Brown J	Storey S	Duthoit J	Thompson R	Collins A	Brigham H	Walker T	Andrews P	Benson R	Birch J	Jackson A	Grant A	Porter L	
1	2	3	4	5	6	7	8	9	10	11															1
1	2	3		5	6	7	8	9	10	11	4														2
1		3		5	6	7	8	9		11	4	2	10												3
1		3		5	6	7	8	9		11	4	2	10												4
1		3		5	6	7		9		11	4			2	8	10									5
1		3		5	6	11	7	9			4				8		2	10							6
1		3		5	6	11	7	9	8		4						2	10							7
1		3		5	6		7	9	8	11	4			2				10							8
1		3		5	6	11	7	9			4		10		8		2								9
1		3		5	6	11	7	9			4			2	8			10							10
1		3		5	6	11	7	9			4		10	2	8										11
1		3		5	6	11	7	9			4		10	2	8										12
1	5				6	7	10	9			4				8		2	11	3						13
1	5				6			9			4		8			10	2		3	7	11				14
1	5				6			9			4		8			10	2		3	7	11				15
1	5		4		8			9			6		10				2		3	7	11				16
1	5				6	7	8				4		10				2	9	3		11				17
1	5					7	8				6		10				2	9	3		11	4			18
1	5				6	7	8	9			4						2	10	3		11				19
1	5				6	7	8	9			4						2	10	3		11				20
1	5				6	11	8	9			4						2	10	3	7					21
1	5				6	11	8	9			4						2	10	3	7					22
1	5				6		8	9			4		11				2	10	3	7					23
1	5				6	11	8	9			4						2	10	3	7					24
1				5	6		11				4		10			8	2	9	3	7					25
1				5	6		11				4		10			8	2	9	3	7					26
1					6	7	11				5					10	2	9	3	8		4			27
1	5	3	8		6		11	9			4		10						2	7					28
1	5	3	8		6		11	9			4		10						2	7					29
1	5	3	8		6		11	9			4		10						2	7					30
1	5	3	8		6		11	9			4		10						2	7					31
1	5	3			6		11	9			4		10		8				2	7					32
1	5				6		11	9			4		8			10	2		3	7					33
	5				6		11	9			4		8			10	2		3	7			1		34
	5						11	9			4		8			10	2		3	7			1	6	35
	5	3					11	9			4		8			10	2			7			1	6	36
1	5	3			10		11	9			4		8				2			7				6	37
1	5					7	11	9			4		8				2		3			10		6	38
1	5					7	11	9			4		8				2		3			10		6	39
1	5	3				7	10	9		11	4		8						2					6	40
1	5	3				7	10	9		11	4		8						2					6	41
1	5	3			6	7	10	9		11	4		8				2								42
39	29	22	6	14	35	25	38	37	4	9	41	2	28	5	8	10	26	16	27	20	7	4	3	7	
			4		3	2	9	14		4	1		1			1		9		3	1				

Middleton M	Stewart A	Simpson J	Spence R	Burgin E	Allen W	Ivey G	Patrick M	Patrick A	Hindle T	Coop J	Brenen A	Brown J	Storey S	Duthoit J	Thompson R	Collins A	Brigham H	Walker T	Andrews P	Benson R	Birch J	Jackson A	Grant A	Porter L	
1	5	3				7	8	9			6		10				2				11	4			1
1	1	1				1	1	1			1		1				1				1	1			
																					1				

1950-51

Manager: Dick Duckworth

1	Aug	19	(a)	Tranmere R	L 2-7	Brown, M.Patrick	10,079
2		21	(h)	Hartlepools U	W 3-0	Daniels 2, Storey	10,522
3		26	(h)	Bradford	L 1-3	Storey	12,572
4		28	(a)	Hartlepools U	L 1-4	M.Patrick	8,648
5	Sep	2	(a)	Oldham A	D 2-2	Linaker, M.Patrick	12,393
6		4	(h)	Accrington S	W 3-0	M.Patrick 2, Linaker	7,417
7		9	(h)	Wrexham	W 3-0	Ivey 2, Brenen	8,480
8		16	(a)	Scunthorpe U	W 1-0	M.Patrick	12,101
9		23	(h)	Mansfield T	D 1-1	Ivey	9,273
10		26	(a)	Accrington S	L 0-2		7,237
11		30	(a)	Rotherham U	L 1-3	A.Patrick	6,807
12	Oct	7	(a)	Rochdale	W 1-0	Linaker	8,123
13		14	(h)	Chester	D 2-2	Linaker, M.Patrick	8,852
14		21	(a)	New Brighton	D 0-0		3,839
15		28	(h)	Bradford C	L 1-2	A.Patrick	8,863
16	Nov	4	(a)	Gateshead	L 0-3		7,614
17		11	(h)	Crewe A	L 1-2	Brenen	7,003
18		18	(a)	Shrewsbury T	L 0-1		8,567
19	Dec	2	(a)	Darlington	W 3-0	Linaker, Brown, Storey	4,428
20		23	(a)	Bradford	L 0-4		9,348
21		25	(h)	Southport	W 2-0	Linaker, Brown	7,873
22		26	(a)	Southport	D 1-1	Brown	5,703
23		30	(h)	Oldham A	D 2-2	Brown, M.Patrick	5,283
24	Jan	13	(a)	Wrexham	L 3-4	A.Patrick 2, R.Spence (pen)	5,159
25		20	(h)	Scunthorpe U	D 0-0		7,187
26		27	(h)	Carlisle U	D 1-1	Storey	7,677
27	Feb	3	(a)	Mansfield T	L 1-3	Storey	10,247
28		10	(a)	Halifax T	W 3-1	R.Spence (pen), Brown, M.Patrick	8,299
29		17	(h)	Rotherham U	D 3-3	M.Patrick 2, A.Patrick	9,184
30		24	(h)	Rochdale	D 2-2	Linaker, Brown	7,664
31	Mar	3	(a)	Chester	L 1-3	Linaker	4,828
32		10	(h)	New Brighton	W 2-0	Linaker 2	6,386
33		17	(a)	Bradford C	L 2-5	R.Spence, Brown	10,840
34		23	(h)	Barrow	L 0-2		9,714
35		24	(h)	Gateshead	D 1-1	Ivey	5,848
36		26	(a)	Barrow	L 0-2		4,920
37		31	(a)	Crewe A	W 4-2	A.Patrick 2, R.Spence, Storey	4,236
38	Apr	7	(h)	Shrewsbury T	W 2-0	A.Patrick, Linaker	5,426
39		11	(h)	Stockport C	D 0-0		5,520
40		14	(a)	Lincoln C	L 1-2	A.Patrick	8,363
41		16	(h)	Lincoln C	D 2-2	Linaker, Brenen	6,623
42		21	(h)	Darlington	D 1-1	Linaker	6,214
43		25	(h)	Tranmere R	W 4-0	M.Patrick 2, R.Spence, Storey	6,416
44		28	(a)	Stockport C	L 0-1		5,658
45	May	3	(a)	Carlisle U	L 2-3	R.Spence, Storey	7,335
46		5	(h)	Halifax T	D 0-0		2,791

FINAL LEAGUE POSITION: 17th in Division Three North

Appearances

Goals

FA Cup

1	Nov	25	(a)	Bishop Auckland	D 2-2	M.Patrick, Brenen	10,000
R		29	(h)	Bishop Auckland	W 2-1	A.Patrick 2	6,836
2	Dec	9	(h)	Tranmere R	W 2-1	A.Patrick 2	10,096
3	Jan	6	(a)	Bolton W	L 0-2		26,652

Appearances

Goals

Pegg J	Andrews P	Simpson J	Horton L	Stewart A	Daniels H	Linaker J	Brown G	Patrick A	Patrick M	Coop J	Frost J	Thompson K	Woodward B	Storey S	Brenen A	Ivey G	Spence R	Spence J	Ashley J	Burgin E	Medd G	Thompson D	Porter L	Lloyd D	
1	2	3	4	5	6	7	8	9	10	11															1
		3	4	5	6	7	8		11		1	2	9	10											2
		3	4	5	6	7	8		11		1	2	9	10											3
	3		4	5	6	7	8		11		1	2	9	10											4
		3	4	5		7			8		1	2	9	10	6	11									5
		3	4	5		7		9	8		1	2		10	6	11									6
		3	4	5		7		9	8		1	2		10	6	11									7
		3	4	5		7		9	8		1	2		10	6	11									8
		3	4	5		7		9	8	10	1	2			6	11									9
	2	3	4	5		7	10	9	8		1					11	6								10
	2	3	4	5		7	10	9	8		1				6	11									11
	3		4	5		7	10	9	8		1				2	11	6								12
	3		4	5		7	10	9	8		1				2	11	6								13
		3	4	5		7	10		9		1			8	6	11		2							14
		3	4	5		7	10	9						8	6	11		2	1						15
		3	4	5		7		9	8					10	6	11		2	1						16
		3	4	5		7	8	9	11		1			10	6			2							17
	2	3	4	5		7		9	11	8	1				10		6								18
	2	3	4	5		7	8	9	11					10			6		1						19
	2	3		5		7	8	9	11					10	4		6		1						20
	2	3		5		7	8	9	11					10	4		6		1						21
	2	3		5		7	8	9	11					10	4		6		1						22
	2	3	4	5		7	8	9	11		1			10			6								23
	2	3	4			7	8	9	11					10	5		6		1						24
	2	3		5		7	8	9	11		1			10	4		6								25
	2	3				7		9	8					10	4		6		1	5	11				26
	2	3				7	8	9	11					10	4		6		1	5					27
		3				7	8	9	11			2		10	4		6			5		1			28
		3				7	8	9	11			2		10	4		6			5		1			29
		3				7	8	9	11			2		10	4		6			5		1			30
	2	3				7	8	9	11					10	4		6			5		1			31
	2	3				7	8		11					10	5		6					1	4	9	32
	2	3				7	8	9	11					10	5		6					1	4		33
	2	3				7	8		11				9	10	5		6					1	4		34
	2	3				7		9	8					10	5	11	6					1	4		35
		3				7	11	9	8			2		10	5		6					1	4		36
		3				7		9	8			2		10	5	11	6			4		1			37
		3				7		9	8			2		10	5	11	6					1	4		38
		3				7		9	8			2		10		11	6			5		1	4		39
		3				7		9	8			2		10		11	6			5		1	4		40
		3		5		7			8					10	9	11	6	2				1	4		41
		3		5		7			8					10	9	11	6	2				1	4		42
				5		7	8		11			3		10	6		9	2				1	4		43
				5		7	8		11			3		10	6		9	2				1	4		44
		3		5		7	8		11			6		10			9	2				1	4		45
		3		5		7	8		11					10	6		9	2				1	4		46
1	21	41	21	30	4	46	31	33	45	3	17	19	5	39	36	19	32	10	9	9	1	19	14	1	
					2	13	8	9	13					8	3	4	6								

Pegg J	Andrews P	Simpson J	Horton L	Stewart A	Daniels H	Linaker J	Brown G	Patrick A	Patrick M	Coop J	Frost J	Thompson K	Woodward B	Storey S	Brenen A	Ivey G	Spence R	Spence J	Ashley J	Burgin E	Medd G	Thompson D	Porter L	Lloyd D	
	2	3	4	5		7		9	11	8					10		6		1						1
		3	4	5		7	8	9	11					10			6	2	1						R
	2	3		5		7	8	9	11					10	4		6		1						2
	2	3		5		7	8	9	10						4	11	6		1						3
	3	4	2	4		4	3	4	4	1				2	3	1	4	1	4						
								4	1						1										

1951-52

Manager: Dick Duckworth

1	Aug	18	(a)	Lincoln C	L 1-3	Slater	12,016
2		20	(h)	Tranmere R	D 1-1	Linaker	9,298
3		25	(h)	Chester	W 4-2	Fenton 2, Linaker, Opp own-goal	8,095
4		28	(a)	Tranmere R	L 0-2		8,400
5	Sep	1	(h)	Chesterfield	W 1-0	Fenton	8,969
6		3	(h)	Southport	L 0-2		7,976
7		8	(a)	Bradford C	D 3-3	Brown, M.Patrick, Fenton	14,840
8		11	(a)	Southport	L 1-2	M.Patrick	5,646
9		15	(h)	Hartlepools U	W 3-1	A.Patrick 2, Fenton	5,935
10		22	(a)	Oldham A	L 0-2		23,083
11		29	(h)	Darlington	W 2-1	Slater 2	6,710
12	Oct	6	(a)	Halifax T	D 1-1	A.Patrick	6,087
13		13	(h)	Mansfield T	W 3-0	Fenton 2, Linaker	7,577
14		20	(a)	Rochdale	W 2-0	R.Spence, Fenton	4,994
15		27	(h)	Accrington S	W 6-1	Fenton 3, Brown, Griffiths, A.Patrick	7,538
16	Nov	3	(a)	Carlisle U	L 1-2	Fenton	10,662
17		10	(h)	Stockport C	L 0-1		10,782
18		17	(a)	Workington	L 0-1		4,812
19	Dec	1	(a)	Grimsby T	D 0-0		12,398
20		8	(h)	Wrexham	W 4-2	Fenton 2, Griffiths, A.Patrick	5,543
21		22	(a)	Chester	W 1-0	Fenton	2,998
22		25	(h)	Bradford	W 1-0	Fenton	8,786
23		26	(a)	Bradford	L 1-2	R.Spence	15,125
24		29	(a)	Chesterfield	L 1-2	Hughes	8,748
25	Jan	5	(h)	Bradford C	W 3-1	Brown, Griffiths, Fenton	8,068
26		17	(a)	Scunthorpe U	D 1-1	Fenton	4,046
27		19	(a)	Hartlepools U	L 2-3	Griffiths, A.Patrick	9,168
28		26	(h)	Oldham A	W 5-0	A.Patrick 3, Fenton 2	9,027
29	Feb	9	(a)	Darlington	L 0-1		5,397
30		16	(h)	Halifax T	W 6-2	Hughes, A.Patrick 3, Fenton 2	7,902
31		23	(a)	Crewe A	D 0-0		6,513
32	Mar	1	(a)	Mansfield T	D 1-1	Griffiths	7,953
33		8	(h)	Rochdale	D 1-1	Griffiths	8,136
34		15	(a)	Accrington S	L 1-2	Fenton	6,439
35		22	(h)	Carlisle U	D 0-0		7,577
36		29	(a)	Stockport C	L 1-3	Fenton	6,334
37		31	(h)	Lincoln C	W 1-0	Storey	6,736
38	Apr	5	(h)	Workington	W 5-1	Brown, A.Patrick 2, Fenton 2	4,229
39		11	(h)	Gateshead	W 1-0	Hughes	12,166
40		12	(a)	Barrow	D 0-0		5,703
41		14	(a)	Gateshead	D 1-1	Fenton	3,916
42		19	(h)	Grimsby T	D 1-1	A.Patrick	11,335
43		21	(h)	Barrow	W 2-1	Fenton 2	6,670
44		26	(a)	Wrexham	D 1-1	Fenton	5,425
45		28	(h)	Scunthorpe U	L 0-1		7,827
46	May	3	(h)	Crewe A	W 3-0	Hughes, Dunmore, Fenton	6,370

FINAL LEAGUE POSITION: 10th in Division Three North — Appearances / Goals

FA Cup

1	Nov	24	(h)	Bradford	D 1-1	A.Patrick	12,015
R		28	(a)	Bradford	D 1-1*	A.Patrick	8,659
2R	Dec	3	(n†)	Bradford	L 0-4		10,000

†Played at Elland Road, Leeds. *After extra-time — Appearances / Goals

Thompson D	Thompson K	Simpson J	Porter L	Stewart A	Spence R	Linaker J	Griffiths S	Slater F	Storey S	Fenton W	Frost J	Spence J	Brown G	Patrick M	Patrick A	Hughes W	Kelly W	Andrews P	Desmond P	Dunmore D	
1	2	3	4	5	6	7	8	9	10	11											1
1	2	3	4	5	6	7	8	9	10	11											2
1	2	3	4	5	6	7	8	9	10	11											3
		3		5	6	7	8	9	10	11	1	2	4								4
		3		5	6	7	8	9	10	11	1	2	4								5
		3		5	6	7	8	9	10	11	1	2	4								6
		3		5	6	7	10			11	1	2	4	8	9						7
1		3	4	5	6	7				11		2	8	10	9						8
1		3		5	6	7			8	11		2	4	10	9						9
1		3		5	6	7			8	11		2	4	10	9						10
1		3		5	6	7		8	10	11		2	4		9						11
1		3		5	6	7		8	10	11		2	4		9						12
1		3		5	6	7		8	10	11		2	4		9						13
1		3		5	6		8		10	11		2	4		9	7					14
1		3		5	6		8		10	11		2	4		9	7					15
1		3		5	6		8		10	11		2	4		9	7					16
1		3		5	6		8		10	11		2	4		9	7					17
1		3		5	6		8		10	11		2	4		9	7					18
1		3	4	5	6		8	10		11		2			9	7					19
1		3		5	6		8		10	11		2	4		9	7					20
1		3			6		8		10	11		5	4		9	7		2			21
1		3			6		8	9	10	11		5	4			7		2			22
1		3			6		8	9	10			5	4	11		7		2			23
1		3			6		8	9		11		5	4			7		2	10		24
1		3			6		8		10	11		5	4		9	7		2			25
1		3			6		8		10	11		5	4		9	7		2			26
1		3			6		8		10	11		5	4		9	7		2			27
1		3			6		8		10	11		5	4		9	7		2			28
1		3			6		8		10	11		5	4		9	7		2			29
1		3			6		8		10	11		5	4		9	7		2			30
1		3			6		8		10	11		5	4		9	7		2			31
1		3			6		8		10	11		5	4		9	7		2			32
1		3			6		8		10	11		5	4		9	7		2			33
1		3			6		8		10	11		5	4		9	7		2			34
1		3			6		8		10	11		5	4		9	7		2			35
1		3			6		8		10	11		5	4		9	7		2			36
1					6		8		10	11		5	4	3	9	7		2			37
1					6		8		10	11		5	4	3	9	7		2			38
1		3			6		8			11		5	4	10	9	7		2			39
1		3			6		8			11		5	4	10	9	7		2			40
1		3			6		8			11		5	4	10	9	7		2			41
1		3	6				8		10	11		5	4		9	7		2			42
1		3	6				8		10	11		5	4		9	7		2			43
1		3			6		8		10	11		5	4		9	7		2			44
1		3			6		8		10	11		5	4		9	7		2			45
1		3			6		8		10	11		5	4			7		2		9	46
42	3	44	7	20	44	13	40	13	39	45	4	43	42	10	36	33		26	1	1	
					2	3	6	3	1	31			4	2	15	4				1	

1 own-goal

Thompson D	Thompson K	Simpson J	Porter L	Stewart A	Spence R	Linaker J	Griffiths S	Slater F	Storey S	Fenton W	Frost J	Spence J	Brown G	Patrick M	Patrick A	Hughes W	Kelly W	Andrews P	Desmond P	Dunmore D	
1		3		5	6		8		10	11		2	4	7	9						1
1		3		5	6		8		10	11		2	4	7	9						R
1		3			6		8	7	10	11		2	4		9		5				2R
3		3		2	3		3	1	3	3		3	3	2	3		1				
															2						

1952-53

Manager: Dick Duckworth until October, then Charles Spencer from November 1952 until February 1953, then vacant.

1	Aug	23	(h)	Bradford	W 3-1	Griffiths (pen), A.Patrick, Fenton	10,246
2		28	(a)	Chester	D 1-1	A.Patrick	6,530
3		30	(a)	Oldham A	L 1-2	A.Patrick	16,632
4	Sep	1	(h)	Chester	D 0-0		8,759
5		6	(h)	Mansfield T	W 2-0	Hughes, Opp own-goal	8,645
6		10	(a)	Wrexham	D 1-1	Fenton	9,583
7		13	(a)	Halifax T	D 0-0		9,970
8		15	(h)	Wrexham	W 2-1	Griffiths, A.Patrick	7,502
9		20	(h)	Accrington S	W 2-0	A.Patrick, Storey	8,232
10		22	(a)	Hartlepools U	L 1-2	Griffiths	9,626
11		27	(a)	Workington	W 3-1	Fenton 2, A.Patrick	5,629
12		29	(h)	Port Vale	W 1-0	R.Spence	7,289
13	Oct	4	(h)	Chesterfield	D 0-0		9,594
14		11	(a)	Scunthorpe U	L 0-2		7,850
15		18	(h)	Stockport C	W 3-0	Fenton 2, Dunmore	9,222
16		25	(a)	Bradford C	D 1-1	Fenton	11,417
17	Nov	1	(h)	Rochdale	W 2-0	Warrender, Griffiths	9,430
18		8	(a)	Darlington	W 1-0	Fenton	7,238
19		15	(h)	Gateshead	L 1-2	Fenton	9,013
20		29	(h)	Carlisle U	W 1-0	Storey	6,589
21	Dec	6	(a)	Crewe A	L 0-3		6,041
22		13	(h)	Crewe A	W 2-1	A.Patrick, Fenton	6,717
23		20	(a)	Bradford	W 3-2	Hughes, A.Patrick, Fenton	6,506
24		26	(h)	Tranmere R	W 2-0	Griffiths (pen), Fenton	11,380
25	Jan	3	(h)	Oldham A	L 1-2	Fenton	15,222
26		10	(h)	Barrow	D 1-1	Fenton	7,698
27		17	(a)	Mansfield T	D 1-1	Fenton	6,960
28		24	(h)	Halifax T	D 2-2	Fenton 2	9,604
29		31	(a)	Barrow	L 0-1		4,949
30	Feb	7	(a)	Accrington S	L 0-1		4,336
31		14	(h)	Workington	L 1-3	Brown	7,110
32		21	(a)	Chesterfield	W 2-1	R.Spence, Hughes	8,736
33		28	(h)	Scunthorpe U	L 0-2		7,480
34	Mar	7	(a)	Stockport C	D 1-1	Griffiths (pen)	8,811
35		14	(h)	Bradford C	D 0-0		7,108
36		21	(a)	Rochdale	W 3-0	Fenton 2, Hughes	6,373
37		28	(h)	Darlington	W 3-0	Fenton 2, A.Patrick	5,453
38	Apr	3	(a)	Grimsby T	L 1-2	Fenton	18,551
39		4	(a)	Gateshead	D 1-1	Fenton	5,745
40		6	(h)	Grimsby T	W 2-0	Hughes, Warrender	12,414
41		11	(h)	Hartlepools U	W 1-0	Hughes	7,939
42		14	(a)	Southport	L 0-2		4,863
43		18	(a)	Carlisle U	D 1-1	Fenton	4,805
44		20	(a)	Port Vale	L 0-2		11,379
45		25	(h)	Southport	W 3-1	Warrender, Dunmore, Storey	6,394
46		28	(a)	Tranmere R	W 3-1	Dunmore 2, Fenton	4,991

FINAL LEAGUE POSITION: 4th in Division Three North

Appearances
Goals

FA Cup

1	Nov	22	(h)	Barrow	L 1-2	A.Patrick	9,586

Appearances
Goals

Thompson D	Andrews P	Simpson J	Brown G	Spence J	Spence R	Hughes W	Griffiths S	Patrick A	Storey S	Fenton W	Wheat A	Patrick M	Dunmore D	Warrender R	Kirby E	Granger M	Searson H	Barritt R	Ryan J	
1	2	3	4	5	6	7	8	9	10	11										1
1	2	3	4	5	6	7	8	9	10	11										2
1	2	3	4	5	6	7	8	9	10	11										3
1	2	3	4	5	6	7	8	9		11	10									4
1	2	3	4	5	6	7	8	9	10	11										5
1	2	3	4	5	6	7	8	9	10	11										6
1	2		4	5	6	7	8	9	10	11		3								7
1	2		4	5	6	7	8	9	10	11		3								8
1	2		4	5	6	7	8	9	10		11	3								9
1	2		4	5	6	7	8	9	10		11	3								10
1	2		4	5	6		8	9	10	11		3	7							11
1	2		4	5	6		8	9	10	11		3	7							12
1	2		4	5	6		8	9	10	11		3	7							13
1	2	3	4	5	6	7	8	9	10	11										14
1	2	3	4	5	6		8		10	11			9	7						15
1	2	3	4	5	6		8		10	11			9	7						16
1	2	3	4	5	6		8		10	11			9	7						17
1	2	3	4	5	6		8		10	11			9	7						18
1	2	3		5	6		8		10	11			9	7	4					19
	2		4	5	6		8	7	10	11		3					1	9		20
	2		4	5	6	7	8		10	11		3					1	9		21
	2		4	5	6	7	8	9	10	11		3					1			22
	2		4	5	6	7	8	9	10	11		3					1			23
	2		4	5	6	7	8	9	10	11		3					1			24
	2		4	5	6	7	8	9	10	11		3					1			25
	2		4	5	6	7	8	9	10	11		3					1			26
	2	3	4	5	6		8		10	11			9	7			1			27
	2	3	4	5	6		8		10	11			9				1		7	28
	2	3	4	5	6		8		10	11			9				1		7	29
	2	3	4	5	6		8		10	11			9				1		7	30
	2		4	5	6					11	10	3	8				1	9	7	31
	2		4	5	6	7			10	11		3	8				1	9		32
	2		4	5	6	7	8		10	11		3					1	9		33
	2	3	4	5	6	7	8	9	10	11							1			34
	2	3	4	5	6	7	8	9	10	11							1			35
	2	3	4	5	6	7		9	10	11				8			1			36
	2	3	4	5	6	7		9	10	11				8			1			37
	2	3	4	5	6	7		9	10	11				8			1			38
	2	3	4	5	6	7	8	9	10	11							1			39
	2	3	4	5	6	7		9	10	11				8			1			40
	2	3	4	5	6	7		9	10	11				8			1			41
	5	3	4		6	7		9	10	11		2		8			1			42
	2	3	4	5	6	7		9	10	11				8			1			43
	2	3	4	5	6	7		9	10	11				8			1			44
	2	3	4	5	6	7			10	11			9	8			1			45
	2	3	4	5	6	7			10	11			9	8			1			46
19	46	29	45	45	46	32	34	31	44	44	4	18	16	16	1		27	5	4	
			1		2	6	6	9	3	25			4	3						

1 own-goal

Thompson D	Andrews P	Simpson J	Brown G	Spence J	Spence R	Hughes W	Griffiths S	Patrick A	Storey S	Fenton W	Wheat A	Patrick M	Dunmore D	Warrender R	Kirby E	Granger M	Searson H	Barritt R	Ryan J	
	2	3	4	5	6		8	7	10	11			9			1				1
	1	1	1	1	1		1	1	1	1			1			1				
								1												

1953-54

Jim McCormick

1	Aug	19	(a)	Grimsby T	L 0-3		16,320
2		22	(h)	Workington	D 0-0		7,868
3		24	(a)	Hartlepools U	D 2-2	R.Spence (pen), Fenton	11,854
4		29	(a)	Scunthorpe U	L 0-3		7,494
5		31	(h)	Hartlepools U	W 5-0	Burgess 2, Porter, Brown, Dunmore	3,645
6	Sep	5	(h)	Stockport C	D 0-0		8,573
7		7	(a)	Gateshead	L 0-3		6,781
8		12	(h)	Southport	W 2-1	Dunmore 2	7,463
9		14	(h)	Gateshead	D 1-1	Dunmore (pen)	7,777
10		19	(a)	Chester	L 1-3	Dunmore (pen)	5,571
11		21	(h)	Darlington	D 3-3	Dunmore 2, Linaker	4,582
12		26	(h)	Crewe A	L 0-3		7,115
13	Oct	3	(a)	Port Vale	L 0-5		18,778
14		10	(a)	Wrexham	D 1-1	Fenton	9,614
15		17	(h)	Mansfield T	W 5-1	Dunmore 3, Storey, Fenton	6,294
16		24	(a)	Barrow	L 1-4	Fenton	6,355
17		31	(h)	Bradford C	W 3-2	Linaker, Dunmore, Opp own-goal	5,849
18	Nov	7	(a)	Chesterfield	L 2-3	Linaker, Fenton	6,770
19		14	(h)	Tranmere R	D 0-0		5,245
20		28	(h)	Carlisle U	L 1-3	Dunmore (pen)	5,752
21	Dec	5	(a)	Accrington S	L 0-2		7,557
22		19	(a)	Workington	L 2-5	Dunmore, Fenton	6,774
23		25	(h)	Barnsley	L 0-2		5,160
24		26	(a)	Barnsley	L 1-2	Dunmore (pen)	9,631
25	Jan	1	(a)	Darlington	W 3-1	Dunmore 2, Burgess	5,996
26		2	(h)	Scunthorpe U	W 2-0	Storey, Burgess	5,355
27		9	(a)	Rochdale	W 2-1	Storey, Dunmore	5,575
28		16	(a)	Stockport C	W 1-0	Dunmore	5,559
29		23	(a)	Southport	D 1-1	Dunmore	3,068
30		30	(h)	Rochdale	L 1-2	Burgess	5,650
31	Feb	6	(h)	Chester	W 2-1	Dunmore, Burgess	3,960
32		13	(a)	Crewe A	D 1-1	Burgess	4,683
33		24	(h)	Port Vale	L 0-1		7,131
34		27	(h)	Wrexham	W 5-2	R.Spence 2, Linaker, Burgess, Fenton	5,276
35	Mar	6	(a)	Mansfield T	L 2-7	Burgess, R.Spence	6,783
36		13	(h)	Barrow	W 5-2	Burgess 2, R.Spence 2 (1 pen), Fenton	3,858
37		20	(a)	Bradford C	L 0-1		12,682
38		27	(h)	Chesterfield	L 1-3	Burgess	4,769
39	Apr	3	(a)	Tranmere R	D 1-1	Burgess	4,264
40		10	(h)	Halifax T	D 1-1	Stewart	3,860
41		12	(h)	Grimsby T	L 1-2	R.Spence (pen)	3,826
42		16	(h)	Bradford	D 0-0		6,362
43		17	(a)	Carlisle U	D 1-1	Burgess	4,411
44		19	(a)	Bradford	L 0-2		5,378
45		24	(h)	Accrington S	L 1-2	Hughes	4,252
46		27	(a)	Halifax T	W 3-2	Warrender 2, Hughes	3,792

FINAL LEAGUE POSITION: 22nd in Division Three North

Appearances
Goals

FA Cup

1	Nov	21	(a)	Barnsley	L 2-5	Dunmore, Fenton	14,755

Appearances
Goals

Searson H	Andrews P	Simpson J	Brown G	Spence J	Spence R	Hughes W	Burgess C	Dunmore D	Warrender R	Fenton W	Porter L	Linaker J	Storey S	Ware C	Marlow F	Stewart A	Jukes N	Patrick M	Williams K	Maddison G	Bainbridge R	
1	2	3	4	5	6	7	8	9	10	11												1
1	2	3	4	5	6	7	8	9	10	11												2
1	2	3	4	5	6	7	8	9	10	11												3
1	2	3	4	5	6	7	8	9	10	11												4
1	2	3	8	5	6		10	9	7	11	4											5
1	2	3	8	5	6		10	9	7	11	4											6
1	2	3	4	5			10	9	8	11	6	7										7
1	2	3	4	5			8	9		11	6	7	10									8
1	2	3	4	5			8	9			6	7	10	11								9
1	2	3	8	5	6			9		11	4	7	10									10
1	2	3	8	5	6			9		11	4	7	10									11
1	2	3	8	5	6			9		11	4	7	10									12
1	2	3			6	8		9		11		7	10		4	5						13
1	5	3			6	8		9		11		7	10		4		2					14
1	5	3			6	8		9		11		7	10					2	4			15
1	5	3	4		6	8		9		11		7	10					2				16
1	5	3	4		6	8		9		11		7	10					2				17
1	5	3	4		6	8		9		11		7	10					2				18
1	5	3	4		6	8		9		11		7	10					2				19
	3		4		6	7	8	9		11			10			5		2		1		20
	2		4		6	7	8	9		11			10			5		3		1		21
	2	3	4		6	8		9		11		7	10			5				1		22
1	2	3	4		6	8		9		11		7	10			5						23
1	2	3	4		6	8		9		11		7	10			5						24
1	2		4				10	9				7	8	11	6	5		3				25
1	2		4				10	9				7	8	11	6	5		3				26
1	2		4				10	9				7	8	11	6	5		3				27
1	2		4			8	10	9				7		11	6	5		3				28
1	2		4			8	10	9				7		11	6	5		3				29
1	2		4				10	9				7	8	11	6	5		3				30
1	2		4				10	9				7	8	11	6	5		3				31
1	2		4			8	9			11		7	10		6	5		3				32
1	2		4			8	9			11		7	10		6	5		3				33
1	2		4		10		9			11		7	8		6	5		3				34
1	2		4		10		9			11		7	8		6	5		3				35
1	2		4		10		9			11		7	8		6	5		3				36
1	2		4		10		9			11		7	8		6	5		3				37
1	2		4		10		9			11		7	8		6	5		3				38
	2		4		10		9			11		7	8		6	5		3		1		39
	2		4		10	8	9			11		7			6	5		3		1		40
	2		4		10		9			11		7	8		6	5		3		1		41
	2		4		10		9			11		7	8		6	5		3		1		42
	2		4		10	7	9			11			8		6	5		3		1		43
	2		4		10	7	9			11			8		6	5		3		1		44
	2		4		10	7	9						8	11	6	5		3		1		45
	2		4		6	7			8	11			10			5		3		1	9	46
35	46	22	43	12	34	25	32	31	8	37	8	34	36	9	23	28	1	29	1	11	1	
			1		7	2	14	20	2	8	1	4	3			1						

1 own-goal

Searson H	Andrews P	Simpson J	Brown G	Spence J	Spence R	Hughes W	Burgess C	Dunmore D	Warrender R	Fenton W	Porter L	Linaker J	Storey S	Ware C	Marlow F	Stewart A	Jukes N	Patrick M	Williams K	Maddison G	Bainbridge R	
1	5	3	4		6	8		9		11		7	10					2				1
1	1	1	1		1	1		1		1		1	1					1				
								1		1												

1954-55

Manager: J.McCormick — then vacant from 8 September

1	Aug	21	(a)	Wrexham	W 6-2	Bottom 3, Wilkinson 2, McNab	11,695
2		23	(h)	Hartlepools U	W 1-0	McNab	10,156
3		28	(h)	Scunthorpe U	L 2-3	Wilkinson, Fenton	12,911
4		30	(a)	Hartlepools U	L 0-1		8,103
5	Sep	4	(a)	Barnsley	L 0-1		11,446
6		6	(h)	Workington	D 0-0		5,940
7		11	(h)	Bradford C	L 0-1		9,285
8		15	(a)	Workington	L 1-2	Bottom	6,493
9		18	(a)	Oldham A	L 2-3	Brown, Bottom	8,700
10		20	(h)	Southport	D 1-1	Bottom (pen)	5,121
11		25	(h)	Halifax T	W 2-1	Bottom, McNab	6,233
12		28	(a)	Southport	D 2-2	Bottom 2	3,206
13	Oct	2	(h)	Stockport C	W 4-0	Brown, Spence, Bottom, Fenton	6,523
14		9	(a)	Gateshead	D 1-1	Bottom	6,926
15		16	(h)	Darlington	W 3-1	Wilkinson, Storey, Fenton	11,964
16		23	(a)	Chesterfield	W 3-0	Fenton 2, Hughes	10,395
17		30	(h)	Crewe A	W 3-1	Bottom 2, Wilkinson	9,401
18	Nov	6	(a)	Carlisle U	W 5-4	Fenton 4, Bottom	5,616
19		13	(h)	Chester	W 5-0	Hughes, Bottom 2, Fenton 2	6,824
20		27	(h)	Bradford	L 1-2	Wilkinson	8,727
21	Dec	4	(a)	Rochdale	D 1-1	Wilkinson	4,051
22		18	(h)	Wrexham	D 3-3	Bottom 2 (2 pens), Storey	6,382
23		25	(h)	Mansfield T	W 3-1	Bottom, Storey, Fenton	10,272
24		27	(a)	Mansfield T	W 2-1	Bottom, Wilkinson	9,725
25	Jan	1	(a)	Scunthorpe U	W 2-1	Wilkinson, Fenton	10,593
26		15	(h)	Barnsley	L 1-3	Spence	7,810
27	Feb	5	(h)	Oldham A	W 2-1	Wilkinson 2	9,752
28		12	(a)	Halifax T	D 3-3	Brown, Bottom, Storey	6,202
29		21	(a)	Stockport C	W 2-1	Bottom 2	2,933
30		26	(h)	Gateshead	W 2-1	Bottom, Wilkinson	13,246
31	Mar	5	(a)	Darlington	L 0-1		10,242
32		16	(h)	Chesterfield	W 3-2	Bottom 2 (1 pen), Fenton	10,614
33		19	(a)	Crewe A	W 3-2	Wilkinson 2, Bottom	7,171
34	Apr	2	(a)	Chester	W 2-1	Bottom, Fenton	6,456
35		4	(a)	Bradford C	W 3-2	Bottom, Wilkinson, Fenton	6,199
36		8	(h)	Accrington S	D 1-1	Bottom	19,843
37		9	(h)	Grimsby T	D 0-0		12,436
38		11	(a)	Accrington S	D 2-2	Bottom, Wilkinson	15,598
39		13	(h)	Carlisle U	W 2-1	Hughes, Wilkinson	8,874
40		16	(a)	Bradford	W 3-1	Phillips (pen), Fenton 2	9,993
41		18	(h)	Tranmere R	W 1-0	Brown	10,996
42		23	(h)	Rochdale	W 2-0	Fenton 2	9,981
43		27	(a)	Grimsby T	L 1-2	Fenton	7,184
44		30	(a)	Tranmere R	L 0-1		6,165
45	May	2	(h)	Barrow	L 1-4	Wilkinson	8,192
46		5	(a)	Barrow	W 5-1	Brown, Wilkinson, Hughes 2, Fenton	4,307

FINAL LEAGUE POSITION: 4th in Division Three North

Appearances
Goals

FA Cup

1	Nov	24	(h)	Scarborough	W 3-2	Wilkinson, Bottom, Spence	10,155
2	Dec	11	(a)	Dorchester T	W 5-2	Bottom 3, Wilkinson, Fenton	5,191
3	Jan	8	(a)	Blackpool	W 2-0	Storey, Fenton	26,030
4		29	(a)	Bishop Auckland	W 3-1	Bottom 2 (1 pen), Storey	15,000
5	Feb	19	(h)	Tottenham H	W 3-1	Wilkinson 2, Fenton	21,000
6	Mar	12	(a)	Notts C	W 1-0	Bottom	47,301
SF	Mar	26	(n*)	Newcastle U	D 1-1	Bottom	65,000
R	Mar	30	(n†)	Newcastle U	L 0-2		58,239

*Played at Hillsborough, Sheffield. †Played at Roker Park, Sunderland.

Appearances
Goals

	Forgan T	Phillips E	Howe G	Brown G	Stewart A	Spence R	Slatter L	Bottom A	Wilkinson N	McNab S	Fenton W	Charlesworth A	Storey S	Linaker J	Bainbridge R	Andrews P	Hughes W	Whiteside K	Granger M	Marlow F	Wardle E	Jones W	Smith R
1	1	2	3	4	5	6	7	8	9	10	11												
2	1	2	3	4	5	6	7	8	9	10	11												
3	1	2	3	4	5	6	7	8	9	10	11												
4	1	2	3	4	5	6	7	8	9		11	10											
5	1	2	3	4	5	6	7	8	9		11		10										
6	1	2	3	4	5	6	7	8	9		11		10										
7	1	2	3	4	5	6	7	8	9		11		10										
8	1	2	3	4	5	6		8		11			10	7	9								
9	1	2	3	4	5	6		8	9	10	11			7									
10	1	2	3	4	5	6		8		11			10	7	9								
11	1	2	3	4		6	7	9		10	11		8			5							
12	1	2	3	4		6	7	9		10	11		8			5							
13	1	2	3	4		6		8	9		11		10			5	7						
14	1	2	3	4		6		9			11		10			5	7	8					
15	1	2	3	4	5	6		8	9		11		10				7						
16	1	2	3	4	5	6	7	8	9		11						10						
17	1	2	3	4	5	6		8	9		11		10				7						
18		2	3	4	5	6		8	9		11		10				7		1				
19		2	3	4	5	6		8	9		11		10				7		1				
20		2	3	4	5	6		8	9		11		10				7		1				
21		2	3		5	6		8	9		11		10				7		1	4			
22		2	3	4	5	6		8	9		11		10				7		1				
23	1	2	3	4	5	6		8	9		11		10				7						
24	1	2	3	4	5	6		8	9		11		10				7						
25	1	2	3	4	5	6		8	9		11		10				7						
26	1	2	3	4	5	6	7	8	9		11		10										
27	1	2	3	4		6		8	9	10	11						7				5		
28	1	2	3	4	5	6		8	9		11		10				7						
29	1	2	3	4	5	6		8	9		11		10				7						
30	1	2	3	4	5	6		8	9		11		10				7						
31	1	2	3	4	5	6	7	9		10	11						8						
32	1	2	3	4		6		8	9		11		10				7				5		
33	1	2	3	4	5	6		8	9		11		10				7						
34	1	2	3			6		8	9		11		10				7				5	4	
35	1	2	3	4		6		8	9		11		10				7				5		
36	1	2	3	4	5	6		8	9		11		10				7						
37	1	2	3	4	5	6		8	9	10	11						7						
38	1	2	3	4	5	6		8	9	10	11						7						
39		2	3	4	5	6			9	10	11						7	8	1				
40		2	3	4	5	6			9	10	11						7	8	1				
41	1	2	3	4	5	6			9	10	11						7	8					
42	1	2	3	4	5	6				10	11				9		7	8					
43	1	2	3	4	5	6			9	10	11						7	8					
44	1	2	3	4		6	8		9	10	11						7				5		
45	1	2	3	4		6			9	10	11						7	8			5		
46	1	2	3	4		6			9		11			7			10	8					5
	39	46	46	44	35	46	13	38	39	19	44	1	28	4	3	4	33	8	7	1	6	1	1
		1		5		2		31	19	3	22		4				5						

	Forgan T	Phillips E	Howe G	Brown G	Stewart A	Spence R	Slatter L	Bottom A	Wilkinson N	McNab S	Fenton W	Charlesworth A	Storey S	Linaker J	Bainbridge R	Andrews P	Hughes W	Whiteside K	Granger M	Marlow F	Wardle E	Jones W	Smith R
1		2	3	4	5	6		8	9		11		10				7		1				
2		2	3	4	5	6		8	9		11		10				7		1				
3	1	2	3	4	5	6		8	9		11		10				7						
4	1	2	3	4	5	6		8	9		11		10				7						
5	1	2	3	4	5	6		8	9		11		10				7						
6	1	2	3	4	5	6		8	9		11		10				7						
SF	1	2	3	4	5	6		8	9	10	11						7						
R	1	2	3	4	5	6		8	9		11		10				7						
	6	8	8	8	8	8		8	8	1	8		7				8		2				
						1		8	4		3		2										

1955-56

Manager: Vacant until 12 March 1956, then Sam Bartram.

1	Aug	20	(h)	Wrexham	L	1-3	Wilkinson	12,332
2		24	(a)	Crewe A	W	2-1	Bottom, Opp own-goal	6,470
3		27	(a)	Halifax T	W	4-2	Fenton 2, Hughes, Bottom	8,603
4		29	(h)	Crewe A	D	1-1	Fenton	11,068
5	Sep	3	(h)	Bradford C	L	0-2		11,960
6		5	(a)	Hartlepools U	W	1-0	Fenton	9,184
7		10	(a)	Scunthorpe U	D	1-1	Fenton	9,720
8		12	(h)	Hartlepools U	W	3-0	Colbridge, Tait, Fenton	10,171
9		17	(h)	Oldham A	W	2-0	Bottom 2	11,094
10		19	(h)	Stockport C	W	1-0	Bottom	10,908
11		24	(a)	Workington	D	0-0		5,895
12		28	(a)	Derby C	L	2-3	Bottom, Prescott	13,136
13	Oct	1	(a)	Tranmere R	L	1-2	Bottom	6,888
14		8	(h)	Rochdale	L	1-2	Brown	9,742
15		15	(a)	Southport	D	3-3	Hughes, Bottom, Prescott	3,937
16		22	(h)	Grimsby T	L	3-4	Colbridge 2, Wilkinson	14,566
17		29	(a)	Carlisle U	L	1-3	Wilkinson	6,240
18	Nov	5	(h)	Chester	W	3-0	Bottom 2, Storey	8,176
19		12	(a)	Barrow	W	1-0	Fenton	5,434
20		26	(a)	Darlington	W	4-1	Fenton 2, Hughes, Bottom	8,752
21	Dec	3	(h)	Gateshead	W	1-0	Bottom	9,714
22		17	(a)	Wrexham	W	5-4	Wilkinson 3, Fenton 2	5,685
23		24	(h)	Halifax T	W	5-0	Hughes 2, Bottom, Wilkinson, Colbridge	9,623
24		26	(a)	Mansfield T	L	1-3	Spence	6,296
25		27	(h)	Mansfield T	D	1-1	Bottom (pen)	14,209
26		31	(a)	Bradford C	L	1-3	Bottom	13,636
27	Jan	21	(a)	Oldham A	D	2-2	Hughes, Wilkinson	5,224
28	Feb	4	(h)	Workington	D	1-1	Bottom (pen)	6,790
29		11	(h)	Tranmere R	L	2-4	Brown, Spence	6,593
30		18	(a)	Rochdale	L	1-3	Fenton	3,923
31		25	(h)	Southport	L	0-1		9,544
32	Mar	3	(a)	Grimsby T	L	1-2	Bottom	14,695
33		10	(h)	Carlisle U	W	3-1	Bottom 2, Hughes	9,782
34		14	(a)	Bradford	L	1-2	Hobson	3,055
35		17	(a)	Accrington S	W	3-1	Colbridge 2, Bottom	9,905
36		24	(h)	Barrow	W	3-2	Bottom, Storey, Colbridge	8,459
37		30	(h)	Chesterfield	W	3-1	Colbridge 2, Bottom	13,476
38		31	(a)	Chester	D	2-2	Prescott, Bottom	6,016
39	Apr	2	(a)	Chesterfield	L	1-3	Bottom	9,486
40		7	(h)	Darlington	W	4-0	Bottom 2 (1 pen), Prescott, Colbridge	8,435
41		9	(h)	Scunthorpe U	D	0-0		9,045
42		14	(a)	Gateshead	L	2-3	Bottom 2	2,301
43		16	(h)	Accrington S	L	0-1		8,016
44		21	(h)	Bradford	W	5-0	Wilkinson 2, Bottom, Prescott, Colbridge	8,006
45		23	(h)	Derby C	W	1-0	Bottom	14,976
46		28	(a)	Stockport C	L	1-4	Bottom	9,724

FINAL LEAGUE POSITION: 11th in Division Three North

Appearances
Goals

FA Cup

1	Nov	19	(a)	Rochdale	W	1-0	Wilkinson	9,000
2	Dec	10	(h)	Mansfield T	W	2-1	Bottom, Hughes	13,326
3	Jan	7	(a)	Swansea T	W	2-1	Colbridge, Bottom	25,636
4		28	(h)	Sunderland	D	0-0		22,000
R	Feb	1	(a)	Sunderland	L	1-2	Fenton	43,928

Appearances
Goals

Forgan T	Phillips E	Howe G	Brown G	Stewart A	Spence R	Hughes W	Bottom A	Wilkinson N	Storey S	Fenton W	Prescott J	Colbridge C	Tait P	Wardle E	Mollatt R	Linaker J	Hobson A	Granger M	
1	2	3	4	5	6	7	8	9	10	11									1
1	2	3	4	5	6	7	8	9	10	11									2
1	2	3	4	5	6	7	8	9	10	11									3
1	2	3	4	5	6	7	8	9	10	11									4
1	2	3	4	5	6	7	8		10	11	9								5
1	2	3	4	5	6	7	8		10	11	9								6
1	2	3	4	5	6	7	8	9	10	11									7
1	2	3	4	5	6		8		10	11		7	9						8
1	2	3	4	5	6		8		10	11		7	9						9
1	2		4	5	6		8		10	11		7	9	3					10
1	2	3	4	5	6	7	8		10	11	9								11
1	2	3	4	5	6	7	8		10	11	9								12
1	2	3	4	5	6	7	8	9		11	10								13
1	2	3	4	5	6	7	8	9		11	10								14
1	2	3	4	5	6	7	8	9		11	10								15
1	2	3	4	5	6	7	8	9	10			11							16
1	2	3	4	5	6	7	8	9	10			11							17
1	2	3	4	5	6	7	8	9	10	11									18
1	2	3	4	5	6	7	8	9	10	11									19
1	2	3	4	5	6	7	8	9	10	11									20
1	2	3		5	6	7	8	9	10	11					4				21
1	2	3	4	5	6		8	9	10	11						7			22
1	2	3	4	5	6	7	8	9	10			11							23
1	2	3	4	5	6	7	8	9	10			11							24
1	2	3	4	5	6	7	8	9	10	11									25
1	2	3		5	6	7	8	9	10	11					4				26
1	2	3	4	5	6	7		9	10		8	11							27
1	2		4	5	6	7	8	9	10	11				3					28
1	2	3	4	5	6	7		9	10	11	8								29
1	2	3	4	5	6	10		9		11	8	7							30
1	2	3	4	5	6	7	8		10	11	9								31
1	2	3	4	5	6		8	9	10	11		7							32
1	2	3	4	5	6	7	9		10	11							8		33
1	2	3	4	5	6	7	9		10	11							8		34
	2	3	4	5	6	7	9		10			11					8	1	35
	2	3	4	5	6	7	9		10			11			8			1	36
	2	3	4	5		7	9		10		8	11			6			1	37
	2	3	4	5		7	9		10		8	11			6			1	38
	2	3	4	5		7	9		10		8	11			6			1	39
1	2	3		5		10	9				8	11		4	6		7		40
1	2	3		5		8	9		10			11		4	6		7		41
1	2	3	4	5		8	9		10			11			6		7		42
1	2	3	4	5		10	9				8	11			6		7		43
1	2	3	4	5			8	9			10	11			6		7		44
1	2	3	4	5		10	8	9				11			6		7		45
1	2	3	4	5			8	9			10	11			6		7		46
41	46	44	42	46	36	39	43	27	37	29	18	22	3	4	13	1	10	5	
			2		2	7	31	10	2	12	5	11	1				1		

1 own-goal

Forgan T	Phillips E	Howe G	Brown G	Stewart A	Spence R	Hughes W	Bottom A	Wilkinson N	Storey S	Fenton W	Prescott J	Colbridge C	
1	2	3	4	5	6	7	8	9	10	11			1
1	2	3	4	5	6	7	8	9	10	11			2
1	2	3	4	5	6	7	8	9	10			11	3
1	2	3	4	5	6	7	8	9	10	11			4
1	2	3	4	5	6	7	8	9	10	11			R
5	5	5	5	5	5	5	5	5	5	4		1	
						1	2	1		1		1	

1956-57

Manager: Sam Bartram

No	Month	Day	Venue	Opponent	Result	Scorers	Attendance
1	Aug	18	(a)	Accrington S	L 0-3		11,026
2		20	(h)	Workington	D 2-2	Monkhouse, Colbridge	15,318
3		25	(h)	Tranmere R	W 1-0	Wragg	12,291
4		29	(a)	Workington	L 2-3	Wilkinson, Wragg (pen)	9,542
5	Sep	1	(a)	Halifax T	D 0-0		8,192
6		3	(h)	Carlisle U	W 2-0	Bottom, Fenton	11,709
7		8	(a)	Oldham A	L 1-3	Hughes	8,608
8		15	(h)	Mansfield T	W 2-0	Colbridge, Fenton	9,835
9		17	(h)	Chester	L 0-1		9,234
10		22	(a)	Southport	D 1-1	Bottom	4,019
11		26	(a)	Chester	W 4-3	Hughes, Wilkinson, Wragg, Fenton	4,258
12		29	(h)	Chesterfield	L 1-2	Bottom	8,820
13	Oct	6	(h)	Hull C	W 2-1	Wilkinson, Fenton	10,763
14		13	(a)	Barrow	W 2-1	Brown, Hughes	5,908
15		20	(h)	Scunthorpe U	L 0-2		8,881
16		27	(a)	Bradford	W 2-0	Wilkinson 2	9,206
17	Nov	3	(h)	Gateshead	W 1-0	Wilkinson	7,325
18		10	(a)	Wrexham	D 1-1	Fenton	12,577
19		24	(a)	Crewe A	D 1-1	Bottom	4,699
20	Dec	1	(h)	Darlington	W 1-0	Bottom	8,153
21		15	(h)	Accrington S	W 3-1	Bottom (pen), Wilkinson, Opp own-goal	8,161
22		22	(a)	Tranmere R	D 3-3	Bottom, Wilkinson, Wragg	3,045
23		25	(h)	Hartlepools U	D 3-3	Bottom (pen), Wilkinson, Fenton	8,663
24		26	(a)	Hartlepools U	L 0-2		6,954
25		29	(h)	Halifax T	L 1-2	Fenton	8,102
26	Jan	1	(a)	Carlisle U	L 0-2		7,838
27		5	(h)	Bradford C	W 3-1	Bottom, Wilkinson, Fenton	10,492
28		12	(h)	Oldham A	W 2-1	Bottom 2	9,166
29		19	(a)	Mansfield T	L 1-4	Wragg	6,941
30		26	(a)	Bradford C	W 2-0	Hughes, Fenton	13,281
31	Feb	2	(h)	Southport	W 9-1	Bottom 4 (1 pen), Wilkinson 2, Brown, Wragg, Fenton	8,801
32		9	(a)	Chesterfield	W 4-3	Bottom 2, Hill, Fenton	16,160
33		16	(a)	Hull C	D 1-1	Wragg	15,697
34		23	(h)	Barrow	W 1-0	Fenton	8,004
35	Mar	2	(a)	Scunthorpe U	L 1-2	Fenton	7,848
36		9	(h)	Bradford	L 1-2	Bottom	8,857
37		16	(a)	Gateshead	W 2-0	Brown, Bottom (pen)	4,934
38		23	(h)	Wrexham	W 1-0	Bottom	8,374
39		30	(a)	Derby C	L 0-1		21,614
40	Apr	6	(h)	Crewe A	W 2-1	Bottom, Wilkinson	7,271
41		13	(a)	Darlington	W 4-2	Hill 2, Wilkinson, Fenton	4,543
42		19	(h)	Stockport C	D 0-0		11,681
43		20	(h)	Rochdale	W 4-0	Wilkinson 3, Wragg	7,203
44		22	(a)	Stockport C	L 0-3		7,193
45		27	(a)	Rochdale	L 0-1		4,215
46		29	(h)	Derby C	D 1-1	Fenton	9,413

FINAL LEAGUE POSITION: 7th in Division Three North

Appearances
Goals

FA Cup

Round	Month	Day	Venue	Opponent	Result	Scorers	Attendance
1	Nov	17	(a)	Southport	D 0-0		5,560
R		21	(h)	Southport	W 2-1	Wragg, Wilkinson	8,409
2	Dec	8	(a)	Hull C	L 1-2	Bottom	24,155

Appearances
Goals

Forgan T	Phillips E	Howe G	Brown G	Stewart A	Mollatt R	Hughes W	Bottom A	Monkhouse A	Wragg P	Colbridge C	Hobson A	Wilkinson N	Cairney J	Fenton W	Powell J	Wardle E	Stoddart T	Stewart J	Hill W	Steel R	
1	2	3	4	5	6	7	8	9	10	11											1
1	2	3	4	5	6		8	9	10	11	7										2
1	2	3	4	5	6		8	9	10	11	7										3
1	2	3	4	5	6			8	10	11	7	9									4
1	2	3	4	5	6	7		8	10	11		9									5
1	2	3	4		6	7	8	9	10				5	11							6
1	2	3	4		6	7	8	9	10				5	11							7
1	2	3	4	5	6		8	9	10	7				11							8
1	2	3	4	5	6		8	9	10	7				11							9
1	2	3	4	5	6	7	8		10			9		11							10
1	2	3	4	5	6	7	8		10			9		11							11
1	2	3	4	5	6	7	8		10			9		11							12
1		3	4			7		8	6			9	5	11	10	2					13
1		3	4			7	8	9	6			9	5		11	2					14
1			4	5		7	8	9	6	11					10	2				3	15
1		3	4	5		7	8		10			9		11		2	6				16
1		3	4	5		7	8		10			9		11		2	6				17
1		3	4	5			8		10			9		11		2	6		7		18
1		3	4	5			8		10	11	7	9	6			2					19
1		3		5	4	7	8		10		11	9	6			2					20
1	2	3	4	5			8		10		7	9	6	11							21
1	2	3	4	5			8		10		7	9	6	11							22
1	2	3	4	5			8		10		7	9	6	11							23
1	2	3	4	5	8				10		7	9	6	11							24
1		3	4		6		8		10	7		9	5	11		2					25
1		3	4		6		8		10			9	5	11		2		7			26
1	2	3	4		6		8		10		7	9	5	11							27
1	2	3	4		6		8		10		7	9	5	11							28
1	2	3	4		6		8		10		7	9	5	11							29
1	2	3	4		6	7	8		10			9	5	11							30
1	2	3	4		6		8		10			9	5	11					7		31
1	2	3	4		6		8		10			9	5	11					7		32
1	2	3	4		6		8		10			9	5	11					7		33
1	2	3	4		6		8		10			9	5	11					7		34
1	2	3	4		6		8		10			9	5	11					7		35
1	2	3	4		6		8		10			9	5	11					7		36
1	2	3	4		6	7	8		10			9	5	11							37
1	2	3	4		6	7	8		10			9	5	11							38
1	2	3	4		6	7	8		10			9	5	11							39
1	2	3	4		6	7	8		10			9	5	11							40
1	2	3	4		6	7			10			8	5	11					9		41
1	2	3	4		6	7			10			8	5	11					9		42
1	2	3	4		6	7			10			8	5	11					9		43
1	2	3	4		6	7			10			8	5	11					9		44
1	2	3			6	7	8		4			10	5	11					9		45
1	2	3			6	7			4	10		8	5	11					9		46
46	36	45	43	20	36	24	37	12	46	11	12	38	32	37	3	10	3	1	13	1	
			3			4	21	1	8	2		17		15					3		

1 own-goal

Forgan T	Phillips E	Howe G	Brown G	Stewart A	Mollatt R	Hughes W	Bottom A	Monkhouse A	Wragg P	Colbridge C	Hobson A	Wilkinson N	Cairney J	Fenton W	Powell J	Wardle E	Stoddart T	Stewart J	Hill W	Steel R	
1	2		4	5		7	8		10			9	6	11		3					1
1		3	4	5			8		10	11	7	9	6			2					2
1		3	4	5		7	8		10	11		9	6			2					3
3	1	2	3	3		2	3		3	2	1	3	3	1		3					
							1		1			1									

1957-58

Manager: Sam Bartram

No	Month	Day	Venue	Opponents	Result	Scorers	Attendance
1	Aug	24	(a)	Hull C	W 1-0	Hughes	17,671
2		26	(h)	Bradford C	W 2-0	Bottom 2	12,272
3		31	(h)	Barrow	D 0-0		9,861
4	Sep	4	(a)	Bradford C	L 2-3	Wragg (pen), Fenton	19,749
5		7	(a)	Oldham A	W 3-2	Wilkinson 2, Colbridge	8,431
6		10	(a)	Carlisle U	L 1-2	Fenton	9,557
7		14	(h)	Bury	W 2-1	Bottom, Fenton	10,943
8		16	(h)	Carlisle U	L 0-5		6,711
9		21	(a)	Accrington S	L 0-3		6,082
10		25	(a)	Bradford	W 2-0	Bottom, Wragg	5,045
11		28	(h)	Chester	L 1-2	Fenton	7,103
12		30	(h)	Bradford	W 3-0	Hughes, Robertson, Wragg	4,407
13	Oct	5	(a)	Chesterfield	L 0-2		8,831
14		12	(h)	Halifax T	D 1-1	Robertson	6,878
15		19	(a)	Mansfield T	L 1-2	Robertson	7,913
16		26	(h)	Gateshead	D 2-2	Wragg, Metcalfe	6,898
17	Nov	2	(a)	Darlington	L 0-2		7,538
18		9	(h)	Scunthorpe U	D 0-0		8,276
19		23	(h)	Crewe A	W 3-1	Wragg, Hughes, Robertson	6,322
20		30	(a)	Rochdale	L 1-2	Metcalfe	6,297
21	Dec	14	(a)	Stockport C	L 1-2	Robertson	10,503
22		21	(h)	Hull C	W 3-1	Wilkinson, Bottom, Fenton	7,031
23		25	(a)	Hartlepools U	D 2-2	Brown, Hughes	6,837
24		26	(h)	Hartlepools U	D 2-2	Bottom, Powell	10,785
25		28	(a)	Barrow	L 0-1		6,235
26	Jan	1	(a)	Tranmere R	L 1-6	Bottom	6,865
27		11	(h)	Oldham A	D 2-2	Bottom, Wilkinson	8,502
28		18	(a)	Bury	L 1-4	Farmer	8,434
29	Feb	1	(h)	Accrington S	L 0-3		7,896
30		8	(a)	Chester	L 2-9	Phillips, Farmer	5,212
31		15	(h)	Chesterfield	D 3-3	Bottom (pen), Farmer, Hughes	4,813
32		22	(a)	Crewe A	W 4-3	Farmer 2, Wilkinson, Wragg	3,332
33	Mar	1	(h)	Mansfield T	W 3-1	Hughes, Wilkinson, Wragg	6,002
34		22	(a)	Halifax T	L 1-2	Wragg	5,813
35		24	(a)	Gateshead	D 0-0		3,971
36		29	(h)	Wrexham	L 1-2	Wragg	4,485
37	Apr	4	(a)	Southport	W 1-0	Hughes	4,386
38		5	(a)	Workington	D 0-0		4,361
39		7	(h)	Southport	W 1-0	Wilkinson	6,417
40		12	(h)	Rochdale	W 1-0	Wardle	5,123
41		16	(a)	Wrexham	D 2-2	Wilkinson, Opp own-goal	7,371
42		19	(a)	Scunthorpe U	W 2-1	Farmer 2	10,083
43		23	(h)	Tranmere R	W 4-0	Farmer 3, Patterson	7,205
44		26	(h)	Stockport C	D 0-0		8,005
45		28	(h)	Workington	W 3-0	Wilkinson 2, Wragg	5,731
46	May	1	(h)	Darlington	W 3-0	Farmer 2, Wragg	5,570

FINAL LEAGUE POSITION: 13th in Division Three North

Appearances
Goals

FA Cup

Round	Month	Day	Venue	Opponents	Result	Scorers	Attendance
1	Nov	16	(h)	Chesterfield	W 1-0	Fenton	8,615
2	Dec	7	(a)	South Shields	W 3-1	Robertson, Wilkinson, Bottom	18,500
3	Jan	8	(h)	Birmingham C	W 3-0	Bottom, Wragg, Wilkinson	19,750
4		25	(h)	Bolton W	D 0-0		23,600
R		29	(a)	Bolton W	L 0-3		34,062

Appearances
Goals

Forgan T	Phillips E	Howe G	Wragg P	Cairney J	Mollatt R	Hughes W	Bottom A	Wilkinson N	Robertson J	Fenton W	Colbridge C	Brown G	Johnson H	Longden C	Addison C	Hill W	Granger M	Patterson G	Powell J	Boyes K	Metcalfe J	Spence R	Greensmith R	Farmer T	Steel R	Wardle E	
1	2	3	4	5	6	7	8	9	10	11																	1
1	2	3	4	5	6	7	8	9		11	10																2
1	2	3	4	5	6	7	8	9		11	10																3
1	2	3	8	5	6	7		9	10	11		4															4
1	2	3	8	5		7		9		11	10	4	6														5
1	2	3	8	5				9		11	10	4	6	7													6
1	2	3	6	5		7	8	9		11		4			10												7
1	2	3	6	5		7	8			11		4			10	9											8
	2		10	5	6	7			9	11		4	3		8		1										9
	2	3	10	5	6	7	8	9		11		4					1										10
	2	3	10		6	7	8	9		11		4	5				1										11
	2	3	10		6	7		9	8	11		4	5				1										12
	2	3		5	6	7		9		11		4					1	8	10								13
	2	3		5	6	7		8	9	11		4			10		1										14
	2	3	10	5	6	7		8	9	11		4					1										15
	2	3	10	5	6			8	9							7	1			4	11						16
	2	3	10			7		8	9				5				1			4	11	6					17
	2	3	6			7	8	9	10	11		4	5				1										18
	2	3	6			7	8	9	10	11		4	5				1										19
	2	3	6			7	8	9	10			4					1			5	11						20
	2	3	6			7	8	9	10			4	5				1		11								21
	2	3	6			7	9	8	10	11		4	5				1										22
	2	3	6			7	9	8	10			4	5				1		11								23
	2	3	6				9	8	10			4	5			7	1		11								24
	2	3	6		10		9	8				4		7	11		1			5							25
	2	3					9	8		11		4				7	1		10	5		6					26
	2	3	10			7	9	8				4	5				1					6	11				27
	2	3	10			7		9				4	5				1					6	11	8			28
	2		10	5		7		9				4					1					6	11	8	3		29
	2	3	6	5		7	9		10			4					1						11	8			30
		3	6	5		10	9			11		4					1						7	8		2	31
	2	3	10	6		7		9				4	5				1						11	8			32
	2	3	10	6		7		9				4	5				1						11	8			33
	2	3	4	6		7		9					5				1						11	8	10		34
	2	3	10	5		7		9				4			8		1					6	11				35
	2	3	10			7		9				4	5				1					6	11	8			36
		3			6	7			9				5		10		1	4					11	8		2	37
		3	10		6			9					5		11		1	4					7	8		2	38
		3	10		6			9		11			5				1	4					7	8		2	39
		3	10		6			9					5			7	1	4					11	8		2	40
	2	3	10		6			9					5				1	4					11	8		7	41
		3	10		6			9					5			7	1	4					11	8		2	42
1		3	10		6			9					5			7		4					11	8		2	43
1		3	10		6			9					5			7		4					11	8		2	44
1		3	10					9				4	5			7						6	11	8		2	45
1		3	10					9				4	5			7						6	11	8		2	46
12	36	44	42	21	21	32	19	41	17	21	4	32	28	2	8	10	34	9	5	5	3	9	20	18	2	11	
	1		11			7	9	10	5	5	1	1						1	1		2			12		1	

1 own-goal

Forgan T	Phillips E	Howe G	Wragg P	Cairney J	Mollatt R	Hughes W	Bottom A	Wilkinson N	Robertson J	Fenton W	Colbridge C	Brown G	Johnson H	Longden C	Addison C	Hill W	Granger M	Patterson G	Powell J	Boyes K	Metcalfe J	Spence R	Greensmith R	Farmer T	Steel R	Wardle E	
	2	3	6			7	8	9	10	11		4	5				1										1
	2	3	6			7	8	9	10			4	5				1		11								2
	2	3	10			7	8	9		11		4	5				1					6					3
	2	3	10			7	8	9		11		4	5				1					6					4
	2	3	10			7	8	9				4	5				1					6	11				R
	5	5	5			5	5	5	2	3		5	5				5		1			3	1				
			1				2	2	1	1																	

1958-59

Manager: Sam Bartram

1	Aug	23	(a)	Oldham A	W 1-0	Greensmith	8,400
2		25	(h)	Southport	W 2-0	Wilkinson 2	8,783
3		30	(h)	Bradford	W 4-0	Farmer 2, Wilkinson, Wragg	8,497
4	Sep	2	(a)	Southport	L 0-1		3,612
5		6	(a)	Port Vale	D 2-2	Farmer 2	10,104
6		8	(h)	Torquay U	W 1-0	Farmer	8,194
7		13	(h)	Crystal P	D 1-1	Addison	8,368
8		17	(a)	Torquay U	D 1-1	Boyes	5,887
9		20	(a)	Chester	D 2-2	Addison, Opp own-goal	8,536
10		22	(h)	Crewe A	W 4-0	Addison 2, Hughes, Farmer	6,989
11		27	(h)	Watford	D 0-0		8,629
12	Oct	1	(a)	Crewe A	W 4-2	Wragg 2, Hughes, Addison	8,540
13		4	(a)	Hartlepools U	W 5-1	Wragg 3, Hughes, Addison	9,799
14		9	(a)	Northampton T	W 2-1	Wragg, Addison	5,826
15		11	(h)	Carlisle U	D 1-1	Wilkinson	9,373
16		18	(a)	Gillingham	D 2-2	Patterson 2	12,023
17		25	(h)	Exeter C	L 0-2		9,793
18	Nov	1	(a)	Coventry C	L 0-2		24,462
19		8	(h)	Shrewsbury T	W 2-0	Addison, Hartnett	7,725
20		22	(h)	Walsall	W 3-2	Farmer 2, Wilkinson	7,454
21		29	(a)	Millwall	L 2-5	Wragg, Addison	13,128
22	Dec	13	(a)	Gateshead	L 0-1		2,825
23		20	(h)	Oldham A	W 3-1	Wragg, Brownlee, Twissell	6,292
24		26	(h)	Barrow	W 1-0	Wardle	10,382
25		27	(a)	Barrow	W 3-2	Hughes, Addison, Powell	5,732
26	Jan	3	(a)	Bradford	L 1-2	Mollatt	7,715
27		24	(h)	Aldershot	D 0-0		7,961
28		31	(a)	Crystal P	D 0-0		16,175
29	Feb	7	(h)	Chester	D 1-1	Wragg	5,414
30		14	(a)	Watford	W 3-2	Twissell, Farmer, Brownlee	5,779
31		21	(h)	Hartlepools U	D 1-1	Wragg	5,339
32		28	(a)	Carlisle U	D 0-0		3,076
33	Mar	7	(h)	Gillingham	W 3-1	Hughes, Tait, Wragg (pen)	5,246
34		14	(a)	Exeter C	W 2-0	Tait, Twissell	9,330
35		18	(a)	Darlington	W 1-0	Tait	2,594
36		21	(h)	Coventry C	D 0-0		8,684
37		27	(h)	Workington	D 2-2	Wilkinson, Wragg	10,278
38		28	(a)	Shrewsbury T	D 2-2	Patterson, Twissell	9,833
39		30	(a)	Workington	D 2-2	Wragg, Wilkinson	4,764
40	Apr	4	(h)	Darlington	W 2-1	Wilkinson, Twissell	7,896
41		11	(a)	Walsall	L 0-5		8,202
42		15	(h)	Port Vale	D 0-0		9,755
43		18	(h)	Millwall	D 3-3	Hughes, Farmer, Opp own-goal	7,654
44		20	(h)	Northampton T	W 2-1	Wilkinson, Farmer	9,123
45		25	(a)	Aldershot	W 1-0	Farmer	2,862
46		27	(h)	Gateshead	W 1-0	Hughes	9,033

FINAL LEAGUE POSITION: 3rd in Division Four

Appearances
Goals

FA Cup

1	Nov	18	(a)	Bury	L 0-1		13,552

Appearances
Goals

Forgan T	Wardle E	Howe G	Patterson G	Jackson B	Mollatt R	Hughes W	Wilkinson N	Wragg P	Farmer T	Greensmith R	Addison C	Hartnett J	Boyes K	Spence R	Powell J	Ramsey R	Twissell C	Middleton D	Brownlee T	Tait B	
1	2	3	4	5	6	7	8	9	10	11											1
1	2	3	4	5	6	7	8	9	10	11											2
1	2	3	4	5	6	7	8	9	10	11											3
1	2	3	4	5	6	7	8	9	10	11											4
1	2	3	4	5	6	7		9	8	11	10										5
1	2	3	4	5	6	7		9	8	11	10										6
1	2	3	4	5	6	7		9	8		10	11									7
1	2	3		5	6	7	8		9	11	10		4								8
1	2	3		5	6	7	8		9	11	10		4								9
1	2	3		5	6	7	8		9	11	10			4							10
1	2	3		5	6	7	8		9	11	10			4							11
1	2	3	4	5		7		9	8	11	10			6							12
1	2	3	4	5		7		9	8	11	10			6							13
1	2	3	4	5		7	8	9		11	10			6							14
1	2	3	4	5		7	8	9		11	10			6							15
1	2	3	4	5		7	8	9		11	10			6							16
1	2	3	4	5		7		9	8	11				6	10						17
1	2	3	4			7		9	8		10		5	6	11						18
1	2	3	4	5		7		9	8		10	11		6							19
1		3		5		7	8	4	9		10			6		2	11				20
1		3		5		7	8	4	9		10					2	11	6			21
1	2		4	5		7		6	8		10					3	11		9		22
1	2		4			7		6	8		10		5			3	11		9		23
1	2		4			7	8	6			10		5			3	11		9		24
1	2		4		6	7	8	3	9		10		5		11						25
1	2				6	7	8	4			10		5			3	11		9		26
1	2			5	6	7		4			10					3	11		9	8	27
1	2		4	5	6			8		11	10					3	7		9		28
1	2		4	5	6			10	8	11						3	7		9		29
1	2		4	5	6			10	8	11						3	7		9		30
1	2		4	5	6			10	8	11						3	7		9		31
1		3	4	5	6	7		10	9							2	11			8	32
1		3	4	5	6	7		10	9							2	11			8	33
1		3	4	5	6	7		10	9							2	11			8	34
1		3	4	5	6	7		10	9							2	11			8	35
1		3	4	5	6	7	9	10			11					2				8	36
1		3	4	5	6	7	9	10								2	11			8	37
1		3	4		6	7	8	10	9				5			2	11				38
1		3	4		6	7	8	9					5		10	2	11				39
1		3	4		6	7	8	10	9				5			2	11				40
1		3	4		6	7	8		9	11	10		5			2					41
1		3	4	5	6	7	8	10	9						11	2					42
1		3	4	5	6	7	8	10	9						11	2					43
1		3	4		6	7	8	10	9				5		11	2					44
1		3	4		6	7	8	10	9				5		11	2					45
1		3	4		6	7	8	10	9				5		11	2					46
46	29	36	38	34	33	42	27	41	36	21	25	2	14	11	9	26	19	1	9	7	
	1		3		1	7	9	14	12	1	10	1	1		1		5		2	3	

2 own-goals

Forgan T	Wardle E	Howe G	Patterson G	Jackson B	Mollatt R	Hughes W	Wilkinson N	Wragg P	Farmer T	Greensmith R	Addison C	Hartnett J	Boyes K	Spence R	Powell J	Ramsey R	Twissell C	Middleton D	Brownlee T	Tait B	
1		3		5		7	8	4	9		10	11		6		2					1
1		1		1		1	1	1	1		1	1		1		1					

1959-60

Manager: Sam Bartram

1	Aug	22	(a)	Bradford C	L 0-2		12,592
2		24	(h)	Bury	W 1-0	Edgar	9,715
3		29	(h)	Coventry C	D 1-1	Twissell	9,412
4	Sep	1	(a)	Bury	L 0-2		14,666
5		5	(h)	Halifax T	L 1-2	Farmer	8,649
6		7	(h)	Queen's Park R	W 2-1	Edgar, Powell	10,593
7		12	(a)	Swindon T	D 1-1	Wilkinson	12,934
8		14	(a)	Queen's Park R	D 0-0		11,857
9		19	(h)	Chesterfield	W 1-0	Wilkinson	9,673
10		21	(h)	Grimsby T	D 3-3	Wilkinson 2, Powell	11,846
11		26	(a)	Newport C	L 2-3	Edgar 2	7,367
12		28	(a)	Grimsby T	D 2-2	Hughes, Wilkinson	10,345
13	Oct	3	(h)	Accrington S	W 3-0	Edgar 3	7,997
14		7	(a)	Bournemouth	L 0-2		2,055
15		10	(a)	Barnsley	D 1-1	Farmer	9,411
16		12	(h)	Bournemouth	W 3-2	Farmer, Wragg, Twissell	8,278
17		17	(h)	Southampton	D 2-2	Wilkinson 2	8,423
18		24	(a)	Reading	L 0-1		11,561
19		31	(h)	Mansfield T	W 2-1	Addison, Wilkinson	6,953
20	Nov	7	(a)	Port Vale	L 0-2		8,425
21		21	(a)	Brentford	W 2-1	Wragg, Wilkinson	13,118
22		28	(h)	Colchester U	L 2-3	Boyes, Addison	6,924
23	Dec	12	(a)	Shrewsbury T	L 0-4		7,686
24		19	(h)	Bradford C	D 1-1	Tait	4,851
25		26	(a)	Tranmere R	D 2-2	Tait, Edgar	10,077
26		28	(h)	Tranmere R	W 3-0	Edgar 2, Opp own-goal	8,920
27	Jan	2	(a)	Coventry C	L 2-5	Hughes, Edgar	14,407
28		16	(a)	Halifax T	W 2-1	Wilkinson, Twissell	3,812
29		23	(h)	Swindon T	W 1-0	Addison	6,031
30		30	(a)	Southend U	D 1-1	Wilkinson	8,825
31	Feb	6	(a)	Chesterfield	L 0-2		6,652
32		12	(h)	Newport C	W 2-0	Edgar 2	7,795
33		27	(h)	Barnsley	D 0-0		6,920
34	Mar	5	(a)	Southampton	L 1-3	Edgar	20,844
35		12	(h)	Reading	L 2-3	Hughes, Wilkinson	5,452
36		16	(h)	Norwich C	L 1-2	Farmer	6,510
37		19	(a)	Colchester U	D 2-2	Wilkinson 2	6,599
38		26	(h)	Port Vale	W 2-0	Hughes, Edgar	6,415
39		30	(a)	Accrington S	L 0-4		925
40	Apr	2	(a)	Norwich C	L 0-1		26,952
41		9	(h)	Brentford	L 0-1		4,751
42		15	(h)	Wrexham	W 3-0	Hughes, Wragg, Addison	6,751
43		16	(a)	Mansfield T	L 0-2		7,234
44		18	(a)	Wrexham	L 1-3	Powell	4,922
45		23	(h)	Southend U	L 2-3	Hughes 2	4,952
46		30	(h)	Shrewsbury T	L 0-1		4,801

FINAL LEAGUE POSITION: 21st in Division Three

Appearances
Goals

FA Cup

1	Nov	14	(h)	Barrow	W 3-1	Addison, Edgar, Hughes	7,631
2	Dec	5	(a)	Crook T	W 1-0	Edgar	8,309
3	Jan	9	(a)	Bournemouth	L 0-1		14,749

Appearances
Goals

Forgan T	Ramsey R	Howe G	Patterson G	Boyes K	Mollatt R	Hughes W	Edgar J	Wilkinson N	Alexander A	Twissell C	Granger M	Battye J	Farmer T	Jackson B	Wragg P	Powell J	Addison C	Hill W	Greensmith R	Tait B	Jones B	
1	2	3	4	5	6	7	8	9	10	11												1
	2	3			6	7	8		10	11	1	4	9	5								2
	2	3			6	7	8		10	11	1	4	9	5								3
	2	3			6	7	8		10		1	4		5	9	11						4
	2	3				7	8		10		1	4	9	5	6	11						5
	2	3				7	8	9			1	4		5	6	11	10					6
	2	3				7	8	9			1	4		5	6	11	10					7
	2	3				7	8	9			1	4		5	6	11	10					8
1	2	3				7	8	9				4		5	6	11	10					9
1	2	3				7	8	9				4		5	6	11	10					10
1	2	3				7	8	9				4		5	6	11	10					11
	2	3				7	8	9		11	1	4		5	6		10					12
	2	3				7	8	9		11	1	4		5	6		10					13
	2	3				7	8			11	1	4	9	5	6		10					14
	2	3	4			7	8			11	1	6	9	5	10							15
	2	3	4			7	8			11	1	6	9	5	10							16
	2	3	4		6	7	8	9		11	1			5	10							17
	2	3	4	5		7	10	8		11	1				6			9				18
1	2	3	4			7	10	9		11				5	6		8					19
1	2	3		4		7	10	9		11				5	6		8					20
1	2	3		4		7	10	9		11				5	6		8					21
1	2	3	4	5		7	10	9		11					6		8					22
1	2	3		4		7	10	9						5	6		8		11			23
1	2	3			6	7	10	9		11				5	4					8		24
1	2	3			6	7	10	9		11				5	4					8		25
1	2	3			6	7	10	9		11				5	4					8		26
1	2	3			6	7	10	9		11				5	4					8		27
1	2	3			6	7	10	9		11				5	4		8					28
1	2	3		5	6	7		8		11					4		10	9				29
1	2	3		5		7	10	9		11		4			6		8					30
1	2	3		5		7	10	9		11		4			6		8					31
1	2	3			6	7	9		10	11				5	4		8					32
1	2	3			6	7	9	8	10	11				5	4							33
1	2	3			6	7	10							5	4	11	8	9				34
1	2	3			6	7	10	8		11				5	4			9				35
1	2	3		5	6	7	10	8					9		4		11					36
1	2	3		5	6	7	10	8					9		4		11					37
1	2	3		4		7	10	8					9	5	6		11					38
1	2	3			6	7	10	5		11			9		6		11					39
1	2	3		4		7	10	8						5	6		11			9		40
1	2	3		4		7		8		11			9	5	6		10					41
1	2	3		4	6	7	10	8						5	6		11					42
1	2	3		4	6	7		10					9	5			11			8		43
1	2	3	4		6	7		8						5		10	11	9				44
1	2	3	4			7	10	8						5			11	9			6	45
1	2	3	6	4		7	10	9		11				5			8					46
32	46	46	10	17	21	46	42	37	7	28	14	17	12	37	39	10	31	6	1	6	1	
				1		7	15	14		3			4		3	3	4			2		

1 own-goal

Forgan T	Ramsey R	Howe G	Patterson G	Boyes K	Mollatt R	Hughes W	Edgar J	Wilkinson N	Alexander A	Twissell C	Granger M	Battye J	Farmer T	Jackson B	Wragg P	Powell J	Addison C	Hill W	Greensmith R	Tait B	Jones B	
1	2	3		4		7	10	9		11				5	6		8					1
1	2	3		4		7	10	9		11				5	6		8					2
1	2	3			6	7	10	9		11				5	4					8		3
3	3	3		2	1	3	3	3		3				3	3		2			1		
						1	2										1					

1960-61

Manager: Tom Lockie

1	Aug	20	(h)	Millwall	W 3-2	Wragg 2, Woods	7,242
2		22	(a)	Barrow	D 1-1	Wragg	7,009
3		29	(h)	Barrow	W 2-0	Weir 2	8,586
4	Sep	3	(h)	Doncaster R	D 1-1	Wilkinson	7,758
5		5	(a)	Bradford	D 3-3	Weir 2, Wragg (pen)	7,782
6		10	(h)	Crewe A	W 3-1	Addison, Scott, Wilkinson	6,160
7		12	(h)	Bradford	W 2-0	Addison, Wragg	9,704
8		17	(a)	Chester	L 1-2	Scott	5,567
9		21	(a)	Gillingham	L 2-3	Wragg, Addison	5,081
10		24	(h)	Workington	W 4-0	Addison 3, Opp own-goal	6,104
11		26	(h)	Gillingham	D 0-0		8,577
12	Oct	1	(a)	Oldham A	L 1-3	Addison	9,284
13		3	(h)	Aldershot	W 4-1	Wragg 3, Weir	7,508
14		8	(a)	Wrexham	L 0-4		5,184
15		15	(h)	Carlisle U	W 4-0	Fountain, Hughes, Wilkinson, Wragg	4,957
16		22	(a)	Rochdale	D 0-0		4,889
17		29	(h)	Mansfield T	W 3-2	Wragg 2, Addison	5,389
18	Nov	12	(h)	Exeter C	W 6-1	Addison 2, Hughes, Wilkinson, Wragg (pen), Weir	5,418
19		19	(a)	Peterborough U	D 1-1	Wilkinson	11,992
20	Dec	3	(a)	Darlington	L 1-2	Addison	8,481
21		10	(h)	Crystal P	L 0-2		6,538
22		17	(a)	Millwall	L 2-3	Wilkinson 2	6,884
23		26	(h)	Northampton T	L 0-1		7,291
24		27	(a)	Northampton T	L 0-3		18,384
25		31	(h)	Accrington S	W 1-0	Addison	4,725
26	Jan	2	(a)	Hartlepools U	W 3-1	Addison 2, Wragg	5,337
27		14	(a)	Doncaster R	W 2-0	Hughes, Hoggart	5,330
28		21	(a)	Crewe A	W 5-1	Wragg 4, Wilkinson	8,272
29	Feb	4	(h)	Chester	W 2-0	Hughes, Wragg	4,867
30		10	(a)	Workington	L 0-2		3,041
31		18	(h)	Oldham A	W 1-0	Wragg	8,311
32		25	(h)	Wrexham	W 2-1	Hughes, Wragg	4,304
33	Mar	4	(a)	Carlisle U	D 1-1	Jackson	3,050
34		11	(h)	Rochdale	W 2-0	Wragg (pen), Opp own-goal	5,477
35		13	(a)	Stockport C	L 0-2		5,263
36		18	(a)	Mansfield T	W 3-1	Hoggatt 2, Wilkinson	5,060
37		20	(h)	Southport	W 2-0	Wilkinson, Weir	6,587
38		25	(h)	Stockport C	D 0-0		8,221
39		31	(h)	Hartlepools U	W 4-0	Jackson (pen), Hoggart, Weir, Gould	8,933
40	Apr	1	(a)	Exeter C	L 1-2	Hoggart	5,093
41		8	(h)	Peterborough U	L 0-1		11,768
42		15	(a)	Southport	D 2-2	Wilkinson, Weir	3,880
43		19	(a)	Accrington S	L 0-2		1,801
44		22	(h)	Darlington	W 4-1	Gould 2, Hoggart, Weir	4,271
45		26	(a)	Aldershot	L 1-6	Edgar	4,926
46		29	(a)	Crystal P	L 0-1		17,885

FINAL LEAGUE POSITION: 5th in Division Four

Appearances
Goals

FA Cup

1	Nov	5	(h)	Bradford	D 0-0		7,808
R		9	(a)	Bradford	W 2-0	Wilkinson, Addison	5,813
2		30	(a)	Tranmere R	D 1-1	Wilkinson	11,226
R	Dec	5	(h)	Tranmere R	W 2-1	Wilkinson 2	10,724
3	Jan	7	(h)	Norwich C	D 1-1	Hughes	9,463
R		11	(a)	Norwich C	L 0-1		27,438

Appearances
Goals

League Cup

1	Oct	10	(h)	Blackburn R	L 1-2	Addison	10,933

Appearances
Goals

Forgan T	Bingley W	Howe G	Woods A	Jackson B	Jordan B	Hughes W	Scott J	Wragg P	Addison C	Weir J	Twissell C	Wilkinson N	Granger M	Tait B	Hoggart D	Fountain J	Boyes K	Edgar J	Ramsey R	Gould W	
1	2	3	4	5	6	7	8	9	10	11											1
1	2	3	4	5	6	7	8	9	10	11											2
1	2	3	4	5	6	7	8	9		11		10									3
1	2	3	4	5	6		8	9		11	7	10									4
1	2	3	4	5	6		8	9		11	7	10									5
1	2	3	4	5	6		8	9	7	11		10									6
	2	3	4	5	6		8	10	7	11			1	9							7
	2	3	4	5	6		8	9	7	11			1		10						8
		3	4	5		7	8	9	10	11			1			6			2		9
1	2	3	4	5		7	8	9	10	11						6					10
1	2	3	4	5		7	8		10	11				9		6					11
1	2	3	4	5		7	8	9	10	11						6					12
1	2	3	4	5		7	8	9	10	11						6					13
1	2	3	4	5		7	8	9	10	11						6					14
1	2	3	4	5		7		9	10	11		8				6					15
1	2	3	4	5		7		9	10	11		8				6					16
1	2	3	4	5		7		9	10	11		8				6					17
1	2	3	4			7		10	8	11		9				6	5				18
1	2	3	4	5		7		10	8	11		9				6					19
1	2	3	4	5		7		10	8	11		9				6					20
1	2	3	4	5		7		10	8	11		9				6					21
1	2	3	4			7			8	11		9				6	5	10			22
	2	3	4			7	8		11			9	1			6	5	10			23
	2	3	4	5		7	8	9	11			10	1			6					24
1	2	3	4	5		7		10	8	11		9				6					25
1	2	3	4	5		7		10	8	11		9				6					26
1	2	3	4	5		7		8			11				10	6		9			27
1	2	3	4	5		7		9			11	8			10	6					28
1	2	3	4	5		7		9			11	8			10	6					29
1		3	4	5		7		9			11	8			10	6			2		30
1	2	3	4	5		7		9				10			8	6				11	31
1	2	3	4	5		7		9				10			8	6				11	32
1	2	3	4	5		7		9				10			8	6				11	33
1	2	3	4	5		7		10				9			8	6				11	34
1	2	3	4	5		7		10		11		9			8	6					35
1	2	3	4	5		7				10		9			8	6				11	36
1	2	3	4	5		7				10		9			8	6				11	37
1	2	3	4	5		7				10		9			8	6				11	38
1	2	3	4	5		7				10		9			8	6				11	39
1	2	3	4	5		7				10		9			8	6				11	40
1	2	3	4	5		7				10		8				6			9	11	41
1	2	3	4	5		7				10		9			8	6				11	42
1	2	3	4	5		7				10		9			8	6				11	43
1	2	3	4	5		7				10		9			8	6				11	44
1	2	3	4	5		7				11		9			8	6		10			45
1	2	3	4	5		7	8			11		10				6		9			46
41	44	46	46	43	8	41	17	32	23	36	6	35	5	2	19	38	3	5	3	13	
			1	2		5	2	22	14	10		11			6	1		1		3	

2 own-goals

Forgan T	Bingley W	Howe G	Woods A	Jackson B	Jordan B	Hughes W	Scott J	Wragg P	Addison C	Weir J	Twissell C	Wilkinson N	Granger M	Tait B	Hoggart D	Fountain J	Boyes K	Edgar J	Ramsey R	Gould W	
1	2	3	4	5		7		9	10	11		8				6					1
1	2	3	4	5		7		10	8	11		9				6					R
1	2	3	4				7	10	8	11		9				6	5				2
1	2	3	4	5		7		10	8	11		9				6					R
1	2	3	4	5		7		10	8	11		9				6					3
1	2	3	4	5		7		10	8	11		9				6					R
6	6	6	6	5		5	1	6	6	6		6				6	1				
						1			1			4									

Forgan T	Bingley W	Howe G	Woods A	Jackson B	Jordan B	Hughes W	Scott J	Wragg P	Addison C	Weir J	Twissell C	Wilkinson N	Granger M	Tait B	Hoggart D	Fountain J	Boyes K	Edgar J	Ramsey R	Gould W	
1	2	3	4			7	8	9	11			10				6	5				1
1	1	1	1			1	1	1	1			1				1	1				
									1												

1961-62

Manager: Tom Lockie

1	Aug	19	(a)	Bradford C	D 2-2	Weir, Opp own-goal	7,549
2		21	(h)	Wrexham	W 3-2	Weir 2, Stainsby	8,290
3		26	(h)	Chesterfield	W 4-0	Weir 2, Wragg 2 (1 pen)	6,621
4		30	(a)	Wrexham	L 1-2	Pierce	13,849
5	Sep	2	(a)	Gillingham	W 2-1	Weir, Pierce	5,222
6		4	(h)	Exeter C	W 2-1	Wragg, Pierce	9,334
7		9	(h)	Millwall	L 0-1		6,945
8		16	(a)	Mansfield T	L 1-3	Gould	8,884
9		18	(h)	Carlisle U	D 1-1	Wragg (pen)	8,171
10		23	(h)	Barrow	W 5-0	Woods, Wragg, Stainsby, Pierce, Gould	5,433
11		27	(a)	Carlisle U	L 2-3	Hughes, Weir	8,171
12		30	(a)	Rochdale	L 1-3	Weir	4,201
13	Oct	2	(h)	Crewe A	W 4-2	Weir 3, Stainsby	6,947
14		7	(h)	Colchester U	W 5-0	Weir 2, Wragg (pen), Stainsby, Gould	5,708
15		11	(a)	Crewe A	D 0-0		7,171
16		14	(a)	Chester	D 1-1	Pierce	6,399
17		21	(h)	Tranmere R	L 1-2	Weir	7,066
18		28	(a)	Southport	L 1-3	Stainsby	4,934
19	Nov	11	(a)	Darlington	D 0-0		5,413
20	Dec	2	(h)	Stockport C	W 1-0	Weir	4,697
21		9	(a)	Aldershot	L 0-2		5,388
22		16	(h)	Bradford C	W 4-0	Wragg 2, Stainsby, Wilkinson	4,473
23		23	(a)	Chesterfield	D 1-1	Weir	3,207
24		26	(a)	Doncaster R	W 2-1	Stainsby 2	6,321
25	Jan	13	(h)	Gillingham	W 4-0	Stainsby 3, Rudd	5,456
26		20	(a)	Millwall	L 1-2	Stainsby	11,881
27	Feb	3	(h)	Mansfield T	W 2-1	Stainsby, Wragg	5,874
28		10	(a)	Barrow	D 0-0		4,190
29		17	(h)	Rochdale	W 2-1	Jackson, Weir	5,168
30		24	(a)	Colchester U	L 1-3	Fountain	4,633
31	Mar	3	(h)	Chester	W 5-1	Weir 2, Gould, Wragg, Stainsby	4,600
32		9	(a)	Tranmere R	D 2-2	Stainsby, Weir	7,933
33		13	(a)	Oldham A	L 0-1		11,952
34		16	(h)	Southport	D 2-2	Wragg, Weir	6,772
35		19	(h)	Hartlepools U	W 2-0	Rudd, Weir	6,613
36		24	(a)	Hartlepools U	W 2-0	Francis, Rudd	3,130
37		31	(h)	Darlington	W 2-1	Francis 2	9,579
38	Apr	2	(h)	Doncaster R	W 5-2	Wragg 3, Weir, Opp own-goal	6,264
39		11	(a)	Exeter C	L 1-2	Weir	2,919
40		14	(h)	Oldham A	W 4-1	Francis, Wragg, Wilkinson, Weir	5,279
41		20	(h)	Workington	W 4-0	Weir 3, Gould	9,767
42		21	(a)	Stockport C	L 1-2	Wilkinson	2,739
43		23	(a)	Workington	D 0-0		2,368
44		28	(h)	Aldershot	L 0-1		7,321

FINAL LEAGUE POSITION: 6th in Division Four

Appearances
Goals

FA Cup

1	Nov	4	(a)	Bradford C	L 0-1		7,676

Appearances
Goals

League Cup

1	Sep	13	(h)	Bristol C	W 3-0	Weir, Stainsby, Wragg	8,379
2	Oct	9	(h)	Leicester C	W 2-1	Wragg, Stainsby	13,273
3	Nov	15	(h)	Watford	D 1-1	Gould	8,504
R		21	(a)	Watford	D 2-2*	Wragg, Stainsby	7,095
2R	Dec	4	(h)	Watford	W 3-2	Francis, Wragg, Jackson	7,019
4		13	(h)	Bournemouth	W 1-0	Stainsby	8,709
5	Feb	7	(a)	Rochdale	L 1-2	Wragg (pen)	7,312

*After extra-time

Appearances
Goals

Forgan T	Bingley W	Heron T	Woods A	Jackson B	Fountain J	Weir J	Wragg P	Stainsby J	Pierce B	Gould W	Boyes K	Wilkinson N	Hughes W	Hoggart D	Francis G	Rudd W	Granger M	Hamilton A	
1	2	3	4	5	6	7	8	9	10	11									1
1	2	3	4	5	6	7	8	9	10	11									2
1	2	3	4	5	6	7	8	9	10	11									3
1	2	3	4	5	6	7	8	9	10	11									4
1	2	3	4	5	6	7	8	9	10	11									5
1	2	3	4		6	7	8	9	10	11	5								6
1	2	3	4	5	6	7	8	9	10	11									7
1	2	3	4	5	6	7	8	9		11		10							8
1	2	3	4	5	6	7	8	9	10	11									9
1	2	3	4	5	6	7	8	9	10	11									10
1	2	3	4	5	6	10	9		8	11			7						11
1	2	3	4	5	6	10	9			11		8	7						12
1	2	3	4	5	6	7	8	9		11		10							13
1	2	3	4	5	6	7	8	9		11		10							14
1	2	3	4		6	7	8	9		11	5			10					15
1	2	3	4	5	6	7		9	8	11		10							16
1	2	3		5	6	7	4	9		11		10			8				17
1	2	3		5	6	7	4	9		11		10			8				18
1	2	3	4	5	6	10	8	9		11					7				19
1	2	3	4	5	6	10	8	9		11					7				20
1	2	3	4	5	6	10	8	9		11					7				21
1	2	3	4	5	6	11	8	9		7		10							22
1	2	3	4	5	6	11	8	9		7		10							23
1	2	3	4	5	6	11	8	9		7		10							24
1	2	3	4	5	6		8	9		11					7	10			25
1	2	3	4	5	6		8	9		11					7	10			26
1	2	3	4	5	6		10	9		11					7	8			27
	2	3	4	5	6	11	10	9		7						8	1		28
	2	3	4	5	6	11	8	9		7						10	1		29
	2	3	4	5	6	11	8	9		7						10	1		30
	2	3	4	5	6	11	8	9		7		10					1		31
	2	3	4	5	6	11	8	9		7		10					1		32
	2	3	4	5	6	11	8	9	10	7							1		33
1	2	3	4	5		11	8	9		7		10						6	34
1	2	3	4	5		11	8	9							7	10		6	35
1	2	3	4	5		11	8	9							7	10		6	36
1	2	3	4	5		11	8	9							7	10		6	37
1	2	3	4	5		11	8	9		7						10		6	38
1	2	3	4	5		11	8	9		7						10		6	39
1	2	3	4	5		11	8					9			7	10		6	40
1	2	3	4	5		10	8			11		9			7			6	41
1	2	3	4	5		10		9		11		8			7			6	42
1	2	3	4	5		10	8			11		9			7			6	43
1	2	3	4	5		10	8			11		9			7			6	44
38	44	44	42	42	33	41	42	38	12	40	2	18	2	1	16	12	6	11	
			1	1	1	28	15	15	5	5		3	1		4	3			

Forgan T	Bingley W	Heron T	Woods A	Jackson B	Fountain J	Weir J	Wragg P	Stainsby J	Pierce B	Gould W	Boyes K	Wilkinson N	Hughes W	Hoggart D	Francis G	Rudd W	Granger M	Hamilton A	
1	2	3	4	5	6	7	9			11		10			8				1
1	1	1	1	1	1	1	1			1		1			1				

Forgan T	Bingley W	Heron T	Woods A	Jackson B	Fountain J	Weir J	Wragg P	Stainsby J	Pierce B	Gould W	Boyes K	Wilkinson N	Hughes W	Hoggart D	Francis G	Rudd W	Granger M	Hamilton A	
1	2	3	4	5	6	7	8	9		11		10							1
1	2	3	4	5	6	7	8	9		11		10							2
1	2	3	4	5	6	7	8	9		11		10							3
1	2	3	4	5	6	11	8	9		7		10							R
	2	3	4	5	6	10	8	9		11					7		1		2R
1	2	3	4	5	6	10	8	9		11					7				4
	2	3	4	5	6		10	9		11					7	8	1		5
5	7	7	7	7	7	6	7	7		7		4			3	1	2		
				1		1	5	4		1					1				

1962-63

Manager: Tom Lockie

1	Aug	18	(a)	Stockport C	D 1-1	Rudd	4,461
2		20	(h)	Crewe A	W 2-0	Wragg 2 (1 pen)	7,360
3		25	(h)	Doncaster R	W 1-0	Gould	5,885
4		29	(a)	Crewe A	L 0-1		6,835
5	Sep	1	(a)	Mansfield T	L 0-2		10,864
6		8	(h)	Workington	L 1-2	Hoggart	4,522
7		12	(a)	Chester	D 0-0		5,277
8		15	(a)	Exeter C	L 1-2	Jackson	3,646
9		17	(h)	Gillingham	L 0-3		5,417
10		22	(h)	Chesterfield	L 3-4	Gould, Stainsby, Wilkinson	2,986
11		26	(a)	Gillingham	D 0-0		6,240
12		29	(a)	Rochdale	L 0-1		3,030
13	Oct	1	(h)	Darlington	W 5-1	Wilkinson 2, Gould, Hoggart, Rudd	4,455
14		6	(a)	Southport	L 1-2	Wilkinson	3,124
15		13	(h)	Aldershot	D 0-0		3,494
16		18	(a)	Newport C	W 3-1	Hoggart, Rudd, Opp own-goal	5,406
17		26	(h)	Oxford U	L 1-2	Jackson	5,215
18	Nov	10	(h)	Tranmere R	L 1-2	Wilkinson	3,784
19		12	(h)	Chester	D 0-0		3,645
20		17	(a)	Torquay U	L 0-1		3,618
21	Dec	1	(a)	Oldham A	L 2-3	Bingley (pen), Ambler	11,836
22		8	(h)	Barrow	D 1-1	Wragg	2,511
23		15	(h)	Stockport C	W 3-1	Gould 2, Wragg	2,610
24		22	(a)	Doncaster R	L 2-3	Bingley (pen), Ambler	4,030
25	Mar	8	(h)	Newport C	W 2-0	Bingley (pen), Wilkinson	4,083
26		11	(a)	Darlington	L 1-2	Wragg	3,377
27		16	(a)	Oxford U	W 2-0	Rudd, Heron	5,518
28		18	(h)	Exeter C	D 3-3	Bingley (pen), Gould, Rudd	4,477
29		22	(h)	Bradford C	W 3-0	Wilkinson, Stainsby, Heron	4,904
30		25	(h)	Hartlepools U	W 2-0	Wilkinson, Heron	4,558
31		29	(a)	Lincoln C	W 4-2	Gould, Wilkinson, Stainsby, Opp own-goal	2,227
32	Apr	1	(a)	Chesterfield	D 1-1	Rudd	8,354
33		5	(h)	Torquay U	W 1-0	Bingley (pen)	4,901
34		8	(a)	Aldershot	L 1-4	Opp own-goal	4,965
35		12	(h)	Brentford	D 1-1	Fountain	7,904
36		13	(a)	Tranmere R	L 1-2	Ambler	5,671
37		15	(a)	Brentford	L 1-2	Stainsby	15,070
38		20	(h)	Oldham A	W 5-2	Stainsby 2, Gould, Wilkinson, Rudd	4,367
39		22	(h)	Lincoln C	W 3-1	Wilkinson 3	5,082
40		27	(a)	Barrow	L 1-2	Hoggart	3,218
41		29	(a)	Hartlepools U	D 1-1	Wilkinson	2,659
42	May	4	(h)	Rochdale	W 1-0	Gould	4,442
43		11	(h)	Mansfield T	W 2-1	Rudd, Gould	5,043
44		15	(a)	Bradford C	W 2-1	Wilkinson, Gould	1,733
45		18	(a)	Workington	L 0-3		1,181
46		20	(h)	Southport	D 1-1	Opp own-goal	3,590

FINAL LEAGUE POSITION: 14th in Division Four

Appearances
Goals

FA Cup

1	Nov	3	(h)	Rochdale	D 0-0		4,663
R		6	(a)	Rochdale	W 2-1	Wragg, Wilkinson	6,225
2		24	(h)	Crewe A	W 2-1	Wragg, Wilkinson	6,163
3	Feb	13	(a)	Southampton	L 0-5		11,722

Appearances
Goals

League Cup

1	Sep	5	(h)	Lincoln C	D 2-2	Gould, Fountain	6,756
R		19	(a)	Lincoln C	L 0-2		4,790

Appearances
Goals

Forgan T	Bingley W	Heron T	Woods A	Jackson B	Fountain J	Gould W	Wragg P	Stainsby J	Rudd W	Weir J	Moor A	Boyes K	Moore A	Wilkinson N	Hoggart D	Perry P	Ambler R	Ashworth J	Popely P	Barmby J	
1	2	3	4	5	6	7	8	9	10	11											1
	2	3	4	5	6	7	8	9	10	11	1										2
	2	3	4	5	6	7	8	9	10	11	1										3
	2	3	4	5	6	7	8	9	10	11	1										4
	2	3	4		6	7			10	11	1	5	9	8							5
	2	3	4	5	6	11	8		10		1		9		7						6
	2	3	4	5	6	11	8	9			1			10	7						7
	2	3	4	5	6	11	8	9			1			10	7						8
	2	3	4	9	6	7	10	8	11		1	5									9
		3	4	5	6	7		8	11		1			9	10	2					10
	2	3	4	5	6		7	8	11		1			9	10						11
		3	4	5	6	7	8		11		1			9	10	2					12
		3	4	5	6	7		8	11		1			9	10	2					13
	2	3	4	5	6	7		8	11		1			9	10						14
	2	3	4	5	6	7		8	11		1			9	10						15
	2	3	4	5	6	7	8		11		1			9	10						16
	2	3	4	5	6	7	8		11		1			9	10						17
1	2	3	4	5	6	7	8		11					9			10				18
1	2		4	5	6	7	9		11						8	3	10				19
1	2	3	4	5	6	7	8		11					9			10				20
1	2	3	4	5	6	7	8		11					9			10				21
1	2	3	4	5	6	7	8		11					9			10				22
1	2	3	4	5	6	7	8		11					10			9				23
1	2	3	4	5	6	7	8		11					10			9				24
1	2	3	4	5	6	7	8	9	11					10							25
1	2	3	4	5	6	7	8	9	11					10							26
1	2	11	4	5	6	7		9	10					8		3					27
1	2	11	4	5	6	7		9	10					8		3					28
1	2	11	4	5	6	7		9	10					8		3					29
1	2	11	4	5	6	7		9	10					8		3					30
1	2	11	4	5	6	7		9	10					8		3					31
1	2		4	5	6	7		9	10					8		3	11				32
1	2		4	5	6	7		9	10					8		3	11				33
1	2		4	5	6	7	11	9	10					8		3					34
1	2	11	4	5	6	7		9	10					8		3					35
1	2	11	4	5	6			9	10					8		3	7				36
1	2	11	4	5	6			9	10					8		3	7				37
1	2	11		5	6	7		9	10					8		3		4			38
1	2	11		5	6	7		9	10					8		3		4			39
1	2	11		5	6	7		9	10						8	3		4			40
1	2	11		5	6			9	10					8	7	3		4			41
1	2			5	6	11		9	10					8	7	3		4			42
1	2			5	6	11			10					8	7	3	9	4			43
1	2			5	6	11		9	10					8	7	3		4			44
1	2	11		5	6	11			10					9	8	3		4			45
1		3	4	5	6	11			8					9	7				2	10	46
30	42	39	38	45	46	42	22	31	44	5	16	2	2	38	19	23	12	8	1	1	
	5	3		2	1	11	5	6	8					15	4		3				

4 own-goals

1	2	3	4	5	6		7	8	11					10				9			1
1	2	3	4	5	6	7	8		11					9	10						R
1	2	3	4	5	6	7	8		11					9			10				2
1	2	3	4	5	6	7	8		11					10			9				3
4	4	4	4	4	4	3	4	1	4					4	1		2	1			
							2							2							

	2	3	4		6	11	8		10		1	5	9		7						1
	2	3	4	9	6	7	10	8	11		1	5									R
	2	2	2	1	2	2	2	1	2		2	2	1		1						
					1	1															

1963-64

Manager: Tom Lockie

1	Aug	24	(h)	Rochdale	L 0-3		5,446
2		26	(a)	Tranmere R	L 0-1		9,667
3		31	(a)	Oxford U	D 4-4	Goldie 2, J.Scott (pen), Rudd	6,986
4	Sep	7	(h)	Workington	L 0-1		5,158
5		9	(h)	Tranmere R	L 1-2	Peyton	4,417
6		14	(a)	Newport C	D 0-0		5,238
7		16	(h)	Barrow	L 1-2	Woods	4,466
8		20	(h)	Stockport C	W 2-0	Woods, Gould	3,956
9		28	(a)	Bradford	W 3-1	Peyton 2, Rudd	5,843
10		30	(a)	Barrow	W 2-1	Hoggart, Rudd	2,745
11	Oct	5	(h)	Chesterfield	W 2-0	Gould, Wilkinson	4,456
12		7	(h)	Brighton & HA	L 2-3	Gould, Rudd	4,711
13		12	(h)	Hartlepools U	L 0-1		5,460
14		17	(a)	Brighton & HA	L 0-3		9,534
15		19	(a)	Exeter C	L 0-1		5,549
16		22	(a)	Doncaster R	D 0-0		4,974
17		25	(h)	Southport	W 4-1	Lang 2, Gould, Wilkinson	3,865
18		28	(h)	Doncaster R	W 3-1	Gould, Wilkinson, Rudd	4,981
19	Nov	2	(a)	Gillingham	L 0-1		9,548
20		9	(h)	Lincoln C	D 0-0		4,346
21		23	(h)	Aldershot	L 1-2	Gould	2,368
22		30	(a)	Carlisle U	L 0-4		5,884
23	Dec	14	(a)	Rochdale	L 0-2		2,203
24		21	(h)	Oxford U	L 0-2		1,653
25		28	(a)	Darlington	L 2-4	Wilkinson, Opp own-goal	3,409
26	Jan	4	(a)	Bradford C	L 2-3	Wilkinson, Goldie (pen)	4,781
27		10	(a)	Workington	L 0-1		4,229
28		18	(h)	Newport C	W 3-0	Baker 2, Goldie	2,114
29		25	(h)	Torquay U	D 1-1	Goldie	2,877
30	Feb	1	(a)	Stockport C	L 0-2		2,558
31		8	(h)	Bradford	W 2-0	Heron, Rudd	4,344
32		15	(a)	Chesterfield	L 0-1		3,527
33		22	(a)	Hartlepools U	W 1-0	Rudd	3,278
34		28	(h)	Exeter C	L 1-2	J.Scott (pen)	3,817
35	Mar	7	(a)	Southport	W 3-0	Wilkinson 2, Goldie	1,904
36		20	(a)	Lincoln C	L 2-3	Wilkinson, Goldie	5,222
37		27	(h)	Chester	W 1-0	J.Scott (pen)	4,437
38		28	(h)	Halifax T	L 1-3	Wilkinson	3,546
39		30	(a)	Chester	D 1-1	Wilkinson	4,326
40	Apr	4	(a)	Aldershot	L 2-5	Baker 2	3,021
41		6	(h)	Darlington	W 3-1	Peyton, Heron, Opp own-goal	2,844
42		11	(h)	Carlisle U	D 0-0		3,151
43		17	(a)	Torquay U	W 1-0	Baker	4,131
44		20	(a)	Halifax T	L 0-2		2,910
45		25	(h)	Bradford C	W 1-0	Heron	4,824
46		27	(h)	Gillingham	L 0-1		3,317

FINAL LEAGUE POSITION: 22nd in Division Four

Appearances
Goals

FA Cup

1	Nov	16	(h)	Carlisle U	L 2-5	Wilkinson 2	7,342

Appearances
Goals

League Cup

1	Sep	4	(a)	Doncaster R	D 0-0		8,020
R		23	(h)	Doncaster R	W 3-0	Lang, Rudd, Baker	5,345
2		25	(h)	Lincoln C	D 1-1	Peyton	5,598
R	Oct	14	(a)	Lincoln C	L 0-2		5,055

Appearances
Goals

Forgan T	Wealthall B	Heron T	Ashworth J	Jackson B	Fountain J	Scott J	Peyton N	Goldie J	Rudd W	Gould W	Baker G	Boyes K	Moor A	Hoggart D	Meecham D	Woods A	Wilkinson N	Lang M	Scott M	Barmby J	Popely P	Wolstenholme I	
1	2	3	4	5	6	7	8	9	10	11													1
1		3	4		6	7	8	9	10	11	2	5											2
1		3	4	5	6	7	8	9	10	11	2												3
1		3	4	5	6	7	8	9	10	11	2												4
		3	6	5			8		10	11	2		1	7	9	4							5
		3	6	5			8		10	11	2		1	7	9	4							6
		3	6	5			8		10	11	2		1	7	9	4							7
		3	6	5				9	10	7	2		1			4	8	11					8
	2	3		5	6		8		10	7			1			4	9	11					9
	2	3		5	6				10	7			1	8	9	4		11					10
	2	3		5	6		8		10	7			1			4	9	11					11
	2	3		5	6		8		10	7			1			4	9	11					12
1		3		5					10	7	2	6		8		4	9	11					13
1		3	6	5					10	7	2				9	4	8	11					14
1		3	6	5					10	7	2				9	4	8	11					15
1	2	3	6	5			8		10	7						4	9	11					16
1	2	3	6	5			8		10	7						4	9	11					17
1	2	3	6	5			8	11	10	7						4	9						18
1	2	3	6	5			8	11	10	7						4	9						19
1		3	6	5			8		10	7	2					4	9	11					20
1	2	3	6	5		7	8		10	11						4	9						21
1	2	3	4	5		7	10		8	9								11	6				22
	2	3	4	5		7	8		10	11			1				9		6				23
1		3	4	5		7	8		10	11	2								6	9			24
1		3		5			8	9	11	7	2					4	10		6				25
	2	3		5			7	10	11		9		1			4	8		6				26
	2	3		5			7	10	11		9		1			4	8		6				27
	2	3		5			7	10	11		9		1			4	8		6				28
	2	3		5			7	10	11		9		1			4	8		6				29
	2	3					7	10	11		9	5	1			4	8		6				30
	2	11				7	8	9	10		3	5	1			4			6				31
	2	11				7	8	9	10		3	5	1			4			6				32
	2	11				7	8	9	10		3	5	1			4			6				33
	2	11				7	8	9	10		3	5	1			4			6				34
	2	11				7		10	8		3	5	1			4	9		6				35
	2	11				7		10	8		3	5	1			4	9		6				36
	2	11		5		7		10	8		3		1			4	9		6				37
	2	11		5		7		10	8		3		1			4	9		6				38
	2	11		5	4		7	10	8				1				9		6		3		39
	2	11		5	4	7	8		10		9		1						6		3		40
	2	11		5	6	7	8		10		9					4					3	1	41
		11	2	5	6		8		10		9			7		4					3	1	42
1	2	11	7	5	6		8		10		9					4					3		43
1	2	11	6	5		7	8		10		9					4					3		44
1	2	11	6	5		7			10		9					4	8				3		45
1	2	11	6	5		7			10		9					4	8				3		46
20	32	46	24	38	13	21	35	22	46	25	33	9	24	6	6	37	27	12	19	1	8	2	
		3				3	4	7	7	6	5			1		2	10	2					

2 own-goals

Forgan T	Wealthall B	Heron T	Ashworth J	Jackson B	Fountain J	Scott J	Peyton N	Goldie J	Rudd W	Gould W	Baker G	Boyes K	Moor A	Hoggart D	Meecham D	Woods A	Wilkinson N	Lang M	Scott M	Barmby J	Popely P	Wolstenholme I	
1		3	6	5		7	8		10	11	2					4	9						1
1		1	1	1		1	1		1	1	1					1	1						
																	2						

Forgan T	Wealthall B	Heron T	Ashworth J	Jackson B	Fountain J	Scott J	Peyton N	Goldie J	Rudd W	Gould W	Baker G	Boyes K	Moor A	Hoggart D	Meecham D	Woods A	Wilkinson N	Lang M	Scott M	Barmby J	Popely P	Wolstenholme I	
1		3	4	5	6		8	9	10	11	2			7									1
		3	6	5					10	7	2		1	8		4	9	11					R
		3	6	5			8		10	7	2		1			4	9	11					2
1		3	6	5					10	7	2			8		4	9	11					R
2		4	4	4	1		2	1	4	4	4		2	3		3	3	3					
							1		1		1							1					

1964-65

Manager: Tom Lockie

1	Aug	22	(h)	Rochdale	W 2-1	Aimson, Provan	4,348
2		24	(a)	Hartlepools U	D 2-2	Walker 2 (2 pens)	6,473
3		29	(a)	Millwall	D 1-1	Walker	8,872
4		31	(h)	Hartlepools U	D 0-0		5,601
5	Sep	5	(h)	Bradford C	W 5-2	Walker 2 (1 pen), Aimson 2, Provan	3,752
6		7	(a)	Barrow	W 2-0	Weddle, Aimson	4,712
7		12	(a)	Chester	L 1-4	Provan	6,095
8		14	(h)	Barrow	W 2-0	Walker, Aimson	5,202
9		18	(h)	Torquay U	L 1-2	Aimson	6,473
10		25	(a)	Stockport C	W 2-1	Walker, Aimson	4,156
11		28	(h)	Brighton & HA	W 2-1	Walker 2	8,937
12	Oct	3	(a)	Notts C	L 1-3	Opp own-goal	6,490
13		6	(a)	Brighton & HA	L 1-3	Walker	14,813
14		9	(h)	Doncaster R	W 4-2	Walker 2, Provan, Aimson	11,898
15		12	(h)	Oxford U	W 2-1	Provan, Aimson	8,108
16		17	(a)	Aldershot	L 0-1		4,309
17		21	(a)	Oxford U	L 0-2		6,830
18		24	(h)	Bradford	L 0-1		7,604
19		27	(a)	Halifax T	D 1-1	Walker	2,933
20		31	(a)	Southport	W 1-0	Aimson	2,876
21	Nov	7	(h)	Wrexham	W 2-1	Aimson, Provan	4,225
22		21	(h)	Darlington	W 2-1	Wilkinson, Provan	4,904
23		28	(a)	Crewe A	W 3-2	Weddle, Wilkinson, Aimson	2,415
24	Dec	12	(a)	Rochdale	W 2-1	Wilkinson, Rudd	3,051
25		19	(h)	Millwall	W 3-1	Aimson 2, Weddle	4,694
26		26	(h)	Chesterfield	W 7-1	Aimson 2, Provan 2, Weddle, Rudd, Wilkinson	6,216
27		28	(a)	Chesterfield	D 1-1	Provan	6,029
28	Jan	2	(a)	Bradford C	W 2-1	Wilkinson, Aimson	4,303
29		16	(h)	Chester	W 3-2	Provan 2, Walker	5,118
30		23	(a)	Torquay U	W 3-1	Wilkinson, Aimson, Provan	6,033
31		29	(a)	Tranmere R	L 1-2	Aimson	13,035
32	Feb	6	(h)	Stockport C	W 3-0	Weddle, Aimson, Rudd	5,778
33		13	(h)	Notts C	W 2-1	Walker (pen), Rudd	6,188
34		20	(a)	Doncaster R	L 3-4	Wilkinson, Aimson, Rudd	8,578
35		27	(h)	Aldershot	W 1-0	Provan (pen)	5,688
36	Mar	1	(h)	Newport C	W 5-1	Provan 2, Wilkinson, Aimson, Opp own-goal	5,957
37		6	(a)	Bradford	D 0-0		13,745
38		12	(h)	Southport	W 3-2	Weddle 2, Aimson	9,534
39		20	(a)	Wrexham	L 0-2		3,215
40		26	(h)	Tranmere R	W 4-0	Weddle 3, Baker	13,444
41	Apr	3	(a)	Darlington	L 0-1		6,083
42		9	(h)	Crewe A	W 3-1	Rudd 2, Aimson	8,071
43		16	(a)	Lincoln C	W 1-0	Weddle	6,478
44		17	(a)	Newport C	L 0-2		2,329
45		19	(h)	Lincoln C	W 3-0	Wilkinson, Rudd, Provan	10,800
46		24	(h)	Halifax T	W 4-0	Aimson 2, Rudd, Provan	12,719

FINAL LEAGUE POSITION: 3rd in Division Four

Appearances

Goals

FA Cup

1	Nov	14	(h)	Bangor C	W 5-1	Aimson 3, Provan, Weddle	5,808
2	Dec	5	(a)	Chesterfield	L 1-2	Aimson	7,870

Appearances

Goals

League Cup

1	Sep	2	(a)	Bradford C	L 0-2		2,331

Appearances

Goals

Moor A	Wealthall B	Heron T	Woods A	Jackson B	Ashworth J	Weddle D	Walker D	Aimson P	Rudd W	Provan A	Povey W	Wilkinson N	Peyton N	Baker G	Hamstead G	Forgan T	
1	2	3	4	5	6	7	8	9	10	11							1
1	2	3		5	6		4	9	10	11	7	8					2
1	2	3		5	6	7	4	9	10	11		8					3
1	2	3	4	5	6	7		9	10	11			8				4
1	2	3	4	5	6	7	8	9	10	11							5
1		3	4	5	6	7	8	9	10	11				2			6
1		3	4	5	6	7	8	9	10	11				2			7
1	2	3	4		6		8	9	10	7				5	11		8
1	2	3	4		6		8	9	10	7				5	11		9
1		3	4	5	6		8	9	10	7				2	11		10
1		3	4	5	6		8	9	10	7				2	11		11
1		3	4	5	6		8	9	10	7				2	11		12
		3	4	5	6		8	9	10	7				2	11	1	13
		3	4	5	6		8	9	10	7				2	11	1	14
		3	4	5	6		8	9	10	7				2	11	1	15
		3	4	5	6		8	9	10	7				2	11	1	16
		3	4	5	6		8	9	10	7				2	11	1	17
		3	4	5	6		8	9	10	11	7			2		1	18
1		3	4	5	6		8	9	10	11	7			2			19
1		3	4	5	6		8	9	10	7				2	11		20
1		3	4	5	6	7	8	9	10	11				2			21
1		3	4	5	6	7		9	10	11		8		2			22
1		3	4	5		7	6	9	10	11		8		2			23
		3	4	5		7	6	9	10	11		8		2		1	24
		3	4	5		7	6	9	10	11		8		2		1	25
		3	4	5		7	6	9	10	11		8		2		1	26
		3	4	5		7	6	9	10	11		8		2		1	27
		3	4	5			6	9	10	7		8		2	11	1	28
		3	4	5		7	6	9	10	11		8		2		1	29
		3	4	5		7	6	9	10	11		8		2		1	30
		3	4	5			6	9	10	7		8		2	11	1	31
		3	4	5		7	6	9	10	11		8		2		1	32
		3	4	5		7	6	9	10	11		8		2		1	33
		3	4	5		7	6	9	10	11		8		2		1	34
		3	4	5		7	6	9	10	11		8		2		1	35
		3	4	5		7	6	9	10	11		8		2		1	36
		3	4	5		7	6	9	10	11		8		2		1	37
		3	4	5		7	6	9	10	11		8		2		1	38
		3	4	5		7	6	9	10	11		8		2		1	39
	2	3	4	5		7	6		10	11		8		9		1	40
		3	4	5		7	6	9	10	11			8	2		1	41
		3	4	5	8	7	6	9	10	11				2		1	42
		3	4	5	8	7	6	9	10	11				2		1	43
		3	4	5	8	7	6	9	10	11				2		1	44
		3	4	5		7	6	9	10	11		8		2		1	45
		3	4	5		7	6	9	10	11		8		2		1	46
17	8	46	44	44	25	30	44	45	46	46	3	23	2	41	13	29	
						11	15	26	9	18		9		1			

2 own-goals

Moor A	Wealthall B	Heron T	Woods A	Jackson B	Ashworth J	Weddle D	Walker D	Aimson P	Rudd W	Provan A	Povey W	Wilkinson N	Peyton N	Baker G	Hamstead G	Forgan T	
1		3	4	5	6	7		9	10	11		8		2			1
1		3	4	5		7	6	9	10	11		8		2			2
2		2	2	2	1	2	1	2	2	2		2		2			
						1		4		1							

Moor A	Wealthall B	Heron T	Woods A	Jackson B	Ashworth J	Weddle D	Walker D	Aimson P	Rudd W	Provan A	Povey W	Wilkinson N	Peyton N	Baker G	Hamstead G	Forgan T	
1	2	3	4	5	6	7		9	10	11			8				1
1	1	1	1	1	1	1		1	1	1			1				

1965-66

Manager: Tom Lockie

1	Aug	21	(a)	Shrewsbury T	L 1-4	Aimson	5,226
2		23	(h)	Swindon T	L 0-2		9,228
3		27	(h)	Grimsby T	D 1-1	Aimson	8,764
4	Sep	4	(a)	Brentford	W 1-0	Dunphy	10,457
5		10	(h)	Bristol R	L 1-5	Aimson	9,594
6		13	(a)	Southend U	W 3-2	Aimson 2, Pearson	10,530
7		18	(a)	Hull C	W 4-1	Aimson 3, Dunmore	20,554
8		25	(a)	Oxford U	L 1-4	Pearson	6,810
9	Oct	1	(h)	Swansea T	W 5-1	Provan 2, Pearson, Aimson, Rudd	8,782
10		4	(h)	Southend U	L 0-3		9,751
11		9	(h)	Queen's Park R	D 2-2	Pearson, Rudd	6,553
12		15	(a)	Brighton & HA	L 1-3	Aimson	14,281
13		19	(a)	Swindon T	L 0-6		12,482
14		30	(a)	Watford	L 2-3	Aimson, Opp own-goal	8,641
15	Nov	5	(h)	Oldham A	D 2-2	Walker, Dunmore	5,726
16		19	(h)	Millwall	W 2-1	Dunmore, Aimson (pen)	5,604
17		27	(a)	Peterborough U	L 0-1		6,196
18	Dec	4	(h)	Scunthorpe U	L 1-3	Walker	4,175
19		11	(a)	Reading	L 0-3		6,191
20		17	(h)	Brighton & HA	L 0-1		3,914
21		27	(h)	Workington	D 3-3	Dunphy 2, Aimson	6,388
22	Jan	1	(a)	Queen's Park R	L 2-7	Aimson 2	7,811
23		8	(h)	Gillingham	L 1-2	Aimson	4,006
24		15	(a)	Scunthorpe U	L 1-4	Opp own-goal	3,680
25		21	(h)	Watford	W 1-0	Weddle	4,003
26		29	(h)	Shrewsbury T	D 2-2	Weddle, Cunliffe	4,523
27	Feb	5	(a)	Grimsby T	L 1-3	Aimson	7,549
28		12	(h)	Bournemouth	L 0-2		3,693
29		26	(a)	Bristol R	D 0-0		8,946
30	Mar	5	(a)	Bournemouth	L 0-1		5,709
31		12	(h)	Hull C	L 1-2	Rudd	19,372
32		15	(a)	Workington	L 1-2	Cunliffe	3,235
33		18	(h)	Oxford U	L 1-4	Dunmore (pen)	4,076
34		25	(a)	Swansea T	L 2-7	Morton, Opp own-goal	6,646
35		28	(h)	Brentford	D 1-1	Morton	2,702
36	Apr	8	(h)	Mansfield T	W 2-1	Hawksby, Dunmore (pen)	3,398
37		9	(h)	Exeter C	W 2-0	Dunmore 2 (1 pen)	2,837
38		11	(a)	Mansfield T	L 1-4	Hawksby	4,232
39		16	(a)	Millwall	L 0-2		14,183
40		23	(h)	Peterborough U	D 1-1	Dunmore	3,196
41		25	(h)	Walsall	L 0-3		2,998
42		30	(a)	Exeter C	W 2-0	Burden 2	3,985
43	May	6	(h)	Reading	L 1-2	Hamstead	2,732
44		10	(a)	Oldham A	L 0-3		9,584
45		17	(a)	Walsall	L 0-2		6,931
46		21	(a)	Gillingham	D 0-0		5,812

FINAL LEAGUE POSITION: 24th in Division Three

Appearances
Sub Appearances
Goals

FA Cup

1	Nov	12	(a)	South Shields	L 1-3	Aimson (pen)	7,000

Appearances
Goals

League Cup

1	Sep	1	(a)	Lincoln C	D 2-2	Dunphy, Aimson	3,725
R		7	(h)	Lincoln C	W 4-2	Dunmore 2, Aimson 2	7,987
2		22	(a)	Millwall	L 1-4	Provan	7,619

Appearances
Goals

Forgan T	Baker G	Heron T	Woods A	Jackson B	Walker D	Weddle D	Dunmore D	Aimson P	Rudd W	Provan A	Dunphy E	Pearson J	Fallon H	Cunliffe R	Hamstead G	Wealthall B	Morton K	Popely P	Wilkinson N	Hawksby J	Boyes K	Hague K	Burden I	Wolstenholme I	
1	2	3	4	5	6	7	8	9	10	11															1
1	2	3	4	5	6	7	8	9	10	11															2
1	2	3*	4	5	6		7	9	10	11	8	12													3
1	2	3		5	6	7	8	9	10	11	4														4
1*	2	3	12	5	6	7	8	9	10	11	4														5
	2	3		5	6		8	9	10	11	4	7	1												6
	2		4	5	3		8	9	10	11	6	7	1												7
	2		4	5	3		8	9	10	11	6	7	1												8
	2	3		5	6		8	9	10	11	4	7	1												9
	2	3		5	6		8	9	10	11	4	7	1												10
	2	3		5	6			9	10	11	4	7	1*	8	12										11
			4	5	3		8	9	10	11	6	7	1			2									12
		3	4	5	6			9	10	11	8	7	1			2									13
	2	3	4	5	6			9	10	11	8	7	1												14
	2	3*	4	5	6		9	9	7	11	10		1				12								15
	2			5	6		8	9	10	7	4		1				11	3							16
			2	5	6		8	9	10	7	4		1				11	3							17
	2	3		5	6		8	9	10		4	7	1				11								18
	3		2	5			9	11	10		4	7*	1	12	6				8						19
	3	11	2	5				9	10	7	4		1		6				8						20
	2	3	4	5	6	7		9	10		8		1		11										21
	2	3	4	5	6	7		9	10		8		1		11										22
	2			5	6	7	4	9	10		8		1		11	3									23
	2		4	5		7	6	9	10		8		1		11	3									24
1	2		4	5	8	7	6	9	10						11	3									25
1	2		4	5	8	7	6	9						10	11	3									26
1	2		4	5		7	6	9	10					8	11	3									27
1	2		4	5		7	6	9	10	11				8		3									28
1	2			5	6	7	4	9	10	11				8		3									29
1	2			5	6	7	4	9	10	11				8		3									30
1	2			5	6		4	9	10	7*				8	12	3				11					31
1	2			5	6		4	9	10					8		3	7			11					32
1	2			5	4		9		10					8	6	3	7			11					33
	2	11	4	5	6		9		10				1			3	7			8					34
	4				6		9		10	7*			1			2	11	3		8	5	12			35
	4			5	6		9		10				1		11	2	7	3		8					36
	4			5	6		9		10			7	1		11	2		3		8					37
	4			5	6		9		10			7	1		11	2		3		8					38
	4			5	6		9		10			7	1		11	2		3		8					39
	4			5	6		9		10	7			1		11	2		3		8					40
	4			5	6		9		10	7			1		11	2		3		8					41
	4			5	6				10	7*			1		12	2		3	8	11			9		42
	4			5	6		12		10				1		11	2		3	8*	7			9		43
	4			5	6		8		10				1	7		2		3		11			9		44
	4			5	6		9		10				1	7	11	2		3		8					45
	4			5	6		9		10				1		7	2	11	3		8					46
14	43	17	20	45	41	14	38	32	45	26	22	14	32	11	19	26	9	14	4	16	1		3		
			1				1					1		1	3		1					1			
					2	2	8	17	3	2	3	4		2	1		2			2			2		

3 own-goals

Forgan T	Baker G	Heron T	Woods A	Jackson B	Walker D	Weddle D	Dunmore D	Aimson P	Rudd W	Provan A	Dunphy E	Pearson J	Fallon H	
	2		4	5	3	7		9	10	11	6	8	1	1
	1		1	1	1	1		1	1	1	1	1	1	
								1						

Forgan T	Baker G	Heron T	Woods A	Jackson B	Walker D	Weddle D	Dunmore D	Aimson P	Rudd W	Provan A	Dunphy E	Pearson J	Wolstenholme I	
1	2	3	4	5	6			9	10	11	8	7		1
1	2	3		5	6	7	8	9	10	11	4			R
	2		4	5	3		8	9	10	11	6	7	1	2
2	3	2	2	3	3	1	2	3	3	3	3	2	1	
							2	3		1	1			

1966-67

Manager: Tom Lockie

1	Aug	20	(h)	Chesterfield	D 1-1	Hawksby	5,957
2		26	(a)	Stockport C	L 1-3	Spencer (pen)	7,897
3	Sep	2	(h)	Rochdale	D 1-1	Provan	5,046
4		4	(h)	Halifax T	W 4-3	Provan 2, Jackson, Opp own-goal	4,206
5		10	(a)	Southport	L 0-2		4,502
6		16	(h)	Notts C	W 4-1	Dunmore 2 (1 pen), Burrows, Spencer	4,909
7		24	(a)	Chester	L 1-3	Spencer	5,315
8		27	(a)	Halifax T	L 1-2	Goodchild	2,869
9		30	(h)	Bradford	W 3-1	Horrey, Dunmore (pen), Provan	5,453
10	Oct	7	(h)	Hartlepools U	D 1-1	Horrey	5,203
11		15	(a)	Exeter C	L 1-3	Hawksby	4,174
12		17	(a)	Barrow	D 1-1	Dunmore	4,621
13		22	(h)	Bradford C	W 4-1	Horrey, Dunmore, Spencer, Provan	5,376
14		28	(a)	Tranmere R	L 1-2	Horrey	6,043
15	Nov	4	(h)	Southend U	W 2-1	Opp own goal, Spencer	4,079
16		12	(a)	Wrexham	D 1-1	Spencer	9,437
17		14	(h)	Barrow	L 1-2	Opp own-goal	4,152
18		19	(h)	Aldershot	L 1-2	Provan	2,643
19	Dec	3	(h)	Barnsley	L 0-3		3,413
20		10	(a)	Newport C	L 2-4	Spencer, Goodchild	1,872
21		17	(a)	Chesterfield	L 0-1		3,967
22		26	(a)	Crewe A	L 0-2		5,434
23		27	(h)	Crewe A	L 0-2		2,871
24		31	(h)	Stockport C	L 1-2	Goodchild	2,446
25	Jan	14	(h)	Southport	W 2-0	Burrows, Spencer	3,072
26		21	(a)	Notts C	L 0-2		4,718
27	Feb	4	(h)	Chester	D 1-1	Spencer	3,094
28		11	(a)	Bradford	L 0-1		4,572
29		18	(a)	Brentford	D 1-1	Provan	7,629
30		25	(a)	Hartlepools U	L 2-4	Caulfield, Provan (pen)	6,638
31	Mar	3	(h)	Exeter C	L 2-4	Horrey, Goodchild	3,254
32		11	(h)	Brentford	D 0-0		1,933
33		18	(a)	Bradford C	L 0-1		4,870
34		24	(a)	Lincoln C	D 2-2	Turner, Spencer	7,389
35		25	(h)	Luton T	W 5-1	Provan 2, Collinson, Spencer, Goodchild	1,912
36		27	(h)	Lincoln C	W 3-1	Spencer, Caulfield, Opp own-goal	3,923
37		31	(a)	Southend U	L 1-2	Provan	8,513
38	Apr	7	(h)	Wrexham	W 4-0	Spencer 2, Turner (pen), Provan	3,084
39		10	(h)	Port Vale	W 3-1	Provan, Spencer, Hawksby	3,834
40		15	(a)	Aldershot	D 0-0		3,671
41		21	(h)	Tranmere R	L 0-1		4,323
42		24	(a)	Port Vale	L 1-4	Spencer	2,554
43		28	(a)	Barnsley	W 1-0	Spencer	5,213
44	May	2	(a)	Rochdale	D 2-2	Provan, Spencer	2,017
45		5	(h)	Newport C	W 2-1	Provan, Goodchild	2,674
46		13	(a)	Luton T	L 1-5	Hawksby	5,196

FINAL LEAGUE POSITION: 22nd in Division Four

Appearances
Sub Appearances
Goals

FA Cup

1	Nov	26	(h)	Morecambe	D 0-0		5,596
R	Dec	5	(a)	Morecambe	D 1-1	Spencer	6,234
2R		8	(n*)	Morecambe	W 1-0	Spencer	4,283
2	Jan	7	(a)	Middlesbrough	D 1-1	Provan	20,573
R		11	(h)	Middlesbrough	D 0-0‡		14,531
2R		16	(n†)	Middlesbrough	L 1-4	Horrey	21,347

*Played at Maine Road, Manchester. ‡After extra-time. †Played at St James' Park, Newcastle.

Appearances
Sub Appearances
Goals

League Cup

1	Aug	24	(a)	Middlesbrough	D 0-0		9,758
R		29	(h)	Middlesbrough	W 2-1	Provan, Spencer (pen)	4,970
2	Sep	13	(h)	Chesterfield	W 3-2	Spencer 2, Provan	4,743
3	Oct	4	(h)	Blackburn R	L 0-2		8,593

Appearances
Sub Appearances
Goals

Fallon H	Wealthall B	Turner K	Wolstenholme	Jackson B	Burrows P	Horrey R	Walker D	Spencer T	Hawksby J	Goodchild J	Dunmore D	Provan A	Baker G	Brookes J	Walker M	Popely P	Coyne G	Caulfield G	Collinson L	
1	2	3	4	5	6	7	8	9	10	11										1
1	2	3	4	5	6	7	8	9	10	11										2
1	2	3	4	5	6	7		9	10		8	11								3
1	2	3		5	6		4	9	10	7	8	11								4
1	2	3		5	6		4	9	10	7	8	11								5
1		3		5	6	7	4	9	10		8	11	2							6
1		3		5	6	7	4	9	10			11	2	8						7
1		3		5	6		4	9	10	7	8	11	2							8
1		3	4	5	6	7		9	10		8	11	2							9
1		3	4	5	6	7		9	10		8	11	2							10
1	4	3		5	6	7		9	10		8	11	2							11
	4	3		5	6	7		9	10		8	11	2		1					12
	4	3		5	6	7		9	10		8	11*	2		1	12				13
	4	3		5	6	7		9	10		8	11	2		1					14
		3		5	6	7	4	9	10		8	11	2		1					15
		3		5	6	7	4	9	10		8	11	2		1					16
		3		5	6	7	4	9	10		8	11	2		1					17
		3	4	5	6			9	10	7	8	11			1	2				18
		3		5	6	7	4	9	10		8	11	2		1					19
		3		5	6	7	4	9	11	10	8		2		1					20
		3		5	6	7	4	9	11	10	8		2		1					21
		3		5	6	7	4		11*	10	8	12	2		1		9			22
		3	4	5	6	7				10	8	11	2		1		9			23
		3	4	5	6	7		9	8	10		11	2		1					24
		3		5	6	7	4	8		10	9	11	2		1					25
		3	4	5	10	7	6	8	11		9		2		1					26
		3	4	5	6	7	8	12		10		11	2		1			9*		27
		3	4	5	6	7		9		10		11	2		1			8		28
		3		5	6	7		9		10		11	2		1			8	4	29
		3		5	6	7		9*		10	12	11	2		1			8	4	30
		3		5	6	7				9	10	11	2		1			8	4	31
1		3		5		7	6		10	9		11	2					8	4	32
1		3		5	6*	7	8	12	10			11	2					9	4	33
1		3		5		7	6	9	10	8		11	2						4	34
1		3		5		7	6	9	8	10		11	2						4	35
1		3		5		7	6	9	10			11	2					8	4	36
1		3		5		7	6	9	10			11	2					8	4	37
1		3		5		7	6	9	10	8		11	2						4	38
1		3		5		7	6	9	10	8		11	2						4	39
1		3		5		7	6	9	10	8		11	2						4	40
1		3		5		7	6	9	10	8		11	2						4	41
1		3		5		7	6	9	10	8		11	2						4	42
1		3		5		7	6	9	10	8		11	2						4	43
1		3		5	12	7	6	9	10	8		11*	2						4	44
1		3		5		7	6	9	10	8		11	2						4	45
1		3		5		7	6	9	10	8		11	2						4	46
26	9	46	11	46	32	42	32	40	39	29	23	40	40	1	20	1	2	9	18	
					1			2			1	1				1				
		2		1	2	5		18	4	6	5	15						2	1	

4 own-goals

Fallon H	Wealthall B	Turner K	Wolstenholme	Jackson B	Burrows P	Horrey R	Walker D	Spencer T	Hawksby J	Goodchild J	Dunmore D	Provan A	Baker G	Brookes J	Walker M	Popely P	Coyne G	Caulfield G	Collinson L	
		3		5	6		4	9	10	7	8	11			1	2				1
		3		5	6	7	4	9		10	8	11	2		1					R
		3		5	6	7	4	9		10	8	11	2		1					2R
		3	4	5	6	7	8			10	9	11	2		1					2
		3	4	5	6	7	8			10	9	11	2		1					R
	2	3	4	5	6	7	8			10	9	11			1					2R
	1	6	3	6	6	5	6	3	1	6	6	6	4		6	1				
						1		2				1								

Fallon H	Wealthall B	Turner K	Wolstenholme	Jackson B	Burrows P	Horrey R	Walker D	Spencer T	Hawksby J	Goodchild J	Dunmore D	Provan A	Baker G	Brookes J	Walker M	Popely P	Coyne G	Caulfield G	Collinson L	
1	2	3	4	5	6	7	8	9	10	11										1
1	2	3	4	5	6	7	8	9	10			11								R
1		3		5	6	7	4	9	10		8	11	2							2
1		3	4	5	6	7		9	10		8	11	2							3
4	2	4	3	4	4	4	3	4	4	1	2	3	2							
								3				2								

1967-68

Manager: Tom Lockie until 16 October, then Joe Shaw from 6 November 1967.

1	Aug	19	(h)	Workington	D 1-1	MacDougall	5,297
2		26	(a)	Rochdale	L 2-3	Spencer, Provan	2,536
3	Sep	2	(h)	Brentford	L 0-1		4,682
4		5	(a)	Newport C	L 1-2	Alderson	4,108
5		9	(a)	Bradford	D 1-1	Provan	3,664
6		16	(h)	Doncaster R	L 1-2	Alderson	5,679
7		23	(a)	Luton T	L 1-3	MacDougall	7,977
8		25	(h)	Newport C	L 0-1		3,223
9		30	(h)	Southend U	D 2-2	Provan 2	4,170
10	Oct	3	(a)	Swansea T	D 1-1	MacDougall	4,241
11		7	(a)	Halifax T	L 1-2	Provan	4,480
12		14	(h)	Bradford C	L 0-1		4,860
13		21	(a)	Crewe A	D 0-0		6,931
14		23	(h)	Swansea T	W 2-1	Horrey, Opp own-goal	4,036
15		28	(h)	Notts C	W 4-2	Burrows, Horrey, Ross, Walker	4,982
16	Nov	4	(a)	Port Vale	L 0-1		4,786
17		11	(h)	Chester	W 4-1	Ross 2, MacDougall, Provan	5,226
18		14	(a)	Brentford	L 1-3	MacDougall	7,968
19		18	(a)	Chesterfield	L 1-3	Hawksby	10,994
20		25	(h)	Exeter C	W 4-0	Ross 2, Burrows, MacDougall	2,914
21	Dec	2	(a)	Darlington	L 1-3	Horrey	4,538
22		16	(a)	Workington	D 1-1	Provan	1,767
23		23	(h)	Rochdale	W 4-1	MacDougall 2, Provan, Opp own-goal	3,329
24		26	(h)	Barnsley	D 1-1	MacDougall	8,132
25		30	(a)	Barnsley	L 0-1		10,175
26	Jan	19	(a)	Doncaster R	L 0-2		7,921
27		27	(a)	Lincoln C	W 3-1	Collinson, Ross, Spencer	6,398
28	Feb	3	(h)	Luton T	D 1-1	Ross	2,747
29		10	(a)	Southend U	W 1-0	Spencer	9,134
30		17	(h)	Wrexham	W 3-1	Ross 2, Provan	3,316
31		24	(h)	Chesterfield	L 0-2		5,210
32	Mar	2	(a)	Bradford C	D 0-0		6,040
33		9	(h)	Lincoln C	W 1-0	Ross	4,716
34		16	(h)	Crewe A	D 1-1	Walker (pen)	4,418
35		23	(a)	Notts C	D 1-1	Jackson	4,174
36		25	(h)	Bradford	W 6-2	Ross 2, MacDougall 2, Horrey, Provan	4,009
37		30	(h)	Port Vale	W 5-1	MacDougall 3, Baker, Opp own-goal	5,153
38	Apr	6	(a)	Chester	D 1-1	Provan	4,170
39		12	(a)	Hartlepools U	L 0-1		9,128
40		13	(h)	Halifax T	L 1-2	Ross	5,837
41		15	(h)	Hartlepools U	L 0-2		5,916
42		20	(a)	Exeter C	L 1-3	Alderson	3,526
43		22	(h)	Aldershot	L 2-3	Alderson, Provan	3,482
44		27	(h)	Darlington	D 1-1	Ross	3,963
45	May	4	(a)	Aldershot	D 2-2	MacDougall, Provan	3,348
46		11	(a)	Wrexham	L 1-3	Alderson	3,564

FINAL LEAGUE POSITION: 21st in Division Four

Appearances
Sub Appearances
Goals

FA Cup

1	Dec	9	(h)	Doncaster R	L 0-1		6,403

Appearances
Sub Appearances
Goals

League Cup

1	Aug	23	(a)	Darlington	L 0-1		4,346

Appearances
Sub Appearances
Goals

Fallon H	Joy D	Turner K	Collinson L	Jackson B	Burrows P	Alderson S	Ross T	Spencer T	MacDougall E	Provan A	Walker D	Hawksby J	Baker G	Horrey R	Fellows S	Walker M	Hodgson W	Spratt T	Woodall J	
1	2	3	4	5	6	7	8	9	10	11										1
1	2	3		5	6	7	10	9	8	11	4									2
1	2	3	4	5		7	8	9	10	11	6									3
1	2	3	4	5		7	8	9	10	11	6									4
1		3		5	6	7	8		9	11	4	10	2							5
1		3		5	6	7	9		10	11	4	8	2							6
1		3		5	6	7		9	8		4	10	2	11						7
1		3		5	6	7		9	8		4*	10	2	11	12					8
1		3	4	5	6		8		9	11		10	2	7						9
		3	4	5	6		8		9	11	12	10	2*	7		1				10
		3	4	5*	6		8		9	11	12	10	2	7		1				11
		3		5	6		8		9	11	4	10	2	7		1				12
		3	4	5	6	12			9	11	8	10*	2	7		1				13
		3	4	5	6		10	9	8	11			2	7		1				14
		3	4	5	6		8		9	11	12	10*	2	7		1				15
		3	4	5	6		10		9	11	8		2	7		1				16
		3	4	5	6		8		9	11	10		2	7		1				17
		3	4*	5	6		8		9	11	10	12	2	7		1				18
	2	3			4		8	12	9	11	6	10*	5	7		1				19
	12	3		5*	4		8	10	9	11	6		2	7		1				20
	2	3			4		8		9	11	6	10	2	7		1				21
	2	3			6	7		9		11	4	8	5			1	10			22
	2	3		5	6	7			9	11	4	8	5			1	10			23
	2*	3			6	7	12		9	11	4	8				1	10			24
		3		5	6	7			9	11	4	8	5			1	10			25
		3		5	6				9	11	4	8*	2	7	12	1	10			26
		3	4	5	6		8	9		11			2	7		1	10			27
		3	4	5	6		8	9		11			2	7		1	10			28
	12	3	4	5			8	9		11	6		2	7*		1	10			29
		3	4	5	12		8	9		11	6		2	7*		1	10			30
		3	4	5			8	9	7	11	6		2			1	10			31
		3		5			8		9	11	6		2	7		1	10	4		32
		3		5			8		9	11	6		2	7		1	10	4		33
		3		5			8		9	11	6		2	7		1	10	4		34
		3		5			8		9	11	6		2	7		1	10	4		35
		3		5			8		9	11	6		2	7		1	10	4		36
		3		5			8		9	11	6		2	7		1	10	4		37
		3		5			8		9	11	6		2	7		1	10	4		38
	9	3		5			8			11	6		2	7		1	10	4		39
		3*		5	12		8		9	11	6		2	7		1	10	4		40
				5	6	3	8		9	11			2	7		1	10	4		41
	3			5	6	7	8			11	12		2			1	10	4	9*	42
	3			5	6	7	8			11	12		2			1	10	4	9*	43
	3			5	6	7*	8		9	11		12	2			1	10	4		44
		3		5	6	12	8*		9	11			2	7		1	10	4		45
		3		5	6	8			9	11			2	7		1	10	4		46
9	13	42	17	42	32	17	37	14	38	44	32	17	41	32		37	25	15	2	
	2				2	2	1	1			5	2			2					
			1	1	2	5	14	3	15	13	2	1	1	4						

3 own-goals

Fallon H	Joy D	Turner K	Collinson L	Jackson B	Burrows P	Alderson S	Ross T	Spencer T	MacDougall E	Provan A	Walker D	Hawksby J	Baker G	Horrey R	Fellows S	Walker M	Hodgson W	Spratt T	Woodall J	
		3		5	4		8		9	11	6	10	2	7		1				1
		1		1	1		1		1	1	1	1	1	1		1				

Fallon H	Joy D	Turner K	Collinson L	Jackson B	Burrows P	Alderson S	Ross T	Spencer T	MacDougall E	Provan A	Walker D	Hawksby J	Baker G	Horrey R	Fellows S	Walker M	Hodgson W	Spratt T	Woodall J	
1	2	3	4	5	6	7	8	9	10	11										1
1	1	1	1	1	1	1	1	1	1	1										

1968-69

Manager: Joe Shaw until 16 August, then Tom Johnston from 31 October 1968.

1	Aug	10	(a)	Chester	L 0-2		7,104
2		17	(h)	Doncaster R	D 1-1	Ross	5,559
3		24	(a)	Chesterfield	D 1-1	Provan	7,036
4		26	(h)	Bradford C	D 1-1	Coleman	5,478
5		31	(h)	Peterborough U	W 2-1	Boyer, Hodgson	4,385
6	Sep	7	(a)	Colchester U	L 0-1		3,756
7		14	(h)	Scunthorpe U	W 2-1	MacDougall, Hodgson	5,071
8		16	(a)	Port Vale	L 0-3		3,466
9		21	(a)	Brentford	L 1-5	Boyer	8,360
10		28	(h)	Rochdale	D 0-0		3,509
11	Oct	5	(h)	Bradford	W 4-2	MacDougall 2, Taylor, Sweenie	5,250
12		9	(a)	Bradford C	L 0-5		5,519
13		12	(a)	Lincoln C	L 0-3		7,247
14		19	(h)	Southend U	D 1-1	Ross	3,911
15		26	(a)	Newport C	D 1-1	Boyer	2,920
16		28	(h)	Exeter C	L 0-2		2,870
17	Nov	4	(h)	Aldershot	W 2-1	Ross 2	2,462
18		9	(a)	Grimsby T	L 0-3		3,627
19		23	(a)	Notts C	D 0-0		3,295
20		30	(h)	Darlington	D 1-1	Ross	5,398
21	Dec	14	(h)	Lincoln C	D 1-1	Ross	2,577
22		20	(a)	Southend U	W 2-1	MacDougall, Boyer	9,268
23		28	(h)	Newport C	D 0-0		2,983
24	Jan	11	(a)	Halifax T	W 4-0	MacDougall, Carr, Coleman, Boyer	5,512
25		18	(h)	Grimsby T	L 2-5	MacDougall (pen), Coleman	3,807
26		25	(a)	Aldershot	L 0-2		6,384
27	Feb	24	(h)	Wrexham	W 1-0	Spratt	3,154
28	Mar	7	(a)	Doncaster R	L 1-2	MacDougall	12,482
29		10	(h)	Workington	W 2-1	Topping, MacDougall	3,395
30		15	(h)	Chesterfield	W 3-1	MacDougall 2 (1 pen), Boyer	3,686
31		18	(a)	Swansea T	L 1-2	Boyer	2,539
32		22	(a)	Peterborough U	L 1-2	MacDougall	4,668
33		26	(a)	Bradford	L 0-1		2,449
34		29	(h)	Colchester U	W 2-0	Boyer 2	3,350
35	Apr	4	(h)	Port Vale	W 3-1	Sibbald 2 (1 pen), Taylor	4,999
36		5	(a)	Rochdale	L 1-2	MacDougall	6,886
37		9	(a)	Exeter C	L 0-5		4,983
38		12	(h)	Brentford	W 2-1	MacDougall, Hewitt	3,767
39		16	(a)	Wrexham	L 1-2	MacDougall	3,826
40		18	(a)	Scunthorpe U	L 1-2	MacDougall	2,300
41		21	(a)	Darlington	L 2-3	MacDougall, Taylor	4,095
42		23	(h)	Notts C	W 2-0	Burrows, MacDougall	3,095
43		28	(h)	Chester	W 4-2	MacDougall 2, Jackson, Hewitt	3,397
44		30	(a)	Workington	L 0-2		1,518
45	May	2	(h)	Swansea T	L 0-2		3,204
46		5	(h)	Halifax T	D 0-0		4,012

FINAL LEAGUE POSITION: 21st in Division Four

Appearances
Sub Appearances
Goals

FA Cup

1	Nov	16	(a)	South Shields	W 6-0	Ross 3, MacDougall 2, Baker (pen)	6,000
2	Dec	7	(h)	Morecambe	W 2-0	MacDougall 2	5,071
3	Jan	4	(h)	Stoke C	L 0-2		11,129

Appearances
Sub Appearances
Goals

League Cup

1	Aug	14	(h)	Barnsley	L 3-4	MacDougall 2, Spratt	5,280

Appearances
Sub Appearances
Goals

Widdowson R	Baker G	Kelly B	Carr G	Jackson B	Burrows P	Boyer P	Hodgson W	MacDougall E	Ross T	Provan A	Spratt T	Walker M	Coleman J	Shepherd J	Dale C	Taylor A	Sweenie T	Richardson W	Topping C	Tunks R	Sibbald R	Hewitt R	Andrews J	Pennick R	
1	2	3	4	5	6	7	8	9	10	11															1
1		3	2	5	6	7	8	9	10	11	4														2
		3	2	5	6	7	8	9	10	11	4	1													3
	2	3	4	5		7	11	9	8		10	1	6												4
	2	3	4	5		7	11	9	8		10	1	6												5
1	2	3	4	5		7	11	9			10		6	8											6
1	2	3		5	6	11	10	9	8				4	7											7
1	2	3		5	6	11	10	9	8				4	7											8
1	2	3	4	5	6	11	10	9	8		12			7*											9
1	2	3	4	5	6	7	10*	9	8				12		11										10
1	2	3	5		6	8	4	9							11	7	10								11
1	2	3	5		6	8	4	9							11	7	10								12
1		2	5	12	6	8	10	9			4				11*	7		3							13
1		2	4	5	6	8		9	10						11	7		3							14
1	2		4	5	6	11	8	9								7	10	3							15
1	2		4*	5	6	11	8	9	12							7	10	3							16
1	2		4	5	6	11	10	9	8							7		3							17
1	2		4	5	6	11	10	9*	8		12					7		3							18
1	2		4	5	6	11	10	9	8							7		3							19
1	2		4	5	6	11	10	9	8							7		3							20
1		2	4	5	6	11	10	9	8							7		3							21
1		2	4	5	6	11	10	9								7	8	3							22
1		2			6	11	10	9	12		4					7*	8	3	5						23
1		2	4		6	11	10	9					8			7		3	5						24
1		2	4	7	6	11	10	9			12		8*					3	5						25
1		2	4	5	6	11	10	9	7		8							3							26
		2		5	6	11	10	9			8					7*		3	4	1	12				27
		2		5	6	11	10	9			8*					7		3	4	1	12				28
				5	6	11	10	9	7		8							3	4	1	2				29
			8	5	6	11	10	9								7		3	4	1	2				30
1		3	8	5	6	11		9								7			4		2	10			31
1		12	8	5	6	11	7	9										3	4		2	10*			32
1			4	5	6	11	8	9								7		3			2	10			33
1			4	5		11	8	9								7		3	6		2	10			34
1*			4	5		11	8	9					12			7		3	6		2	10			35
			4	5		11	8	9					12			7*		3	6		2	10	1		36
			12	5	6	11	8	9					7					3	4		2	10*	1		37
		3		5	6	11	8	9								7			4		2	10	1		38
		3		5	6	11	8	9								7			4		2	10	1		39
		3	4		6	11	8	9*	12					10		7			4		2		1		40
		3		5	6	11	8	9	10							7			4		2		1		41
		3		5	6	11	8	9								7			4		2	10	1		42
		3		5	6	11	8	9	12							7*			4		2	10	1		43
		3		5	6	11	8	9	7										4		2	10	1		44
		3		5	6	11	8	9								7			4		2	10	1		45
			4	5	3	11	8	9								7*			6		2	10	1	12	46
28	16	31	32	40	40	46	44	46	19	3	11	3	8	5	5	30	6	24	22	4	18	14	11		
		1	1	1					4		3		3								2			1	
			1	1	1	9	2	19	6	1	1		3			3	1		1		2	2			

Widdowson R	Baker G	Kelly B	Carr G	Jackson B	Burrows P	Boyer P	Hodgson W	MacDougall E	Ross T	Provan A	Spratt T	Walker M	Coleman J	Shepherd J	Dale C	Taylor A	Sweenie T	Richardson W	Topping C	Tunks R	Sibbald R	Hewitt R	Andrews J	Pennick R	
1	2		4	5	6	11	10	9	8							7		3							1
1	2		4	5	6	11	10	9	8							7		3							2
1		2	4		6	11	10	9	8							7		3	5						3
3	2	1	3	2	3	3	3	3	3							3		3	1						
	1							4	3																

Widdowson R	Baker G	Kelly B	Carr G	Jackson B	Burrows P	Boyer P	Hodgson W	MacDougall E	Ross T	Provan A	Spratt T	Walker M	Coleman J	Shepherd J	Dale C	Taylor A	Sweenie T	Richardson W	Topping C	Tunks R	Sibbald R	Hewitt R	Andrews J	Pennick R	
1		2	4	5	6	7	8	9	10	11	12							3*							1
1		1	1	1	1	1	1	1	1	1								1							
											1														
								2			1														

1969-70

Manager: Tom Johnston

1	Aug	9	(a)	Newport C	W 2-1	Mahon 2	4,206
2		16	(h)	Lincoln C	W 2-0	McMahon, Jackson	3,233
3		23	(a)	Hartlepool	D 2-2	Hewitt, Topping	2,976
4		25	(h)	Exeter C	W 1-0	Mahon	6,200
5		30	(h)	Swansea T	W 3-0	McMahon 2, Aimson	5,191
6	Sep	6	(a)	Wrexham	L 0-4		7,741
7		13	(h)	Bradford	W 4-1	Hodgson, McMahon, Burrows, Mahon	4,523
8		15	(a)	Chesterfield	L 1-3	Opp own-goal	7,190
9		20	(a)	Workington	D 1-1	Aimson	1,819
10		27	(h)	Scunthorpe U	W 3-2	McMahon 2, Mahon	4,610
11		29	(h)	Darlington	W 2-1	Aimson, McMahon	6,700
12	Oct	4	(a)	Notts C	W 2-0	Mahon, McMahon	5,883
13		8	(a)	Lincoln C	L 0-4		7,525
14		11	(h)	Port Vale	L 0-1		6,639
15		18	(h)	Colchester U	W 4-2	Opp own-goal, Boyer 2, Mahon	3,981
16		25	(a)	Peterborough U	L 1-3	Mahon	7,756
17	Nov	1	(h)	Northampton T	D 1-1	Boyer	4,449
18		8	(a)	Oldham A	L 1-3	Hewitt	3,174
19		22	(h)	Southend U	W 1-0	Stainwright	3,018
20		26	(a)	Aldershot	L 1-4	Mahon	4,867
21		29	(a)	Chester	L 0-3		4,201
22	Dec	13	(a)	Bradford	L 0-2		3,084
23		26	(h)	Hartlepool	D 0-0		4,274
24		27	(a)	Swansea T	L 1-2	Sibbald	10,800
25	Jan	17	(a)	Scunthorpe U	D 1-1	Boyer	4,740
26		31	(h)	Notts C	L 1-2	Sibbald (pen)	3,482
27	Feb	7	(a)	Port Vale	D 1-1	Sibbald	3,955
28		9	(h)	Workington	W 1-0	McMahon	3,343
29		21	(h)	Oldham A	D 0-0		3,102
30		28	(a)	Colchester U	L 0-3		3,803
31	Mar	2	(h)	Grimsby T	D 1-1	Mahon	2,729
32		9	(a)	Brentford	D 0-0		8,120
33		13	(h)	Chester	D 0-0		2,803
34		18	(a)	Crewe A	L 0-3		2,683
35		21	(a)	Grimsby T	D 0-0		3,016
36		27	(h)	Peterborough U	W 3-0	Boyer 2, Aimson	3,153
37		28	(h)	Brentford	W 4-2	Aimson 3, Boyer	2,496
38		31	(a)	Northampton T	D 2-2	Aimson, Hewitt	4,128
39	Apr	4	(a)	Exeter C	L 1-2	McMahon	4,111
40		7	(h)	Aldershot	W 2-0	Taylor, Sibbald	3,014
41		13	(h)	Chesterfield	D 1-1	Boyer	4,994
42		17	(h)	Crewe A	D 0-0		2,689
43		21	(h)	Newport C	W 2-1	Swallow 2	1,888
44		24	(h)	Wrexham	W 2-1	Swallow, Boyer	2,852
45		27	(a)	Darlington	L 0-1		1,794
46	May	1	(a)	Southend U	L 0-1		5,546

FINAL LEAGUE POSITION: 13th in Division Four

Appearances
Sub Appearances
Goals

FA Cup

1	Nov	15	(h)	Whitby T	W 2-0	Aimson, Sibbald (pen)	6,007
2	Dec	6	(a)	Bangor C	D 0-0		5,324
R		10	(h)	Bangor C	W 2-0	Mahon, Boyer	6,418
3	Jan	3	(h)	Cardiff C	D 1-1	Boyer	8,439
R		12	(a)	Cardiff C	D 1-1†	Taylor	21,263
2R		15	(n*)	Cardiff C	W 3-1†	Swallow 2, Aimson	7,347
4		24	(a)	Middlesbrough	L 1-4	Boyer	38,283

*Played at St Andrew's, Birmingham. †After extra-time.

Appearances
Sub Appearances
Goals

League Cup

1	Aug	13	(a)	Darlington	L 0-3		3,878

Appearances
Sub Appearances
Goals

Gadsby M	Sibbald R	Kelly B	Davidson I	Jackson B	Burrows P	Mahon M	Stainwright D	McMahon K	Hodgson W	Hewitt R	Topping C	Taylor A	Boyer P	Widdowson R	Aimson P	Mackin J	Hillyard R	Morritt G	Swallow B	McArthur B	Maloney P	
1	2	3	4	5	6	7*	8	9	10	11	12											1
1	2		4	5	3	11*		9	10	12	6	7	8									2
	2		4	5	3			9	10	11	6	7	8	1								3
1	2			5	3	11		8	4	10	6		7		9							4
1	2		4	5	3	11		8	10		6		7		9							5
1	2		4	5	3	11*		8	10	12	6		7		9							6
1	2		4	5	3	11	12	8*	10		6		7		9							7
1	2		4	5	3	11			10		6	7	8		9							8
1	2		4	5	6	11	8		10				7		9	3						9
1	2		4	5	6	11		8	10				7		9	3						10
1	2		4	5	6	11		8	10				7		9	3						11
1	2			5	6	11	12	8*	10		4		7		9	3						12
1	2		12	5	6	11		8	10		4*		7		9	3						13
1*	2		4	5	6			8	10		12	7	11		9	3						14
	2		4	5	12	11		7	10		6*		8	1	9	3						15
	2		4	5	6	11		8	10				7		9	3	1					16
	2		4	5	6	11*		8	10	12			7		9	3	1					17
	2		4	5	6	12		8	10	11*			7		9	3		1				18
	2		4	5	3		8	9	11			7				10		1	6			19
	2		4	5	3	8		9	11		7					10		1	6			20
	2		4	5	3	7		9	11				8			10		1	6			21
	2		4	5	3	11		9*	10			7	8			12		1	6			22
	2		4	5	3	11		9	10			7			8			1	6			23
	2		10		3	11*	9	12			5	7	8			4		1	6			24
	4		10	5	3					11		7	8		9	2		1	6			25
	4		10	5	3	11		8				7			9	2		1	6			26
	4		10		3	11		9			6	7	8			2		1	5			27
	4		10		3			9		11	6	7*	8		12	2		1	5			28
	4		10		3			9*		11	6	7	8		12	2		1	5			29
	4		12		3			9		11	6	7*	8		10	2		1	5			30
			4		3	11					6	7	8		10	2		1	5	9		31
	4				3	11*	9		10	12	6	7	8			2		1	5			32
	4				3	11	9		10		6	7	8			2		1	5			33
	4		8		3			9	10		6	7*	11		12	2		1	5			34
	4		8		3				10		6	7	11		9	2		1	5			35
	4		8		3				10		6	7	11		9	2		1	5			36
	4		8		3				10		6	7	11		9	2		1	5			37
	4		8		3					10	6	7	11		9	2		1	5			38
	4		8		3			12		10	6	7	11*		9	2		1	5			39
	4		8		3					10	6	7	11		9	2		1	5			40
	4		8		3					10	6	7	11		9	2		1	5			41
	4		12		3	8		9		10	6	7*	11			2		1	5			42
	4		8		3	7		9		11	6		12			2	1		5		10*	43
	4		10		3	12		7		11*	6		8		9	2		1	5			44
	4		8		3			10		7	6		11		9*	2		1	5		12	45
	4		10		3			9		8*	6	7	11		12	2		1	5			46
13	45	1	39	25	45	27	6	32	29	17	32	27	40	2	29	36	3	28	28	1	1	
			3		1	2	2	2		4	2		1		4	1					1	
	4			1	1	10	1	10	1	3	1	1	9		8				3			

2 own-goals

Gadsby M	Sibbald R	Kelly B	Davidson I	Jackson B	Burrows P	Mahon M	Stainwright D	McMahon K	Hodgson W	Hewitt R	Topping C	Taylor A	Boyer P	Widdowson R	Aimson P	Mackin J	Hillyard R	Morritt G	Swallow B	McArthur B	Maloney P	
				5	3	7		8	10	11					9	4		1	6			1
	2			5	3	11	8	9	10		4		7					1	6			2
	2		4	5	3	11		9	10			7	8					1	6			R
	4		10	5	3				12	11*		7	8		9	2		1	6			3
	4		10	5	3				12	11*		7	8		9	2		1	6			R
	4		10*	5	3				11	12		7	8		9	2		1	6			2R
	4		10	5	3				11			7	8		9	2		1	6			4
	7		5	7	7	3	1	3	5	3	1	5	6		5	5		7	7			
									2	1												
	1					1						1	3		2				2			

Gadsby M	Sibbald R	Kelly B	Davidson I	Jackson B	Burrows P	Mahon M	Stainwright D	McMahon K	Hodgson W	Hewitt R	
1	2	3	4	5	6	7	8	9	10	11	1
1	1	1	1	1	1	1	1	1	1	1	

1970-71

Manager: Tom Johnston

1	Aug	15	(h)	Notts C	D 0-0		4,216
2		22	(a)	Crewe A	W 4-3	Aimson 2, Taylor, Boyer	2,334
3		29	(h)	Lincoln C	W 2-0	Aimson, Boyer	4,160
4		31	(h)	Workington	W 1-0	Boyer	5,373
5	Sep	5	(a)	Northampton T	L 2-3	Aimson, Boyer	7,038
6		12	(h)	Chester	D 1-1	Boyer	3,251
7		19	(a)	Scunthorpe U	W 1-0	Davidson	3,723
8		23	(a)	Peterborough U	L 1-2	Sibbald	4,854
9		26	(h)	Bournemouth	D 1-1	Boyer	3,858
10	Oct	3	(a)	Darlington	L 0-2		2,689
11		9	(h)	Southport	W 2-0	Johanneson, Boyer	3,694
12		12	(h)	Barrow	W 4-3	Taylor, Aimson 2, Topping	4,142
13		17	(a)	Notts C	L 1-2	Johanneson	7,690
14		19	(a)	Colchester U	L 0-1		4,457
15		24	(a)	Grimsby T	L 1-3	Hewitt	4,052
16		30	(h)	Newport C	W 1-0	Aimson	3,174
17	Nov	6	(a)	Stockport C	L 0-1		4,217
18		9	(a)	Brentford	L 4-6	Aimson 2, Hewitt, Opp own-goal	5,950
19		13	(h)	Aldershot	W 3-1	Boyer, Aimson 2	3,099
20		27	(h)	Southend U	W 3-0	Johanneson, Swallow, Boyer	3,288
21	Dec	5	(a)	Exeter C	W 2-0	Mackin (pen), Aimson	4,403
22		19	(h)	Crewe A	W 1-0	Aimson	3,102
23		26	(a)	Hartlepool	L 1-2	McMahon	2,365
24	Jan	9	(a)	Barrow	W 2-0	Taylor, Davidson	2,558
25		16	(h)	Colchester U	D 1-1	McMahon	3,951
26		29	(a)	Southend U	L 0-1		5,125
27	Feb	6	(h)	Exeter C	D 2-2	McMahon 2	3,364
28		13	(a)	Cambridge U	D 1-1	Swallow	4,293
29		20	(h)	Brentford	D 0-0		3,158
30		26	(a)	Newport C	W 3-0	Henderson 2, Aimson	1,753
31	Mar	1	(h)	Cambridge U	W 3-0	McMahon 2, Aimson	2,821
32		5	(h)	Grimsby T	W 4-1	Swallow, Mackin (pen), Aimson, McMahon	3,514
33		8	(h)	Peterborough U	W 2-1	Aimson 2	5,254
34		13	(a)	Aldershot	W 1-0	Topping	4,813
35		15	(a)	Oldham A	D 1-1	Aimson	9,084
36		19	(h)	Stockport C	W 2-1	McMahon, Aimson	6,251
37		27	(h)	Northampton T	W 4-1	McMahon 2, Aimson, Swallow	7,089
38	Apr	3	(a)	Lincoln C	W 5-4	McMahon, Burrows, Swallow, Aimson, Davidson	4,226
39		9	(h)	Darlington	W 2-0	Aimson, Taylor	10,623
40		10	(h)	Hartlepool	W 4-0	Swallow, McMahon, Topping, Aimson	7,407
41		12	(a)	Chester	D 1-1	Aimson	7,898
42		16	(a)	Southport	D 2-2	Davidson, McMahon	2,058
43		19	(h)	Oldham A	L 0-1		14,321
44		24	(h)	Scunthorpe U	W 2-0	Aimson, Chambers	5,021
45		27	(a)	Workington	L 0-1		1,874
46	May	1	(a)	Bournemouth	L 0-4		12,627

FINAL LEAGUE POSITION: 4th in Division Four (Promoted)

Appearances
Sub Appearances
Goals

FA Cup

1	Nov	21	(a)	Tamworth	D 0-0		4,650
R		23	(h)	Tamworth	W 5-0	Aimson 3, Boyer, Hewitt	5,390
2	Dec	12	(a)	Boston U	W 2-1	Davidson, Mackin (pen)	6,500
3	Jan	2	(h)	Bolton W	W 2-0	Davidson 2	10,882
4		23	(h)	Southampton	D 3-3	McMahon, Hewitt, Aimson	13,775
R	Feb	1	(a)	Southampton	L 2-3	Aimson, Johanneson	25,034

Appearances
Sub Appearances
Goals

League Cup

1	Aug	14	(a)	Hartlepool	W 3-2	Boyer 2, Johanneson	3,734
2	Sep	9	(h)	Northampton T	D 0-0		5,265
R		14	(a)	Northampton T	D 1-1*	Davidson	7,247
2R		28	(n†)	Northampton T	L 1-2	Boyer	2,561

*After extra-time. †Played at Villa Park, Birmingham.

Appearances
Sub Appearances
Goals

Morritt G	Mackin J	Burrows P	Sibbald R	Swallow B	Topping C	Taylor A	Boyer P	McMahon K	Davidson I	Johanneson A	Aimson P	Maloney P	Hewitt R	Hillyard R	Newman K	Henderson T	Jones D	Smith A	Chambers D	Thompson T	
1	2	3	4	5	6	7*	8	12	10	11	9										1
1	2	6	4	5		7	8		10	11	9									3	2
1	2	6	4	5		7	8		10	11	9									3	3
1	2	6	4	5		7	8		10	11	9									3	4
1	2	6	4	5		8*	7	12	10	11	9									3	5
1	2	3	4	5	6	7	8	9	10	11											6
1	2	3	4	5	6	7	8	9	10	11											7
1	2	3	4	5	6	7	8	12	10	11*	9										8
1	2	3	4	5	6	7	8	9	10	11											9
1	2	3		5	6	7	8	9*	4	11		12	10								10
	2	3		5	6	7	8		4	11	9		10	1							11
	2	3		5	6	7	8		4	11	9		10	1							12
	2	3	12	5	6	7	8		4*	11	9		10	1							13
	2	3		5	6	7	8		4	11	9		10	1							14
	2	3*	12	5	6	7	8		10	11	9		4	1							15
	2	3	4	5	6	7	8			11	9		10	1							16
1	2	3		5	6		8		12		9		10		4	7*	11				17
1	2	3		5*	6		8				9	12	10		4	7	11				18
	2	3			5		8		4		9		10	1	6	7	11				19
	2	3		5	6	7	8		4	11*	9		10	1	12						20
	2	3		5	6	7	8		4		9		10	1		11					21
	2	3		5	6	7	8		10		9		4	1		11					22
	2	3		5	6			10	8		9		4	1		7		11			23
	2	3		5	6	11		9	4		10		8	1		7					24
	2	3		5	6	7		9	4		10		8	1		11					25
	2	3		5	6			8	4	11	9	12	10*	1		7					26
	2	3		5	6	12		8	4	11	9		10	1		7*					27
	2	3		5	6	7		8	4	11	9		10	1							28
	2	3		5	6	7		8	4	11	9		10	1							29
	2	3	12	5	6			8	4	11	9*		10	1		7					30
	2	3		5	6	12		8	4	11*	9		10	1		7					31
	2	3		5	6	11		8	4		9		10*	1		7		12			32
	2	3		5	6	11		8	4		9		10	1		7					33
	2	3		5	6	11		8	4		9		10	1		7*			12		34
	2	3		5	6	11		8	4		9		10	1		7					35
	2	3*		5	6	11		8	4		9		10	1		7			12		36
	2	3		5	6	11		8	4		9		10	1		7					37
	2	3		5	6	11		8	4		9		10	1		7*			12		38
	2	3		5	6	11		8	4		9		10	1		7					39
	2	3		5	6	11		8	4		9		10	1		7					40
	2	3		5	6	11		8	4		9		10	1		7					41
	2	3		5	6	11		8	4		9		10	1		7					42
	2	3		5	6	7		8*	4	11	9		10	1					12		43
	2	3		5	6			8	4	11*	9		10	1		7			12		44
	2	3		5*	6	12		8	4		9		10	1		7			11		45
	2	3	6		5	11		12	8		9		10	1		7			4*		46
12	46	46	11	44	42	36	22	27	43	25	42		37	34	3	26	3	1	2	4	
			3			3		4	1			3			1			1	5		
	2	1	1	6	3	4	9	13	4	3	26		2			2			1		

1 own-goal

Morritt G	Mackin J	Burrows P	Sibbald R	Swallow B	Topping C	Taylor A	Boyer P	McMahon K	Davidson I	Johanneson A	Aimson P	Maloney P	Hewitt R	Hillyard R	Newman K	Henderson T	Jones D	Smith A	Chambers D	Thompson T	
	2	3			5		8		4		9		10	1	6	7	11				1
	2	3		5	6	7	8		4		9		10	1			11				R
	2	3		5	6	11	8		4		9		10	1		7					2
	2	3		5	6			8	4	11	9		10	1		7					3
	2	3		5	6	7		8	4	11	9		10	1							4
	2	3		5	6	7*		8	4	11	9		10	1		12					R
	6	6		5	6	4	3	3	6	3	6		6	6	1	3	2				
																1					
	1						1	1	3	1	5		2								

Morritt G	Mackin J	Burrows P	Sibbald R	Swallow B	Topping C	Taylor A	Boyer P	McMahon K	Davidson I	Johanneson A	Aimson P	Maloney P	Hewitt R	Hillyard R	Newman K	Henderson T	Jones D	Smith A	Chambers D	Thompson T	
1	2	3	4	5	6*	7	8	12	10	11	9										1
1	2	3	4	5	6	7	8	9	10	11											2
1	2	3	4	5	6	7	8		10	11	9										R
1	2	3	4	5	6	7	8	9	10	11											2R
4	4	4	4	4	4	4	4	2	4	4	2										
								1													
							3		1	1											

1971-72

Manager: Tom Johnston

1	Aug	14	(h)	Bristol R	D 0-0		6,360
2		21	(a)	Halifax T	L 1-3	McMahon	4,930
3		28	(h)	Plymouth A	L 2-3	Henderson, Aimson	5,352
4		31	(a)	Oldham A	L 0-1		7,695
5	Sep	4	(a)	Brighton & HA	W 2-0	Aimson 2	14,360
6		11	(h)	Wrexham	D 1-1	Aimson	4,732
7		18	(a)	Bolton W	W 1-0	Calloway	12,192
8		25	(h)	Walsall	W 2-0	McMahon 2	5,294
9		29	(a)	Bradford C	L 1-3	Aimson	5,169
10	Oct	2	(a)	Rotherham U	D 1-1	Opp own-goal	7,024
11		9	(h)	Shrewsbury T	D 1-1	Henderson	5,017
12		16	(a)	Bristol R	L 4-5	McMahon, Aimson, Mackin 2 (2 pens)	6,876
13		18	(h)	Torquay U	W 3-1	Aimson, McMahon, Calloway	5,672
14		23	(a)	Port Vale	L 3-4	Henderson, Mackin, McMahon	4,484
15		30	(h)	Notts C	L 0-2		7,303
16	Nov	5	(a)	Tranmere R	L 0-2		2,953
17		13	(h)	Barnsley	D 1-1	McMahon	5,699
18		27	(h)	Mansfield T	L 1-2	Swallow	3,921
19	Dec	4	(a)	Bournemouth	D 2-2	Rowles, Swallow	11,244
20		18	(h)	Brighton & HA	L 1-2	Rowles	3,451
21		27	(a)	Chesterfield	L 1-2	Burluraux	9,467
22	Jan	1	(h)	Bolton W	D 0-0		4,467
23		8	(a)	Plymouth A	L 0-4		6,943
24		15	(a)	Blackburn R	L 0-3		7,273
25		21	(h)	Bradford C	W 3-1	McMahon, Henderson, Aimson	3,678
26		24	(h)	Swansea C	D 1-1	Burrows	4,795
27		29	(a)	Torquay U	W 1-0	Aimson	2,793
28	Feb	5	(a)	Aston Villa	L 0-1		26,905
29		12	(h)	Port Vale	W 2-1	Aimson 2	3,902
30		19	(a)	Notts C	D 2-2	Rowles, Lally	12,351
31		26	(h)	Tranmere R	W 5-0	Rowles 2, Wann, Lally, Aimson	4,227
32	Mar	4	(a)	Barnsley	L 1-2	Mackin (pen)	3,279
33		10	(a)	Shrewsbury T	L 1-2	Opp own-goal	3,487
34		14	(a)	Swansea C	L 1-2	Burrows	3,749
35		18	(h)	Halifax T	D 1-1	Mackin (pen)	3,943
36		20	(h)	Rochdale	W 2-0	Swallow, Calloway	4,170
37		25	(a)	Wrexham	L 0-2		3,830
38		31	(h)	Rotherham U	W 2-0	Rowles 2	6,117
39	Apr	1	(h)	Chesterfield	W 4-1	Aimson 3, Swallow	4,272
40		4	(a)	Walsall	L 1-2	Aimson	7,061
41		8	(h)	Aston Villa	L 0-1		9,620
42		15	(a)	Mansfield T	D 0-0		5,006
43		17	(a)	Rochdale	W 2-1	Burrows, Henderson	2,776
44		22	(h)	Bournemouth	L 0-2		6,846
45		24	(h)	Oldham A	D 0-0		5,770
46		29	(h)	Blackburn R	L 0-1		5,099

FINAL LEAGUE POSITION: 19th in Division Three

Appearances
Sub Appearances
Goals

FA Cup

1	Nov	20	(h)	Grimsby T	W 4-2	Opp own-goal, Henderson, Swallow, McMahon	6,578
2	Dec	11	(a)	Rotherham U	D 1-1	Rowles	8,252
R		13	(h)	Rotherham U	L 2-3*	McMahon, Chambers	10,010

*After extra-time

Appearances
Sub Appearances
Goals

League Cup

1	Aug	18	(a)	Darlington	W 1-0	Henderson	4,661
2	Sep	8	(h)	Middlesbrough	D 2-2	McMahon, Henderson	10,700
R		14	(a)	Middlesbrough	W 2-1	Calloway, Henderson	21,121
3	Oct	5	(a)	Sheffield U	L 2-3	Swallow, Topping	29,828

Appearances
Sub Appearances
Goals

Hillyard R	Mackin J	Burrows P	Calloway L	Swallow B	Topping C	Chambers D	Henderson T	McMahon K	Aimson P	Hewitt R	Johanneson A	Rowles E	Lally P	Woodward J	Crawford G	Burluraux D	Morritt G	Maloney P	Murray A	Wann D	Rioch N	Yeats W	Pollard B	De Placido M	
1	2	3	4	5	6	7*	12	8	9	10	11														1
1	2	3	4	5	6	7	11	9	10	8															2
1	2	3	4	5	6	7	11*	9	10	8		12													3
1	2	3	4	5	6		11	8	9	10			7												4
1	2	3	4	5	6		11	9	10	8			7												5
1	2	3	8	5	6		7	9	10	11			4												6
1	2	3	10	5	6		7	8	9	11			4												7
1	2	3	8	5	6		7	9	10	11			4												8
1	2	3	10	5	6		7	8	9	11			4												9
1	2	3	10	5	6		7	8	9	11			4												10
1	2	3	10	5	6		7	8	9	11			4												11
1	2	3	10	5	6		7	8	9	11			4*	12											12
1	2	3	10	5	6	12	7	8	9	11*				4											13
1	2	3	11	5	6	8	7*	9	10				12	4											14
1	2	3	10	5	6		7	8	9	11			4												15
	2	3	10	5	6		7	8	9	11*			4	12	1										16
	2	3	10	5	6	12	7*	9	8			11	4		1										17
	2	3	10	5	6	12	7*	8	9			11	4		1										18
1	2	3		5	6	7	11	9	10			8	4												19
1	2	3		5	6	10*	7	12	9			8	4			11									20
	2	3	10	5	6				9	11*		8	4			7	1	12							21
	2	3	10	5	6			9		11		8	4		1	7									22
	2	3		5	4		7	9	8*	11		12		6	1			10							23
	2	3	10	5	6		7		9			8*	4	12	1				11						24
	2	3	10	5	6		7	8	9				4		1				11						25
	2	3	10	5	6		7	8	9				4		1				11						26
	2	3	8	5	6		7	9	10				4		1					11					27
	2	3	10	5	6			8	9*			12	4		1				7	11					28
	2	3	8	5	6		7		9			10	4		1					11					29
	2	3	8*	5	6		7		9			10	4		1					11	12				30
	2	3	10	5	6		7		9			8	4		1					11					31
	2	3		5	6		7	9				8	4	12	1			10*		11					32
	2	3	10	5	6		7					8	4		1					11		9			33
	2	3	10	5	6		7		12			8	4		1					11		9*			34
	2	3	10	5	6		7		9			8		4	1					11					35
	2	3	10	5	6		7		9			8		4	1					11					36
	2	3	10	5	6		7*		9			8	12	4	1					11					37
	2	3	10	5	6				9			8	4		1					11			7*	12	38
	2	3	10	5	6				9			8	4		1					11			7*	12	39
	2	3	10	5	6				9			8	4		1					11			7*	12	40
	2	3	10	5	6				9			8	4		1					11			7		41
	2	3	10	5	6		7		9			8	4		1					11					42
	2	3	10	5	6		7	12	9			8		4	1					11*					43
	2	3	10	5	6		7		9			8	12	4	1					11*					44
	2	3	10	5	6		7*		9			8		4	1					11				12	45
	2	3	10	5	6				9	11		8	12	4	1									7*	46
17	46	46	42	46	46	6	37	26	42	19	1	25	33	10	28	3	1	2	4	19		2	4	1	
						3	1	2	1			3	4	4				1			1			4	
	5	3	3	4			5	8	16			7	2			1				1					

2 own-goals

Hillyard R	Mackin J	Burrows P	Calloway L	Swallow B	Topping C	Chambers D	Henderson T	McMahon K	Aimson P	Hewitt R	Johanneson A	Rowles E	Lally P	Woodward J	Crawford G	Burluraux D	Morritt G	Maloney P	Murray A	Wann D	Rioch N	Yeats W	Pollard B	De Placido M	
1	2	3	10	5	6		7	8	9			11	4												1
1	2	3		5	6	7	11	9	10			8	4												2
1	2	3		5	6	7	11	9*	10			8	4	12											R
3	3	3	1	3	3	2	3	3	3			3	3												
														1											
				1		1	1	2				1													

1 own-goal

Hillyard R	Mackin J	Burrows P	Calloway L	Swallow B	Topping C	Chambers D	Henderson T	McMahon K	Aimson P	Hewitt R	Johanneson A	Rowles E	Lally P	Woodward J	Crawford G	Burluraux D	Morritt G	Maloney P	Murray A	Wann D	Rioch N	Yeats W	Pollard B	De Placido M	
1	2	3	4	5	6	7	11	8	9*	10				12											1
1	2	3	10	5	6		7	8	9	11			4												2
1	2	3	10	5	6		7	8	9	11			4												R
1	2	3	10	5	6		7	8*	9	11		12	4												3
4	4	4	4	4	4	1	4	4	4	4			3												
												1		1											
			1	1	1		3	1																	

1972-73

Manager: Tom Johnston

1	Aug	12	(h)	Grimsby T	D 0-0		6,437
2		19	(a)	Port Vale	L 1-2	Rowles	4,112
3		26	(h)	Notts C	D 1-1	Taylor	4,059
4		28	(h)	Rotherham U	L 0-1		4,090
5	Sep	2	(a)	Charlton A	L 0-1		5,378
6		9	(h)	Bournemouth	D 0-0		3,225
7		15	(a)	Tranmere R	L 0-1		3,378
8		18	(h)	Watford	D 0-0		3,066
9		23	(h)	Oldham A	D 0-0		2,668
10		26	(a)	Shrewsbury T	L 0-1		2,362
11		30	(a)	Wrexham	L 1-3	Wann	5,398
12	Oct	7	(a)	Bristol R	W 2-1	Stone, Aimson	7,601
13		9	(h)	Blackburn R	W 1-0	Swallow	3,428
14		14	(h)	Chesterfield	W 2-0	Burrows, Rowles	3,489
15		21	(a)	Scunthorpe U	L 0-1		3,538
16		24	(a)	Plymouth A	D 1-1	Seal	8,424
17		28	(h)	Walsall	D 0-0		3,530
18	Nov	4	(h)	Shrewsbury T	W 2-1	Seal, Rowles	2,407
19		11	(a)	Watford	D 2-2	Rowles, Lally	6,864
20		25	(a)	Brentford	L 0-2		7,110
21	Dec	2	(h)	Southend U	W 2-0	Pollard, Wann	2,538
22		23	(h)	Swansea C	W 3-0	Pollard 2, Wann	2,218
23		26	(a)	Oldham A	D 1-1	Wann	9,800
24		30	(h)	Port Vale	D 0-0		3,118
25	Jan	6	(a)	Notts C	L 0-1		6,202
26		20	(h)	Charlton A	D 1-1	Pollard	2,239
27		27	(a)	Bournemouth	W 3-2	Aimson, Stone 2	11,964
28		29	(a)	Swansea C	W 3-1	Rowles, Aimson, Opp own-goal	3,269
29	Feb	3	(a)	Blackburn R	L 0-2		8,259
30		10	(h)	Tranmere R	W 4-1	Woodward (pen), Swallow, Pollard, Aimson	3,318
31		17	(a)	Grimsby T	W 2-1	Rowles, Aimson	12,899
32		24	(h)	Halifax T	W 2-1	Rowles, Woodward	3,515
33	Mar	3	(h)	Bristol R	D 0-0		4,363
34		5	(h)	Bolton W	L 0-1		9,611
35		10	(a)	Chesterfield	D 0-0		3,942
36		13	(a)	Halifax T	L 0-1		1,918
37		17	(h)	Scunthorpe U	W 3-1	Pollard, Lally, Taylor	2,848
38		19	(a)	Rochdale	L 0-1		2,100
39		24	(a)	Walsall	D 0-0		4,051
40		26	(h)	Plymouth A	L 1-2	Pollard	3,488
41		31	(h)	Brentford	L 0-1		2,107
42	Apr	7	(a)	Southend U	L 0-3		7,341
43		14	(h)	Rochdale	L 1-2	Stone	2,144
44		20	(h)	Wrexham	D 1-1	Lally	2,966
45		21	(a)	Bolton W	L 0-3		19,999
46		28	(a)	Rotherham U	W 2-1	Stone, Seal	3,936

FINAL LEAGUE POSITION: 18th in Division Three

Appearances
Sub Appearances
Goals

FA Cup

1	Nov	18	(h)	Mansfield T	W 2-1	Rowles, Seal	4,316
2	Dec	9	(a)	Bangor C	W 3-2	Rowles, Burrows, Pollard	3,785
3	Jan	13	(h)	Oxford U	L 0-1		8,116

Appearances
Sub Appearances
Goals

League Cup

1	Aug	16	(a)	Notts C	L 1-3	Calloway	8,078

Appearances
Sub Appearances
Goals

Crawford G	Mackin J	Burrows P	Calloway L	Swallow B	Topping C	Pollard B	Seal J	Aimson P	Wann D	Taylor R	Lally P	Woodward J	Rowles E	Hillyard R	Yeats W	Stone J	Crangle J	De Placido M	Thompson B	Calvert C	
1	2	3	4	5	6	7	8	9	10	11											1
1	2	3	4	5	6		9		10	11	12	7*	8								2
1	2	3	4	5	6			9	10	11	7*	12	8								3
1	2	3	4	5	6		7*	9	10	11	12		8								4
	2	3	11	5	6	7		9	10		4	12	8*	1							5
1	2	3		5	6			9	10	11	4	7			8						6
1		3	8	12	6		7*	9	10	11	4	5				2					7
1		3	4		6		8	9	11	10		5				2	7				8
1	12	3	4		6		8*	9	10	11		5				2	7				9
1	7	3		4	6		9		10	11		5	8			2					10
1	4	3		5	6		8	9	11	10*	12		7			2					11
1	2	6	4	5	8		10*	9	11				7		12	3					12
1	2	10	4	5	6		8	9	11				7			3					13
1	2	3	10	5	6		8		11				7		9	4					14
1	2	10	4	5	6		8		11			12	7		9*	3					15
1		3		5	6	7	8		11		4	10	9			2					16
1		3		5	6	7*	9		11	12	4	8	10			2					17
1		3		5	6	7	8		11		4	9	10			2					18
1		3		5	6	7	8		11		4	9	10			2					19
1		3	12	5	6	7	9		11		4	8*	10			2					20
1		3		5	6	7	8	12	11		4	10	9*			2					21
1	12	3		5	6	7	8		11		4*	10	9			2					22
1	4	3		5	6	7	8*	12	11			10	9			2					23
1	10	3		5	6	7	8				11	4	9			2					24
1	4	3		5	6	7	8	12			11	10	9*			2					25
1		3		5	6	8		10		11	4		9			2		7			26
1		3		5	6	7		10		11	4	8	9			2					27
1		3		5	6	7		10		11	4	8	9			2					28
1		3		5	6	7	12	10		11	4	8	9			2*					29
1	2	3		5	6	7		10		11	4	8	9								30
1	2	3		5	6	7		10		11	4	8	9								31
1	2	3		5	6	7		10		11	4	8	9								32
1	2	3		5	6	7		10		11	4	8	9								33
1		3		5	6	7		10		11	4	8	9			2					34
		3		5	6	7	10			11*	4	8	9	1		2			12		35
		3		5	6	7	10			11	4	8	9	1		2*			12		36
	2	3		5	6	7				11	4	8		1	9				10		37
1	2	3		5	6	7				11	4	8	12		9*				10		38
1	2	3		5	6	7				11*	4	8	12		9				10		39
1	2	3		5	6	7	11					8	9					12	10*	4	40
1*	2	3		5	6	8	10			12		11	9					7		4	41
1	2	3		5	6		11			10		8	9*			7		12		4	42
1	2	3		5	6	7	10*			11	4	9				8				12	43
1	2	3		5	6						4	8*	9			10	11	12		7	44
1	2	3		5	6		12				8		10			9	7	11*		4	45
1	2	3		5	6	7	10*				8	11	12			9				4	46
42	29	46	12	43	46	30	29	20	23	26	31	35	36	4	6	31	4	3	4	6	
	2		1	1			2	3		2	3	3	3		1			3	2	1	
		1		2		7	3	5	4	2	3	2	7			5					

1 own-goal

Crawford G	Mackin J	Burrows P	Calloway L	Swallow B	Topping C	Pollard B	Seal J	Aimson P	Wann D	Taylor R	Lally P	Woodward J	Rowles E	Hillyard R	Yeats W	Stone J	Crangle J	De Placido M	Thompson B	Calvert C	
1		3		5	6	7	8		11		4	10	9			2					1
1		3		5	6	7	8*	12	11		4	10	9			2					2
1	4*	3		5	6	7	8	12			11	10	9			2					3
3	1	3		3	3	3	3		2		3	3	3			3					
								2													
		1				1	1						2								

Crawford G	Mackin J	Burrows P	Calloway L	Swallow B	Topping C	Pollard B	Seal J	Aimson P	Wann D	Taylor R	Lally P	Woodward J	Rowles E	Hillyard R	Yeats W	Stone J	Crangle J	De Placido M	Thompson B	Calvert C	
1	2	3	4	5	6		8		10	11	12				9		7*				1
1	1	1	1	1	1		1		1	1					1		1				
											1										
			1																		

1973-74

Manager: Tom Johnston

1	Aug	25	(a)	Charlton A	W 4-2	Woodward 2, Seal, Jones	4,925
2	Sep	1	(h)	Halifax T	D 1-1	Jones	4,120
3		8	(a)	Blackburn R	L 0-4		8,057
4		10	(h)	Walsall	D 1-1	Butler	3,710
5		15	(h)	Port Vale	W 3-1	Swallow 2, Seal	3,172
6		19	(a)	Chesterfield	W 2-0	Pollard, Jones	5,759
7		22	(a)	Watford	D 1-1	Pollard	6,452
8		29	(h)	Aldershot	W 3-1	Seal, Lyons 2	3,121
9	Oct	1	(h)	Chesterfield	D 0-0		5,405
10		6	(a)	Cambridge U	D 0-0		4,396
11		12	(h)	Wrexham	W 1-0	Peachey	5,154
12		16	(a)	Walsall	D 0-0		5,569
13		20	(a)	Bristol R	D 0-0		8,706
14		27	(h)	Tranmere R	W 2-0	Swallow, Seal	4,650
15	Nov	3	(a)	Brighton & HA	D 0-0		16,017
16		10	(h)	Southend U	W 1-0	Jones	8,153
17		12	(h)	Hereford U	D 0-0		7,450
18		17	(a)	Shrewsbury T	W 2-0	Jones, Peachey	1,891
19	Dec	8	(h)	Southport	W 4-0	Seal, Jones, Pollard, Peachey	2,712
20		22	(a)	Aldershot	D 2-2	Seal, Woodward	3,214
21		26	(h)	Grimsby T	D 1-1	Woodward (pen)	5,890
22		29	(h)	Blackburn R	W 1-0	Pollard	6,274
23	Jan	5	(h)	Rochdale	W 2-1	Jones, Seal	3,727
24		12	(a)	Port Vale	D 2-2	Burrows, Holmes	3,537
25		19	(h)	Charlton A	L 0-1		4,699
26	Feb	3	(a)	Rochdale	W 3-1	Jones 2, Seal	2,205
27		10	(h)	Watford	D 2-2	Seal, Holmes	7,638
28		20	(a)	Wrexham	L 0-1		6,618
29		24	(h)	Cambridge U	W 2-0	Seal, Opp own-goal	7,149
30	Mar	2	(a)	Grimsby T	W 2-1	Seal, Lyons (pen)	7,410
31		6	(h)	Bournemouth	W 4-1	Topping, Lyons 2 (1 pen), Seal	10,392
32		9	(a)	Tranmere R	D 0-0		2,391
33		12	(a)	Oldham A	L 1-2	Burrows	15,806
34		16	(h)	Bristol R	W 2-1	Jones, Holmes (pen)	11,066
35		24	(a)	Southend U	D 3-3	Jones 2, Seal	6,584
36		27	(a)	Bournemouth	W 3-1	Jones, Seal, Holmes	7,404
37		30	(h)	Brighton & HA	W 3-0	Burrows, Jones 2	7,252
38	Apr	3	(h)	Plymouth A	D 1-1	Seal	8,931
39		6	(a)	Hereford U	D 0-0		7,866
40		12	(h)	Huddersfield T	W 2-1	Holmes (pen), Jones	9,938
41		13	(h)	Shrewsbury T	L 0-1		7,001
42		16	(a)	Huddersfield T	W 1-0	Seal	7,737
43		19	(a)	Southport	D 1-1	Lyons	1,901
44		27	(h)	Oldham A	D 1-1	Jones	15,583
45		30	(a)	Halifax T	L 1-2	Hunter	4,275
46	May	6	(a)	Plymouth A	W 2-0	Seal, Opp own-goal	5,125

FINAL LEAGUE POSITION: 3rd in Division Three (Promoted)

Appearances
Sub Appearances
Goals

FA Cup

1	Nov	24	(h)	Mansfield T	D 0-0		4,254
R	Dec	10	(a)	Mansfield T	L 3-5	Jones 2, Swallow	4,733

Appearances
Sub Appearances
Goals

League Cup

1	Aug	29	(h)	Huddersfield T	W 1-0	Opp own-goal	6,497
2	Oct	9	(h)	Aston Villa	W 1-0	Peachey	7,981
3		31	(a)	Orient	D 1-1	Swallow	12,061
R	Nov	6	(h)	Orient	W 2-1*	Holmes, Butler	11,152
4		21	(h)	Manchester C	D 0-0		15,360
R	Dec	5	(a)	Manchester C	L 1-4	Pollard	17,972

*After extra-time

Appearances
Sub Appearances
Goals

Crawford G	Stone J	Burrows P	Taylor P	Swallow B	Topping C	Holmes I	Woodward J	Seal J	Jones C	Butler I	Pollard B	Hillyard R	Calvert C	Lyons B	Wilson K	Peachey J	Hunter G	Wann D	Robb I	
1	2	3	4	5	6	7	8	9	10	11										1
1	2	3	11	5	4	8		9	10	7	6									2
1	2	3	7	5	6	4*	8	9	10	11	12									3
	2	3	4*	5	6		8	9	10	11	7	1	12							4
	2	3		5	6		8	9	10		7	1	4	11						5
1	2	3		5	6		8	9	10		7		4	11						6
1	2	3		5	6		8	9	10		7		4	11						7
1	2	3		5	6		8	9	10	12	7		4*	11						8
1	2	3		5	6		8	9		11	7			4	10					9
1	2	3		5	6		8	9*		11	7		12	4	10					10
1	2	3		5	6		8			11	7		10	4		9				11
1	2	3		5	6		8	12		11	7		10*	4		9				12
1	2	3		5	6		10	9		11	7		8*	4		12				13
1	2	3		5	6		8	9	10	11	7			4						14
1	2	3		5	6		8	9	10		7		11	4						15
1	2	3		5	6		8	9	10	11	7			4						16
1	2	3		5	6	12	8	9	10	11	7*			4						17
1	2	3		5	6	7*	8		10	11	12			4		9				18
1	2	3		5	6	12	8	9	10*		7		4			11				19
1	2	3		5	6	12	8	9	10		7		11*	4						20
1	2	3		5	6		8	9	10		7		11	4						21
1		3		5	6		8	9	10		7		11	4			2			22
1	2	3		5	6	12	8	9	10		7*		11	4						23
1	2	3		5	6	7	8	9	10				11	4						24
1	2	3		5	6	7*	8	9	10		12		11	4						25
1	2	3		5	6	4	11	9	10				8	7						26
1	2	3		5	6	4	11*	9	10		12		8	7						27
	2	3		5	6	4	11	9	10		12	1	8	7*						28
1	2	3		5	6	4		9	10				8	7				11		29
1	2	3		5	6	4	12	9	10				8	7				11*		30
1	2	3		5	6	4		9	10				8	7				11		31
1	2	3		5	6	7		9	10				8	4				11		32
1	2	3		5	6	4	12	9	10				8	7				11*		33
1	2	3		5	6	4	11	9	10				8	7						34
1	2	3		5	6	4	11*	9	10		12		8	7						35
1	2	3		5	6	4	11	9	10				8	7*		12				36
1	2	3		5	6	4	11	9	10				8	7						37
1	2	3		5	6	4	11	9	10				8	7						38
1	2	3		5	6	4	11	9	10	12	7*		8							39
1	2	3		5	6	4	11*	9	10	12			8	7						40
1	2	3		5	6	4		9	10	11			8	7						41
1	2	3		5	6	4	8	9	10	11				7						42
1	2	3		5	6	4	8	9	10	11				7						43
1		3		5	6	4	8	9	10	11			2	7						44
1		3		5	6	4	8	9	10	11				7			2			45
1	2	3		5	6	4		9	10	11				7					8	46
43	43	46	4	46	46	27	38	43	41	19	21	3	32	40	2	4	2	5	1	
						4	2	1		3	6		2			2				
		3		3	1	5	4	17	17	1	4			6		3	1			

2 own-goals

Crawford G	Stone J	Burrows P	Taylor P	Swallow B	Topping C	Holmes I	Woodward J	Seal J	Jones C	Butler I	Pollard B	Hillyard R	Calvert C	Lyons B	Wilson K	Peachey J	Hunter G	Wann D	Robb I	
1	2	3		5	6	12	8	9	10		7			4*		11				1
1	2	3		5	6		8	9	10		7		4	11						R
2	2	2		2	2		2	2	2		2		1	2		1				
						1														
				1					2											

Crawford G	Stone J	Burrows P	Taylor P	Swallow B	Topping C	Holmes I	Woodward J	Seal J	Jones C	Butler I	Pollard B	Hillyard R	Calvert C	Lyons B	Wilson K	Peachey J	Hunter G	Wann D	Robb I	
1	2	3	4	5	6	7	8*	9	10	11	12									1
1	2	3		5	6		8			11	7		10	4		9				2
1	2	3		5	6		8	9	10	11	7			4						3
1	2	3		5	6	12	8	9	10*	11	7			4						R
1	2	3		5	6	12	8	9*	10		7			4		11				4
1	2	3		5	6		8	9*	10		7		12	4		11				R
6	6	6	1	6	6	1	6	5	5	4	5		1	5		3				
						2					1		1							
				1		1				1	1					1				

1 own-goal

1974-75

Manager: Tom Johnston until January, then Wilf McGuinness from February 1975.

1	Aug	17	(h)	Aston Villa	D 1-1	Lyons	9,396
2		24	(a)	Oxford U	L 1-3	Jones	6,249
3		27	(h)	Cardiff C	W 1-0	Jones	6,321
4		31	(h)	Notts C	D 2-2	Seal 2	6,558
5	Sep	7	(a)	Fulham	W 2-0	Jones 2	7,628
6		14	(h)	Sunderland	L 0-1		14,974
7		17	(h)	Oxford U	D 1-1	Holmes (pen)	7,020
8		21	(a)	Blackpool	D 1-1	Seal	7,927
9		24	(a)	Bristol C	D 0-0		11,867
10		28	(h)	Portsmouth	W 3-0	Seal, Holmes, Wann	6,771
11	Oct	5	(a)	West Brom A	L 0-2		11,707
12		12	(h)	Bristol R	W 3-0	Seal 2, Hinch	6,470
13		16	(a)	Cardiff C	L 2-3	Holmes 2 (2 pens)	5,887
14		19	(a)	Oldham A	W 3-2	Lyons, Holmes, Seal	12,141
15		26	(h)	Bolton W	L 1-3	Holmes (pen)	9,581
16	Nov	1	(h)	Orient	L 0-1		8,538
17		9	(a)	Sheffield W	L 0-3		12,495
18		16	(h)	Millwall	W 2-1	Jones, Seal	6,391
19		23	(a)	Nottingham F	L 1-2	Jones	10,471
20		30	(h)	Norwich C	W 1-0	Seal	7,887
21	Dec	7	(a)	Southampton	L 1-2	Seal	13,500
22		14	(a)	Aston Villa	L 0-4		15,840
23		21	(h)	Manchester U	L 0-1		15,314
24		26	(a)	Sunderland	L 0-2		35,367
25		28	(h)	Hull C	W 3-0	Holmes 2 (2 pens), Swallow	10,619
26	Jan	10	(h)	Southampton	D 1-1	Topping	9,562
27		18	(a)	Norwich C	W 3-2	Seal, Jones 2	23,382
28		31	(h)	Sheffield W	W 3-0	Lyons 2, Butler	10,552
29	Feb	8	(a)	Orient	L 0-1		6,454
30		14	(h)	Nottingham F	D 1-1	Seal	7,666
31		22	(a)	Millwall	W 3-1	Jones 2, Cave	9,018
32	Mar	1	(a)	Notts C	L 1-2	Seal	8,835
33		8	(h)	Bristol C	W 1-0	Pollard	7,251
34		15	(a)	Portsmouth	L 0-1		9,906
35		22	(h)	Fulham	W 3-2	Jones 2, Holmes (pen)	7,495
36		29	(a)	Manchester U	L 1-2	Seal	46,802
37		31	(a)	Hull C	L 0-2		10,095
38	Apr	1	(h)	Blackpool	D 0-0		8,744
39		5	(a)	Bolton W	D 1-1	Seal	7,876
40		12	(h)	West Brom A	L 1-3	Seal	8,181
41		19	(a)	Bristol R	W 3-1	Topping, Swallow, Seal	11,841
42		26	(h)	Oldham A	D 0-0		10,101

FINAL LEAGUE POSITION: 15th in Division Two

Appearances
Sub Appearances
Goals

FA Cup

3	Jan	4	(a)	Arsenal	D 1-1	Seal	27,029
R		7	(h)	Arsenal	L 1-3*	Lyons	15,362

*After extra-time

Appearances
Sub Appearances
Goals

League Cup

1	Aug	21	(h)	Huddersfield T	L 0-2		5,570

Appearances
Sub Appearances
Goals

Crawford G	Stone J	Oliver P	Holmes I	Swallow B	Topping C	Lyons B	Cave M	Seal J	Jones C	Butler I	Hinch J	Wann D	Peachey J	Hunter G	Ogden A	Woodward J	Calvert C	Pollard B	Robb I	Coop M	Taylor P	
1	2	3	4	5	6	7	8	9*	10	11	12											1
1	2	3	4	5	6	7	8		10		9	11										2
1	2	3	4	5	6	7	8	9	10			11										3
1	2	3	4	5	6	7	8*	9	10		12	11										4
1	2	3	4	5	6	7	8	9	10	11												5
1	2*	3	4	5	6	7	8	9	10	11	12											6
1		2	4	5	6	7	8	9	10	11			3									7
1		3	4	5*	6	7	8	9	10	11	12			2								8
1		3	4	5	6	7	8	9	10*		12	11		2								9
1		3	4	5	6	7	8	9			10	11		2								10
1		3	4	5	6	7	8	9			10	11		2								11
1		2	4	5	6	7	8	9			10	11			3							12
1		2	4	5	6	7	8	9			10	11*			3		12					13
1		2	4	5	6	7	8	9			10	11*			3	12						14
1		3	4	5	6	7	8	9	12		10*	11					2					15
1		3	4	5	6	7*	8	9	10	11						12	2					16
1			4*		6		8	9	10	11			3			7	2	12	5			17
1		3*	4		6		8	9	10	11						12		7	5	2		18
1			4	5	6	11	8	9	10					3		7				2		19
1			4	5	6	7	8	9	10					2		11				3		20
1			4	5	6	11	8	10	9					2		7*	12			3		21
1			4	5	6	7	11	9*	10		12			2	3	8						22
1			4	5	6	12	8	9	10		11			2	3	7*						23
1			4	5	6	12	11	9	10*		7			2	3	8						24
1			4	5	6	7		9	10	11					3	8	2					25
1		3	4	5	6	7	8	9	10*	11	12						2					26
1		3	4	5	6	7	8	9	10	11*						12	2					27
1		3	4	5	6	7	8	9	10	11							2					28
1		2	4	5	6	7	8	9	10	11							3					29
1		3	4		6	7	8	9	10	11							2		5			30
1		3	4	5*	6		8	9	10	11						12	2	7				31
1		3	4		6		8*	9	10	11		12				5	2	7				32
1		3	4		6	11	8	9	10							5	2	7				33
1		3	4	5	6	11	8	9	10								2	7				34
1		3	4	5	6		8	9	10	11							2	7				35
1		3	4	5	6	12	8	9	10*	11							2	7				36
1		3	4	5	6	12	8	9	10*	11							2	7				37
1		3	4	5	6		8	9	10	11							2	7				38
1		3	4	5	6		8	9	10	11							2	7				39
1		3	4	5	6	12	8*	9	10	11							2	7				40
1		3	4	5	6	7		9	10	11						8	2					41
1		3	4	5*	6	7		9	10	11						8	2				12	42
42	6	34	42	37	42	30	39	41	36	24	9	10	2	10	7	12	21	11	3	4		
						5			1		7	1				5	2	1			1	
			9	2	2	4	1	17	12	1	1	1						1				

Crawford G	Stone J	Oliver P	Holmes I	Swallow B	Topping C	Lyons B	Cave M	Seal J	Jones C	Butler I	Hinch J	Wann D	Peachey J	Hunter G	Ogden A	Woodward J	Calvert C	Pollard B	Robb I	Coop M	Taylor P	
1			4	5	6	7		9	10	11					3	8	2					3
1		12	4	5	6	7		9	10	11					3	8*	2					R
2			2	2	2	2		2	2	2					2	2	2					
		1																				
						1		1														

Crawford G	Stone J	Oliver P	Holmes I	Swallow B	Topping C	Lyons B	Cave M	Seal J	Jones C	Butler I	Hinch J	Wann D	Peachey J	Hunter G	Ogden A	Woodward J	Calvert C	Pollard B	Robb I	Coop M	Taylor P	
1	2	3	4	5	6	7	8	9		11	10											1
1	1	1	1	1	1	1	1	1		1	1											

1975-76

Manager: Wilf McGuinness

1	Aug	16	(h)	Portsmouth	W 2-1	Lyons, McMordie	4,702
2		23	(a)	Bristol R	L 1-2	Downing	8,142
3		30	(h)	Bolton W	L 1-2	Jones	5,640
4	Sep	6	(a)	West Brom A	D 2-2	Seal, Jones	11,028
5		13	(h)	Notts C	L 1-2	McMordie	5,807
6		20	(a)	Plymouth A	D 1-1	Seal	12,818
7		23	(a)	Orient	L 0-1		4,290
8		27	(h)	Oxford U	W 2-0	Swallow, Wann	4,235
9	Oct	4	(a)	Chelsea	D 0-0		15,323
10		11	(a)	Oldham A	L 0-2		8,704
11		18	(h)	Bristol C	L 1-4	Cave	5,073
12		21	(h)	Charlton A	L 1-3	Jones	4,808
13		25	(a)	Southampton	L 0-2		13,501
14	Nov	1	(h)	Sunderland	L 1-4	Jones	15,225
15		4	(a)	Luton T	L 0-4		7,982
16		8	(a)	Carlisle U	L 0-1		7,021
17		15	(h)	Fulham	W 1-0	Holmes (pen)	3,857
18		22	(a)	Bristol C	L 1-4	Seal	11,228
19		29	(a)	Nottingham F	L 0-1		13,108
20	Dec	6	(h)	Hull C	L 1-2	Seal	7,037
21		13	(h)	Bristol R	D 0-0		3,112
22		20	(a)	Portsmouth	W 1-0	Hinch	7,093
23		26	(h)	Blackburn R	W 2-1	Holmes (pen), Hosker	7,295
24		27	(a)	Blackpool	D 0-0		7,939
25	Jan	10	(a)	Notts C	L 0-4		10,156
26		17	(h)	West Brom A	L 0-1		5,628
27		31	(a)	Charlton A	L 2-3	Cave, Pollard	6,916
28	Feb	7	(h)	Luton T	L 2-3	Holmes (pen), Pollard	3,166
29		14	(h)	Carlisle U	L 1-2	Holmes	3,958
30		21	(a)	Fulham	L 0-2		6,686
31		24	(h)	Orient	L 0-2		2,857
32		28	(h)	Southampton	W 2-1	Cave, Hinch	3,848
33	Mar	13	(h)	Oldham A	W 1-0	Cave	4,542
34		20	(h)	Nottingham F	W 3-2	Hinch, Pollard 2	5,750
35		27	(a)	Hull C	D 1-1	Cave	6,306
36		30	(a)	Sunderland	L 0-1		33,462
37	Apr	3	(a)	Oxford U	L 0-1		4,926
38		10	(h)	Plymouth A	W 3-1	Holmes, Pollard, Cave	3,646
39		13	(a)	Bolton W	W 2-1	Hinch, Cave	19,048
40		17	(a)	Blackburn R	L 0-4		8,952
41		19	(h)	Blackpool	D 1-1	Holmes	3,871
42		24	(h)	Chelsea	D 2-2	Seal, Cave	4,914

FINAL LEAGUE POSITION: 21st in Division Two (Relegated)

Appearances
Sub Appearances
Goals

FA Cup

3	Jan	3	(h)	Hereford U	W 2-1	Seal, Hosker	5,358
4		24	(h)	Chelsea	L 0-2		10,089

Appearances
Sub Appearances
Goals

League Cup

1	Aug	20	(a)	Bradford C	L 0-2		3,120
		26	(h)	Bradford C	W 3-0	Seal 2, Jones	4,495
2	Sep	10	(h)	Liverpool	L 0-1		11,897

Appearances
Sub Appearances
Goals

Crawford G	Oliver P	Downing D	Holmes I	Swallow B	Topping C	Lyons B	Cave M	Seal J	Jones C	McMordie E	Woodward J	Calvert C	Stone J	Pollard B	Wann D	Hinch J	Hunter G	Creamer P	Hosker R	Scott P	Taylor P	James S	
1	2	3	4	5	6	7	8	9	10	11													1
1	2	3	4*	5	6	7	8	10	9	11	12												2
1		3	4	5	6	7	8	9	10	11		2											3
1		3		5	6	7	8	9	10	11	4	2											4
1		3	12	5	6	7	8	9	10	11	4*	2											5
1		3		5	6			9	10	7	8		2	4	11								6
1		3		5	6			9	10	11*	4		2	7	8	12							7
1		3		5	6		7	9	10	11			2	4	8								8
1		3		5	6		8	9	10	7			2	4	11								9
1		3		5	6		8	9	10*	7			2	4	11	12							10
1	2	3	4*	5	6	11	8	9		10				7			12						11
1	2	3			5		4	9	10	11	8			7			6						12
1	2	3			5		8	9	10		4			7	11		6						13
1	2	3			5		8	9	10		7			4	11		6						14
1	2	3	8	5	6		4	9	10					7	11								15
1		11	4	5	6	8		9	10*	7	3							2	12				16
1		11	4	5	6	8		9	10	7	3							2					17
1		11	4	5	6	8*		9		7	3					10		2	12				18
1		11	4	5	6	8*		9		7	3					10		2	12				19
1		11	4	5	6			9	10*	7	3					12			8	2			20
1		11*	4	5	6		12	9		7	3					10			8	2			21
1			8	5	6		11	9		4	3					10	2		7				22
1		11	8	5	6		12	9		4	3*					10	2		7				23
1		3*		5	6		8	9		7				12		10	2		4		11		24
1		11	4	5	6			9		7	3					10			8	2			25
1					6		10	12		4*	3			8		9	11		7	2		5	26
1			8*	6	11		10	9		4	3			7			12			2		5	27
1			8*	5	6		10	9		11	3		2	7					12			4	28
1			4		6		8	9		10	3			7					11	2		5	29
1			8		5		6	9		10	3			7					11	2		4	30
1			8		5		6	9		10	3			7		12			11*	2		4	31
1		3	4		6		8			10	11			7		9				2		5	32
1		3	4		6		8			11	10			7		9				2		5	33
1		3	4		6		8			10	11			7		9				2		5	34
1		2	4*		6		8	12		10	11			7		9				3		5	35
1		3	8		5		10	12		11	6			7*		9				2		4	36
1		3	4*		5		8	12		11	6			7		9			10	2			37
1		3	4*		6		8	12		11	10			7		9				2		5	38
1		3	8		5		10	4		11	6			7		9				2			39
1		3	4		5		8	10		11*	6			7		9			12	2			40
1		3	8		5		10	11			6			7		9				2		4	41
1		3	8		5		10	11			6			7		9				2		4	42
42	7	35	30	24	42	10	32	34	17	37	33	3	6	27	8	19	7	4	11	19	1	14	
			1				2	5			1			1		4	2		5				
		1	6	1		1	8	5	4	2				5	1	4			1				

Crawford G	Oliver P	Downing D	Holmes I	Swallow B	Topping C	Lyons B	Cave M	Seal J	Jones C	McMordie E	Woodward J	Calvert C	Stone J	Pollard B	Wann D	Hinch J	Hunter G	Creamer P	Hosker R	Scott P	Taylor P	James S	
1		11	8	5	6			9		4	3					10			7	2			3
1				5	6		4	9		12	3			11		10*	8		7	2			4
2		1	1	2	2		1	2		1	2			1		2	1		2	2			
										1													
								1											1				

Crawford G	Oliver P	Downing D	Holmes I	Swallow B	Topping C	Lyons B	Cave M	Seal J	Jones C	McMordie E	Woodward J	Calvert C	
1	2	3	4	5	6	7	8	9	10	11			1
1		3	4	5	6	7	8	9	10	11		2	
1		3		5	6	7	8	9	10	11	4	2	2
3	1	3	2	3	3	3	3	3	3	3	1	2	
								2	1				

1976-77

Manager: Wilf McGuinness

1	Aug	21	(a)	Crystal P	L 0-1		14,426
2		28	(h)	Bury	D 2-2	Cave, Seal	2,786
3	Sep	4	(a)	Peterborough U	L 0-3		6,281
4		7	(h)	Tranmere R	W 1-0	Cave	2,608
5		11	(h)	Mansfield T	L 0-1		2,481
6		18	(a)	Brighton & HA	L 2-7	Hinch, Pollard	15,605
7		25	(h)	Oxford U	W 2-1	Young, Hinch	2,213
8	Oct	2	(a)	Preston NE	L 2-4	Holmes, Hinch	6,380
9		9	(h)	Rotherham U	D 1-1	Holmes	3,811
10		16	(a)	Grimsby T	L 0-1		4,237
11		23	(h)	Chester	L 0-2		2,182
12		26	(h)	Northampton T	L 1-4	Cave	2,328
13		30	(a)	Chesterfield	L 0-2		4,115
14	Nov	1	(a)	Wrexham	D 1-1	Cave	6,000
15		6	(h)	Port Vale	W 1-0	Pollard	1,882
16		13	(a)	Walsall	W 2-1	Downing, Hope	5,297
17		27	(h)	Shrewsbury T	L 0-3		2,514
18	Dec	18	(h)	Portsmouth	L 1-4	Pollard	2,058
19		27	(a)	Sheffield W	L 2-3	Holmes, Pollard	22,004
20	Jan	8	(h)	Gillingham	D 2-2	Pollard 2	2,030
21		22	(h)	Crystal P	W 2-1	Galvin 2	3,427
22		25	(h)	Chesterfield	W 2-1	Staniforth, Galvin	2,579
23		31	(a)	Tranmere R	D 4-4	Staniforth 2, Opp own-goal, Hope	2,106
24	Feb	5	(a)	Bury	L 2-4	Opp own-goal, Pollard	4,400
25		7	(a)	Port Vale	W 2-0	James, Pollard	4,686
26		12	(h)	Peterborough U	W 2-1	Hinch, Pollard	3,224
27		16	(a)	Reading	D 1-1	Galvin	4,560
28		19	(a)	Mansfield T	L 1-4	Pollard	7,576
29		22	(h)	Lincoln C	D 2-2	Galvin, Holmes	2,644
30		26	(h)	Brighton & HA	L 0-1		4,415
31	Mar	5	(a)	Oxford U	W 2-0	Pollard, Opp own-goal	4,377
32		12	(h)	Preston NE	L 0-2		3,577
33		19	(a)	Rotherham U	D 1-1	Holmes	7,409
34		26	(h)	Grimsby T	D 1-1	Hinch	2,798
35		29	(a)	Swindon T	L 1-5	Holmes	5,874
36	Apr	2	(a)	Chester	L 0-1		3,045
37		9	(a)	Lincoln C	L 0-2		6,920
38		11	(h)	Sheffield W	L 0-2		5,568
39		12	(h)	Wrexham	D 0-0		2,425
40		16	(a)	Northampton T	L 0-3		5,427
41		19	(h)	Swindon T	W 4-2	Galvin, Hinch, Pollard, Hope	1,848
42		23	(h)	Walsall	D 0-0		2,279
43		30	(a)	Shrewsbury T	L 1-2	Hinch	2,352
44	May	3	(a)	Gillingham	L 0-2		3,094
45		7	(h)	Reading	D 1-1	Holmes	1,748
46		14	(a)	Portsmouth	L 1-3	Hope	14,288

FINAL LEAGUE POSITION: 24th in Division Three (Relegated)

Appearances
Sub Appearances
Goals

FA Cup

1	Nov	20	(a)	Dudley T	D 1-1	Cave	5,019
R		23	(h)	Dudley T	W 4-1	Holmes 2 (1 pen), Cave, Pollard	2,933
2	Dec	11	(a)	Rotherham U	D 0-0		7,076
R		14	(h)	Rotherham U	D 1-1*	Holmes (pen)	3,996
2R		21	(a)	Rotherham U	L 1-2*	Hinch	6,714

*After extra-time

Appearances
Sub Appearances
Goals

League Cup

1	Aug	14	(h)	Barnsley	D 0-0		3,157
		17	(a)	Barnsley	D 0-0*		4,965
R		24	(h)	Barnsley	L 1-2*	Holmes (pen)	3,643

*After extra-time

Appearances
Sub Appearances
Goals

Crawford G	Scott P	Hunter G	James S	Topping C	Woodward J	Pollard B	Holmes I	Seal J	Cave M	Hosker R	Taylor P	Hinch J	Joy B	Downing D	Walker S	Young T	McMordie E	Hope G	Galvin C	Staniforth G	Hutt G	Bell R	Morris D	Neenan J	
1	2	3	4	5	6	7	8	9	10	11															1
1	2	3	4	5	6	7	8	9	10	11*	12														2
1	2	3	4	5	6	7	8*		10	11	12	9													3
1	2		4	5	6	7	8		10	11		9	3												4
1	2		4	5	6	7	8	12	10	11*		9	3												5
1	2		4	5	3	7	8	11	10			9	6*	12											6
	2	3	4	5	6	7			8			9	10		1	11									7
	2	3	4	5	6*	7	12		10			9	11		1	8									8
1	2	3	4	5		7	6		10			9	11			8									9
1	2	3		5	6	7		10*	11			9	4	12		8									10
1	2	3		5	6	7	4		10	12		9		11		8*									11
1	2	3		5	6	7	4		10			9		11		8									12
1	2	3*		5	6		12		10			9	4	11		8	7								13
1	2		6	5		12	4	9	10				3	11		8	7*								14
1	2		6	5		12	4		10			9	3	11		7*	8								15
1	2*		6	5		12	4		10				3	11		8	7	9							16
1	2		6	5		7	4						3	11		10	8	9							17
1		2	6	5		7	4		10	12			3*	11		8		9							18
1	2	6		5		7	4							3		8		9	10	11					19
1		6		5		7	4		8				3			2		9	10	11					20
1			5	6		7	4		8				3			2		9	10	11					21
1	12		6	5		7	4		8				3			2		9	10	11*					22
1			6	5		7	4		8				3			2		9	11	10					23
1			6	5		7	4		8			12	3			2		9*	10	11					24
1			6	4		7	8		9							2			11	10	3	5			25
1			6	4		7	8					9				2			10	11	3	5			26
1			6	4		7	8					9				2			11	10	3	5			27
1			6	4		7	8					9				2			11	10	3	5			28
1			6	4		7	8					9				2			11	10	3	5			29
1		5	6	4		7	8					9				2			11	10	3				30
1	2	5	6	4		7	8					9							11	10	3				31
1	2	5	6*	4		7	8					9							11	10	3		12		32
1	2	5	6	4		7	8					9							11	10	3				33
1		5	6	4		7	8					9				2			11*	10	3		12		34
1		5*	6	4		7	8					9				2			11	10	3		12		35
1	2	5	4	6			8*							12		7			11	10	3		9		36
1	2	5	6	4		7*	11									8		9		10	3		12		37
1	2*	5	6	4		7	8					9				10				11	3		12		38
1		2	6	5		7	8					9				4			10	11	3				39
1		2	5*	4	6	7						9				8		12	11	10	3				40
		4		5	6	7						9				2		8	11	10	3			1	41
		5		6	4	7						9*				2		8	11	10	3		12	1	42
		5		6	4	7	8					9				2		10		11	3			1	43
		2	6	5	4*	7	10			12	11							8		9	3			1	44
		2	6	5		7	10				11					4		8		9	3			1	45
		2*	6	5		7	8			12	11					4		9		10	3			1	46
38	24	30	37	46	17	41	39	5	23	5	3	28	18	9	2	36	5	16	22	28	22	5	1	6	
	1					3	2	1		4	2	1		3				1					6		
			1			12	7	1	4			7		1		1		4	6	3					

3 own-goals

Crawford G	Scott P	Hunter G	James S	Topping C	Woodward J	Pollard B	Holmes I	Seal J	Cave M	Hosker R	Taylor P	Hinch J	Joy B	Downing D	Walker S	Young T	McMordie E	Hope G	Galvin C	Staniforth G	Hutt G	Bell R	Morris D	Neenan J	
1	2		6	5		12	4		10			9	3	11		8	7*								1
1	2		6	5		7	4		9				3	11		10	8								R
1		2	6	5		7	4		10	12			3	11*		8		9							2
1		2	6	5		7	4		10				3	11		8		9							R
1	2	3	6*	5		7	4		10	11		12				8		9							2R
5	3	3	5	5		4	5		5	1		1	4	4		5	2	3							
						1				1		1													
						1	3		2			1													

Crawford G	Scott P	Hunter G	James S	Topping C	Woodward J	Pollard B	Holmes I	Seal J	Cave M	Hosker R	Taylor P	Hinch J	Joy B	Downing D	Walker S	Young T	McMordie E	Hope G	Galvin C	Staniforth G	Hutt G	Bell R	Morris D	Neenan J	
1	2		4	5	6	7	8	9	10					3			11								1
1	2	3	4	5	6	7	8	9	10	11															
1	2	3	4	5	6	7	8	9	10	11															R
3	3	2	3	3	3	3	3	3	3	2				1			1								
							1																		

1977-78

Manager: Wilf McGuinness until October, then Charlie Wright from November 1977.

1	Aug	20	(h)	Aldershot	L 1-2	Opp own-goal	1,852
2		27	(a)	Watford	W 3-1	Pollard, Hope, Taylor	7,743
3	Sep	2	(h)	Stockport C	W 2-1	Staniforth, Holmes (pen)	2,046
4		6	(a)	Newport C	L 1-2	Hope	2,987
5		10	(h)	Grimsby T	L 1-2	Opp own-goal	1,872
6		13	(a)	Bournemouth	L 1-2	Holmes	2,863
7		16	(a)	Southend U	D 0-0		7,079
8		24	(h)	Huddersfield T	D 1-1	Hoy	2,595
9		27	(h)	Reading	W 2-0	Staniforth, Pollard	1,551
10	Oct	1	(a)	Barnsley	L 1-2	Pollard	4,592
11		5	(a)	Crewe A	L 0-1		2,380
12		7	(h)	Darlington	L 1-2	Pollard	2,383
13		15	(a)	Swansea C	D 1-1	Hope	5,346
14		21	(h)	Rochdale	D 2-2	Hutt, Holmes	1,579
15		28	(h)	Doncaster R	W 2-1	Randall 2	3,001
16	Nov	5	(a)	Brentford	L 0-1		5,980
17		12	(h)	Southport	W 2-1	Pollard, Opp own-goal	2,011
18		19	(a)	Wimbledon	L 1-2	Topping	2,056
19	Dec	3	(h)	Torquay U	D 0-0		1,284
20		10	(a)	Northampton T	D 1-1	Staniforth	3,108
21		26	(h)	Hartlepool U	W 1-0	Novacki	3,367
22		27	(a)	Scunthorpe U	L 1-2	Scott	3,242
23		31	(h)	Brentford	W 3-2	Staniforth, Randall, Young	2,145
24	Jan	2	(a)	Halifax T	L 0-2		3,744
25		7	(h)	Newport C	W 2-0	Scott, Staniforth (pen)	1,971
26		14	(a)	Aldershot	D 1-1	Randall	3,798
27		21	(h)	Watford	L 0-4		4,001
28		27	(a)	Stockport C	L 0-2		4,558
29	Feb	4	(a)	Grimsby T	L 2-3	Staniforth, Scott	3,282
30		24	(h)	Barnsley	L 1-2	Randall	3,269
31		28	(h)	Southend U	L 1-2	Staniforth (pen)	1,586
32	Mar	4	(a)	Darlington	W 2-0	Topping 2	1,965
33		7	(h)	Bournemouth	D 0-0		1,531
34		11	(h)	Swansea C	W 2-1	Staniforth 2 (2 pens)	2,008
35		14	(a)	Hartlepool U	L 2-4	Randall, Staniforth	3,446
36		18	(a)	Rochdale	W 2-1	Randall 2	1,046
37		24	(h)	Scunthorpe U	L 0-2		2,408
38		28	(a)	Doncaster R	D 1-1	Hope	2,385
39		31	(h)	Halifax T	D 1-1	Novacki	1,526
40	Apr	4	(h)	Crewe A	D 1-1	McDonald	1,415
41		7	(a)	Southport	L 1-4	Novacki	1,296
42		11	(a)	Huddersfield T	W 2-1	Staniforth (pen), McDonald	2,037
43		15	(h)	Wimbledon	D 1-1	Staniforth (pen)	1,617
44		22	(a)	Torquay U	L 0-3		1,958
45		26	(a)	Reading	L 0-1		2,212
46		29	(h)	Northampton T	L 0-3		1,339

FINAL LEAGUE POSITION: 22nd in Division Four

Appearances
Sub Appearances
Goals

FA Cup

1	Nov	26	(a)	Wigan A	L 0-1		6,289

Appearances
Sub Appearances
Goals

League Cup

1	Aug	13	(a)	Rotherham U	L 0-3		2,475
		16	(h)	Rotherham U	W 3-0	Topping, Hoy, Staniforth	1,720
R		23	(h)	Rotherham U	D 1-1*	James	2,518

*Rotherham United won 6-5 on penalties

Appearances
Sub Appearances
Goals

Neenan J	Scott P	Hutt G	Young T	Topping C	James S	Pollard B	Holmes I	Hope G	Staniforth G	Woodward J	Hoy R	Taylor P	Hunter G	Mitchell B	Brown G	Randall K	Clements A	McDonald I	Novacki J	Bainbridge P	
1	2	3	4	5	6	7	8	9	10	11*	12										1
1	2	3		4	5	7	8	9	10		6	11									2
1	2	3		5	6	7	8	9*	11		4	10	12								3
1	2	3		5	6	7	8	9	11		4*	10	12								4
1	2	3*	6	4	5	7	8	9	11			10	12								5
1	2			5	6	7	8	10	11	4	12		3	9*							6
1	2		3	5	6	7	8	9	11	4	10										7
1	2	3	12	5	6	7	8	9*	11	4	10										8
1	2	3*	9	5	6	7	8		11	4	10			12							9
1	2	3	9	5	6	7	8*		11	4	10			12							10
	2	3		5	6	7	8		11	4*	12	10	9		1						11
	2	3	4	5	6	7	8		11		12	10*	9		1						12
	2	3	5	4	6	7	8	9	11				10		1						13
	2	3	4	5	6	7	8		11		10		9		1						14
	2	3	4	5	6	7			11		10		8		1	9					15
	2	3	4	5	6	7			11		10		8		1	9					16
	4	3	12	5	6*	7		8	10						1	9	2	11			17
	6	3	7	4	5			9*	11				12		1	10	2	8			18
	4	3	7	5	6				10			8			1	9	2	11			19
	4	3	7	5	6				10			8			1	9	2	11			20
	4	3	8	5	6				11						1	9	2	10	7		21
	4	3	8	5	6				11						1	9	2	10	7		22
	4	3	8	5	6				11						1	9	2	10	7		23
	4	3	8	5	6				11						1	9	2	10	7		24
	4	3		5	6			12	11			8*			1	9	2	10	7		25
	4	3	8	5	6			12	11						1	9	2	10	7*		26
	4	3		5	6			12	11				8		1	9	2	10	7*		27
	4	3		5	6			12	11				8		1	9	2	10	7*		28
	4	3		5	6			12	11				8		1	9	2	10	7*		29
		3	8	5				4	11				6		1	9	2	10	7		30
	4	3	8	5				7	11				6		1	9	2	10			31
	4	3	8	5	6			9	11						1		2	10	7		32
	4	3	8	5	6			9	11						1		2	10	7		33
	4	3	8	5	6			9	11						1	12	2	10	7*		34
	4	3	8	5	6			9*	11						1	7	2	10	12		35
	4	3	8	5	6*				11				12		1	9	2	10	7		36
	4	3	8	5					11				6		1	9	2	10	7		37
	4	3		5				12	11				8		1	9	2	10	7	6*	38
	4	3		5					11			12	8		1	9	2	10*	7	6	39
	4	3		5					11				8		1	9	2	10	7	6	40
	4	3		5	6			8	11			12			1	9*	2	10	7		41
	4	3		5					11				8		1	9	2	10	7	6	42
	4*	3		5				12	11				8		1	9	2	10	7	6	43
1	4		6	5					11			12	8			9	2*	10	7	3	44
1	4		8	5	6*				11			12	3			9	2	10	7		45
1	4		2	5					11			8	3			9		10	7	6	46
13	45	41	29	46	36	17	14	18	46	7	10	10	21	1	33	29	29	30	24	7	
			2					7			4	4	5	2		1			1		
	3	1	1	3		5	3	4	12		1	1				8		2	3		

3 own-goals

Neenan J	Scott P	Hutt G	Young T	Topping C	James S	Pollard B	Holmes I	Hope G	Staniforth G	Woodward J	Hoy R	Taylor P	Hunter G	Mitchell B	Brown G	Randall K	Clements A	McDonald I	Novacki J	Bainbridge P	
	4	3	8	5	6				10			12	7*		1	9	2	11			1
	1	1	1	1	1				1				1		1	1	1	1			
												1									

Neenan J	Scott P	Hutt G	Young T	Topping C	James S	Pollard B	Holmes I	Hope G	Staniforth G	Woodward J	Hoy R	Taylor P	Hunter G	Mitchell B	Brown G	Randall K	Clements A	McDonald I	Novacki J	Bainbridge P	
1	2	3	8	4	5	7	6	9	10	11											1
1	2	3	4	5	6	7	8	9	11	10*	12										
1	2	3		5	6	7	8	9	11	10*	4	12									R
3	3	3	2	3	3	3	3	3	3	3	1										
											1	1									
				1	1				1		1										

1978-79

Manager: Charlie Wright

1	Aug	19	(a)	Rochdale	W 2-1	Staniforth, Randall	1,241
2		22	(h)	Portsmouth	W 5-3	Staniforth 2, Randall 2, Loggie	2,513
3		26	(h)	Doncaster R	D 1-1	Randall	3,609
4	Sep	2	(a)	Barnsley	L 0-3		8,599
5		9	(h)	Northampton T	W 1-0	Staniforth	2,358
6		12	(a)	Halifax T	W 1-0	Randall	1,701
7		15	(a)	Stockport C	L 0-2		6,103
8		23	(h)	Wigan A	L 0-1		3,307
9		26	(h)	Hereford U	W 1-0	Randall	2,358
10		30	(a)	Newport C	D 1-1	Loggie	3,021
11	Oct	7	(h)	Wimbledon	L 1-4	Loggie	3,329
12		14	(a)	Bradford C	L 1-2	Randall	4,026
13		17	(h)	Torquay U	D 0-0		2,084
14		21	(a)	Reading	L 0-3		12,031
15		28	(h)	Scunthorpe U	W 1-0	Staniforth	1,970
16	Nov	4	(a)	Huddersfield T	L 0-1		3,696
17		11	(h)	Barnsley	L 0-1		6,900
18		18	(a)	Doncaster R	W 2-1	Randall, Wellings	2,479
19	Dec	9	(a)	Bournemouth	W 2-1	Clements, Staniforth	3,323
20		23	(a)	Grimsby T	L 0-3		4,339
21		26	(h)	Hartlepool U	D 1-1	Faulkner	3,825
22	Feb	3	(a)	Hereford U	L 0-1		3,107
23		24	(h)	Bradford C	D 2-2	Staniforth, Loggie	4,022
24		28	(a)	Wigan A	D 1-1	Loggie	5,896
25	Mar	3	(h)	Reading	L 0-1		2,654
26		6	(a)	Darlington	W 1-0	Staniforth	1,173
27		10	(a)	Scunthorpe U	W 3-2	Randall 2, Clements	2,261
28		13	(h)	Halifax T	W 2-0	Loggie, Staniforth	2,196
29		20	(h)	Newport C	L 1-2	Staniforth	2,156
30		24	(a)	Portsmouth	D 1-1	Loggie	9,353
31		27	(h)	Rochdale	W 2-1	Opp own-goal, McDonald	2,295
32		31	(h)	Aldershot	D 1-1	McDonald	2,110
33	Apr	3	(a)	Northampton T	L 0-1		1,628
34		7	(a)	Port Vale	D 0-0		2,712
35		13	(h)	Grimsby T	D 0-0		5,401
36		14	(a)	Hartlepool U	D 1-1	McDonald	2,343
37		16	(h)	Darlington	W 5-2	Staniforth, Ford, Loggie, Stronach, McDonald	2,973
38		21	(a)	Crewe A	W 1-0	Stronach	1,428
39		25	(a)	Torquay U	L 0-3		1,724
40		28	(h)	Bournemouth	W 2-1	McDonald, Staniforth (pen)	2,171
41	May	1	(h)	Crewe A	W 1-0	Ford	2,009
42		5	(a)	Aldershot	L 0-1		3,675
43		7	(h)	Port Vale	W 4-0	Staniforth 3 (1 pen), McDonald	2,344
44		11	(a)	Wimbledon	L 1-2	Ford	3,897
45		14	(h)	Stockport C	W 1-0	Wellings	2,089
46		19	(h)	Huddersfield T	L 1-3	Ford	2,664

FINAL LEAGUE POSITION: 10th in Division Four

Appearances
Sub Appearances
Goals

FA Cup

1	Nov	25	(h)	Blyth Spartans	D 1-1	Pugh	5,088
R		28	(a)	Blyth Spartans	W 5-3*	Wellings, Clements, Ford, Randall, Staniforth	3,543
2	Dec	16	(h)	Scarborough	W 3-0	Faulkner, Staniforth 2	7,870
3	Jan	9	(h)	Luton T	W 2-0	Staniforth, Randall	6,730
4		27	(a)	Nottingham F	L 1-3	Wellings	25,228

*After extra-time

Appearances
Sub Appearances
Goals

League Cup

1	Aug	12	(a)	Grimsby T	L 0-2		3,054
		15	(h)	Grimsby T	L 0-3		2,668

Appearances
Sub Appearances
Goals

Neenan J	Scott P	Kay R	Young T	Faulkner S	Clements A	Stronach P	Randall K	Loggie D	McDonald I	Staniforth G	Warnock N	Wellings B	Bainbridge P	Collier G	Walsh J	Brown G	Ford G	Pugh D	
1	2	3	4	5	6	7	8	9	10	11*	12								1
1	2	3	7	5	6	4	8	9	10	11									2
1	2	3	7	5	6	4	8	9	10	11									3
1	2	3	7	5	6	4*	8	9	10	11		12							4
1	2	3	7	5	6	4	8	9	10	11									5
1	2	3	7		6	4	8	9	10	11			5						6
1	2	3	7		6	4	8	9	10	11			5						7
1	2*	3	7	5	6	10	8	9		11				4	12				8
1		2	7	5	6		8	9	10	11				4	3				9
1		3	7	5	6	12	8	9	10	11*				4	2				10
1		2	7	5	6	8*	9	10		11		12		4	3				11
1	4	2		5	6		8	9	10	11				7	3				12
	7	2		5	6	4	8	9	10	11					3	1			13
	10	2		5	6	4	8	9*		11	12				3	1	7		14
		2		5	6	4	8	9	10	11					3	1	7		15
		2		5	6		8	9	10	11	12				3*	1	7	4	16
		2		5	6		8	9	10	11	7*				3	1	12	4	17
		2		5	6		8		10	11		9			3	1	7	4	18
		2		5	6		8		10	11		9			3	1	7	4	19
		2		5	6		8		10	11		9			3	1	7	4	20
		2		5	6		8	12	10	11		9*			3	1	7	4	21
		2		5	6		8		10	11		9			3	1	7	4	22
		2		5	6		12	8	10	11		9*			3	1	7	4	23
1		2		5	6		8	9	10	11					3		7	4	24
1		2		5	6		8	9	10	11		12			3		7*	4	25
1		2		5	6		8	9*	10	11		12			3		7	4	26
1		2		5	6		8	9	10	11					3		7	4	27
1		2		5	6		8	9	10	11					3		7	4	28
1		2		5	6		8	9	10	11					3		7	4	29
1		2		5	6			9	10	11		8			3		7	4	30
1		2		5	6	12	8*	9	10	11					3		7	4	31
1		2		5	6		8	9	10	11					3		7	4	32
1		2		5	6	12	8	9*	10	11					3		7	4	33
		2		5	6		8	9	10	11					3	1	7	4	34
		2		5	6		8	9	10	11					3	1	7	4	35
		2		5	6	12	8*	9	10	11					3	1	7	4	36
		2		5	6	8		9	10	11					3	1	7	4	37
		2		5	6	8		9	10	11					3	1	7	4	38
		2		5	6	8		9	10	11					3	1	7	4	39
		2		5	6	8	12	9*	10	11					3	1	7	4	40
		2		5	6	8	9*	12	10	11					3	1	7	4	41
		2		5	6	8*	12	9	10	11					3	1	7	4	42
		2		5	6	8	9*		10	11		12			3	1	7	4	43
		2		5	6	8	12		10	11		9*			3	1	7	4	44
		2		5	6	8	11		10			9			3	1	7	4	45
		2		5	6	8*	12		10	11		9			3	1	7	4	46
22	11	46	11	44	46	22	37	36	43	45	1	10	2	5	38	24	32	31	
						4	5	2			3	5			1		1		
				1	2	2	10	8	6	15		2					4		

1 own-goal

Neenan J	Scott P	Kay R	Young T	Faulkner S	Clements A	Stronach P	Randall K	Loggie D	McDonald I	Staniforth G	Warnock N	Wellings B	Bainbridge P	Collier G	Walsh J	Brown G	Ford G	Pugh D	
		2		5	6		9		8	11		10			3	1	7	4	1
		2		5	6		9		8	11		10			3	1	7	4	R
		2		5	6		7		10	11		9			3	1	7	4	2
		2		5	6		7	9	10	11					3	1	7	4	3
		2		5	6		7	9*	10	11		12			3	1	7	4	4
		5		5	5		5	2	5	5		3			5	5	5	5	
												1							
				1	1		2			4		2					1	1	

Neenan J	Scott P	Kay R	Young T	Faulkner S	Clements A	Stronach P	Randall K	Loggie D	McDonald I	Staniforth G	Warnock N	Wellings B	Bainbridge P	Collier G	Walsh J	Brown G	Ford G	Pugh D	
1	2	3	8	5	6	4		9		11	7				10				1
1	2	3	4	5	6	7		9	10	11		12			8*				
2	2	2	2	2	2	2		2	1	2	1				2				
												1							

1979-80

Manager: Charlie Wright until March 1980, then Barry Lyons.

1	Aug	18	(a)	Hereford U	L 1-3	Randall	3,149
2		21	(h)	Darlington	W 3-1	McDonald 2, Ford	2,537
3		25	(h)	Lincoln C	L 0-2		2,716
4	Sep	1	(a)	Newport C	L 0-2		3,818
5		8	(h)	Peterborough U	L 0-2		3,102
6		15	(a)	Wigan A	W 5-2	Staniforth 3, Loggie, Lorimer	5,900
7		18	(a)	Scunthorpe U	L 1-6	McDonald	2,365
8		22	(h)	Stockport C	D 2-2	Wellings, Lorimer	2,443
9		29	(a)	Portsmouth	L 2-5	Eccles, Kay	14,917
10	Oct	2	(h)	Scunthorpe U	W 2-0	Byrne, Eccles	2,397
11		6	(h)	Rochdale	W 3-2	Eccles, Byrne, Wellings	2,462
12		9	(a)	Darlington	L 1-2	Wellings	2,072
13		12	(h)	Bournemouth	D 1-1	Lorimer	2,840
14		19	(a)	Tranmere R	W 2-1	Randall, Lorimer	2,197
15		23	(h)	Doncaster R	L 1-3	Eccles	4,707
16		27	(a)	Huddersfield T	D 2-2	Eccles 2	7,547
17	Nov	3	(h)	Hereford U	W 3-1	Lorimer, Eccles, Randall	2,226
18		6	(a)	Doncaster R	L 0-2		6,683
19		10	(a)	Torquay U	L 3-4	Randall, Eccles, Wellings	3,963
20		17	(h)	Bradford C	D 2-2	Randall, Kay	3,832
21	Dec	1	(h)	Port Vale	W 5-1	Lorimer 2, Clements, Randall, McDonald	2,402
22		8	(a)	Aldershot	D 2-2	Randall, Wellings	3,610
23		21	(h)	Walsall	L 0-1		1,990
24		26	(a)	Hartlepool U	L 1-3	Loggie	2,936
25		29	(a)	Lincoln C	D 1-1	Clements	3,492
26	Jan	5	(a)	Northampton T	L 0-2		2,095
27		12	(h)	Newport C	W 2-1	Kay, Lorimer	2,248
28		26	(h)	Crewe A	D 2-2	McDonald (pen), Loggie	2,460
29	Feb	2	(h)	Wigan A	L 1-2	Opp own-goal	2,400
30		8	(a)	Stockport C	L 0-1		2,500
31		12	(h)	Halifax T	D 2-2	Faulkner 2	2,124
32		16	(h)	Portsmouth	W 1-0	Hood	2,509
33		23	(a)	Bournemouth	D 0-0		3,201
34	Mar	1	(h)	Tranmere R	L 0-1		2,327
35		5	(a)	Peterborough U	L 1-2	Faulkner	3,434
36		8	(h)	Huddersfield T	L 0-4		5,742
37		14	(a)	Rochdale	W 2-0	Wellings, McDonald	1,151
38		22	(h)	Torquay U	W 1-0	Eccles	1,791
39		29	(a)	Bradford C	W 2-1	McDonald, Ford	5,035
40	Apr	1	(a)	Walsall	L 1-3	Faulkner	4,897
41		5	(h)	Hartlepool U	W 2-1	Walsh 2	2,711
42		7	(a)	Halifax T	D 1-1	Pugh	1,778
43		12	(h)	Northampton T	L 1-2	Faulkner	2,161
44		19	(a)	Port Vale	W 2-1	Clements, Wellings	2,640
45		26	(h)	Aldershot	D 1-1	McDonald (pen)	2,051
46	May	3	(a)	Crewe A	L 0-2		2,651

FINAL LEAGUE POSITION: 17th in Division Four

Appearances
Sub Appearances
Goals

FA Cup

1	Nov	24	(h)	Mossley	W 5-2	Randall, Eccles, Byrne, Lorimer, McDonald (pen)	3,872
2	Dec	15	(a)	Bury	D 0-0		4,195
R		18	(h)	Bury	L 0-2		4,932

Appearances
Sub Appearances
Goals

League Cup

1	Aug	11	(a)	Mansfield T	L 0-1		3,117
		14	(h)	Mansfield T	W 3-2*	Randall, Clements, Staniforth	2,590

*After extra-time. Mansfield Town won on away-goals rule.

Appearances
Sub Appearances
Goals

Brown G	Kay R	Walsh J	Pugh D	Faulkner S	Clements A	Ford G	Randall K	Stronach P	McDonald I	Staniforth G	Byrne J	James S	Wellings B	Lorimer P	Loggie D	Neenan J	Kamara A	Eccles T	Harrison J	McGhie W	Ferebee S	Crawford G	Hood D	Taylor R	Leaf A	
1	2	3	4	5	6	7	8	9	10	11																1
1	2	3	4	5	6	7	8	9	10	11																2
1	2	3	4	5	6	7	8	9*	10	11	12															3
1	2	3	4		6	7	8	9	10	11		5														4
1	2	3	4*	5		7	9		10	11		6	12	8												5
1	2	3	4	5		7			10	11			9	8	6											6
1	2	3	6	5	12	7			10	11			9	8	4*											7
	3		12	5	6				10	11	7*		9	8	4	1	2									8
	3		4	5					10	11		6	9	7		1	2	8								9
	3		4		5		12		10		7*	6	11	8		1	2	9								10
	3		4		5				10		7	6	11	8		1	2	9								11
	3		4		5				10		7	6	11	8		1	2	9								12
	3	2	4		5		12		10		7*	6	11	8		1		9								13
	3		4		5		7		10			6	11	8		1	2	9								14
	3		4		5		7		10			6	11	8		1	2	9								15
	3		4*		5		12	8	10			6	11	7		1	2	9								16
1	3				5	12	7	4	10			6*	11	8			2	9								17
1	3			6	5	7	12	4	10				11	8			2*	9								18
1	3			5	2	12	7	4	10			6*	11	8				9								19
	2			5	6	4	7		10				11	8		1		9	3							20
	2				5	4*	7		10		12	6	11	8		1		9	3							21
	2				6	4	7		10		12	6	11	8		1		9*	3							22
	2				6	4	7		10			5	11	8	9	1			3							23
	2		12		6	4	7		10			5	11*	8	9	1			3							24
1	2		4		6				10			5		8	11			9	3	7*	12					25
1	2		6		5				10			4		8	11			9	3	7*	12					26
	2	3	4	5	6		7		10					8	11	1		9								27
	2	3	4	5	6		7		10				12	8	11			9*				1				28
	2	3		5	6		7		10					8	11*			9		4	12	1				29
	2	3	4	5	6		7*		10					8	12			9		11		1				30
		3	4	5	6				10					8				9		11	7	1	2			31
		3	4*	5	6		12		10					8				9		11	7	1	2			32
		3		5	6	4	7		10									9		11	8	1	2			33
		3		5	6	12	7		10					8				9		4	11*	1	2			34
	3		12	5	6	4	8*		10				7					9		11		1	2			35
	3			6	6	4			10		12		11		8*			9		4		1	2			36
	3		8	5	6	4			10				7					9		11		1	2			37
	3		7	5	6	4			10				11					9*		8	12	1	2			38
	3		8	5	6	4			10				11					9		7		1	2			39
	3		8	5	6	4			10				7					9		11		1	2			40
	3	12	7	5	6	4			10				11					9		8*		1	2			41
	3	11	8	5	6	4			10				7					9				1	2			42
	3	8	7	5	6	4			10				11*					9			12	1	2			43
	3		7	5	6	4			10				11					9		8		1	2			44
			7	5	6	4			10				11					9		8			2	1	3	45
	3	6	12	5*		8			10									9	4	7	11		2	1		46
12	41	19	31	31	41	26	21	8	46	9	5	18	30	29	11	15	10	36	8	18	5	17	16	2	1	
		1	4		1	3	5				4		2		1						5					
	3	2	1	5	3	2	7		8	3	2		7	8	3			9					1			

1 own-goal

Brown G	Kay R	Walsh J	Pugh D	Faulkner S	Clements A	Ford G	Randall K	Stronach P	McDonald I	Staniforth G	Byrne J	James S	Wellings B	Lorimer P	Loggie D	Neenan J	Kamara A	Eccles T	Harrison J	
	2			5*	6	4	7		10		12		11	8		1		9	3	1
	2				6	4	7		10			5	11	8	9	1			3	2
	2			12	6	4	7		10		9*	5	11	8		1			3	R
	3			1	3	3	3		3		1	2	3	3	1	3		1	3	
				1							1									
							1		1		1			1				1		

Brown G	Kay R	Walsh J	Pugh D	Faulkner S	Clements A	Ford G	Randall K	Stronach P	McDonald I	Staniforth G	Byrne J	James S	Wellings B	Lorimer P	Loggie D	
1	2	3	4	5	6	7	8	12	10	11					9*	1
1	2	3	4	5	6	7	8	9	10	11						
2	2	2	2	2	2	2	2	1	2	2					1	
								1								
					1		1			1						

1980-81

Manager: Barry Lyons

1	Aug	16	(h)	Bournemouth	W 4-0	Eccles, McDonald, Ford, Byrne	2,195
2		18	(a)	Mansfield T	W 1-0	Eccles	4,080
3		23	(h)	Torquay U	D 0-0		2,892
4		30	(a)	Hereford U	D 1-1	Ford	2,757
5	Sep	5	(a)	Southend U	L 0-3		5,124
6		13	(h)	Hartlepool U	L 0-1		2,504
7		19	(a)	Northampton T	L 0-2		1,843
8		23	(h)	Tranmere R	W 4-1	Kay, Ford, Faulkner, Eccles	2,322
9		27	(h)	Doncaster R	L 0-1		4,641
10		29	(a)	Tranmere R	L 0-5		1,595
11	Oct	4	(h)	Port Vale	W 4-1	McDonald 2, Byrne, Eccles	2,025
12		7	(a)	Halifax T	L 1-3	Smith	1,088
13		11	(a)	Lincoln C	D 1-1	Smith	4,026
14		18	(h)	Stockport C	W 1-0	McDonald	2,135
15		21	(h)	Darlington	L 1-2	Smith	2,534
16		25	(a)	Wimbledon	L 0-3		2,082
17		29	(a)	Wigan A	L 0-1		3,668
18	Nov	1	(h)	Scunthorpe U	W 1-0	Eccles	1,959
19		4	(h)	Halifax T	D 1-1	Eccles	1,837
20		8	(a)	Crewe A	D 1-1	McGhie	2,798
21		11	(h)	Mansfield T	W 2-0	Smith, Byrne	2,204
22		15	(a)	Bournemouth	D 1-1	Clements	2,203
23	Dec	6	(a)	Bradford C	D 1-1	Opp own-goal	3,638
24		20	(h)	Aldershot	W 4-1	McDonald, Eccles 2, Ford	1,583
25		26	(a)	Bury	L 0-2		3,224
26		27	(h)	Rochdale	L 1-2	Smith	2,828
27	Jan	3	(a)	Darlington	D 0-0		3,209
28		10	(h)	Wigan A	W 2-1	McDonald, Richards	2,028
29		17	(a)	Peterborough U	L 0-3		3,954
30		24	(h)	Hereford U	L 1-2	Craig	1,924
31	Feb	7	(a)	Hartlepool U	L 0-1		3,119
32		14	(h)	Southend U	L 0-1		2,129
33		20	(a)	Doncaster R	L 2-3	Opp own-goal, Eccles	5,839
34	Mar	7	(a)	Port Vale	L 0-2		2,319
35		14	(h)	Lincoln C	W 1-0	Pugh	2,222
36		20	(a)	Stockport C	L 0-2		1,903
37		24	(h)	Peterborough U	L 1-2	Randall	1,725
38		28	(h)	Wimbledon	L 0-1		2,026
39	Apr	4	(a)	Scunthorpe U	L 2-3	Byrne, Randall	1,694
40		8	(a)	Torquay U	W 2-1	Smith, McDonald	1,406
41		11	(h)	Crewe A	W 2-0	McDonald (pen), Byrne	1,602
42		14	(h)	Bury	L 0-1		1,786
43		18	(a)	Rochdale	L 2-3	McDonald 2 (1 pen)	1,651
44		25	(a)	Aldershot	D 1-1	McDonald	1,831
45	May	2	(h)	Bradford C	L 0-3		1,481
46		5	(h)	Northampton T	L 1-2	Byrne	1,167

FINAL LEAGUE POSITION: 24th in Division Four

Appearances
Sub Appearances
Goals

FA Cup

1	Nov	22	(a)	Tranmere R	D 0-0		2,687
R		25	(h)	Tranmere R	L 1-2*	Byrne	3,036

*After extra-time

Appearances
Sub Appearances
Goals

League Cup

1	Aug	9	(h)	Hartlepool U	W 2-1	Ford, McDonald	2,444
		11	(a)	Hartlepool U	D 0-0		3,496
2		27	(h)	Bristol R	W 2-1	Richards, Opp own-goal	3,405
	Sep	3	(a)	Bristol R	L 0-1*		3,047

*After extra-time. Bristol Rovers won on away-goals rule.

Appearances
Sub Appearances
Goals

Blackburn E	Kay R	Faulkner S	Craig D	Ford G	Richards L	McGhie W	McDonald I	Eccles T	Byrne J	Walsh J	Smith M	Hood D	Ferebee S	Millar A	Clements A	Astbury M	Stanley T	Randall K	Pugh D	Senior S	
1	2	5	6	7	4	10	11	9	8	3											1
1	2	5	6	7	4	10	11	9		3	8										2
1	2	5	6	7	4	10	11	9		3	8										3
1	2	5	6	7	4	10	11	9		3	8										4
1	2	5	6	7	4		11	9*	12	3	8	10									5
1	2	5	6	7	4		11	9	8*	3		10	12								6
1	2	5	6	7*	4		11	9		3	8	10		12							7
1	3	5	6	7	4		11	9			8	2		10							8
1	3	5	6	7	4		11	9			8	2		10							9
1	3	5	6	7	4		11	9			8	2		10*	12						10
1	3		6	7			11	9	8*	12	4	2		10	5						11
1	3		6	7			11	9	8	12	4	2*		10	5						12
1	3		6	7			11	9*	8	12	4	2		10	5						13
1	3		6	7			11		8*	12	4	2	9	10	5						14
1	3		6	7			11		8	12	4	2	9*	10	5						15
1	3		6				11	9	8	7	4	2		10	5						16
1	3		6	12			11*	9	8	7	4	2		10	5						17
1	3		6	4	11		10	9	8	7		2			5						18
1	3		6	4	11		10	9	8	7		2			5						19
1	3		6	12		7*	10	9	8	11	4	2			5						20
1	3		6			11	10	9	8	12	4*	2		7	5						21
	3		6	7		11	10	9	8	4		2			5	1					22
1	3		6	7		4*	10	9	8	11	12	2			5						23
1	3		6	7		4	10	9		11	8	2			5						24
1	3		6	7*		4	10	9	12	11	8	2			5						25
1	3		6	7			10	9	8	11	4	2			5						26
1	3		6	7	12	4	10		8	11	9*	2			5						27
1	3		6	7	9	4	10		8	11		2			5						28
1	3		6	7*	9	4	10		8	11	12	2			5						29
1	3		6	7	9	4	10		8	11*	12	2			5						30
1	3		6	7		4	10	9	8		11	2			5						31
1	3		6	7	4		10	9	8		11	2			5						32
1	3	4	6				10	9	8	11	7	2			5						33
1		4	6	7	11		10	9	8	3		2			5						34
1		5	6*	7		12	10		8	3		2					4	9	11		35
1		5	6	7			10		8	3		2					4	9	11		36
1		5	6	7			10		8	3		2					4	9	11		37
1			6	7			10		8	3		2			5		4	9	11		38
1			6	7		12	10		8	3		2			5		4*	9	11		39
1			6	7		4	10		8	3	12	2			5			9*	11		40
1			6	7		4	10		8	3	12	2			5			9*	11		41
1			6	7		4	10		8	3	12	2			5*			9	11		42
1			6	7		4	10		8*	3	12	2			5			9	11		43
1	5		6	7		11*	10		8	3	9	2					4			12	44
1	2		6	7			10*		8	3	9	5					4		11	12	45
1	3		6	7			10		8		9	5					4		11	2	46
45	36	15	46	41	17	20	46	28	36	34	27	42	2	11	30	1	8	9	11	1	
				2	1	2			2	6	7		1	1	1					2	
	1	1	1	4	1	1	11	9	6		6				1			2	1		

2 own-goals

Blackburn E	Kay R	Faulkner S	Craig D	Ford G	Richards L	McGhie W	McDonald I	Eccles T	Byrne J	Walsh J	Smith M	Hood D	Ferebee S	Millar A	Clements A	Astbury M	Stanley T	Randall K	Pugh D	Senior S	
1	3		6	7		11	10	9	8	4		2			5						1
1	3		6	7		11	10	9	8*	4		2		12	5						R
2	2		2	2		2	2	2	2	2		2			2						
														1							
									1												

Blackburn E	Kay R	Faulkner S	Craig D	Ford G	Richards L	McGhie W	McDonald I	Eccles T	Byrne J	Walsh J	Smith M	Hood D	Ferebee S	Millar A	Clements A	Astbury M	Stanley T	Randall K	Pugh D	Senior S	
1	2	5	6	7	4	10	11	9		3	8										1
1	2	5	6	7	4	10	11	9		3	8										
1	2	5	6	7	4	10*	11	9	12	3	8										2
1	2	5	6	7*	4		11	9	12	3	8	10									
4	4	4	4	4	4	3	4	4		4	4	1									
									2												
				1	1		1														

1 own-goal

1981-82

Manager: Barry Lyons until December 1981, then Kevin Randall until March, Barry Swallow until May 1982 (caretaker managers).

No	Month	Day	Venue	Opponent	Result	Scorers	Attendance
1	Aug	29	(a)	Tranmere R	W 2-0	Walwyn, Hood	1,850
2	Sep	4	(h)	Northampton T	W 2-1	Waldron, Walwyn	2,086
3		12	(a)	Bradford C	L 2-6	Walwyn, Byrne	3,601
4		18	(h)	Hartlepool U	L 1-2	Walwyn	2,244
5		22	(h)	Bournemouth	L 0-1		2,252
6		26	(a)	Torquay U	L 2-3	Walwyn, Pollard	2,853
7		29	(a)	Aldershot	W 1-0	Pollard	2,056
8	Oct	3	(h)	Sheffield U	L 3-4	Walwyn, Ford, McDonald (pen)	5,557
9		9	(h)	Darlington	D 2-2	McDonald, Walwyn	2,407
10		16	(a)	Colchester U	L 0-4		3,139
11		20	(h)	Blackpool	L 0-4		2,657
12		24	(a)	Peterborough U	W 1-0	Walwyn	4,220
13		31	(h)	Hereford U	L 3-4	Pollard, Ford, Hedley	1,600
14	Nov	3	(a)	Hull C	L 0-2		3,340
15		7	(a)	Scunthorpe U	W 3-0	Ford, Walwyn 2	1,622
16		14	(h)	Wigan A	D 0-0		2,780
17		28	(a)	Crewe A	D 1-1	Walwyn	1,881
18	Dec	5	(h)	Stockport C	D 2-2	Walwyn, Kay	1,762
19	Jan	23	(h)	Tranmere R	L 1-3	Senior	1,594
20		30	(a)	Hartlepool U	L 2-3	Crosby 2	2,291
21	Feb	2	(h)	Bury	D 0-0		1,713
22		6	(h)	Bradford C	L 0-3		3,093
23		9	(a)	Bournemouth	L 1-5	Hood	4,373
24		13	(a)	Sheffield U	L 0-4		12,901
25		19	(h)	Torquay U	D 1-1	Kay	1,660
26		22	(h)	Port Vale	W 2-0	Ford, Hood (pen)	1,938
27		28	(a)	Darlington	L 1-3	Aitken	3,212
28	Mar	5	(h)	Colchester U	W 3-0	Hood (pen), Walwyn 2	1,854
29		10	(a)	Blackpool	L 1-3	Walwyn	2,164
30		13	(h)	Peterborough U	W 4-3	Kay 2, Laverick, Byrne	2,178
31		16	(h)	Hull C	L 1-3	Walwyn	4,771
32		20	(a)	Hereford U	L 1-2	Aitken	2,703
33		23	(a)	Northampton T	L 0-5		2,452
34		26	(h)	Scunthorpe U	W 3-1	Walwyn, Hood (pen), Opp own-goal	2,189
35	Apr	2	(a)	Wigan A	L 2-4	Byrne, D.Smith	6,029
36		5	(a)	Mansfield T	W 2-0	Laverick, Ford	2,388
37		10	(h)	Mansfield T	W 2-1	Walwyn, Ford	2,155
38		12	(a)	Rochdale	L 0-2		1,421
39		16	(a)	Stockport C	L 1-4	Laverick	1,938
40		23	(h)	Crewe A	W 6-0	Laverick, Walwyn 2, Ford, Byrne, Hood (pen)	1,753
41		27	(h)	Rochdale	L 1-2	Walwyn	2,089
42	May	1	(a)	Port Vale	D 0-0		1,924
43		4	(h)	Aldershot	W 4-0	Walwyn, Ford, Byrne, Hood	1,571
44		7	(h)	Halifax T	W 4-0	Opp own-goal, Walwyn, Byrne, Hood (pen)	2,423
45		11	(a)	Halifax T	D 0-0		1,903
46		15	(a)	Bury	L 1-3	Opp own-goal	2,002

FINAL LEAGUE POSITION: 17th in Division Four

Appearances
Sub Appearances
Goals

FA Cup

Rd	Month	Day	Venue	Opponent	Result	Scorers	Attendance
1	Nov	20	(a)	Stafford R	W 2-1	Ford, Walwyn	2,289
2	Dec	12	(h)	Altrincham	D 0-0		3,786
R	Jan	2	(a)	Altrincham	L 3-4	Pollard 2, Walwyn	3,088

Appearances
Sub Appearances
Goals

League Cup

Rd	Month	Day	Venue	Opponent	Result	Scorers	Attendance
1	Sep	1	(a)	Sheffield U	L 0-1		6,702
	Sep	15	(h)	Sheffield U	D 1-1	Byrne	4,750

Appearances
Sub Appearances
Goals

Blackburn E	Kay R	Flood E	Hood D	Croft S	Dawson R	Ford G	Byrne J	Walwyn K	McDonald I	Waldron A	McGhie W	Craig D	Senior S	Pollard B	Bentham J	Smith M	Stanley T	Hedley G	Crosby M	Czuczman M	Laverick M	Astbury M	Sweeney G	Aitken P	Fell G	Smith D	
1	2	3	4	5	6	7	8	9	10	11																	1
1	2	3	4	5	6	7	8*	9	10	11	12																2
1	2	3	4	5	6	7	8	9	10	11*	12																3
1	2	3	4		6	7	8	9	10		6*	5	12														4
1	2	3	4	5	6		8*	9					12	7	11	10											5
1	3		4	5	6		8	9	10				2	7	11												6
1	3		4	5	6		8	9	10				2*	7	11		12										7
1	2	3	4	5	6	8		9	10					7	11												8
1	2	3	4	5	6	8		9	10					7	11												9
1		3	2	5	6		8	9	10					7	11			4									10
1		3	2	5	6	12	8*	9	10					7	11			4									11
1	3		2	5	6	8		9				10		7	11			4									12
1	3		2	5	6	8	9*					10	12	7	11			4									13
1	3		8	5	6	10						4	2	9	11			7									14
1		3	8	5	6	10		9					2	7	11				4								15
1	6	3	5			10		9					2	7	11		4		8								16
1	6	3	4			10	12	9					2	7	11*				8	5							17
1	6	3	4			10		9					2	7	11				8	5							18
1	3		5		6	10		9					2	7	11				8		4						19
	3		6		5	10		9					2	7	11*		12		8		4	1					20
	3		6		5	10		9					2	7	11				8		4	1					21
	3		5		6	7	10	9					2		11				8		4	1					22
	3		6		5	7	10*	9					2		11		12		8		4	1					23
1	3	12	4		6	7	10	9				5	2				11		8*								24
1	8		4		3	10		9							11		7			5			2	6			25
1	8		4		3	10		9									7			5	11		2	6			26
1	4		2		3	10		9									7		8	5	11			6			27
1			4		3	10		9											8	5	11		2	6	7		28
1	6		4*		3	10	8	9				5			12		2				11				7		29
1	7		4		3	10	8	9				5									11		2*	6	12		30
	7*		4		3	10	8	9													11	1	2	6	12	5	31
	7		4		3	10	8	9													11	1	2	6		5	32
	7		5		3		8	9											10	4*	11	1	2	6	12		33
			7		3	9	10*	11											12	4	6	1	2	8		5	34
			4		3	7	10	9											12	6	11*	1	2	8		5	35
			4		3	7	10	9											12	5*	11	1	2	8		6	36
			4		3	8		9						7					10		11	1	2	6		5	37
			4		3	8		9						7					10		11	1	2	6		5	38
	4		6		5	10		9					2	7	3				8		11	1					39
1	3		4		2	7	11	9											10	5	8			6			40
1	6		4		2	7	8	9						12	3				10	5*	11						41
1	6	12	4		3	10	8	9						7					2*	5	11						42
1	3		4		2	10	8	9						7						5	11			6			43
1	3		4		2	10	8	9						7						5	11			6			44
	3		4		2	10	8	9						7						5	11	1		6			45
	3*		4		2	10	8	9						7					12	5	11	1		6			46
31	37	13	46	14	43	40	28	44	10	3	1	7	14	25	22	1	6	5	19	17	26	15	12	18	2	7	
		2				1	1				2		3	1	1		3		4						3		
	4		8			8	6	23	2	1			1	3				1	2		4			2		1	

3 own-goals

Blackburn E	Kay R	Flood E	Hood D	Croft S	Dawson R	Ford G	Byrne J	Walwyn K	McDonald I	Waldron A	McGhie W	Craig D	Senior S	Pollard B	Bentham J	Smith M	Stanley T	Hedley G	Crosby M	Czuczman M	Laverick M	Astbury M	Sweeney G	Aitken P	Fell G	Smith D	
1	6	3	5			10		9					2	7	11		4		8								1
1	6	3	4			10		9					2	7	11				8	5							2
1	6	3	4		5	10		9					2	7	11				8								R
3	3	3	3		1	3		3					3	3	3		1		3	1							
						1		2						2													

Blackburn E	Kay R	Flood E	Hood D	Croft S	Dawson R	Ford G	Byrne J	Walwyn K	McDonald I	Waldron A	McGhie W	Craig D	Senior S	Pollard B	Bentham J	Smith M	Stanley T	Hedley G	Crosby M	Czuczman M	Laverick M	Astbury M	Sweeney G	Aitken P	Fell G	Smith D	
1	2	3	4	5	6	7	8	9	10	11																	1
1	2	3	4		6	7	8	9	10		11	5															
2	2	2	2	1	2	2	2	2	2	1	1	1															
							1																				

1982-83

Manager: Denis Smith

1	Aug	28	(h)	Torquay U	D 1-1	Hood (pen)	1,737
2	Sep	4	(a)	Northampton T	D 1-1	Laverick	2,254
3		7	(a)	Hull C	L 0-4		3,769
4		11	(h)	Tranmere R	W 2-1	Hood (pen), Walwyn	1,632
5		19	(a)	Scunthorpe U	D 0-0		2,436
6		25	(h)	Peterborough U	D 1-1	Ford	1,872
7		28	(h)	Halifax T	W 3-2	Laverick, Ford, Busby	1,772
8	Oct	2	(a)	Hereford U	D 0-0		2,037
9		9	(a)	Bristol C	D 2-2	Byrne, Ford	3,680
10		16	(h)	Wimbledon	L 1-4	Pollard	2,064
11		19	(a)	Blackpool	D 1-1	Walwyn	2,765
12		22	(a)	Stockport C	L 1-2	Walwyn	2,014
13		30	(h)	Hartlepool U	W 5-1	Hood, Crosby, Walwyn, Ford, Pollard	1,971
14	Nov	2	(a)	Crewe A	L 1-2	Smith	1,633
15		6	(h)	Aldershot	W 4-0	Pollard 2 (1 pen), Byrne 2	1,743
16		13	(a)	Swindon T	L 2-3	Ford, Walwyn	4,081
17		27	(h)	Mansfield T	W 6-1	Walwyn 3, Pollard 2, Crosby	2,119
18	Dec	3	(a)	Colchester U	D 0-0		2,204
19		18	(a)	Chester	W 1-0	Walwyn	1,185
20		27	(h)	Bury	W 3-1	Opp own-goal, Pollard (pen), Walwyn	5,174
21		28	(a)	Rochdale	L 0-1		2,127
22	Jan	1	(h)	Darlington	W 5-2	Smith 2, Busby, Byrne 2	3,679
23		3	(a)	Port Vale	L 1-2	Busby	6,056
24		15	(a)	Torquay U	W 3-1	Byrne, Walwyn, Pollard	2,738
25		23	(h)	Scunthorpe U	W 2-1	Walwyn, Ford	7,097
26		29	(a)	Tranmere R	L 0-3		1,802
27	Feb	5	(a)	Peterborough U	D 2-2	Hood, Pollard (pen)	2,652
28		15	(h)	Blackpool	W 2-0	Ford, Byrne	2,937
29		19	(h)	Bristol C	W 3-0	Byrne 2, Pollard (pen)	2,879
30		26	(a)	Wimbledon	L 3-4	Opp own-goal, Walwyn, Hay	2,168
31	Mar	1	(h)	Crewe A	W 2-0	Smith, Walwyn	2,975
32		5	(h)	Stockport C	W 3-1	Ford, Pollard 2 (1 pen)	2,883
33		12	(a)	Hartlepool U	L 0-2		1,604
34		15	(h)	Northampton T	W 5-2	Ford 2, Walwyn, Pollard, Hood	2,802
35		19	(a)	Aldershot	W 3-2	Byrne, Walwyn 2	1,528
36		26	(h)	Swindon T	D 0-0		3,256
37	Apr	2	(h)	Rochdale	W 1-0	Walwyn	3,357
38		4	(a)	Bury	L 1-2	Walwyn	3,543
39		9	(h)	Colchester U	W 3-0	Busby, Pollard (pen), Senior	2,538
40		15	(a)	Halifax T	D 2-2	Pollard (pen), Sbragia	2,117
41		19	(h)	Hull C	W 1-0	Byrne	9,909
42		23	(h)	Chester	W 1-0	MacPhail	3,264
43		30	(a)	Mansfield T	D 2-2	Ford, Walwyn	2,288
44	May	2	(h)	Port Vale	D 0-0		4,814
45		7	(h)	Hereford U	W 5-1	Pollard 2, Opp own-goal, Hood, MacPhail	2,106
46		14	(a)	Darlington	W 3-1	Byrne, Hood, Walwyn	1,668

FINAL LEAGUE POSITION: 7th in Division Four

Appearances
Sub Appearances
Goals

FA Cup

1	Nov	20	(h)	Bury	W 3-1	Hood, Ford, Walwyn	3,057
2	Dec	11	(a)	Hartlepool U	D 1-1	Pollard	3,334
R		14	(h)	Hartlepool U	W 4-0	Hood, Pollard, Byrne, Ford	4,206
3	Jan	8	(a)	Crystal P	L 1-2	Walwyn	7,837

Appearances
Sub Appearances
Goals

League Cup

1	Aug	31	(h)	Lincoln C	W 2-1	Walwyn, Byrne	1,982
	Sep	15	(a)	Lincoln C	L 1-3	Opp own-goal	2,716

Appearances
Sub Appearances
Goals

Jones R	Evans C	Hay A	Sbragia R	Hood D	Laverick M	Pollard B	Ford G	Busby V	Byrne J	Crosby M	Senior S	Smith D	Walwyn K	Dawson R	Stanley T	Astbury M	MacPhail J	King D	Match
1	2	3	4	5	6	7	8	9*	10	11	12								1
1	2	3	4	6	11	7	8		10			5	9						2
1	2	3	4	6	11	8	7		10			5	9						3
1	2	3	4	6	11	6	8		10			5	9						4
1	2	3	4	6	11	7*	8		10	5	12		9						5
1	2	3	4	6	11	7*	8		10	5	12		9						6
1	2	3	4	6	11	7	8	12	10*	5			9						7
1	2	3	4	6	11	7	8		10	5			9						8
1	2		4	6		7	8	12	10	5	11*		9	3					9
1	2		4	6	11	7	8	12	10	5			9	3*					10
1	2		4	3	11	7	8	10		5		6	9						11
1	2		4	3	11	7	8	10*	12	5		6	9						12
1	2	3	4	6		11	7		10	8		5	9						13
1	2	3	4	6		11	7		10	8		5	9						14
1	2	3	4	6		11	7		10	8		5	9						15
1	2	3	4	6		11	7		10	8		5	9						16
1	2	3	4	6		11	7		10	8		5	9						17
1	2	3	4	6		11	7		10	8		5	9						18
1	2	3	4	6	7	11	10			8		5	9						19
1	2	3	4	6	12	11	7	10		8		5	9*						20
1	2	3	4	6		11	7	10*	9	8		5			12				21
	2	3	4	6	12	11	7	9	10	8*		5				1			22
	2*	3	4	6	12	11	7	9	10	8		5				1			23
1	2	3	4	6		11	7		10	8		5	9						24
1	2	3	4	6		11	7		10	8		5	9						25
1	2	3	4*	6		11	7	12	10	8		5	9						26
1	2*	3	4	6		12	7		10	8		5	9				11		27
1	2	3	4	6		11	7		10	8		5*	9				12		28
1	2	3	4	6		11	7		10	8		5	9						29
1	2	3	4	6		12	7		10	8		5	9				11*		30
1	2	3	4	6		11	7		10	8		5	9						31
1	2	3	4	6		11	7		10	8		5	9						32
	2	3	4	6		11	7		10	8		5	9			1			33
	2	3	4	6		11	7		10	8		5	9			1			34
1	2	3	4	6		11	7		10	8		5	9						35
1	2	3	4	6		11	7		10	8		5	9						36
1	2	3	4	6		11	7	12	10	8*		5	9						37
1	2	3	4	6		11	7	12	10		8*		9				5		38
1	2	3	4	6		11	7	9	10		8						5		39
1	2	3	4	6		11		7	10		8*		9				5	12	40
1	2	3	4	6		11	7		10		8		9				5		41
1	2	3	4	6		11	7		10		8		9				5		42
1	2	3	4	6		11	7		10	8			9				5		43
1	2	3	4	6		11	7*	12	10	8			9				5		44
1	2	3	4	6		11	7		10	8			9				5		45
1	2	3	4	6		11	7		10*	8	12		9				5		46
42	46	42	46	46	12	44	45	9	42	38	6	30	41	2		4	11		
					3	2		7	1		4				1		1	1	
		.	1	7	2	17	11	4	12	2	1	4	21				2		

3 own-goals

Jones R	Evans C	Hay A	Sbragia R	Hood D	Laverick M	Pollard B	Ford G	Busby V	Byrne J	Crosby M	Senior S	Smith D	Walwyn K	Dawson R	Stanley T	Astbury M	MacPhail J	King D	Match
1	2	3	4	6		11	7		10	8		5	9						1
1	2	3	4	6		11	7		10	8		5	9						2
1	2	3	4	6		11	7		10	8		5	9						R
	2	3	4	6		11	7		10	8		5	9			1			3
3	4	4	4	4		4	4		4	4		4	4			1			
				2		2	2		1				2						

Jones R	Evans C	Hay A	Sbragia R	Hood D	Laverick M	Pollard B	Ford G	Busby V	Byrne J	Crosby M	Senior S	Smith D	Walwyn K	Dawson R	Stanley T	Astbury M	MacPhail J	King D	Match
1	2	3	4	6	11	7	8		10			5	9						1
1	2	3	4	6	11	7	8		10			5	9						
2	2	2	2	2	2	2	2		2			2	2						
									1				1						

1 own-goal

1983-84

Manager: Denis Smith

1	Aug	27	(a)	Stockport C	W 2-0	MacPhail, Byrne	2,185
2	Sep	3	(h)	Rochdale	W 2-0	Ford, Walwyn	2,772
3		6	(h)	Peterborough U	W 2-0	Pollard, Byrne	3,709
4		10	(a)	Chesterfield	L 1-2	Walwyn	4,041
5		17	(h)	Chester C	W 4-1	Byrne 3, MacPhail	3,037
6		24	(a)	Darlington	D 0-0		2,181
7		27	(a)	Doncaster R	D 2-2	Byrne, Walwyn	4,996
8	Oct	1	(h)	Blackpool	W 4-0	Byrne 2, Walwyn 2	4,058
9		7	(h)	Colchester U	W 3-0	MacPhail, Pollard (pen), Walwyn	6,207
10		15	(a)	Swindon T	L 2-3	Walwyn 2	2,457
11		18	(a)	Bristol C	L 0-1		10,827
12		22	(h)	Reading	D 2-2	Pollard, Sbragia	4,315
13		29	(a)	Northampton T	W 2-1	Walwyn 2	2,956
14	Nov	1	(h)	Wrexham	W 3-2	Sbragia, Pollard 2 (1 pen)	5,641
15		5	(a)	Crewe A	W 3-0	Walwyn 2, Byrne	2,785
16		12	(h)	Torquay U	L 2-3	Hood, Ford	4,609
17		26	(a)	Hartlepool U	W 3-2	Byrne 2, Sbragia	2,022
18	Dec	3	(h)	Aldershot	W 2-0	Byrne, Pearce	3,951
19		17	(h)	Hereford U	W 4-0	Ford 2, Pearce, Byrne	2,722
20		26	(a)	Halifax T	W 2-1	Walwyn 2	2,457
21		27	(h)	Tranmere R	D 1-1	Senior	6,357
22		31	(a)	Bury	W 3-1	Walwyn, Byrne 2	3,864
23	Jan	2	(h)	Mansfield T	W 2-1	Ford, Hay	5,682
24		14	(h)	Stockport C	W 3-1	Hood (pen), MacPhail, Walwyn	3,570
25		31	(h)	Chesterfield	W 1-0	Byrne	4,782
26	Feb	4	(a)	Blackpool	L 0-3		6,010
27		11	(h)	Darlington	W 2-0	MacPhail, Ford	4,773
28		18	(h)	Northampton T	W 3-0	Walwyn, Pollard (pen), Byrne	3,941
29		25	(a)	Reading	L 0-1		4,548
30		28	(a)	Wrexham	D 0-0		1,199
31	Mar	3	(h)	Bristol C	D 1-1	Opp own-goal	5,096
32		6	(h)	Crewe A	W 5-2	Walwyn 2, Byrne, Sbragia, Pearce	4,106
33		10	(a)	Torquay U	W 3-1	Ford, Walwyn, Byrne	2,836
34		19	(a)	Colchester U	W 3-1	MacPhail, Walwyn, Pearce	3,032
35		24	(h)	Swindon T	W 2-0	Walwyn, Ford	3,341
36		27	(a)	Rochdale	W 2-0	Byrne 2	1,756
37	Apr	1	(a)	Peterborough U	W 2-0	MacPhail, Byrne	5,216
38		8	(h)	Doncaster R	D 1-1	Ford	11,297
39		14	(a)	Aldershot	W 4-1	MacPhail, Houchen, Byrne, Pearce	5,071
40		18	(a)	Chester C	D 1-1	Hood	1,850
41		20	(h)	Halifax T	W 4-1	Byrne 3, Walwyn	7,120
42		23	(a)	Tranmere R	W 1-0	Ford	3,527
43		28	(h)	Hartlepool U	W 2-0	Walwyn 2	6,063
44	May	5	(a)	Mansfield T	W 1-0	MacPhail	3,355
45		7	(h)	Bury	W 3-0	Byrne, Hood, Ford	8,026
46		12	(a)	Hereford U	L 1-2	MacPhail	4,333

FINAL LEAGUE POSITION: 1st in Division Four

Appearances
Sub Appearances
Goals

FA Cup

1	Nov	19	(a)	Macclesfield T	D 0-0		3,407
R		22	(h)	Macclesfield T	W 2-0	Sbragia, Byrne	4,963
2	Dec	13	(h)	Rochdale	L 0-2		5,203

Appearances
Sub Appearances
Goals

League Cup

1	Aug	30	(h)	Grimsby T	W 2-1	Ford, Pollard	3,505
	Sep	13	(a)	Grimsby T	L 0-2*		3,529

*After extra-time

Appearances
Sub Appearances
Goals

Jones R	Senior S	Hay A	Sbragia R	MacPhail J	Hood D	Ford G	Crosby M	Walwyn K	Byrne J	Pollard B	Haslegrave S	Evans C	Astbury M	Busby V	Pearce A	Chippendale B	Houchen K	
1	2	3	4	5	6	7	8	9	10	11								1
1	2	3	4	5		7	8	9	10	11	6							2
1	2	3	4	5		7	8	9	10	11	6							3
	2	3	4	5		7	8	9	10	11	6		1					4
	2	3	4	5		7	8	9	10	11	6		1					5
1	2	3	4	5		7*	8	9	10	11	6	12						6
1	2	3	4	5		7	8	9	10	11	6							7
1	2	3	4	5		7	8	9	10	11	6							8
1	2	3	4	5		7	8	9	10	11	6							9
	2	3	4	5		7	8	9	10	11	6		1					10
	6	3	4	5		7	8	9*	10	11		2	1	12				11
1	6	3	4	5	12	7	8	9	10	11		2*						12
1	2*	3	4	5	6	7	8	9	10	11		12						13
1	3		4	5	6	7	8	9*	10	11		2		12				14
1	3		4	5	6	7	8*	9	10	11		2		12				15
1	8	3	4	5	6	7		9	10	11		2						16
1	9	3	4	5	6	7	8		10			2			11*	12		17
1	2	3	4	5		7	8	9	10		6*	12			11			18
1	2	3	4	5	6	7	8	9	10						11			19
1	2	3	4	5	6*	7	8	9	10	11						12		20
1	6	3	4	5		7	8	9	10			2			11			21
1	2	3	4	5	6*	7	8	9	10	11						12		22
1	2	3	4	5	6	7	8	9	10	11*					12			23
1	2	3	4	5	6	7	8	9	10						11			24
1	2	3	4	5	6	7*	8	9	10	11	12							25
1	2	3	4	5	6	7	8	9	10	11								26
	2	3	4	5	6	7	8	9	10	11			1					27
1	3		4	5	6	7	8	9	10	11		2						28
1	3		4	5	6	7	8	9	10	11*	12	2						29
1	2	3	4	5	6	7	8	9	10						11			30
1	2	3	4	5	6	7	8	9	10						11			31
1	2	3	4	5	6	7		9	10		8				11			32
1	2	3	4	5	6	7		9	10		8				11			33
1	2	3	4	5	6	7		9	10		8				11			34
1	2	3	4	5	6	7		9	10		8				11			35
1	2	3	4	5	6	7		9	10	12	8				11*			36
1	2	3	4	5	6	7		9	10	11	8							37
1	2	3	4	5	6	7		9	10		8				11			38
1	2*	3	4	5	6	7		9	10		8				11		12	39
1		3	4	5	6	7		9	10		8	2			11			40
1		3	4	5	6	7		9	10	11	8*	2					12	41
1		3	4	5	6	7		9	10	11	8*	2					12	42
1		3	4	5	6	7		9	10	11*	8	2					12	43
1		3	4	5	6	7	8	9*	10	11		2					12	44
1		3		5	4	7		9	10		8	2			11	12	6*	45
1		3	4	5	6	7		9	10*		8	2			11		12	46
41	39	42	45	46	33	46	31	45	46	29	24	16	5		17		1	
					1					1	2	3		3	1	4	6	
	1	1	4	10	4	11		25	27	6					5		1	

1 own-goal

Jones R	Senior S	Hay A	Sbragia R	MacPhail J	Hood D	Ford G	Crosby M	Walwyn K	Byrne J	Pollard B	Haslegrave S	Evans C	Astbury M	Busby V	Pearce A	Chippendale B	Houchen K	
1	2	3	4	5	6	7	8		10	11				9				1
1	2	3	4	5	6	7	8		10	11*		12		9				R
1	2	3	4	5	6	7	8	9	10	11								2
3	3	3	3	3	3	3	3	1	3	3				2				
												1						
			1						1									

Jones R	Senior S	Hay A	Sbragia R	MacPhail J	Hood D	Ford G	Crosby M	Walwyn K	Byrne J	Pollard B	Haslegrave S	Evans C	Astbury M	Busby V	Pearce A	Chippendale B	Houchen K	
1	2	3	4	5	6*	7	8	9	10	11	12							1
	2	3	4	5		7	8	9	10*	11	6	12	1					
1	2	2	2	2	1	2	2	2	2	2	1		1					
											1	1						
						1				1								

1984-85

Manager: Denis Smith

1	Aug	25	(h)	Walsall	D 1-1	Walwyn	4,364
2	Sep	1	(a)	Swansea C	W 3-1	Walwyn 2, Byrne	4,211
3		8	(h)	Newport C	W 2-0	MacPhail (pen), Houchen	4,194
4		15	(a)	Orient	W 3-1	Walwyn, Byrne, Nicholson	2,473
5		18	(a)	Plymouth A	D 1-1	Walwyn	4,537
6		25	(h)	Cambridge U	W 3-2	Opp own-goals 2, Ford	4,064
7		29	(a)	Wigan A	W 2-1	Walwyn, Houchen	3,219
8	Oct	2	(h)	Bristol R	W 1-0	Walwyn	7,197
9		6	(h)	Bristol C	L 0-2		4,890
10		13	(a)	Bradford C	L 0-1		5,697
11		20	(h)	Millwall	D 1-1	Sbragia	4,774
12		23	(a)	Bournemouth	L 0-4		2,987
13		27	(a)	Brentford	L 1-2	Ford	4,261
14	Nov	3	(h)	Gillingham	W 7-1	Houchen 3, Opp own-goal, Pearce 2, Walwyn	2,921
15		6	(a)	Bolton W	L 1-2	Hood	4,672
16		11	(h)	Doncaster R	W 3-1	Houchen 2, Ford	8,540
17		24	(a)	Lincoln C	L 1-2	Banton	2,864
18	Dec	1	(h)	Reading	D 2-2	Houchen, Hood	4,015
19		15	(a)	Rotherham U	L 1-4	Banton	4,716
20		19	(a)	Preston NE	W 4-2	MacPhail, Houchen, Pearce, Banton	2,864
21		26	(h)	Burnley	W 4-0	Banton 2, Houchen, Ford	6,397
22		29	(h)	Hull C	L 1-2	Walwyn	9,665
23	Jan	1	(a)	Derby C	L 0-1		16,113
24		12	(h)	Swansea C	W 1-0	Nicholson	5,544
25	Feb	2	(h)	Wigan A	W 2-0	Ford, Pearce	10,948
26		9	(a)	Cambridge U	W 4-0	Banton 2, MacPhail (pen), Sbragia	1,925
27		12	(h)	Plymouth A	D 0-0		4,820
28		23	(a)	Gillingham	L 0-1		5,193
29		26	(a)	Walsall	L 0-3		5,031
30	Mar	2	(h)	Brentford	W 1-0	Canham	4,288
31		5	(h)	Bournemouth	W 4-1	Hood, MacPhail (pen), Banton, Opp own-goal	4,532
32		9	(a)	Millwall	L 0-1		7,542
33		17	(h)	Bradford C	L 1-2	Butler	10,442
34		20	(a)	Newport C	D 1-1	Nicholson	1,535
35		23	(a)	Bristol C	L 0-1		8,655
36		29	(h)	Bolton W	L 0-3		4,363
37	Apr	2	(h)	Orient	W 2-1	Banton, Hood	3,626
38		6	(a)	Burnley	D 1-1	Houchen	3,607
39		8	(h)	Derby C	D 1-1	MacPhail	6,797
40		15	(a)	Doncaster R	L 0-3		3,816
41		21	(h)	Lincoln C	W 2-1	Houchen, Butler	3,309
42		27	(a)	Reading	W 2-1	Banton, Nicholson	2,433
43	May	3	(h)	Rotherham U	W 3-0	Ward 2, Banton	3,551
44		6	(a)	Hull C	W 2-0	Banton, Ward	15,795
45		11	(h)	Preston NE	L 0-1		4,523
46		14	(a)	Bristol R	D 1-1	Butler	3,692

FINAL LEAGUE POSITION: 8th in Division Three

Appearances
Sub Appearances
Goals

FA Cup

1	Nov	17	(h)	Blue Star	W 2-0	Walwyn, Houchen	3,836
2	Dec	8	(a)	Hartlepool U	W 2-0	MacPhail, Houchen	8,554
3	Jan	5	(h)	Walsall	W 3-0	Butler, Walwyn, Hay	5,493
4		26	(h)	Arsenal	W 1-0	Houchen (pen)	10,840
5	Feb	16	(h)	Liverpool	D 1-1	Sbragia	13,485
R		20	(h)	Liverpool	L 0-7		43,010

Appearances
Sub Appearances
Goals

League Cup

1	Aug	28	(a)	Doncaster R	W 3-2	Byrne 2, Ford	4,632
	Sep	4	(h)	Doncaster R	W 5-0	MacPhail 2 (1 pen), Byrne, Houchen, Ford	5,554
2		25	(h)	Queen's Park R	L 2-4	Houchen, Walwyn	10,012
	Oct	9	(a)	Queen's Park R	L 1-4	Chippendale	7,544

Appearances
Sub Appearances
Goals

Jones R	Evans C	Hay A	Sbragia R	MacPhail J	Haslegrave S	Ford G	Houchen K	Walwyn K	Byrne J	Nicholson G	Hood D	Pearce A	Atkinson H	Chippendale	Senior S	Butler M	Banton D	Crosby M	Astbury M	Richards S	Canham T	Gabbiadini M	Ward W	
1	2	3	4	5	6	7	8*	9	10	11	12													1
1	2	3	4	5	6	7	8*	9	10	11	12													2
1	2	3	4	5	6	7	8	9	10	11														3
1	2	3	4	5	6	7	8	9	10	11														4
1	2	3	4	5	6	7	8	9	10	11*	12													5
1	2	3	4	5	6	7	8	9	10	11														6
1	2	3	4		6	7	8	9	10		5	11												7
1	2	3		5	6	7	8*	9	10		4	11	12											8
1	2	3	4	5	6	7		9	10	11	8*		12											9
1	2	3		5	6	7		9	10	11			4	8										10
1	2	3	4	5	8	7	10	9			6	11*				12								11
1	2	3	4	5	6	7	10	9			8*	11				12								12
1	2	3*	4	5	8	7	10	9			6	11				12								13
1	2	3	4	5	8	7	10	9			6	11												14
1	2	3	4	5	8	7	10	9		12	6	11*												15
1	2	3	4	5	8	7	10	9			6	11												16
1	2	3	4	5	8	7	10	9				11					6							17
1	2	3	4		6	7	10	9			5	11					8							18
1		3	4	5	6	7	10	9				11			2		12	8*						19
1		3	4	5	6	7	10	9				11			2		8							20
		3	4	5	6	7	10	9				11			2		8		1					21
		3	4		6	7	10	9				11			2		8		1	5				22
		3	4		6	7	10	9				11			2		8		1	5				23
		3	4	5	6	7	10	9*		11			12		2		8		1					24
		3	4	5	6	7	10*	9				11	12		2		8		1					25
		3	4	5	6	7						11	10		2	9	8		1					26
		3	4	5	6	7						11	10		2	9	8		1					27
1		3		5	6	7		9			10	11			2		8			4				28
1		3		5	6	7		9*			10	11			2	12	8			4				29
1		3		5	6	7					10			12	2	9	8			4*	11			30
1		3		5	6	7					4				2	9	8	10			11			31
1		3		5	6	7					4			12	2	9	8	10			11*			32
1		3		5	6	7	10			11	4				2	9	8							33
1		3		5	6					11	4			7	2	9	8	10						34
1		3		5	6*					11	4	7			2	9	8	10		12				35
1		3		5	6	7	10			11	9				2		8*			4		12		36
1		3		5	6	7	10			11	4	9			2		8							37
1		3		5		7	10			11	4	8*			2	12	9	6						38
1		3		5	6	7	10			11	4				2	12	8*	9						39
1		3		5	6	7	10			11	4				2	12	8	9*						40
1	3	12		5	6	7	10			11*	4				2	9	8							41
1	3			5	6	7	10			11	4				2	9	8							42
1	3	12		5	6	7	10			11	4				2		8						9*	43
1	3	12		5		7	10			11	4*				2		8	6					9	44
1	3	4		5		7	10			11					2	12	8	6					9*	45
1	3	4		5		7	10			11*					2	12	8	6					9	46
39	24	42	25	42	42	44	35	27	10	23	27	23	3	2	28	10	29	11	7	6	3		4	
		3								1	3		4	2		9	1			1		1		
			2	5		5	12	9	2	4	4	4				3	12				1		3	
																								4 own-goals
1	2	3	4	5	6	7	10	9			8	11												1
1		3	4	5	6	7	10	9				11			2			8						2
		3	4	5	6	7	10	9		11					2	8			1					3
		3	4	5	6	7	10	9				11			2	8			1					4
		3	4	5	6	7		9			10	11			2	8			1					5
		3	4	5	6	7	10*	9			12	11			2	8			1					R
2	1	6	6	6	6	6	5	6		1	2	5			5	4		1	4					
											1													
		1	1	1			3	2								1								
1	2	3	4	5	6	7	8	9	10	11														1
1	2	3	4	5	6*	7	8	9	10	11	12													
1	2	3	4	5	6	7	8	9	10	11*	12													2
1	2	3		5	6*	7		9	10	11			4	8	12									
4	4	4	3	4	4	4	3	4	4	4			1	1										
											2				1									
				2		2	2	1	3					1										

1985-86

Manager: Denis Smith

1	Aug	17	(h)	Plymouth A	W 3-1	Canham, Walwyn, Gabbiadini	4,242
2		24	(a)	Bury	L 2-4	MacPhail (pen), Walwyn	2,782
3		26	(h)	Wigan A	W 4-1	Walwyn 2, Ford 2	4,067
4		31	(a)	Wolves	L 2-3	MacPhail (pen), Walwyn	4,400
5	Sep	7	(h)	Cardiff C	D 1-1	Evans	3,760
6		14	(a)	Blackpool	W 2-0	Walwyn, Canham	4,053
7		17	(a)	Notts C	L 1-3	Walwyn	3,708
8		21	(h)	Bristol C	D 1-1	MacPhail (pen)	3,904
9		28	(a)	Gillingham	W 2-1	Banton, McAughtrie	3,509
10	Oct	1	(h)	Bolton W	W 3-0	Houchen 2, Banton	4,680
11		5	(h)	Darlington	W 7-0	Canham 3 (1 pen), Walwyn 2, Houchen, Senior	5,039
12		12	(a)	Chesterfield	L 0-1		3,723
13		19	(a)	Derby C	L 1-2	Houchen (pen)	11,157
14		22	(h)	Bournemouth	W 2-1	Walwyn, Ford	4,194
15		26	(h)	Rotherham U	W 2-1	Banton 2	4,444
16	Nov	2	(a)	Bristol R	W 1-0	Banton	4,174
17		6	(a)	Newport C	D 1-1	Ford	1,529
18		9	(h)	Reading	L 0-1		6,045
19		24	(a)	Lincoln C	W 4-3	Banton 2, Senior, Walwyn	2,295
20		30	(h)	Brentford	W 1-0	Walwyn	3,674
21	Dec	14	(a)	Swansea C	L 0-1		2,779
22		20	(h)	Bury	D 0-0		3,645
23		26	(h)	Doncaster R	L 0-1		5,472
24	Jan	1	(a)	Walsall	L 1-3	MacPhail	5,643
25		11	(h)	Wolves	W 2-1	Houchen, Banton	4,290
26		18	(a)	Plymouth A	D 2-2	Walwyn 2	5,942
27		31	(a)	Cardiff C	L 1-2	Walwyn	2,051
28	Feb	4	(a)	Bournemouth	L 0-2		2,476
29		8	(h)	Derby C	L 1-3	Houchen (pen)	5,994
30		22	(a)	Bristol C	D 2-2	MacPhail (pen), Canham	6,409
31	Mar	1	(h)	Gillingham	W 2-0	Opp own-goals 2	4,351
32		4	(a)	Bolton W	D 1-1	Walwyn	3,589
33		9	(a)	Darlington	L 0-1		4,255
34		12	(h)	Bristol R	W 4-0	Canham 2, Walwyn, Gabbiadini	2,857
35		15	(h)	Chesterfield	W 2-0	Hood, Gabbiadini	3,580
36		18	(a)	Wigan A	L 0-1		4,307
37		22	(a)	Rotherham U	L 1-4	Gabbiadini	3,240
38		29	(h)	Walsall	W 1-0	Walwyn	3,695
39		31	(a)	Doncaster R	D 1-1	Hay	3,319
40	Apr	5	(h)	Newport C	W 3-1	Walwyn 2, Canham	3,038
41		12	(a)	Reading	D 0-0		6,133
42		19	(h)	Lincoln C	W 2-1	Canham, MacPhail (pen)	3,874
43		22	(h)	Notts C	D 2-2	Walwyn, MacPhail (pen)	3,211
44		26	(a)	Brentford	D 3-3	Banton (pen), Mills, Senior	2,364
45	May	3	(h)	Swansea C	W 3-1	Walwyn, Banton, Canham	3,132
46		6	(h)	Blackpool	W 3-0	Canham 2, Banton	3,370

FINAL LEAGUE POSITION: 7th in Division Three

Appearances
Sub Appearances
Goals

FA Cup

1	Nov	16	(h)	Morecambe	D 0-0		3,696
R		19	(n*)	Morecambe	W 2-0	Sbragia, Walwyn	1,305
2	Dec	7	(h)	Whitby T	W 3-1	Ford, Walwyn, Pearce	6,229
3	Jan	4	(h)	Wycombe W	W 2-0	Walwyn 2	5,546
4		25	(h)	Altrincham	W 2-0	Banton, Ford	8,842
5	Feb	15	(h)	Liverpool	D 1-1	Ford	12,752
R		18	(a)	Liverpool	L 1-3†	Canham	29,362

*Played at Maine Road, Manchester. †After extra-time.

Appearances
Sub Appearances
Goals

League Cup

1	Aug	20	(h)	Lincoln C	W 2-1	Walwyn, McAughtrie	3,630
	Sep	4	(a)	Lincoln C	W 2-1	MacPhail (pen), Walwyn	2,259
2		24	(a)	Grimsby T	D 1-1	Walwyn	2,908
	Oct	8	(h)	Grimsby T	L 2-3	Houchen (pen), Banton	5,030

Appearances
Sub Appearances
Goals

Astbury M	Hood D	Evans C	McAughtrie D	MacPhail J	Haslegrave S	Ford G	Gabbiadini M	Walwyn K	Houchen K	Canham T	Mills S	Banton D	Senior S	Hay A	Leaning A	Sbragia R	Pearce A	Butler M	McKenzie S	
1	2	3	4	5	6	7	8*	9	10	11	12									1
1	2	3	4	5	6	7		9	10*	11		8	12							2
1	2	3	4*	5	6	7	12	9		11	10	8								3
1	2	3	4	5	6	7		9	12	11*	10	8								4
1	2	3	4	5	6*	7		9	12	11	10	8								5
1	2	3	4	5	6	7		9		11	10	8								6
1	2	3	4	5	6*	7		9	12	11	10	8								7
1			4	5	6	7	12	9	10	11	8		2*	3						8
1			4	5	6	7		9	10	11		8	2	3						9
1			4	5	6	7		9	10	11		8	2	3						10
1	12		4*	5	6	7		9	10	11		8	2	3						11
1			4	5	6	7		9	10	11		8	2	3						12
1			4	5	6	7		9	10	11		8	2	3						13
1			4	5	6	7	12	9		11	10*	8	2	3						14
1			4	5	6	7		9		11	10	8	2	3						15
1*			4	5	6	7		9	12	11	10	8	2	3						16
			4	5	6	7		9		11	10	8	2	3	1					17
				5	6	7		9	12	11*	10	8	2	3	1	4				18
	12			5		7		9*	10		6	8	2	3	1	4	11			19
				5		7		9	10		6	8	2	3	1	4	11			20
			4	5		7		9	10		6	8	2	3	1		11			21
	2		4	5		7	12	9	10		6	8		3	1		11*			22
			4	5		7	12	9	10		6	8	2	3	1		11*			23
	3		4	5	6	7	12	9	10	11		8*	2		1					24
	3		4	5	12	7		9*	10	11	6	8	2		1					25
	3		4	5		7		9	10	11	6	8	2		1					26
	3		4	5		7		9	10	11	6	8	2		1					27
	3		4	5	12	7		9	10	11*	6	8	2		1					28
	3		4	5	11	7		9	10	12	6	8*	2		1					29
	3		4	5	10	7		9		11	6	8*	2		1			12		30
	3		4	5	10	7	12	9		11	6		2		1			8*		31
	3		4		10	7	12	9		11	6		2	5	1			8*		32
	3		4		10	7	12	9	8	11	6		2*	5	1					33
	3		4	5	10*	7	8	9		11	6				1			12	2	34
	3		4	5	10	7	8	9		11	6				1				2	35
	3		4	5	10	7	8*	9		11	6				1			12	2	36
	3		4	5	10	7	8	9		11*	6				1			12	2	37
	3*		4	5	10	7	8	9		11	6		2		1			12		38
			4	5	10	7	8	9		11*	6		2	3	1			12		39
	2		4		10		8	9		11	6	12		3	1	5		7*		40
			4	5	10	7	8*	9		11	6	12	2	3	1					41
	3		4	5	10		12	9		11		8*	2		1		6	7		42
	3			5	10		12	9		11		8	2		1	4	6*	7		43
	3		5		10			9		11	6	8	2		1	4		7		44
	3			5	10		12	9		11	6*	8	2		1	4		7		45
	3		4	5	6		8	9		11		10	2		1			7		46
16	29	7	41	42	37	40	10	46	20	40	35	33	33	21	30	7	7	8	4	
	2				2		12		5	1	1	2	1					6		
	1	1	1	7		4	4	22	6	13	1	11	3	1						

2 own-goals

Astbury M	Hood D	Evans C	McAughtrie D	MacPhail J	Haslegrave S	Ford G	Gabbiadini M	Walwyn K	Houchen K	Canham T	Mills S	Banton D	Senior S	Hay A	Leaning A	Sbragia R	Pearce A	Butler M	McKenzie S	
				5	6	7		9	12	11*	10	8	2	3	1	4				1
				5		7		9	10		6	8	2	3	1	4	11			R
	2		4	5		7		9	10		6	8		3	1		11			2
	3		4	5	6	7		9	10	11		8	2		1					3
	3		4	5		7		9	10	11	6	8	2		1					4
	3		4	5	10	7		9		11	6	8	2		1					5
	3		4	5	10*	7		9	12	11	6	8	2		1					R
	5		5	7	4	7		7	4	5	6	7	6	3	7	2	2			
									2											
						3		4		1		1				1	1			

Astbury M	Hood D	Evans C	McAughtrie D	MacPhail J	Haslegrave S	Ford G	Gabbiadini M	Walwyn K	Houchen K	Canham T	Mills S	Banton D	Senior S	Hay A	Leaning A	Sbragia R	Pearce A	Butler M	McKenzie S	
1	2	3	4	5	6	7	12	9	10	11		8*								1
1	2	3	4	5	6	7		9		11	10	8								
1	12		4	5	6	7		9	10	11	8*		2	3						2
1			4	5	6	7		9	10	11		8	2	3						
4	2	2	4	4	4	4		4	3	4	2	3	2	2						
	1						1													
			1	1				3	1			1								

1986-87

Manager: Denis Smith

1	Aug	23	(h)	Darlington	W 3-1	Hood (pen), Canham, Ford	4,382
2		30	(a)	Carlisle U	D 2-2	Banton, Walwyn	3,593
3	Sep	6	(h)	Bristol R	W 1-0	Canham	3,795
4		13	(a)	Port Vale	W 3-2	Walwyn 2, Gabbiadini	4,843
5		16	(a)	Gillingham	L 0-2		4,115
6		20	(h)	Bury	W 1-0	Hood	3,800
7		27	(a)	Doncaster R	L 1-3	Gabbiadini	3,358
8		30	(h)	Bournemouth	W 2-0	Walwyn 2	3,770
9	Oct	4	(h)	Mansfield T	L 1-3	Ford	4,158
10		11	(a)	Bristol C	L 0-3		7,951
11		18	(a)	Brentford	L 1-3	Banton	3,457
12		21	(h)	Chester C	D 1-1	Canham	3,322
13		25	(h)	Rotherham U	W 2-1	Walwyn, Banton	3,216
14	Nov	1	(a)	Swindon T	L 1-3	Banton	6,297
15		4	(a)	Newport C	D 1-1	Walwyn	2,079
16		8	(h)	Chesterfield	D 1-1	Gabbiadini	3,225
17		22	(h)	Walsall	L 1-5	Hood (pen)	3,149
18		29	(a)	Bolton W	L 1-3	Gabbiadini (pen)	4,528
19	Dec	13	(a)	Notts C	L 1-5	Canham	3,614
20		20	(h)	Fulham	D 1-1	Gabbiadini (pen)	2,670
21		26	(a)	Blackpool	L 1-2	Gabbiadini (pen)	4,515
22		27	(h)	Wigan A	D 1-1	Canham	3,238
23	Jan	1	(h)	Middlesbrough	W 3-1	Butler, Walwyn 2	8,611
24		23	(a)	Bristol R	L 0-1		2,597
25	Feb	7	(h)	Gillingham	W 2-1	Walwyn, Gabbiadini	2,845
26		14	(a)	Bury	L 0-1		2,521
27		21	(h)	Doncaster R	D 1-1	Banton	2,807
28		24	(a)	Darlington	D 2-2	Ford, Gabbiadini	1,648
29		28	(a)	Bournemouth	L 0-3		5,804
30	Mar	3	(h)	Swindon T	L 0-3		2,561
31		7	(a)	Rotherham U	D 0-0		2,465
32		14	(h)	Brentford	W 2-1	Walwyn, Gabbiadini	2,426
33		18	(a)	Chester C	L 1-2	Canham	2,325
34		21	(h)	Bristol C	D 1-1	Canham	2,874
35		24	(a)	Walsall	L 2-3	Canham, Mills	3,811
36		28	(a)	Mansfield T	D 1-1	Walwyn	2,326
37		31	(h)	Carlisle U	W 2-0	Walwyn 2	2,557
38	Apr	4	(a)	Chesterfield	L 0-1		2,120
39		11	(h)	Newport C	W 3-0	Ford, Walwyn 2	2,202
40		14	(h)	Port Vale	L 1-4	Banton (pen)	2,804
41		18	(a)	Middlesbrough	L 1-3	Walwyn	10,546
42		20	(h)	Blackpool	D 1-1	Pickering	2,694
43		25	(a)	Fulham	L 0-1		4,107
44	May	2	(h)	Bolton W	W 2-1	Butler, Canham	4,079
45		4	(a)	Wigan A	L 2-3	Walwyn 2	3,816
46		9	(h)	Notts C	D 1-1	Butler	3,760

FINAL LEAGUE POSITION: 20th in Division Three

Appearances
Sub Appearances
Goals

FA Cup

1	Nov	15	(h)	Crewe A	W 3-1	Mills, Banton, Walwyn	3,889
2	Dec	6	(a)	Caernarfon	D 0-0		1,976
R		9	(h)	Caernarfon	L 1-2	Canham	3,851

Appearances
Sub Appearances
Goals

League Cup

1	Aug	26	(a)	Sunderland	W 4-2	Mills, Walwyn 3	9,162
	Sep	2	(h)	Sunderland	L 1-3*	Walwyn	6,524
2		23	(h)	Chelsea	W 1-0	Canham	7,436
	Oct	7	(a)	Chelsea	L 0-3		9,927

* After extra-time, won on away-goals rule

Appearances
Sub Appearances
Goals

Leaning A	Senior S	Hood D	Sbragia R	Pickering M	Haslegrave S	Ford G	Banton D	Walwyn K	Mills S	Canham T	Gabbiadini M	McAughtrie D	Butler M	McKenzie S	Murray S	Whitehead A	Pearce A	Smallwood N	Costello N	Lowey J	
1	2	3	4	5	6	7	8	9	10	11											1
1	2	3	4	5	6		8	9	10	11			7								2
1		3	4	5	6*	7		9	10	11	8		12	2							3
1		3	4	5		7	8	9	10	11	6			2							4
1	2	3	4	5		7	8	9	10	11	6										5
1	2	3	4	5		7	8	9	10	11	6*			12							6
1	2	3	4	5		7	8	9	10	11	6										7
1	2	3	4	5		7	8	9	10	11	6*				12						8
1	2	3	4	5		7	8*		10	11	6		12		9						9
1	2	6	4			7	8		10	11	9*	5	12	3							10
1	2	6		5*		7	8		10	11	9	4	12	3							11
1	2	3				7	8		10	11	12	4	9		6*	5					12
1	2	3				7	8	9	10	11		4				5	6				13
1	2	3			6	7	8	9	10	11		4				5					14
1	2	3			6	7	8*	9	10		12	4				5	11				15
1	2	3			6	7	8*	9	10		12	4				5	11				16
1	2	3			6	7	8*	9	10	11	12	4				5					17
	2				7*	11		9	10	12	8	4		3		5	6	1			18
	2	3	4		12	7		9	10	11	8*	5					6	1			19
1	2		4		6	7		9	10	11	8*	5	12				3				20
1	2		4		6	7		9	10	11	8	5					3				21
1	2		4		6	7		9	10	11	8	5*	12				3				22
1	2*	12	4	5	6	7		9	10	11			8				3				23
1	2	12	4	5	6	7		9		11	10		8*				3				24
1	2	11	4	5	6	7		9	10		8						3				25
1	2	11	4	5*	6	7	12	9	10		8						3				26
1	2	11	4	5*	6	7	12	9	10		8						3				27
1	2	11	4	5	6	7*	12	9	10		8						3				28
1	2	11	4	5	6	7*	12	9	10		8						3				29
1	2		4		6	7	8	9	10	11						5	3				30
1	2		4	12	6	7		9	10	11	8					5	3*				31
1				4	6	7		9	10	11	8			2		5	3				32
1				4	6	7		9	10	11	8			2		5	3				33
1	3	12		4	6	7		9	10	11	8*	5		2							34
1	3			4	6	7	8	9	10	11*		5		2			12				35
1	2			4	6	7	8	9	10	11		5					3				36
1	2			4	6	7	8	9	10	11		5					3				37
1	2			4	6	7	8	9	10	11*		5					3			12	38
1	2			4	6	7	8	9	10	11		5					3				39
1	2		4	5	6	7	8	9	10	11*							3			12	40
1			5	4	6	7	8*	9	10	12				2			3			11	41
	3		4	5	6*	7		9	10	11			8	2				1		12	42
				4		7	12	9	10			5	8	2			3	1	11*	6	43
				4	6	7		9	10	11		5	8	2			3	1			44
				4	6	7		9	10	11	12	5	8	2*			3	1			45
		4			6	7		9	10	11		5	8				3	1		2	46
39	37	24	26	31	34	45	24	42	45	36	24	23	9	14	2	11	29	7	1	3	
		3		1	1		5			2	5		6	1	1		1			3	
		3		1		4	6	19	1	9	9		3								

Leaning A	Senior S	Hood D	Sbragia R	Pickering M	Haslegrave S	Ford G	Banton D	Walwyn K	Mills S	Canham T	Gabbiadini M	McAughtrie D	Butler M	McKenzie S	Murray S	Whitehead A	Pearce A	Smallwood N	Costello N	Lowey J	
1	2	3			6	7	8	9	10	11		4				5					1
	2	3	4			7	8*	9	10	11		5	12				6	1			2
	2	3	4			7	8*	9	10	11		5	12				6	1			R
1	3	3	2		1	3	3	3	3	3		3				1	2	2			
													2								
							1	1	1	1											

Leaning A	Senior S	Hood D	Sbragia R	Pickering M	Haslegrave S	Ford G	Banton D	Walwyn K	Mills S	Canham T	Gabbiadini M	McAughtrie D	Butler M	McKenzie S	Murray S	Whitehead A	Pearce A	Smallwood N	Costello N	Lowey J	
1	2	3	4	5	6	7*	8	9	10	11	12										1
1	2*	3	4†	5	6	7	8	9	10	11	12	13									
1		3	4	5		7	8	9	10	11	6			2							2
1	2	3	4	5		7	8*	9	10	11	6†		13	12							
4	3	4	4	4	2	4	4	4	4	4	2			1							
											2	1	1	1							
								4	1	1											

1987-88

Manager: Bobby Saxton

1	Aug	15	(a)	Brighton & HA	L 0-1		6,068
2		22	(h)	Notts C	L 3-5	Whitehead, Canham, Banton	2,878
3		29	(a)	Chester C	L 0-1		2,010
4		31	(h)	Walsall	L 1-3	Banton	2,661
5	Sep	5	(a)	Port Vale	L 1-2	Canham	2,711
6		12	(h)	Preston NE	D 1-1	Hood (pen)	3,237
7		16	(a)	Bristol R	L 1-2	Banton	3,177
8		19	(a)	Gillingham	L 1-3	M.Gabbiadini	5,507
9		26	(h)	Doncaster R	D 1-1	Cook (pen)	2,702
10		29	(h)	Blackpool	L 1-3	Buchanan	2,559
11	Oct	3	(a)	Wigan A	D 1-1	Banton (pen)	2,878
12		10	(a)	Fulham	L 1-3	Buchanan	4,057
13		17	(h)	Aldershot	D 2-2	Banton 2	1,984
14		20	(h)	Rotherham U	L 1-2	Hood (pen)	1,932
15		24	(a)	Sunderland	L 2-4	Banton, Mills	19,314
16		31	(h)	Chesterfield	W 1-0	Banton	2,316
17	Nov	4	(a)	Northampton T	D 0-0		4,960
18		7	(h)	Bury	D 1-1	Helliwell	2,641
19		21	(a)	Grimsby T	L 1-5	Mills	2,500
20		28	(h)	Southend U	L 0-3		2,225
21	Dec	12	(a)	Bristol C	L 2-3	Banton 2	6,328
22		18	(h)	Brentford	D 1-1	Clegg	1,801
23		26	(a)	Doncaster R	L 0-2		2,409
24		28	(h)	Mansfield T	D 2-2	Banton (pen), Helliwell	2,781
25	Jan	1	(h)	Chester C	W 2-0	Clegg, Wilson	2,686
26		2	(a)	Preston NE	L 0-3		6,302
27		9	(a)	Notts C	L 0-3		5,924
28		16	(h)	Gillingham	L 0-2		2,129
29		30	(a)	Walsall	L 1-2	Banton	4,371
30	Feb	6	(h)	Port Vale	L 2-3	Himsworth, Banton (pen)	2,420
31		13	(a)	Mansfield T	L 1-2	Helliwell	2,749
32		20	(h)	Brighton & HA	L 0-2		2,576
33		27	(h)	Wigan A	W 3-1	Helliwell, Banton 2	2,366
34	Mar	1	(a)	Blackpool	L 1-2	Bradshaw	2,249
35		5	(a)	Aldershot	W 2-1	Helliwell, Hood	2,672
36		12	(h)	Fulham	L 1-3	Hood	2,560
37		19	(a)	Chesterfield	L 1-2	Himsworth	1,966
38		26	(h)	Sunderland	W 2-1	Helliwell, Banton	9,183
39	Apr	2	(a)	Bury	W 1-0	Clegg	2,277
40		4	(h)	Grimsby T	L 0-2		3,215
41		8	(a)	Rotherham U	W 1-0	Branagan	2,942
42		15	(h)	Bristol R	L 0-4		1,834
43		25	(h)	Northampton T	D 2-2	Howlett 2	2,048
44		29	(a)	Southend U	L 1-3	Helliwell	3,768
45	May	2	(h)	Bristol C	L 0-1		2,616
46		7	(a)	Brentford	W 2-1	Helliwell, Staniforth	4,180

FINAL LEAGUE POSITION: 23rd in Division Three

Appearances
Sub Appearances
Goals

FA Cup

1	Nov	14	(h)	Burton A	D 0-0		3,140
R		18	(a)	Burton A	W 2-1	Hood (pen), Mills	4,381
2	Dec	5	(h)	Hartlepool U	D 1-1	Wilson	3,394
R		9	(a)	Hartlepool U	L 1-3	Banton	4,067

Appearances
Sub Appearances
Goals

League Cup

1	Aug	18	(a)	Halifax T	D 1-1	M.Gabbiadini	1,359
		25	(h)	Halifax T	W 1-0	Hood (pen)	2,382
2	Sep	23	(a)	Leeds U	D 1-1	Buchanan	11,527
	Oct	6	(h)	Leeds U	L 0-4		6,059

Appearances
Sub Appearances
Goals

Endersby S	McKenzie S	Johnson P	Wilson P	Whitehead A	Clegg T	Himsworth G	Hood D	Gabbiadini M	Butler M	Canham T	Banton D	Kitching P	Tutill S	Smallwood N	Cook M	Costello N	Mills S	Buchanan D	Branagan J	Spofforth D	Downing D	Helliwell I	Staniforth G	Brough P	Bradshaw D	Stowell M	McMillan A	Rogers L	Gabbiadini R	Howlett G	
1	2	3	4	5	6	7†	8	9	10*	11	12	13																			1
1	2	3	4	5	6		8	9*	7	11	10	12																			2
1	2	3	4	5	6		8	9	7	11*	10		12																		3
	2	3	4	5	6		12	9	7*	11	10			1	8																4
	7*	3	4	5	6		2	9		11	10			1	8		12														5
1		3	4	5	6		2	9		11	10				8		7														6
1	7	3	4*	5	6		2	9		12	10				8		11														7
1	11	3		5	6	12	2	9			10	4*			8		7														8
1	12	3	4	5		11					10*		6		8		7	9	2												9
1	9*	3	4	5		11	8					12	6				7	10	2												10
1		3	4	5	6						10	8	11				7	9	2												11
1		3	4	5	6				12		10		11			7*	8	9	2												12
1		3	4	5	6						10		11				8	9	2		7										13
1	7	3	4		6		5				10		11				8	9	2												14
1	7†	3	4	5	6		12				10		11				8		2*			9	13								15
1		3	4	5	6						10		11				8		2			9	7								16
1		3	4	5	6		2						11				8	10				9	7								17
1		3	4	5	6		2				10		11				8					9	7								18
1				5	6		3*				10	4	11				8		2			9	7†	13	12						19
1			4	5		11*	2				10		6				7		3			9	12		8						20
		3	4	5	12	13	2†			11	10		6*	1			7					9			8						21
		3*	4	5	6	13				11†	10			1			8		12			9	7		2						22
			4	5	6	7	3				10	12							2			9	11		8*	1					23
			4	5	6	7					10*	8				12			2	3†		9	11			1	13				24
			4	5*	6	7						10							2			9	11		8	1	12	3			25
			4		6	7*						10				12			2			9	11†		8	1	5	3	13		26
			4	5	12	7					10								2			9	11		8	1	6	3*			27
		3	4	5	6	7						10										9	11		8	1	2				28
		3	4	5		7*				11	10			1								9	12		8†		2	13		6	29
		3	4	5		8				11*	10	13		1								9†	12				2	6		7	30
1		3	4			8	5			11	10											9					2	6		7	31
1		3	4†	5		11*				12	10								6			9			8		2	13		7	32
1		4				11	5			12	10								3	6*		9			8		2			7	33
1		3				11*	5			12	10								6	4		9			8		2			7	34
1		3			4	11	5				10								6			9			8		2			7	35
1		3			4	11	5				10								6			9			8		2			7	36
1		3	13		6	11	5†			12	10								4			9*			8		2			7	37
1		3			4	11					10		5						6			9			8		2			7	38
1		3	12		4	11	13			10			5†						6			9			8*		2			7	39
1		3	12	13	4	11	5			10†									6			9			8*		2			7	40
1		3	10		4	11	5												6			9			8		2			7	41
1		3	10		4	11	12						5						6*			9			8		2			7	42
1		3	10*		4	11	6					12	5									9	2		8					7	43
1		3			4	11							5						2			9	10		8		6			7	44
1	6	3			4	11							5									9	10		8		2			7	45
1	6	3			4	11							5									9	10		8		2			7	46
34	12	39	33	29	35	28	24	8	4	13	32	7	20	6	6	1	17	7	27	3	1	32	15		24	6	20	5		18	
	1		3	1	2	3	4		1	5	1	6	1			2	1		1				4	1	1		2	2	1		
			1	1	3	2	4	1		2	16				1		2	2	1			8	1		1					2	

Endersby S	McKenzie S	Johnson P	Wilson P	Whitehead A	Clegg T	Himsworth G	Hood D	Gabbiadini M	Butler M	Canham T	Banton D	Kitching P	Tutill S	Smallwood N	Cook M	Costello N	Mills S	Buchanan D	Branagan J	Spofforth D	Downing D	Helliwell I	Staniforth G	Brough P	Bradshaw D	
1		3	4		6		5				10	2	11				8						7	9		1
1			4	5	6		11				10		3				8		2				7	9		R
		3	4	5							10		6	1			7		2				11	9	8	2
		3	4	5			12				10		6	1			7		2*				11	9	8	R
2		3	4	3	2		2				4	1	4	2			4		3				4	4	2	
							1																			
			1				1				1						1									

Endersby S	McKenzie S	Johnson P	Wilson P	Whitehead A	Clegg T	Himsworth G	Hood D	Gabbiadini M	Butler M	Canham T	Banton D	Kitching P	Tutill S	Smallwood N	Cook M	Costello N	Mills S	Buchanan D	
1	2	3		5	6		8	9	7	11	10	4							1
1	2	3	4	5	6		8	9	7	11	10								
1	9	3	4	5		11	2				10	7*	6				8	12	2
1		3	4	5	6		2				10	8	11				7	9	
4	3	4	3	4	3	1	4	2	2	2	4	3	2				2	1	
																		1	
							1	1										1	

1988-89

Manager: Bobby Saxton until 17 September, Barry Swallow (caretaker manager), then John Bird from 10 October 1988.

1	Aug	27	(a)	Colchester U	L 0-1		1,664
2	Sep	3	(h)	Carlisle U	D 1-1	Banton (pen)	2,303
3		10	(a)	Burnley	L 0-6		7,238
4		17	(h)	Scunthorpe U	L 1-2	Howlett	2,735
5		20	(h)	Hartlepool U	L 2-3	Bradshaw, Banton	2,611
6		24	(a)	Peterborough U	W 1-0	Helliwell	2,756
7	Oct	1	(h)	Halifax T	W 5-3	Butler, Bradshaw, Canham, Banton (pen), Howlett	2,238
8		4	(a)	Leyton O	L 0-4		2,467
9		7	(a)	Tranmere R	W 1-0	Canham	3,054
10		15	(h)	Darlington	W 4-1	Butler 2, Canham, Banton	2,851
11		22	(a)	Grimsby T	L 0-2		2,825
12		25	(h)	Doncaster R	D 1-1	Dunn	2,957
13		29	(a)	Wrexham	L 1-2	Smith	2,014
14	Nov	5	(h)	Torquay U	D 1-1	Eli	2,007
15		8	(h)	Crewe A	W 3-0	Dunn, Johnson, Wilson	1,980
16		11	(a)	Stockport C	L 2-3	Dunn, Smith	2,477
17		26	(a)	Rochdale	L 0-2		1,880
18	Dec	3	(h)	Hereford U	W 4-1	Helliwell 2, Canham, Himsworth	1,698
19		16	(h)	Rotherham U	D 1-1	Spooner	2,656
20		26	(a)	Scarborough	D 0-0		5,057
21		31	(a)	Exeter C	L 0-2		3,092
22	Jan	2	(h)	Lincoln C	W 2-1	Smith, Dixon	3,589
23		14	(a)	Carlisle U	D 0-0		3,462
24		21	(h)	Colchester U	W 2-0	Dixon, Howlett	2,219
25		28	(a)	Scunthorpe U	L 2-4	Canham 2	4,196
26	Feb	4	(a)	Hartlepool U	W 1-0	Helliwell	2,863
27		11	(h)	Peterborough U	W 5-1	Helliwell 2, Spooner, Canham, Dixon	2,438
28		18	(h)	Tranmere R	L 0-1		2,923
29		25	(a)	Darlington	D 2-2	Dixon, Helliwell	2,504
30		28	(a)	Doncaster R	W 2-1	Greenough, Smith	1,526
31	Mar	4	(h)	Grimsby T	L 0-3		3,481
32		14	(h)	Wrexham	W 1-0	Spooner (pen)	2,006
33		18	(h)	Burnley	D 0-0		3,164
34		25	(a)	Lincoln C	L 1-2	Himsworth	3,710
35		27	(h)	Scarborough	D 0-0		4,872
36	Apr	1	(a)	Rotherham U	W 1-0	Canham	5,926
37		4	(a)	Cambridge U	D 1-1	Reid	2,668
38		8	(h)	Exeter C	W 3-1	Spooner, Dunn, Helliwell	2,052
39		14	(a)	Halifax T	D 0-0		1,875
40		22	(h)	Leyton O	D 1-1	Dunn	2,744
41		25	(a)	Torquay U	L 0-2		2,015
42		29	(h)	Rochdale	D 3-3	Canham, Tutill, Dunn	1,920
43	May	1	(a)	Crewe A	W 2-1	Reid, Helliwell	3,693
44		6	(a)	Hereford U	W 2-1	Smith, Howlett	1,819
45		9	(h)	Cambridge U	L 1-2	Spooner (pen)	2,336
46		13	(h)	Stockport C	W 2-0	Helliwell 2	2,327

FINAL LEAGUE POSITION: 11th in Division Four

Appearances
Sub Appearances
Goals

FA Cup

1	Nov	19	(a)	Halifax T	L 0-1		2,894

Appearances
Sub Appearances
Goals

League Cup

1	Aug	30	(h)	Sunderland	D 0-0		4,204
	Sep	6	(a)	Sunderland	L 0-4		9,388

Appearances
Sub Appearances
Goals

Marples C	Bradshaw D	Johnson P	Wilson P	Fazackerley D	Smith K	Howlett G	Spooner S	Helliwell I	Banton D	Himsworth G	Canham T	Branagan J	Tutill S	Butler M	Clegg T	Hotte T	Dunn I	Shaw A	McMillan A	Morris N	Eli R	Greenough R	Dixon K	Hay A	Reid S	Endersby S	Hurlstone G	Barratt T	Hall W	
1	2	3	4*	5	6	7	8	9	10	11	12	2																		1
1				6		7	8	9	10	11*	4	2	5	12	3															2
1	4	3	12	6	5	7		9	10†	11		2		13	8*															3
1	4	3		6		7		9	10*	11		3	5	12		8														4
1	2	4		6		8		9	10		11	3	5*	7	12															5
1	2	4		6	5	8		9	10		11	3		7																6
1	2	4		6		8		9	10		11*	3	5	7		12														7
1	2	4		6	12	8		9	10		11	3	5*	7																8
1	2	4		6		8		9	10		11	3	5	7																9
1	2	4	12	6		8		9†	10		11	3	5*	7			13													10
1	2	4	13	6		8†		9*	10		11	3		7	5		12													11
1	2	4†	12	6	5					10*	11	3		7			9	8	13											12
1	2	4	13	6	5					10†	11	3		7*			9	8	12											13
1	2	3	8	6	5					7*	11						10	4		9	12									14
1	2	3	8	6	5						11						10	4		9	7									15
1	2	3	8	6	5*					13	11	12					10	4		9	7†									16
1		3	8		6			9		7	11		5							12	4	2	10*							17
1	4	3			5		8	9		7	11		6									2	10							18
1	4				6		8	9		7	11	2										5	10	3						19
1	2	3			6		8	9		7	11											5	10		4					20
1	2	3			6		8	9		7	11											5	10		4					21
1	2	3			6		8	9		7*	11						12					5	10		4					22
1	2	3			6		8	9			11						7					5	10		4					23
1	2	3			6	12	8	9			11						7*					5	10		4					24
1	2	3			6	7*	8	9		12	11											5	10		4					25
1	2	3			6		8	9		7	11											5	10		4					26
1	2	3			6	4	8	9		7	11											5	10							27
1	2	3			6	4	8	9		7*	11						12					5	10							28
1	2	3			6	4	8	9		7	11											5	10							29
1	2	3			6		8	9		7	11											5	10		4					30
1	2	3			6	11	8	9		7†			13				12					5	10*		4					31
	2	3			6		8	9		7							11					5	10*		4	1	12			32
1	2	3			6		8	9		7							12					5	10		4		11*			33
1	2	3			6		8	9		7	11											5	10		4					34
1	2	3					8	9		10	11*		6				12					5			4			7		35
1	2	3					8	9		10*	11		6				12					5			4			7		36
1		3					8	9		10	11		6				7					5			4			2		37
1		3					8	9		10	11		6				7*					5	12		4			2		38
1		3					8	9		10	11		6				7					5			4			2		39
1		3					8	9		10	11		6				7					5			4			2		40
1		3				12	8	9		10	11		6				7*					5			4			2		41
1		3				12	8	9		10	11		6				7*					5			4			2		42
1		3			5	10	8	9			11		6				7								4			2		43
1		3			5	10	8	9			11		6				7								4			2		44
1		3			5	10	8	9			11		6				7*								4			2	12	45
1		3			5	10	8	9			11		6				7*								4			2	12	46
45	34	44	5	16	30	20	31	41	11	30	40	13	21	9	3	1	18	5		3	3	26	18	1	24	1	1	12		
			5		1	3				2	1	1	1	3	1	1	8		2	1	1		1				1		2	
	2	1	1		5	4	5	11	4	2	9		1	3			6				1	1	4		2					

Marples C	Bradshaw D	Johnson P	Wilson P	Fazackerley D	Smith K	Howlett G	Spooner S	Helliwell I	Banton D	Himsworth G	Canham T	Branagan J	Tutill S	Butler M	Clegg T	Hotte T	Dunn I	Shaw A	McMillan A	Morris N	Eli R	Greenough R	Dixon K	Hay A	Reid S	Endersby S	Hurlstone G	Barratt T	Hall W	
1		3	8	6		12		9			11	2	5	7			10*				4									1
1		1	1	1				1			1	1	1	1			1				1									
						1																								

Marples C	Bradshaw D	Johnson P	Wilson P	Fazackerley D	Smith K	Howlett G	Spooner S	Helliwell I	Banton D	Himsworth G	Canham T	Branagan J	Tutill S	Butler M	Clegg T	Hotte T	Dunn I	Shaw A	McMillan A	Morris N	Eli R	Greenough R	Dixon K	Hay A	Reid S	Endersby S	Hurlstone G	Barratt T	Hall W	
1	2	3		6		7	8	9	10	11		4	5																	1
1	2			5		7	8	9	10	11		3		6	4															
2	2	1		2		2	2	2	2	2		2	1	1	1															

1989-90

Manager: John Bird

1	Aug	19	(a)	Southend U	L 0-2		2,725
2		26	(h)	Peterborough U	W 1-0	Hall	2,569
3	Sep	1	(a)	Stockport C	D 2-2	Howlett, Helliwell	2,793
4		9	(h)	Rochdale	W 1-0	Spooner (pen)	2,250
5		16	(a)	Lincoln C	D 0-0		4,149
6		23	(h)	Grimsby T	L 0-1		3,366
7		26	(a)	Burnley	D 1-1	Warburton	7,896
8		30	(h)	Wrexham	W 1-0	Dunn	2,196
9	Oct	7	(h)	Cambridge U	W 4-2	Barratt, Dixon, Helliwell, Spooner	2,061
10		13	(a)	Colchester U	W 2-0	Himsworth 2	3,274
11		17	(h)	Aldershot	D 2-2	Helliwell, Dixon	2,788
12		21	(a)	Hartlepool U	W 2-1	Himsworth, Howlett	2,325
13		28	(h)	Doncaster R	W 2-1	Dixon, Warburton	2,978
14		31	(a)	Scunthorpe U	D 1-1	Helliwell	3,800
15	Nov	4	(h)	Torquay U	D 1-1	Kelly (pen)	2,496
16		11	(a)	Maidstone U	L 0-1		2,043
17		24	(a)	Scarborough	W 3-1	Helliwell, Howlett, Barratt	3,602
18	Dec	9	(h)	Gillingham	W 1-0	Canham	2,134
19		16	(a)	Chesterfield	D 0-0		3,383
20		26	(h)	Halifax T	L 0-2		3,665
21		30	(h)	Hereford U	L 1-2	Dixon	2,405
22	Jan	1	(a)	Carlisle U	L 1-2	Kelly (pen)	6,510
23		13	(a)	Peterborough U	D 1-1	Hall	3,678
24		20	(h)	Southend U	W 2-1	Helliwell 2	2,397
25		27	(h)	Colchester U	W 3-1	Longhurst 2, Reid	2,311
26	Feb	3	(a)	Grimsby T	L 0-3		5,049
27		6	(a)	Rochdale	W 1-0	Helliwell	1,821
28		10	(h)	Lincoln C	D 0-0		2,687
29		13	(h)	Stockport C	L 0-3		2,256
30		17	(a)	Gillingham	D 0-0		3,653
31		24	(h)	Scarborough	L 1-2	Helliwell	3,551
32	Mar	3	(a)	Exeter C	L 1-3	Reid	4,632
33		6	(a)	Wrexham	L 0-2		1,780
34		10	(h)	Burnley	L 1-3	Reid (pen)	3,216
35		16	(a)	Cambridge U	D 2-2	Howlett, Hall	4,621
36		24	(a)	Aldershot	D 2-2	Spooner, Helliwell	1,556
37		31	(h)	Hartlepool U	D 1-1	Reid	2,891
38	Apr	2	(h)	Exeter C	W 3-0	Barratt, Canham, Helliwell	2,091
39		7	(a)	Doncaster R	W 2-1	Spooner, Himsworth	2,185
40		10	(h)	Scunthorpe U	L 0-1		2,232
41		14	(h)	Carlisle U	L 0-1		2,805
42		16	(a)	Halifax T	D 2-2	Canham, Helliwell	1,605
43		21	(h)	Chesterfield	W 4-0	Barratt, Helliwell, Dunn, Spooner	2,374
44		25	(a)	Hereford U	W 2-1	Helliwell, Barratt	2,007
45		28	(h)	Maidstone U	D 0-0		2,362
46	May	5	(a)	Torquay U	D 1-1	Spooner	1,564

FINAL LEAGUE POSITION: 13th in Division Four

Appearances
Sub Appearances
Goals

FA Cup

1	Nov	18	(h)	Grimsby T	L 1-2	Warburton	4,128

Appearances
Sub Appearances
Goals

League Cup

1	Aug	23	(a)	Hartlepool U	D 3-3	Colville 2, Helliwell	1,507
		29	(h)	Hartlepool U	W 4-1	Warburton, Spooner 3	2,236
2	Sep	20	(h)	Southampton	L 0-1		4,526
	Oct	3	(a)	Southampton	L 0-2		8,096

Appearances
Sub Appearances
Goals

Marples C	Barratt T	Kelly T	Reid S	Greenough R	Warburton R	Howlett G	Spooner S	Helliwell I	Colville R	Hall W	Dunn I	Tutill S	Dixon K	McMillan A	Canham T	Himsworth G	Heathcote M	Longhurst D	Naylor G	Ord R	Madden C	Crossley R	
1	2	3	4	5	6	7	8	9	10	11*	12												1
1	2	3	4	12	6	7	8	9	10	11		5*											2
1	2	3	4		6	7	8	9	10	11*	12	5											3
1	2	3	4*		6	7	8	9	10	12		5	11										4
1	2	3	4		6	7	8	9	10		11	5											5
1	2	3	4		6	7	8	9	10	12	11*	5											6
1	2	3			6	7	8	9	10	11†	13	5		12	4*								7
1	4	3			6	7	8	9	10*		11	5	12	2									8
1	2	3	4		6	7	8	9				5	10			11							9
1	4	3			6	7	8	9				5	10	2	12	11*							10
1	4	3			6	7	8	9				5	10	2	12	11*							11
1	4	3			6	7	8	9				5	10	2		11							12
1	4	3			6	7	8	9				5	10	2	12	11*							13
1	4	3			6	7	8	9	12		10*	5		2		11							14
1	4	3			6	7	8	9	10†		13	5		2	12	11*							15
1	4*	3			6	7	8	9				5	12	2	10	11							16
1	4	3			6	7	8	9				5	11	2	10								17
1	4	3			6	7	8	9				5	11	2	10								18
1	4	3			6	7	8	9				5	11	2	10*	12							19
1	4	3			6	7†	8	9		13		5	11*	2	10	12							20
1	2*	3			6	7	8	9†	13			5	11	12	10	4							21
1	2	3			6	7	8	12	9			5	11		10	4*							22
1	2	3				7		12	9*	8	13	5	11		10	4†	6						23
1	2	3			6	7		9	12	8†		5	13		11*		4	10					24
1	8	3	4*		6	7		9		12		5			11		2	10					25
1	2	3	4		6	7	8	9				5			11			10					26
1	2	3	4		6	7	8	9	12			5			11			10*					27
1	2	3	4		6	7	8	9	10			5			11								28
1	2	3	4*		6	7	8	9	10†	12	13	5			11								29
1	2	3			6	7	8	9	10*	4		5			11				12				30
1	2	3	4		6	7		9	10	8					11*	12				5			31
1	2	3	4	6		7*		9		8			10		12	11				5			32
1	2	3	4†			13	8	9		11*		5	12		7					6	10		33
1	2	3	4		6	7	8	9				5*		12	11	13					10†		34
1	2	3	4		6	7	8	9		11		5				10							35
1	2				6	7	8	9		3		5	4		11	10*					12		36
1	2		4		6	7*	8	9		3	13	5		12	11	10†							37
1	7		4		6		8	9		3	10	5		2	11								38
1	7		4		6		8	9		3	10*	5		2	11	12							39
1	7		4		6		8	9		3	10*	5		2	11	12							40
1	7		4*		6	12	8	9	13	3				2	11						10†	5	41
1	7				6	4	8	9	10†	3	13	5		2	11*	12							42
1	7		12		6	4	8	9		3	10	5		2	11*								43
1	7		4		6	11	8	9	12	3	10*	5		2									44
1	7		4		6	11*	8	9	13	3	10†	5		2	12								45
1	7				6	4	8	9	10*	3		5		2	11	12							46
46	46	35	24	2	43	41	41	44	17	22	10	42	15	21	28	15	3	4		3	3	1	
			1	1		2		2	7	5	8		4	4	6	8			1		1		
	5	2	4		2	4	6	14		3	2		4		3	4		2					

Marples C	Barratt T	Kelly T	Reid S	Greenough R	Warburton R	Howlett G	Spooner S	Helliwell I	Colville R	Hall W	Dunn I	Tutill S	Dixon K	McMillan A	Canham T	
1	4	3			6	7	8*	9		12		5	11	2	10	1
1	1	1			1	1	1	1				1	1	1	1	
										1						
					1											

Marples C	Barratt T	Kelly T	Reid S	Greenough R	Warburton R	Howlett G	Spooner S	Helliwell I	Colville R	Hall W	Dunn I	Tutill S	Dixon K	McMillan A	
1	2	3	4	5	6	7	8	9	10		11				1
1	2	3	4		6	7	8	9	10	11		5			
1	2	3	4		6	7	8	9	10*		11	5	12		2
1	4	3			6	7	8	9*	12		11	5	10	2	
4	4	4	3	1	4	4	4	4	3	1	3	3	1	1	
									1				1		
					1		3	1	2						

York Against Other League Clubs

City have played 90 clubs in the Football League since their election in 1929-30. Below is City's home and away record against each club. Some clubs changed their name (eg South Shields became Gateshead) and some clubs modified their titles (eg Clapton Orient became Leyton Orient then just Orient then Leyton Orient again). In all cases the last name used by each club covers all games under previous names.

			HOME					*AWAY*				
	First pld	*P*	*W*	*D*	*L*	*F*	*A*	*W*	*D*	*L*	*F*	*A*
Accrington S	1929-30	48	13	6	5	46	25	3	3	18	22	60
AFC Bournemouth	1959-60	28	7	4	3	23	13	3	3	8	13	30
Aldershot	1958-59	42	10	6	5	40	21	6	7	8	27	39
Aston Villa	1971-72	4	0	1	1	1	2	0	0	2	0	5
Barnsley	1932-33	22	1	4	6	10	19	1	2	8	6	15
Barrow	1929-30	60	16	5	9	57	37	11	8	11	37	39
Blackburn R	1971-72	8	3	0	1	4	2	0	0	4	0	13
Blackpool	1974-75	16	3	3	2	12	9	1	3	4	7	12
Bolton W	1971-72	14	2	1	4	7	10	2	2	3	7	11
Bradford	1950-51	32	11	1	4	40	15	5	3	8	20	24
Bradford C	1937-38	56	11	7	10	46	39	8	6	14	39	59
Brentford	1959-60	28	6	5	3	16	12	3	3	8	18	30
Brighton & HA	1963-64	14	2	0	5	8	10	1	1	5	6	17
Bristol C	1974-75	16	2	3	3	8	10	0	3	5	7	16
Bristol R	1965-66	20	5	3	2	12	10	3	3	4	13	13
Burnley	1984-85	6	1	1	1	5	3	0	2	1	2	8
Bury	1957-58	20	5	4	1	13	6	2	0	8	11	23
Cambridge U	1970-71	10	4	0	1	13	6	1	4	0	8	4
Cardiff C	1974-75	4	1	1	0	2	1	0	0	2	3	5
Carlisle U	1929-30	60	14	10	6	64	34	3	12	15	37	60
Charlton A	1972-73	6	0	1	2	2	5	1	0	2	6	6
Chelsea	1975-76	2	0	1	0	2	2	0	1	0	0	0
Chester C	1931-32	72	19	11	6	74	39	6	10	20	40	99
Chesterfield	1929-30	60	15	10	5	57	31	4	7	19	28	51
Colchester U	1959-60	20	8	1	1	28	7	2	2	6	8	16
Coventry C	1958-59	4	0	2	0	1	1	0	0	2	2	7
Crewe A	1929-30	78	24	7	8	96	49	12	10	17	62	83
Crystal P	1958-59	6	1	1	1	3	4	0	1	2	0	2
Darlington	1929-30	84	28	9	5	107	45	10	9	23	47	73
Derby C	1955-56	8	1	2	1	4	5	0	0	4	3	7
Doncaster R	1929-30	58	9	9	11	47	47	7	6	16	34	48
Exeter C	1958-59	26	7	2	4	29	18	3	0	10	13	25
Fulham	1974-75	8	2	1	1	6	6	1	0	3	3	6
Gateshead	1929-30	46	12	8	3	43	29	4	10	9	25	39
Gillingham	1958-59	24	6	2	4	22	13	2	4	6	9	16
Grimsby T	1951-52	36	2	9	7	21	28	2	3	13	14	39
Halifax T	1929-30	80	21	13	6	98	47	12	13	15	54	61
Hartlepool U	1929-30	82	23	10	8	84	39	9	9	23	56	85
Hereford U	1973-74	18	5	1	3	22	11	2	3	4	8	11
Huddersfield T	1973-74	8	1	1	2	4	9	2	1	1	5	4
Hull C	1930-31	34	7	3	7	25	22	5	4	8	21	29
Leyton O	1974-75	8	1	1	2	3	5	1	0	3	3	7
Lincoln C	1929-30	56	14	8	6	40	28	5	8	15	38	60
Luton T	1966-67	6	1	1	1	8	5	0	0	3	2	12
Maidstone U	1989-90	2	0	1	0	0	0	0	0	1	0	1
Manchester U	1974-75	2	0	0	1	0	1	0	0	1	1	2
Mansfield T	1932-33	58	20	5	4	68	38	8	5	16	31	61

	First pld	P	HOME W	D	L	F	A	AWAY W	D	L	F	A
Middlesbrough	1986-87	2	1	0	0	3	1	0	0	1	1	3
Millwall	1958-59	14	4	2	1	14	10	1	1	5	9	15
Nelson	1929-30	4	2	0	0	4	0	1	0	1	6	5
New Brighton	1929-30	30	14	0	1	36	9	4	2	9	22	29
Newport C	1959-60	30	12	1	2	30	8	3	6	6	19	22
Northampton T	1958-59	26	6	2	5	23	20	2	4	7	10	25
Norwich C	1959-60	4	1	0	1	2	2	1	0	1	3	3
Nottingham F	1974-75	4	1	1	0	4	3	0	0	2	1	3
Notts C	1964-65	26	4	5	4	23	21	1	3	9	10	28
Oldham A	1935-36	54	15	9	3	49	20	3	7	17	32	68
Oxford U	1962-63	14	3	1	3	9	11	2	1	4	10	14
Peterborough U	1960-61	26	8	2	3	24	14	3	3	7	12	20
Plymouth A	1971-72	12	2	2	2	10	8	1	4	1	7	9
Portsmouth	1974-75	10	4	0	1	12	8	1	1	3	5	10
Port Vale	1929-30	44	12	4	6	41	22	3	7	12	23	42
Preston NE	1976-77	6	0	1	2	1	4	1	0	2	6	9
Queen's Park R	1959-60	4	1	1	0	4	3	0	1	1	2	7
Reading	1959-60	16	1	3	4	10	12	1	2	5	3	11
Rochdale	1929-30	84	22	9	11	80	59	17	6	19	61	65
Rotherham United	1929-30	46	13	4	6	50	28	5	4	14	26	51
Scarborough	1988-89	4	0	1	1	1	2	1	1	0	3	1
Scunthorpe U	1950-51	42	10	3	8	25	22	6	5	10	25	37
Sheffield U	1981-82	2	0	0	1	3	4	0	0	1	0	4
Sheffield W	1974-75	4	1	0	1	3	2	0	0	2	2	6
Shrewsbury T	1950-51	16	3	2	3	9	9	1	1	6	7	16
Southampton	1959-60	6	1	2	0	5	4	0	0	3	2	7
Southend U	1959-60	26	6	2	5	17	17	3	3	7	12	22
Southport	1929-30	64	17	6	9	62	36	9	11	12	43	47
Stockport C	1929-30	74	20	10	7	60	36	5	6	26	35	78
Sunderland	1974-75	6	1	0	2	3	6	0	0	3	2	7
Swansea C	1965-66	18	7	1	1	20	7	2	2	5	13	18
Swindon T	1959-60	12	3	1	2	7	7	0	1	5	7	21
Torquay U	1958-59	28	4	8	2	14	11	6	2	6	20	22
Tranmere R	1929-30	74	21	5	11	63	28	7	10	20	44	80
Walsall	1931-32	32	6	6	4	22	21	2	3	11	15	39
Watford	1958-59	10	1	3	1	3	6	2	2	1	11	9
West Bromwich A	1974-75	4	0	0	2	1	4	0	1	1	2	4
Wigan A	1978-79	16	4	2	2	13	7	2	2	4	13	14
Wigan Bor	1929-30	4	1	0	1	6	3	1	0	1	3	3
Wimbledon	1977-78	8	0	1	3	3	10	0	0	4	5	11
Wolverhampton W	1985-86	2	1	0	0	2	1	0	0	1	2	3
Workington	1951-52	34	7	7	3	31	17	1	6	10	13	27
Wrexham	1929-30	74	22	9	6	75	43	4	11	22	44	77
		2416	606	301	301	2198	1384	253	290	665	1387	2325

FULL RECORD:

	First pld		P	HOME W	D	L	F	A	AWAY W	D	L	F	A
Division Two	Sns	2	84	17	10	15	56	52	7	8	27	34	74
Division Three	Sns	10	460	96	70	64	338	268	42	51	137	238	435
Division Three Nth	Sns	22	954	241	117	119	953	591	104	113	260	620	1026
Division Four	Sns	20	918	252	104	103	851	473	100	118	241	495	790

York City in the Leyland Daf Cup (previously Associate Members' Cup, Freight/Rover Trophy and Sherpa Van Trophy)

1983-4
Round 1
21 February v Hull City (h) 1-2
Senior
Jones; Evans, Senior, Sbragia, MacPhail, Hood, Ford(Haslegrave), Crosby, Walwyn, Byrne, Pollard(Pearce).
Att: 5,837

1984-5
Round 1 (lst leg)
22 January v Doncaster Rovers (a) 0-0
Astbury; Senior, Hay, Richards, MacPhail, Atkinson, Chippendale, Banton, Butler, Houchen, Nicholson (Canham).
Att: 1,892
(2nd leg)
5 February v Doncaster Rovers (h) 2-0
Butler, Banton
Jones; Senior, Hay, Richards, MacPhail, Hood, Ford (Chippendale), Banton, Butler, Atkinson, Canham.
Att: 4,397
Round 2
12 March v Chesterfield (h) 1-0
Butler
Jones; Senior, Hay, Richards, Hood, Haslegrave, Ford, Banton, Butler(Pearce), Chippendale, Nicholson (Evans).
Att: 3,891
Round 3
22 April v Lincoln City (h) 2-3
MacPhail, Houchen (pen)
Jones; Senior, Hay, Hood, MacPhail, Hastlegrave, Ford, Banton, Butler, Houchen, Nicholson(Ward).
Att: 4,010

1985-6
Group Match
14 January v Rotherham United (h) 0-0
Leaning; Senior, Hood, McAughtrie, MacPhail, Mills, Ford, Banton, Gabbiadini(Hay), Houchen, Canham (Haslegrave).
Att: 2,122
Group Match
29 January v Hartlepool United 2-3
Houchen (pen), Butler
Leaning; Senior, Hay, McAughtrie, Murphy (McKenzie), Mills, Ford, Banton, Gabbiadini(Butler), Houchen, Canham.
Att: 1,080

1986-7
Group Match
25 November v Darlington (h) 4-1
Gabbiadini 3, Walwyn
Leaning; McKenzie, Senior, McAughtrie, Whitehead, Pearce, Haslegrave(Hood), Gabbiadini, Walwyn (Canham), Mills, Ford.
Att: 1,630
Group Match
6 January v Rochdale (a) 1-1
Canham
Leaning; Senior(Tutill), Pearce, Pickering, Whitehead, Haslegrave, Ford, Hood, Walwyn(Costello), Mills, Canham.
Att: 783
Round 1
27 January v Mansfield Town (h) 0-1
Leanir‿, Senior, Pearce, Sbragia, Pickering, Haslegrave, Ford, Butler(Hood), Walwyn, Gabbiadini, Canham.
Att: 2,061

1987-8
Group Match
13 October v Darlington (h) 3-4
Mills, Banton, Whitehead
Endersby; Branagan, Johnson, Wilson, Whitehead, Clegg, Butler(Tutill), Mills, Banton, Buchanan, Hood.
Att: 1,296
Group Match
24 November v Chesterfield (a) 0-2
Endersby; Tutill, Branagan, Wilson, Whitehead, Clegg, Mills, Bradshaw, Helliwell, Banton, Himsworth.
Att: 1,197

1988-9
Group Match
22 November v Burnley (h) 0-2
Marples; Greenough, Johnson, Wilson, Tutill, Fazackerley, Eli, Shaw(Himsworth), Helliwell, Dixon, Canham.
Att: 1,648
Group Match
13 December v Hartlepool United (a) 2-0
Dixon 2
Marples; Branagan, Johnson, Bradshaw, Greenough, Smith, Himsworth, Spooner, Helliwell, Dixon, Canham.
Att: 1,396
Round 1
7 January v Scarborough (a) 1-3
Canham
Marples; Bradshaw, Johnson, Wilson, Greenough, Smith, Himsworth(Dunn), Spooner, Helliwell, Dixon, Canham.
Att: 2,779

1989-90
Group Match
7 November v Hartlepool United (h) 7-1
Helliwell 3, Canham 2, Spooner, Tutill
Marples; McMillan, Kelly, Barratt(Colville), Tutill, Warburton, Howlett, Spooner, Helliwell, Canham, Himsworth(Dunn)
Att: 1,443
Group Match
12 December v Rotherham United (a) 1-3
Kelly (pen)
Marples; McMillan(Himsworth), Kelly, Barratt, Tutill, Warburton, Howlett, Spooner, Helliwell(Colville), Canham, Dixon.
Att: 1,996
Round 1
9 January v Halifax Town (a) 1-1
Helliwell
Marples; Barratt, Kelly, Himsworth(Dunn), Tutill, Heathcote, Howlett, Hall, Colville, Canham, Dixon (Helliwell).
Att: 1,063
(Halifax Town won 7-6 on penalties)

The Football League Third Division Cup (1933-39)

The Third Division North and Third Division South Cups were inaugurated in 1933-4. City's record in the North Section was as follows:

1933-4
Round 1
13 January v Hartlepools United (h) 2-1
Lax, Dando
Fawcett; Wass, Dawson, Scott, Lockie, Wilcockson, Jenkinson, Fox, Dando, Hathway, Lax.
Att: 3,000
Round 2
7 March v Carlisle United (h) 2-1
Dando, Wilcockson
Fawcett; Wass, Strain, Fox, Lockie, Wilcockson, Jenkinson, Ivory, Dando, Hathway, Lax.
Att: 2,500
Round 3
21 March v Darlington (a) 3-4
Dando 2, Hathway
Fawcett; Wass, Strain, Scott, Lockie, Wilcockson, Jenkinson, Ivory, Dando, Hathway, Lax.
Att: 2,000

1934-5
Round 1
2 January v Gateshead (a) 2-2
Dando, Jenkins
Cunningham; Pinder, A.Turner, Fox, Routledge, Speed, Jenkins, Eyres, Dando, Hathway, Bowater.
Att: 2,000
Replay
30 January v Gateshead (h) 3-1
Dando, Hughes, Bowater
Cunningham; Pinder, A.Turner, Fox, Routledge, Hathway, Jenkins, Eyres, Dando, Hughes, Bowater.
Att: 2,000
Round 2
20 February v Hartlepools United (a) 0-4
Cunningham; Pinder, Wass, Fox, Routledge, Speed, Jenkins, Eyres, Dando, Hathway, Bowater.
Att: 1,700

1935-6
Round 1
9 October v Darlington (a) 2-3
Speed, Lawie
Wilson; Fox, Wass, Hathway, Routledge, Speed, Green, Banfield, Graham, Lawie, Spooner.
Att: 1,500

1936-7
Round 1
16 September v Hull City (h) 3-2
Hughes 2, Fox
Wharton; Wass, Young, Fox, Duckworth, Hathway, Agar, Hughes, Nicol, Comrie, Spooner.
Att: 7,022
Round 2
17 March v Hartlepools United (h) 5-0
Whitelaw 2, Thompson, Comrie, Hathway
Wharton; Fox, Legge, Duckworth, Wass, Whitelaw, Scott, Hathway, Thompson, Comrie, Spooner.
Att: 1,600
Round 3
7 April v Darlington (a) 2-3
Hathway, Scott
Wharton; Fox, Legge, Duckworth, Wass, Whitelaw, Scott, Hathway, Thompson, Comrie, Spooner.
Att: 1,004

1937-8
Round 1
20 September v Halifax Town (a) 1-4
Gledhill
Wharton; Pinder, Legge, Duckworth, Wass, Fox, Scott, Earl, Gledhill, Milner, Spooner.
Att: 1,300

City did not enter the competition in 1938-9 as clubs that were in the third round of the FA Cup were exempt this season.

City in the FA Cup 1923-1928

1923-4
Extra Preliminary Round
Sep 8 v Castleford & Allerton U (h) 2-1
Rippon, Middlemiss
Boot; Shaw, MacMurray, Reed, Smith, Middlemiss, Tindale, Elliott, Charlesworth, Rippon, Davison.
Att: 2,000
Preliminary Round
Sep 22 v Cudworth (a) 1-0
Davison
Boot; Shaw, MacMurray, Reed, Smith, Middlemiss, Charlesworth, Elliott, Dennis, Rippon, Davison.
Att: 1,500
First Qualifying Round
Oct 6 v Mexborough T (h) 1-1
Elliott
Boot; Shaw, MacMurray, Reed, Smith, Middlemiss, Hulme, Elliott, Charlesworth, Rippon, Davison.
Att: 2,500
Replay
Oct 11 v Mexborough T (a) 1-1 (aet)
Elliott
Boot; Shaw, MacMurray, Reed, Smith, Middlemiss, Tindale, Elliott, Charlesworth, Rippon, Davison.
Att: 2,000
Second Replay
Oct 15 v Mexborough T (at Doncaster) 1-3
Rippon
Boot; W.A.Kay, MacMurray, Reed, Smith, Middlemiss, Tindale, Elliott, Charlesworth, Rippon, Davison.
Att: 2,000

1924-5
Extra Preliminary Round
Sep 6 v Guiseley (h) 1-0
Cleasby
Smith; Wood, J.Baines, G.Maskill, Rutherford, Middlemiss, Elliott, Acklam, Miller, Cleasby, Cobain.
Att: 3,000
Preliminary Round
Sep 20 v Horsforth (h) 7-1
Marshall 5, Miller 2
Smith; Sayles, J.Baines, Albrecht, Rutherford, Middlemiss, Elliott, Miller, Marshall, Cleasby, Cobain.
Att: 3,000
First Qualifying Round
Oct 4 v Wombwell (h) 1-2
Miller
Smith; Glover, J.Baines, G.Maskill, Rutherford, Albrecht, Elliott, Miller, Marshall, Brooke, Cobain.
Att: 4,500

1925-6
Preliminary Round
Sep 23 v Maltby Main (h) 5-3 §
Cleasby 2, Holland 2, Laws
Furnell; Sayles, Drew, Albrecht, Loughran, Middlemiss, Harron, Ranby, Holland, Cleasby, Laws.
Att: 1,500
§Match at Maltby on 19 September abandoned after 71 minutes owing to rainstorm, with City leading 7-0.
First Qualifying Round
Oct 3 v Wombwell (h) 5-0
Holland 3, Ranby, Loughran (pen)
Furnell; Sayles, J.Baines, G.Maskill, Loughran, Middlemiss, Harron, Ranby, Holland, Cleasby, Laws.
Att: 3,000
Second Qualifying Round
Oct 17 v Castleford T (h) 3-0
Cleasby, Holland, Ranby
Furnell; Sayles, Drew, G.Maskill, Loughran, Middlemiss, Harron, Ranby, Holland, Cleasby, Laws.
Att: 4,300
Third Qualifying Round
Oct 31 v Wath A (a) 1-4
Loughran
Furnell; Sayles, Drew, G.Maskill, Loughran, Middlemiss, Harron, Ranby, Holland, Albrecht, Laws.
Att: 2,000

1926-7
First Qualifying Round
Oct 2 v Guisborough Belmont A (h) 5-0
Clayton 3, Ranby, Loughran
Thompson; Flynn, Daniels, G.Maskill, Loughran, Middlemiss, Harvey, Ranby, Clayton, Duckham, Merritt.
Att: 2,500
Second Qualifying Round
Oct 16 v South Bank (h) 4-0
Merritt 2, Flood, Duckham
Thompson; Flynn, Daniels, O'Cain, Loughran, Middlemiss, Harvey, Flood, Duckham, Ranby, Merritt.
Att: 3,000
Third Qualifying Round
Oct 31 v Whitby U (h) 0-0
Thompson; Flynn, Daniels, Redfearn, Loughran, Middlemiss, Harvey, Flood, O'Cain, Ranby, Merritt.
Att: 3,000
Replay (at York)
Nov 3 v Whitby U (h) 2-1
Flood, Ranby
Thompson; Flynn, Shanks, Redfearn, Loughran, Middlemiss, Clayton, Flood, Duckham, Ranby, Merritt.
Att: 2,000
Fourth Qualifying Round
Nov 13 v Ilkeston T (a) 5-1
Clayton 2, Ranby, Loughran, Duckham
Thompson; Flynn, Shanks, Redfearn, Loughran, Middlemiss, Harvey, Duckham, Clayton, Ranby, Merritt.
Att: 3,000
First Round
Dec 1 v Worksop T (h) 4-1 §
Merritt 2, Ranby, Harvey
Thompson; Flynn, Shanks, Redfearn, Loughran, Middlemiss, Harvey, Flood, Clayton, Ranby, Merritt.
Att: 2,931
§Match on 27 November abandoned after 70 minutes because of fog with the score at 1-1.

Second Round
Dec 11 v Grimsby T (a) 1-2
Harvey
Thompson; Flynn, Shanks, Redfearn, Loughran, Middlemiss, Harvey, Duckham, Clayton, Ranby, Merritt.
Att: 11,000

1927-8
First Qualifying Round
Oct 1 v Whitby U (h) 4-0
Hammerton 2, Waite, Ranby
Crowther; Flynn, Page, Loughran, Levick, Middlemiss, Waite, Fenoughty, Hammerton, Ranby, Merritt.
Att: 2,500
Second Qualifying Round
Oct 15 v Scarborough (h) 1-1
Hammerton
Crowther; Flynn, Page, Loughran, Levick, Middlemiss, Waite, Fenoughty, Hammerton, Ranby, Merritt.
Att: 6,422
Replay
Oct 19 v Scarborough (a) 4-0
Albrecht, Merritt 2, Clayton
Crowther; Flynn, Page, Loughran, Levick, Middlemiss, Waite, Clayton, Albrecht, Ranby, Merritt.
Att: 4,073
Third Qualifying Round
Oct 29 v Stockton Malleable (h) 7-1
Merritt 2, Albrecht 2, Ranby 2, Levick
Crowther; Flynn, Page, Loughran, Levick, Middlemiss, Waite, Fenoughty, Albrecht, Ranby, Merritt.
Att: 2,685
Fourth Qualifying Round
Nov 12 v Shildon (a) 1-1
Fenoughty
Crowther; Flynn, Page, Loughran, Levick, Middlemiss, Waite, Fenoughty, Albrecht, Ranby, Merritt.
Att: 3,500
Replay
Nov 16 v Shildon (h) 1-2
Ranby
Crowther; Flynn, Page, Loughran, Levick, Middlemiss, Waite, Fenoughty, Albrecht, Ranby, Merritt.
Att: 4,541

1928-9
First Qualifying Round
Sep 29 v Stockton (h) 7-1
Cowie 6, Ranby 1
Robertson; Brown, Marshall, Precious, Charnley, Middlemiss, Forrest, Duthie, Cowie, Ranby, Roberts.
Att: 3,370
Second Qualifying Round
Oct 13 v Normanby Magnestie (h) 2-1
Forrest, Charnley
Robertson; Brown, Marshall, Duthie, Charnley, Middlemiss, Forrest, Fenoughty, Cowie, Ranby, Roberts.
Att: 2,000
Third Qualifying Round
Oct 27 v Bridlington (h) 3-0
Duthie 2, Ranby
Robertson; Brown, Marshall, Middlemiss, Charnley, Duthie, Merritt, Fenoughty, Cowie, Ranby, Roberts.
Att: 2,000
Fourth Qualifying Round
Nov 10 v Jarrow (a) 0-0
Robertson; Brown, Marshall, Middlemiss, Charnley, Duthie, Merritt, Fenoughty, Cowie, Ranby, Roberts.
Att: 5,541
Replay
Nov 14 v Jarrow (h) 2-2 (aet)
Merritt, Cowie
Robertson; Brown, Marshall, Middlemiss, Charnley, Duthie, Merritt, Fenoughty, Cowie, Forrest, Roberts.
Att: 4,370
Second Replay
Nov 19 v Jarrow (at Newcastle) 3-2
Roberts, Merritt, Fenoughty
Robertson; Brown, Albrecht, Middlemiss, Charnley, Duthie, Merritt, Fenoughty, Cowie, Forrest, Roberts.
Att: 6,843
First Round
Nov 24 v Barrow (h) 0-1
Robertson; Brown, Marshall, Middlemiss, Charnley, Duthie, Merritt, Fenoughty, Cowie, Forrest, Roberts.
Att: 6,957

City in World War Two

1939-40

Acting Manager: J.A.Wright

1	Oct	21	(h)	Middlesbrough	L 1-3	Stockill	4,500
2		28	(a)	Newcastle U	L 2-9	Allen, Lee	5,300
3	Nov	11	(h)	Hull C	W 3-1	Lee 2, Stockill	3,000
4		18	(a)	Halifax T	W 4-1	Allen, Stockill (pen), Lee, Sherwood	
5		25	(h)	Leeds U	D 1-1	Lee	4,000
6	Dec	2	(a)	Bradford C	L 1-2	Stockill	1,635
7		9	(h)	Darlington	W 2-1	Lee, Porritt	
8		25	(a)	Hartlepools U	W 2-1	Lee, Opp own-goal	
9	Mar	16	(h)	Halifax T	W 3-1	Porritt 2, Hodgson	
10		23	(a)	Leeds U	L 1-3	Brenen	3,000
11		25	(a)	Hull C	L 1-4	Brenen	5,000
12		30	(h)	Bradford C	L 0-1		3,000
13	Apr	6	(a)	Darlington	L 3-5	Stockill, Lee, Hawkins	
14		17	(h)	Newcastle	L 2-4	Hydes 2	3,000
15	May	4	(h)	Bradford	W 3-2	Lee 2, Hodgson	
16		18	(h)	Hartlepools U	W 2-1	Lee, Hydes	
17		25	(a)	Bradford	W 3-2	Gledhill, Hydes, Stockill	
*18		29	(h)	Huddersfield T	L 1-2	Hydes (pen)	3,000
19	Jun	1	(a)	Middlesbrough	L 1-6	Lee	1,500
20		3	(a)	Huddersfield T	L 0-1		332

FINAL LEAGUE POSITION: 8th in League North-East — Appearances

*Abandoned after 58 minutes (storm), result stood. — Goals

League North War Cup

P	Apr	13	(h)	Bradford C	W 6-4	Hydes 3, Lee, Roberts, Wardle	3,375
1		20	(h)	Hull C	D 1-1	Gallacher	3,980
R		27	(a)	Hull C	L 0-1		6,000

Appearances

Goals

1940-41

Acting Manager: J.A.Wright

1	Aug	31	(h)	Middlesbrough	W 4-3	Porritt 2, Brenen, M.Patrick	3,000
2	Sep	7	(a)	Middlesbrough	L 1-2	Brenen	2,000
3		14	(h)	Hull C	W 4-1	Brenen 2, M.Patrick 2	3,500
4		21	(a)	Rotherham U	L 0-3		2,600
5		28	(a)	Hull C	W 3-1	Brenen 2, M.Patrick	1,500
6	Oct	5	(h)	Lincoln C	L 1-2	Lee	3,000
7		12	(a)	Lincoln C	L 2-4	M.Patrick, Little	2,500
8		19	(h)	Rotherham U	W 3-1	M.Patrick, Brenen, Lee	2,000
9		26	(a)	Halifax T	L 1-2	Lee	3,000
10	Nov	2	(a)	Bradford C	L 2-8	M.Patrick, Robinson (pen)	661
11		9	(a)	Newcastle U	L 0-3		3,000
12		16	(a)	Middlesbrough	L 4-6	Little, Halton, Dawson, Gledhill	1,700
13		23	(h)	Newcastle U	W 3-0	Lee 2, Robinson (pen)	2,000
14		30	(h)	Halifax T	D 2-2	Robinson, Brenen	1,500
15	Dec	7	(h)	Bradford C	W 5-2	Lee 2, Gledhill 2, Walsh	1,000
16		14	(h)	Doncaster R	L 1-4	Walsh	2,000
17		21	(a)	Doncaster R	L 2-9	Mennie 2	2,075
18		25	(a)	Chesterfield	L 0-2		3,000
19		28	(h)	Bradford	D 0-0		2,000

20	Jan	11	(a)	Bradford	L 2-4	Brenen, Lee	2,265
21		25	(h)	Hull C	D 3-3	Lee 3	2,000
22	Apr	12	(h)	Grimsby T	W 3-2	Brenen 2, Dawson	3,000
23		14	(a)	Barnsley	D 1-1	Dawson	2,724
24		28	(a)	Grimsby T	L 0-2		2,000
25	May	24	(h)	Middlesbrough	L 2-4	Lee, Brenen	2,000

FINAL LEAGUE POSITION: 32nd out of 36 in League North

Appearances

Goals

League North War Cup

P	Feb	1	(h)	Sheffield W	W 7-0	Brenen 4, Lee 2, Dawson	2,500
		8	(a*)	Sheffield W	L 1-2	Halton	1,800
1		15	(h)	Bradford	W 3-2	Dawson 2, Little	2,600
		22	(a*)	Bradford	W 4-3	Lee 2, Flint, Gledhill	1,200
2	Mar	1	(h)	Newcastle U	D 1-1	Robinson	4,935
		8	(a)	Newcastle U	L 1-4	Dawson	6,520

*Played at the Old Show Ground, Scunthorpe.

Appearances

Goals

1941-42

Acting Manager: J.A.Wright

1	Aug	30	(a)	Leeds U	L 0-2		3,000
2	Sep	6	(h)	Leeds U	W 1-0	Brenen	4,000
3		13	(h)	Middlesbrough	W 9-5	Lee 4, Brenen 2, Brown (pen), Bradley, Dawson	3,600
4		20	(a)	Middlesbrough	L 2-5	Brown, Dawson	4,900
5		27	(a)	Newcastle U	L 3-5	Brenen 3	7,900
6	Oct	4	(h)	Newcastle U	D 2-2	Dawson 2	4,500
7		11	(h)	Bradford C	D 3-3	Dawson 2, Gledhill	3,500
8		18	(a)	Bradford C	W 2-0	Lee, Marshall	647
9		25	(a)	Huddersfield T	L 1-5	Lee	2,141
10	Nov	1	(h)	Huddersfield T	L 1-5	Bentall	4,000
11		8	(a)	Lincoln C	D 3-3	Lee 2, Brenen	
12		15	(h)	Lincoln C	W 4-2	Lee 2, Brenen 2	
13		22	(h)	Gateshead	L 3-4	Lee 2, Dean	
14		29	(a)	Gateshead	L 0-1		
15	Dec	6	(a)	Sunderland	L 2-4	Porritt, Jones	
16		13	(h)	Sunderland	L 1-4	Melaniphy	
17		20	(h)	Bradford	L 2-3	Melaniphy, Rudd	
18		25	(a)	Bradford	D 2-2	Marshall, Bradley	

FINAL LEAGUE POSITION: 32nd out of 38 in League North

Appearances

Goals

League North War Cup (Qualifying Group)

19	Dec	27	(a)	Grimsby T	D 0-0		2,600
20	Jan	3	(h)	Grimsby T	W 3-2	Lee 2, Brown	5,157
21		10	(a)	Gateshead	L 2-3	Sargent 2	3,404
22		17	(h)	Gateshead	D 3-3	Lee 2 (2 pens), Dryden	4,161
23		31	(a)	Middlesbrough	D 3-3	Livingstone, W.Jones, Brown	2,400
24	Feb	14	(a)	Sunderland	L 3-8	A.Jones, Lee, Brenen	5,600
25		28	(a)	Bolton W	L 3-4	Lee 2, Brenen	2,109
26	Mar	14	(h)	Sunderland	D 2-2	Brenen, Lee	4,288
27		21	(h)	Middlesbrough	D 1-1	McGarry	4,058
28		28	(h)	Bolton W	W 2-1	Sargent, Lee	3,762

York City failed to qualify

Appearances

Goals

Combined Counties Cup

Q	Apr	11	(h)	Chesterfield	W 3-1	Lee, Brenen 2	3,500
Q		18	(a)	Halifax T	D 1-1	Livingstone	2,000
Q		25	(h)	Huddersfield T	D 2-2	Livingstone 2	3,347
1	May	9	(h)	Bradford C	W 2-1	Brenen 2	2,796
SF		16	(h)	Middlesbrough	W 4-1	Lee, Brenen, O'Donnell 2	4,011
F		23	(h)	Halifax T	W 2-0	Lee 2	4,710
		30	(a)	Halifax T	L 3-4	Lee, Brenen, O'Donnell	4,311

York City won 5-4 on aggregate

Appearances

Goals

1942-43

Acting Managers: J.A.Wright/Tom Lockie

1	Aug	29	(h)	Gateshead	L 1-2	Knight	3,200
2	Sep	5	(a)	Gateshead	W 4-1	Knight 2, O'Donnell 2	3,280
3		12	(a)	Sunderland	D 0-0		7,480
4		19	(h)	Sunderland	L 0-3		4,250
5		26	(h)	Middlesbrough	D 2-2	Lee, O'Donnell	3,348
6	Oct	3	(a)	Middlesbrough	W 3-2	Brown, Lee, F.Scott	3,500
7		10	(h)	Newcastle U	W 4-3	O'Donnell 4	4,460
8		17	(a)	Newcastle U	D 3-3	F.Scott, Gledhill, Brown	5,967
9		24	(h)	Grimsby T	W 5-2	F.Scott, Lee, O'Donnell, L.Compton 2	3,901
10		31	(a)	Grimsby T	W 1-0	Knight	2,300
11	Nov	7	(a)	Bradford C	W 3-1	Lee, Brown, O'Donnell	3,500
12		14	(h)	Bradford C	W 9-1	Knight 3, O'Donnell, Brown, Lee, Gledhill, F.Scott, Opp own-goal	4,415
13		21	(a)	Leeds U	L 1-2	Lee	4,500
14		28	(h)	Leeds U	W 3-1	Lee 2 (1 pen), O'Donnell	4,656
15	Dec	5	(h)	Bradford	L 3-6	Lee 2 (1 pen), Tutill	2,288
16		12	(a)	Bradford	L 1-3	Brown	2,400
17		19	(h)	Rotherham U	W 2-1	Brown, Lee	2,369
18		25	(a)	Rotherham U	L 2-3	Lee, Marshall	6,000

FINAL LEAGUE POSITION: 17th out of 47 in League North

Appearances
Goals

League North War Cup (Qualifying Competition)

19	Dec	26	(h)	Doncaster R	D 3-3	Lee 2, A.Scott	4,552
20	Jan	2	(a)	Doncaster R	W 5-3	F.Scott 3, Lee (pen), Brenen	2,000
21		16	(a)	Newcastle U	L 1-3	Brenen	5,203
22		23	(h)	Sunderland	W 4-0	Lee 2 (1 pen), Knight, Brown	5,494
23		30	(a)	Sunderland	W 5-4	Lee 2 (1 pen), Knight, Brenen, Campbell	7,413
24	Feb	6	(a)	Gateshead	L 2-3	Brenen, Shinwell	4,026
25		13	(h)	Gateshead	W 2-0	Lee (pen), Campbell	5,065
26		20	(a)	Middlesbrough	W 5-1	Lee 2, Brenen, F.Scott, Hodgson	2,500
27		27	(h)	Middlesbrough	W 6-0	Brenen 3 (1 pen), Lee, Brown, Hodgson	5,241

Appearances
Goals

League North War Cup (Competition Proper)

1	Mar	6	(a)	Newcastle U	L 2-3	Lee, Brown	19,989
		13	(h)	Newcastle U	W 2-0	Wilson, Brenen	11,385
2		20	(h)	Bradford	W 2-1	Brenen, Lee	10,827
		27	(a)	Bradford	W 3-0	F.Scott, Dawson, Brenen	12,899
3	Apr	3	(h)	Chesterfield	W 2-0	Brown, McCormack	14,007
		10	(a)	Chesterfield	W 2-0	McCormack, F.Scott	16,225
SF		17	(a)	Sheffield W	L 0-3		35,253
		24	(h)	Sheffield W	D 1-1	Lee (pen)	16,350

Appearances
Goals

Additional League North Match

	May	1	(h)	Newcastle U	D 5-5	Brenen 2 (1 pen), Campbell 2, Stone	2,308

Appearances
Goals

1943-44

Acting Manager: Tom Lockie

No	Month	Day	Venue	Opponents	Res	Score	Scorers	Att
1	Aug	28	(a)	Grimsby T	L	2-3	Woodgate, Stone	1,600
2	Sep	4	(h)	Grimsby T	W	2-0	Dawson, Dunn	4,982
3		11	(a)	Gateshead	L	0-3		3,253
4		18	(h)	Gateshead	W	5-1	Billington 3, Woodgate, Fenton	4,036
5		25	(h)	Newcastle U	W	2-0	Lee, Dawson	5,938
6	Oct	2	(a)	Newcastle U	D	1-1	Lee	9,877
7		9	(h)	Hartlepools U	W	2-0	Dunn, Scott	5,686
8		16	(a)	Hartlepools U	L	1-4	Dawson	5,200
9		23	(a)	Darlington	L	2-4	Wilson (pen), Brenen	8,210
10		30	(h)	Darlington	W	5-2	Billington 3, Lee (pen), Fenton	4,590
11	Nov	6	(a)	Middlesbrough	D	1-1	O'Donnell	3,000
12		13	(h)	Middlesbrough	W	5-3	Walker 3, Dawson, Killourhy	5,036
13		20	(h)	Leeds U	L	1-3	Dawson	4,708
14		27	(a)	Leeds U	L	0-1		4,500
15	Dec	4	(a)	Bradford	L	1-6	Dawson	4,056
16		11	(h)	Bradford	L	2-4	McDonald, Billington	4,119
17		18	(a)	Rotherham U	L	1-3	McDonald	3,000
18		25	(h)	Rotherham U	W	2-1	Woodgate, Dawson	3,948

FINAL LEAGUE POSITION: 31st out of 50 in Football League North (First Competition)

Appearances
Goals

League North War Cup (Qualifying Competition)

No	Month	Day	Venue	Opponents	Res	Score	Scorers	Att
19	Dec	27	(h)	Huddersfield T	W	2-1	Billington 2	8,475
20	Jan	1	(a)	Huddersfield T	W	3-0	Brown, Billington 2	4,184
21		8	(a)	Bradford C	L	1-4	Billington	3,008
22		15	(h)	Bradford C *	W	3-1	Lee, Killourhy, Billington	2,384
23		22	(a)	Barnsley	L	1-2	Killourhy	4,363
24		29	(h)	Barnsley	W	2-0	Killourhy 2	5,851
25	Feb	5	(h)	Bradford	L	0-1		6,500
26		12	(a)	Bradford	L	1-4	Lee	6,966
27		19	(a)	Leeds U	L	1-2	Hawkins	7,000
28		26	(h)	Leeds U	W	8-1	Lee 2, Billington 2, Hawkins 2, Killourhy, Litchfield	5,176

*Abandoned after 60 minutes (fog), result allowed to stand.

Appearances
Goals

League North War Cup (Competition Proper)

Rd	Month	Day	Venue	Opponents	Res	Score	Scorers	Att
1	Mar	4	(h)	Barnsley	W	4-1	Lee 2, Litchfield, Killourhy	7,653
		11	(a)	Barnsley	L	1-3	Hawkins	14,001
2		18	(h)	Bradford	L	1-5	Billington	11,977
		25	(a)	Bradford	L	1-2	Billington	12,393

Appearances
Goals

Combined Counties Cup

Rd	Month	Day	Venue	Opponents	Res	Score	Scorers	Att
1	Apr	1	(a)	Halifax T	L	1-4	Hawkins	2,800
		8	(h)	Halifax T	D	1-1	Hawkins	5,110

Appearances
Goals

Additional League Matches

No	Month	Day	Venue	Opponents	Res	Score	Scorers	Att
29	Apr	15	(a)	Chesterfield	L	0-2		2,356
30		22	(h)	Chesterfield	D	1-1	A.Brown	3,423
31		29	(a)	Sheffield W	L	1-2	Scott	5,000
32	May	6	(h)	Sheffield W	W	4-3	T.Brown 2, Wilson (pen), Dawson	2,919

Appearances
Goals

1944-45

Acting Manager: Tom Lockie

1	Aug	26	(h)	Hartlepools U	W 3-1	Dawson, Wrigglesworth, Taylor	4,485
2	Sep	2	(a)	Hartlepools U	L 0-5		4,000
3		9	(a)	Huddersfield T	L 1-2	Haddington	4,885
4		16	(h)	Huddersfield T	L 1-3	Dawson	5,251
5		23	(a)	Hull C	L 0-1		7,000
6		30	(h)	Hull C	W 1-0	Hawkins	4,351
7	Oct	7	(h)	Darlington	W 2-0	Hawkins, Dix	4,540
8		14	(a)	Darlington	L 4-6	Dawson 2, Dix, Sutherland	6,794
9		21	(a)	Gateshead	L 2-4	Scott 2	1,500
10		28	(h)	Gateshead	W 10-2	Hawkins 4, Dix 3, Scott 2, Dawson	4,100
11	Nov	4	(h)	Bradford	W 4-1	Dix, Thompson 2, Dawson (pen)	6,064
12		11	(a)	Bradford	L 3-5	Thompson 2, Dawson	7,956
13		18	(h)	Sunderland	L 3-5	Dawson 2 (1 pen), Riddle	8,197
14		25	(a)	Sunderland	D 3-3	M.Wilson, J.Wilson, Thompson	11,000
15	Dec	2	(h)	Middlesbrough	W 5-1	Dawson 2, Hawkins 2, Thompson	4,941
16		9	(a)	Middlesbrough	L 3-4	Dawson 3	3,349
17		16	(a)	Leeds U	L 1-3	Dix	5,000
18		23	(h)	Leeds U	L 3-6	Dawson, Hawkins, Bowden	4,871

FINAL LEAGUE POSITION: 42nd out of 54 in Football League North (First Championship) — Appearances

Goals

League North War Cup (Qualifying Competition)

19	Dec	25	(h)	Hull C	W 5-1	Bowden 2, Dawson, Hawkins, Woollett	2,043
20		30	(a)	Hull C	L 1-6	J.Wilson (pen)	4,300
21	Jan	6	(a)	Bradford	L 2-4	Thompson, J.Wilson (pen)	7,456
22		20	(h)	Leeds U	L 0-5		1,279
23		27	(a)	Leeds U	L 3-4	Bates, Riddle, Opp own-goal	6,000
24	Feb	3	(a)	Barnsley	L 1-2	J.Wilson (pen)	10,238
25		10	(h)	Barnsley	W 5-1	Hawkins 3, Nettleton, Johnson	4,465
26		17	(h)	Bradford C	D 2-2	Johnson 2	4,602
27		24	(a)	Bradford C	L 0-3		6,776
28	Mar	3	(h)	Bradford	W 6-1	Dawson 3, Scott, Nettleton, Bartram (pen)	3,997

Appearances

Goals

Additional League Games

29	Mar	10	(a)	Hartlepools U	D 1-1	Johnson	2,000
30		24	(h)	Huddersfield T	W 1-0	Nettleton	3,635
31		31	(a)	Huddersfield T	L 0-1		3,297
32	Apr	2	(a)	Darlington	L 3-7	Hawkins 2, Dix	3,000
33		7	(a)	Sunderland	D 0-0		5,000
34		14	(h)	Sunderland	W 4-2	Johnson 2, J.Wilson (pen), Nettleton	2,682
35	May	19	(a)	Darlington	L 2-4	Maddison, Johnson	3,243
36		21	(h)	Middlesbrough	W 5-3	Hawkins 2, Nettleton, Dawson, Maddison	3,104

FINAL LEAGUE POSITION: 36th out of 60 in Football League North (Second Championship) — Appearances

Goals

Tyne, Wear & Tees Cup

1	Apr	21	(h)	Darlington	W 2-0	Bartram 2 (2 pens)	4,004
		28	(a)	Darlington	D 2-2	Hawkins 2	4,790
SF	May	5	(h)	Sunderland	W 2-1	Hawkins 2	4,147
		12	(a)	Sunderland	L 1-6	Dawson	6,000

Appearances

Goals

1945-46

Acting Manager: Tom Lockie

1	Aug	25	(h)	Carlisle U	D 3-3	Winters, Gledhill, Nettleton	4,664
2	Sep	1	(a)	Carlisle U	W 2-0	Winters, Dawson	6,500
3		8	(a)	Gateshead	W 3-1	Winters 3	5,364
4		15	(h)	Gateshead	W 2-1	Dawson, Winters	5,825
5		22	(h)	Darlington	L 3-4	Maddison, Winters, Dawson	5,758
6		29	(a)	Darlington	L 1-3	Winters	7,449
7	Oct	6	(h)	Halifax T	D 0-0		5,044
8		13	(a)	Halifax T	L 1-3	Nettleton	4,000
9		20	(h)	Lincoln C	W 3-0	Winters 2, Nettleton	4,754
10		27	(a)	Lincoln C	D 2-2	Winters, Dawson	5,635
11	Nov	3	(a)	Hartlepools U	W 2-0	Winters 2	4,000
12		10	(h)	Hartlepools U	W 5-2	Porritt, Routledge, Dawson, Gledhill, Opp own-goal	5,055
13	Dec	1	(a)	Doncaster R	D 1-1	Robbins	5,523
14		22	(a)	Rotherham U	L 2-3	Cooke, Scott	6,706
15		25	(h)	Bradford C	D 2-2	Robbins, Winters	6,611
16		26	(a)	Bradford C	L 0-6		8,569
17		29	(h)	Doncaster R	L 1-2	Cooke	5,953
18	Feb	20	(h)	Rotherham U	D 1-1	Allen	1,813

FINAL LEAGUE POSITION: 5th out of 10 in Football League North (East Region) — Appearances

Goals

Third Division Cup (Qualifying Group East)

19	Jan	12	(h)	Carlisle U	L 1-2	Winters	4,930
20		19	(a)	Carlisle U	L 1-3	Scott	6,900
21	Feb	2	(h)	Doncaster R	L 1-3	Gledhill	4,000
22		9	(a)	Bradford C	D 0-0		4,797
23		16	(h)	Bradford C	D 2-2	Allen, Iddon	5,454
24		23	(a)	Halifax T	W 1-0	Allen	2,200
25	Mar	2	(h)	Halifax T	D 1-1	Allen	4,738
26		9	(h)	Lincoln C	W 6-2	Thompson 3, Mahon 2, Winters	4,823
27		13	(a)	Lincoln C	D 2-2	Allen, Iddon	1,643
28		16	(a)	Doncaster R	L 1-3	Pinder (pen)	9,000

Appearances

Goals

Third Division Cup (Competition Proper East)

1	Mar	23	(a)	Accrington S	L 0-1		4,000
		30	(h)	Accrington S	W 3-1	Allen 2, Scott	6,433
2	Apr	6	(a)	Chester	L 0-4		6,000
		13	(h)	Chester	W 1-0	Allen	5,225

Appearances

Goals

Additional League Games

29	Apr	19	(h)	Doncaster R	W 5-1	Scott 2, Brenen, Allen 2	5,946
30		22	(a)	Doncaster R	D 1-1	Allen	6,961
31		27	(h)	Hartlepools U	L 2-3	Opp own-goal, Allen	2,106
32	Mar	4	(a)	Hartlepools U	L 2-6	Porritt 2	4,150

FINAL LEAGUE POSITION: 12th out of 20 in Football League North (Second Championship) — Appearances

Goals

FA Cup

1	Nov	17	(a)	Halifax T	L 0-1		5,849
		24	(h)	Halifax T	W 4-2	Lee, Gledhill (pen), Scott 2	7,573
2	Dec	8	(a)	B.Auckland	W 2-1	Maddison, Winters	5,674
		15	(h)	B.Auckland	W 3-0	Winters, Brenen, Robbins	8,651
3	Jan	5	(a)	Chesterfield	D 1-1	Mahon	15,025
		9	(h)	Chesterfield	W 3-2	Winters 2, Opp own-goal	14,267
4		26	(a)	Sheffield W	L 1-5	Scott (pen)	33,363
		30	(h)	Sheffield W	L 1-6	Allen	10,447

Appearances

Goals

High Scoring Games

League

6 or more goals

For

1929-30	Rochdale (home)	6-0
1931-32	Halifax Town (home)	7-2
1932-33	Darlington (home)	6-1
1933-34	Barrow (home)	6-1
	Rochdale (away)	6-3
	Rochdale (home)	6-1
1934-35	Crewe Alex (home)	7-3
	Carlisle United (home)	7-0
1935-36	Mansfield Town (home)	7-5
1947-48	Halifax Town (home)	6-0
1948-49	Carlisle United (home)	6-0
	Rotherham United (home)	6-1
1951-52	Accrington S (home)	6-1
	Halifax Town (home)	6-2
1954-55	Wrexham (away)	6-2
1956-57	Southport (home)	9-1
1960-61	Exeter City (home)	6-1
1964-65	Chesterfield (home)	7-1
1967-68	Bradford (home)	6-2
1981-82	Crewe Alex (home)	6-0
1982-83	Mansfield Town (home)	6-1
1984-85	Gillingham (home)	7-1
1985-86	Darlington (home)	7-0

Against

1931-32	Gateshead (away)	0-6
	Crewe Alex (away)	1-8
	Hartlepools U (away)	2-7
1932-33	Rochdale (home)	2-6
1935-36	Oldham Athletic (away)	2-6
	Walsall (away)	0-6
	Accrington S (away)	2-7
	Chester (away)	0-12
1936-37	Stockport County (away)	0-6
1937-38	Oldham Athletic (away)	2-6
1938-39	Bradford City (away)	0-6
	Crewe Alex (away)	2-8
	Rochdale (home)	0-7
	Oldham Athletic (away)	0-6
1946-47	Chester (away)	0-6
	Rotherham United (away)	1-6
1950-51	Tranmere Rovers (away)	2-7
1953-54	Mansfield Town (away)	2-7
1957-58	Tranmere Rovers (away)	1-6
	Chester (away)	2-9
1960-61	Aldershot (away)	1-6
1965-66	Swindon Town (away)	0-6
	Queen's Park R (away)	2-7
	Swansea Town (away)	2-7
1970-71	Brentford (away)	4-6
1976-77	Brighton & HA (away)	2-7
1979-80	Scunthorpe United (away)	1-6
1981-82	Bradford City (away)	2-6
1988-89	Burnley (away)	0-6

FA Cup

For

1924-25	Horsforth (home	7-1
1927-28	Stockton Malleable (home)	7-1
1928-29	Stockton (home)	7-1
1968-69	South Shields (away)	6-0

Against

1945-46	Sheffield Wednesday (home)	1-6
1984-85	Liverpool (away)	0-7

FL Cup

Biggest Victory

1984-85	Doncaster Rovers (home)	5-0

Biggest Defeats

1987-88	Leeds United (home)	0-4
1988-89	Sunderland (away)	0-4

Other Cups

For

1989-90	Hartlepool United (home)	7-1

Against

1987-88	Darlington (home)	3-4

York City Hat-tricks

League

Player	Gls	Opponents	Date
Bottrill	3	Wigan Borough	28 Dec 1929
Millar	3	Crewe Alex	1 Feb 1930
Cowie	3	Hartlepools U	4 Feb 1931
Baines	3	New Brighton	27 Feb 1932
Baines	3	Rochdale	28 Mar 1932
Baines	3	Halifax T	23 Apr 1932
Baines	3	Mansfield T	17 Sep 1932
Baines	3	Barrow	5 Apr 1933
Hathway	3	Barrow	3 Feb 1934
Dando	3	Rochdale	24 Mar 1934
Dando	3	Rotherham U	10 Nov 1934
Hughes	3	Walsall	30 Mar 1935
Dando	3	Carlisle U	27 Apr 1935
Thompson	3	Darlington	13 Mar 1937
Thompson	3	Carlisle U	1 May 1937
Baines	3	Chester	11 Sep 1937
A.Patrick	4	Halifax T	30 Aug 1947
A.Patrick	3	Chester	27 Dec 1947
A.Patrick	5	Rotherham U	28 Nov 1948
A.Patrick	3	Stockport C	15 Jan 1949
Spence	3	Wrexham	4 Feb 1950
Fenton	3	Accrington S	27 Oct 1951
A.Patrick	3	Oldham A	26 Jan 1952
A.Patrick	3	Halifax T	16 Feb 1952
Dunmore	3	Mansfield T	17 Oct 1953
Bottom	3	Wrexham	21 Aug 1954
Fenton	4	Carlisle U	28 Nov 1954
Wilkinson	3	Wrexham	17 Dec 1955
Bottom	4	Southport	2 Feb 1957
Wilkinson	3	Rochdale	20 Apr 1957
Farmer	3	Tranmere R	23 Apr 1958
Wragg	3	Hartlepools U	4 Oct 1958
Edgar	3	Accrington S	3 Oct 1959
Addison	3	Workington	24 Sep 1960
Wragg	3	Aldershot	3 Oct 1960
Wragg	4	Crewe Alex	21 Jan 1961
Weir	3	Crewe Alex	2 Oct 1961
Stainsby	3	Gillingham	13 Jan 1962
Wragg	3	Doncaster R	2 Apr 1962
Weir	3	Workington	20 Apr 1962
Wilkinson	3	Lincoln C	22 Apr 1963
Weddle	3	Tranmere R	26 Mar 1965
Aimson	3	Hull City	18 Sep 1965
MacDougall	3	Port Vale	30 Mar 1968
Aimson	3	Brentford	28 Mar 1970
Aimson	3	Chesterfield	1 Apr 1972
Staniforth	3	Port Vale	7 May 1979
Staniforth	3	Wigan A	15 Sep 1979
Walwyn	3	Mansfield T	27 Nov 1982
Byrne	3	Chester C	17 Sep 1983
Byrne	3	Halifax T	20 Apr 1984
Houchen	3	Gillingham	3 Nov 1984
Canham	3	Darlington	5 Oct 1985

FA Cup

Player	Gls	Opponents	Date
Marshall	5	Horsforth	20 Sep 1924
Holland	3	Wombwell	3 Oct 1925
Clayton	3	Guisborough	2 Oct 1926
Cowie	6	Stockton	29 Sep 1928
Agar	3	Hull C	28 Nov 1936
Baines	3	West Brom	22 Jan 1938
Bottom	3	Dorchester	11 Dec 1954
Aimson	3	Bangor C	14 Nov 1964
Ross	3	Sth Shields	16 Nov 1968
Aimson	3	Tamworth	23 Nov 1970

FL Cup

Player	Gls	Opponents	Date
Walwyn	3	Sunderland	26 Aug 1986
Spooner	3	Hartlepool U	29 Aug 1989

Other Cups

Player	Gls	Opponents	Date
Gabbiadini	3	Darlington	25 Nov 1986
Helliwell	3	Hartlepool U	7 Nov 1989

YORK CITY CAREER RECORDS
FOOTBALL LEAGUE 1929-1990

*The following list features the career records of all those players who have played for York City in the Football League and FA Cup since 1929, the Football League Cup since 1960, other competitions (Associate Members Cup, Freight/Rover, Sherpa Van and Leyland Daf Trophy) since 1983. Not included are Wartime league and cup appearances 1939-40 to 1945-6 inclusive or players who only appeared for the club during this period. *Denotes also played for the club in the Midland League.*

		League		FA Cup		FL Cup		Others		Total	
Player	Played	App	Gls	App	Gls	App	Gls	App	Gls	App	Gls
ADDISON, Colin	1957-61	87	28	9	2	1	1	0	0	97	31
AGAR, Alfred	1936-37	24	4	3	3	0	0	0	0	27	7
AIMSON, Paul	1964-66										
	1969-73	210/9	98	17/2	12	9	3	0	0	236/11	113
AITKEN, James	1929-30	4	1	0	0	0	0	0	0	4	1
AITKEN, Peter	1982	18	2	0	0	0	0	0	0	18	2
ALDERSON, Stuart	1967-68	17/2	5	0	0	1	0	0	0	18/2	5
ALEXANDER, Gus	1959-60	7	0	0	0	0	0	0	0	7	0
ALLEN, William	1945-50	129	23	6	1	0	0	0	0	135	24
AMBLER, Roy	1962-63	12	3	2	0	0	0	0	0	14	3
ANDREWS, John	1969	11	0	0	0	0	0	0	0	11	0
ANDREWS, Percy	1947-54	176	0	5	0	0	0	0	0	181	0
ARCHIBALD, David	1929-33	85	0	1	0	0	0	0	0	86	0
ASHLEY, Joe	1950-51	9	0	4	0	0	0	0	0	13	0
ASHWORTH, Joe	1962-65	57	0	3	0	5	0	0	0	65	0
ASTBURY, Michael	1980-85	48	0	5	0	5	0	1	0	59	0
ATKINSON, Hugh	1984-85	3/4	0	0	0	1	0	2	0	6/4	0
BAINBRIDGE, Peter	1978	9	0	0	0	0	0	0	0	9	0
BAINBRIDGE, Robert	1954-55	4	0	0	0	0	0	0	0	4	0
BAINES, Reg	1931-33										
	1937-38	110	81	11	5	0	0	0	0	121	86
BAKER, Gerry	1963-68	214	7	11	1	9	1	0	0	234	9
BANFIELD, Albert	1935-36	30	10	0	0	0	0	0	0	30	10
BANTON, Dale	1984-88	129/9	49	14	3	13	1	8	2	164/9	55
BARMBY, Jeff	1963	2	0	0	0	0	0	0	0	2	0
BARNES, John	1934-35	15	1	0	0	0	0	0	0	15	1
BARRATT, Tony	1989-90	58	5	1	0	4	0	3	0	66	5
BARRETT, Claude	1937-38	41	0	9	0	0	0	0	0	50	0
BARRITT, Ronald	1952-53	5	0	0	0	0	0	0	0	5	0
BATTYE, John	1959-60	17	0	0	0	0	0	0	0	17	0
BECK, Harold	1929-32	119	12	12	0	0	0	0	0	131	12
BELL, Robert	1977	5	0	0	0	0	0	0	0	5	0
BENSON, Ron	1949-50	20	3	0	0	0	0	0	0	20	3
BENTALL, Edward	1945-47	1	0	3	0	0	0	0	0	4	0
BENTHAM, John	1981-82	22/1	0	0	0	0	0	0	0	22/1	0
BINGLEY, Walter	1960-63	130	5	11	0	10	0	0	0	151	5
BIRCH, Jeff	1949	7	1	1	1	0	0	0	0	8	2
BLACKBURN, Eddie	1980-82	76	0	5	0	6	0	0	0	87	0
BLACKBURN, Stanley	1931	1	0	0	0	0	0	0	0	1	0
BOLTON, James*	1932-33	7	0	0	0	0	0	0	0	7	0
BONASS, Albert	1933-34	6	0	0	0	0	0	0	0	6	0
BOTTOM, Arthur	1954-58	137	92	21	13	0	0	0	0	158	105
BOTTRILL, William	1929-30	39	18	6	2	0	0	0	0	45	20

Player	Played	League App	League Gls	FA Cup App	FA Cup Gls	FL Cup App	FL Cup Gls	Others App	Others Gls	Total App	Total Gls
BOWATER, George	1934-35	30	11	3	1	0	0	0	0	33	12
BOYER, Philip	1968-70	108/1	27	12	4	5	3	0	0	125/1	34
BOYES, Ken	1957-66	53	2	3	0	3	0	0	0	59	2
BRADLEY, Charles	1946-47	10	2	0	0	0	0	0	0	10	2
BRADSHAW, Darren	1987-89	58/1	3	2	0	2	0	3	0	65/1	3
BRANAGAN, Jim	1987-89	40/2	1	4	0	2	0	3	0	49/2	1
BRENEN, Bert	1939-51	206	13	14	2	0	0	0	0	220	15
BREWIS, Thomas	1930-32	26	11	2	1	0	0	0	0	28	12
BRIGHAM, Harry	1948-50	86	5	4	1	0	0	0	0	90	6
BROOKES, John	1929-32	82	0	11	0	0	0	0	0	93	0
BROOKES, John	1966	1	0	0	0	0	0	0	0	1	0
BROUGH, Paul	1987	0/1	0	4	0	0	0	0	0	4/1	0
BROWN, Gordon	1950-58	322	25	29	0	0	0	0	0	351	25
BROWN, Graham	1977-80	69	0	6	0	4	0	0	0	79	0
BROWN, John	1948-49	22	0	0	0	0	0	0	0	22	0
BROWNE, Robert	1947	5	0	0	0	0	0	0	0	5	0
BROWNLEE, Tommy	1958-59	9	2	0	0	0	0	0	0	9	2
BUCHANAN, David	1987	7	2	0	0	1/1	1	1	0	9/1	3
BULLOCK, Arthur	1934-35	6	0	1	0	0	0	0	0	7	0
BURDEN, Ian	1966	3	2	0	0	0	0	0	0	3	2
BURGESS, Campbell	1953-54	32	14	0	0	0	0	0	0	32	14
BURGIN, Eric	1949-51	23	0	0	0	0	0	0	0	23	0
BURLURAUX, Don	1971-72	3	1	0	0	0	0	0	0	3	1
BURROWS, Philip	1966-74	333/4	14	31	1	22	0	0	0	386/4	15
BURROWS, Wilfred	1933-34	3	0	0	0	0	0	0	0	3	0
BUSBY, Viv	1982-83	9/10	4	2	0	0	0	0	0	11/10	4
BURTON, Ernie	1948	3	0	0	0	0	0	0	0	3	0
BUTLER, Ian	1973-75	43/3	2	2	0	5	1	0	0	50/3	3
BUTLER, Martin	1984-88	40/25	9	5/2	1	3/1	0	6/1	3	54/29	13
BUTT, Len	1947	25	2	0	0	0	0	0	0	25	2
BYRNE, John	1979-84	167/8	55	10/1	4	10/2	5	1	0	188/11	64
CAIRNEY, Jim	1956-58	53	0	3	0	0	0	0	0	56	0
CALLOWAY, Laurie	1971-72	54/1	3	1	0	5	2	0	0	60/1	5
CALVERT, Cliff	1972-75	62/5	0	3	0	3/1	0	0	0	68/7	0
CAMIDGE, William	1932-33	2	0	0	0	0	0	0	0	2	0
CANHAM, Tony	1984-90	160/15	37	10	2	10	1	11/2	4	191/17	44
CARR, Frank	1946-47	7	3	0	0	0	0	0	0	7	3
CARR, Graham	1968-69	32/1	1	3	0	1	0	0	0	36/1	1
CARR, James	1938	2	2	0	0	0	0	0	0	2	2
CAULFIELD, Graham	1967	9	2	0	0	0	0	0	0	9	2
CAVE, Michael	1974-77	94/2	13	6	2	7	0	0	0	107/2	15
CHAMBERS, David	1971	8/8	1	2	1	1	0	0	0	11/8	2
CHAPPELL, Sydney	1939	1	0	0	0	0	0	0	0	1	0
CHARLESWORTH, Arnold	1954	1	0	0	0	0	0	0	0	1	0
CHIPPENDALE, Brian	1984-85	2/6	0	0	0	1	1	2/1	0	5/7	1
CLAYSON, William	1933-34	7	0	0	0	0	0	0	0	7	0
CLEGG, Tony	1987-88	38/3	3	2	0	4	0	2	0	46/3	3
CLEMENTS, Andy	1977-81	146/2	6	11	1	4	1	0	0	161/2	8
COLBRIDGE, Clive	1955-57	37	14	3	1	0	0	0	0	40	15
COLEMAN, John	1968-69	8/1	3	0	0	0	0	0	0	8/1	3
COLLIER, Austin	1946	10	0	0	0	0	0	0	0	10	0
COLLIER, Graham	1978	5	0	0	0	0	0	0	0	5	0
COLLINS, Tony	1949-50	10	1	0	0	0	0	0	0	10	1
COLLINSON, Les	1967-68	35	2	0	0	1	0	0	0	36	2
COMRIE, Malcolm	1936-38	79	20	16	3	0	0	0	0	95	23
COLVILLE, Robert	1989-90	17/7	0	0	0	3/1	2	1/1	0	21/10	2
COOK, Mike	1987	6	1	0	0	0	0	0	0	6	1

Player	Played	League App	Gls	FA Cup App	Gls	FL Cup App	Gls	Others App	Gls	Total App	Gls
COOP, Jim	1949-50	12	4	1	0	0	0	0	0	13	4
COOP, Michael	1974	4	0	0	0	0	0	0	0	4	0
COSTELLO, Nigel	1987-88	2/2	0	0	0	0	0	0/1	0	2/3	0
COWIE, James*	1929-31	18	9	3	1	0	0	0	0	21	10
COYNE, George	1966	2	0	0	0	0	0	0	0	2	0
CRAIG, Derek	1980-82	53	1	2	0	5	0	0	0	60	1
CRANGLE, Jimmy	1972-73	4	0	0	0	1	0	0	0	5	0
CRAVEN, George	1936	3	0	0	0	0	0	0	0	3	0
CRAWFORD, Graeme	1971-77 1980	252	0	14	0	14	0	0	0	280	0
CREAMER, Peter	1975	4	0	0	0	0	0	0	0	4	0
CROFT, Stuart	1981	14	0	0	0	0	0	0	0	14	0
CROSBY, Malcolm	1981-85	99/4	4	11	0	2	0	1	0	113/4	4
CROSSLEY, Richard	1990	1	0	0	0	0	0	0	0	1	0
CUNLIFFE, Robert	1965-66	11/1	2	0	0	0	0	0	0	11/1	2
CUNNINGHAM, Joseph	1934-35	42	0	3	0	0	0	0	0	45	0
CZUCZMAN, Michael	1981-82	17	0	1	0	0	0	0	0	18	0
DALE, Chris	1968	5	0	0	0	0	0	0	0	5	0
DANDO, Maurice	1933-35	82	46	4	0	0	0	0	0	86	46
DANIELS, Harold	1950	4	2	0	0	0	0	0	0	4	2
DAVIDSON, Ian	1969-71	82/4	4	11	3	5	1	0	0	98/4	8
DAVIS, Charles	1929-31	61	1	11	1	0	0	0	0	72	2
DAWSON, Richard	1981-82	45	0	1	0	2	0	0	0	48	0
DAWSON, William	1933-34	28	1	1	0	0	0	0	0	29	1
DENHOLME, George	1936-39	8	0	0	0	0	0	0	0	8	0
DE PLACIDO, Michael	1972-73	4/7	0	0	0	0	0	0	0	4/7	0
DESMOND, Peter	1951	1	0	0	0	0	0	0	0	1	0
DIXON, Kevin	1988-90	33/5	8	1	0	1/1	0	5	2	40/6	10
DONALDSON, David	1932-33	18	1	1	0	0	0	0	0	19	1
DOWNING, David	1987	1	0	0	0	0	0	0	0	1	0
DOWNING, Derek	1975-77	44/3	2	5	0	4	0	0	0	54/2	2
DUCKWORTH, Joseph	1932	7	0	0	0	0	0	0	0	7	0
DUCKWORTH, Dick	1936-39	88	0	17	0	0	0	0	0	105	0
DUNMORE, David	1952-54 1965-67	109/2	38	8	1	4	2	0	0	121/2	41
DUNN, Iain	1988-90	28/16	8	1	0	2	0	0/3	0	31/19	8
DUNPHY, Eamonn	1965-66	22	3	1	0	3	1	0	0	26	4
DUTHIE, John*	1930-31	22	0	1	0	0	0	0	0	23	0
DUTHOIT, Jack	1946-49	36	0	1	0	0	0	0	0	37	0
EARL, Sam	1937-39	58	9	6	1	0	0	0	0	64	10
ECCLES, Terry	1979-81	64	18	3	1	4	0	0	0	71	19
EDGAR, John	1959-61	47	16	3	2	0	0	0	0	50	18
ELI, Roger	1988	3/1	1	1	0	0	0	1	0	5/1	1
ELLIS, William	1930	3	1	1	0	0	0	0	0	4	1
ENDERSBY, Scott	1987-89	35	0	2	0	4	0	2	0	43	0
EVANS, Chris	1982-85	93/3	1	5/1	0	8/1	0	2/1	0	108/6	1
EVANS, Sam	1929-31	66	12	9	2	0	0	0	0	75	14
EYRES, Jack	1934-35	37	13	3	0	0	0	0	0	40	13
FALLON, Harry	1965-67	67	0	1	0	5	0	0	0	73	0
FARMER, Terry	1958-60	66	28	1	0	0	0	0	0	67	28
FARMERY, John	1929-31	67	0	11	0	0	0	0	0	78	0
FAULKNER, Steve	1978-81	90	7	6/1	1	8	0	0	0	104/1	8
FAWCETT, Desmond	1932-34	74	0	2	0	0	0	0	0	76	0
FAZACKERLEY, Derek	1988	16	0	1	0	2	0	1	0	20	0
FELL, Gerry	1982	2/3	0	0	0	0	0	0	0	2/3	0
FELLOWS, Stuart	1967-68	0/2	0	0	0	0	0	0	0	0/2	0
FENOUGHTY, Thomas*	1929-34	147	56	12	5	0	0	0	0	159	61

Player	Played	League App	Gls	FA Cup App	Gls	FL Cup App	Gls	Others App	Gls	Total App	Gls
FENTON, Billy	1951-58	258	118	21	6	0	0	0	0	279	124
FEREBEE, Stuart	1980	7/6	0	0	0	0	0	0	0	7/6	0
FERGUSON, Bob	1945-47	26	0	9	0	0	0	0	0	35	0
FIRTH, Joe	1938	6	1	0	0	0	0	0	0	6	1
FLATLEY, Albert	1939	4	0	0	0	0	0	0	0	4	0
FLOOD, Eddie	1981-82	13/2	0	3	0	2	0	0	0	18/2	0
FORD, Gary	1978-87	359/7	53	36	7	24	4	9	0	428/7	64
FORGAN, Tommy	1954-66	388	0	30	0	10	0	0	0	428	0
FORSTER, Leslie	1946-47	10	2	0	0	0	0	0	0	10	2
FOUNTAIN, Jack	1960-64	130	3	11	0	11	1	0	0	152	4
FOX, Stanley	1932-38	136	4	5	0	0	0	0	0	141	4
FRANCIS, Gerry	1961-62	16	4	1	0	2	1	0	0	19	5
FROST, John	1948-51	45	0	3	0	0	0	0	0	48	0
GABBIADINI, Marco	1984-87	42/18	14	0	0	4/3	1	4	3	50/21	18
GABBIADINI, Ricardo	1988	0/1	0	0	0	0	0	0	0	0/1	0
GADSBY, Michael	1969	13	0	0	0	1	0	0	0	14	0
GALE, Tom	1947-49	76	0	4	0	0	0	0	0	80	0
GALLACHER, Samuel	1929	3	0	0	0	0	0	0	0	3	0
GALVIN, Chris	1976-77	22	6	0	0	0	0	0	0	22	6
GARDNER, William	1929-31	51	26	6	2	0	0	0	0	57	28
GARGAN, John	1947	1	0	0	0	0	0	0	0	1	0
GLEDHILL, Sam	1936-48	123	6	11	1	0	0	0	0	134	7
GLIDDEN, Sidney	1929	2	0	0	0	0	0	0	0	2	0
GOLDIE, Jim	1963-64	22	7	0	0	1	0	0	0	23	7
GOODCHILD, John	1966-67	29	6	6	0	1	0	0	0	36	6
GOULD, Walter	1961-63	120	25	5	0	13	2	0	0	138	27
GRAHAM, James	1935	7	0	0	0	0	0	0	0	7	0
GRANGER, Michael	1952-62	71	0	8	0	2	0	0	0	81	0
GRANT, Alec	1950	3	0	0	0	0	0	0	0	3	0
GRAY, Robert	1935-36	4	1	0	0	0	0	0	0	4	1
GREEN, Harold	1935-36	42	8	1	0	0	0	0	0	43	8
GREENER, Robert	1932-33	24	0	1	0	0	0	0	0	25	0
GREENOUGH, Richard	1988-90	28/1	1	0	0	1	0	3	0	32/1	1
GREENSMITH, Ron	1958-59	42	1	1	0	0	0	0	0	43	1
GREENWELL, Don	1947	1	0	0	0	0	0	0	0	1	0
GRIFFITHS, Stephen	1951-53	74	12	4	0	0	0	0	0	78	12
HAGUE, Keith	1966	0/1	0	0	0	0	0	0	0	0/1	0
HALL, Wayne	1989-90	22/7	3	0/1	0	1	0	1	0	24/8	3
HAMER, Arnold	1938	8	0	0	0	0	0	0	0	8	0
HAMILTON, Alec	1962	11	0	0	0	0	0	0	0	11	0
HAMSTEAD, George	1964-66	32/3	1	0	0	0	0	0	0	32/3	1
HARNBY, Don	1947	1	0	0	0	0	0	0	0	1	0
HARRIS, Joseph	1931-33	62	0	2	0	0	0	0	0	64	0
HARRISON, John	1979-80	8	0	3	0	0	0	0	0	11	0
HARTNETT, James	1958	2	1	1	0	0	0	0	0	3	1
HASLEGRAVE, Sean	1983-87	137/5	0	11	0	11/1	0	5/2	0	164/8	0
HATHWAY, Ted	1933-39	218	38	21	2	0	0	0	0	239	40
HAWKINS, Joseph	1938-39	21	1	0	0	0	0	0	0	21	1
HAWKSBY, John	1966-68	72/2	7	2	0	4	0	0	0	78/2	7
HAY, Alan	1982-86 1988	148/3	2	16	1	10	0	4/1	0	178/4	3
HEATHCOTE, Micky	1990	3	0	0	0	0	0	1	0	4	0
HEDLEY, Graham	1981	5	1	0	0	0	0	0	0	5	1
HELLIWELL, Ian	1987-90	117/2	33	2	0	6	1	6/1	4	131/3	38
HENDERSON, Tom	1970-72	63/1	7	3	1	4	3	0	0	71	11
HERON, Tommy	1961-66	192	6	8	0	16	0	0	0	216	6
HEWITSON, William	1936	2	1	0	0	0	0	0	0	2	1

Player	Played	League App	League Gls	FA Cup App	FA Cup Gls	FL Cup App	FL Cup Gls	Others App	Others Gls	Total App	Total Gls
HEWITT, Richard	1969-72	87/4	7	9/1	2	5	0	0	0	101/5	9
HILL, William	1956-60	29	3	0	0	0	0	0	0	29	3
HILLYARD, Ron	1969-74	61	0	9	0	4	0	0	0	74	0
HIMSWORTH, Garry	1987-90	73/13	8	0	0	3	0	5/3	0	81/16	8
HINCH, Jim	1974-77	56/12	12	3/1	1	1	0	0	0	60/13	13
HINDLE, Thomas	1949	19	3	0	0	0	0	0	0	19	3
HOBSON, Albert	1956-57	22	1	1	0	0	0	0	0	23	1
HODGSON, Billy	1967-70	98	3	8/2	0	2	0	0	0	108/2	3
HOGGART, Dennis	1960-64	45	11	1	0	4	0	0	0	50	11
HOLMES, Ian	1973-77	152/7	30	8/1	3	10/2	2	0	0	170/10	35
HOOD, Derek	1980-88	287/13	32	24/2	3	16/3	1	7/2	0	334/20	36
HOPE, George	1976-78	34/8	9	3	0	3	0	0	0	40/8	9
HORREY, Rowland	1966-68	74	9	6	1	4	0	0	0	84	10
HORTON, Leslie	1950-51	21	0	2	0	0	0	0	0	23	0
HOSKER, Robert	1975-77	16/9	1	3/1	1	2	0	0	0	21/10	2
HOTTE, Tim	1988	1/1	0	0	0	0	0	0	0	1/1	0
HOUCHEN, Keith	1984-86	56/11	19	9/2	3	6	3	4	2	75/13	27
HOWE, George	1954-61	307	0	30	0	1	0	0	0	338	0
HOWLETT, Gary	1988-90	79/4	10	1/1	0	6	0	3	0	89/5	10
HOY, Robert	1977	10/4	1	0	0	1/1	1	0	0	11/5	2
HUGHES, James	1934-39	106	30	20	3	0	0	0	0	126	33
HUGHES, Billy	1951-61	349	55	30	3	1	0	0	0	380	58
HUNTER, Gordon	1973-78	70/7	1	5	0	2	0	0	0	77/7	1
HURLSTONE, Gary	1989	1/1	0	0	0	0	0	0	0	1/1	0
HUTT, Geoff	1977-78	63	1	1	0	3	0	0	0	67	1
IVEY, George	1948-51	79	13	5	1	0	0	0	0	84	14
IVORY, George	1933-34	31	9	1	0	0	0	0	0	32	9
JACKSON, Alec	1946-50	50	5	3	0	0	0	0	0	53	5
JACKSON, Barry	1958-70	481/1	9	34	0	23	1	0	0	538/1	10
JAMES, Steve	1976-80	105	1	8	0	6	1	0	0	119	2
JENKINS, Evan	1934-35	28	10	3	1	0	0	0	0	31	11
JENKINSON, Matt	1930-34	72	20	1	1	0	0	0	0	73	21
JOHANNESON, Albert	1970-71	26	3	3	1	4	1	0	0	33	5
JOHNSON, Clifford	1935	4	2	0	0	0	0	0	0	4	2
JOHNSON, Howard	1957-58	28	0	5	0	0	0	0	0	33	0
JOHNSON, Paul	1987-89	83	1	4	0	5	0	4	0	96	1
JOHNSON, Sam	1929-33	124	0	13	0	0	0	0	0	137	0
JONES, Brian	1960	1	0	0	0	0	0	0	0	1	0
JONES, Chris	1973-76	94/1	34	4	2	8	1	0	0	106/1	37
JONES, David	1970	3	0	2	0	0	0	0	0	5	0
JONES, Roger	1982-85	122	0	8	0	7	0	4	0	141	0
JONES, Walter	1955	1	0	0	0	0	0	0	0	1	0
JONES, William	1931-32	12	0	0	0	0	0	0	0	12	0
JORDAN, Brian	1960	8	0	0	0	0	0	0	0	8	0
JOWETT, Jim	1946	1	0	0	0	0	0	0	0	1	0
JOY, Brian	1976-77	18	0	4	0	0	0	0	0	22	0
JOY, David	1967-68	13/1	0	0	0	1	0	0	0	14/1	0
JUKES, Norman	1953	1	0	0	0	0	0	0	0	1	0
KAMARA, Alan	1979	10	0	0	0	0	0	0	0	10	0
KAY, Rob	1978-82	160	8	13	0	10	0	0	0	183	8
KELLY, Brian	1968-69	32/1	0	1	0	2	0	0	0	35/1	0
KELLY, Daniel	1930-32	48	12	3	0	0	0	0	0	51	12
KELLY, James	1938-39	24	0	1	0	0	0	0	0	25	0
KELLY, John	1930-31	6	4	2	0	0	0	0	0	8	4
KELLY, Tom	1989-90	35	2	1	0	4	0	3	1	43	3
KELLY, William	1951	0	0	1	0	0	0	0	0	1	0
KING, Dave	1983	0/1	0	0	0	0	0	0	0	0/1	0

Player	Played	League App	League Gls	FA Cup App	FA Cup Gls	FL Cup App	FL Cup Gls	Others App	Others Gls	Total App	Total Gls
KING, Herbert	1933	1	0	0	0	0	0	0	0	1	0
KIRBY, Eric	1952	1	0	0	0	0	0	0	0	1	0
KITCHING, Phil	1987-88	7/6	0	1	0	3	0	0	0	11/6	0
KUBICKI, Eryk	1946	5	0	0	0	0	0	0	0	5	0
LALLY, Pat	1971-73	64/7	5	6	0	3/1	0	0	0	73/8	5
LANG, Malcolm	1963	12	2	0	0	3	1	0	0	15	3
LAVERICK, Michael	1982-83	38/3	6	0	0	2	0	0	0	40/3	6
LAWIE, Charles	1935-36	10	1	1	0	0	0	0	0	11	1
LAWSON, John	1947	1	0	0	0	0	0	0	0	1	0
LAX, Walter	1933-34	28	5	1	1	0	0	0	0	29	6
LAYCOCK, Frederick	1930-31	27	12	5	5	0	0	0	0	32	17
LEAF, Andrew	1980	1	0	0	0	0	0	0	0	1	0
LEANING, Andy	1985-87	69	0	8	0	4	0	5	0	86	0
LEE, George	1937-46	37	11	2	1	0	0	0	0	39	12
LEGGE, Edward	1935-38	82	2	11	0	0	0	0	0	93	2
LINAKER, John	1950-51										
	1953-55	98	20	5	0	0	0	0	0	103	20
LINDSAY, Duncan	1935-36	25	8	1	1	0	0	0	0	26	9
LITTLE, George	1947-48	15	2	0	0	0	0	0	0	15	2
LLOYD, David	1951	1	0	0	0	0	0	0	0	1	0
LOCKIE, Tom	1933-34	29	1	0	0	0	0	0	0	29	1
LOGGIE, David	1978-80	47/3	11	3	0	3	0	0	0	53/3	11
LONGDEN, Colin	1957	2	0	0	0	0	0	0	0	2	0
LONGHURST, David	1990	4	2	0	0	0	0	0	0	4	2
LORIMER, Peter	1979-80	29	8	3	1	0	0	0	0	32	9
LOUGHRAN, James*	1931	1	0	0	0	0	0	0	0	1	0
LOWEY, John	1987	3/3	0	0	0	0	0	0	0	3/3	0
LYONS, Barry	1973-76	80/5	10	4	1	9	0	0	0	93/5	11
McARTHUR, Barry	1970	1	0	0	0	0	0	0	0	1	0
McAUGHTRIE, David	1985-87	64	1	8	0	4/1	1	3	0	79/1	2
McCABE, Bernard	1931	21	10	0	0	0	0	0	0	21	10
McCARTNEY, Charles	1937	1	0	0	0	0	0	0	0	1	0
McDERMOTT, Maurice	1947	7	0	0	0	0	0	0	0	7	0
McDONALD, Ian	1977-81	175	29	11	1	9	1	0	0	195	31
McDONALD, Thomas	1931-35	75	11	2	1	0	0	0	0	77	12
MacDOUGALL, Ted	1967-69	84	34	4	4	2	2	0	0	90	40
McGHIE, William	1979-81	39/4	1	2	0	4	0	0	0	45/4	1
McKENZIE, Stuart	1986-88	30/2	0	0	0	4/1	0	1/1	0	35/4	0
MACKIN, John	1969-73	157/3	6	15	1	9	0	0	0	181/3	7
McMAHON, Kevin	1969-72	85/8	30	9	3	7/1	1	0	0	101/9	34
McMILLAN, Andy	1987-90	41/8	0	1	0	1	0	2	0	45/8	0
McMORDIE, Eric	1975-76	42	2	3	0	4	0	0	0	49	2
McNAB, Sam	1954-55	19	3	1	0	0	0	0	0	20	3
MacPHAIL, John	1983-86	141/1	24	16	1	10	3	5	1	172/1	29
MADDEN, Craig	1990	3/1	0	0	0	0	0	0	0	3/1	0
MADDISON, George	1953-54	11	0	0	0	0	0	0	0	11	0
MAHON, Michael	1969-70	27/2	10	3	1	1	0	0	0	31/2	11
MALONEY, Paul	1970-72	3/5	0	0	0	0	0	0	0	3/5	0
MARLOW, Fred	1953-54	24	0	0	0	0	0	0	0	24	0
MARPLES, Chris	1988-90	91	0	2	0	6	0	6	0	105	0
MASKILL, George*	1932	3	0	0	0	0	0	0	0	3	0
MASKILL, Thomas*	1932-33	29	3	1	0	0	0	0	0	30	3
MEDD, Gordon	1951	1	0	0	0	0	0	0	0	1	0
MEECHAN, David	1963	6	0	0	0	0	0	0	0	6	0
METCALFE, John	1957	3	2	0	0	0	0	0	0	3	2
MIDDLETON, Derek	1958	1	0	0	0	0	0	0	0	1	0
MIDDLETON, Matt	1949-50	55	0	1	0	0	0	0	0	56	0

Player	Played	League App	League Gls	FA Cup App	FA Cup Gls	FL Cup App	FL Cup Gls	Others App	Others Gls	Total App	Total Gls
MILLAR, Alistair	1980	11/1	0	0	0	0	0	0	0	11/1	0
MILLAR, William	1929-31	58	12	6	0	0	0	0	0	64	12
MILLS, Simon	1985-87	97/1	4	13	2	8	1	6	1	124/1	8
MILNER, Leonard	1938-39	11	4	0	0	0	0	0	0	11	4
MILTON, Stanley	1938-39	9	0	0	0	0	0	0	0	9	0
MITCHELL, Barry	1977	1/2	0	0	0	0	0	0	0	1/2	0
MITCHELL, Tom	1931-33	23	5	1	0	0	0	0	0	24	5
MOLLATT, Ron	1955-60	124	1	1	0	0	0	0	0	125	1
MONKHOUSE, Alan	1956	12	1	0	0	0	0	0	0	12	1
MOOR, Tony	1962-64	57	0	2	0	5	0	0	0	64	0
MOORE, Tony	1962	2	0	0	0	1	0	0	0	3	0
MOORE, William	1933	2	0	0	0	0	0	0	0	2	0
MORRIS, David	1977	1/6	0	0	0	0	0	0	0	1/6	0
MORRIS, Neil	1988	3/1	0	0	0	0	0	0	0	3/1	0
MORRITT, Gordon	1969-71	41	0	7	0	4	0	0	0	52	0
MORTIMER, Robert	1938-39	35	22	1	0	0	0	0	0	36	22
MORTON, Ken	1965-66	9/1	2	0	0	0	0	0	0	9/1	2
MURPHY, Nick	1986	0	0	0	0	0	0	1	0	1	0
MURRAY, Alan	1972	4	0	0	0	0	0	0	0	4	0
MURPHY, Steven	1986	2/1	0	0	0	0	0	0	0	2/1	0
NAYLOR, Glen	1990	0/1	0	0	0	0	0	0	0	0/1	0
NEENAN, Joe	1977-80	56	0	3	0	3	0	0	0	62	0
NETTLETON, Ernie	1946-47	7	2	0	0	0	0	0	0	7	2
NEWMAN, Keith	1970	3/1	0	1	0	0	0	0	0	4/1	0
NICHOLSON, Gary	1984-85	23/1	4	1	0	4	0	3	0	31/1	4
NICOL, James	1936-37	11	3	3	1	0	0	0	0	14	4
NOVACKI, Jan	1977-78	24/1	3	0	0	0	0	0	0	24/1	3
OGDEN, Alan	1974-75	7	0	2	0	0	0	0	0	9	0
OLIVER, Peter	1974-75	41	0	0/1	0	2	0	0	0	43/1	0
ORD, Richard	1990	3	0	0	0	0	0	0	0	3	0
PARK, William	1946-47	22	1	1	0	0	0	0	0	23	1
PATRICK, Alf	1946-53	228	109	13	8	0	0	0	0	241	117
PATRICK, Matt	1946-54	249	47	13	1	0	0	0	0	262	48
PATTERSON, George	1957-60	57	4	0	0	0	0	0	0	57	4
PAWSON, Thomas	1935	1	1	0	0	0	0	0	0	1	1
PEACHEY, John	1973-74	6/2	3	1	0	3	1	0	0	10/2	4
PEARCE, Alan	1983-87	76/2	9	9	1	0	0	3/2	0	88/4	10
PEARS, Jeff	1948-49	3	0	0	0	0	0	0	0	3	0
PEARSON, John	1965-66	14/1	4	1	0	2	0	0	0	17/1	4
PEART, Ron	1948	5	0	0	0	0	0	0	0	5	0
PEGG, James	1950	1	0	0	0	0	0	0	0	1	0
PENNICK, Ray	1969	0/1	0	0	0	0	0	0	0	0/1	0
PERRY, Peter	1962-63	23	0	0	0	0	0	0	0	23	0
PEYTON, Noel	1963-65	37	4	1	0	3	1	0	0	41	5
PHILLIPS, Ernie	1954-58	164	2	19	0	0	0	0	0	183	2
PICKERING, Mike	1986-87	31/1	1	0	0	4	0	2	0	37/1	1
PICKERING, Peter	1947-48	49	0	1	0	0	0	0	0	50	0
PIERCE, Barry	1961-62	12	5	0	0	0	0	0	0	12	5
PINDER, Jack	1932-48	199	4	26	0	0	0	0	0	225	4
POLLARD, Brian	1972-77										
	1981-84	249/15	60	20/1	6	15	2	1	0	285/16	68
POPELY, Peter	1963-66	24/1	0	1	0	0	0	0	0	25/1	0
PORRITT, William	1936-47	40	5	2	0	0	0	0	0	42	5
PORTEOUS, Joe	1946-47	23	0	0	0	0	0	0	0	23	0
PORTER, Les	1949-53	39	1	0	0	0	0	0	0	39	1
POVEY, William	1964	3	0	0	0	0	0	0	0	3	0
POWELL, John	1956-60	27	5	1	0	0	0	0	0	28	5

Player	Played	League App	League Gls	FA Cup App	FA Cup Gls	FL Cup App	FL Cup Gls	Others App	Others Gls	Total App	Total Gls
PRESCOTT, Jimmy	1955-56	18	5	0	0	0	0	0	0	18	5
PRICE, John	1948-49	2	2	0	0	0	0	0	0	2	2
PROVAN, Andy	1964-68	159/1	49	10	2	9	3	0	0	178/1	54
PUGH, David	1978-81	73/4	2	5	1	2	0	0	0	80/4	3
PYLE, Elijah	1947-48	10	3	0	0	0	0	0	0	10	3
RAMSEY, Bob	1958-61	75	0	4	0	0	0	0	0	79	0
RANDALL, Kevin	1977-81	96/11	27	9	2	2	1	0	0	107/11	30
REAGAN, Martin	1945-46	1	0	2	0	0	0	0	0	3	0
REID, Shaun	1988-90	48/1	6	0	0	3	0	0	0	51/1	6
REYNOLDS, Walter	1938	3	0	0	0	0	0	0	0	3	0
RICHARDS, Lloyd	1980-81	17/1	1	0	0	4	1	0	0	21/1	2
RICHARDS, Steve	1984-85	6/1	0	0	0	0	0	3	0	9/1	0
RICHARDSON, William	1968-69	24	0	3	0	1	0	0	0	28	0
RIDLEY, Ralph	1930-32	46	0	1	0	0	0	0	0	47	0
RIOCH, Neil	1972	0/1	0	0	0	0	0	0	0	0/1	0
ROBB, Ian	1974-75	4	0	0	0	0	0	0	0	4	0
ROBERTS, Arthur	1946	1	0	0	0	0	0	0	0	1	0
ROBERTSON, John	1957-58	17	5	2	1	0	0	0	0	19	6
ROBINSON, A	1936	3	0	0	0	0	0	0	0	3	0
RODGERS, Cliff	1945-47	26	0	9	0	0	0	0	0	35	0
ROGERS, Lee	1988	5/2	0	0	0	0	0	0	0	5/2	0
ROSS, Tommy	1967-69	56/5	20	4	3	2	0	0	0	62/5	23
ROUTLEDGE, William	1934-36	78	1	4	0	0	0	0	0	82	1
ROWLES, Eddie	1971-73	61/6	15	6	3	0/1	0	0	0	67/7	18
RUDD, Jimmy	1947-49	83	23	4	1	0	0	0	0	87	24
RUDD, Billy	1962-66	193	30	8	0	11	1	0	0	212	31
RYAN, Michael	1953	4	0	0	0	0	0	0	0	4	0
SBRAGIA, Ricky	1982-87	149	7	17	3	11	0	2	0	179	10
SCOTT, Fred	1937-46	74	16	12	4	0	0	0	0	86	20
SCOTT, John	1933-34	34	1	1	0	0	0	0	0	35	1
SCOTT, John	1963-64	21	3	1	0	0	0	0	0	22	3
SCOTT, Joe	1960-61	17	2	1	0	1	0	0	0	19	2
SCOTT, Malcolm	1963-64	19	0	0	0	0	0	0	0	19	0
SCOTT, Peter	1975-78	99/1	3	6	0	8	0	0	0	113/1	3
SEAL, Jimmy	1972-76	152/9	43	9	3	13	2	0	0	174/9	48
SEARSON, Harold	1952-54	62	0	1	0	0	0	0	0	63	0
SENIOR, Steve	1981-87	158/10	6	20	0	7/1	0	10	1	195/11	7
SHARPE, George*	1929-30	24	2	1	1	0	0	0	0	25	3
SHAW, Adrian	1988	5	0	0	0	0	0	1	0	6	0
SHEPHERD, John	1968-69	5	0	0	0	0	0	0	0	5	0
SIBBALD, Bob	1969-71	74/5	7	7	1	5	0	0	0	86/5	8
SIMPSON, John	1948-53	207	0	13	0	0	0	0	0	220	0
SLATER, Fred	1951	13	3	1	0	0	0	0	0	14	3
SLATTER, Les	1954-55	13	0	0	0	0	0	0	0	13	0
SLICER, Jack	1933	6	0	0	0	0	0	0	0	6	0
SMALLWOOD, Neil	1986-88	13	0	4	0	0	0	0	0	17	0
SMILES, Thomas	1929-30	8	0	0	0	0	0	0	0	8	0
SMITH, Alan	1970-71	1/1	0	0	0	0	0	0	0	1/1	0
SMITH, Denis	1982-83	37	5	4	0	2	0	0	0	43	5
SMITH, Kevan	1988-89	30/1	5	0	0	0	0	2	0	32/1	5
SMITH, Malcolm	1980-81	28/7	6	0	0	4	0	0	0	32/7	6
SMITH, Ron	1955	1	0	0	0	0	0	0	0	1	0
SPARGO, Stephen	1932-33	35	0	1	0	0	0	0	0	36	0
SPEED, Fred	1934-36	79	15	4	1	0	0	0	0	83	16
SPENCE, Joe	1950-53	110	0	5	0	0	0	0	0	115	0
SPENCE, Ron	1948-58	280	25	26	1	0	0	0	0	306	26
SPENCER, Tom	1966-68	54/3	21	3	2	5	3	0	0	62/3	26

Player	Played	League App	League Gls	FA Cup App	FA Cup Gls	FL Cup App	FL Cup Gls	Others App	Others Gls	Total App	Total Gls
SPOFFORTH, David	1987-88	3	0	0	0	0	0	0	0	3	0
SPOONER, Peter	1931-33										
	1935-39	189	42	18	6	0	0	0	0	207	48
SPOONER, Steve	1988-90	72	11	1	0	6	3	4	1	83	15
SPRATT, Tommy	1968-69	26/2	1	0	0	0/1	1	0	0	26/3	2
SPRINGETT, Fred	1938-39	17	0	0	0	0	0	0	0	17	0
STAINSBY, John	1961-63	69	21	1	0	8	4	0	0	78	25
STAINWRIGHT, David	1969-70	6/2	1	1	0	1	0	0	0	8/2	1
STANIFORTH, Gordon	1976-79										
	1987-88	143/4	34	10	4	7	2	0	0	160/4	40
STANLEY, Tommy	1981-82	14/4	0	1	0	0	0	0	0	15/4	0
STEEL, Richard	1956-58	3	0	0	0	0	0	0	0	3	0
STEWART, Alan	1949-56	208	1	23	0	0	0	0	0	231	1
STEWART, James	1957	1	0	0	0	0	0	0	0	1	0
STOCKILL, Reg	1929-30	2	1	2	0	0	0	0	0	4	1
STODDART, Terry	1956	3	0	0	0	0	0	0	0	3	0
STONE, John	1972-76	86	5	5	0	7	0	0	0	98	5
STOREY, Sid	1947-56	328	40	24	2	0	0	0	0	352	42
STOWELL, Michael	1987-88	6	0	0	0	0	0	0	0	6	0
STRAIN, David	1934	13	0	0	0	0	0	0	0	13	0
STRONACH, Peter	1978-79	30/4	2	0	0	3/1	0	0	0	33/5	2
SWALLOW, Barry	1969-76	268/1	21	24	4	19	2	0	0	311/1	27
SWEENEY, Gerry	1982	12	0	0	0	0	0	0	0	12	0
SWEENIE, Tom	1968	6	1	0	0	0	0	0	0	6	1
TAIT, Barry	1959-60	15	5	1	0	0	0	0	0	16	5
TAIT, Peter	1955	3	1	0	0	0	0	0	0	3	1
TAYLOR, Archie	1968-71	93/3	9	12	0	4	0	0	0	109/3	10
TAYLOR, Paul	1873	4	0	0	0	1	0	0	0	5	0
TAYLOR, Philip	1975-78	14/7	1	0/1	0	0/1	0	0	0	14/9	1
TAYLOR, Richard	1973-74	26/2	2	0	0	1	0	0	0	27/2	2
TAYLOR, Dick	1980	2	0	0	0	0	0	0	0	2	0
THOMPSON, Brian	1973	4/2	0	0	0	0	0	0	0	4/2	0
THOMPSON, Des	1951-52	80	0	3	0	0	0	0	0	83	0
THOMPSON, Albert	1936-37	24	24	5	4	0	0	0	0	29	28
THOMPSON, Ken	1950-51	21	0	0	0	0	0	0	0	21	0
THOMPSON, Oliver	1929-32	121	2	12	0	0	0	0	0	133	2
THOMPSON, Ron	1949-50	8	0	0	0	0	0	0	0	8	0
THOMPSON, Tommy	1970	4	0	0	0	0	0	0	0	4	0
THORNTON, Richard	1932	11	0	0	0	0	0	0	0	11	0
TOMLINSON, Bob	1930	3	1	0	0	0	0	0	0	3	1
TOPPING, Chris	1968-78	410/2	10	26	0	25	2	0	0	461/2	12
TUCKER, William	1935	2	1	0	0	0	0	0	0	2	1
TUNKS, Roy	1969	4	0	0	0	0	0	0	0	4	0
TURNBULL, John	1932	1	0	0	0	0	0	0	0	1	0
TURNER, Arthur	1934-35	12	0	0	0	0	0	0	0	12	0
TURNER, Ken	1966-68	88	2	7	0	5	0	0	0	100	2
TURNER, Robert	1934-35	9	0	0	0	0	0	0	0	9	0
TUTILL, Steve	1987-90	83/2	1	6	0	6	0	5/2	1	100/4	2
TWISSELL, Charlie	1958-61	53	8	3	0	0	0	0	0	56	8
WALDRON, Alan	1981	3	1	0	0	1	0	0	0	4	1
WALKER, Dennis	1964-68	149/5	19	9	0	6	0	0	0	164/5	19
WALKER, Mike	1966-68	60	0	7	0	0	0	0	0	67	0
WALKER, Stuart	1976	2	0	0	0	0	0	0	0	2	0
WALKER, Terry	1949-50	16	9	0	0	0	0	0	0	16	9
WALSH, Jimmy	1978-81	91/8	2	7	0	8	0	0	0	106/8	2
WALWYN, Keith	1981-87	245	119	24	11	18	9	4	1	291	140
WANN, Denis	1972-75	65/1	7	2	0	1	0	0	0	68/1	7

Player	Played	League App	League Gls	FA Cup App	FA Cup Gls	FL Cup App	FL Cup Gls	Others App	Others Gls	Total App	Total Gls
WARBURTON, Ray	1989-90	43	2	1	1	4	1	2	0	50	4
WARD, Warren	1985	4	3	0	0	0	0	0/1	0	4/1	3
WARDLE, Ernest	1955-59	60	2	3	0	0	0	0	0	63	2
WARE, Charlie	1953-54	9	0	0	0	0	0	0	0	9	0
WARNOCK, Neil	1978	1/3	0	0	0	1	0	0	0	2/3	0
WARRENDER, Robert	1952-54	24	5	0	0	0	0	0	0	24	5
WASS, Ted	1932-39	222	0	22	0	0	0	0	0	244	0
WEALTHALL, Barry	1963-66	75	0	1	0	3	0	0	0	79	0
WEDDLE, Derek	1964-66	44	13	3	1	2	0	0	0	49	14
WEIR, Jimmy	1960-62	82	38	7	0	6	1	0	0	95	39
WELLINGS, Barry	1978-80	40/7	9	6/1	3	0/1	0	0	0	46/9	12
WHARTON, Norman	1936-39	117	0	17	0	0	0	0	0	134	0
WHEAT, Arthur	1952-53	4	0	0	0	0	0	0	0	4	0
WHITEHEAD, Alan	1986-88	40/1	1	4	0	4	0	4	1	52/1	2
WHITELAW, John	1937	10	4	0	0	0	0	0	0	10	4
WHITELAW, William	1934	2	0	0	0	0	0	0	0	2	0
WHITESIDE, Ken	1954-55	8	0	0	0	0	0	0	0	8	0
WIDDOWSON, Bob	1968-69	30	0	3	0	1	0	0	0	34	0
WIGHTMAN, John	1933-34	5	0	1	0	0	0	0	0	6	0
WILCOCKSON, Stanley	1933-34	39	5	0	0	0	0	0	0	39	5
WILKINSON, Norman	1954-66	354	127	39	16	9	0	0	0	402	143
WILLIAMS, Leslie	1932-33	7	0	0	0	0	0	0	0	7	0
WILLIAMS, Ken	1953	1	0	0	0	0	0	0	0	1	0
WILSON, George	1935-36	39	0	1	0	0	0	0	0	40	0
WILSON, Ken	1973	2	0	0	0	0	0	0	0	2	0
WILSON, Phil	1987-89	38/8	2	5	1	3	0	4	0	50/8	3
WINTERS, Ian	1945-47	27	10	8	4	0	0	0	0	35	14
WOJTCZAK, Edward	1946-47	8	0	0	0	0	0	0	0	8	0
WOLSTENHOLME, Ian	1964-65	2	0	0	0	1	0	0	0	3	0
WOLSTENHOLME, Trevor	1966-67	11	0	3	0	3	0	0	0	17	0
WOODALL, John	1968	2	0	0	0	0	0	0	0	2	0
WOODS, Alan	1960-66	227/1	4	15	0	16	0	0	0	258/1	4
WOODWARD, Brian	1950-51	5	0	0	0	0	0	0	0	5	0
WOODWARD, John	1971-77	152/15	7	9/1	0	13/1	0	0	0	174/17	7
WOOLLETT, Charles	1949	4	0	0	0	0	0	0	0	4	0
WRAGG, Peter	1956-63	264	78	23	4	10	5	0	0	297	87
YEATS, William	1972-73	8/1	0	0	0	1	0	0	0	9/1	0
YOUNG, Harold	1935-37	10	0	0	0	0	0	0	0	10	0
YOUNG, Tony	1976-78	76/2	2	6	0	4	0	0	0	86/2	2

SUBSCRIBERS

Presentation Copies
1 York City Football Club
2 The Football League • 3 The Football Association

4 J R Greenway MP
5 Michael Sinclair
6 John Bird
7 Dave Batters
8 J A Harris
9 Raymond Shaw
10 A N Other
11 K P Wood
12 John Lathan
13 Derek Hyde
14 Harry Kay
15 William James Grier
16 Dave Parine
17 Roberto J Gamble
18 Malcolm Ferguson
19 David Earnshaw
20 Errick Peterson
21 Peter Lunn
22 R K Shoesmith
23 Douglas Lamming
24 Harald Löhr
25 B H Standish
26 Moira & Frederick Furness
27 John Motson
28 Duncan Watt
29 Richard J Moor
30 P H Whitehead
31 D T Bryant
32 L Burgess
33 Sports Marketing (Australia)
34 Brian H Hobbs
35 Ian Willott
36 Chris Minchin
37 Gordon Small
38 David Downs
39 Angus W Rodger
40 Colin Cameron
41 Paul H Bannister
42 J Ringrose
43 Douglas Bidgood
44 David J Godfrey
45 Lars-Olof Wendler
46 John Treleven
47 J Mulrennan
48 P Marks
49 David Keats
50 J D M Whitaker
51 Kevin C Wyatt
52 Paul Vibert
53 Christer Svensson
54 David Bagshaw
55 Richard D N Wells
56 Barry Watson
57 Keith Coburn
58 Roger Hudson
59 W D Phillips
60 Stephen Gartside
61 John W T Megson
62 Kevin Dagwell
63 Gordon Martin
64 Andrew Darbyshire
65 D J Cundell
66 Roger Dawson
67 Neil James Smith
68 Rob McGill
69 Jason McGill
70 Richard Bunday
71 John Pamplin
72 David Atkinson
73 T M Bagley
74 Darrell Crouch
75 William L Richardson
76 Edwin Nelson
77 J H Miller
78 Ian Harper
79 Paul Bowser
80 Alan David Starkie
81 Lt-Col R K Cooley
82 Donald J Fearnley
83 Stuart Kilvington
84 S W Blythe
85 Martin A Berridge
86 David Scaife
87 N E S Petty
88 Roger Wash
89 Gilbert Monnereau
90 Diamant Yosef
91 Ron Sheppeard
92 Anthony Charles Long
93 Sandra Woodcock
94 June Dixon
95 Andrew Briggs
96 R Benton
97 P M Benton
98 Terry Bland
99 Margaret Andrew
100 Kevin Andrew
101 Alf Cumberland
102 Geir Juva
103 M Thompson
104 D J Lawson
105 David P Thomas
106 John Gerald Hansom
107 Backhouse Joiners
108 Backhouse Joiners
109 Harry Thompson
110 Fred Lee
111 G M Puckering
112 F A Dibb
113 Ian Hey
114 T Burnett
115 W G Lewis
116 Howard L Lewis
117 Stephen J Bradley
118 Patrick McCauley
119 A H Sanderson
120 Ian Clough
121 Paul Grewer
122 Mark Grewer
123 Michael Dunham
124 John A Brough

125 Marcus Piggin
126 Phil Hutchinson
127 Peter Owston
128 Robert Long
129 Graham Smith
130 Keith B Ducker
131 Richard Coaker
132 Frank Kenneth Ward
133 Alan J Musgrave
134 Alan P Beecroft
135 Keith Houlston
136 Keith Till
137 David Carr
138 Karen Chappell
139 Philip Scoble
140 J Gardiner
141 John Raw
142 K H Marshall
143 S P Varley
144 P W S De Silva
145 Paul Bunce
146 Trond Isaksen
147 W Gittons
148 Gordon Neale
149 Garry Cummings
150 Gordon R Knaggs
151 Raymond A Kelly
152 I Watts
153 F K Sherwood
154 Paul Adrian Brewer
155 N Gonsalves
156 Tom Mitchell
157 C S Johnson
158 T D Culshaw
159 Alan Davies
160 M A Tiplady
161 Richard Webb
162 M Heather
163 Stephen J Mann
164 Patrick H Blundy
165 Robert Johnson
166 D Cade
167 Nicholas H D Brown
168 John van den Elsen
169 J S Pyke
170 C J Morton
171 Terry Frost
172 Garry Beckett
173 Helen Elsworth
174 Malcolm J Ferguson
175 Gary James - 'The Blue'
176 David Gregg
177 Peter Baxter
178 Dave Harrison
179 Bruce D Bottomley
180 Douglas M Craig
181 Duncan Kirk
182 Tim Milburn
183 P H Beck
184 Ruth Page
185 L A Zammit
186 J P Robinson
187 Andy Meek
188 Brian Tabner
189 Stuart M Robertson
190 P H Needham
191 D A Howarth
192 J B Tate
193 Michael McHugh
194 Ken Shaw
195 Trevor A Hutchinson
196 David R Allison
197 Gordon S Winters
198 D A Cooper
199 David Coulson
200 L C & P Gallagher
201 Tony M Hopper
202 Richard White
203 Richard J Moor
204 M Wiles
205 Tim Waugh
206 Graham Kilby
207 Richard Wiles
208 James Hutchinson
209 Terry Doyle
210 Mick Parker
211 David M S Quickfall
212 George Dunn
213 F Beale
214 Chris Forth
215 Christopher K Wishart
216 Paul Jerome
217 Dave Hillam
218 Paul Brookes
219 David J Smith
220 Alan Wheatley
221 B R Butler
222 Eric Heesom
223 Elizabeth Joyce
224 Jon Robinson
225 Mike Purkiss
226 Paul Michael Rawnsley
227 Jonathan Rawnsley
228 Andrew Anderson
229 David Dansie
230 Stanley A Robinson
231 Alan Hindley
232 Mark Race
233 Andrew Barry Heppell
234 Jim Walker
235 M R Pearce
236 Geoffrey Wright
237 Tony Bluff
238 Filippo Rossi
239 Phillip Blacker
240 Dave Green
241 Mervyn Powell
242 Dale L Richardson
243 John Snowdon
244 John Snowdon
245 P M Shepherd
246 Richard Stocken
247 Norman Green
248 A N Davis
249 Ruth Pease
250 Peter Pickup
251 Keith Druggitt
252 Neal Druggitt
253 M Robson
254 Mark White
255 Lawrence A Fray
256 A N Peace
257 David J Smith
258 J Buitenga
259 Iain Symes
260 Tony Milner
261 Stan Taylor
262 N M Clay
263 Peter Rookes
264 Michael Briggs
265 H Petler
266 H Petler
267 H Petler
268 Andrew Cowl
269 Dave Wake
270 Robert Mills
271 Henry Mills
272 M Winn
273 Andrew J Ives
274 Gerald Hill

275 Tasos Botsis
276 Kostas Fotopoulos
277 Ian Griffiths
278 Surapot Saengchote
279 Peter Overton
280 Kenneth Baxter
281 A J Saunders
282 Robert Horsman
283 Desmond Dowker
284 Peter G Rowe
285 Kevin Robert Morgan
286 Colin Benson
287 A & A S Hirst
288 John Uttley
289 Ian L E Birch
290 James Hutchinson
291 Michael R Brown
292 Peter Stokell
293 Geoff Allman
294 Paul Wilson
295 R S Godfrey
296 Darren Brookes
297 Tim Bentall
298 Anthony Jones
299 S P Tomlin
300 A H Atkins
301 A Young
302 M Swart
303 P W Stevenson
304 Anders Johansson
305 Q C M Olsthoorn
306 G D Painter
307 Tonny Otten
308 Patricia Arthur
309 R G Woolman
310 R W Lane
311 Simons Martin
312 David Lumb
313 David Helliwell
314 John Taylor
315 P Whiteoak
316 John Wherrett
317 John Griffin
318 Neil Griffin
319 Stuart Powell
320 Ronald Knox
321 Mrs H Sleightholm
322 Mrs H Sleightholm
323 D Stewart
324 M G Wood
325 Anthony Brewer
326 Catherine Parker
327 William Wells
328 Simon Bell
329 Sophie Bell
330 David Craggs
331 D N Lilley
332 M E Ward
333 John Russell Taylor
334 Roy W Dewhirst
335 Mark Scarr
336 Raymond Kendal
337 Mark Cowling
338 Chris Moffatt
339 Donald Horsfield
340 Kenneth Smith
341 Nicholas Beilby
342 The Taylor Family
343 Donald Burns
344 M Haffenden
345 G K & P Rowe
346 Sarah Pullon
347 Owen Robson
348 Dave Windross
349 Judith Wardell
350 C R Nutbrown
351 Paul Coultate
352 Graham P Oglesby
353 Jim Tindell
354 Jim Lacey
355 Tony Mason
356 Steve Cook
357 John H Clarke
358 C J Bowes
359 Trevor Pullan
360 Phil Reed
361 Michael Boggitt
362 Chris Salmon
363 Michael K Swales
364 David Quinn
365 Marc Chappell
366 Peter W Broderick
367 David M S Rhodes
368 Frank Ormston
369 David Goldsmith
370 J Geelan
371 Paul Coxon
372 R M Blenkinsop
373 D Pearson
374 Hugh F W Kitchin
375 Charles & Jean Lang
376 Edward Lang
377 Jonathan Hall
378 Stewart M Pearson
379 Geoff Marshall
380 Kevin Crick
381 David Crawford
382 Mrs D Ainscow
383 N Wilkinson
384 R V Calmels
385 Esa Kautonen
386 Paul Wilson